PERSONALITY DISORDERS AND PATHOLOGY

PERSONALITY DISORDERS AND PATHOLOGY

Integrating Clinical Assessment and
Practice in the **DSM-5** and **ICD-11** Era

Edited by Steven K. Huprich

AMERICAN PSYCHOLOGICAL ASSOCIATION

Copyright © 2022 by the American Psychological Association. All rights reserved. Except as permitted under the United States Copyright Act of 1976, no part of this publication may be reproduced or distributed in any form or by any means, including, but not limited to, the process of scanning and digitization, or stored in a database or retrieval system, without the prior written permission of the publisher.

The opinions and statements published are the responsibility of the authors, and such opinions and statements do not necessarily represent the policies of the American Psychological Association.

The Editor has worked to ensure that all information in this book is accurate at the time of publication and consistent with general mental health care standards. As research and practice continue to advance, however, therapeutic standards may change. Moreover, particular situations may require a particularized therapeutic response not addressed or included in this book.

Published by
American Psychological Association
750 First Street, NE
Washington, DC 20002
https://www.apa.org

Order Department
https://www.apa.org/pubs/books
order@apa.org

In the U.K., Europe, Africa, and the Middle East, copies may be ordered from Eurospan
https://www.eurospanbookstore.com/apa
info@eurospangroup.com

Typeset in Meridien and Ortodoxa by Circle Graphics, Inc., Reisterstown, MD

Printer: Gasch Printing, Odenton, MD
Cover Designer: Gwen J. Grafft, Minneapolis, MN

Library of Congress Cataloging-in-Publication Data

Names: Huprich, Steven Ken, 1966- editor.
Title: Personality disorders and pathology : integrating clinical
   assessment and practice in the DSM-5 and ICD-11 era / edited by
   Steven K. Huprich.
Description: Washington, DC : American Psychological Association, [2022] |
   Includes bibliographical references and index.
Identifiers: LCCN 2022004005 (print) | LCCN 2022004006 (ebook) |
   ISBN 9781433835766 (paperback) | ISBN 9781433835773 (ebook)
Subjects: LCSH: Personality disorders--Pathophysiology. | Personality
   disorders--Diagnosis. | Personality disorders--Treatment. | BISAC:
   PSYCHOLOGY / Personality | PSYCHOLOGY / Assessment, Testing &
   Measurement
Classification: LCC RC554 .P4717 2022 (print) | LCC RC554 (ebook) |
   DDC 616.85/81--dc23/eng/20220224
LC record available at https://lccn.loc.gov/2022004005
LC ebook record available at https://lccn.loc.gov/2022004006

https://doi.org/10.1037/0000310-000

Printed in the United States of America

10 9 8 7 6 5 4 3 2 1

CONTENTS

Introduction: The Changing Landscape of Personality Disorders **3**
Steven K. Huprich

I. EMPIRICAL FOUNDATIONS AND CLINICAL UTILITY OF THE *DSM-5* ALTERNATIVE MODEL AND *ICD-11* MODEL **7**

1. The Alternative *DSM-5* Model for Personality Disorders and Its Empirical Support **9**
Nicole M. Cain and Abby L. Mulay

2. Empirical Foundation of the *ICD-11* Classification of Personality Disorders **27**
Bo Bach and Roger Mulder

3. Clinical Utility of Proposed Dimensional Personality Disorder Models: Considerations and Opportunities **53**
Caleb J. Siefert, John Porcerelli, Kevin B. Meehan, and Barry Dauphin

II. ASSESSMENT AND TREATMENT WITHIN THE NEWEST PARADIGMS **75**

4. Principles of Psychological Assessment for Personality Disorders **77**
Emily A. Dowgwillo, JoAnna Molina, and Kathryn R. Forche

5. The Assessment of Personality Function in Adolescents **109**
Carla Sharp, Kiana Cano, Sune Bo, and Joost Hutsebaut

6. Principles of Treating Personality Pathology **135**
Steven K. Huprich

vi *Contents*

7. The Alternative *DSM* Model for Personality Disorders in Psychological Assessment and Treatment — 159
Mark H. Waugh, Jeremy M. Ridenour, and Katie C. Lewis

8. Assessment and Treatment of Personality Disorders Within the *ICD-11* Framework — 183
Roger Mulder and Bo Bach

III. COMMON FRAMEWORKS TREATING PERSONALITY PATHOLOGY — 209

9. Transference-Focused Psychotherapy — 211
Kenneth N. Levy, Frank E. Yeomans, and Daniel S. Spina

10. Mentalization-Based Treatment — 237
Anthony W. Bateman

11. Dialectical Behavior Psychotherapy — 259
Sharon M. Nelson, Chelsea D. Cawood, Takakuni Suzuki, Elizabeth Chapman, and Rebecca Lusk

12. Schema Therapy: Conceptualization and Treatment of Personality Disorders — 281
Joan Farrell and Ida A. Shaw

13. Pharmacotherapy for Personality Disorders — 305
Lea K. Marin, Celia Foster, and Marianne Goodman

14. Neuroscience and Personality Disorders — 323
Sabine C. Herpertz and Katja Bertsch

IV. TREATMENT FOR SPECIFIC PERSONALITY DISORDERS — 351

15. Borderline Personality Disorder — 353
Kenneth N. Levy, Johannes C. Ehrenthal, and Jacob A. Martin

16. Narcissistic Personality Disorder — 375
Elsa Ronningstam

17. Antisocial Personality Disorder — 391
Daniel Mark, Sandeep Roy, Hannah Walsh, and Craig S. Neumann

18. Higher Level Personality Disorders — 413
Benjamin McCommon, Julia F. Sowislo, and Eve Caligor

Index — 435
About the Editor — 467

CONTRIBUTORS

Bo Bach, PhD, Center for Personality Disorder Research, Mental Health Services, Region Zealand, Denmark

Anthony W. Bateman, MA, FRCPsych, University College London, London, England

Katja Bertsch, PhD, Ludwig-Maximilians-University Munich, Munich, Germany

Sune Bo, PhD, Child and Adolescent Psychiatry and Psychiatric Research Unit, Copenhagen, Denmark

Nicole M. Cain, PhD, Rutgers, The State University of New Jersey, Piscataway, NJ, United States

Eve Caligor, MD, Columbia University, New York, NY, United States

Kiana Cano, MA, University of Houston, Houston, TX, United States

Chelsea D. Cawood, PhD, VA Ann Arbor Healthcare System, Ann Arbor, MI, and University of Michigan, Ann Arbor, MI, United States

Elizabeth Chapman, LMSW, DBT-LBC, VA Ann Arbor Healthcare System, Ann Arbor, MI, United States

Barry Dauphin, PhD, ABPP, University of Detroit Mercy, Detroit, MI, United States

Emily A. Dowgwillo, PhD, University of Detroit Mercy, Detroit, MI, United States

Johannes C. Ehrenthal, PhD, University of Cologne, Cologne, Germany

Joan Farrell, PhD, Indiana University–Purdue University, Indianapolis, IN, United States

Kathryn R. Forche, BA, University of Detroit Mercy, Detroit, MI, United States

Celia Foster, MD, Icahn School of Medicine at Mount Sinai, New York, NY, United States

Marianne Goodman, MD, Icahn School of Medicine at Mount Sinai, New York, NY, and James J. Peters VA Medical Center, Bronx, NY, United States

Sabine C. Herpertz, MD, Heidelberg University, Heidelberg, Germany

Steven K. Huprich, PhD, University of Detroit Mercy, Detroit, MI, and Michigan State University College of Human Medicine, Lansing, MI, United States

Joost Hutsebaut, PhD, de Viersprong, Halsteren, Netherlands, and Tilburg University, Tilburg, Netherlands

Kenneth N. Levy, PhD, The Pennsylvania State University, University Park, PA, United States

Katie C. Lewis, PhD, Austen Riggs Center, Stockbridge, MA, United States

Rebecca Lusk, PsyD, ABPP, DBT-LBC, VA Ann Arbor Healthcare System, Ann Arbor, MI, and University of Michigan, Ann Arbor, MI, United States

Lea K. Marin, MD, MPH, Icahn School of Medicine at Mount Sinai, New York, NY, and James J. Peters VA Medical Center, Bronx, NY, United States

Daniel Mark, PhD, Northwest Forensic Institute, Portland, OR

Jacob A. Martin, MS, The Pennsylvania State University, University Park, PA, United States

Benjamin McCommon, MD, Columbia University, New York, NY, United States

Kevin B. Meehan, PhD, Long Island University–Brooklyn, New York, NY, United States

JoAnna Molina, MS, University of Detroit Mercy, Detroit, MI, United States

Abby L. Mulay, PhD, Medical University of South Carolina, Charleston, SC, United States

Roger Mulder, MBChB, PhD, FRANZCP, University of Otago, Christchurch, New Zealand

Sharon M. Nelson, PhD, Serious Mental Illness Treatment Resource and Evaluation Center, VA Ann Arbor Health Care System, Ann Arbor, MI, United States

Craig S. Neumann, PhD, University of North Texas, Denton, TX, United States

John Porcerelli, PhD, ABPP, University of Detroit Mercy, Detroit, MI, United States

Jeremy M. Ridenour, PsyD, Austen Riggs Center, Stockbridge, MA, United States

Elsa Ronningstam, PhD, McLean Hospital, Harvard Medical School, Belmont, MA, United States

Sandeep Roy, PhD, Patton State Hospital, Patton, CA, United States

Carla Sharp, PhD, University of Houston, Houston, TX, United States

Ida A. Shaw, MA, Schema Therapy Institute Midwest, Indianapolis, IN, United States

Caleb J. Siefert, PhD, University of Michigan–Dearborn, Dearborn, MI, United States

Julia F. Sowislo, PhD, New York–Presbyterian Weill Cornell Medical College, New York, NY, United States

Daniel S. Spina, MA, The Pennsylvania State University, University Park, PA, United States

Takakuni Suzuki, PhD, University of Michigan, Ann Arbor, MI, United States

Hannah Walsh, PhD, University of North Texas, Denton, TX, United States

Mark H. Waugh, PhD, ABPP, University of Tennessee, Knoxville, TN, United States

Frank E. Yeomans, MD, PhD, Joan and Sanford I. Weill Medical College, Cornell University, New York, NY, United States

PERSONALITY DISORDERS AND PATHOLOGY

Introduction

The Changing Landscape of Personality Disorders

Steven K. Huprich

Over the past several years, psychology has increasingly shifted from a categorical model of diagnosis and treating personality disorders (PDs) to a more dimensional model. The shift began in 2007, when Widiger and Trull (2007) published a seminal article in *American Psychologist* that suggested that a radical shift was necessary in the ways in which psychologists assess and diagnose PDs. This article was preceded by a white paper by Widiger and Simonsen (2005), who challenged the field to move toward a dimensional model by which to understand, assess, and diagnose personality pathology. These concerns were heeded, and their voices reflected those of many researchers and clinicians who argued that the science did not support the retention of PD categories (e.g., Clark, 2007; Krueger & Eaton, 2010).

Indeed, with the publication of the *Diagnostic and Statistical Manual of Mental Disorders* (5th ed.; *DSM-5*; American Psychiatric Association, 2013), research output on the proposed, dimensionalized Alternative *DSM-5* Model for Personality Disorders (AMPD) exploded. In this model, six traditional PD categories are retained—antisocial, avoidant, borderline, narcissistic, obsessive–compulsive, and schizotypal—although they are described on a continuum by both their level of personality functioning and their constellation of pathological personality traits. Levels of personality functioning is classified as Criterion A of the AMPD description of PDs and assesses personality pathology by its expressions in the sense of self and interpersonal relatedness. Self-functioning is assessed by the maturity of an individual's level of self-directedness and identity, while interpersonal functioning is assessed by an individual's capacity for

---

https://doi.org/10.1037/0000310-001

Personality Disorders and Pathology: Integrating Clinical Assessment and Practice in the DSM-5 *and* ICD-11 *Era*, S. K. Huprich (Editor)

Copyright © 2022 by the American Psychological Association. All rights reserved.

empathy and intimacy. Criterion B of the AMPD describes 25 trait facets that fall more broadly into five superordinate trait domains: negative affectivity, detachment, antagonism, disinhibition, and psychoticism. Patients are rated along a continuum to describe the extent to which they possess each trait.

But it was not just within American psychiatry and psychology that the transition to a dimensional model was being proposed. Tyrer et al. (2011) made an even bolder suggestion, writing that all PD categories should be eliminated and that patients should be assessed for the severity of their PD and for their broad personality trait domains. The World Health Organization (WHO, 2019) proceeded along this pathway for the revision of the *International Statistical Classification of Diseases and Related Health Problems* (11th ed.; *ICD-11*). The final version of *ICD-11* asks providers to rate their patients along a continuum of personality pathology severity, ranging from "none" to "severe." Patients also are to be evaluated for the extent to which they exhibit certain trait domains, labeled as negative affectivity, detachment, disinhibition, dissociability, and anankastia. In addition, when WHO agreed on the final version of *ICD-11*, a borderline pattern specifier became an option for those patients who resemble past categorical descriptions of borderline PD.

Thus, much has changed since Widiger and Trull's (2007) now clairvoyant paper. Clinicians throughout the world are asked to utilize a dimensionalized method of diagnosis and assessment. In an earlier edited text, I (Huprich, 2015) described the evolution of the diagnostic system. In 6 short years, a considerable body of research and discussion has arisen. The PD field is now embracing a dimensionalized approach to understanding personality pathology. Consequently, I believed it was time to produce another edited text on this matter—but one that had a focus on clinical utility and application of the dimensionalized models described by *DSM-5* and *ICD-11*. While some concerns remain about the utility of a fully dimensionalized system (see Huprich, 2018), I have found much of this approach more congruent with my thinking when I assess and treat patients with personality pathology. The authors of this edited volume have most aptly described research on the dimensional systems of both *ICD-11* and *DSM-5*. They also have described major treatment approaches and have discussed some of the well-established PD categories and how to consider them within a dimensionalized model. Thus, this book has something for both the researcher and the clinician.

Part I of this book lays out the empirical foundation of both *DSM-5* and *ICD-11* dimensional models. Cain and Mulay as well as Bach and Mulder, the authors of the first two chapters, respectively, make compelling arguments for the need and usefulness of these dimensional models. In the third chapter, Siefert and colleagues offer both important content related to the clinical utility of the dimensionalized systems and ideas for how to enhance clinical utility beyond what is currently known.

Part II of this book focuses on assessment and treatment within the dimensionalized models. Dowgwillo and colleagues present an up-to-date, comprehensive discussion of principles that guide personality pathology assessment, reviewing what has historically been known in the PD literature but also linking current assessment research into the newer paradigms. Specific applications of assessing and treating patients with these models are presented by Waugh and colleagues for *DSM-5* and Mulder and Bach for *ICD-11*. Sharp and colleagues present the value and necessity of assessing and treating adolescents for PDs and pathology, offering clear reasons for evaluating adolescents more carefully than is typically done and then providing a case application of how the dimensionalized models can be clinically helpful. I also provide a chapter on guiding principles of how to use these dimensionalized systems in treating personality pathology, something that hopefully will help clinicians rooted in categorical models of PD as they transition into a dimensional framework.

Part III is organized around major treatment paradigms for personality pathology that arguably have the most empirical support and clinical utility. While each of these chapters presents a concise and helpful overview of the treatment model, the authors also discuss how dimensionalized models can be used within these frameworks. What I believe is especially helpful in this section is that these chapters demonstrate that existing treatments all can be implemented with newer, dimensionalized models. The authors review challenges that exist in transitioning older models into newer frameworks yet send the strong message that PDs and pathology are treatable conditions.

Part IV offers specific guidelines for those PD for which we know the most from the evidence base and clinical applications. The authors of these chapters review these conditions in depth as well as offer clinical examples of what it is like to work with such patients. Again, these authors send a strong message about the treatability of most of these conditions and the challenges that remain in how to best intervene with very challenging patients. I am especially pleased to present a chapter on higher level PDs that is written by McCommon and colleagues. These disorders, although originally rooted in a categorical framework, have always been placed within a dimensional understanding of personality pathology in general. This chapter provides clear guidelines for how to understand this set of disorders and conditions and what clinical approaches are required for such patients.

In closing, I express my deepest and most sincere appreciation for all the authors who contributed to this book. Engaging in a project such as this during a pandemic came with more challenges than one typically experiences when writing chapters like these. All authors were thoughtful and collaborative, demonstrating high levels of professionalism and competency. The field is fortunate to have such good individuals help shape the future.

I also am grateful for the support I received from the American Psychological Association to put together this book. Emily Ekle and Beth Hatch were attentive to the process and details, and I could not have asked for better individuals to help develop and produce this book.

And I express my deepest appreciation to my family (Donna, Chris, and Katie) and for the many patients I have had the privilege of treating over the years. The love of my family and their presence in my life have allowed me to enjoy a profession that is fruitful and satisfying. My patients' commitment to therapy and their honest desire for a better life have allowed me to understand their inner worlds with a level of insight that I could not have attained if they did not have faith in me and the psychotherapy process. Ultimately, it is for them and patients everywhere that this book has been created.

REFERENCES

American Psychiatric Association. (2013). *Diagnostic and statistical manual of mental disorders* (5th ed.). https://doi.org/10.1176/appi.books.9780890425596

Clark, L. A. (2007). Assessment and diagnosis of personality disorder: Perennial issues and an emerging reconceptualization. *Annual Review of Psychology, 58*(1), 227–257. https://doi.org/10.1146/annurev.psych.57.102904.190200

Huprich, S. K. (Ed.). (2015). *Personality disorders: Moving toward theoretical and empirical integration in assessment and diagnosis.* American Psychological Association. https://doi.org/10.1037/14549-000

Huprich, S. K. (2018). Moving beyond categories and dimensions in personality pathology diagnosis and assessment. *The British Journal of Psychiatry, 213*(6), 685–689. https://doi.org/10.1192/bjp.2018.149

Krueger, R. F., & Eaton, N. R. (2010). Personality traits and the classification of mental disorders: Toward a more complete integration in *DSM-5* and an empirical model of psychopathology. *Personality Disorders, 1*(2), 97–118. https://doi.org/10.1037/a0018990

Tyrer, P., Crawford, M., Mulder, R., Blashfield, R., Farnam, A., Fossati, A., Kim, Y.-R., Koldobsky, N., Lecic-Tosevski, D., Ndetei, D., Swales, M., Clark, L. A., & Reed, G. M. (2011). The rationale for the classification of personality disorder in the 11th revision of the *International Classification of Diseases (ICD-11). Personality and Mental Health, 5*(4), 246–259. https://doi.org/10.1002/pmh.190

Widiger, T. A., & Simonsen, E. (2005). Alternative dimensional models of personality disorder: Finding a common ground. *Journal of Personality Disorders, 19*(2), 110–130. https://doi.org/10.1521/pedi.19.2.110.62628

Widiger, T. A., & Trull, T. J. (2007). Plate tectonics in the classification of personality disorder: Shifting to a dimensional model. *American Psychologist, 62*(2), 71–83. https://doi.org/10.1037/0003-066X.62.2.71

World Health Organization. (2019). *International statistical classification of diseases and related health problems* (11th ed.). https://icd.who.int/

I

EMPIRICAL FOUNDATIONS AND CLINICAL UTILITY OF THE *DSM-5* ALTERNATIVE MODEL AND *ICD-11* MODEL

1

The Alternative *DSM-5* Model for Personality Disorders and Its Empirical Support

Nicole M. Cain and Abby L. Mulay

The introduction of operationally defined categories of personality disorder (PD) in the third edition of the *Diagnostic and Statistical Manual of Mental Disorders* (*DSM-III*; American Psychiatric Association, 1980) sparked years of interest and study in the assessment and treatment of personality pathology. *DSM-III* was innovative in that it separated PDs from other clinical disorders, thus highlighting their importance for case conceptualization and treatment. Yet, over time and with increased empirical scrutiny, it has become clear that there are several problematic issues with categorical PD diagnosis. These issues include

- high rates of diagnostic comorbidity (i.e., individuals who meet diagnostic criteria for one PD are likely to meet diagnostic criteria for another PD);

- arbitrary thresholds (e.g., why does borderline personality disorder [BPD] have nine criteria when five are required for the diagnosis);

- heterogeneity within PD category (i.e., wide variation in how a PD may clinically manifest); and the frequent use of the "not otherwise specified" (NOS) label (i.e., PD-NOS; the label does not highlight specific personality dysfunction that should be targeted in treatment and only serves to alert that *some* personality dysfunction is present in *some* capacity).

As Krueger (2019) aptly noted, "Human personality is too rich of a phenomenon to be readily segmented into categories" (p. 63). However, across decades and several iterations, from *DSM-III* (American Psychiatric Association, 1980) to

---

https://doi.org/10.1037/0000310-002

Personality Disorders and Pathology: Integrating Clinical Assessment and Practice in the DSM-5 *and* ICD-11 *Era,* S. K. Huprich (Editor)

Copyright © 2022 by the American Psychological Association. All rights reserved.

DSM-III-R (3rd ed., rev.; American Psychiatric Association, 1987), to *DSM-IV* (4th ed.; American Psychiatric Association, 1994), to *DSM-IV-TR* (4th ed., text rev.; American Psychiatric Association, 2000), PD diagnosis has remained categorical.

As such, across the fields of psychology and psychiatry, many researchers and clinicians sought to make significant revisions to PD classification for *DSM-5* (5th ed.; American Psychiatric Association, 2013). In response, the *DSM-5* Personality and Personality Disorder Work Group initially proposed a thoroughly revised PD diagnostic system (Skodol et al., 2011) that would include two dimensional aspects: (a) a severity continuum assessing deficits in self- and interpersonal functioning that are ubiquitous to all PDs, referred to as "Criterion A"; and (b) pathological personality traits, which included 25 trait facets (e.g., Anxiousness, Emotional Lability) across five trait domains (e.g., Negative Affectivity, Detachment, Antagonism, Disinhibition, and Psychoticism), referred to as "Criterion B."

In addition, the Work Group provided diagnostic inclusion criteria for six specific PD categories (e.g., Antisocial, Borderline, Avoidant, Narcissistic, Obsessive-Compulsive, and Schizotypal) as well as PD-Trait Specified (PD-TS), which would be used instead of PD-NOS (Morey, 2019). These six PDs were selected to be retained because of their clinical and empirical significance as well as their reported prevalence rates (Waugh et al., 2017). While this hybrid model was approved by the *DSM-5* Task Force, the American Psychiatric Association board of trustees rejected this proposal. The PD categories from *DSM-IV* were included in the main section (Section II) of *DSM-5* essentially verbatim, whereas the proposed hybrid model was included in *DSM-5* Section III as "emerging"—the Alternative *DSM-5* Model for Personality Disorders (AMPD)—with the recommendation that this model warrants further study (for a comprehensive review of the development of the AMPD and its inclusion in Section III of *DSM-5*, refer to Zachar et al., 2016). The *DSM-5* allows for an AMPD diagnosis using the *DSM-5* code "Other Specific Personality Disorder" (American Psychiatric Association, 2013).

OVERVIEW OF THE AMPD

Diagnosis with the AMPD requires fulfilling seven general criteria for PD. Waugh et al. (2017) argued that Criterion A and Criterion B are the most innovative criteria. Based on the proposal by the Work Group, Criterion A assesses disturbances in self-functioning (on the domains of identity and self-direction) and interpersonal functioning (on the domains of empathy and intimacy with others), and Criterion B assesses 25 pathological personality trait facets, which may be organized into five trait domains. The remaining criteria for the *DSM-5* AMPD are as follows: Criterion C, inflexibility; Criterion D, stability across time; Criterion E, the PD is not better explained by another mental disorder; Criterion F, the PD is not better explained by the effects of a substance or medical condition;

and Criterion G, the PD is not normative for the person's developmental stage or sociocultural environment (American Psychiatric Association, 2013).

By recreating six of the *DSM-IV* (American Psychiatric Association, 1994) PD categories within the AMPD, the aim was to show how certain PD types could be understood as specific combinations of personality functioning and pathological traits rather than as simply categorical symptom lists. In addition, the inclusion of PD-TS was designed to capture clinical presentations that would not fit neatly into a specific category. PD-TS allows the clinician to describe and specify PD using levels of personality functioning and maladaptive traits rather than as "NOS." Thus, this approach makes the PD-TS diagnosis more helpful for clinical conceptualization and treatment planning (Krueger & Hobbs, 2020).

Waugh and colleagues (2017) argued that many clinicians and personality researchers would already be familiar with AMPD concepts, specifically Criterion A and Criterion B, because they integrate perspectives from different theoretical orientations and across different paradigms of personality assessment. This pantheoretical approach reintroduces theory into the traditional medical model of *DSM*, which is atheoretical, and should appeal to clinicians and researchers of differing theoretical backgrounds.

There has been an explosion of research examining the AMPD since the *DSM-5* was published in 2013. A recent review by Zimmermann and colleagues (2019) found more than 300 citations for the AMPD. The remaining sections of this chapter highlight the development of and the research findings relevant to Criteria A and B, the conceptual and empirical overlap between Criteria A and B, and how the AMPD may be used in clinical practice.

CRITERION A

Criterion A refers to impairments in self- (on the domains of self-direction and self-identity) and interpersonal (on the domains of empathy and intimacy with others) functioning. The *DSM-5* Level of Personality Functioning Scale (LPFS; Bender et al., 2011) is used to define Criterion A with five levels of impairment (ranging from *little to none* to *extreme impairment*) specified for each aspect of functioning. The LPFS renders a single rating of the severity of PD and can be used to decide whether a PD diagnosis is appropriate (a score of greater than moderate impairment on any domain of personality functioning indicates the presence of PD). Deficits in personality functioning are thought to cut across all PDs, regardless of the specific PD type.

Bender et al. (2011) drew on the psychodynamic, attachment, and social-cognitive perspectives to develop Criterion A and the LPFS. Waugh et al. (2017) further noted that Criterion A represents the psychodynamic, interpersonal, and personological paradigms of personality assessment. In this way, the LPFS incorporates constructs that may be familiar to many clinicians, such as self-esteem stability, ways of thinking about self and others, identity, interpersonal functioning, mentalization, and reflective functioning (Waugh et al., 2017).

Although the AMPD Criterion A differentiates self- and interpersonal impairments, Pincus et al. (2020) noted that self and other are intertwined throughout Criterion A's diagnostic features (e.g., "depends excessively on others for identity, self-esteem, and emotion regulation with compromised boundaries" [p. 134]; "hyper-attuned to others, but only with respect to perceived relevance to self" [p. 134]). In this way, the AMPD offers several advantages. Most notably, it highlights self- and interpersonal impairment as a core feature of PD; it allows PD to be distinguished from other types of psychopathology, such as depression and anxiety; and it provides fertile avenues for theoretical and treatment integration (Pincus et al., 2020).

Assessment of Criterion A

The assessment of Criterion A was initially conceptualized as an expert rating on the 5-point impairment scale of the LPFS (Morey et al., 2013). However, researchers have recently begun rating the LPFS in different ways, such as separately rating the four domains (Few et al., 2013), 12 subdomains within the four domains (Roche, 2018; Zimmermann et al., 2014), or as 60 prototypical descriptors (Zimmermann et al., 2015), and aggregating the ratings afterward. In addition, researchers have begun to develop structured interviews, such as the Semi-Structured Interview for Personality Functioning *DSM-5* (Hutsebaut et al., 2017) and the Structured Clinical Interview for the Level of Personality Functioning Scale (Bender et al., 2018). Moving beyond expert clinician ratings, self-report measures have also been developed that ask individuals to rate themselves according to prototypical descriptions on 12 subdomains within the four domains. These self-report measures include the Level of Personality Functioning Scale–Self Report (LPFS-SR; Morey, 2017), the Level of Personality Functioning Scale–Brief Form (Hutsebaut et al., 2016; Weekers et al., 2019), and the *DSM-5* Levels of Personality Functioning Questionnaire (Huprich et al., 2018; Nelson et al., 2018; Siefert et al., 2020). Research has also suggested that the LPFS can be accurately rated by laypersons (Morey, 2018; Zimmermann et al., 2015), thus providing evidence for its use for informant ratings as well as clinical training.

Reliability and Validity of Criterion A

Studies of Criterion A have examined both clinician ratings of the LPFS and self-report measures. For example, studies have found that when clinicians use the LPFS to rate clinical material stemming from vignettes, interviews, or case narratives, the interrater reliability is largely acceptable (ranging from .42 to .67), including for those raters who may lack clinical training (Cruitt et al., 2019; Few et al., 2013; Morey, 2019; Roche et al., 2018; Zimmermann et al., 2014). Importantly, Zimmermann et al. (2019) noted that interrater reliability tends to improve significantly with training and when based on clinical interviews that specifically assess information relevant to Criterion A (Buer Christensen et al.,

2018; Cruitt et al., 2019; Hutsebaut et al., 2017). Research also shows that the internal consistency of the LPFS total score is acceptable when computed based on ratings of the 12 subdomains (Bach & Hutsebaut, 2018; Hutsebaut et al., 2017). With regard to the self-report measures of Criterion A, the four domains and the 12 subdomains also show high internal consistency (Huprich et al., 2018; Morey, 2017; Zimmermann et al., 2014, 2015).

Zimmermann et al. (2015) examined the structure of Criterion A using ratings from both laypersons and clinicians. Results showed that the four subdomains of Criterion A can be empirically derived and that it is also possible to use global LPFS scores to indicate general personality severity. However, Zimmermann and colleagues also noted some issues with the structure of Criterion A. Most notably, not all items loaded most strongly on their hypothesized domain, and not all items met the threshold for severity to indicate the presence of a PD. Nonetheless, these results broadly support the hypothesized structure of Criterion A. Subsequent studies have shown that the structure of Criterion A includes two highly correlated factors (Hutsebaut et al., 2016; Roche, 2018; Weekers et al., 2019), which is consistent with a strong general factor of PD severity.

Several studies have also demonstrated the criterion validity of Criterion A. For example, Criterion A predicted the presence of PD as well as the number of PD diagnoses across different samples (Few et al., 2013; Morey et al., 2013). In addition, Morey et al. (2014) found that an LPFS score of at least moderate impairment showed high sensitivity and specificity for identifying patients who met criteria for a PD diagnosis and also incremented the existing PD categories in predicting functional impairment, prognosis, and treatment intensity. Studies of convergent and discriminant validity have also shown that the LPFS is associated with, to name a few, psychosocial functioning (Morey et al., 2013); measures of symptom distress (Hutsebaut et al., 2016; Weekers et al., 2019); risk for dropout from inpatient treatment (Busmann et al., 2019), poor well-being (Huprich et al., 2018); interpersonal problems, sensitivities, motives, and efficacies (Dowgwillo et al., 2018; Roche et al., 2018); attachment styles and interpersonal dependency (Huprich et al., 2018); and personality traits (Hopwood, Good, & Morey, 2018; Morey, 2018; for a comprehensive review of all convergent and discriminant validity results for Criterion A and the LPFS, see Zimmermann et al., 2019).

CRITERION B

In contrast to Criterion A, Criterion B draws on the multivariate and empirical paradigms of personality assessment with a particular emphasis on the five-factor model (Waugh et al., 2017). There is a long-standing body of empirical support for the five-factor model, including its relationship to traditional *DSM* PD categories (Trull & Widiger, 2013). However, before the development of the AMPD, there was no stated goal to base Criterion B on five-factor models of personality. During its development, personality scholars distinguished Criterion B from the five-factor model, given it was believed some aspects of the two models did not align with one another (e.g., the domain that became Psychoticism, Schizotypy, did not align with the five-factor trait of Openness; see Widiger & McCabe, 2020). The five broad domains of Criterion B (i.e., Negative Affectivity, Detachment, Antagonism, Disinhibition, and Psychoticism), which are described in detail shortly, are now considered the antithesis of the "normal" traits of Neuroticism, Extraversion, Agreeableness, Conscientiousness, and Openness to experience (Rodriguez-Seijas et al., 2019).

Krueger et al. (2012) described the way in which the 25 pathological trait facets of the AMPD were developed in conjunction with its assessment instrument, the 220-item, self-report measure Personality Inventory for *DSM-5* (PID-5; Krueger et al., 2012). In the initial stages, members of the *DSM-5* Work Group offered suggestions of what clinical constructs they found most pertinent in their work with patients with personality dysfunction, which led to the identification of 37 facets and corresponding definitions. Multiple items were then developed to assess the characteristics of each facet using a questionnaire format, at which point item data were gathered within a national sample of community members who were seeking mental health treatment. Some facets were highly correlated with one another and thus collapsed into single facets, and items that underperformed were removed and replaced with new items. Through analyses, the initial 37 facets were subsequently reduced to 25 and are as follows: Anhedonia, Anxiousness, Attention Seeking, Callousness, Cognitive and Perceptual Dysregulation, Deceitfulness, Depressivity, Distractibility, Eccentricity, Emotional Lability, Grandiosity, Hostility, Impulsivity, Intimacy Avoidance, Irresponsibility, Manipulativeness, Perseveration, Separation Insecurity, Submissiveness, Suspiciousness, Restricted Affectivity, Rigid Perfectionism, Risk Taking, Unusual Beliefs and Experiences, and Withdrawal. The maladaptive trait facets of Criterion B are intended to describe the content of an individual's personality in connection with the level of personality functioning outlined by Criterion A (Krueger, 2019).

Through factor analyses, 25 maladaptive trait facets were identified that could be arranged into the five broad trait domains (Krueger et al., 2012). As such, the trait facets are subordinate to five high-order factors, which include Negative Affectivity (i.e., the experience of a wide range of upsetting emotions), Detachment (i.e., the preference to avoid engaging with others), Antagonism (i.e., the tendency to disagree with others though callous/manipulative behaviors), Disinhibition (i.e., a lack of restraint), and Psychoticism (i.e., unusual perceptual experiences and other odd behavioral attributes).

Assessment of Criterion B

In addition to the 220-item PID-5, which was developed in parallel with Criterion B, shorter versions are also currently available for use and demonstrate good psychometric properties. For example, the PID-5–Brief Form (American Psychiatric Association, 2013) comprises 25 items and assesses the five broad trait domains as opposed to the individual 25 pathological trait facets.

The PID-5–Informant Report Form (Markon et al., 2013) is a 218-item measure that may be used to rate an individual by a knowledgeable informant. Structured clinical interviews for the personality traits of the AMPD have also been developed for use by clinicians or researchers (e.g., Skodol et al., 2017).

Reliability and Validity of Criterion B

Criterion B has been the subject of significant research since its inception (see Hopwood, 2019), generally through the examination of the PID-5. A recent Google Scholar search produced more than 1,208 citations using the PID-5 (Krueger & Hobbs, 2020), suggesting a wealth of empirical support for Criterion B. As such, a comprehensive review of all of the empirical support for Criterion B and the PID-5 is beyond the scope of this chapter (refer to Zimmermann et al., 2019, for a comprehensive review). However, this section highlights considerations regarding the reliability and validity of Criterion B and the PID-5.

Internal consistency estimates for the PID-5 suggest that the trait facets have acceptable reliability, whereas the trait domain scores show higher internal consistency that likely relates to the longer length of the domain scales relative to facet scales (Al-Dajani et al., 2016). The higher order structure of the PID-5 has been supported in the literature (for a discussion, see Al-Dajani et al., 2016; Krueger & Markon, 2014). However, a meta-analysis of 14 studies of the PID-5 (Watters & Bagby, 2018) suggests that some facets demonstrate sizable cross-loadings on factors and/or strongly load onto factors that differed from that of Krueger et al. (2012). For example, Hostility was found to load on Antagonism rather than on Negative Affectivity, Restricted Affectivity only loaded on Detachment rather than on Negative Affectivity, Depressivity loaded on Negative Affectivity but also more strongly on Detachment, and Rigid Perfectionism only loaded on Negative Affectivity but not on Disinhibition.

In a follow-up study, Watters et al. (2019) used the PID-5 and the Revised Neuroticism, Extraversion, Openness Personality Inventory (Costa & McCrae, 1992) to examine the lower order structure of the PID-5 using an ethnically diverse undergraduate sample and a clinical sample. Results revealed a five-factor solution in the undergraduate sample in which the Openness facets did not load onto any of the factors but a six-factor solution in the clinical sample, with Openness forming its own factor. In addition, Watters et al. (2019) found that their model supported several modifications to the PID-5, including moving Restricted Affectivity to Detachment from Negative Affectivity, moving Hostility to Antagonism from Negative Affectivity, moving Suspiciousness to Negative Affectivity from Detachment, and removing Submissiveness altogether. Given these questions about the optimal PID-5 structure as well as the continued development of measures designed to assess the trait facets, further research is warranted.

Central to the validity of self-report measures is their ability to accurately assess a given construct, with consideration given to an individual's response style (e.g., whether they endorse an accurate view of themselves or engage in the over- or underreporting of problems or symptoms). Research suggests that, like other self-report measures, response bias likely inflates scores on the PID-5 (Krueger et al., 2012; McGee Ng et al., 2016); however, the PID-5 was not designed with built-in measures of response style. Given this criticism (e.g., Al-Dajani et al., 2016), recent efforts have been underway to develop these tools with PID-5 items.

For example, Keeley et al. (2016) created an inconsistency scale by identifying pairs of items that were not redundant with one another but were similar in item content based on correlations of .60 or greater. To calculate the scale score, the value of the discrepancy for each item in each item pair is summed, which creates a score from 0 to 60. Higher scores are representative of a greater probability of inconsistent responding. Using discriminant function analysis, the authors then created "cut scores" (i.e., 17 within the student sample [$n = 989$] and 18 within the clinical sample [$n = 131$]) that may be used to determine the presence of inconsistent responding. Bagby and Sellbom (2018) attempted to cross-validate the results of Keeley et al.; the authors found that the cut scores established by Keeley et al. performed well across the study samples. As such, preliminary evidence suggests the scale developed by Keeley et al. offers promising results in the detection of inconsistent responding.

Similarly, Sellbom et al. (2018) developed a scale using PID-5 items to detect the overreporting of symptoms. The authors identified items that were rarely endorsed within three distinct university samples (total of the three samples $n = 1,370$) and a psychiatric sample ($n = 194$). The overreporting scale, with 10 items, demonstrated adequate-to-good internal reliability and was significantly correlated with the overreporting scales of the Minnesota Multiphasic Personality Inventory–2–Restructured Form (MMPI-2-RF; Ben-Porath & Tellegen, 2008/2011). To assess criterion validity, students who were instructed to inflate their symptoms ($n = 80$) scored higher on the overreporting scale when compared with a group of psychiatric patients and students who were instructed to be honest when completing the scale ($n = 161$).

Studies have also focused on the ability of Criterion B to identify personality pathology. For example, Fowler and colleagues (2018) examined the ability of the PID-5 to successfully screen for the presence of BPD. Patients ($N = 1,000$) of the Menninger Clinic completed the research version of the Structured Clinical Interview for *DSM-IV* Axis II Personality Disorders (SCID-II; First et al., 2002) and the PID-5. Based on the results of the SCID-II, 19% of the patients in the sample were diagnosed with BPD. Results of the PID-5 algorithm for BPD revealed scores of 11 or greater that were associated with 81% sensitivity, 76% specificity, and an odds ratio of 13.26. The authors therefore concluded that the PID-5 could be used as a screening tool for BPD. Similarly, Drislane and colleagues (2019) demonstrated that items from the PID-5 could be used to measure the triarchic psychopathy constructs of boldness, meanness, and disinhibition (see Patrick et al., 2009).

Other studies have questioned the predictive validity of Criterion B. For example, Stone and Segal (2021) administered the PID-5 (Krueger et al., 2012), the LPFS-SR (Morey, 2017), and the Coolidge Axis II Inventory (CATI; Coolidge, 2020) to a sample of older adults. The authors found that the PID-5 trait facets correlated significantly with *all* PD scales of the CATI, suggesting that the PID-5 lacks sensitivity among older adults and may instead represent general personality dysfunction rather than specific trait dysfunction. The authors also conducted a series of hierarchical regressions while controlling for gender, with the trait facets of the PID-5 predicting PDs, as assessed by the CATI. Results were variable: Some traits were predictive of their intended scales and some were not predictive of their intended scales. Some traits were also found to be predictive despite not being predicted by the AMPD prototypes. The authors noted that, of the 10 regression models, eight (i.e., Antisocial, Avoidant, Borderline, Histrionic, Narcissistic, Obsessive-Compulsive, Paranoid, and Schizotypal) had more nonpredicted traits occur than predicted traits. Only two models (i.e., Dependent and Schizoid) had more significantly predicted traits occur than nonpredicted traits. Given the differing results in the PID-5's ability to accurately predict personality pathology, further research is warranted to examine the predictive validity of Criterion B.

A plethora of research is examining the convergent and discriminant validity of the PID-5 with other psychological constructs. For example, research has shown strong relationships of PID-5 trait domain scores with other measures of pathological personality traits, such as the Computer Adaptive Test of Personality Disorder (Simms et al., 2011) as well as with more broadband clinical measures, such as the MMPI-2-RF. In addition, maladaptive traits have been found to relate to variables, including general symptom distress, problematic alcohol use, self-harm, posttraumatic stress disorder, quality of life, maladaptive schemas, emotion dysregulation, and relationship satisfaction (refer to Al-Dajani et al., 2016, and Zimmermann et al., 2019, for a thorough review of the convergent and discriminant validity of Criterion B and the PID-5).

OVERLAP BETWEEN CRITERION A AND CRITERION B

Researchers have recently begun to question whether Criteria A and B provide discrete or redundant data (for a discussion, refer to Widiger et al., 2019). It has been argued that from a purely semantic perspective, Criteria A and B simply describe socially undesirable aspects of personality and that many of their differences are likely because of differing theoretical paradigms (Waugh et al., 2017). Thus, it could be argued that their separate assessment is not parsimonious. Some research indicates that measures of Criteria A and B are highly correlated (Bach & Hutsebaut, 2018; Few et al., 2013; Hopwood, Kotov, et al., 2018; Huprich et al., 2018; Nelson et al., 2018; Roche et al., 2018). In addition, one study to date has conducted a factor analysis of both Criteria A and B and found overlap: Some Criterion A domains load onto Criterion B traits (e.g., depth and duration of connections loaded onto detachment), and some Criterion B traits load onto Criterion A domains (e.g., callousness loaded onto impairments in interpersonal functioning; Zimmermann et al., 2015).

Results are also variable for studies examining the incremental validity of the AMPD. For example, while some research has shown support for the incremental validity of severity (Criterion A) over pathological traits (Criterion B) when predicting the presence of a PD diagnosis (e.g., Cruitt et al., 2019), personality dynamics in daily life (Roche, 2018; Roche et al., 2018), symptom distress and maladaptive schemas (Bach & Hutsebaut, 2018), substance use and physical health (Cruitt et al., 2019), well-being (Bach & Hutsebaut, 2018; Huprich et al., 2018), and interpersonal dependency (Huprich et al., 2018), the effect sizes were small. In contrast, other studies were unable to find significant incremental validity for severity ratings (Criterion A) over pathological personality traits (Criterion B) when predicting PD diagnosis (Few et al., 2013) and problematic alcohol use (Creswell et al., 2016).

Interestingly, Rodriguez-Seijas et al. (2019) argued that the utility of both Criterion A and Criterion B might be in their differential consequences for treatment. For example, attending to impairments in self- and interpersonal functioning (Criterion A) may have important implications for the formation of a therapeutic alliance, whereas specific maladaptive personality traits (Criterion B) may suggest specific therapeutic intervention techniques are necessary. As such, further research is necessary to examine the relative importance and distinctiveness of Criteria A and B for clinical practice.

THE AMPD IN CLINICAL PRACTICE

When the AMPD was first introduced, many clinicians worried that a dimensional model would be burdensome and less clinically relevant (e.g., Clarkin & Huprich, 2011). Shedler and colleagues (2010) commented, "The proposed system for classifying PD is too complicated, includes a trait-based approach to diagnosis without a clinical rationale, and omits personality syndromes that have clinical utility" (p. 1026). However, as Mullins-Sweatt et al. (2016) noted, there is limited research supporting the clinical usefulness of the traditional categorical PD model.

To address the initial concerns from clinicians, Morey et al. (2013) conducted a study in which they surveyed 337 mental health professionals (63% psychologists, 26% psychiatrists, and 11% other professionals) and asked them to provide both *DSM-IV* PD ratings and *DSM-5* AMPD ratings on one of their patients. Clinicians were then asked to rate the clinical utility of each diagnostic system on the following dimensions: communication with patients and other professionals, comprehensiveness, descriptiveness, ease of use, and utility for treatment planning. Results showed that AMPD Criterion B was rated as more clinically helpful than the *DSM-IV* PD model for all dimensions except ease of use. This result has been supported by more recent research showing that dimensional models of personality are often rated as more clinically useful than PD categories (Bornstein & Natoli, 2019). However, Morey et al. (2013) also found that AMPD Criterion A was rated as less easy to use and less useful for communication with other professionals than the *DSM-IV* PD categories, which is likely because of the novelty of Criterion A ratings for most mental health professionals at the time that *DSM-5* was published, and that study was conducted in 2013.

Subsequent research has shown that the AMPD, including Criterion A, is easily understood and can be learned and used reliably with minimal training (Few et al., 2013; Zimmermann et al., 2014). In addition, one of the strengths of the AMPD is that it is structured around the major paradigms of personality assessment (Waugh et al., 2017), which are already familiar to most mental health professionals and facilitate the learning and application of the model. Mulay and colleagues (2018) examined the inclusion of the five major personality assessment paradigms (e.g., psychodynamic, interpersonal, personological, empirical, multivariate) within the AMPD model and found that Criterion A had strong representation from the psychodynamic and personological paradigms, and the multivariate and empirical paradigms were represented in Criterion B. Results also indicated that the interpersonal paradigm could be found across both Criterion A and Criterion B. This supports the work of Hopwood et al. (2013), who argued that PD is fundamentally interpersonal in nature. The Mulay et al. study also provided additional support for Waugh and colleagues (2017), who noted that the AMPD retains a traditional foundation of psychological knowledge while also moving PD diagnosis forward.

As Cain (2019) noted, another significant contribution of the AMPD is that clinicians and researchers can move away from existing PD categories to more accurately diagnose personality pathology. For example, there have been a plethora of critiques of the *DSM-IV/DSM-5* Section II diagnosis of narcissistic personality disorder (NPD; see Cain et al., 2008, for a review). Clinicians and researchers have long argued that the NPD diagnosis does not cover the full scope of impairment associated with pathological narcissism. Specifically, pathological narcissism is thought to encompass two broad phenotypic expressions: *narcissistic grandiosity*, which reflects grandiose fantasies, exploitation, and entitlement; and *narcissistic vulnerability*, which reflects contingent self-esteem, shame, and hiding the self when expectations for self and others are not met. Cain and colleagues (2008) noted that while narcissistic grandiosity is well represented by the categorical NPD diagnosis, features of narcissistic vulnerability are left out of the traditional *DSM* criteria for NPD.

One of the advantages of the AMPD is that through its emphasis on self- and interpersonal impairment as well as on pathological traits, it allows for the diagnosis of NPD when narcissistic vulnerability is prominent, which fits more closely with the typical clinical presentation of pathological narcissism. For example, Cain (2019) noted that Criterion A provides an opportunity for clinicians to diagnose pathological narcissism when self-esteem is either too high or too low as well as when expectations for others are either too high or too low based on entitled needs. Cain (2019) further noted that Criterion B allows for trait-level grandiosity that may be both overt or covert (Pincus et al., 2016). Because the AMPD allows clinicians to better diagnose pathological narcissism, much of the clinical literature on the AMPD often includes NPD as an example of improved clinical utility (e.g., Morey & Stagner, 2012; Pincus et al., 2016; Waugh et al., 2017).

Cain (2019) argued that the AMPD can also have a key impact on treatment planning. Mullins-Sweatt and colleagues (2016) highlighted that one limitation of the *DSM* categorical model is that there has never been a strong pathway between diagnosis and treatment planning. Because the AMPD incorporates aspects of many different theoretical models for PD, it offers an exciting opportunity for more transdiagnostic treatments for PD (Cain, 2019). For example, Pincus et al. (2020) noted that many psychodynamic (e.g., transference-focused psychotherapy and mentalization-based therapy) and cognitive behavior (e.g., schema-focused therapy) treatments for PD focus on clarifying how a patient thinks about self and other, which are directly related to Criterion A. Dialectical behavior therapy also involves the teaching of skills, such as mindfulness, validation, acceptance, emotion regulation, distress tolerance, and interpersonal effectiveness, to promote better self- and interpersonal functioning. With regard to Criterion B, Hopwood (2018) noted that understanding maladaptive personality traits could also lead to the differential selection of treatments for PD. For example, a behavioral approach may be considered favorable for a PD profile high in negative affectivity, whereas skills related to interpersonal effectiveness might be warranted for those with elevated antagonism and detachment.

Cain (2019) argued that the AMPD is also consistent with psychotherapy integration. Specifically, Clarkin et al. (2015) articulated an integrated modular treatment for PD that emphasizes the needs of the individual patient over the categorical diagnosis; the severity of impairment and the specific trait-level manifestation of impairment similar to Criteria A and B, respectively; the use of evidence-based treatment models; and the importance of the therapeutic alliance. As an increasing number of clinicians begin to use the AMPD for treatment planning for PD patients, it will be necessary for empirical investigations to examine how to best target Criteria A and B using new and existing treatment models (Cain, 2019).

FUTURE DIRECTIONS AND CONCLUDING COMMENTS

To date, Criteria A and B of the AMPD have offered a psychometrically strong and clinically useful alternative to the *DSM* categorical diagnosis of PD. Clinical experience and empirical evidence highlight the difficulties posed by the traditional categorical approach, including diagnostic comorbidity, arbitrary diagnostic thresholds, heterogeneity within PD categories, and the frequent use of the NOS label. Although diagnostic categories are undoubtedly useful for ease of communication within health care settings, such an approach tends to distill personality dysfunction to a simple diagnostic impression rather than to a nuanced understanding of specific personality dysfunction (e.g., the severity of personality disturbance) and the presence maladaptive personality traits. Furthermore, the use of categories in health care settings appears to be dictated by health insurance companies and health care institutions, which forces the clinician into using a diagnostic scheme that has minimal research support. As Hopwood,

Kotov, et al. (2018) noted, the fields of psychology and psychiatry should be concerned about continuing to propagate a diagnostic approach that has significant empirical and clinical limitations.

Future research should continue to assess the psychometric properties of Criteria A and B of the AMPD across community and clinical settings as a way to encourage the use of this emerging diagnostic model. An additional important line of research would be to examine the real-time use of this model in health care settings, including clinician reactions to the ease (or difficulty) of using the model in the "real world." At this point, theoretical papers offer the clinician useful ways to integrate the AMPD with psychotherapy intervention techniques (e.g., Hopwood, 2018; Pincus et al., 2020; Rodriguez-Seijas et al., 2019); thus, a continued dialogue and empirical examination of clinical outcomes using the AMPD would be beneficial. Measures of Criteria A and B would also benefit from further examination and the creation of validity scales, which would allow for the use of these measures in broader contexts, such as forensic evaluations in which a respondent might be motivated to respond in socially desirable ways.

The *DSM-5* AMPD has significantly addressed the many limitations of *DSM* categorical PD diagnosis. The theoretical and empirical support for the AMPD, as well as its clinical applications, suggests that it offers a pantheoretical approach to the complexity of personality pathology. As such, the AMPD has advanced the fields of psychology and psychiatry.

REFERENCES

Al-Dajani, N., Gralnick, T. M., & Bagby, R. M. (2016). A psychometric review of the Personality Inventory for *DSM-5* (PID-5): Current status and future directions. *Journal of Personality Assessment, 98*(1), 62–81. https://doi.org/10.1080/00223891.2015.1107572 (Erratum published 2018, *Journal of Personality Assessment, 100*(4), p. 448)

American Psychiatric Association. (1980). *Diagnostic and statistical manual of mental disorders* (3rd ed.).

American Psychiatric Association. (1987). *Diagnostic and statistical manual of mental disorders* (3rd ed., rev.).

American Psychiatric Association. (1994). *Diagnostic and statistical manual of mental disorders* (4th ed.).

American Psychiatric Association. (2000). *Diagnostic and statistical manual of mental disorders* (4th ed., text rev.).

American Psychiatric Association. (2013). *Diagnostic and statistical manual of mental disorders* (5th ed.). https://doi.org/10.1176/appi.books.9780890425596

Bach, B., & Hutsebaut, J. (2018). Level of Personality Functioning Scale–Brief Form 2.0: Utility in capturing personality problems in psychiatric outpatients and incarcerated addicts. *Journal of Personality Assessment, 100*(6), 660–670. https://doi.org/10.1080/00223891.2018.1428984

Bagby, R. M., & Sellbom, M. (2018). The validity and clinical utility of the Personality Inventory for *DSM-5* Response Inconsistency Scale. *Journal of Personality Assessment, 100*(4), 398–405. https://doi.org/10.1080/00223891.2017.1420659

Bender, D. S., Morey, L. C., & Skodol, A. E. (2011). Toward a model for assessing level of personality functioning in *DSM-5*, Part I: A review of theory and methods. *Journal of Personality Assessment, 93*(4), 332–346. https://doi.org/10.1080/00223891.2011.583808

Bender, D. S., Skodol, A., First, M. B., & Oldham, J. (2018). Module I: Structured Clinical Interview for the Level of Personality Functioning Scale. In M. B. First, A. Skodol, D. S. Bender, & J. Oldham (Eds.), *Structured Clinical Interview for the* DSM-5 *Alternative Model for Personality Disorders (SCID-AMPD)* (pp. 5–56). American Psychiatric Association.

Ben-Porath, Y. S., & Tellegen, A. (2011). *Minnesota Multiphasic Personality Inventory–2– Restructured Form: Manual for administration, scoring, and interpretation.* University of Minnesota Press. (Original work published 2008)

Bornstein, R. F., & Natoli, A. P. (2019). Clinical utility of categorical and dimensional perspectives on personality pathology: A meta-analytic review. *Personality Disorders, 10*(6), 479–490. https://doi.org/10.1037/per0000365

Buer Christensen, T., Paap, M. C. S., Arnesen, M., Koritzinsky, K., Nysaeter, T.-E., Eikenaes, I., Germans Selvik, S., Walther, K., Torgersen, S., Bender, D. S., Skodol, A. E., Kvarstein, E., Pedersen, G., & Hummelen, B. (2018). Interrater reliability of the Structured Clinical Interview for the *DSM-5* Alternative Model of Personality Disorders module I: Level of Personality Functioning Scale. *Journal of Personality Assessment, 100*(6), 630–641. https://doi.org/10.1080/00223891.2018.1483377

Busmann, M., Wrege, J., Meyer, A. H., Ritzler, F., Schmidlin, M., Lang, U. E., Gaab, J., Walter, M., & Euler, S. (2019). Alternative Model of Personality Disorders (*DSM-5*) predicts dropout in inpatient psychotherapy for patients with personality disorder. *Frontiers in Psychology, 10,* Article 952. https://doi.org/10.3389/fpsyg.2019.00952

Cain, N. M. (2019). Concluding comments: The value of AMPD diagnosis. In C. J. Hopwood, A. Mulay, & M. Waugh (Eds.), *The* DSM-5 *Alternative Model for Personality Disorders: Integrating multiple paradigms of personality assessment* (pp. 221–228). Taylor & Francis. https://doi.org/10.4324/9781315205076-10

Cain, N. M., Pincus, A. L., & Ansell, E. B. (2008). Narcissism at the crossroads: Phenotypic description of pathological narcissism across clinical theory, social/personality psychology, and psychiatric diagnosis. *Clinical Psychology Review, 28*(4), 638–656. https://doi.org/10.1016/j.cpr.2007.09.006

Clarkin, J. F., Cain, N., & Livesley, W. J. (2015). An integrated approach to treatment of patients with personality disorders. *Journal of Psychotherapy Integration, 25*(1), 3–12. https://doi.org/10.1037/a0038766

Clarkin, J. F., & Huprich, S. K. (2011). Do *DSM-5* personality disorder proposals meet criteria for clinical utility? *Journal of Personality Disorders, 25*(2), 192–205. https://doi.org/10.1521/pedi.2011.25.2.192

Coolidge, F. L. (2020). *Coolidge Axis II Inventory: Manual.* Author.

Costa, P. T., & McCrae, R. R. (1992). *Revised NEO Personality Inventory: Professional manual.* Psychological Assessment Resources.

Creswell, K. G., Bachrach, R. L., Wright, A. G. C., Pinto, A., & Ansell, E. (2016). Predicting problematic alcohol use with the *DSM-5* alternative model of personality pathology. *Personality Disorders, 7*(1), 103–111. https://doi.org/10.1037/per0000131

Cruitt, P. J., Boudreaux, M. J., King, H. R., Oltmanns, J. R., & Oltmanns, T. F. (2019). Examining Criterion A: *DSM-5* level of personality functioning as assessed through life story interviews. *Personality Disorders, 10*(3), 224–234. https://doi.org/10.1037/per0000321

Dowgwillo, E. A., Roche, M. J., & Pincus, A. L. (2018). Examining the interpersonal nature of Criterion A of the *DSM-5* Section III Alternative Model for Personality Disorders using bootstrapped confidence intervals for the interpersonal circumplex. *Journal of Personality Assessment, 100*(6), 581–592. https://doi.org/10.1080/00223891.2018.1464016

Drislane, L. E., Sellbom, M., Brislin, S. J., Strickland, C. M., Christian, E., Wygant, D. B., Krueger, R. F., & Patrick, C. J. (2019). Improving characterization of psychopathy within the *Diagnostic and Statistical Manual of Mental Disorders,* fifth edition (*DSM–5*), Alternative Model for Personality Disorders: Creation and validation of Personality

Inventory for *DSM–5* Triarchic scales. *Personality Disorders: Theory, Research, Treatment, 10*(6), 511–523. https://doi.org/10.1037/per0000345

Few, L. R., Miller, J. D., Rothbaum, A. O., Meller, S., Maples, J., Terry, D. P., Collins, B., & MacKillop, J. (2013). Examination of the Section III *DSM-5* diagnostic system for personality disorders in an outpatient clinical sample. *Journal of Abnormal Psychology, 122*(4), 1057–1069. https://doi.org/10.1037/a0034878

First, M. B., Gibbon, M., Spitzer, R. L., & Williams, J. B. (2002). *Structured Clinical Interview for DSM-IV Axis II Personality Disorders (SCID-II).* American Psychiatric Association.

Fowler, J. C., Madan, A., Allen, J. G., Patriquin, M., Sharp, C., Oldham, J. M., & Frueh, B. C. (2018). Clinical utility of the *DSM-5* alternative model for borderline personality disorder: Differential diagnostic accuracy of the BFI, SCID-II-PQ, and PID-5. *Comprehensive Psychiatry, 80*, 97–103. https://doi.org/10.1016/j.comppsych.2017.09.003

Hopwood, C. J. (2018). A framework for treating *DSM-5* alternative model for personality disorder features. *Personality and Mental Health, 12*(2), 107–125. https://doi.org/10.1002/pmh.1414

Hopwood, C. J. (2019). Research and assessment with the AMPD. In C. J. Hopwood, A. L. Mulay, & M. H. Waugh (Eds.), *The DSM-5 Alternative Model for Personality Disorders: Integrating multiple paradigms of personality assessment* (pp. 77–95). Routledge. https://doi.org/10.4324/9781315205076-4

Hopwood, C. J., Good, E. W., & Morey, L. C. (2018). Validity of the *DSM-5* Levels of Personality Functioning Scale–Self Report. *Journal of Personality Assessment, 100*(6), 650–659. https://doi.org/10.1080/00223891.2017.1420660

Hopwood, C. J., Kotov, R., Krueger, R. F., Watson, D., Widiger, T. A., Althoff, R. R., Ansell, E. B., Bach, B., Michael Bagby, R., Blais, M. A., Bornovalova, M. A., Chmielewski, M., Cicero, D. C., Conway, C., De Clercq, B., De Fruyt, F., Docherty, A. R., Eaton, N. R., Edens, J. F., . . . Zimmermann, J. (2018). The time has come for dimensional personality disorder diagnosis. *Personality and Mental Health, 12*(1), 82–86. https://doi.org/10.1002/pmh.1408

Hopwood, C. J., Wright, A. G., Ansell, E. B., & Pincus, A. L. (2013). The interpersonal core of personality pathology. *Journal of Personality Disorders, 27*(3), 270–295. https://doi.org/10.1521/pedi.2013.27.3.270

Huprich, S. K., Nelson, S. M., Meehan, K. B., Siefert, C. J., Haggerty, G., Sexton, J., Dauphin, V. B., Macaluso, M., Jackson, J., Zackula, R., & Baade, L. (2018). Introduction of the *DSM-5* Levels of Personality Functioning Questionnaire. *Personality Disorders, 9*(6), 553–563. https://doi.org/10.1037/per0000264

Hutsebaut, J., Feenstra, D. J., & Kamphuis, J. H. (2016). Development and preliminary psychometric evaluation of a brief self-report questionnaire for the assessment of the *DSM-5* Level of Personality Functioning Scale: The LPFS Brief Form (LPFS-BF). *Personality Disorders, 7*(2), 192–197. https://doi.org/10.1037/per0000159

Hutsebaut, J., Kamphuis, J. H., Feenstra, D. J., Weekers, L. C., & De Saeger, H. (2017). Assessing *DSM-5*-oriented level of personality functioning: Development and psychometric evaluation of the Semi-Structured Interview for Personality Functioning *DSM-5* (STiP-5.1). *Personality Disorders, 8*(1), 94–101. https://doi.org/10.1037/per0000197

Keeley, J. W., Webb, C., Peterson, D., Roussin, L., & Flanagan, E. H. (2016). Development of a response inconsistency scale for the Personality Inventory for *DSM-5*. *Journal of Personality Assessment, 98*(4), 351–359. https://doi.org/10.1080/00223891.2016.1158719

Krueger, R. F. (2019). Criterion B of the AMPD and the interpersonal, multivariate, and empirical paradigms of personality assessment. In C. J. Hopwood, A. L. Mulay, & M. H. Waugh (Eds.), *The DSM-5 Alternative Model for Personality Disorders: Integrating multiple paradigms of personality assessment* (pp. 60–76). Routledge. https://doi.org/10.4324/9781315205076-3

Krueger, R. F., Derringer, J., Markon, K. E., Watson, D., & Skodol, A. E. (2012). Initial construction of a maladaptive personality trait model and inventory for *DSM-5*. *Psychological Medicine, 42*(9), 1879–1890. https://doi.org/10.1017/S0033291711002674

Krueger, R. F., & Hobbs, K. A. (2020). An overview of the *DSM-5* Alternative Model of Personality Disorders. *Psychopathology, 53*(3-4), 126–132. https://doi.org/10.1159/000508538

Krueger, R. F., & Markon, K. E. (2014). The role of the *DSM-5* personality trait model in moving toward a quantitative and empirically based approach to classifying personality and psychopathology. *Annual Review of Clinical Psychology, 10*(1), 477–501. https://doi.org/10.1146/annurev-clinpsy-032813-153732

Markon, K. E., Quilty, L. C., Bagby, R. M., & Krueger, R. F. (2013). The development and psychometric properties of an informant-report form of the Personality Inventory for *DSM-5* (PID-5). *Assessment, 20*(3), 370–383. https://doi.org/10.1177/1073191113486513

McGee Ng, S. A., Bagby, R. M., Goodwin, B. E., Burchett, D., Sellbom, M., Ayearst, L. E., Dhillon, S., Yiu, S., Ben-Porath, Y. S., & Baker, S. (2016). The effect of response bias on the Personality Inventory for *DSM-5* (PID-5). *Journal of Personality Assessment, 98*(1), 51–61. https://doi.org/10.1080/00223891.2015.1096791

Morey, L. C. (2017). Development and initial evaluation of a self-report form of the *DSM-5* Level of Personality Functioning Scale. *Psychological Assessment, 29*(10), 1302–1308. https://doi.org/10.1037/pas0000450

Morey, L. C. (2018). Application of the *DSM-5* Level of Personality Functioning Scale by lay raters. *Journal of Personality Disorders, 32*(5), 709–720. https://doi.org/10.1521/pedi_2017_31_305

Morey, L. C. (2019). Interdiagnostician reliability of the *DSM-5* Section II and Section III alternative model criteria for borderline personality disorder. *Journal of Personality Disorders, 33*(6), 721–S18. https://doi.org/10.1521/pedi_2019_33_362

Morey, L. C., Bender, D. S., & Skodol, A. E. (2013). Validating the proposed *Diagnostic and Statistical Manual of Mental Disorders*, 5th edition, severity indicator for personality disorder. *Journal of Nervous and Mental Disease, 201*(9), 729–735. https://doi.org/10.1097/NMD.0b013e3182a20ea8

Morey, L. C., Skodol, A. E., & Oldham, J. M. (2014). Clinician judgments of clinical utility: A comparison of *DSM-IV-TR* personality disorders and the Alternative Model for *DSM-5* Personality Disorders. *Journal of Abnormal Psychology, 123*(2), 398–405. https://doi.org/10.1037/a0036481

Morey, L. C., & Stagner, B. H. (2012). Narcissistic pathology as core personality dysfunction: Comparing the *DSM-IV* and the *DSM-5* proposal for narcissistic personality disorder. *Journal of Clinical Psychology, 68*(8), 908–921. https://doi.org/10.1002/jclp.21895

Mulay, A. L., Cain, N. M., Waugh, M. H., Hopwood, C. J., Adler, J. M., Garcia, D. J., Kurtz, J. E., Lenger, K. A., & Skadberg, R. (2018). Personality constructs and paradigms in the Alternative *DSM-5* Model of Personality Disorder. *Journal of Personality Assessment, 100*(6), 593–602. https://doi.org/10.1080/00223891.2018.1477787

Mullins-Sweatt, S. N., Lengel, G. J., & DeShong, H. L. (2016). The importance of considering clinical utility in the construction of a diagnostic manual. *Annual Review of Clinical Psychology, 12*(1), 133–155. https://doi.org/10.1146/annurev-clinpsy-021815-092954

Nelson, S. M., Huprich, S. K., Meehan, K. B., Siefert, C., Haggerty, G., Sexton, J., Dauphin, V. B., Macaluso, M., Zackula, R., Baade, L., & Jackson, J. (2018). Convergent and discriminant validity and utility of the *DSM-5* Levels of Personality Functioning Questionnaire (DLOPFQ): Associations with medical health care provider ratings and measures of physical health. *Journal of Personality Assessment, 100*(6), 671–679. https://doi.org/10.1080/00223891.2018.1492415

Patrick, C. J., Fowles, D. C., & Krueger, R. F. (2009). Triarchic conceptualization of psychopathy: Developmental origins of disinhibition, boldness, and meanness. *Development and Psychopathology, 21*(3), 913–938. https://doi.org/10.1017/S0954579409000492

Pincus, A. L., Cain, N. M., & Halberstadt, A. L. (2020). Importance of self and other in defining personality pathology. *Psychopathology, 53*(3-4), 133–140. https://doi.org/10.1159/000506313

Pincus, A. L., Dowgwillo, E. A., & Greenberg, L. S. (2016). Three cases of narcissistic personality disorder through the lens of *DSM-5* Alternative Model for Personality Disorders. *Practice Innovations, 1*(3), 164–177. https://doi.org/10.1037/pri0000025

Roche, M. J. (2018). Examining the Alternative Model for Personality Disorder in daily life: Evidence for incremental validity. *Personality Disorders, 9*(6), 574–583. https://doi.org/10.1037/per0000295

Roche, M. J., Jacobson, N. C., & Phillips, J. J. (2018). Expanding the validity of the Level of Personality Functioning Scale observer report and self-report versions across psychodynamic and interpersonal paradigms. *Journal of Personality Assessment, 100*(6), 571–580. https://doi.org/10.1080/00223891.2018.1475394

Rodriguez-Seijas, C., Ruggero, C., Eaton, N. R., & Krueger, R. F. (2019). The *DSM-5* Alternative Model for Personality Disorders and clinical treatment: A review. *Current Treatment Options in Psychiatry, 6*(4), 284–298. https://doi.org/10.1007/s40501-019-00187-7

Sellbom, M., Dhillon, S., & Bagby, R. M. (2018). Development and validation of an Overreporting Scale for the Personality Inventory for *DSM-5* (PID-5). *Psychological Assessment, 30*(5), 582–593. https://doi.org/10.1037/pas0000507

Shedler, J., Beck, A., Fonagy, P., Gabbard, G. O., Gunderson, J., Kernberg, O., Michels, R., & Westen, D. (2010). Personality disorders in *DSM-5*. *The American Journal of Psychiatry, 167*(9), 1026–1028. https://doi.org/10.1176/appi.ajp.2010.10050746

Siefert, C. J., Sexton, J., Meehan, K., Nelson, S., Haggerty, G., Dauphin, B., & Huprich, S. (2020). Development of a short form for the *DSM-5* Levels of Personality Functioning Questionnaire. *Journal of Personality Assessment, 102*(4), 516–526. https://doi.org/10.1080/00223891.2019.1594842

Simms, L. J., Goldberg, L. R., Roberts, J. E., Watson, D., Welte, J., & Rotterman, J. H. (2011). Computerized adaptive assessment of personality disorder: Introducing the CAT-PD project. *Journal of Personality Assessment, 93*(4), 380–389. https://doi.org/10.1080/00223891.2011.577475

Skodol, A. E., Clark, L. A., Bender, D. S., Krueger, R. F., Morey, L. C., Verheul, R., Alarcon, R. D., Bell, C. C., Siever, L. J., & Oldham, J. M. (2011). Proposed changes in personality and personality disorder assessment and diagnosis for *DSM-5* Part I: Description and rationale. *Personality Disorders, 2*(1), 4–22. https://doi.org/10.1037/a0021891

Skodol, A. E., First, M. B., Bender, D. S., & Oldham, J. M. (2017). *Structured Clinical Interview for the* DSM-5 *Alternative Model for Personality Disorders*. American Psychiatric Association.

Stone, L. E., & Segal, D. L. (2021). An empirical evaluation of the *DSM-5* Alternative Model for Personality Disorders in later life. *The International Journal of Aging and Human Development, 93*(3), 904–926. https://doi.org/10.1177/0091415020980762

Trull, T. J., & Widiger, T. A. (2013). Dimensional models of personality: The five-factor model and the *DSM-5*. *Dialogues in Clinical Neuroscience, 15*(2), 135–146. https://doi.org/10.31887/DCNS.2013.15.2/ttrull

Watters, C. A., & Bagby, R. M. (2018). A meta-analysis of the five-factor internal structure of the Personality Inventory for *DSM-5*. *Psychological Assessment, 30*(9), 1255–1260. https://doi.org/10.1037/pas0000605

Watters, C. A., Sellbom, M., Uliaszek, A. A., & Bagby, R. M. (2019). Clarifying the interstitial nature of facets from the Personality Inventory for *DSM-5* using the five factor model of personality. *Personality Disorders, 10*(4), 330–339. https://doi.org/10.1037/per0000327

Waugh, M. H., Hopwood, C. J., Krueger, R. F., Morey, L. C., Pincus, A. L., & Wright, A. G. C. (2017). Psychological assessment with the *DSM-5* Alternative Model for Personality Disorders: Tradition and innovation. *Professional Psychology: Research and Practice, 48*(2), 79–89. https://doi.org/10.1037/pro0000071

Weekers, L. C., Hutsebaut, J., & Kamphuis, J. H. (2019). The Level of Personality Functioning Scale–Brief Form 2.0: Update of a brief instrument for assessing level of personality functioning. *Personality and Mental Health, 13*(1), 3–14. https://doi.org/10.1002/pmh.1434

Widiger, T. A., Bach, B., Chmielewski, M., Clark, L. A., DeYoung, C., Hopwood, C. J., Kotov, R., Krueger, R. F., Miller, J. D., Morey, L. C., Mullins-Sweatt, S. N., Patrick, C. J., Pincus, A. L., Samuel, D. B., Sellbom, M., South, S. C., Tackett, J. L., Watson, D., Waugh, M. H., . . . Thomas, K. M. (2019). Criterion A of the AMPD in HiTOP. *Journal of Personality Assessment, 101*(4), 345–355. https://doi.org/10.1080/00223891.2018.1465431

Widiger, T. A., & McCabe, G. A. (2020). The Alternative Model of Personality Disorders (AMPD) from the perspective of the five-factor model. *Psychopathology, 53*(3-4), 149–156. https://doi.org/10.1159/000507378

Zachar, P., Krueger, R. F., & Kendler, K. S. (2016). Personality disorder in *DSM-5*: An oral history. *Psychological Medicine, 46*(1), 1–10. https://doi.org/10.1017/S0033291715001543

Zimmermann, J., Benecke, C., Bender, D. S., Skodol, A. E., Schauenburg, H., Cierpka, M., & Leising, D. (2014). Assessing *DSM-5* level of personality functioning from videotaped clinical interviews: A pilot study with untrained and clinically inexperienced students. *Journal of Personality Assessment, 96*(4), 397–409. https://doi.org/10.1080/00223891.2013.852563

Zimmermann, J., Böhnke, J. R., Eschstruth, R., Mathews, A., Wenzel, K., & Leising, D. (2015). The latent structure of personality functioning: Investigating criterion a from the Alternative Model for Personality Disorders in *DSM-5*. *Journal of Abnormal Psychology, 124*(3), 532–548. https://doi.org/10.1037/abn0000059

Zimmermann, J., Kerber, A., Rek, K., Hopwood, C. J., & Krueger, R. F. (2019). A brief but comprehensive review of research on the Alternative *DSM-5* Model for Personality Disorders. *Current Psychiatry Reports, 21*(9), Article 92. https://doi.org/10.1007/s11920-019-1079-z

2

Empirical Foundation of the *ICD-11* Classification of Personality Disorders

Bo Bach and Roger Mulder

The *International Statistical Classification of Diseases and Related Health Problems* (11th ed.; *ICD-11*; World Health Organization [WHO], 2019) classifies personality disorders (PD) according to severity, followed by the option of coding one or more trait domain specifiers that contribute to the individual expression of personality dysfunction (see the outline in Table 2.1). Thus, the *ICD-11* PD classification can be said to abolish all type-specific PD categories apart from the main one—the presence of PD itself. Nevertheless, the practitioner is also allowed to specify a borderline pattern specifier consistent with the historically well-established Borderline PD type. (Note: For this chapter, we have used the full clinical version of *ICD-11*'s specific section for mental disorders, titled the *ICD-11 Clinical Descriptions and Diagnostic Guidelines for Mental and Behavioural Disorders* [WHO, 2022], which is intended specifically for clinical practitioners.)

After a brief historical–scientific record of how the model has evolved, this chapter focuses on the now official *ICD-11* PD model and the emerging research that has been conducted in relation to it. We specifically aim to provide an overview of the empirical validity and utility of the *ICD-11* PD classification. Based on its similarities (and boundaries) with the *Diagnostic and Statistical Manual of Mental Disorders* (5th ed.; *DSM-5*; American Psychiatric Association, 2013) Alternative *DSM-5* Model of Personality Disorders (AMPD), we derive some of its empirical support from the large body of existing research on the AMPD framework. In other words, the empirical foundation for the *ICD-11* PD classification goes far beyond the limited but emerging research that is explicitly devoted to the *ICD-11*.

---

https://doi.org/10.1037/0000310-003
Personality Disorders and Pathology: Integrating Clinical Assessment and Practice in the DSM-5 *and* ICD-11 *Era*, S. K. Huprich (Editor)
Copyright © 2022 by the American Psychological Association. All rights reserved.

TABLE 2.1. Alignment Between *ICD-11* and *DSM-5* AMPD Personality Disorder Models

ICD-11 severity of personality dysfunction	*DSM-5* Criterion A: Level of personality functioning
None	0) No impairment (healthy functioning)
Personality Difficulty	1) Some impairment
Mild PD	2) Moderate impairment
Moderate PD	3) Severe impairment
Severe PD	4) Extreme impairment
ICD-11 trait domain specifiers	***DSM-5* Criterion B: Trait domains**
Negative Affectivity	Negative Affectivity
Detachment	Detachment
Disinhibition	Disinhibition
Dissociality	Antagonism
Anankastia	(Rigid Perfectionism)
(Schizotypal Disorder)	Psychoticism
Continuity with clinical practice	**Hybrid types**
Borderline pattern specifier	Antisocial, Avoidant, Borderline, Narcissistic, Obsessive-Compulsive, Schizotypal, Trait-Specified

Note. The dashed line represents the threshold for a PD diagnosis. *ICD-11* = *International Statistical Classification of Diseases and Related Health Problems* (11th ed.); *DSM-5* = *Diagnostic and Statistical Manual of Mental Disorders* (5th ed.). Data from World Health Organization (2019) and American Psychiatric Association (2013).

REASONS FOR A NEW CLASSIFICATION OF PERSONALITY DISORDERS IN *ICD-11*

The shortcomings of the established classification of PD types have been recognized since at least the 1970s, while the *DSM-II* and *ICD-9* were employed (Frances, 1980; Tyrer & Alexander, 1979). These shortcomings were empirically corroborated in the subsequent years, suggesting that a dimensional approach to PDs is most appropriate (Ekselius et al., 1993; Frances, 1982; Fyer et al., 1988). It is now well established that the categorical PD diagnoses suffer from excessive co-occurrence, heterogeneity, and pseudoaccurate thresholds, among other issues (Hopwood et al., 2018; Skodol, 2012). Thus, when the WHO released the 10th revision of the *International Statistical Classification of Diseases* (*ICD-10* ["Blue Book"]; 1994), certain nosological issues with "disorder of adult personality (F60)" were emphasized, and it was explicitly acknowledged that "a new approach to the description of personality disorders is required" (p. 20).

Consequently, in recent years, the WHO PD working group has drawn the obvious conclusions of *DSM-5*'s movement toward dimensions (see Chapter 1, this volume) by including a fully dimensional classification system for PDs in *ICD-11*, which has been approved by the World Health Assembly and must be used for coding purposes by WHO member states. As we highlight in the present chapter, the aforementioned *DSM-5* AMPD framework can, to a large extent, be converted or translated into the *ICD-11* PD model. Thus, the large body of research on the AMPD is being highlighted as part of the empirical foundation of the *ICD-11* PD approach.

FROM INITIAL DRAFTS TO THE FINALLY APPROVED MODEL

The earliest foundation of the initial proposal for a revision of the *ICD-10* PD classification was centered on the Personality Assessment Schedule (PAS; Tyrer & Alexander, 1979), originally developed in 1976, which allowed the user to evaluate both trait-like features and overall severity of personality dysfunction. Later, Tyrer and Johnson (1996) developed an algorithm for *DSM-IV* that allowed practitioners to estimate PD severity primarily based on the complexity or constellation of co-occurring *DSM-IV* PDs. To further support routine PD assessment, another British group developed a screening instrument for general PD features, entitled the Standardized Assessment of Personality–Abbreviated Scale (SAPAS; Moran et al., 2003).[1]

In December 2004, a conference was cosponsored by the WHO, the American Psychiatric Association, and the National Institute of Mental Health to review the limitations of the *DSM-IV* and *ICD-10* classification systems and to recommend a research agenda aimed at incorporating a dimensional approach in the future (E. Simonsen & Tyrer, 2005). Six years later, the World Psychiatric Association Section on PDs examined new ways of classifying PDs, using a simpler dimensional approach based on overall severity and specific domain specifiers that could be applied across all cultural settings (Tyrer et al., 2010). For this purpose, the appointed *ICD-11* work group members conducted a systematic review of the scientific literature on classifying PD according to severity (Crawford et al., 2011) and trait domains (Mulder et al., 2011).

Between 2011 and 2015, an initial draft of the *ICD-11* PD classification was presented in scientific journals (Tyrer, Crawford, Mulder, et al., 2011; Tyrer, Crawford, Mulder, & the *ICD-11* Working Group for the Revision of Classification of Personality Disorders, 2011; Tyrer et al., 2015). Between 2014 and 2016, preliminary studies were conducted and published, however, with different methodological approaches and mixed findings (Kim et al., 2014, 2015, 2016; Mulder et al., 2016; Tyrer et al., 2014). For example, it was not straightforward to identify distinct trait domain features of Disinhibition and Negative Affectivity, apparently because the research relied on data from SCID-II interviews (First et al., 1997) with insufficient indicators of such features (Mulder et al., 2016). Simultaneously, this initial draft received both negative and positive feedback from clinicians and researchers (Bateman, 2011; Bornstein, 2016; Davidson, 2011; Ekselius, 2016; Fineberg et al., 2014; E. Simonsen, 2011). For example, some considered it to be too minimalistic and thought that dropping the established categories was "throwing out the baby with the bath water" (e.g., Bateman, 2011).

---

[1]The SAPAS later served as the foundation for the Standardized Assessment of Severity of Personality Disorder (SASPD; Olajide et al., 2018), which was specifically developed for the initial *ICD-11* PD proposal.

Again, just before the World Health Assembly's final approval of the entire *ICD-11* draft, representatives from the European Society for the Study of Personality Disorders, the International Society for the Study of Personality Disorders, and the North American Society for the Study of Personality Disorders expressed their concern about this initial proposal (Herpertz et al., 2017). Among the most critical concerns was the missing possibility of diagnosing Borderline PD. As a result of further dialogues between *ICD-11* work group members and representatives from the aforementioned societies, a further modified solution was finally agreed upon (Huprich et al., 2018; Reed, 2018). Essentially, the model changed from focusing on interpersonal aspects of personality disturbance to focusing on both self- and interpersonal functioning, including the option of specifying a borderline pattern specifier. This final solution was also better aligned with the more comprehensive and detailed AMPD framework, including its growing body of research. In other words, the scientific foundation of the now approved *ICD-11* PD model is closely linked to the extensive scientific foundation of the AMPD model (Krueger & Hobbs, 2020). Thus, it is important to distinguish the initially proposed drafts from the finally approved version of the *ICD-11* PD classification.

For a more detailed overview of the entire scientific and political process, including the initial drafts of the proposed model, we refer to Tyrer et al. (2019) and Huprich (2020).

SIMILARITIES AND BOUNDARIES BETWEEN *ICD-11* AND *DSM-5* AMPD

As illustrated in Table 2.1, the *ICD-11* and *DSM-5* AMPD approaches to PDs are comparable overall with respect to both severity and trait descriptors (except for the trait domain of Psychoticism), which is analogous to the overall comparability between *ICD-10* and *DSM-IV* categorical approaches to PDs. These similarities (and differences) are important for allowing the large body of research supporting the *DSM-5* AMPD model to be generalized to the *ICD-11* PD model. Table 2.2 organizes all capacities of personality functioning across *ICD-11* and *DSM-5* AMPD according to their affiliations with identity, self-direction, empathy, and intimacy. Table 2.3 shows a tentative crosswalk between *ICD-11*, *DSM-5* AMPD, and Kernberg's traditional model of personality organization (Caligor et al., 2018), exemplified with specific impairments of identity functioning.

Beyond the overall similarities, the *ICD-11* model provides elaborated and empirically informed guidelines for the determination of PD severity (Crawford et al., 2011; Sleep et al., 2021), which do not contradict the AMPD features of personality functioning but seem to expand them. Accordingly, the *ICD-11* provides a separate list of explicit emotional manifestations (e.g., ability to recognize unwanted emotions), cognitive manifestations (e.g., accuracy of situational and interpersonal appraisals under stress), and behavioral manifestations (e.g., appropriate behavioral responses to intense emotions) of personality dysfunction that contribute to the severity determination. Thus, the *ICD-11* determination

Empirical Foundation of the ICD-11 Classification of Personality Disorders   31

TABLE 2.2. Comparative Overview of Personality Functioning Across *ICD-11* and *DSM-5* AMPD

	ICD-11	*DSM-5* AMPD
Self		
Identity	Stability and coherence of one's sense of identity (e.g., extent to which identity or sense of self is variable and inconsistent or overly rigid and fixed); ability to maintain an overall positive and stable sense of self-worth; accuracy of one's view of one's characteristics, strengths, limitations.	Experience of oneself as unique, with clear boundaries between self and others; stability of self-esteem and accuracy of self-appraisal; capacity for, and ability to regulate, a range of emotional experience.
Self-direction	Capacity for self-direction (ability to plan, choose, and implement appropriate goals).	Pursuit of coherent goals and meaningful short-term life goals; utilization of constructive and prosocial internal standards of behavior; ability to self-reflect productively.
Interpersonal		
Empathy	Ability to understand and appreciate others' perspectives.	Comprehension and appreciation of others' experiences and motivations; tolerance of differing perspectives; understanding the effects of one's own behavior on others.
Intimacy	Interest in engaging in relationships with others; ability to develop and maintain close and mutually satisfying relationships.	Depth and duration of connection with others; desire and capacity for closeness; mutuality of regard reflected in interpersonal behavior.

Note. ICD-11 = International Statistical Classification of Diseases and Related Health Problems (11th ed.); *DSM-5 = Diagnostic and Statistical Manual of Mental Disorders* (5th ed.); AMPD = Alternative *DSM-5* Model of Personality Disorders. Data from World Health Organization (2019) and American Psychiatric Association (2013).

of PD severity is also based on the accuracy of situational and interpersonal appraisals, especially under stress. Accordingly, Severe PD may include stress-related distortions in the individual's situational and interpersonal appraisals, which may involve dissociative states or psychotic-like beliefs and perceptions (e.g., extreme paranoid reactions). Such features of *ICD-11* PD severity typically apply to individuals with a highly vulnerable inner structure and strongly immature defenses when in unstructured situations or stressed out (Skodol et al., 2002). This may also be viewed as equivalent to the potential difficulties in reality testing and ideational clarity often seen in patients with Severe PD,

TABLE 2.3. Tentative Crosswalk for Severity of Impaired Personality Functioning in the Case of Identity

	ICD-11		*DSM-5* AMPD		STIPO
None	Stability and coherence of one's sense of identity.	0. None Healthy	Has ongoing awareness of a unique self; maintains role-appropriate boundaries.	Consolidated identity	Self-experience is very well integrated—coherent, complex, and continuous across time and situations.
Difficulty	Only intermittent (e.g., during times of stress) or low-intensity identity problems, without notable disruptions in life.	1. Some impairment	Has relatively intact sense of self, with some decrease in clarity of boundaries when strong emotions and mental distress are experienced.	Consolidated identity with some slight deficit	Self-experience is well integrated—coherent but with mild instability across time or mild, relatively stable distortion in sense of self.
Mild PD	The individual's sense of self may be somewhat contradictory and inconsistent with how others view them.	2. Moderate impairment	Depends excessively on others for identity definition, with compromised boundary delineation.	Mild identity pathology	Self-experience is somewhat poorly integrated—somewhat incoherent, superficial, or discontinuous and contradictory, with significant distortion.
Moderate PD	The individual's sense of self may become incoherent in times of crisis.	3. Severe impairment	Has a weak sense of autonomy/agency; experience of a lack of identity, or emptiness. Boundary definition is poor or rigid.	Moderate identity pathology	Self-experience is poorly integrated, unstable, incoherent, extremely superficial, or consistently grandiose or devalued.
Severe PD	The individual's self-view is very unrealistic and typically is highly unstable or internally contradictory.	4. Extreme impairment	Experience of a unique self and sense of agency/autonomy are virtually absent or are organized around perceived external persecution. Boundaries with others are confused or lacking.	Severe identity pathology	Self-experience is unintegrated—highly incoherent, especially superficial, discontinuous, and chaotically unstable with little to no sense of having a core "self."

Note. ICD-11 = International Statistical Classification of Diseases and Related Health Problems (11th ed.); *DSM-5 = Diagnostic and Statistical Manual of Mental Disorders* (5th ed.); AMPD = Alternative *DSM-5* Model of Personality Disorders; STIPO = Structured Interview for Personality Organization. Data from World Health Organization (2019), American Psychiatric Association (2013), Bender et al. (2011), and Krueger et al. (2012).

which has traditionally been characterized using the Perceptual Thinking Index (PTI) from Exner's Rorschach scoring system (Hilsenroth et al., 2007).

Moreover, instead of incorporating the capacity for emotion regulation as an aspect of self-functioning, the *ICD-11* presents this feature as a general emotional manifestation of personality disturbance (e.g., tendency to be emotionally over- or underreactive). As an aspect of behavioral manifestations, the *ICD-11* model also explicitly determines PD severity based on risk of harm to self or others. Finally, the *ICD-11* also determines global PD severity based on the complexity and pervasiveness of the disturbance. For example, manifestations of a Severe PD may affect most, if not all, areas of personality functioning (i.e., few healthy capacities), whereas a Mild PD may involve only some areas of functioning (i.e., more healthy capacities).

WHY INCLUDE A SEPARATE DOMAIN SPECIFIER OF ANANKASTIA?

The *ICD-11* trait domain of Anankastia corresponds to compulsivity, which was originally proposed as a distinct domain for the *DSM-5* trait model (Skodol et al., 2011). Eventually, the separate inclusion of this domain in *DSM-5* was abandoned in favor of parsimony (Krueger et al., 2012). Instead, the *DSM-5* AMPD defines features of Anankastia (e.g., rigid perfectionism) in terms of low Disinhibition, which is partially supported by empirical evidence (Bach & Zine El Abiddine, 2020; Watters & Bagby, 2018). Accordingly, emerging and compelling research on the *ICD-11* trait domains supports the bipolarity of one single Disinhibition-versus-Anankastia dimension (e.g., Gutiérrez et al., 2020; Oltmanns & Widiger, 2018). Nevertheless, other studies support a five-factor solution in which Anankastia and Disinhibition are two separate domains (e.g., Bach et al., 2017; Mulder et al., 2016; Sellbom et al., 2020). Some research reveals that there is not always a significant negative association between Disinhibition and Anankastia as would be expected (Bach, Kerber, et al., 2020). This seems consistent with the clinical reality, where rather complex PD patterns may be characterized by both Disinhibition and Anankastia at the same time (Chamberlain et al., 2018).

Perhaps most important, it might not be straightforward or intuitive for practitioners to specify a code for "lack of Disinhibition" or "low Disinhibition," because lack of something does not necessarily say anything about the presence of something else. When *ICD-11* trait domains are being employed for research and screening purposes, it would not be possible to measure both Disinhibition and Anankastia at the same time if each were only represented by polar opposites within one single dimension. Moreover, despite the fact that trait domains are dimensional rather than categorical in nature, *ICD-11* only allows them to be coded categorically in terms of "prominent" versus "not prominent," which makes it necessary to have two separate codes for Disinhibition and Anankastia, respectively.

Taken together, from both clinical and scientific perspectives, it should be possible to specify prominent features of Anankastia and Disinhibition at the same time using two separate codes. This does not contradict the fact that the two domains may be better conceptualized as two opposite poles, psychometrically and dimensionally speaking.

EMPIRICAL FOUNDATION OF *ICD-11* PERSONALITY DISORDER SEVERITY

The *ICD-11* approach to global PD severity is supported by a large body of scientific literature (Bender et al., 2011; Clark et al., 2018; Crawford et al., 2011; Hopwood et al., 2011; Morey et al., 2013; Sharp et al., 2015; Sleep et al., 2021). Moreover, the initial preparation of the *ICD-11* PD classification has involved numerous discussions and studies on how to classify PD according to severity (e.g., Kim et al., 2014; Tyrer, 2005; Yang et al., 2010). For example, a method of estimating four levels of PD severity based on the complexity and number of categorical PD criteria has been developed (Tyrer & Johnson, 1996; Yang et al., 2010), which largely corresponds to the four *ICD-11* levels of personality disturbance (i.e., personality difficulty, Mild PD, Moderate PD, and Severe PD). As illustrated in Table 2.3, the now official *ICD-11* classification of PD severity is closely aligned with the *DSM-5* AMPD and Kernberg's model of personality organization (Clarkin et al., 2020).

Clinical Utility of a Global Severity Dimension

Preliminary studies on its perceived clinical utility and diagnostic accuracy indicate that the *ICD-11* PD severity classification is at least as promising as the familiar *ICD-10* PD approach. A survey among Danish mental health professionals suggests that the *ICD-11* PD classification is considered slightly more useful than the *ICD-10* approach (Hansen et al., 2019). This particularly applied to utility for treatment planning, communication with patients, comprehensiveness, and ease of use. Notably, the perceived utility for treatment planning was particularly pronounced for subgroups of physicians and psychologists. Likewise, a survey by Morey and Hopwood (2019) also indicated that experts generally prefer the dimensional *ICD-11* PD approach over PD categories.

However, a randomized WHO field study on the perceived clinical utility and diagnostic accuracy (i.e., whether mental health professionals derive the correct *ICD-11* diagnosis) showed no significant differences between *ICD-10* and *ICD-11* PD models with respect to diagnostic accuracy, ease of use, clarity, goodness of fit, and time required for diagnosis (Gaebel et al., 2020). A potential limitation of this study was that it included only Moderate PD, which is not the same as the entire PD classification. Moreover, the interpretation of these findings should take into account that health professionals might naturally face greater difficulty in determining an *ICD-11* PD diagnosis because they are more strongly accustomed to *ICD-10*.

In a broader sense, the clinical relevance of classifying personality disturbance by severity has been demonstrated in several studies (Bach & Simonsen,

2021; Gordon et al., 2019; Koelen et al., 2012). Individuals with more severe personality disturbance are more likely to self-harm (Blasco-Fontecilla et al., 2009), to have a disorganized attachment (Beeney et al., 2017), to suffer from psychosocial impairment over time (Buer Christensen et al., 2020; Wright et al., 2016), to have a greater degree of comorbidity and suicide risk (Conway et al., 2016), to be more prone to alexithymia (S. Simonsen et al., 2021), to have low-quality alliance and treatment engagement (Papamalis et al., 2020), and to have higher risk of treatment dropout (Eurelings-Bontekoe et al., 2009). Moreover, a Cochrane meta-analysis suggests that total Borderline PD symptom severity is an important indicator of treatment outcome (Storebø et al., 2020). For these reasons, among others, global severity of personality disturbance is expected to be useful for clinical management and decision making (e.g., prognosis and optimal treatment intensity).

Significance of Subthreshold Personality Difficulty

Several studies have shown the importance of subthreshold personality difficulty in mental health care. Not surprisingly, when the full range of personality disturbance is taken into account, a majority of the general population will have some personality disturbance (Yang et al., 2010). This is also consistent with research showing that the residual diagnosis of Personality Disorder Not Otherwise Specified (PDNOS), which includes subsyndromal PD, is among the most frequently used PD diagnoses (Verheul & Widiger, 2004). Although there are obvious reservations about attributing personality pathology to normal human variation, data suggest that personality difficulty creates significant distress, increases health service use, and impairs social functioning (Karukivi et al., 2017; Sanatinia et al., 2016). Subthreshold personality difficulty may also be important for detecting and treating early personality pathology or accentuated personality traits in adolescents (Jørgensen et al., 2020; Thompson et al., 2019).

Measurement of *ICD-11* Personality Disorder Severity

In contrast to the *DSM-5* framework of diagnostic criteria and official instruments (e.g., the Personality Inventory for *DSM-5* [PID-5]), the *ICD-11* first and foremost operates with diagnostic guidelines without any sanctioned or mandatory instruments. In other words, health practitioners in WHO member countries should be able to diagnose a PD using the available *ICD-11* clinical descriptions and guidelines per se without having to employ additional measures or instruments. Therefore, PD severity may be determined based on clinical observations and other available information. Nevertheless, for scientific purposes, it is desired to have a standardized measure to operationalize the diagnostic PD features.

In contrast to the *DSM-5* AMPD approach to PD severity, there are no published measures of the *ICD-11* PD severity model. However, it is important to acknowledge that the Standardized Assessment of Severity of Personality

Disorders (SASPD; Olajide et al., 2018) was developed for measuring the initial proposal for the *ICD-11* PD classification (Tyrer et al., 2015). The SASPD may appropriately be considered an index of severity in terms of PD complexity (i.e., features from different PD categories) rather than a unidimensional scale of impairment. As highlighted by Oltmanns and Widiger (2019), the nine SASPD items refer explicitly to each of the five *ICD-11* trait domain specifiers, including Negative Affectivity (e.g., constant worrying), Detachment (e.g., avoiding other persons), Dissociality (e.g., callousness), Disinhibition (e.g., acting on impulse), and Anankastia (e.g., excessively organized). Thus, the SASPD was not constructed to capture the psychodynamic self- and interpersonal core capacities of personality functioning as described in the *DSM-5* AMPD and the now official *ICD-11* PD framework. For example, the SASPD does not cover the specific features of self-functioning (e.g., sense of identity, self-directedness, sense of self-worth) that also comprise essential aspects of the now official *ICD-11* classification of PD severity (Bach & First, 2018; Reed, 2018). Moreover, comparative studies clearly indicate that the SASPD does not align well with other established measures of personality dysfunction and that it does not capture problems related to sense of identity (Bach & Anderson, 2020; Waugh et al., 2020; Zimmermann et al., 2020). Additionally, a large study of SASPD in both clinical- and nonclinical samples concluded that SASPD is a psychometrically questionable measure of PD severity (Rek et al., 2020). Nevertheless, it has been employed in initial studies of the *ICD-11* PD severity model, where findings have generally suggested that this operationalization of PD severity may be improved (Bach & Anderson, 2020; Gutiérrez et al., 2020; McCabe & Widiger, 2020).

As a temporary solution to the current need for an appropriate measure of the now official *ICD-11* PD severity model, the use of established instruments for the AMPD model to operationalize the *ICD-11* PD severity dimension has been suggested (Bach & First, 2018). For example, some of the *ICD-11* aspects of self- and interpersonal functioning could potentially be operationalized using the Level of Personality Functioning Scale–Brief Form (LPFS-BF; Bach & Hutsebaut, 2018; Weekers et al., 2019) or the Structured Clinical Interview for the *DSM-5* Alternative Model for Personality Disorders (SCID-5-AMPD) Module I (Bender et al., 2018). Yet, such AMPD instruments were originally developed to assess the four subdomains and 12 specific capacities of the *DSM-5* AMPD approach, which are similar but not identical to the *ICD-11* PD core features (i.e., eight impaired capacities along with emotional, cognitive, and behavioral manifestations). Thus, we expect the development of an instrument that captures all of the aforementioned and unique *ICD-11* PD features, including specific capacities of self- and interpersonal functioning along with manifestations and global impairment. As a preliminary attempt to fill in this gap, an international research group has developed the 14-item Personality Disorder Severity *ICD-11* (PDS-ICD-11) scale, which has demonstrated promising utility for capturing a variety of PD severity features and manifestations (Bach et al., 2021).

EMPIRICAL FOUNDATION OF TRAIT DOMAIN SPECIFIERS

About the same time as the *DSM-5* AMPD trait model was constructed (Krueger et al., 2011), a similar trait domain model was under construction for the *ICD-11* (Tyrer, Crawford, Mulder, et al., 2011). This *ICD-11* proposal was guided by a systematic review of the PD literature, which identified 1,408 studies potentially revealing the central empirical domains of PDs (Mulder et al., 2011). These studies generally indicated the presence of four higher order trait domains, including externalizing, internalizing, aloof/schizoid, and compulsivity. However, Mulder et al. (2011) also acknowledged that predominant externalizing traits such as callousness and lack of remorse may represent a more specific domain of Dissociality. Eventually, the *ICD-11* PD work group decided to include and validate the trait domains of Negative Affectivity, Detachment, Dissociality, Disinhibition, and Anankastia, which are nearly concordant with the *DSM-5* trait model (Mulder et al., 2016; Oltmanns, 2021; Tyrer et al., 2015).

As shown in Table 2.1 and Table 2.4, the *ICD-11* and AMPD trait domains are conceptually aligned with one another (Mulder et al., 2011; Widiger & Simonsen, 2005), and research clearly indicates that the AMPD and *ICD-11* trait domains converge and largely capture the same external features (Bach et al., 2018; Crego & Widiger, 2020; Oltmanns & Widiger, 2018; Somma et al., 2020). Thus, it should be safe to say that the extensive research on the AMPD traits (except for Psychoticism) may be generalized to *ICD-11* trait domains

TABLE 2.4. Convergence of *ICD-11* Trait Domains With Well-Established Trait Models

ICD-11	Negative Affectivity	Detachment	Disinhibition versus Anankastia	Dissociality
PID-5	Negative Affectivity	Detachment	Disinhibition	Antagonism
FFM	Neuroticism	Extraversion	Conscientiousness	Agreeableness
CAT-PD	Negative Emotionality	Detachment	Disconstraint	Antagonism
DAPP-BQ	Emotional Dysregulation	Inhibitedness	Compulsivity	Dissocial Behavior
PSY-5	Negative Emotionality	Positive Emotionality	Constraint	Aggressiveness
SNAP	Negative Affectivity	Positive Affectivity	Disinhibition	
EPQ	Neuroticism	Extraversion		

Note. The presented convergences with *ICD-11* trait domains are conceptually and empirically supported (Carnovale et al., 2020; Crego & Widiger, 2020; Gutiérrez et al., 2020; Kerber et al., 2020; Kim et al., 2020; McCabe & Widiger, 2020; Oltmanns & Widiger, 2018, 2019, 2020; Sellbom et al., 2020; Somma et al., 2020; Tarescavage & Menton, 2020). *ICD-11* = *International Statistical Classification of Diseases and Related Health Problems* (11th ed.); PID-5 = Personality Inventory for *DSM-5*; FFM = five-factor model; CAT-PD = Computerized Adaptive Test of Personality Disorder; DAPP-BQ = Dimensional Assessment of Personality Pathology–Brief Questionnaire; PSY-5 = MMPI-2-RF Personality Psychopathology 5; SNAP = Schedule for Nonadaptive and Adaptive Personality; EPQ = Eysenck Personality Questionnaire. Data from World Health Organization (2019).

with respect to clinical information and guidelines. As illustrated in Table 2.4, the *ICD-11* trait domains have also been found to converge with other well-established trait models.

Measuring *ICD-11* Trait Domains Using an Algorithm for PID-5

As the first published operationalization of the now official *ICD-11* trait domain specifiers, Bach et al. (2017) developed an algorithm for delineating all five *ICD-11* trait domains (including a separate domain of Anankastia) by means of the well-established PID-5 (Krueger et al., 2012). More specifically, 16 PID-5 facets were designated to generate the five *ICD-11* domain scores, and the five-factor structure was supported across U.S. and Danish data.

Since its release, a number of studies have employed and validated this *ICD-11* algorithm for PID-5 in different populations (Bach et al., 2018; Lotfi et al., 2018; Lugo et al., 2019; Sellbom et al., 2020). The five-factor structure of the *ICD-11* domains has been replicated in an Iranian sample, which supports its potential utility in Middle Eastern culture (Lotfi et al., 2018). A Brazilian study demonstrated the utility of the *ICD-11* domain scores to differentiate between community-dwelling individuals and psychiatric inpatients in a conceptually meaningful way (Lugo et al., 2019). A study among psychiatric patients indicates that the *ICD-11* trait domain scores show meaningful continuity with categorical PDs and captured a substantial amount of their variance, suggesting that little information is lost in the transition from *ICD-10* to *ICD-11* (Bach et al., 2018). Moreover, the *ICD-11* algorithm was superior in capturing obsessive-compulsive PD relative to the *DSM-5* AMPD trait operationalization.

Finally, Sellbom et al. (2020) further improved the *ICD-11* algorithm by including two more PID-5 facets (i.e., Suspiciousness and Attention Seeking), which were expected to capture additional nuances of Negative Affectivity and Dissociality. The empirical structure of this revised 18-facet *ICD-11* algorithm was supported in a sample of Canadian psychiatric patients, and overall it demonstrated expected associations with categorical PD criterion-count scores and five-factor model (FFM) traits.

As Bach and First (2018) suggested, it seems reasonable to employ this *ICD-11* algorithm for the *DSM-5* AMPD trait system in general, including the SCID-5-AMPD Module II for the trait criterion (Skodol et al., 2018) and the PID-5 Informant Report Form (Markon et al., 2013).

Measuring Trait Domain Specifiers Using the Personality Inventory for *ICD-11*

Oltmanns and Widiger (2018) introduced the first instrument that is exclusively developed for the *ICD-11* trait domains: the Personality Inventory for *ICD-11* (PiCD). The PiCD comprises 60 items, which are used to calculate the five *ICD-11* trait domain scores (i.e., 12 items per domain). The PiCD has already been evaluated in a number of studies, supporting the validity of the *ICD-11* trait domains. In the initial construction study, which was based on a combined

Empirical Foundation of the ICD-11 *Classification of Personality Disorders*   39

sample of 525 community participants, the *ICD-11* trait domains showed meaningful convergence with external criteria including FFM traits and Eysenck's trait model. The domain of Negative Affectivity converged with Neuroticism, Detachment converged with low Extraversion, Dissociality converged with Insensitivity, Anankastia converged with high Orderliness, and Disinhibition converged with low Orderliness. Likewise, the five PiCD domains also converged with expected domain scales from the PID-5 and the Computerized Adaptive Test of Personality Disorder (CAT-PD; Oltmanns & Widiger, 2018). This pattern of convergence with FFM measures was later corroborated in a subsequent study among 269 individuals who were currently or had previously been in mental health treatment (Oltmanns & Widiger, 2019).

A study by Crego and Widiger (2020), based on a sample of 323 persons with a history of mental health treatment, found expected and meaningful convergence of PiCD scales with the Schedule for Nonadaptive and Adaptive Personality (SNAP; Clark, 1993), the Dimensional Assessment of Personality Pathology–Basic Questionnaire (DAPP-BQ; Livesley & Larstone, 2008), and the PID-5 scales (Krueger et al., 2012), which supports alignment with these historically important frameworks (see Table 2.4). This was demonstrated by means of joint factor analysis and zero-order correlations. The authors particularly highlighted the strength of delineating a separate *ICD-11* trait domain of Anankastia, which is consistent with both SNAP and DAPP-BQ (i.e., Compulsivity) but not the PID-5.

Carnovale et al. (2020) generally supported the empirical structure and criterion validity of the PiCD in a sample of 518 students. The five PiCD trait domains generally showed expected convergence with another important framework, the Minnesota Multiphasic Personality Inventory-2-Restructured Form (MMPI-2-RF) Personality Psychopathology 5 (PSY-5). Both four- and five-factor solutions were considered appropriate in this study, but the four-factor model was deemed most interpretable. Along the same lines, Tarescavage and Menton (2020) also investigated structural convergence with the aforementioned MMPI-2-RF PSY-5 using a sample of 328 college students. Consistent with previous findings, they overall found an expected pattern of convergence and discrimination, in particular for Negative Affectivity, Disinhibition, and Dissociality.

Gutiérrez et al. (2020) investigated the structural validity of PiCD trait domains in a large mixed Spanish–Catalonian sample composed of 2,522 community volunteers and 797 psychiatric outpatients. This study also yielded a conceptually coherent hierarchical structure, including one higher order global factor of personality pathology followed by an internalizing–externalizing metastructure and finally an expected four-factor solution corresponding to the one identified in the initial PiCD construction study (Oltmanns & Widiger, 2018). In this study, the four-factor solution comprised a bipolar Disinhibition–Anankastia factor, whereas a lower level five-factor solution did not allow two separate factors of Disinhibition and Anankastia.

Somma et al. (2020) also explored the PiCD's joint factor structure with FFM traits and PID-5 traits using a large Italian community sample of 1,203 adults.

Findings were consistent with previous studies in terms of expected and meaningful convergence with the PiCD trait domains. Moreover, the authors also investigated the association between PiCD domains and general impairment of personality functioning using the Measure of Disordered Personality Functioning (MDPF; Parker et al., 2004), which supported the proposition that PiCD captures maladaptive trait expressions. Notably, the PiCD domains of Detachment and Negative Affectivity showed the strongest association with general personality dysfunction, whereas Anankastia was least associated with dysfunction, which is consistent with previous meta-analytic data documenting that PDs in general are most related to neuroticism and least to conscientiousness (Ozer & Benet-Martínez, 2006; Saulsman & Page, 2004). Additionally, Somma et al. (2020) extended previous empirical support of the PiCD's scale reliability by evaluating its test–retest reliability after 2 weeks. They found all reliability values (r) to be greater than .80, indicating that the PiCD operationalization of the *ICD-11* trait domains at least has adequate short-term stability.

Finally, McCabe and Widiger (2020) performed a more comprehensive head-to-head comparison of the *ICD-11* PiCD trait model versus the PID-5 trait model using a sample of 300 individuals who were currently receiving or had received mental health treatment in the past. These findings suggest that the two systems converge within a joint factor structure that includes the bipolar dimension of the Anankastia versus Disinhibition domains. Notably, based on domain intercorrelations, this study showed good discriminant validity for the PiCD trait model—albeit problematic discriminant validity for the PID-5 trait model.

Other Measures of the *ICD-11* Trait Domains

One noteworthy difference between the *ICD-11* and the *DSM-5* AMPD models is that the five *ICD-11* domains do not include any distinct trait facets. Consideration was initially given to the inclusion of subscales within each domain, but the *ICD-11* PD work group felt that such inclusion would provide an unnecessary complexity (Tyrer, Crawford, Mulder, et al., 2011; Tyrer et al., 2015). Nevertheless, several of the aforementioned studies suggested that a facet-level operationalization of the *ICD-11* trait domains is desirable in order to capture more specific qualities and to provide more clinically useful information.

In response to these concerns, Oltmanns and Widiger (2020) developed the 121-item Five-Factor Personality Inventory for *ICD-11* (FFiCD). The FFiCD was initially constructed based on responses from 377 participants who were currently or had previously been in mental health treatment. The FFiCD scales were subsequently validated in samples of 148 and 301 individuals, respectively, with the same clinical characteristics. By means of joint factor analysis, the FFiCD demonstrated expected convergence with both FFM trait domains and PID-5 trait domains, where the domains of Anankastia and Disinhibition comprised two poles of one dimension. The FFiCD portrays 20 facets and 47 nuances, which are organized within five maladaptive domains.

Kerber et al. (2020) developed the 34-item Personality Inventory for *DSM-5*, Brief Form Plus (PID5BF+), which was aimed to capture both *DSM-5* and *ICD-11* trait domains, including both Anankastia and Psychoticism as well as 17 primary facets. The PID5BF+ was constructed from the 220-item PID-5 item pool using a large mixed sample of 2,927 participants, which included both German inpatients and community participants as well as U.S. students. Ant colony optimization, which is a computational method that has been proven to be very effective for item-selection tasks, was employed to designate the optimal set of items to cover *ICD-11* domains and *DSM-5* AMPD domains. Importantly, the association of PID5BF+ with both FFM traits and scales of interpersonal problems demonstrated expected convergent, discriminant, and criterion validity. It also showed good scale reliability and was useful for discriminating PDs from other mental disorders in a clinical subsample.

In order to further adapt the PID5BF+ to efficiently capture the primary facets represented in the *ICD-11* domain of Anankastia, Bach, Kerber, et al. (2020) modified its operationalization by extracting subfacets of rigidity, orderliness, and perfectionism from the composite PID-5 facet of rigid perfectionism. This new six-domain model was initially tested in Danish, German, and U.S. samples, with subsequent replications across 13 samples from France, Italy, the French-speaking part of Switzerland, the French-speaking part of Belgium, the Dutch-speaking part of Belgium, Norway, Portugal, Spain, Poland, Brazil, and the Czech Republic, with an additional U.S. sample. Thus, the study included a total of 16,327 participants (of which 2,347 were clinical) from 16 different samples and 12 different languages. The extraction of the three new Anankastia facets is consistent with the initial 37-facet version of the *DSM-5* trait proposal (Krueger et al., 2012). Moreover, in this modified version of PID5BF+, the facet of perseveration (two items) was omitted as a primary feature of Anankastia because this facet was originally intended to capture features of Negative Affectivity as reflected by its predominant loadings on the Negative Affectivity domain (Watters & Bagby, 2018). Taken together, Bach, Kerber, et al. (2020) developed a modified version of PID5BF+ to operationalize the *DSM-5* and *ICD-11* trait domains using three primary facets per domain, so that all domains are represented by an equal (and comparable) number of trait indicators. The complete modified PID5BF+ comprises 36 items, which delineate 18 facets (two items per facet). The PID5BF+ has demonstrated a robust factor structure across all samples and revealed expected continuity with interview-rated categorical PDs. For practitioners who wish to assess only the *ICD-11* trait domains, a reduced 30-item version may be employed, which omits the *DSM-5* domain of Psychoticism (see Figure 2.1).

Finally, a Korean research group developed the 17-item Personality Assessment Questionnaire for *ICD-11* (PAQ-11; Kim et al., 2020), which was intended as a short and reliable self-report measure. All items were derived from the Personality Assessment Schedule, which was originally developed by Tyrer and Alexander (1979) for the purpose of assessing an early draft of the *ICD-11* PD proposal. The PAQ-11 construction and item selection procedure were initially based on Korean data from 334 female university students and 75 psychiatric

FIGURE 2.1. Five ICD-11 Trait Domains With Primary Facets

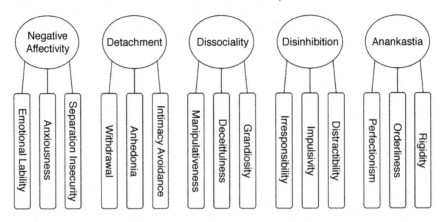

Note. The 5 trait domains and 15 facets are measured using 30 items from the Modified Personality Inventory for *DSM-5*, Brief Form Plus (PID5BF+; Bach, Kerber, et al., 2020).

patients (*n* = 409). Subsequently, the PAQ-11 was validated in a subsample of individuals who were deemed to be at high risk of having a PD (*n* = 210). The PAQ-11 scales demonstrated adequate convergence with expected FFM and PID-5 scales as well as measures of emotional disorders and anger dysregulation. Moreover, most of the five PAQ-11 scales showed a meaningful pattern of continuity with categorical PD scores, largely consistent with previous studies (see overview in Table 2.5).

Other Empirical Sources of *ICD-11* Trait Domain Information

The *ICD-11* trait domain specifiers may be assessed in various ways other than the self-report approaches. For example, a representative sample of psychologists,

TABLE 2.5. Continuity of Categorical Personality Disorders With *ICD-11* Trait Domains

	Negative affectivity	Detachment	Dissociality	Disinhibition	Anankastia
Paranoid	++	+	+		
Schizoid	−	++			
Antisocial	−		++	+	
Borderline	++		+	+	
Histrionic	+	−−	+	+	
Narcissistic	+		++		+
Avoidant	++	++	−	−	
Dependent	++		−		
OCPD		+		−−	++

Note. Present (+); strongly present (++); absent (−); strongly absent (−−). The patterns of the presented associations are overall conceptually and empirically supported (Bach et al., 2018; Bach, Kerber, et al., 2020; Kim et al., 2020; Mulder et al., 2016; Sellbom et al., 2020; Watters et al., 2019). *ICD-11* = International Statistical Classification of Diseases and Related Health Problems (11th ed.); OCPD = obsessive-compulsive personality disorder. Data from World Health Organization (2019).

physicians, and other professionals were asked to apply a clinician-report form of the PiCD to rate one or more of their own patients (Bach, Christensen, et al., 2020). Accordingly, 238 mental health patients were characterized in terms of clinician-reported *ICD-11* traits. The patients were predominantly characterized by personality pathology followed by other common mental disorders. Consistent with research on self-reported *ICD-11* traits (Bach et al., 2017; Oltmanns & Widiger, 2018), the authors identified expected four- and five-factor solutions as empirically appropriate, of which the four-factor solution seemed most robust. The authors also analyzed other levels of the hierarchical taxonomy in which a recognizable two-factor metastructure of internalizing and externalizing features emerged. Essentially, these findings provide evidence that the *ICD-11* trait domain specifiers can be validly reported by clinicians on behalf of their patients.

ICD-11 trait domain information may also be derived from health records, notes, and other documents (Kim et al., 2016). For example, Barroilhet, Pellegrini, et al. (2020) collected health record data from 3,623 adult psychiatric inpatients who had a total of 4,702 hospital admissions. As a particularly innovative approach, they employed natural language processing (i.e., a computerized approach to organizing and analyzing human language) of health record notes to systematically characterize patients according to the five *ICD-11* trait domains. The study concludes that this health record approach can be used to characterize *ICD-11* trait domain features, which are empirically associated with clinically useful information. For example, the presence of Disinhibition and Negative Affectivity were each significantly associated with a longer stay, while Detachment was associated with a shorter stay.

In a similar study, Barroilhet, Bieling, et al. (2020) investigated patterns of *ICD-11* trait domains in electronic health records from 12,274 patients who had been admitted to general hospital treatment. The included cohort of patients had a total of 19,985 admissions, and a total of 2,379 deaths had occurred during the course. The authors concluded that *ICD-11* trait domains can be identified from electronic health records and associated with readmission and mortality risk. For example, Disinhibition was associated with a higher mortality risk, whereas Anankastia was associated with a lower mortality risk. In general, Detachment was the most common trait domain among these hospitalized patients. As the authors of the two studies suggested, practitioners may take advantage of such *ICD-11* trait domain information to target the individual patient and enable more efficient and focused interventions.

CONCLUSION

The now official *ICD-11* PD classification has evolved from decades of research on overall PD severity and specific trait features. The *ICD-11* PD severity diagnosis essentially relies on research indicating that level of personality functioning, PD complexity, and a global p-factor comprise important prognostic and clinical markers (e.g., needed treatment intensity, treatment outcome, quality of alliance, risk of dropout, risk of harm to self and others). The empirical foundation of the *ICD-11* PD model is largely shared with the *DSM-5* AMPD model and other well-established models of personality functioning and traits, which expands its scientific validity substantially. The trait domain specifiers can be evaluated using different measures, algorithms, and sources of information, and to date their reliability and validity have been supported cross-culturally in more than 13 languages and 15 different countries. A number of international studies using the *ICD-11* PD measures, reviewed in this chapter, are currently being carried out, and we therefore expect to see a further accumulated body of research when the present volume is published. The clinical application of the *ICD-11* PD model is further elucidated in Chapter 8.

REFERENCES

American Psychiatric Association. (2013). *Diagnostic and statistical manual of mental disorders* (5th ed.). https://doi.org/10.1176/appi.books.9780890425596

Bach, B., & Anderson, J. L. (2020). Patient-reported *ICD-11* personality disorder severity and *DSM-5* level of personality functioning. *Journal of Personality Disorders*, *34*(2), 231–249. https://doi.org/10.1521/pedi_2018_32_393

Bach, B., Brown, T. A., Mulder, R. T., Newton-Howes, G., Simonsen, E., & Sellbom, M. (2021). Development and initial evaluation of the *ICD-11* personality disorder severity scale: PDS-ICD-11. *Personality and Mental Health*, *15*(3), 223–236. https://doi.org/10.1002/pmh.1510

Bach, B., Christensen, S., Kongerslev, M. T., Sellbom, M., & Simonsen, E. (2020). Structure of clinician-reported *ICD-11* personality disorder trait qualifiers. *Psychological Assessment*, *32*(1), 50–59. https://doi.org/10.1037/pas0000747

Bach, B., & First, M. B. (2018). Application of the *ICD-11* classification of personality disorders. *BMC Psychiatry*, *18*(1), Article 351. https://doi.org/10.1186/s12888-018-1908-3

Bach, B., & Hutsebaut, J. (2018). Level of Personality Functioning Scale–Brief Form 2.0: Utility in capturing personality problems in psychiatric outpatients and incarcerated addicts. *Journal of Personality Assessment*, *100*(6), 660–670. https://doi.org/10.1080/00223891.2018.1428984

Bach, B., Kerber, A., Aluja, A., Bastiaens, T., Keeley, J. W., Claes, L., Fossati, A., Gutierrez, F., Oliveira, S. E. S., Pires, R., Riegel, K. D., Rolland, J.-P., Roskam, I., Sellbom, M., Somma, A., Spanemberg, L., Strus, W., Thimm, J. C., Wright, A. G. C., & Zimmermann, J. (2020). International assessment of *DSM-5* and *ICD-11* personality disorder traits: Toward a common nosology in DSM-5.1. *Psychopathology*, *53*(3-4), 179–188. https://doi.org/10.1159/000507589

Bach, B., Sellbom, M., Kongerslev, M., Simonsen, E., Krueger, R. F., & Mulder, R. (2017). Deriving *ICD-11* personality disorder domains from *DSM-5* traits: Initial attempt to harmonize two diagnostic systems. *Acta Psychiatrica Scandinavica*, *136*(1), 108–117. https://doi.org/10.1111/acps.12748

Bach, B., Sellbom, M., Skjernov, M., & Simonsen, E. (2018). *ICD-11* and *DSM-5* personality trait domains capture categorical personality disorders: Finding a common ground. *Australian & New Zealand Journal of Psychiatry*, *52*(5), 425–434. https://doi.org/10.1177/0004867417727867

Bach, B., & Simonsen, S. (2021). How does level of personality functioning inform clinical management and treatment? Implications for *ICD-11* classification of personality disorder severity. *Current Opinion in Psychiatry*, *34*(1), 54–63. https://doi.org/10.1097/YCO.0000000000000658

Bach, B., & Zine El Abiddine, F. (2020). Empirical structure of *DSM-5* and *ICD-11* personality disorder traits in Arabic-speaking Algerian culture. *International Journal of Mental Health, 49*(2), 186–200. https://doi.org/10.1080/00207411.2020.1732624

Barroilhet, S. A., Bieling, A. E., McCoy, T. H., Jr., & Perlis, R. H. (2020). Association between *DSM-5* and *ICD-11* personality dimensional traits in a general medical cohort and readmission and mortality. *General Hospital Psychiatry, 64*, 63–67. https://doi.org/10.1016/j.genhosppsych.2020.01.003

Barroilhet, S. A., Pellegrini, A. M., McCoy, T. H., & Perlis, R. H. (2020). Characterizing *DSM-5* and *ICD-11* personality disorder features in psychiatric inpatients at scale using electronic health records. *Psychological Medicine, 50*(13), 2221–2229. https://doi.org/10.1017/S0033291719002320

Bateman, A. W. (2011). Throwing the baby out with the bathwater? *Personality and Mental Health, 5*(4), 274–280. https://doi.org/10.1002/pmh.184

Beeney, J. E., Wright, A. G. C., Stepp, S. D., Hallquist, M. N., Lazarus, S. A., Beeney, J. R. S., Scott, L. N., & Pilkonis, P. A. (2017). Disorganized attachment and personality functioning in adults: A latent class analysis. *Personality Disorders: Theory, Research, and Treatment, 8*(3), 206–216. https://doi.org/10.1037/per0000184

Bender, D. S., Morey, L. C., & Skodol, A. E. (2011). Toward a model for assessing level of personality functioning in *DSM-5*, Part I: A review of theory and methods. *Journal of Personality Assessment, 93*(4), 332–346. https://doi.org/10.1080/00223891.2011.583808

Bender, D. S., Skodol, A. E., First, M. B., & Oldham, J. M. (2018). Module I: Structured Clinical Interview for the Level of Personality Functioning Scale. In M. B. First, A. E. Skodol, D. S. Bender, & J. M. Oldham (Eds.), *Structured Clinical Interview for the DSM-5 Alternative Model for Personality Disorders (SCID-5-AMPD)*. American Psychiatric Association Publishing.

Blasco-Fontecilla, H., Baca-Garcia, E., Dervic, K., Perez-Rodriguez, M. M., Saiz-Gonzalez, M. D., Saiz-Ruiz, J., Oquendo, M. A., & De Leon, J. (2009). Severity of personality disorders and suicide attempt. *Acta Psychiatrica Scandinavica, 119*(2), 149–155. https://doi.org/10.1111/j.1600-0447.2008.01284.x

Bornstein, R. F. (2016). Toward a firmer foundation for *ICD-11*: On the conceptualization and assessment of personality pathology. *Personality and Mental Health, 10*(2), 123–126. https://doi.org/10.1002/pmh.1342

Buer Christensen, T., Eikenaes, I., Hummelen, B., Pedersen, G., Nysæter, T.-E., Bender, D. S., Skodol, A. E., & Selvik, S. G. (2020). Level of personality functioning as a predictor of psychosocial functioning—Concurrent validity of Criterion A. *Personality Disorders: Theory, Research, and Treatment, 11*(2), 79–90. https://doi.org/10.1037/per0000352

Caligor, E., Kernberg, O. F., Clarkin, J. F., & Yeomans, F. E. (2018). *Psychodynamic therapy for personality pathology: Treating self and interpersonal functioning*. American Psychiatric Association Publishing.

Carnovale, M., Sellbom, M., & Bagby, R. M. (2020). The Personality Inventory for *ICD-11*: Investigating reliability, structural and concurrent validity, and method variance. *Psychological Assessment, 32*(1), 8–17. https://doi.org/10.1037/pas0000776

Chamberlain, S. R., Stochl, J., Redden, S. A., & Grant, J. E. (2018). Latent traits of impulsivity and compulsivity: Toward dimensional psychiatry. *Psychological Medicine, 48*(5), 810–821. https://doi.org/10.1017/S0033291717002185

Clark, L. A. (1993). *Schedule for Nonadaptive and Adaptive Personality (SNAP): Manual for administration, scoring, and interpretation*. University of Minnesota Press.

Clark, L. A., Nuzum, H., & Ro, E. (2018). Manifestations of personality impairment severity: Comorbidity, course/prognosis, psychosocial dysfunction, and 'borderline' personality features. *Current Opinion in Psychology, 21*, 117–121. https://doi.org/10.1016/j.copsyc.2017.12.004

Clarkin, J. F., Caligor, E., & Sowislo, J. F. (2020). An object relations model perspective on the Alternative Model for Personality Disorders (*DSM-5*). *Psychopathology, 53*(3-4), 141–148. https://doi.org/10.1159/000508353

Clarkin, J. F., Caligor, E., Stern, B. L., & Kernberg, O. F. (2007). *Structured Interview of Personality Organization (STIPO)* [Unpublished manuscript]. Personality Disorders Institute, Weill Medical College of Cornell University.

Conway, C. C., Hammen, C., & Brennan, P. A. (2016). Optimizing prediction of psychosocial and clinical outcomes with a transdiagnostic model of personality disorder. *Journal of Personality Disorders, 30*(4), 545–566. https://doi.org/10.1521/pedi_2015_29_218

Crawford, M. J., Koldobsky, N., Mulder, R., & Tyrer, P. (2011). Classifying personality disorder according to severity. *Journal of Personality Disorders, 25*(3), 321–330. https://doi.org/10.1521/pedi.2011.25.3.321

Crego, C., & Widiger, T. A. (2020). The convergent, discriminant, and structural relationship of the DAPP-BQ and SNAP with the *ICD-11, DSM-5*, and FFM trait models. *Psychological Assessment, 32*(1), 18–28. https://doi.org/10.1037/pas0000757

Davidson, K. (2011). Changing the classification of personality disorders—An *ICD-11* proposal that goes too far? *Personality and Mental Health, 5*(4), 243–245. https://doi.org/10.1002/pmh.180

Ekselius, L. (2016). Reflections of the reconceptualization of *ICD-11*: Empirical and practical considerations. *Personality and Mental Health, 10*(2), 127–129. https://doi.org/10.1002/pmh.1343

Ekselius, L., Lindström, E., von Knorring, L., Bodlund, O., & Kullgren, G. (1993). Personality disorders in *DSM-III-R* as categorical or dimensional. *Acta Psychiatrica Scandinavica, 88*(3), 183–187. https://doi.org/10.1111/j.1600-0447.1993.tb03436.x

Eurelings-Bontekoe, E. H. M., van Dam, A., Luyten, P., Verhulst, W. A. C. M., van Tilburg, C. A., de Heus, P., & Koelen, J. (2009). Structural personality organization as assessed with theory driven profile interpretation of the Dutch short form of the MMPI predicts dropout and treatment response in brief cognitive behavioral group therapy for Axis I disorders. *Journal of Personality Assessment, 91*(5), 439–452. https://doi.org/10.1080/00223890903087927

Fineberg, N. A., Reghunandanan, S., Kolli, S., & Atmaca, M. (2014). Obsessive-compulsive (anankastic) personality disorder: Toward the *ICD-11* classification. *Brazilian Journal of Psychiatry, 36*(Suppl. 1), 40–50. https://doi.org/10.1590/1516-4446-2013-1282

First, M. B., Gibbon, M., Spitzer, R. L., Williams, J. B. W., & Benjamin, L. S. (1997). *Structured Clinical Interview for DSM-IV Axis II Personality Disorders (SCID-II)*. American Psychiatric Press.

Frances, A. (1980). The *DSM-III* personality disorders section: A commentary. *The American Journal of Psychiatry, 137*(9), 1050–1054. https://doi.org/10.1176/ajp.137.9.1050

Frances, A. (1982). Categorical and dimensional systems of personality diagnosis: A comparison. *Comprehensive Psychiatry, 23*(6), 516–527. https://doi.org/10.1016/0010-440X(82)90043-8

Fyer, M. R., Frances, A. J., Sullivan, T., Hurt, S. W., & Clarkin, J. (1988). Comorbidity of borderline personality disorder. *Archives of General Psychiatry, 45*(4), 348–352. https://doi.org/10.1001/archpsyc.1988.01800280060008

Gaebel, W., Stricker, J., Riesbeck, M., Zielasek, J., Kerst, A., Meisenzahl-Lechner, E., Köllner, V., Rose, M., Hofmann, T., Schäfer, I., Lotzin, A., Briken, P., Klein, V., Brunner, F., Keeley, J. W., Brechbiel, J., Rebello, T. J., Andrews, H. F., Reed, G. M., . . . Falkai, P. (2020). Accuracy of diagnostic classification and clinical utility assessment of *ICD-11* compared to *ICD-10* in 10 mental disorders: Findings from a web-based field study. *European Archives of Psychiatry and Clinical Neuroscience, 270*(3), 281–289. https://doi.org/10.1007/s00406-019-01076-z

Gordon, R. M., Spektor, V., & Luu, L. (2019). Personality organization traits and expected countertransference and treatment interventions. *International Journal of Psychology and Psychoanalysis, 5*(1), 1–7. https://doi.org/10.23937/2572-4037.1510039

Gutiérrez, F., Aluja, A., Ruiz, J., García, L. F., Gárriz, M., Gutiérrez-Zotes, A., Gallardo-Pujol, D., Navarro-Haro, M. V., Alabèrnia-Segura, M., Mestre-Pintó, J. I., Torrens, M., Peri, J. M., Sureda, B., Soler, J., Pascual, J. C., Vall, G., Calvo, N., Ferrer, M., Oltmanns, J. R., & Widiger, T. A. (2020). Personality disorders in the *ICD-11*: Spanish validation of the PiCD and the SASPD in a mixed community and clinical sample. *Assessment*. Advance online publication. https://doi.org/10.1177/1073191120936357

Hansen, S. J., Christensen, S., Kongerslev, M. T., First, M. B., Widiger, T. A., Simonsen, E., & Bach, B. (2019). Mental health professionals' perceived clinical utility of the *ICD-10* vs. *ICD-11* classification of personality disorders. *Personality and Mental Health*, *13*(2), 84–95. https://doi.org/10.1002/pmh.1442

Herpertz, S. C., Huprich, S. K., Bohus, M., Chanen, A., Goodman, M., Mehlum, L., Moran, P., Newton-Howes, G., Scott, L., & Sharp, C. (2017). The challenge of transforming the diagnostic system of personality disorders. *Journal of Personality Disorders*, *31*(5), 577–589. https://doi.org/10.1521/pedi_2017_31_338

Hilsenroth, M. J., Eudell-Simmons, E. M., DeFife, J. A., & Charnas, J. W. (2007). The Rorschach Perceptual-Thinking Index (PTI): An examination of reliability, validity, and diagnostic efficiency. *International Journal of Testing*, *7*(3), 269–291. https://doi.org/10.1080/15305050701438033

Hopwood, C. J., Kotov, R., Krueger, R. F., Watson, D., Widiger, T. A., Althoff, R. R., Ansell, E. B., Bach, B., Bagby, R. M., Blais, M. A., Bornovalova, M. A., Chmielewski, M., Cicero, D. C., Conway, C., De Clercq, B., De Fruyt, F., Docherty, A. R., Eaton, N. R., Edens, J. F., . . . Zimmermann, J. (2018). The time has come for dimensional personality disorder diagnosis. *Personality and Mental Health*, *12*(1), 82–86. https://doi.org/10.1002/pmh.1408

Hopwood, C. J., Malone, J. C., Ansell, E. B., Sanislow, C. A., Grilo, C. M., McGlashan, T. H., Pinto, A., Markowitz, J. C., Shea, M. T., Skodol, A. E., Gunderson, J. G., Zanarini, M. C., & Morey, L. C. (2011). Personality assessment in *DSM-5*: Empirical support for rating severity, style, and traits. *Journal of Personality Disorders*, *25*(3), 305–320. https://doi.org/10.1521/pedi.2011.25.3.305

Huprich, S. K. (2020). Personality disorders in the *ICD-11*: Opportunities and challenges for advancing the diagnosis of personality pathology. *Current Psychiatry Reports*, *22*(8), Article 40. https://doi.org/10.1007/s11920-020-01161-4

Huprich, S. K., Herpertz, S. C., Bohus, M., Chanen, A., Goodman, M., Mehlum, L., Moran, P., Newton-Howe, G., Scott, L., & Sharp, C. (2018). Comment on Hopwood et al., "the time has come for dimensional personality disorder diagnosis." *Personality and Mental Health*, *12*(1), 87–88. https://doi.org/10.1002/pmh.1407

Jørgensen, M. S., Storebø, O. J., & Simonsen, E. (2020). Systematic review and meta-analyses of psychotherapies for adolescents with subclinical and borderline personality disorder: Methodological issues. *The Canadian Journal of Psychiatry*, *65*(1), 59–60. https://doi.org/10.1177/0706743719893893

Karukivi, M., Vahlberg, T., Horjamo, K., Nevalainen, M., & Korkeila, J. (2017). Clinical importance of personality difficulties: Diagnostically sub-threshold personality disorders. *BMC Psychiatry*, *17*, Article 16. https://doi.org/10.1186/s12888-017-1200-y

Kerber, A., Schultze, M., Müller, S., Rühling, R. M., Wright, A. G. C., Spitzer, C., Krueger, R. F., Knaevelsrud, C., & Zimmermann, J. (2020). Development of a short and *ICD-11* compatible measure for *DSM-5* maladaptive personality traits using ant colony optimization algorithms. *Assessment*. Advance online publication. https://doi.org/10.1177/1073191120971848

Kim, Y.-R., Blashfield, R., Tyrer, P., Hwang, S.-T., & Lee, H.-S. (2014). Field trial of a putative research algorithm for diagnosing *ICD-11* personality disorders in psychiatric patients: 1. Severity of personality disturbance. *Personality and Mental Health*, *8*(1), 67–78. https://doi.org/10.1002/pmh.1248

Kim, Y.-R., Tyrer, P., & Hwang, S.-T. (2020). Personality Assessment Questionnaire for *ICD-11* personality trait domains: Development and testing. *Personality and Mental Health, 15*(1), 58–71. https://doi.org/10.1002/pmh.1493

Kim, Y.-R., Tyrer, P., Lee, H.-S., Kim, S.-G., Connan, F., Kinnaird, E., Olajide, K., & Crawford, M. (2016). Schedule for personality assessment from notes and documents (SPAN-DOC): Preliminary validation, links to the *ICD-11* classification of personality disorder, and use in eating disorders. *Personality and Mental Health, 10*(2), 106–117. https://doi.org/10.1002/pmh.1335

Kim, Y.-R., Tyrer, P., Lee, H.-S., Kim, S.-G., Hwang, S.-T., Lee, G. Y., & Mulder, R. (2015). Preliminary field trial of a putative research algorithm for diagnosing *ICD-11* personality disorders in psychiatric patients: 2. Proposed trait domains. *Personality and Mental Health, 9*(4), 298–307. https://doi.org/10.1002/pmh.1305

Koelen, J. A., Luyten, P., Eurelings-Bontekoe, L. H. M., Diguer, L., Vermote, R., Lowyck, B., & Bühring, M. E. F. (2012). The impact of level of personality organization on treatment response: A systematic review. *Psychiatry: Interpersonal and Biological Processes, 75*(4), 355–374. https://doi.org/10.1521/psyc.2012.75.4.355

Krueger, R. F., Derringer, J., Markon, K. E., Watson, D., & Skodol, A. E. (2012). Initial construction of a maladaptive personality trait model and inventory for *DSM-5*. *Psychological Medicine, 42*(9), 1879–1890. https://doi.org/10.1017/S0033291711002674

Krueger, R. F., Eaton, N. R., Clark, L. A., Watson, D., Markon, K. E., Derringer, J., Skodol, A., & Livesley, W. J. (2011). Deriving an empirical structure of personality pathology for *DSM-5*. *Journal of Personality Disorders, 25*(2), 170–191. https://doi.org/10.1521/pedi.2011.25.2.170

Krueger, R. F., & Hobbs, K. A. (2020). An overview of the *DSM-5* Alternative Model of Personality Disorders. *Psychopathology, 53*(3-4), 126–132. https://doi.org/10.1159/000508538

Livesley, W. J., & Larstone, R. M. (2008). The Dimensional Assessment of Personality Pathology (DAPP). In G. J. Boyle, G. Matthews, & D. H. Saklofske (Eds.), *The SAGE handbook of personality theory and assessment: Vol. 2. Personality measurement and testing* (pp. 608–625). SAGE Publications.

Lotfi, M., Bach, B., Amini, M., & Simonsen, E. (2018). Structure of *DSM-5* and *ICD-11* personality domains in Iranian community sample. *Personality and Mental Health, 12*(2), 155–169. https://doi.org/10.1002/pmh.1409

Lugo, V., de Oliveira, S. E. S., Hessel, C. R., Monteiro, R. T., Pasche, N. L., Pavan, G., Motta, L. S., Pacheco, M. A., & Spanemberg, L. (2019). Evaluation of *DSM-5* and *ICD-11* personality traits using the Personality Inventory for *DSM-5* (PID-5) in a Brazilian sample of psychiatric inpatients. *Personality and Mental Health, 13*(1), 24–39. https://doi.org/10.1002/pmh.1436

Markon, K. E., Quilty, L. C., Bagby, R. M., & Krueger, R. F. (2013). The development and psychometric properties of an informant-report form of the Personality Inventory for *DSM-5* (PID-5). *Assessment, 20*(3), 370–383. https://doi.org/10.1177/1073191113486513

McCabe, G. A., & Widiger, T. A. (2020). A comprehensive comparison of the *ICD-11* and *DSM-5* Section III personality disorder models. *Psychological Assessment, 32*(1), 72–84. https://doi.org/10.1037/pas0000772

Moran, P., Leese, M., Lee, T., Walters, P., Thornicroft, G., & Mann, A. (2003). Standardised Assessment of Personality—Abbreviated Scale (SAPAS): Preliminary validation of a brief screen for personality disorder. *The British Journal of Psychiatry, 183*(3), 228–232. https://doi.org/10.1192/bjp.183.3.228

Morey, L. C., Bender, D. S., & Skodol, A. E. (2013). Validating the proposed *Diagnostic and Statistical Manual of Mental Disorders*, 5th Edition, severity indicator for personality disorder. *The Journal of Nervous and Mental Disease, 201*(9), 729–735. https://doi.org/10.1097/NMD.0b013e3182a20ea8

Morey, L. C., & Hopwood, C. J. (2019). Brief report: Expert preferences for categorical, dimensional, and mixed/hybrid approaches to personality disorder diagnosis. *Journal of Personality Disorders, 34*(Suppl. C), 1–8. https://doi.org/10.1521/pedi_2019_33_398

Mulder, R. T., Horwood, J., Tyrer, P., Carter, J., & Joyce, P. R. (2016). Validating the proposed *ICD-11* domains. *Personality and Mental Health, 10*(2), 84–95. https://doi.org/10.1002/pmh.1336

Mulder, R. T., Newton-Howes, G., Crawford, M. J., & Tyrer, P. J. (2011). The central domains of personality pathology in psychiatric patients. *Journal of Personality Disorders, 25*(3), 364–377. https://doi.org/10.1521/pedi.2011.25.3.364

Olajide, K., Munjiza, J., Moran, P., O'Connell, L., Newton-Howes, G., Bassett, P., Akintomide, G., Ng, N., Tyrer, P., Mulder, R., & Crawford, M. J. (2018). Development and psychometric properties of the Standardized Assessment of Severity of Personality Disorder (SASPD). *Journal of Personality Disorders, 32*(1), 44–56. https://doi.org/10.1521/pedi_2017_31_285

Oltmanns, J. R. (2021). Personality traits in the *International Classification of Diseases 11th Revision (ICD-11)*. *Current Opinion in Psychiatry, 34*(1), 48–53. https://doi.org/10.1097/YCO.0000000000000656

Oltmanns, J. R., & Widiger, T. A. (2018). A self-report measure for the *ICD-11* dimensional trait model proposal: The Personality Inventory for *ICD-11*. *Psychological Assessment, 30*(2), 154–169. https://doi.org/10.1037/pas0000459

Oltmanns, J. R., & Widiger, T. A. (2019). Evaluating the assessment of the *ICD-11* personality disorder diagnostic system. *Psychological Assessment, 31*(5), 674–684. https://doi.org/10.1037/pas0000693

Oltmanns, J. R., & Widiger, T. A. (2020). The Five-Factor Personality Inventory for *ICD-11*: A facet-level assessment of the *ICD-11* trait model. *Psychological Assessment, 32*(1), 60–71. https://doi.org/10.1037/pas0000763

Ozer, D. J., & Benet-Martínez, V. (2006). Personality and the prediction of consequential outcomes. *Annual Review of Psychology, 57*(1), 401–421. https://doi.org/10.1146/annurev.psych.57.102904.190127

Papamalis, F. E., Kalyva, E., Teare, M. D., & Meier, P. S. (2020). The role of personality functioning in drug misuse treatment engagement. *Addiction, 115*(4), 726–739. https://doi.org/10.1111/add.14872

Parker, G., Hadzi-Pavlovic, D., Both, L., Kumar, S., Wilhelm, K., & Olley, A. (2004). Measuring disordered personality functioning: To love and to work reprised. *Acta Psychiatrica Scandinavica, 110*(3), 230–239. https://doi.org/10.1111/j.1600-0447.2004.00312.x

Reed, G. M. (2018). Progress in developing a classification of personality disorders for *ICD-11*. *World Psychiatry, 17*(2), 227–229. https://doi.org/10.1002/wps.20533

Rek, K., Thielmann, I., Henkel, M., Crawford, M., Piccirilli, L., Graff, A., Mestel, R., & Zimmermann, J. (2020). A psychometric evaluation of the Standardized Assessment of Severity of Personality Disorder (SASPD) in nonclinical and clinical German samples. *Psychological Assessment, 32*(10), 984–990. https://doi.org/10.1037/pas0000926

Sanatinia, R., Wang, D., Tyrer, P., Tyrer, H., Crawford, M., Cooper, S., Loebenberg, G., & Barrett, B. (2016). Impact of personality status on the outcomes and cost of cognitive–behavioural therapy for health anxiety. *The British Journal of Psychiatry, 209*(3), 244–250. https://doi.org/10.1192/bjp.bp.115.173526

Saulsman, L. M., & Page, A. C. (2004). The five-factor model and personality disorder empirical literature: A meta-analytic review. *Clinical Psychology Review, 23*(8), 1055–1085. https://doi.org/10.1016/j.cpr.2002.09.001

Sellbom, M., Solomon-Krakus, S., Bach, B., & Bagby, R. M. (2020). Validation of Personality Inventory for *DSM-5* (PID-5) algorithms to assess *ICD-11* personality trait domains in a psychiatric sample. *Psychological Assessment, 32*(1), 40–49. https://doi.org/10.1037/pas0000746

Sharp, C., Wright, A. G. C., Fowler, J. C., Frueh, B. C., Allen, J. G., Oldham, J., & Clark, L. A. (2015). The structure of personality pathology: Both general ('g') and specific ('s') factors? *Journal of Abnormal Psychology, 124*(2), 387–398. https://doi.org/10.1037/abn0000033

Simonsen, E. (2011). A clinician's view of the proposed changes. *Personality and Mental Health, 5*(4), 286–295. https://doi.org/10.1002/pmh.186

Simonsen, E., & Tyrer, P. (2005). New developments in personality disorder research. In G. N. Christodoulou (Ed.), *Advances in psychiatry* (2nd ed.). World Psychiatric Association.

Simonsen, S., Eikenaes, I. U.-M., Bach, B., Kvarstein, E., Gondan, M., Møller, S. B., & Wilberg, T. (2021). Level of alexithymia as a measure of personality dysfunction in avoidant personality disorder. *Nordic Journal of Psychiatry, 75*(4), 266–274. https://doi.org/10.1080/08039488.2020.1841290

Skodol, A. E. (2012). Personality disorders in *DSM-5*. *Annual Review of Clinical Psychology, 8*(1), 317–344. https://doi.org/10.1146/annurev-clinpsy-032511-143131

Skodol, A. E., Clark, L. A., Bender, D. S., Krueger, R. F., Morey, L. C., Verheul, R., Alarcon, R. D., Bell, C. C., Siever, L. J., & Oldham, J. M. (2011). Proposed changes in personality and personality disorder assessment and diagnosis for *DSM-5* Part I: Description and rationale. *Personality Disorders: Theory, Research, and Treatment, 2*(1), 4–22. https://doi.org/10.1037/a0021891

Skodol, A. E., First, M. B., Bender, D. S., & Oldham, J. M. (2018). Module II: Structured Clinical Interview for Personality Traits. In M. B. First, A. E. Skodol, D. S. Bender, & J. M. Oldham (Eds.), *Structured Clinical Interview for the* DSM-5 *Alternative Model for Personality Disorders (SCID-5-AMPD)*. American Psychiatric Publishing.

Skodol, A. E., Gunderson, J. G., Pfohl, B., Widiger, T. A., Livesley, W. J., & Siever, L. J. (2002). The borderline diagnosis I: Psychopathology, comorbidity, and personality structure. *Biological Psychiatry, 51*(12), 936–950. https://doi.org/10.1016/S0006-3223(02)01324-0

Sleep, C., Lynam, D. R., & Miller, J. D. (2021). Personality impairment in the *DSM-5* and *ICD-11*: Current standing and limitations. *Current Opinion in Psychiatry, 34*(1), 39–43. https://doi.org/10.1097/YCO.0000000000000657

Somma, A., Gialdi, G., & Fossati, A. (2020). Reliability and construct validity of the Personality Inventory for *ICD-11* (PiCD) in Italian adult participants. *Psychological Assessment, 32*(1), 29–39. https://doi.org/10.1037/pas0000766

Storebø, O. J., Stoffers-Winterling, J. M., Völlm, B. A., Kongerslev, M. T., Mattivi, J. T., Jørgensen, M. S., Faltinsen, E., Todorovac, A., Sales, C. P., Callesen, H. E., Lieb, K., & Simonsen, E. (2020). Psychological therapies for people with borderline personality disorder. *Cochrane Database of Systematic Reviews*. https://doi.org/10.1002/14651858.CD012955.pub2

Tarescavage, A. M., & Menton, W. H. (2020). Construct validity of the personality inventory for *ICD-11* (PiCD): Evidence from the MMPI-2-RF and CAT-PD-SF. *Psychological Assessment, 32*(9), 889–895. https://doi.org/10.1037/pas0000914

Thompson, K. N., Jackson, H., Cavelti, M., Betts, J., McCutcheon, L., Jovev, M., & Chanen, A. M. (2019). The clinical significance of subthreshold borderline personality disorder features in outpatient youth. *Journal of Personality Disorders, 33*(1), 71–81. https://doi.org/10.1521/pedi_2018_32_330

Tyrer, P. (2005). The problem of severity in the classification of personality disorder. *Journal of Personality Disorders, 19*(3), 309–314. https://doi.org/10.1521/pedi.2005.19.3.309

Tyrer, P., & Alexander, J. (1979). Classification of personality disorder. *The British Journal of Psychiatry, 135*(2), 163–167. https://doi.org/10.1192/bjp.135.2.163

Tyrer, P., Crawford, M., Mulder, R., Blashfield, R., Farnam, A., Fossati, A., Kim, Y.-R., Koldobsky, N., Lecic-Tosevski, D., Ndetei, D., Swales, M., Clark, L. A., & Reed, G. M. (2011). The rationale for the reclassification of personality disorder in the 11th revision of the *International Classification of Diseases (ICD-11)*. *Personality and Mental Health, 5*(4), 246–259. https://doi.org/10.1002/pmh.190

Tyrer, P., Crawford, M., Mulder, R., & the *ICD-11* Working Group for the Revision of Classification of Personality Disorders. (2011). Reclassifying personality disorders. *The Lancet, 377*(9780), 1814–1815. https://doi.org/10.1016/S0140-6736(10)61926-5

Tyrer, P., Crawford, M., Sanatinia, R., Tyrer, H., Cooper, S., Muller-Pollard, C., Christodoulou, P., Zauter-Tutt, M., Miloseska-Reid, K., Loebenberg, G., Guo, B., Yang, M., Wang, D., & Weich, S. (2014). Preliminary studies of the *ICD-11* classification of personality disorder in practice. *Personality and Mental Health, 8*(4), 254–263. https://doi.org/10.1002/pmh.1275

Tyrer, P., & Johnson, T. (1996). Establishing the severity of personality disorder. *The American Journal of Psychiatry, 153*(12), 1593–1597. https://doi.org/10.1176/ajp.153.12.1593

Tyrer, P., Mulder, R., Crawford, M., Newton-Howes, G., Simonsen, E., Ndetei, D., Koldobsky, N., Fossati, A., Mbatia, J., & Barrett, B. (2010). Personality disorder: A new global perspective. *World Psychiatry, 9*(1), 56–60. https://doi.org/10.1002/j.2051-5545.2010.tb00270.x

Tyrer, P., Mulder, R., Kim, Y.-R., & Crawford, M. J. (2019). The development of the *ICD-11* classification of personality disorders: An amalgam of science, pragmatism, and politics. *Annual Review of Clinical Psychology, 15*, 481–502. https://doi.org/10.1146/annurev-clinpsy-050718-095736

Tyrer, P., Reed, G. M., & Crawford, M. J. (2015). Classification, assessment, prevalence, and effect of personality disorder. *The Lancet, 385*(9969), 717–726. https://doi.org/10.1016/S0140-6736(14)61995-4

Verheul, R., & Widiger, T. A. (2004). A meta-analysis of the prevalence and usage of the personality disorder not otherwise specified (PDNOS) diagnosis. *Journal of Personality Disorders, 18*(4), 309–319. https://doi.org/10.1521/pedi.2004.18.4.309

Watters, C. A., & Bagby, R. M. (2018). A meta-analysis of the five-factor internal structure of the Personality Inventory for *DSM-5*. *Psychological Assessment, 30*(9), 1255–1260. https://doi.org/10.1037/pas0000605

Watters, C. A., Bagby, R. M., & Sellbom, M. (2019). Meta-analysis to derive an empirically based set of personality facet criteria for the alternative *DSM-5* model for personality disorders. *Personality Disorders: Theory, Research, and Treatment, 10*(2), 97–104. https://doi.org/10.1037/per0000307

Waugh, M. H., McClain, C. M., Mariotti, E. C., Mulay, A. L., DeVore, E. N., Lenger, K. A., Russell, A. N., Florimbio, A. R., Lewis, K. C., Ridenour, J. M., & Beevers, L. G. (2020). Comparative content analysis of self-report scales for level of personality functioning. *Journal of Personality Assessment, 103*(2), 161–173. https://doi.org/10.1080/00223891.2019.1705464

Weekers, L. C., Hutsebaut, J., & Kamphuis, J. H. (2019). The Level of Personality Functioning Scale-Brief Form 2.0: Update of a brief instrument for assessing level of personality functioning. *Personality and Mental Health, 13*(1), 3–14. https://doi.org/10.1002/pmh.1434

Widiger, T. A., & Simonsen, E. (2005). Alternative dimensional models of personality disorder: Finding a common ground. *Journal of Personality Disorders, 19*(2), 110–130. https://doi.org/10.1521/pedi.19.2.110.62628

World Health Organization. (1994). *International statistical classification of diseases and related health problems* (10th ed.).

World Health Organization. (2019). *International statistical classification of diseases and related health problems* (11th ed.). https://icd.who.int/

World Health Organization. (2022). *ICD-11 clinical descriptions and diagnostic guidelines for mental and behavioural disorders.* https://gcp.network/en/private/icd-11-guidelines

Wright, A. G. C., Hopwood, C. J., Skodol, A. E., & Morey, L. C. (2016). Longitudinal validation of general and specific structural features of personality pathology. *Journal of Abnormal Psychology, 125*(8), 1120–1134. https://doi.org/10.1037/abn0000165

Yang, M., Coid, J., & Tyrer, P. (2010). Personality pathology recorded by severity: National survey. *The British Journal of Psychiatry, 197*(3), 193–199. https://doi.org/10.1192/bjp.bp.110.078956

Zimmermann, J., Müller, S., Bach, B., Hutsebaut, J., Hummelen, B., & Fischer, F. (2020). A common metric for self-reported severity of personality disorder. *Psychopathology, 53*(3-4), 168–178. https://doi.org/10.1159/000507377

3

Clinical Utility of Proposed Dimensional Personality Disorder Models

Considerations and Opportunities

Caleb J. Siefert, John Porcerelli, Kevin B. Meehan, and Barry Dauphin

There has been considerable discussion regarding the clinical utility of the dimensional approach to personality disorders (PD) outlined for the 11th edition of the *International Statistical Classification of Diseases and Related Health Problems* (*ICD-11*; World Health Organization, 2019) and the Alternative Model of Personality Disorders (AMPD) within the *Diagnostic and Statistical Manual of Mental Disorders* (5th ed.; *DSM-5*; American Psychiatric Association, 2013). Much of this discourse centers on the question "Do proposed dimensional PD diagnostic systems have sufficient clinical utility?" This question frames utility as if it were static, existing within a system. We assert that utility does not exist solely within a system, arguing that it reflects an interaction between the system and the clinicians employing it. In this chapter, we revisit prior discourse and research on the clinical utility of the AMPD and the *ICD-11* PD system to identify areas of tension. We reframe these issues in terms of "next steps" for enhancing utility. If the field is to transition from categorical to dimensional PD systems, then continuing to improve utility is important.

REVISED PERSONALITY DISORDER SYSTEMS FOR *ICD-11* AND *DSM-5*

The AMPD and *ICD-11* PD systems have been extensively described elsewhere (e.g., Bach et al., 2020; McCabe & Widiger, 2020; Tyrer et al., 2019; Waugh et al., 2017; Zimmermann et al., 2019). While similar, the systems do differ. The *ICD-11* system is fully dimensional. The AMPD uses a hybrid approach,

https://doi.org/10.1037/0000310-004
Personality Disorders and Pathology: Integrating Clinical Assessment and Practice in the DSM-5 *and* ICD-11 *Era*, S. K. Huprich (Editor)
Copyright © 2022 by the American Psychological Association. All rights reserved.

organizing patterns of pathological traits into six PD prototypes, while also allowing clinicians to diagnose a PD as an idiographic constellation of the traits not subsumed under the prototypes. In the AMPD, pathological traits are rated dimensionally, while the *ICD-11* has the clinician code traits as being either present or absent.

Despite differences, the systems share many features. Both systems base PD diagnosis on dysfunction at a global level. Criterion A of the AMPD outlines assessment of level of personality functioning (LPF). Steps 1 and 2 of the *ICD-11* system detail assessment of PD severity. Severity and LPF ratings are both based on pervasiveness and intensity of problems in self-functioning (i.e., identity and self-direction) and interpersonal functioning (i.e., empathy and intimacy). LPF and severity are conceptualized dimensionally, with subcomponents viewed as mutually reciprocal (Bender et al., 2011). For example, a chronically negative identity may inhibit intimacy in close relationships. When pathological levels of LPF or severity are present, the patient is diagnosed with a PD.

When a patient is diagnosed with a PD, clinicians can specify the nature of the PD using pathological traits (and PD prototypes in the AMPD). Both systems contain five higher order pathological traits. The AMPD further breaks these down into 25 facets, while the *ICD-11* utilizes only the five higher order traits. The first three pathological traits are the same in both systems: Negative Affectivity, Detachment, and Disinhibition. The *ICD-11*'s fourth trait is Dissociality (self-centeredness, lack of empathy, demand for admiration), which is similar to the AMPD's Antagonism (manipulation, deceitfulness, grandiosity). The fifth trait of the AMPD is Psychoticism (odd or eccentric beliefs, cognitive or perceptual experiences deviating from social norms), whereas the fifth in the *ICD-11* is Anankastia (stubbornness, rigidity, perfectionism). Psychoticism in the AMPD involves features of Schizotypal PD (McCabe & Widiger, 2020). It is not included in the *ICD-11* because schizotypal symptoms are classified as psychotic symptoms (Tyrer et al., 2019). A final similarity is that the AMPD and *ICD-11* model generated strong reactions (Herpertz et al., 2017; Tyrer et al., 2019). Critics and proponents (a) agree that categorical PD approaches have limitations but (b) diverge on whether dimensional PD systems sufficiently address these. Clinical utility has been a central point of contention.

CLINICAL UTILITY AND DIMENSIONAL PERSONALITY DISORDER DIAGNOSTIC SYSTEMS

To achieve widespread adoption, diagnostic systems must be useful. Adopting a construct validity approach, Meehl (1959) argued that diagnoses have utility when they group people in ways that provide information on etiology, prognosis, and treatment course (e.g., risk of relapse). Today, construct validity and clinical utility are viewed as related but conceptually distinct constructs (Kendell & Jablensky, 2003). An invalid system cannot be clinically useful; however, a valid system that is difficult to use, implement, or translate into practice will have limited utility and poor clinical adoption (First, 2005). Clinicians' perceptions of utility influence whether systems are truly adopted (or are employed in a perfunctory way [e.g., to submit claims]; Keeley et al., 2016; Zachar & First, 2015).

Among valid systems, some are more intuitive, more parsimonious, and less demanding of resources than others. These features are indicators of utility (Mullins-Sweatt & Widiger, 2011). Several experts have identified criteria for evaluating the clinical utility of a diagnostic system (Clarkin & Huprich, 2011; Evans et al., 2013; First, 2005; First et al., 2004; First & Westen, 2007; Keeley et al., 2016; Mullins-Sweatt et al., 2016; Reed et al., 2011; Samuel & Widiger, 2006; Verheul, 2005). Across experts, five themes consistently emerge: *Diagnostic functionality* refers to the clarity of decisional criteria for differentiating those *with* from those *without* a disorder (and for differentiating one disorder or style from another). *Goodness of fit* involves the system's comprehensiveness in describing the range of problems clinicians encounter, ease of applying criteria to individual patients, and usefulness for describing a patient's global personality. *Ease of implementation* refers to the costs involved in learning and transitioning to the system. It is impacted by the intuitiveness of the system and the availability of resources for employing the system (e.g., self-report tests, interviews, training materials). *Professional communication* refers to the usefulness of the system for facilitating communication with patients, other professionals, researchers, and third-party administrators. *Clinical direction* refers to the usefulness of the system in planning treatments and for anticipating needs (e.g., likelihood of hospitalization or early drop out), as well as the ease with which the system can be integrated with existing treatment approaches. Elements of these criteria have served as the basis for comparing diagnostic systems with one another in research contexts. We review these comparative studies next.

RESEARCH INTO THE CLINICAL UTILITY OF THE AMPD AND *ICD-11* PD SYSTEMS

A number of studies have compared the clinical utility of dimensional and categorical approaches to PD diagnosis. Early studies focused on the five-factor model (FFM). For example, Blais (1997) and Sprock (2002) found that clinicians were able to effectively apply the FFM to their clinical cases. Eventually, research comparing categorical PD approaches with the FFM was conducted, but findings are mixed. For example, Sprock (2003) found that clinicians preferred categorical diagnoses when rating vignettes; however, Samuel and Widiger (2006) speculated that the use of vignettes from *DSM-IV-TR* (2000) training sources confounded results. They found that clinicians rated FFM approaches more positively than categorical models when clinicians were making ratings based on detailed case histories.

Would these findings hold with actual patients? Spitzer and colleagues (2008) had clinicians apply the FFM to one of their patients and found that clinicians rated the categorical models more highly than the FFM. Lowe and Widiger (2009) criticized this study for using a burdensome FFM rating system. They replicated the study with a less demanding FFM approach and found clinicians to prefer the FFM system. Rottman et al. (2009) had clinicians translate PD categories into the FFM and found clinicians to prefer categorical approaches; however, Glover et al. (2012) replicated this study without requiring clinicians to translate from categorical systems and achieved opposing results (i.e., FFM approaches were preferred). Later studies by Mullins-Sweatt and Widiger (2011) had clinicians rate an existing patient with categorical and FFM models on a single occasion, and Samuel and Widiger (2011) had clinicians rate patients across the course of treatment. In both studies, clinicians' ratings showed slight preferences for the FFM. While this body of research provides some support for dimensional approaches, the FFM is not synonymous with either the AMPD or the *ICD-11* system.

Two recent studies focused directly on the AMPD system. Morey et al. (2014) had a large sample ($N = 337$) of psychologists, psychiatrists, and therapists compare the AMPD with the existing categorical model. The categorical approach was rated easier to use and more useful than the AMPD for communication with clinicians, while the AMPD was rated superior for communication with patients, formulating interventions, comprehensiveness, and descriptive utility. Nelson and colleagues (2017) had graduate students in clinical psychology ($N = 329$) read descriptions of 15 PDs and rate the utility of the categorical approach, the AMPD, and two other approaches. On average, participants rated the AMPD more favorably than other models, though some findings violated this trend. Responses to open-ended questions indicated that all models were viewed as having weaknesses.

Across studies, standard deviations for utility ratings were large. Thus, clinicians evidenced considerable variability in how they applied components of clinical utility to the systems. An excellent feature of the Nelson et al. (2017) study was the analysis of open-ended comments, which revealed (among other things) that 138 participants described the AMPD as useful and 130 described it as not useful (a similar pattern was observed for categorical systems). Thus, even early career professionals evidence differences in how they experience these systems.

TENSION REGARDING DIMENSIONAL PERSONALITY DISORDER SYSTEMS: IMPLICATIONS FOR UTILITY

The clinical utility of the AMPD and *ICD-11* PD systems has been much discussed. Like participants in the studies just described, experts often reach differing conclusions regarding each system's utility. Here, we note tensions underlying some of these disagreements.

Clinicians Think in Categories

Arguably, the most cogent concern raised against dimensional PD systems is that clinicians think in categories. Citing a wealth of evidence from cognitive–affective neuroscience, Bornstein (2019) concluded that humans are "built to classify" (p. 202). Clinicians clearly rely on internal exemplars to assign clinical diagnoses (First et al., 2004; Hayes, 2018). Thus, categorical systems may be more intuitive. By condensing a large amount of clinical information, categorical diagnoses serve as a "shorthand," which may increase efficacies in professional communication. These efficiencies, however, invite heuristics, stereotypes, and bias, which may sometimes be problematic (Bornstein, 2019). If a clinician tells another professional that a patient has Schizotypal PD, this communication is efficient to the degree that both professionals use a similar shorthand to conceptualize this disorder. If they do not, communication may appear easy—when in fact, miscommunication is occurring. It is unclear whether a shift to a dimensional approach alleviates these challenges, worsens them, or is simply a lateral move.

Consistent with the hybrid approach of the AMPD, Bornstein (2019) agreed that diagnostic "types" can be considered trait profiles. Clinicians' tendency, however, to think in categories could lead them to invert the diagnostic process of dimensional PD systems. Clinicians may place patients into well-known types and then assign trait ratings post hoc. Such inversions pose few problems for severity ratings but may threaten the ecological validity of pathological trait ratings. This may also occur in categorical models (e.g., assessment of symptoms is overly guided by confirmation bias).

Proponents of the new models typically grant that people think in categories, but they argue that with sufficient time, training, and experience, clinicians will transition to thinking dimensionally (Bach et al., 2015). In our own work training clinicians in graduate schools, we have found trainees to be as accepting of dimensional PD models as they are of categorical ones. This conforms to the findings of Nelson and colleagues (2017), suggesting that familiarity may play some role in why some seasoned clinicians resist moving away from categories. It seems unlikely, however, that familiarity alone accounts for all criticisms. Beyond thinking in categories, some clinicians argue that PDs inherently involve problematic "if–then" contingencies that are not easily folded into dimensional conceptualizations of PDs.

Personality Pathology and If–Then Contingencies

Some question whether newly proposed systems can account for the if–then contingency patterns observed in PDs (Bornstein, 2019; Huprich, 2020). The dysregulation common in PDs involves dynamic interplay between cognition/affect, perception, and motivation, often giving rise to consistently inconsistent behavior (Meehan et al., 2018a, 2018b; Meehan et al., 2019; Roche, 2018). Mischel and Shoda's (1995) model frames dispositional patterns in relation to cues and contexts that elicit and inhibit them. Bornstein (2019, p. 203) described several empirically supported if–then contingencies that differentiate among PD types, and Huprich and Nelson (2015) offered guidelines on how to utilize if–then contingencies in PD diagnosis. For example, people with Narcissistic PD are hypervigilant for cues of weakness and respond defensively when such cues are observed but may not react defensively in the absence of such cues (Horvath & Morf, 2009).

Experienced clinicians consider dysfunctional relationships between internal states, behavior, and contexts when assessing for PDs. Some are unclear how this form of assessment layers into dimensional approaches (Clarkin & Huprich, 2011). For example, the Intimacy Avoidance facet was expected to be a feature of Avoidant PD. Such associations have not been consistently obtained (Watters et al., 2019), possibly due to discrepancy between motivation and behavior. Those with Avoidant PD desire closeness but inhibit pursuing it due to anxiety and poor self-image (Sellbom et al., 2017). Challenges folding if–then contingencies into dimensional assessments may limit aspects of utility (e.g., diagnostic function, clinical direction) for dimensional PD systems.

Not everyone agrees with this assessment. Proponents argue that facet-level traits in the AMPD offer the granularity necessary to account for inconsistencies in behaviors, motives, and cognitions (e.g., Wright et al., 2015). Others frame dimensional ratings as a starting point (rather than an end point) for thinking about patient dynamics. Hopwood and colleagues (2015) offered a case example in which analysis of the AMPD is augmented with a "structural" interpersonal approach (which serves to identify and address the meaning of if–then contingencies for the patient). While Criterion A of the AMPD and *ICD-11* PD severity ratings do not explicitly target if–then contingencies, they do require clinicians to consider dysfunction in key areas of life likely to occur as a function of problematic discrepancies. Thus, even if the conflicting impulses often observed in PDs are not fully captured by pathological trait ratings, they impact diagnostic status by influencing ratings of LPF and severity (Bach & First, 2018).

Current categorical models also rarely require specific if–then contingencies for PD diagnosis. Only a small number of PD symptoms in categorical models overtly refer to inconsistency (e.g., a pattern of unstable relationships) or dynamics (e.g., unwilling to relate unless certain of being liked). This has not precluded clinicians from focusing on dynamic if–then contingencies to formulate treatment approaches. In the same way, newly developed PD models allow clinicians to identify problematic if–then contingencies (even if these systems do not require them for diagnosis). Overall, the thrust of questions regarding if–then contingencies hints at another oft raised concern: Do the AMPD and *ICD-11* PD systems sufficiently lend themselves to planning treatments?

To What Degree Should Personality Disorder Diagnoses Shape Treatments?

Some question whether dimensional PD models lend themselves to treatment planning and progress monitoring (i.e., the clinical direction component of clinical utility; Clarkin et al., 2020; Huprich, 2020; Meehan & Clarkin, 2015). It is unclear whether pathological traits should be the target of treatment or if they are simply indicators of a condition. Categorical models fare only slightly better in this respect (Kupfer et al., 2002). Still, symptoms of categorical disorders do give clear treatment targets. Clinicians working with patients with borderline personality disorder (BPD) who self-harm, for example, likely agree that reducing the frequency of nonsuicidal self-injurious behavior should be a treatment goal. The specific avenues traversed to achieve this aim vary as a function of clinician, patient, and treatment approach. Thus, even in categorical models, diagnosis provides only a general road map toward treatment targets.

Some disagreements regarding the clinical direction component of utility may reflect differing expectations regarding the degree to which diagnosis *should* inform the treatment plan. Despite different conceptualizations and varying treatment techniques, dialectical behavior therapy, schema therapy, and transference-focused therapy have been shown to effectively treat BPD. This reflects that treatment planning occurs at different levels based upon differing theoretical frameworks. Diagnosis provides general targets, while treatment approach and idiographic assessment of the patient provides more granular objectives. So, not all aspects of treatment planning *should* occur at the level of diagnosis. In fact, the AMPD and *ICD-11* use of theory-neutral language allows for a shared language across differing treatment approaches. Still, it is unclear if the AMPD and *ICD-11* PD systems provide for even a general level of goal agreement. If they do not, then diagnosis with these systems may contribute very little to treatment planning. Regardless of whether one views a diagnostic system as an early or late step to determining treatment targets, diagnoses must make meaningful distinctions among individuals in order to have clinical utility.

Do New Models Have Sufficient Discriminative Power?

A frequent criticism of categorical models is that diagnostic categories show excessive overlap. This limits the diagnostic function and goodness of fit utility components of categorical systems. It is unclear whether dimensional PD models truly improve on this state of affairs. Decreasing the number of PD prototypes will (by necessity) reduce comorbidity. The question remains of whether this movement truly reduces problematic overlaps. For example, Dependent PD will now be coded as PD-Trait Specified, with high ratings on the facets of Submissiveness, Anxiousness, and Separation Insecurity. Clarkin and Huprich (2011) questioned whether this trait pattern meaningfully differentiates Dependent from Avoidant or Borderline PDs (which also include high scores on these facets). Meehan and Clarkin (2015) raised similar concerns, noting that trait profiles for Narcissistic, Antisocial, and Obsessive-Compulsive PDs are similar.

Studies of facet profiles in the AMPD provide mixed support for the differentiation among AMPD prototypes. A recent meta-analysis found the trait profiles underlying the six PD prototypes of the AMPD to be sufficiently independent, though Antisocial and Narcissistic PDs did show problematic overlap (Watters et al., 2019). The discriminative power of the traits and facets, however, was less robust, leading the authors to state that "several nonproposed traits also reached moderate-to-large correlations with the PDs" (p. 102). In considering these data, one must differentiate the models from the measures used to assess them. The meta-analysis relied exclusively on Personality Inventory for *DSM-5* (PID-5) studies, and the PID-5 was not developed to maximize discriminant validity. It has sometimes produced large intertrait correlations

60   *Siefert et al.*

among higher order pathological traits (McCabe & Widiger, 2020) and among facets (Crego et al., 2015). Research with other tools may produce different results.

There has been less research on differentiation among PD styles with the *ICD-11* model. While proponents of the AMPD point to facet-level ratings for differentiating among PD styles, the *ICD-11* employs only higher order traits. While efficient, it is challenging to imagine how differences among PD styles will be sufficiently characterized (e.g., Narcissistic and Antisocial PDs would be expected to involve high Dissociality). Some pathological traits seem to have near one-to-one relationships with PD types. For example, Obsessive-Compulsive PD corresponds to high anankastia, and Avoidant PD is associated with high detachment. It is unclear how simply moving to trait labels (vs. diagnostic categories) clears up problematic overlaps between disorders. Proponents of the *ICD-11* argue that clinical efficiency more than makes up for these challenges (Bach & First, 2018), noting that mental health professionals clearly prefer simple systems with fewer domains (Reed et al., 2011). By sacrificing aspects of diagnostic function and goodness of fit, the *ICD-11*'s system enhances ease of implementation (Keeley et al., 2016, p. 10). Still, some claims are overstated. Bach and First (2018) argued that PD severity replaces comorbidity. This sentence would be equally accurate if rephrased to say "hides comorbidity."[1] While we disagree with the frame of such statements, we agree with their thrust. If existing systems have questionable discriminative power and excessive comorbidity while *requiring considerable time, training, and effort to learn and implement*, then a movement to streamlined rating systems is advisable (even if it does not address underlying difficulties discriminating among personality problems). Arguments for prioritizing utility, such as these, may not be raised enough (though *ICD-11* PD system proponents are more willing than those of the AMPD). This may be due, in part, to fears that such arguments invite criticisms regarding breadth of consideration.

Are Complexity and Efficiency Properly Balanced in Dimensional PD Systems?

Natural tension exists between a system's goodness of fit and ease of implementation. Complex systems may promote goodness of fit even as they reduce ease of implementation. A broad criticism of *DSM-5* (beyond the AMPD) is that the inclusion of increasing numbers of specifiers and diagnoses creates training and implementation burdens on clinicians (and can result in poor ecological validity). Proponents of dimensional PD systems either argue overtly

---

[1]Statements such as this are not uncommon among proponents for newly developed PD systems but can be misleading and contradictory of other arguments. For example, the frequency of the use of PDNOS is typically cited as a problem of existing systems; however, newly proposed systems' use of LPF and PD severity invites a PDNOS-like approach. Further, for all the debate over newly developed systems, both critics and proponents seem to largely ignore that the two-step process implied by the *ICD-11* and AMPD is not so wholeheartedly different from the *DSM-5*'s current two-step approach (in which the clinician must first ascertain if a PD is present using the general criteria and then seek to clarify if criteria are met for any of the 10 PD diagnostic types).

for reductionism or implicitly support it (through heavy reliance on factor-analytic research; see Zimmermann et al., 2019). Limiting the number of underlying dimensions condenses an array of behaviors, motives, characteristics, and patterns into a streamlined nosology.

Efforts to streamline can engender concerns about what has been lost in translation. If too simplistic, goodness of fit suffers (i.e., while simple to rate, the system fails to capture actual PD patients). Bach and First (2018) stated, "The parsimoniousness of the *ICD-11* classification may also frustrate clinicians who desire a more detailed conceptualization of the patient's personality structure" (p. 11). This has been the case for some; however, when diagnostic systems are overly burdensome or complex, clinicians cut corners and show little adherence with diagnostic rules (Garb, 2005). Mullins-Sweatt and colleagues (2016) believe a major contributor to poor clinical utility is excessive complexity in the form of an ever-increasing number of categories, subtypes, and specifiers. Still, there are concerns that dimensional PD systems are streamlined to a degree that harms PD conceptualization (see Clarkin & Huprich, 2011). A goal of diagnostic systems is to group like individuals while also differentiating among groups. When there are many avenues to a rating (e.g., high negative affectivity), the label provides less meaning, as it is unclear which avenues the individual took to arrive at this rating. Still, there are also advantages to broad dimensions.

Criterion A and PD severity have generally been met with praise (Pincus et al., 2020). They are somewhat vaguely defined. This honors clinical judgement while also creating uncertainty. It is not clear if and where some components of personality belong. For example, should internalized moral standards and capacity to regulate aggression be viewed as aspects of self-functioning (Clarkin et al., 2020)? Should such decisions be made on a case-to-case basis depending on the specific motives that underlie the patient's presentation? There is a wealth of evidence that PDs involve a number of defensive and cognitive processes occurring outside of awareness, but it is unclear where these features should be located in newly developed models (Bornstein, 2019; Huprich, 2018a; Meehan & Clarkin, 2015).

Are These the Right Pathological Traits?

The *ICD-11* system's and AMPD's goodness of fit and clinical direction components of utility have also been questioned in terms of the higher order pathological traits for differentiating between personality styles. Factor analysis is routinely applied to study pathological and nonpathological personality, playing a key role in the development of the AMPD and *ICD-11* PD systems. Not all researchers agree on these five pathological traits (Huprich, 2020; Huprich et al., 2010). For example, factor analysis of the 200 items from the Shedler-Westen Assessment Procedure (Shedler & Westen, 1998) suggested 12 factors that loosely reflected the familiar PD categories (e.g., Antisocial PD, Narcissistic PD). Huprich and colleagues (2010) factor analyzed PD symptoms using SCID-II interviews, finding a 10-factor model superior to a five-factor fit.

Research into the neurobiology raises similar questions. While most researchers in this domain are proponents of dimensional approaches, some argue for different dimensions for characterizing PDs. For example, Lenzenweger and Depue (2020) viewed PDs as emergent phenomenon reflecting complex interrelationships among underlying neurobiological systems. These authors suggested three reaction surfaces: Incentive-Anxiety, Affiliative Reward-Rejection Sensitivity, and Neural Constraint. These surfaces reflect dynamic ratios between motivational neurobiological systems. For example, the Incentive-Anxiety surface involves a dopamine-facilitated positive-reward-seeking system in relation to a norepinephrine and stress hormone modulated system regulating negative emotion and avoidance. Ultimately, both camps argued that goodness of fit is hampered by the pathological traits selected.

NEXT STEPS FOR IMPROVING THE CLINICAL UTILITY OF DIMENSIONAL PERSONALITY DISORDER SYSTEMS

Clinical utility involves an interaction between system and clinician. It is not static; it can be improved. As the *ICD-11* moves forward with its dimensional system and the *DSM* considers the AMPD, tensions give direction for improving the utility of both systems.

The Need for Needs Analyses

There is considerable variance in how clinicians perceive and rate diagnostic systems. Comparative research on this topic, especially the AMPD, is framed as an "election" of sorts (i.e., of the candidates, which achieves higher average ratings). While necessary, such studies shed little light on how utility could be improved. The time may be ripe for qualitative efforts in the form of a needs analysis. While we affirm that adoptions of diagnostic systems be based on empirical research, determining how to best structure the system to meet clinicians' needs is also essential. Proponents of the AMPD are working to establish the former, but there is room to improve the latter. The *ICD-11* fairs a bit better in this respect (Reed et al., 2011). Input from real-world clinicians can highlight training and implementation needs that could be addressed through resource development. Such resources could enhance the diagnostic function of new systems by improving clinicians' accuracy in using decision rules and ultimately increasing their confidence in their decisions.

Building Confidence in Diagnostic Decisions Through Training Resources

The success of newly developed PD systems hinges largely on clinician understanding of how to make severity and LPF ratings. In the *ICD-11* model, a significant severity rating equates to a PD diagnosis, and LPF rating plays a similar role for the AMPD. Interrater reliability across clinicians needs to be strong for LPF and severity ratings. For this, experience with the new systems will be necessary (Lambert, 2012). There is a need for clear criteria to establish diagnostic thresholds and examples of how to apply these to case material (i.e., when is severity enough to warrant a diagnosis?; see Morey, Bender, & Skodol, 2013; Morey, Krueger, & Skodol, 2013).

Existing studies support rater agreement for Criterion A (Buer Christensen et al., 2018; Garcia et al., 2018). Research is needed to examine how training resources can improve assessment. We are not advocating studies comparing agreement among well-trained and naive clinicians (see Zimmermann et al., 2014); we are calling for studies examining clinician agreement (and accuracy where possible) before and after exposure to training materials or resources. Prior to conducting such research, development of resources designed to guide clinicians in differentiating among severity and LPF levels would be of benefit and allow for studies assessing how resources contribute to improved rater agreement. As it is increasingly clear that we will transition to dimensional models, research should shift from determining *if* clinicians can achieve agreement toward identifying what *improves* agreement.

While general criteria for severity and LPF have been described, detailed case examples with explanations can assist clinicians in decision making (Bach et al., 2015; Bach & First, 2018). While improved agreement across clinicians is desirable in its own right, we raise it here in relation to clinician confidence. When clinicians feel they are employing a diagnostic system in a manner similar to others, their willingness to employ the system is likely to increase. Clinician confidence may be higher for some cases than others, and developing resources to help clinicians navigate such decisions is also desirable and may further enhance adoption of newly developed systems.

Clarifying Diagnostic Efficiency for Dimensional PD Assessment Tools

In the *ICD-11* system and AMPD, PD ratings are ultimately clinical decisions. Continued development and refinement of clinician rating scales, interviews, and self-report scales will address clinicians' needs (First & Westen, 2007). Existing research supports the reliability and validity of a variety of measures, rating scales, and interviews for use in dimensional PD assessments (Buer Christensen et al., 2018; Fowler et al., 2018; Garcia et al., 2018; Keeley et al., 2016). Correlational and group-based research are important to establish the construct, convergent, and predictive validity of these tools; however, research establishing cut scores and clarifying diagnostic efficiency will have tremendous value for clinicians seeking to make decisions about individual cases.

Determining diagnostic efficiency for decisions related to Criterion A and PD severity (in the *ICD-11*) is particularly important because these ratings establish whether a patient has a PD, has subclinical aspects of a PD, or does not have a PD. While further research is needed, there are studies serving as excellent models on which to build. For example, Morey, Bender, and Skodol (2013) found the Level of Personality Functioning Scale to have good sensitivity (84.6%) and adequate specificity (72.2%) for detecting patients with *DSM-IV-TR* PD diagnoses. Olajide and colleagues (2018) reported cut scores for the Standardized

Assessment of Severity of Personality Disorder, a scale developed for rating PD severity using the *ICD-11* criteria, to have adequate sensitivity (>70%) and specificity (>70%).

Ideally, similar research will be conducted with the pathological traits. While research in this area is largely lacking, a notable exception is a study by Fowler and colleagues (2018). These authors examined the diagnostic efficiency of the Big Five Inventory and the PID-5 for diagnosing BPD in a large clinical sample. They reported specific cut scores yielding good sensitivity (81%) and adequate specificity (76%) for classification based on PID-5 scores. Additional research in this area is particularly important for the AMPD's hybrid model, which has retained PD prototypes. Ideally, as the field transitions to dimensional models, there will be an increase in diagnostic efficiency research for dimensional tools to provide clinicians with direction for when and how to use these scales in order to establish when there is sufficient severity or problematic LPF to require a PD diagnosis and to differentiate among PD prototypes in the AMPD. Beyond supplying clinicians with validated tools and strong recommendations for how to make decisions with them, a transition to new PD systems can be eased by building on what clinicians already do.

Integrating the Old With the New

When transitioning to new systems, it is advantageous to understand how features of the old system are integrated into the new one. There are tensions between critics and proponents of dimensional PD systems in terms of their discriminative power, ability to fold in important if–then contingencies, and capacity to direct treatments. In developing resources for easing clinician transition to dimensional PD systems, it may be wise to consider links between the existing categorical system and newly developed PD systems.

While reasonable criticisms of the current categorical system have been raised, no one is saying that the symptoms contained within this system are useless. In fact, PD symptoms listed in *DSM-5*'s categorical approach may serve as indicators of LPF, PD severity, and pathological traits. Some studies empirically link pathological traits and LPF to specific PD symptoms (Mulay et al., 2019; Mulder et al., 2016). Building on these studies may help clinicians familiar with these symptoms to understand their role in dimensional models. Beyond empirical research, descriptions of case material in which symptoms are linked to LPF/PD severity and pathological traits can highlight how patient dynamics inform decisions. For example, understanding how a specific symptom (e.g., self-harm) corresponds to a pathological trait entails consideration of motives that promote and maintain the symptom. Thus, one patient engages in detailed ritualistic-like self-harm to feel numb and reduce feelings of shame (Negative Affectivity), another threatens and engages in self-harm to manipulate others (Antagonism), and another impulsively self-harms despite explicit desire to avoid this behavior (Disinhibition). Resources that help clinicians understand how symptoms they are familiar with assessing and treating map to dimensional models can ease the transition to new models by reaffirming to clinicians that familiar symptoms remain important. Such resources could enhance diagnostic function, goodness of fit, and ease of implementation. They may also prevent reification of PD assessment measures.

Preventing Reification of Assessment PD Severity and Pathological Trait Measures

Experts in assessment have played a significant role in developing dimensional PD models. Still, a patient's standing on an assessment measure (e.g., the PID-5) should inform clinical decisions but should not be the sole basis for clinical decisions. Just as high scores on measures of attention-deficit/hyperactivity disorder symptoms can be produced by a variety of clinical phenomena (e.g., head trauma, severe depression), scores on measures of LPF, PD severity, and pathological traits must be considered in a broader context.

We are in agreement with Mullins-Sweatt and Widiger (2011), who speculated that increased use of formal instruments in clinical settings is desirable. Still, clinicians retain the burden of acting as a check-and-balance when using such tools. Individuals presenting with acute distress may score highly on indices of LPF/PD severity and pathological traits as a function of their distress (vs. as a result of persistent, ongoing patterns). While useful, self-report measures are limited in their ability to clarify dynamics underlying individuals' dimensional scores. This is especially true for PDs. This is not an attack on self-report measures; we raise this issue to highlight the importance of clinicians learning how to assess, listen for, and link client descriptions of symptoms and problems to PD severity and pathological trait ratings. Clinical case papers and resources cultivating clinicians' capacity to make such decisions prevent reification of assessment measures and promote clinicians' ability to transition from making a dimensional PD diagnosis to developing a treatment plan.

Facilitating Links Between Dimensional PD Models and Treatment Planning

Tensions regarding the extent to which the AMPD and *ICD-11* PD systems fulfill the clinical direction component of utility certainly exist. These are worsened, to a degree, by limited consensus on the extent to which diagnostic systems should direct treatment planning. Correctly categorizing like individuals need not necessarily translate into specific goals for treatment, and treatment plans *should* vary across individuals (even within the same diagnostic category). Still, if diagnosis is based on clinically relevant factors, then there should be overlap, even if at a high level, in terms of treatment targets for individuals sharing a diagnosis (Clark et al., 2020; Vivian et al., 2012).

Clinicians' ability to use dimensional PD systems may be enhanced by improving their understanding of how their specific treatment approach or theory layers into dimensional PD models (Meehan & Clarkin, 2015). The AMPD and *ICD-11* systems employ nontheoretical language; still, real-world clinicians have a reasonable need for resources that help them bridge the gap between these systems and the treatment approaches they utilize. Currently, a few papers link the AMPD and *ICD-11* systems to specific treatment approaches (see Bach & Bernstein, 2019; Hopwood et al., 2015; Pincus et al., 2020). These papers are an excellent start, but more papers of this ilk are needed across the full spectrum of PD approaches (e.g., cognitive behavioral approaches, transference-focused psychotherapy, dialectical behavior therapy). To achieve this aim, proponents of the AMPD and *ICD-11* should partner with influential clinical theorists within specific theoretical treatment domains. Again, special issues in journals or edited books may offer forums for such papers. While generally approached as a feature of the system, clinician perception of a system's clinical utility may increase when clinicians have a clearer sense of how to use the system within their respective treatment framework.

In terms of clinical direction, it is also unclear whether changes to pathological traits should be treatment targets. Right now, existing measures (e.g., PID-5) have been developed with a focus on broad assessment of various components of trait domains and facets. There may be benefit in developing measures focusing on problematic behaviors that correspond to pathological traits. Here, we use the term *behavior* in a broad sense that would include cognitive acts (e.g., "I see myself as worthless"), emotional patterns (e.g., "My emotions overwhelm me"), and overt behaviors (e.g., "I argue too much"). By way of comparison, there are circumplex measures with items written to assess traits, values, strengths, and problematic behaviors (see Locke, 2010). In clinical contexts, indexes of problematic interpersonal behaviors, such as the Inventory of Interpersonal Problems (Horowitz et al., 2000), are often preferred precisely because they can be used as progress measures. Identifying aspects of LPF, PD severity, and pathological traits that can be measured in a manner promoting progress monitoring would also be a boon to clinicians. This may also help clinicians clarify what to focus on clinically when a patient has been determined to possess a pathological trait.

Resources and Decision-Making Models for Gray Area Cases

Concerns about clinicians' challenges differentiating among PD styles, resulting from the tendency to think in categories, are more applicable to cases that providers find hard to classify. These challenges are likely with patients with complex presentations. When case presentations are less clear, diagnostic decisions become more difficult, and it is not readily obvious how the patient should be classified or rated; we refer to such cases as *gray area cases*. Diagnostic systems strive to clarify how criteria should be applied to individuals; still, eliminating gray area cases is impossible. The situation is similar to decision making in complex clinical situations involving ethics and in other complex areas of mental health, such as suicide assessment. Experts in both realms accept that gray areas are unavoidable. The literature in these domains provides decision-making models highlighting what clinicians should consider when navigating gray areas (e.g., Fowler, 2012).

Most current papers applying dimensional PD systems to case examples focus on relatively clean-cut cases (Bach et al., 2015; Bach & First, 2018; Waugh et al., 2017). Such papers are essential for the field, providing a foundation for clinicians to learn to employ new systems in a real-world context. Papers reviewing navigation of gray area cases complement existing work by guiding clinicians through more complex scenarios. Ideally, edited books or special issues of journals would solicit papers applying new systems to gray area cases. With regard to clinical utility, we speculate that such papers would promote ease of implementation and enhance the diagnostic function of dimensional PD systems by increasing clinicians' confidence that they know what steps to take to reach a decision, even in cases that are unclear.

CLINICAL UTILITY: DOES ONE SIZE FIT ALL?

DSM-5's authors noted that a challenge facing all mental health diagnostic systems is balancing the competing needs of insurance providers, patients, primary care providers, nurse practitioners, social workers, psychiatrists, psychologists, and therapists (of all types and traditions). What is simple, intuitive, and useful for one group may be complex, confusing, and burdensome for others. In short, a one-size-fits-all approach to clinical utility may leave much lacking. We have focused on utility primarily from the vantage point of psychotherapists. To provide an illustrative example on how clinical utility may vary across contexts, we briefly consider the needs of those working in primary care settings.

Physicians are often the first health care providers that individuals with mental health concerns present themselves to. The prevalence rates of patients with a diagnosable mental health disorder in the United States range from 42% (Ansseau et al., 2004) to as high as 54% (Roca et al., 2009). Prevalence rates of primary care patients with a PD in the United States, England, Wales, Scotland, Western Europe, Norway, and Australia range from 4% to 22% (Quirk et al., 2016; see Huprich, 2018b, for a review of this issue). These rates suggest that primary care providers (PCPs) would benefit greatly from a diagnostic classification system for PDs that is clear-cut, is easy to implement, provides direction for treatment and referral, and aids in communication with other health care providers and mental health professionals.

Rarely do patients with PDs seek primary health care for the treatment of their PDs. These patients often come to the attention of PCPs for one or more of the following reasons: when (a) the PD complicates the treatment of another mental health condition (e.g., major depression), (b) the PD interferes with compliance with recommendations in the treatment of a physical condition (e.g., diabetes mellitus; Porcerelli & Huprich, 2007), (c) the patient is experienced as being "difficult" to work with by the office staff or by the patient's provider, or (d) a spouse or family member forces the patient with a PD to seek help (Porcerelli & Jones, 2017). In such cases, being able to clearly conceptualize the problem as a PD would help health care providers to develop management strategies (e.g., providing firm limits to patients with BPD when disruptive during clinic visits), provide an appropriate referral for treatment (e.g., dialectical behavior therapy for BPD), or implement psychopharmacological treatment (Porcerelli & Huprich, 2007). Despite the fact that PCPs rely heavily on brief screening measures for identifying psychiatric syndromes and disorders (e.g., Patient Health Questionnaire-2), learning and applying AMPD PD LPF ratings and *ICD-11* severity ratings could prove enormously helpful.

CONCLUSION

The true test of clinical utility for the AMPD and *ICD-11* PD systems will be the degree to which clinicians self-select these systems for use. When a system serves key diagnostic functions, has reasonable goodness of fit for the patients clinicians encounter, is reasonably easy to implement, provides some clinical direction, and is useful for professional communication (with patients and other professionals), it is likely to be viewed as having utility. Research and expert discourse suggest a range of opinions regarding the clinical utility of the AMPD and *ICD-11* systems. Rather than levy an opinion on which side is correct, we have identified key tensions among proponents and critics of the AMPD and *ICD-11* and reframed them in terms of opportunities for improving aspects of clinical utility going forward. We are particularly bullish on research that utilizes "needs analysis" paradigms for highlighting next steps to improve utility. Additionally, future papers illustrating how the models integrate with common approaches for treating PDs and across settings in which PDs are regularly encountered (e.g., primary care) have an important role to play when it comes to clinical application. Together, empirical research and clinical application papers have the potential to enhance the utility of both the AMPD and *ICD-11* PD systems while also serving to ease the transition away from categorical models and into a new direction.

REFERENCES

American Psychiatric Association. (2000). *Diagnostic and statistical manual of mental disorders* (4th ed., text rev.).

American Psychiatric Association. (2013). *Diagnostic and statistical manual of mental disorders* (5th ed.). https://doi.org/10.1176/appi.books.9780890425596

Ansseau, M., Dierick, M., Buntinkx, F., Cnockaert, P., De Smedt, J., Van Den Haute, M., & Vander Mijnsbrugge, D. (2004). High prevalence of mental disorders in primary care. *Journal of Affective Disorders, 78*(1), 49–55. https://doi.org/10.1016/S0165-0327(02)00219-7

Bach, B., & Bernstein, D. P. (2019). Schema therapy conceptualization of personality functioning and traits in *ICD-11* and *DSM-5*. *Current Opinion in Psychiatry, 32*(1), 38–49. https://doi.org/10.1097/YCO.0000000000000464

Bach, B., Christensen, S., Kongerslev, M. T., Sellbom, M., & Simonsen, E. (2020). Structure of clinician-reported *ICD-11* personality disorder trait qualifiers. *Psychological Assessment, 32*(1), 50–59. https://doi.org/10.1037/pas0000747

Bach, B., & First, M. B. (2018). Application of the *ICD-11* classification of personality disorders. *BMC Psychiatry, 18*(1), Article 351. https://doi.org/10.1186/s12888-018-1908-3

Bach, B., Markon, K., Simonsen, E., & Krueger, R. F. (2015). Clinical utility of the *DSM-5* Alternative Model of Personality Disorders: Six cases from practice. *Journal of Psychiatric Practice, 21*(1), 3–25. https://doi.org/10.1097/01.pra.0000460618.02805.ef

Bender, D. S., Morey, L. C., & Skodol, A. E. (2011). Toward a model for assessing level of personality functioning in *DSM-5*, Part I: A review of theory and methods. *Journal of Personality Assessment, 93*(4), 332–346. https://doi.org/10.1080/00223891.2011.583808

Blais, M. A. (1997). Clinician ratings of the five-factor model of personality and the *DSM-IV* personality disorders. *The Journal of Nervous and Mental Disease, 185*(6), 388–394. https://doi.org/10.1097/00005053-199706000-00005

Bornstein, R. F. (2019). The trait–type dialectic: Construct validity, clinical utility, and the diagnostic process. *Personality Disorders: Theory, Research, and Treatment, 10*(3), 199–209. https://doi.org/10.1037/per0000299

Buer Christensen, T., Paap, M. C. S., Arnesen, M., Koritzinsky, K., Nysaeter, T.-E., Eikenaes, I., Germans Selvik, S., Walther, K., Torgersen, S., Bender, D. S., Skodol, A. E., Kvarstein, E., Pedersen, G., & Hummelen, B. (2018). Interrater reliability of the Structured Clinical Interview for the *DSM-5* Alternative Model of Personality Disorders Module i: Level of Personality Functioning Scale. *Journal of Personality Assessment, 100*(6), 630–641. https://doi.org/10.1080/00223891.2018.1483377

Clark, L. A., Nuzum, H., Shapiro, J. L., Vanderbleek, E. N., Daly, E. J., Simons, A. D., & Ro, E. (2020). Personality profiles as potential targets for intervention: Identification and replication. *Personality and Mental Health, 14*(1), 142–163. https://doi.org/10.1002/pmh.1455

Clarkin, J. F., Caligor, E., & Sowislo, J. F. (2020). An object relations model perspective on the Alternative Model for Personality Disorders (*DSM-5*). *Psychopathology, 53*(3-4), 141–148. https://doi.org/10.1159/000508353

Clarkin, J. F., & Huprich, S. K. (2011). Do *DSM-5* personality disorder proposals meet criteria for clinical utility? *Journal of Personality Disorders, 25*(2), 192–205. https://doi.org/10.1521/pedi.2011.25.2.192

Crego, C., Gore, W. L., Rojas, S. L., & Widiger, T. A. (2015). The discriminant (and convergent) validity of the Personality Inventory for *DSM-5*. *Personality Disorders: Theory, Research, and Treatment, 6*(4), 321–335. https://doi.org/10.1037/per0000118

Evans, S. C., Reed, G. M., Roberts, M. C., Esparza, P., Watts, A. D., Correia, J. M., Ritchie, P., Maj, M., & Saxena, S. (2013). Psychologists' perspectives on the diagnostic classification of mental disorders: Results from the WHO-IUPsyS Global Survey. *International Journal of Psychology, 48*(3), 177–193. https://doi.org/10.1080/00207594.2013.804189

First, M. B. (2005). Clinical utility: A prerequisite for the adoption of a dimensional approach in *DSM*. *Journal of Abnormal Psychology, 114*(4), 560–564. https://doi.org/10.1037/0021-843X.114.4.560

First, M. B., Pincus, H. A., Levine, J. B., Williams, J. B. W., Ustun, B., & Peele, R. (2004). Clinical utility as a criterion for revising psychiatric diagnoses. *The American Journal of Psychiatry, 161*(6), 946–954. https://doi.org/10.1176/appi.ajp.161.6.946

First, M. B., & Westen, D. (2007). Classification for clinical practice: How to make *ICD* and *DSM* better able to serve clinicians. *International Review of Psychiatry, 19*(5), 473–481. https://doi.org/10.1080/09540260701563429

Fowler, J. C. (2012). Suicide risk assessment in clinical practice: Pragmatic guidelines for imperfect assessments. *Psychotherapy, 49*(1), 81–90. https://doi.org/10.1037/a0026148

Fowler, J. C., Madan, A., Allen, J. G., Patriquin, M., Sharp, C., Oldham, J. M., & Frueh, B. C. (2018). Clinical utility of the *DSM-5* alternative model for borderline personality disorder: Differential diagnostic accuracy of the BFI, SCID-II-PQ, and PID-5. *Comprehensive Psychiatry, 80*, 97–103. https://doi.org/10.1016/j.comppsych.2017.09.003

Garb, H. N. (2005). Clinical judgment and decision making. *Annual Review of Clinical Psychology, 1*(1), 67–89. https://doi.org/10.1146/annurev.clinpsy.1.102803.143810

Garcia, D. J., Skadberg, R. M., Schmidt, M., Bierma, S., Shorter, R. L., & Waugh, M. H. (2018). It's not that difficult: An interrater reliability study of the *DSM-5* Section III Alternative Model for Personality Disorders. *Journal of Personality Assessment, 100*(6), 612–620. https://doi.org/10.1080/00223891.2018.1428982

Glover, N. G., Crego, C., & Widiger, T. A. (2012). The clinical utility of the five factor model of personality disorder. *Personality Disorders: Theory, Research, and Treatment, 3*(2), 176–184. https://doi.org/10.1037/a0024030

Hayes, B. (2018). The category use effect in clinical diagnosis. *Clinical Psychological Science, 6*(2), 216–227. https://doi.org/10.1177/2167702617712525

Herpertz, S. C., Huprich, S. K., Bohus, M., Chanen, A., Goodman, M., Mehlum, L., Moran, P., Newton-Howes, G., Scott, L., & Sharp, C. (2017). The challenge of transforming the diagnostic system of personality disorders. *Journal of Personality Disorders, 31*(5), 577–589. https://doi.org/10.1521/pedi_2017_31_338

Hopwood, C. J., Zimmermann, J., Pincus, A. L., & Krueger, R. F. (2015). Connecting personality structure and dynamics: Towards a more evidence-based and clinically useful diagnostic scheme. *Journal of Personality Disorders, 29*(4), 431–448. https://doi.org/10.1521/pedi.2015.29.4.431

Horowitz, L. M., Alden, L. E., Wiggins, J. S., & Pincus, A. L. (2000). *Inventory of Interpersonal Problems manual.* The Psychological Corporation.

Horvath, S., & Morf, C. C. (2009). Narcissistic defensiveness: Hypervigilance and avoidance of worthlessness. *Journal of Experimental Social Psychology, 45*(6), 1252–1258. https://doi.org/10.1016/j.jesp.2009.07.011

Huprich, S. K. (2018a). Moving beyond categories and dimensions in personality pathology assessment and diagnosis. *The British Journal of Psychiatry, 213*(6), 685–689. https://doi.org/10.1192/bjp.2018.149

Huprich, S. K. (2018b). Personality pathology in primary care: Ongoing needs for detection and intervention. *Journal of Clinical Psychology in Medical Settings, 25*(1), 43–54. https://doi.org/10.1007/s10880-017-9525-8

Huprich, S. K. (2020). Personality disorders in the *ICD-11*: Opportunities and challenges for advancing the diagnosis of personality pathology. *Current Psychiatry Reports, 22*(8), Article 40. https://doi.org/10.1007/s11920-020-01161-4

Huprich, S. K., & Nelson, S. M. (2015). Advancing the assessment of personality pathology with the Cognitive-Affective Processing System. *Journal of Personality Assessment, 97*(5), 467–477. https://doi.org/10.1080/00223891.2015.1058806

Huprich, S. K., Schmitt, T. A., Richard, D. C. S., Chelminski, I., & Zimmerman, M. A. (2010). Comparing factor analytic models of the *DSM-IV* personality disorders. *Personality Disorders: Theory, Research, and Treatment, 1*(1), 22–37. https://doi.org/10.1037/a0018245

Keeley, J. W., Reed, G. M., Roberts, M. C., Evans, S. C., Medina-Mora, M. E., Robles, R., Rebello, T., Sharan, P., Gureje, O., First, M. B., Andrews, H. F., Ayuso-Mateos, J. L., Gaebel, W., Zielasek, J., & Saxena, S. (2016). Developing a science of clinical utility in diagnostic classification systems: Field study strategies for *ICD-11* mental and behavioral disorders. *American Psychologist, 71*(1), 3–16. https://doi.org/10.1037/a0039972

Kendell, R., & Jablensky, A. (2003). Distinguishing between the validity and utility of psychiatric diagnoses. *The American Journal of Psychiatry, 160*(1), 4–12. https://doi.org/10.1176/appi.ajp.160.1.4

Kupfer, D. J., First, M. B., & Regier, D. A. (Eds.). (2002). *A research agenda for DSM-V.* American Psychiatric Association.

Lambert, M. J. (2012). Helping clinicians to use and learn from research-based systems: The OQ-analyst. *Psychotherapy, 49*(2), 109–114. https://doi.org/10.1037/a0027110

Lenzenweger, M. F., & Depue, R. A. (2020). Personality disturbances as emergent phenomena reflective of underlying neurobehavioral systems: Beyond dimensional measurement, phenotypic trait descriptors, and factor analysis. *Psychopathology,* *53*(3-4), 213–220. https://doi.org/10.1159/000509624

Locke, K. D. (2010). Circumplex measures of interpersonal constructs. In L. M. Horowitz & S. Strack (Eds.), *Handbook of interpersonal psychology: Theory, research, assessment, and therapeutic interventions* (pp. 313–324). John Wiley and Sons.

Lowe, J. R., & Widiger, T. A. (2009). Clinicians' judgments of clinical utility: A comparison of the *DSM-IV* with dimensional models of general personality. *Journal of Personality Disorders, 23*(3), 211–229. https://doi.org/10.1521/pedi.2009.23.3.211

McCabe, G. A., & Widiger, T. A. (2020). A comprehensive comparison of the *ICD-11* and *DSM-5* Section III personality disorder models. *Psychological Assessment, 32*(1), 72–84. https://doi.org/10.1037/pas0000772

Meehan, K. B., & Clarkin, J. F. (2015). A critical evaluation of moving toward a trait system for personality disorder assessment. In S. K. Huprich (Ed.), *Personality disorders: Toward theoretical and empirical integration in diagnosis and assessment* (pp. 85–106). American Psychological Association. https://doi.org/10.1037/14549-005

Meehan, K. B., Clarkin, J. F., & Lenzenweger, M. F. (2018a). Conceptual models of borderline personality disorder, Part 1: Overview of prevailing and emergent models. *Psychiatric Clinics of North America, 41*(4), 535–548. https://doi.org/10.1016/j.psc.2018.08.001

Meehan, K. B., Clarkin, J. F., & Lenzenweger, M. F. (2018b). Conceptual models of borderline personality disorder, Part 2: A process approach and its implications. *Psychiatric Clinics of North America, 41*(4), 549–559. https://doi.org/10.1016/j.psc.2018.08.002

Meehan, K. B., Siefert, C., Sexton, J., & Huprich, S. K. (2019). Expanding the role of levels of personality functioning in personality disorder taxonomy: Commentary on "Criterion A of the AMPD in HiTOP." *Journal of Personality Assessment, 101*(4), 367–373. https://doi.org/10.1080/00223891.2018.1551228

Meehl, P. E. (1959). Some ruminations on the validation of clinical procedures. *Canadian Journal of Psychology/Revue canadienne de psychologie, 13*(2), 102–128. https://doi.org/10.1037/h0083769

Mischel, W., & Shoda, Y. (1995). A cognitive-affective system theory of personality: Reconceptualizing situations, dispositions, dynamics, and invariance in personality structure. *Psychological Review, 102*(2), 246–268. https://doi.org/10.1037/0033-295X.102.2.246

Morey, L. C., Bender, D. S., & Skodol, A. E. (2013). Validating the proposed *Diagnostic and Statistical Manual of Mental Disorders, 5th Edition,* severity indicator for personality disorder. *The Journal of Nervous and Mental Disease, 201*(9), 729–735. https://doi.org/10.1097/nmd.0b013e3182a20ea8

Morey, L. C., Krueger, R. F., & Skodol, A. E. (2013). The hierarchical structure of clinician ratings of proposed *DSM-5* pathological personality traits. *Journal of Abnormal Psychology, 122*(3), 836–841. https://doi.org/10.1037/a0034003

Morey, L. C., Skodol, A. E., & Oldham, J. M. (2014). Clinician judgments of clinical utility: A comparison of *DSM-IV-TR* personality disorders and the alternative model for *DSM-5* personality disorders. *Journal of Abnormal Psychology, 123*(2), 398–405. https://doi.org/10.1037/a0036481

Mulay, A. L., Waugh, M. H., Fillauer, J. P., Bender, D. S., Bram, A., Cain, N. M., Caligor, E., Forbes, M. K., Goodrich, L. B., Kamphuis, J. H., Keeley, J. W., Krueger, R. F., Kurtz, J. E., Jacobsson, P., Lewis, K. C., Rossi, G. M. P., Ridenour, J. M., Roche, M., Sellbom, M., . . . Skodol, A. E. (2019). Borderline personality disorder diagnosis in a new key. *Borderline Personality Disorder and Emotion Dysregulation, 6,* Article 18. https://doi.org/10.1186/s40479-019-0116-1

Mulder, R. T., Horwood, J., Tyrer, P., Carter, J., & Joyce, P. R. (2016). Validating the proposed *ICD-11* domains. *Personality and Mental Health, 10*(2), 84–95. https://doi.org/10.1002/pmh.1336

Mullins-Sweatt, S. N., Lengel, G. J., & DeShong, H. L. (2016). The importance of considering clinical utility in the construction of a diagnostic manual. *Annual Review of Clinical Psychology, 12*, 133–155. https://doi.org/10.1146/annurev-clinpsy-021815-092954

Mullins-Sweatt, S. N., & Widiger, T. A. (2011). Clinician's judgments of the utility of the *DSM-IV* and five-factor models for personality disordered patients. *Journal of Personality Disorders, 25*(4), 463–477. https://doi.org/10.1521/pedi.2011.25.4.463

Nelson, S. M., Huprich, S. K., Shankar, S., Sohnleitner, A., & Paggeot, A. V. (2017). A quantitative and qualitative evaluation of trainee opinions of four methods of personality disorder diagnosis. *Personality Disorders: Theory, Research, and Treatment, 8*(3), 217–227. https://doi.org/10.1037/per0000227

Olajide, K., Munjiza, J., Moran, P., O'Connell, L., Newton-Howes, G., Bassett, P., Akintomide, G., Ng, N., Tyrer, P., Mulder, R., & Crawford, M. J. (2018). Development and psychometric properties of the Standardized Assessment of Severity of Personality Disorder (SASPD). *Journal of Personality Disorders, 32*(1), 44–56. https://doi.org/10.1521/pedi_2017_31_285

Pincus, A. L., Cain, N. M., & Halberstadt, A. L. (2020). Importance of self and other in defining personality pathology. *Psychopathology, 53*(3-4), 133–140. https://doi.org/10.1159/000506313

Porcerelli, J. H., & Huprich, S. K. (2007). Approach to personality disorders in primary care. *Hospital Physician, 43*, 2–11.

Porcerelli, J. H., & Jones, J. R. (2017). Uses of psychological assessment in primary care settings. In M. E. Maruish (Ed.), *Handbook of psychological assessment in primary care settings* (pp. 75–94). Routledge.

Quirk, S. E., Berk, M., Chanen, A. M., Koivumaa-Honkanen, H., Brennan-Olsen, S. L., Pasco, J. A., & Williams, L. J. (2016). Population prevalence of personality disorder and associations with physical health comorbidities and health care service utilization: A review. *Personality Disorders: Theory, Research, and Treatment, 7*(2), 136–146. https://doi.org/10.1037/per0000148

Reed, G. M., Mendonça Correia, J., Esparza, P., Saxena, S., & Maj, M. (2011). The WPA-WHO global survey of psychiatrists' attitudes towards mental disorders classification. *World Psychiatry, 10*(2), 118–131. https://doi.org/10.1002/j.2051-5545.2011.tb00034.x

Roca, M., Gili, M., Garcia-Garcia, M., Salva, J., Vives, M., Garcia Campayo, J., & Comas, A. (2009). Prevalence and comorbidity of common mental disorders in primary care. *Journal of Affective Disorders, 119*(1-3), 52–58. https://doi.org/10.1016/j.jad.2009.03.014

Roche, M. J. (2018). Examining the alternative model for personality disorder in daily life: Evidence for incremental validity. *Personality Disorders: Theory, Research, and Treatment, 9*(6), 574–583. https://doi.org/10.1037/per0000295

Rottman, B. M., Ahn, W.-K., Sanislow, C. A., & Kim, N. S. (2009). Can clinicians recognize *DSM-IV* personality disorders from five-factor model descriptions of patient cases? *The American Journal of Psychiatry, 166*(4), 427–433. https://doi.org/10.1176/appi.ajp.2008.08070972

Samuel, D. B., & Widiger, T. A. (2006). Clinicians' judgments of clinical utility: A comparison of the *DSM-IV* and five-factor models. *Journal of Abnormal Psychology, 115*(2), 298–308. https://doi.org/10.1037/0021-843X.115.2.298

Samuel, D. B., & Widiger, T. A. (2011). Clinicians' use of personality disorder models within a particular treatment setting: A longitudinal comparison of temporal consistency and clinical utility. *Personality and Mental Health, 5*(1), 12–28. https://doi.org/10.1002/pmh.152

Sellbom, M., Carmichael, K. L. C., & Liggett, J. (2017). Examination of *DSM-5* Section III avoidant personality disorder in a community sample. *Personality and Mental Health, 11*(4), 299–313. https://doi.org/10.1002/pmh.1388

Shedler, J., & Westen, D. (1998). Refining the measurement of Axis II: A Q-sort procedure for assessing personality pathology. *Assessment, 5*(4), 333–353. https://doi.org/10.1177/107319119800500403

Spitzer, R. L., First, M. B., Shedler, J., Westen, D., & Skodol, A. E. (2008). Clinical utility of five dimensional systems for personality diagnosis: A "consumer preference" study. *The Journal of Nervous and Mental Disease, 196*(5), 356–374. https://doi.org/10.1097/NMD.0b013e3181710950

Sprock, J. (2002). A comparative study of the dimensions and facets of the five-factor model in the diagnosis of cases of personality disorder. *Journal of Personality Disorders, 16*(5), 402–423. https://doi.org/10.1521/pedi.16.5.402.22122

Sprock, J. (2003). Dimensional versus categorical classification of prototypic and non-prototypic cases of personality disorder. *Journal of Clinical Psychology, 59*(9), 991–1014. https://doi.org/10.1002/jclp.10184

Tyrer, P., Mulder, R., Kim, Y.-R., & Crawford, M. J. (2019). The development of the *ICD-11* classification of personality disorders: An amalgam of science, pragmatism, and politics. *Annual Review of Clinical Psychology, 15*, 481–502. https://doi.org/10.1146/annurev-clinpsy-050718-095736

Verheul, R. (2005). Clinical utility of dimensional models for personality pathology. *Journal of Personality Disorders, 19*(3), 283–302. https://doi.org/10.1521/pedi.2005.19.3.283

Vivian, D., Hershenberg, R., Teachman, B. A., Drabick, D. A. G., Goldfried, M. R., & Wolfe, B. (2012). A translational model of research-practice integration. *Psychotherapy, 49*(2), 143–151. https://doi.org/10.1037/a0027925

Watters, C. A., Bagby, R. M., & Sellbom, M. (2019). Meta-analysis to derive an empirically based set of personality facet criteria for the alternative *DSM-5* model for personality disorders. *Personality Disorders: Theory, Research, and Treatment, 10*(2), 97–104. https://doi.org/10.1037/per0000307

Waugh, M. H., Hopwood, C. J., Krueger, R. F., Morey, L. C., Pincus, A. L., & Wright, A. G. C. (2017). Psychological assessment with the *DSM-5* alternative model for personality disorders: Tradition and innovation. *Professional Psychology: Research and Practice, 48*(2), 79–89. https://doi.org/10.1037/pro0000071

World Health Organization. (2019). *International statistical classification of diseases and related health problems* (11th ed.). https://icd.who.int/

Wright, A. G. C., Hopwood, C. J., & Simms, L. J. (2015). Daily interpersonal and affective dynamics in personality disorder. *Journal of Personality Disorders, 29*(4), 503–525. https://doi.org/10.1521/pedi.2015.29.4.503

Zachar, P., & First, M. B. (2015). Transitioning to a dimensional model of personality disorder in *DSM* 5.1 and beyond. *Current Opinion in Psychiatry, 28*(1), 66–72. https://doi.org/10.1097/YCO.0000000000000115

Zimmermann, J., Benecke, C., Bender, D. S., Skodol, A. E., Schauenburg, H., Cierpka, M., & Leising, D. (2014). Assessing *DSM-5* level of personality functioning from videotaped clinical interviews: A pilot study with untrained and clinically inexperienced students. *Journal of Personality Assessment, 96*(4), 397–409. https://doi.org/10.1080/00223891.2013.852563

Zimmermann, J., Kerber, A., Rek, K., Hopwood, C. J., & Krueger, R. F. (2019). A brief but comprehensive review of research on the alternative *DSM-5* model for personality disorders. *Current Psychiatry Reports, 21*(9), Article 92. https://doi.org/10.1007/s11920-019-1079-z

II

ASSESSMENT AND TREATMENT WITHIN THE NEWEST PARADIGMS

4

Principles of Psychological Assessment for Personality Disorders

Emily A. Dowgwillo, JoAnna Molina, and Kathryn R. Forche

Personality assessment as a field emerged from an enduring awareness of and desire to understand the individual differences in how people think, feel, and behave. While early assessment efforts took an idiographic approach in the form of case histories and psychobiographies (Wiggins, 2003), the field of personality assessment has been influenced by historical events, different theoretical perspectives, and advances in statistics and technology, inspiring a range of methods and related measures (e.g., clinical interviewing, performance-based measures, self- and informant report, person-specific approaches) to assess individual differences. The definitions of personality disorder and personality pathology have also evolved over time. Most recently, the development of the Alternative *DSM-5* Model of Personality Disorders (AMPD; American Psychiatric Association, 2013) and the *International Statistical Classification of Diseases and Related Health Problems* (11th ed.; *ICD-11*; World Health Organization, 2019) has encouraged clinicians to view personality disorders dimensionally by assessing a patient's level of personality functioning (Severity of Impairment, AMPD Criterion A) and maladaptive trait domains (Style of Impairment, AMPD Criterion B). Although this conceptualization of personality disorder contrasts with more traditional categorical approaches, the assessment of these AMPD and *ICD-11* diagnostic dimensions has relied on existing and familiar methods. By understanding the strengths and weaknesses of these methods, we can better understand how they can contribute to our understanding of these new models of personality disorder, help the clinician to select

https://doi.org/10.1037/0000310-005
Personality Disorders and Pathology: Integrating Clinical Assessment and Practice in the DSM-5 *and* ICD-11 *Era*, S. K. Huprich (Editor)
Copyright © 2022 by the American Psychological Association. All rights reserved.

CLINICAL INTERVIEW METHODS

The *clinical interview* is one of the most commonly used methods for observing, evaluating, assessing, and diagnosing patients; in this approach, the clinician gathers information about the patient through a series of direct, verbal questions. The success of this approach depends not only on the content of the responses but also on the therapist's ability to develop rapport and observe the patient's behavior throughout the interview (Mueller & Segal, 2014). As an assessment tool, clinical interviews differ in terms of their level of structure, ranging from unstructured to semistructured to fully structured interviews.

Structured Versus Unstructured Interviews

A *structured interview* relies on a standard set of questions that are asked in a fixed order, using precise wording, and are responded to using a systematic rating system. As such, structured interviews are highly standardized and rely heavily on this consistency to compare responses across patients and over time. Comparatively, a *semistructured interview* begins with a standardized sequence of questions but allows the interviewer to follow up on patient responses as needed to gain insight and clarity into the patient's personal history and symptom experience. A handful of structured and semistructured interviews have been developed to assess level of personality functioning for the AMPD specifically. These include the Structured Clinical Interview for the *DSM-5* Alternative Model for Personality Disorders (SCID-5-AMPD; Bender et al., 2018), the Semi-Structured Interview for Personality Functioning *DSM-5* (STiP-5.1; Berghuis et al., 2013), and the Structured Interview of Personality Organization (STIPO; Clarkin et al., 2007). The trait domains identified by the AMPD are typically assessed using other methods. Given its recent publication, specific interview measures for functional impairment do not yet exist for the *ICD-11*.

Unlike more structured approaches, *unstructured interviews* promote exploration and spontaneity by using nondirective, open-ended questions to gain deeper insight into the patient's history, current functioning, presenting concerns, traits, interpersonal relationships, and life narrative themes. In this way, clinicians can integrate their observations over the course of their interactions with the patient to arrive at AMPD or *ICD-11* ratings. An unstructured approach provides a vivid description of the patient and a genuine sense of their experiences (Ganellen, 2007). Because unstructured interviews do not rely on predetermined questions, clinicians must rely on their theoretical orientation, previous training, and current knowledge base to guide their questioning,

Principles of Psychological Assessment for Personality Disorders 79

which will invariably influence the breadth and depth of information gained by the interview (Mueller & Segal, 2014).

Advantages and Disadvantages of Clinical Interviewing

The advantages and disadvantages of clinical interviewing methods depend on the degree of interview structure. Because of their inherent standardization, structured and semistructured interviews increase reliability by decreasing variability in patient responses across clinicians. Additionally, the use of standardized quantitative ratings highlights the magnitude of impairment and, if applicable, changes in this magnitude across time (Mueller & Segal, 2014). That said, because both structured and unstructured interview methods require patients to report on their experiences, both are limited by patients' level of insight, their willingness to reveal information about themselves, and their ability to accurately judge their experiences (Ganellen, 2007).

Using structured interviews can also increase the validity of the assessment by limiting clinician bias and ensuring a comprehensive assessment across psychological domains (Segal et al., 2006). When left to their own devices, even experienced clinicians can fail to consider certain diagnostic criteria or relevant dimensions, prematurely eliminate diagnoses, fail to acknowledge comorbid pathology, or overlook certain patient concerns (Ganellen, 2007; Mueller & Segal, 2014; Zimmerman & Mattia, 1999). The comprehensiveness of structured interviews increases the accuracy of a diagnosis by ensuring that all domains are assessed (Mueller & Segal, 2014). This is especially important in assessment settings where the credibility or validity of an assessment may be called into question. Conversely, structured interviews have been criticized for their over-reliance on criteria sets. Because these criteria guide the standardized line of questioning, the validity of conclusions from a structured interview can be only as good as the validity of the diagnostic criteria themselves (Rogers, 2001). As diagnostic systems are revised, these structured interviews must also be updated. Because unstructured interviews are guided by patient characteristics, they can flexibly adapt, as the field of clinical psychology and personality progresses, without developing new interviewing protocols.

Structured interviews are also useful as training tools because they provide a framework for learning the specific diagnostic questions used by experienced clinical interviewers (Segal et al., 2006). Critics of more structured approaches, however, have expressed concern that focusing on protocol adherence could devolve into mindless symptom counting that does not integrate the patient's history, context, and behavior over the course of the assessment (Westen, 1997). Further, they argue that more structured approaches could damage rapport with patients by asking about "irrelevant" domains and reducing the empathy and warmth needed for a good therapeutic alliance (Mueller & Segal, 2014; Rogers, 2001). This concern may be unfounded, given recent research suggesting that patients find structured interviews to be helpful,

Reliability and Validity of Clinical Interviews

Reliability of an assessment instrument refers to the stability of scores across raters (*interrater reliability*) and/or across measurement occasions (*test–retest reliability*). Research suggests that unstructured interviews can be quite unreliable (Mellsop et al., 1982; Spitzer et al., 1979) and that diagnoses made in unstructured settings show only modest agreement with those from semistructured interviews (Hyler et al., 1989). Rather, the likelihood of a reliable and replicable assessment increases when interviews are more structured. Research suggests that across measures, structured interviews, including those that assess AMPD level of personality functioning, tend to have good-to-excellent interrater reliability (Buer Christensen et al., 2018; Kampe et al., 2018; Maffei et al., 1997; Pilkonis et al., 1995; Segal & Coolidge, 2003; Zanarini et al., 1987). Research on the test–retest reliability for semistructured and structured interviews is less prevalent but tends to fall in the fair-to-excellent range across measures (Buer Christensen et al., 2018; First et al., 1995; Kampe et al., 2018; Zanarini et al., 1987). Thus, clinical interviews appear to be a reliable way to assess personality pathology more generally and the level of personality functioning dimension of the AMPD specifically.

The *validity* of an assessment instrument refers to the extent to which the instrument measures what it purports to assess. Research examining convergent validity across clinical interviews suggests that diagnostic agreement is variable but tends to fall in the fair-to-moderate range. Agreement is improved when personality pathology is conceptualized dimensionally rather than categorically (Kampe et al., 2018; O'Boyle & Self, 1990; Pilkonis et al., 1995; Skodol, 1991). For example, SCID-5-AMPD and STIPO total scores are strongly correlated ($r = .73–.76$; Kampe et al., 2018). When researchers examine convergence between structured interviews and self-report measures, they find significant associations in the expected direction and that convergence increases as clinical interviews become more structured (Widiger & Coker, 2002). For the SCID-5-AMPD specifically, research has found significant associations with important clinical constructs (suicide attempts, psychiatric hospitalizations, *ICD-10* diagnoses; Kampe et al., 2018) and measures of social impairment (Buer Christensen et al., 2020). Structured interviews have also been shown to have incremental validity. In a study by Samuel and colleagues (2013), semistructured interviews significantly incremented the ability of naturalistic clinician ratings to predict functioning 5 years later (Samuel et al., 2013). The reverse was not true, and greater familiarity with the patient did not improve the predictive ability of a clinician's naturalistic diagnosis. Together, these findings support the use of clinical interview methods and highlight the stronger psychometric properties of semistructured and structured interviews. They also highlight the value and clinical utility of using structured clinical interviews to specifically assess constructs central to AMPD and *ICD-11* conceptualizations of personality disorder.

PERFORMANCE-BASED METHODS

Performance-based (also called *implicit, stimulus attribution,* or *projective*) *methods* provide insight into a patient's personality by having them attribute meaning to ambiguous stimuli. The first—and perhaps most famous—example of performance-based methods is the Rorschach inkblot method (Rorschach, 1921), which asks patients to attribute meaning to a series of standardized inkblots. Other performance-based approaches ask patients to create stories from drawings, provide word associations, complete sentences/phrases, or draw specific scenarios (Ganellen, 2007). Because the clinician does not structure the performance-based task for the patient, the patient is forced to create their own structure and attribute their own unique meaning to the ambiguous stimuli. By examining response characteristics as well as response content, clinicians can better understand a patient's interpersonal dynamics, perceptual organization, associational processes, cognitive functioning, and thought patterns, regardless of whether the patient is aware of these characteristics themself (Ganellen, 2007). This ability of performance-based methods to assess subjective, ideographic, and unconscious material has been identified as a particularly valuable and necessary contribution that performance-based measures make to standard personality assessment practice (Huprich, 2011a, 2011b). More recently, researchers and clinicians have discussed using performance-based methods to assess the level of personality functioning, a core component of the AMPD and *ICD-11* conceptualizations of personality disorder (Bender et al., 2011; Waugh et al., 2017). This application could reintroduce the inclusion of a patient's unique, unconscious experiences to the process of diagnosis (Huprich, 2011b; Waugh et al., 2017).

Advantages and Limitations of Performance-Based Methods

A major advantage of performance-based methods is their lack of transparency. Because "correct" or "favorable" responses are less clear, patients have a harder time engaging in impression management. Additionally, because performance-based measures assess patients implicitly, they are well suited for patients with low levels of self-awareness. Performance-based methods, then, are advantageous because they provide insight into a patient's personality without relying on the patient's willingness or ability to divulge information (Ganellen, 2007). The complexity of these methods, however, requires clinicians to have extensive specialized training in the administration, coding, and interpretation of the performance-based measure. Because errors in administration and scoring can substantially influence the interpretive process (Huprich & Ganellen, 2006), this training is vital to gain insight into a patient's mental functioning. This intensive training and associated supervision may be difficult to acquire outside of formal educational settings.

Performance-based measures are also limited in their ability to provide a detailed patient history, describe presenting symptomology, or link directly to *DSM-5* personality disorder diagnostic criteria. They can, however, provide information about how patients characteristically perceive themselves and others, how they interpret events, and their capacity to regulate intense affect and control their impulses (Huprich & Ganellen, 2006). These concepts are central to understanding a patient's level of personality functioning. Because of this, performance-based approaches may be well suited for assessing patients from an AMPD or *ICD-11* perspective (Bender et al., 2011; Waugh et al., 2017). Research, however, on using performance-based measures to assess the level of personality functioning from the AMPD is limited.

Although performance-based measures are used frequently in clinical settings, they have been criticized for a limited, and at times disjointed, body of research. Because of variability in the administration and scoring procedures used and the content, number, and quality of patient responses, relevant variables are often difficult to systematically study. The development of standardized clinician rating systems such as the Comprehensive System (CS; Exner, 1974), the Rorschach Performance Assessment System (R-PAS; Meyer et al., 2011), and the Social Cognition and Object Relations Scale-Global Rating Method (SCORS-G; Hilsenroth et al., 2004), among others, has allowed researchers to characterize narrative data using quantitative values and standardized indices. Doing this has facilitated research on the reliability, validity, and clinical utility of performance-based measures in general.

Although proponents of performance-based methods suggest that these methods' widespread use across patients and settings is an indication of their validity with diverse patients (Piotrowski, 2015), the empirical evidence supporting this claim is limited (Lilienfeld et al., 2000). Not only are there insufficient normative data on non-American and American minority groups, but research supports the presence of group differences (Lilienfeld et al., 2000). Because it is unclear whether this is due to meaningful group differences or cultural bias, the use of these measures in diverse populations is potentially problematic.

Reliability and Validity of Performance-Based Measures

Given the breadth of methods and measures that encompass performance-based techniques, overarching claims about the reliability and validity of these methods may be inappropriate. For this reason, our discussion of the psychometric properties of performance-based measures will be limited to specific standardized scoring systems, which lend themselves more readily to empirical study.

Perhaps the most widely studied standardized scoring system is Exner's CS (1974). The clinical utility of the CS has been well documented (Kostogianni, 2010; Meloy et al., 2013). Research suggests that interrater reliability values vary across CS indices ($ICC = .16–1.00$), with median values ranging from .78 to .97 (Acklin et al., 2000; Meyer et al., 2002). Importantly, indices with higher base rates tend to be more reliably scored (Pianowski et al., 2021). Similarly, the median test–retest reliability coefficient for CS indices across studies was .79 to .80 (Gronnerod, 2003; Meyer, 1997). These stability values tend to decrease as the time between assessments increases. In terms of validity, Mihura and colleagues (2013) found that across 53 meta-analytic reviews, the average relationship between CS variables and externally assessed criteria was $r = .27$. When criteria were introspectively assessed (across 42 meta-analytic studies), the average validity coefficient was only $r = .08$. This is consistent with a larger body of research that has noted poor convergence between the Rorschach and self-report methods (Archer & Krishnamurthy, 1993). Studies have also provided support for the incremental validity of CS indices (Blasczyk-Schiep et al., 2011; Dao et al., 2008; Hartmann et al., 2003; Meyer, 2000; Mihura et al., 2013; Viglione & Hilsenroth, 2001) and have suggested that indices that assess cognitive and perceptual processes tend to have the most support (Mihura et al., 2013).

The R-PAS (Meyer et al., 2011) is an alternative to and/or extension of the CS designed to address its psychometric limitations. R-PAS developers retained CS variables that had accumulated strong evidence of validity, eliminated variables that have lower levels of empirical support, and introduced an administration procedure that decreased the variability in the number of patient responses. Across studies and indices, the average interrater reliability for the R-PAS was between .78 and .88 with values ranging from .30 to 1.00 (Giromini et al., 2016; Kivisalu et al., 2016; Pianowski et al., 2021; Pignolo et al., 2017; Viglione et al., 2012). When CS and R-PAS scores are compared, research suggests that in most cases, means and standard deviations are equivalent across scoring systems (Meyer et al., 2011; Pianowski et al., 2021). Although they typically focus on a subset of indices, validity studies tend to support the use of the R-PAS. Researchers have found, for example, that stress- and distress-related R-PAS variables were significantly correlated with electrodermal activity during a stress-inducing task (Giromini et al., 2016). Additionally, R-PAS composite variables for thought and perception, vigilance, and suicidality were strongly associated with their CS counterparts (Viglione et al., 2014); space reversal and space integration responses were uniquely associated with oppositionality and cognitive complexity, respectively (Mihura et al., 2018); and R-PAS scales showed expected relationships with psychotic symptomatology and psychiatric severity (Su et al., 2015). Thus, evidence for the validity of R-PAS variables continues to accumulate, supporting its use in clinical practice.

Finally, research has examined the reliability and validity of the Social Cognition and Object Relations Scale (SCORS; Westen et al., 1990) and SCORS-G (Hilsenroth et al., 2004), standardized scoring systems that are used to code narrative data (including Thematic Apperception Test [TAT] narratives, early memories, psychotherapy sessions, etc.) in terms of complexity of object relations, affective tone, capacity for emotional investment in relationships, and understanding social causality, among others. Interrater reliability for the SCORS-G has generally been in the good-to-excellent range across all dimensions (Peters et al., 2006; Porcerelli et al., 2006; Siefert et al., 2016; Stein et al., 2011). Although research does suggest that TAT cards pull for certain kinds of responses and therefore certain SCORS-G codes (Siefert et al., 2016; Stein et al., 2014), TAT-derived SCORS dimensions are significantly related to self-report personality scales, measures of interpersonal behavior and defense mechanisms, psychosocial functioning and other intellectual and cognitive abilities, and important external outcomes (history of childhood trauma, psychiatric hospitalizations, and suicidality; Peters et al., 2006; Porcerelli et al., 2006; Stein et al., 2012, 2015).

Thus, performance-based measures provide an important contribution to the study of personality pathology. Given the unique assessment approach and relevant content assessed by performance-based measures, their role in assessing level of personality impairment central to the AMPD and *ICD-11* appears promising. However, more research is needed to directly examine the clinical utility and validity of performance-based scores for this purpose.

SELF-REPORT METHODS

Self-report methods ask patients to evaluate their own experiences and behaviors using an established set of questions and associated response scales and are one of the most popular methods in personality assessment. Although the breadth of constructs assessed by personality inventories and self-report measures is vast, these measures typically have their theoretical roots in either the empirical paradigm or the multivariate paradigm.

The *empirical paradigm* focuses on categorizing a patient by diagnostic group or class of people rather than understanding the degree to which a trait or characteristic is present in a patient (Loevinger, 1957). Importantly, item content takes a back seat to diagnostic class membership. From this perspective, then, a self-report item works well if it distinguishes people who meet specific diagnostic criteria from nonclinical controls. This approach is consistent with the disease model (or medical model) of mental illness, originating from Emil Kraepelin. Personality assessment efforts from an empirical approach have revolved around the development and revisions of the Minnesota Multiphasic Personality Inventory (MMPI; Hathaway & McKinley, 1943). For a more complete discussion of the empirical paradigm, see Wiggins (2003).

A *multivariate paradigm* approach to personality assessment typically views personality constructs through a *dimensional* lens (degree of a trait or personality feature, rather than its presence vs. absence) and relies heavily on the psychometric properties of items, scales, and measures. From this perspective, an item or scale works well if it (a) has good statistical properties, including strong factor loadings on the parent scale; (b) has good internal consistency values; or (c) provides a substantial amount of psychometric information along the latent trait continuum. Personality assessment efforts to capture AMPD and *ICD-11* dimensions using self-report measures typically rely on a multivariate approach: for example, (a) the Level of Personality Functioning Scale–Self Report (LPFS-SR; Morey, 2017), (b) the *DSM-5* Levels of Personality Functioning Questionnaire (DLOPFQ; Huprich et al., 2018), (c) the Level of Personality Functioning Scale–Brief Form (LPFS-BF; Hutsebaut et al., 2016), (d) the Standardized Assessment of Severity of Personality Disorder (SASPD;

Olajide et al., 2018), (e) the Personality Inventory for *ICD-11* (PiCD; Oltmanns & Widiger, 2018), and (f) the Personality Inventory for *DSM-5* (PID-5; Krueger et al., 2012). For a more complete discussion of the multivariate paradigm, see Wiggins (2003).

Advantages and Disadvantages of Self-Report Methods

Self-report measures are quick, easy to administer and score, and inexpensive, yet they can provide rich information about the patient. Patients not only have access to a breadth of information about themselves, but they also are privy to thoughts, feelings, motives, and sensations that are not readily observable to outsiders (Robins et al., 1999). Furthermore, a patient's self-appraisal, regardless of its accuracy, can have important implications for how the patient navigates the world, interacts with others, sets expectations for themselves, and thinks about their identity (Ickes et al., 1997; Vazire & Gosling, 2004).

Because of the structure and ease of administration, measures that rely on self-report methods (including those that assess the AMPD and *ICD-11* dimensional models) have developed extensive research literatures. These research efforts have added to our understanding of personality scales by expanding their nomological networks and have inspired the development of revisions, alternative forms, and updated norms. These efforts have led to improvements in the reliability, validity, and clinical utility of these scales. Finally, the development of personality inventory translations has facilitated a better understanding of cultural influences on test scores. Although research suggests that for many inventories the relationships between self-reported personality traits are similar across cultures and languages (e.g., the PID-5 has been translated into at least 15 languages; Allik, 2005; Zimmermann, Kerber, et al., 2019), these efforts have been criticized for transporting existing models into new cultural contexts rather than identifying culture-specific personality constructs. Cultural differences and differential item functioning (DIF) have been found for certain measures and cultures (Church et al., 2011; Glass et al., 1996; Krall et al., 1983). Although DIF in self-report measures may seem problematic, the ability to detect and quantify DIF can help guide future research directions and encourage closer examination on commonly used self-report measures.

However, self-report methods have some distinct disadvantages: Because these methods rely on patients to provide honest and accurate self-appraisals, self-report measures are vulnerable to distortion. Distorted responses may be the product of a conscious motivation to manipulate test scores or to use a particular response style characterized by acquiescent, extreme, or socially desirable themes (Alicke, 1985; Galione & Oltmanns, 2014; Ganellen, 2007; Taylor & Brown, 1988). Even when patients are doing their best to respond to self-report items truthfully, they may misinterpret a question, misremember events, make judgements based on flawed heuristic processes, or lack insight into their own experience (Galione & Oltmanns, 2014; Meyer, 2002). Research also suggests that responses on self-report measures can be influenced by the patient's mood and cognitive functioning at the time of testing, limiting the validity and generalizability of the patient's responses (Galione & Oltmanns, 2014). To address these limitations, a number of personality assessment measures have added validity scales to alert the assessor to inconsistent, acquiescent, socially desirable, exaggerated, or false responding. However, self-report measures of AMPD and *ICD-11* personality disorder criteria largely do not include validity scales (the exceptions are an Inconsistency scale [Keeley et al., 2016] and an Overreporting scale [Sellbom et al., 2018], recently developed using PID-5 items). Thus, a self-report approach to AMPD and *ICD-11* dimensional models is not only vulnerable to the distortion inherent to self-report methods but also fails to measure the level of distortion that may be present. Given that distorted perception is characteristic of personality pathology, relying solely on self-report methods could be problematic and bears further discussion. This is particularly true given that self-report methods dominate the research and clinical applications of the AMPD and *ICD-11*.

Reliability and Validity of Self-Report Methods

Because self-report methods allow for large quantities of data to be collected quickly, easily, and inexpensively, research on the psychometric properties of self-report measures is extensive. Reliability and validity indices understandably vary across measures. However, because they are constructed with these properties in mind, self-report measures that have gone through the peer review process generally fall in the acceptable range. For measures assessing AMPD and *ICD-11* models specifically, internal consistency values ranged from .61 to .95 across measures of AMPD level of personality impairment (see Zimmermann, Kerber, et al., 2019, for a review), .76 for the SASPD (Olajide et al., 2018), from .72 to .96 for the PID-5 (see Al-Dajani et al., 2016, for review), and from .77 to .88 for the PiCD (Carnovale et al., 2020; Oltmanns & Widiger, 2018). These values are similar to those found in other commonly used self-report personality inventories (.34–.85 for the Minnesota Multiphasic Personality Inventory–2 clinical scales [MMPI-2; Butcher et al., 2001], .38–.88 for the Minnesota Multiphasic Personality Inventory-2-Restructured Form [MMPI-2-RF; Ben-Porath & Tellegen, 2008], .67–.89 for the Millon Clinical Multiaxial Inventory–III [MCMI-III; Millon et al., 1997], .55–.94 for the Personality Assessment Inventory [PAI; Morey, 1991], and .50–.81 for the NEO Personality Inventory–Revised [NEO-PI-R; McCrae et al., 2011]). Although .70 is often cited as a cutoff value for good reliability, psychometricians have noted that reliability values as low as .50 do not seriously attenuate validity coefficients and have warned that alphas greater than .90 may limit the predictive validity of the scale by artificially narrowing scale content (Loevinger, 1954). For AMPD and *ICD-11* measures, test–retest reliability is similarly high (Hopwood et al., 2018; Olajide et al., 2018; Wright, Calabrese, et al., 2015).

To guard against invalid responding, many self-report inventories have embedded validity indices to identify individuals who are responding in an overly negative, overly positive, random, or inconsistent manner. Research supports the effectiveness of many of these validity indices in identifying individuals who are malingering (Berry et al., 1991; Hawes & Boccaccini, 2009; Morey & Lanier, 1998; Rogers & Bender, 2003), responding defensively (Baer & Wetter, 1997; Morey & Lanier, 1998), and randomly and/or inconsistently responding (Handel et al., 2010; Keeley et al., 2016; Morey, 1991). In terms of criterion validity, self-report trait measures are strongly correlated with self-reported behaviors and clinical outcomes (Grucza & Goldberg, 2007); recidivism and violence (Gardner et al., 2015); life event data (Slavin-Mulford et al., 2012); social, occupational, and recreational dysfunction (Hopwood et al., 2009); and academic performance (Poropat, 2009), among others, providing evidence for the construct validity of self-report measures. For a review of these associations for self-report measures of personality impairment and the PID-5 (concepts central to the AMPD), see Zimmermann, Kerber, and colleagues (2019) and McCabe and Widiger (2020). There is also evidence that self-report methods provide greater information about patients' internal thoughts and feelings than informant reports (Fiedler et al., 2004; Spain et al., 2000) and explain an additional 8% of the variance in personality disorder diagnosis, after accounting for information obtained in a structured interview (Quirk et al., 2003). Maladaptive traits in particular increment *DSM* personality disorder diagnostic categories in predicting treatment planning, disability, social cognition deficits, and aggression (see Zimmermann, Kerber, et al., 2019, for a review).

INFORMANT REPORT METHODS

Informant report methods ask knowledgeable people in the patient's life (e.g., parents, romantic partner, close friends, teachers, therapists) to provide information about the patient from their perspective. This information is typically collected using informant versions of established self-report measures (e.g., the Personality Inventory for *DSM-5*–Informant Report Form [PID-5-IRF; Markon et al., 2013], the Informant-Personality Inventory for *ICD-11* [IPiC; Oltmanns & Widiger, 2021]) or by talking to the informant directly.

Advantages and Limitations of Informant Report Methods

Informant report methods provide a different understanding of the patient's personality. This is particularly useful in light of the distortion inherent to self-report methods. If responses from the patient and informant do differ, it is up to the assessor to describe these differences, and, if they are able, to reconcile these differences to create a more complex understanding of the patient. Informant reports are particularly useful for rating observable behaviors but are somewhat limited for rating the patient's internal experiences (Fiedler et al., 2004; Spain et al., 2000).

One limitation of informant report methods is that the quality of the assessment depends on the informant. A teacher, a parent, a romantic partner, and a friend will all have different access to the patient's experiences and different thoughts and feelings about the behaviors or symptoms the patient displays (Galione & Oltmanns, 2014). Additionally, informants may have different levels of familiarity with the psychological constructs being assessed. A clinician who is providing informant ratings, as is often the case with measures that assess the AMPD and *ICD-11* models, will be much more familiar with the nuances of the assessment measure than a patient's peers will be. While collecting data from multiple informants could help to capture these different perspectives, it could also provide an increasingly conflicting picture of the patient that could be difficult to reconcile.

Although informant reports provide an alternative perspective on patient symptoms, this does not mean they are objective or free from bias. Informants have their own standards of behavior derived from their values, beliefs, experiences, and cultures that will influence their evaluation. Informants may also have their own expectations from an assessment or be motivated to portray the patient in a particular way to qualify for a certain kind of treatment or service (Becker-Haimes et al., 2018). Furthermore, for a patient who is socially isolated or who lacks enduring, deep relationships, informant reports may not be as helpful, as the accuracy of informant ratings is positively associated with the depth and length of a relationship (Kurtz & Sherker, 2003).

Validity and Reliability of Informant Report Methods

Informant report measures are often adaptations of self-report inventories and therefore have similar (and occasionally better) psychometric properties. In particular, research on internal consistency suggests that informant reports of normal-range personality traits have greater internal consistency (α = .61–.94) than their self-report counterparts (α = .53–.93; Balsis et al., 2015; Olino & Klein, 2015). The level of convergence in informant ratings across multiple informants is typically assessed with a cross-informant correlation rather than a measure of interrater reliability. Research on children and adolescents suggests that informant reports provided by parents, teachers, mental health workers, and trained observers were correlated on average r = .28 (Achenbach et al., 1987). Agreement improved (r = .60) when pairs of informants occupied similar roles in relation to the patient (e.g., pairs of parents or teachers). For adults, cross-informant correlations across 108 studies were on average r = .27 (Achenbach et al., 2005). This level of agreement improved when personality traits were directly observable and less evaluative (John & Robins, 1993). Thus, informant ratings depend in part on the relationship between the informant and the patient and in part on the nature of the variables being assessed.

Researchers have also examined the validity of informant report methods. Typically, informant reports are correlated .20 to .67 with self-report ratings (John & Robins, 1993; Markon et al., 2013; Oltmanns & Widiger, 2021; Ready & Clark, 2002; Vazire, 2006; Watson et al., 2000). This association is generally lower (median correlation of .36 across studies) when examining dimensional ratings of *DSM* personality disorders (like the AMPD and *ICD-11*) compared with normal-range personality traits (Klonsky et al., 2002). For example, correlations between self- versus informant reports were .27 for the LPFS (Roche et al., 2018) and ranged from .18 to .67 across PID-5 indices (Markon et al., 2013) and from .28 to .44 across Personality Inventory for *ICD-11* indices (Oltmanns & Widiger, 2021). Research suggests that correspondence can be improved by increasing the level of acquaintance between informants and patients (Connelly & Ones, 2010; Paulhus & Bruce, 1992; Watson et al., 2000). Interestingly, the level of self-informant discrepancy itself predicts poor treatment outcomes and increased behavioral problems (De Los Reyes et al., 2010; Ferdinand et al., 2004).

Research also supports the criterion and incremental validity of informant reports (Kolar et al., 1996; Lawton et al., 2011; Vazire, 2006). In particular, measures associated with the AMPD and *ICD-11* (e.g., LPFS, PID-5-IRF, IPiC) show expected relationships with self-reported personality traits, interpersonal values, psychodynamic outcome measures, life satisfaction, mental health problems, social support and informant-reported relationship satisfaction, health problems, and cognitive problems (Markon et al., 2013; Oltmanns & Widiger, 2021; Roche et al., 2018). In terms of incremental validity, one study estimated that clinicians changed their initial diagnosis of a patient (based on the patient's self-report) in 20% of cases after receiving clinically relevant information on pathological behavior from informants (Zimmerman et al., 1988). Other researchers have found that a combination of informant and self-report methods was a better predictor of interpersonal problems than either method on its own (Rodebaugh et al., 2010) and that informant reports of five-factor model personality traits incrementally predicted academic achievement and job performance over a self-report measure of the same traits (Connelly & Ones, 2010; Oh et al., 2011). Together, these findings suggest a certain level of self-informant agreement but also highlight the unique variance explained by an informant perspective.

TECHNOLOGICAL ADVANCES AND PATIENT-SPECIFIC ASSESSMENT APPROACHES

Psychological assessment has increasingly relied on computers for the administration, scoring, and interpretation of self-report measures of personality and personality pathology (Ben-Porath & Butcher, 1986). These approaches have made psychological testing more efficient by increasing test security and reducing (a) time to administer, score, and interpret item responses; (b) associated labor costs; and (c) scoring errors (Drasgow & Olson-Buchanan, 1999). In recent years, technological advancements have also led to the development of more advanced assessment methods, including computer adaptive testing and ecological momentary assessment, that facilitate a person-specific approach to the assessment process. This emphasis on understanding the individual patient is aligned with efforts from the AMPD and *ICD-11* to comprehensively describe an individual's personality by examining the unique elevations and depressions across their profile of scores and could provide a method for extending the idiographic emphasis of dimensional models of personality pathology.

Computer Adaptive Testing

In *computer adaptive testing* (CAT), the computer selects and administers a person-specific subset of self-report items from a larger item bank (Simms et al., 2011). To do this, the computer estimates a person's level of the latent trait after each item is answered. Based on that estimate, the computer chooses the most informative item to administer next. This iterative process continues until the trait estimate is sufficiently precise. To determine the item characteristics needed for person-specific item selection, CAT procedures have historically relied heavily on parameters (e.g., item difficulty, item discrimination, item information) from item response theory. However, other approaches, including the countdown method (Butcher et al., 1985) and the Full Scores on Elevated Scales (FSES; Ben-Porath et al., 1989) approach, have been used when personality constructs are categorical in nature. These approaches terminate item administration if clinical cutoffs have been reached (countdown method) or are impossible to reach (both countdown and FSES methods). CAT has been widely used in the ability testing literature but thus far has had more limited applications in the field of personality assessment.

Advantages and Limitations of CAT Methods

Given that many existing personality inventories (including those used to assess the AMPD) are hundreds of items long, one of the distinct advantages of CAT is its ability to estimate personality variables more quickly. Research simulating CAT procedures using existing data reports item savings of 20% to 75% across scales and measures (Handel et al., 1999; Reise & Henson, 2000; Roper et al., 1995; Waller & Reise, 1989). When personality assessment measures are adaptively administered to patients, researchers have similarly found substantial time savings (30%–60%) and item savings (mean of 20%–37%; Roper et al., 1995; Simms & Clark, 2005). By decreasing the number of items administered and overall testing time, clinicians can reduce patient fatigue and more efficiently assess their patient's personality.

CAT approaches also help to maintain test security. The personalization that occurs with CAT ensures that patients not only receive fewer items but also receive a unique subset of items. Thus, patients do not access the entire item bank, and if no two people take the same test, copying answers or memorizing a sequence of responses would be less useful. Further, because CAT approaches administer items via computer, hard copies of test booklets are never compromised.

Despite this, CAT methods are not without their disadvantages. First, the reliance on item response theory necessitates (a) the development of large and broad item pools that provide information across the entire latent trait continuum and (b) the recruitment of large standardization samples. At minimum, this is a time-consuming and expensive process. Second, given that existing inventories often don't provide equivalent information across the entire latent trait continuum, it isn't always appropriate to translate existing inventories directly into CAT methods. Instead, researchers have proposed creating new inventories, such as the Computerized Adaptive Test of Personality Disorder (CAT-PD), whose items are optimized for a CAT environment (Simms et al., 2011). These inventories are a prominent advancement for the field but currently lack the rich history and extensive study that existing inventories possess. However, because new models like the AMPD and *ICD-11* are developing an extensive research literature in their own right, CAT applications may be particularly appropriate to consider.

Reliability and Validity of CAT Methods

Research examining the reliability and validity of CAT methods is currently minimal but generally supports the use of CAT methodologies. Test–retest reliability estimates are typically equivalent to or slightly lower than their paper-and-pencil counterparts and tend to fall in the acceptable range (Roper et al., 1991; Simms & Clark, 2005). In particular, mean reliability estimates for the computerized adaptive version of the Schedule for Nonadaptive and Adaptive Personality (SNAP-CAT) and MMPI-2 scales were .84 (ranging from .73 to .89) and .73 (ranging from .55 to .92), respectively (Roper et al., 1991; Simms & Clark, 2005).

In terms of validity, research supports the person-specific nature of CAT administrations. CAT items lower in difficulty and higher in discrimination are administered more frequently than higher difficulty or lower discrimination items (Simms & Clark, 2005). According to one study, the average SNAP-CAT item was administered adaptively to only 62% of participants, and fewer than 10% of items were administered to all participants (Simms & Clark, 2005). With that being said, a CAT approach may not be necessary or appropriate for all measures. Research on the adaptive administration of the NEO-PI-R (McCrae et al., 2011), for example, found that the same four items were administered first for nearly all examinees, suggesting that the development of a short form may be more appropriate for this measure (Reise & Henson, 2000).

Research also supports the criterion validity of CAT methods. CAT scale scores are correlated highly ($r > .76$) with full-scale trait estimates, suggesting that they are assessing the same constructs despite using fewer items (Reise & Henson, 2000; Simms & Clark, 2005). There is also evidence that CAT methods can recover the factor structure suggested by the full-length measure, and these factor scores show expected relationships with a range of criterion variables (Roper et al., 1995; Simms & Clark, 2005). However, the magnitude of these relationships may be attenuated. The SNAP-CAT, for example, ultimately accounted for 6.6% to 24.6% less variance in other personality inventories, compared with the full SNAP. Roper et al. (1995) similarly found that criterion correlations with MMPI Scales 1 and 3 were somewhat attenuated for computer adaptive methods. Simms and Clark (2005) suggested that this attenuation may be expected when using measures whose scales do not include adequate information at all levels of the latent trait. Future measures that are built specifically for CAT methods may not exhibit similar levels of attenuation.

Ecological Momentary Assessment

Ecological momentary assessment (EMA) encompasses a range of methods (daily diary, smartphone applications, passive sensors, etc.) that assess a patient repeatedly in real time, over various periods and at various intensities in their natural environment, to provide a person- specific assessment of the patient (Shiffman et al., 2008). Like content and sequence analyses performed on responses from performance-based measures (Peebles-Kleiger, 2002), EMA methods focus on understanding idiographic dynamic processes. By assessing the patient repeatedly, EMA approaches allow clinicians to quantify how emotions, cognitions, perceptions, and behaviors co-occur for an individual, enabling the creation of an evidence-based and clinically useful conceptualization of a patient's personality pathology and symptom triggers. This focus on so-called precision diagnosis is consistent with a similar push in psychiatry to link assessment to the precise and individualized contexts in which psychopathology manifests (van Os et al., 2013). It is also a direct response to the limitations of nomothetic assessment approaches that risk identifying structures and processes that apply to the population as a whole but fail to apply to any specific person (Allport, 1937).

Advantages and Disadvantages of EMA Methods

EMA approaches minimize recall bias by assessing patients in the moment rather than retrospectively (Bolger et al., 2003; Conner et al., 2009; Shiffman et al., 2008). Research has consistently demonstrated that retrospective accounts of the frequency of an event, the sequence of events, and the experience of an event are often unreliable and inaccurate, even when participants report high confidence in their ratings (Shiffman et al., 2008). By quickly, easily, and inconspicuously collecting data from the individual as they go about their day, EMA approaches maximize the ecological validity of the assessment (Stone & Shiffman, 2002). Furthermore, EMA methods uniquely allow clinicians to quantify and model patient variability over time. This is clinically important given that research suggests that much of the variability in interpersonal behavior and emotional experience is related to fluctuations in daily stress rather than dispositional measures of personality dysfunction (Wright, Hopwood, & Simms, 2015). Although EMA methods have yet to become part of mainstream assessment practice, a number of case studies have been published demonstrating the clinical utility of these approaches (Dowgwillo et al., 2019; Lewis et al., 2021; Roche et al., 2014; Wright et al., 2016).

As employed, this approach is not without its limitations. First, EMA approaches are often limited to a single account of the interaction and do not typically integrate informant ratings or objective data. Thus, clinicians can talk about how the patient is likely to respond when they experience the world in a particular way, but often have no way of knowing how distorted or biased that perception might be or how the patient compares to a normative group. For this reason, it is important to integrate EMA methods with time-invariant measures. In existing applications, this has been accomplished by administering a series of baseline measures that assess maladaptive traits and/or AMPD level of personality functioning prior to the EMA assessment. Research has demonstrated that AMPD level of personality functioning moderates the association between interpersonal perception and psychological symptoms, emotions, and functioning (Dowgwillo et al., 2019). Including a person-specific approach in a larger assessment battery could provide person-specific context to the self and other deficits identified by dimensional models of personality pathology such as the AMPD or *ICD-11*. Additionally, examining how these dynamic patterns may change over the course of therapy and how these changes may be associated with changes in level of personality functioning would be an interesting future application of this approach.

Another limitation of EMA methods is that assessment validity depends on compliance with the assessment protocol, which is more difficult to monitor outside of a formal assessment setting. Finally, because EMA methods require that patients provide data repeatedly over the course of days or weeks, patients have historically been assessed with broad items (e.g., "Please rate your level of anxiety right now") that inquire about the patient's mood, perceptions, symptoms, or behaviors, rather than longer, well-validated personality measures. To address these concerns and facilitate a comprehensive assessment, Zimmermann, Woods, and colleagues (2019) developed the Personality Dynamics Diary (PDD), a 30-item measure of patient behaviors and situational features specifically designed to be administered repeatedly in EMA formats. Although patients have noted that the measure was easy to use and was moderately successful at comprehensively evaluating clinically relevant aspects of daily life, and submitting daily questionnaires was not overly burdensome, more research on the psychometric properties of this and other standardized EMA item batteries is needed.

Reliability and Validity of EMA Methods

In a clinical setting, EMA instruments often use a series of short-form and/or individually tailored, single-item measures to assess the patient over the course of their daily life. Because of this, reliability and validity are difficult to systematically study and assess. When constructs are assessed with brief forms of longer measures, reliabilities are often greater than .7 at the person level (Dowgwillo, 2020; Zimmermann, Woods, et al., 2019). Reliabilities tend to be lower and more variable at the within-person level, ranging from .40 to .99.

When EMA methods are used to study groups of individuals, findings suggest that reports of psychological states are associated with situational features, correlate with independent measures of similar constructs, and distinguish between groups (Csikszentmihalyi & Larson, 2014; Dotterer et al., 2020; Dowgwillo et al., 2018), supporting the validity of an EMA approach. Findings for groups, however, do not necessarily apply to specific individuals. The level of ecological validity for a specific patient depends on adequate sampling of the patient's experience (Ram et al., 2017). To ensure adequate sampling, it is important that patients comply with the assessment protocol. If patients do not provide enough responses, respond only under certain conditions (e.g., only on weekends or only when they are very distressed), or complete surveys retrospectively rather than in the moment, their data may not adequately represent their experience, limiting the validity of conclusions. Reports of compliance in EMA-type studies is variable, ranging from 11% to over 80% or 90% (Hufford et al., 2002; Stone & Shiffman, 2002). Research suggests that compliance is improved when patients are more comfortable (e.g., using smartphones to record their responses), incoming data are monitored in real time, and motivational support is provided (Newcomb et al., 2018; Ram et al., 2017). The ecological validity of EMA is similarly threatened if the repeated assessments characteristic of EMA change the patient's feelings, behavior, or experience. Although some studies have found no evidence of reactivity (Reynolds et al., 2016), others suggest that protocols may have influenced behavior via reflection, social desirability, fatigue, or feedback processes (Barta et al., 2012). In these latter instances, assessment data may no longer represent the patient's natural environment. Given this variability, the effects of reactivity should be considered when assessing patients in clinical settings. Furthermore, although EMA methods help to protect against retrospective bias, patients can still be influenced by the saliency, accessibility, and social desirability biases that characterize self-report methods more generally.

MULTIMETHOD ASSESSMENT

Given their diverse properties, each of the methods described above provides an informative yet incomplete picture of a patient's personality. Rather than place one method in direct competition with another, *multimethod clinical assessment* integrates conclusions derived from different methodologies to more comprehensively describe the patient. This process is one of the hallmarks of personality assessment that helps to distinguish it from psychometric testing.

The benefits of multimethod assessment have been well documented (Bornstein & Hopwood, 2014; Mihura & Graceffo, 2014). Multimethod clinical assessment minimizes threats to reliability and validity by using the strengths of one method to compensate for the weaknesses of another. A multimethod approach also allows clinicians to better understand areas of convergence and divergence in assessment scores. Although initially it was thought that measures of the same trait should be highly convergent, Campbell and Fiske's (1959) multitrait-multimethod matrix provided a framework for considering both measure and method variance. This approach helps to explain why correlations across personality assessment methods are modest at best and why performance-based measures correlate more highly with established self-report measures when they are converted to a self-report format (McCredie & Morey, 2019; Morey & McCredie, 2019). Thus, contemporary thinking suggests that divergences across methods should be viewed as information rather than error. Understanding those divergences can reveal additional aspects of the patient's personality, improving assessment accuracy and clinical recommendations (Hunsley & Meyer, 2003). For these reasons, using a multi-method assessment approach as part of clinical practice is encouraged.

To facilitate its use, Bornstein and Hopwood (2014) described the process of multimethod assessment and test-score integration in six steps. First, they recommended understanding the strengths and limitations of different assessment methods. This can include information on the psychological processes engaged by each method (Bornstein, 2011), evidence of method reliability and validity, and the psychometric properties characteristic of specific assessment measures. Second, they advocated for understanding when a multimethod approach may be most useful. At the most basic level, a multimethod approach is useful when a clinician needs a nuanced and thorough understanding of a particular personality construct, when a clinician's behavioral observations of the patient are at odds with the patient's self-report, when the patient has trouble understanding and communicating their inner experiences, or when the case is complex and the stakes around the assessment decision are particularly high (Lawton et al., 2011; Meyer et al., 2001, 2011; Mihura et al., 2013). The third and fourth steps involve deciding which methods to include in the assessment and selecting appropriate measures. These decisions are guided by the referral question, the patient's history, prior evaluations, the domains of behavior and mental functioning centrally important to the assessment, and the psychometric properties, cost-effectiveness, and clinical utility associated with specific measures (Bornstein & Hopwood, 2014). The clinician may revisit these decisions over the course of an assessment as preliminary results suggest areas that merit additional consideration. Once an assessment battery is administered and scored, the clinician must implement a framework for integrating assessment findings across methods to create a comprehensive understanding of the patient (Step 5) and use this understanding to make treatment recommendations (Step 6).

A number of frameworks for understanding method convergences and divergences have been established. Some of these frameworks are specific to particular constructs, measures, or methods. Bornstein's four-cell model of interpersonal dependency, for example, focuses on integrating self-report and performance-based data to classify patients into one of four groups: low dependency, high dependency, unacknowledged dependency, and dependent self-presentation (Bornstein, 2012). Shedler and colleagues (1993), using self-report neuroticism data and constructed early memories, provided a similar framework for classifying patients as genuinely healthy, genuinely distressed, experiencing an illusion of mental illness, or experiencing an illusion of mental health.

Other frameworks have focused on integrating data across domains of interest. Carr and Goldstein (1981) described a framework for understanding borderline pathology through the lens of personality structure, response to confrontation, severity of illness, symptom diagnosis, and differential responses based on each test's level of structure, while Huprich (2008) discussed how personality pathology could be understood by integrating (a) intrapsychic (internal conflicts, object relations, and unconscious motivations commonly assessed via performance-based techniques), (b) behavioral (situational determinants and cross-situational similarities and discrepancies assessed by observing behaviors), (c) dimensional (personality factors/traits assessed with self-report methods), and (d) genetic (genetic or biological basis of personality and psychopathology) perspectives.

More recently, Blais and Smith (2014) proposed a transtheoretical model of personality, one of the most comprehensive integration frameworks to date. They identified five interrelated "systems," based on work by Mayer (2005), that are central to understanding personality processes across theoretical perspectives: emotional processing, the nature and quality of thinking, sense of self, sense of others, and ability to cope. Each of these systems relies upon neurocognitive processes such as attention, concentration, and memory. Additionally, each system is composed of *explicit processes* that are within the patient's awareness and *implicit processes* that operate outside of conscious awareness. Because different assessment methods target these systems at different levels (implicit vs. explicit), this transtheoretical model is ideally suited to a multimethod assessment approach.

In particular, Blais and Smith's (2014) transtheoretical model can be used to guide the integration of multimethod assessment data that assess concepts central to the AMPD and *ICD-11*. Self- and informant scores for the Emotional Lability domain (and the Depressivity, Anxiousness, Hostility, and Restricted Affectivity indices) of the PID-5 and the Negative Affectivity trait domain specifier of the PiCD and IPiC can be used to explicitly assess the emotional processing domain of the transtheoretical model. If used to assess level of personality functioning, Rorschach and SCORS-G indices could also implicitly provide information about a patient's ability to experience, express, and regulate painful affect.

Although the PID-5 Psychoticism domain (particularly the Cognitive and Perceptual Dysregulation and Unusual Beliefs and Experiences scales) can speak to the nature and quality of a patient's thinking, the overall ability of AMPD and *ICD-11* self-report and interview measures to assess a patient's thought processes is limited. Using indices from the Rorschach and SCORS-G to implicitly assess level of personality functioning has the added benefit of providing information about a patient's perceptual accuracy, associational quality, and information processing ability, providing a more comprehensive view of the patient's functioning.

The self and other domains of the transtheoretical model can be explicitly assessed with LPFS-assessed deficits in self- and interpersonal functioning; self- and informant report ratings of the PID-5 Detachment (particularly the Withdrawal, Intimacy Avoidance and Suspiciousness facets) and Antagonism (with associated facets) domains; self- and informant reports of the PID-5 facets of Submissiveness, Separation Insecurity, and Eccentricity; and the Detachment and Dissociality trait domain specifiers of the PiCD and IPiC. Rorschach and SCORS-G indices can implicitly add information about a patient's level of egocentricity and narcissistic defenses, self-esteem, and identity and coherence of self.

Finally, a patient's coping strategies can be explicitly assessed using the self- and informant PID-5 Disinhibition dimension (including facets of Impulsivity, Risk Taking, Irresponsibility, and Rigid Perfectionism) and the Disinhibition and Anankastic trait domain specifiers of the PiCD and IPiC. Coping can also be assessed implicitly with Rorschach and SCORS-G indices associated with coping ability, ideational versus emotional problem-solving strategies, the experience of stressors, and tendencies toward aggression or intellectualization to add a more nuanced perspective to a clinician's understanding of the patient. In this way, existing models for integration could be used to better understand multimethod data from a dimensional assessment of personality pathology.

CONCLUSION

Personality assessment as a field relies on a number of methods to better understand a patient's personality traits and dynamics. These methods have served the field well and are equally as applicable to the new dimensional conceptualizations of personality pathology identified in the AMPD and *ICD-11*. Rather than place one method in direct competition with another, a multimethod assessment approach encourages clinicians to view divergences as clinical information rather than noise. By means of (a) examination of how self-report information differs from a patient's behavior in a clinical interview, (b) information provided by informants, and/or (c) conclusions derived from performance-based measures, clinicians can develop a more nuanced view of the patient's personality. It is our hope that with further development, person-specific assessment methods will play a key role in the multimethod assessment batteries of the future, allowing clinicians to tailor assessment measures to the individual and discover ideographic contextual information that will more specifically inform patient conceptualization and treatment planning.

REFERENCES

Achenbach, T. M., Krukowski, R. A., Dumenci, L., & Ivanova, M. Y. (2005). Assessment of adult psychopathology: Meta-analyses and implications of cross-informant correlations. *Psychological Bulletin, 131*(3), 361–382. https://doi.org/10.1037/0033-2909.131.3.361

Achenbach, T. M., McConaughy, S. H., & Howell, C. T. (1987). Child/adolescent behavioral and emotional problems: Implications of cross-informant correlations for situational specificity. *Psychological Bulletin, 101*(2), 213–232. https://doi.org/10.1037/0033-2909.101.2.213

Acklin, M. W., McDowell, C. J., II, Verschell, M. S., & Chan, D. (2000). Interobserver agreement, intraobserver reliability, and the Rorschach Comprehensive System. *Journal of Personality Assessment, 74*(1), 15–47. https://doi.org/10.1207/S15327752JPA740103

Al-Dajani, N., Gralnick, T. M., & Bagby, R. M. (2016). A psychometric review of the Personality Inventory for *DSM-5* (PID-5): Current status and future directions. *Journal of Personality Assessment, 98*(1), 62–81. https://doi.org/10.1080/00223891.2015.1107572

Alicke, M. D. (1985). Global self-evaluation as determined by the desirability and controllability of trait adjectives. *Journal of Personality and Social Psychology, 49*(6), 1621–1630. https://doi.org/10.1037/0022-3514.49.6.1621

Allik, J. (2005). Personality dimensions across cultures. *Journal of Personality Disorders, 19*(3), 212–232. https://doi.org/10.1521/pedi.2005.19.3.212

Allport, G. W. (1937). *Personality: A psychological interpretation.* Holt.

American Psychiatric Association. (2013). *Diagnostic and statistical manual of mental disorders* (5th ed.). https://doi.org/10.1176/appi.books.978089042559

Archer, R. P., & Krishnamurthy, R. (1993). A review of MMPI and Rorschach interrelationships in adult samples. *Journal of Personality Assessment, 61*(2), 277–293. https://doi.org/10.1207/s15327752jpa6102_9

Baer, R. A., & Wetter, M. W. (1997). Effects of information about validity scales on underreporting of symptoms on the Personality Assessment Inventory. *Journal of Personality Assessment, 68*(2), 402–413. https://doi.org/10.1207/s15327752jpa6802_10

Balsis, S., Cooper, L. D., & Oltmanns, T. F. (2015). Are informant reports of personality more internally consistent than self reports of personality? *Assessment, 22*(4), 399–404. https://doi.org/10.1177/1073191114556100

Barta, W. D., Tennen, H., & Litt, M. D. (2012). Measurement reactivity in diary research. In M. R. Mehl & T. S. Conner (Eds.), *Handbook of research methods for studying daily life* (pp. 108–123). Guilford Press.

Becker-Haimes, E. M., Jensen-Doss, A., Birmaher, B., Kendall, P. C., & Ginsburg, G. S. (2018). Parent–youth informant disagreement: Implications for youth anxiety treatment. *Clinical Child Psychology and Psychiatry, 23*(1), 42–56. https://doi.org/10.1177/1359104516689586

Bender, D. S., Morey, L. C., & Skodol, A. E. (2011). Toward a model for assessing level of personality functioning in *DSM-5*, part I: A review of theory and methods. *Journal of Personality Assessment, 93*(4), 332–346. https://doi.org/10.1080/00223891.2011.583808

Bender, D. S., Skodol, A. E., First, M. B., & Oldham, J. M. (2018). Module I: Structured Clinical Interview for the Level of Personality Functioning Scale. In M. B. First, A. E. Skodol, D. S. Bender, & J. M. Oldham (Eds.), *Structured Clinical Interview for the DSM-5 Alternative Model for Personality Disorders (SCID-5-AMPD).* American Psychiatric Association Publishing.

Ben-Porath, Y. S., & Butcher, J. N. (1986). Computers in personality assessment: A brief past, an ebullient present, and an expanding future. *Computers in Human Behavior, 2*(3), 167–182. https://doi.org/10.1016/0747-5632(86)90001-4

Ben-Porath, Y. S., Slutske, W. S., & Butcher, J. N. (1989). A real-data simulation of computerized adaptive administration of the MMPI. *Psychological Assessment, 1*(1), 18–22. https://doi.org/10.1037/1040-3590.1.1.18

Ben-Porath, Y. S., & Tellegen, A. (2008). *MMPI-2-RF (Minnesota Multiphasic Personality Inventory-2-Restructured Form): Manual for administration, scoring, and interpretation.* University of Minnesota Press.

Berghuis, H., Hutsebaut, J., Kaasenbrood, A., de Saeger, H., & Ingenhoven, T. (2013). Semi-structured interview for personality functioning *DSM-5* (STiP-5). The Podium *DSM-5* research group of the Netherlands Centre of Expertise on Personality Disorders. Trimbos Institute.

Berry, D. T. R., Baer, R. A., & Harris, M. J. (1991). Detection of malingering on the MMPI: A meta-analysis. *Clinical Psychology Review, 11*(5), 585–598. https://doi.org/10.1016/0272-7358(91)90005-F

Blais, M. A., & Smith, S. R. (2014). Improving the integration process in psychological assessment: Data organization and report writing. In R. P. Archer & S. R. Smith (Eds.), *Personality assessment* (pp. 433–469). Routledge.

Blasczyk-Schiep, S., Kazén, M., Kuhl, J., & Grygielski, M. (2011). Appraisal of suicidal risk among adolescents and young adults through the Rorschach test. *Journal of Personality Assessment, 93*(5), 518–526. https://doi.org/10.1080/00223891.2011.594130

Bolger, N., Davis, A., & Rafaeli, E. (2003). Diary methods: Capturing life as it is lived. *Annual Review of Psychology, 54*, 579–616. https://doi.org/10.1146/annurev.psych.54.101601.145030

Bornstein, R. F. (2011). Toward a process-focused model of test score validity: Improving psychological assessment in science and practice. *Psychological Assessment, 23*(2), 532–544. https://doi.org/10.1037/a0022402

Bornstein, R. F. (2012). From dysfunction to adaptation: An interactionist model of dependency. *Annual Review of Clinical Psychology, 8*, 291–316. https://doi.org/10.1146/annurev-clinpsy-032511-143058

Bornstein, R. F., & Hopwood, C. J. (2014). Introduction to multimethod clinical assessment. In C. J. Hopwood & R. F. Bornstein (Eds.), *Multimethod clinical assessment* (pp. 1–18). Guilford Press.

Buer Christensen, T., Eikenaes, I., Hummelen, B., Pedersen, G., Nysæter, T.-E., Bender, D. S., Skodol, A. E., & Selvik, S. G. (2020). Level of personality functioning as a predictor of psychosocial functioning—Concurrent validity of Criterion A. *Personality Disorders: Theory, Research, and Treatment, 11*(2), 79–90. https://doi.org/10.1037/per0000352

Buer Christensen, T., Paap, M. C. S., Arnesen, M., Koritzinsky, K., Nysaeter, T.-E., Eikenaes, I., Germans Selvik, S., Walther, K., Torgersen, S., Bender, D. S., Skodol, A. E., Kvarstein, E., Pedersen, G., & Hummelen, B. (2018). Interrater reliability of the Structured Clinical Interview for the *DSM-5* Alternative Model of Personality Disorders Module i: Level of Personality Functioning Scale. *Journal of Personality Assessment, 100*(6), 630–641. https://doi.org/10.1080/00223891.2018.1483377

Butcher, J. N., Graham, J. R., Ben-Porath, Y. S., Tellegen, A., Dahlstrom, W. G., & Kaemmer, B. (2001). *MMPI-2: Manual for administration and scoring* (Rev. ed.). University of Minnesota Press.

Butcher, J. N., Keller, L. S., & Bacon, S. F. (1985). Current developments and future directions in computerized personality assessment. *Journal of Consulting and Clinical Psychology, 53*(6), 803–815. https://doi.org/10.1037/0022-006X.53.6.803

Campbell, D. T., & Fiske, D. W. (1959). Convergent and discriminant validation by the multitrait-multimethod matrix. *Psychological Bulletin, 56*(2), 81–105. https://doi.org/10.1037/h0046016

Carnovale, M., Sellbom, M., & Bagby, R. M. (2020). The Personality Inventory for *ICD-11*: Investigating reliability, structural and concurrent validity, and method variance. *Psychological Assessment, 32*(1), 8–17. https://doi.org/10.1037/pas0000776

Carr, A. C., & Goldstein, E. G. (1981). Approaches to the diagnosis of borderline conditions by use of psychological tests. *Journal of Personality Assessment, 45*(6), 563–574. https://doi.org/10.1207/s15327752jpa4506_1

Church, A. T., Alvarez, J. M., Mai, N. T. Q., French, B. F., Katigbak, M. S., & Ortiz, F. A. (2011). Are cross-cultural comparisons of personality profiles meaningful? Differential item and facet functioning in the Revised NEO Personality Inventory. *Journal of Personality and Social Psychology, 101*(5), 1068–1089. https://doi.org/10.1037/a0025290

Clarkin, J. F., Caligor, E., Stern, B. L., & Kernberg, O. F. (2007). *Structured Interview of Personality Organization (STIPO)* [Unpublished manuscript]. Personality Disorders Institute, Weill Medical College of Cornell University.

Connelly, B. S., & Ones, D. S. (2010). An other perspective on personality: Meta-analytic integration of observers' accuracy and predictive validity. *Psychological Bulletin, 136*(6), 1092–1122. https://doi.org/10.1037/a0021212

Conner, T. S., Tennen, H., Fleeson, W., & Barrett, L. F. (2009). Experience sampling methods: A modern idiographic approach to personality research. *Social and Personality Psychology Compass, 3*(3), 292–313. https://doi.org/10.1111/j.1751-9004.2009.00170.x

Csikszentmihalyi, M., & Larson, R. (2014). Validity and reliability of the experience-sampling method. In M. Csikszentmihalyi (Ed.), *Flow and the foundations of positive psychology: The collected works of Mihaly Csikszentmihalyi* (pp. 35–54). Springer. https://doi.org/10.1007/978-94-017-9088-8_3

Dao, T. K., Prevatt, F., & Horne, H. L. (2008). Differentiating psychotic patients from nonpsychotic patients with the MMPI-2 and Rorschach. *Journal of Personality Assessment, 90*(1), 93–101. https://doi.org/10.1080/00223890701693819

De Los Reyes, A., Alfano, C. A., & Beidel, D. C. (2010). The relations among measurements of informant discrepancies within a multisite trial of treatments for childhood social phobia. *Journal of Abnormal Child Psychology, 38*(3), 395–404. https://doi.org/10.1007/s10802-009-9373-6

Dotterer, H. L., Beltz, A. M., Foster, K. T., Simms, L. J., & Wright, A. G. C. (2020). Personalized models of personality disorders: Using a temporal network method to understand symptomatology and daily functioning in a clinical sample. *Psychological Medicine, 50*(14), 2397–2405. https://doi.org/10.1017/S0033291719002563

Dowgwillo, E. A. (2020). *Within person covariation of narcissistic grandiosity and vulnerability in daily life and the construct validity of the Super Brief-Pathological Narcissism Inventory* [Unpublished doctoral dissertation]. Pennsylvania State University.

Dowgwillo, E. A., Dawood, S., Bliton, C. F., & Pincus, A. L. (2018, March). *Within person covariation of narcissistic grandiosity and vulnerability in daily life* [Poster presentation]. Society for Personality Assessment 80th Annual Meeting, Washington, DC, United States.

Dowgwillo, E. A., Pincus, A. L., Newman, M. G., Wilson, S. J., Molenaar, P. C. M., & Levy, K. N. (2019). Two methods for operationalizing the interpersonal situation to investigate personality pathology and interpersonal perception in daily life. In L. I. Truslow & J. M. Rahmaan (Eds.), *Personality disorders: What we know and future directions for research* (pp. 31–106). Nova Science Publishers. https://drive.google.com/file/d/19mRLPkPWmZuhhLHqDsauEI8QpEg83f3L/view

Drasgow, F., & Olson-Buchanan, J. B. (Eds.). (1999). *Innovations in computerized assessment.* Psychology Press. https://doi.org/10.4324/9781410602527

Exner, J. E. (1974). *The Rorschach: A comprehensive system.* John Wiley & Sons.

Ferdinand, R. F., van der Ende, J., & Verhulst, F. C. (2004). Parent–adolescent disagreement regarding psychopathology in adolescents from the general population as a risk factor for adverse outcome. *Journal of Abnormal Psychology, 113*(2), 198–206. https://doi.org/10.1037/0021-843X.113.2.198

Fiedler, E. R., Oltmanns, T. F., & Turkheimer, E. (2004). Traits associated with personality disorders and adjustment to military life: Predictive validity of self and peer reports. *Military Medicine, 169*(3), 207–211. https://doi.org/10.7205/MILMED.169.3.207

First, M. B., Spitzer, R. L., Gibbon, M., Williams, J. B. W., Davies, M., Borus, J., Howes, M. J., Kane, J., Pope, H. G., Jr., & Rounsaville, B. (1995). The structured clinical interview for *DSM-III-R* personality disorders (SCID-II). Part II: Multi-site test-retest reliability study. *Journal of Personality Disorders, 9*(2), 92–104. https://doi.org/10.1521/pedi.1995.9.2.92

Galione, J., & Oltmanns, T. F. (2014). Multimethod assessment of traits. In C. J. Hopwood & R. F. Bornstein (Eds.), *Multimethod clinical assessment* (pp. 21–50). Guilford Press.

Ganellen, R. J. (2007). Assessing normal and abnormal personality functioning: Strengths and weaknesses of self-report, observer, and performance-based methods. *Journal of Personality Assessment, 89*(1), 30–40. https://doi.org/10.1080/00223890701356987

Gardner, B. O., Boccaccini, M. T., Bitting, B. S., & Edens, J. F. (2015). Personality Assessment Inventory scores as predictors of misconduct, recidivism, and violence: A meta-analytic review. *Psychological Assessment, 27*(2), 534–544. https://doi.org/10.1037/pas0000065

Giromini, L., Ando', A., Morese, R., Salatino, A., Di Girolamo, M., Viglione, D. J., & Zennaro, A. (2016). Rorschach Performance Assessment System (R-PAS) and vulnerability to stress: A preliminary study on electrodermal activity during stress. *Psychiatry Research, 246*, 166–172. https://doi.org/10.1016/j.psychres.2016.09.036

Glass, M. H., Bieber, S. L., & Tkachuk, M. J. (1996). Personality styles and dynamics of Alaska Native and nonnative incarcerated men. *Journal of Personality Assessment, 66*(3), 583–603. https://doi.org/10.1207/s15327752jpa6603_8

Gronnerod, C. (2003). Temporal stability in the Rorschach method: A meta-analytic review. *Journal of Personality Assessment, 80*(3), 272–293. https://doi.org/10.1207/S15327752JPA8003_06

Grucza, R. A., & Goldberg, L. R. (2007). The comparative validity of 11 modern personality inventories: Predictions of behavioral acts, informant reports, and clinical indicators. *Journal of Personality Assessment, 89*(2), 167–187. https://doi.org/10.1080/00223890701468568

Handel, R. W., Ben-Porath, Y. S., Tellegen, A., & Archer, R. P. (2010). Psychometric functioning of the MMPI-2-RF VRIN-r and TRIN-r scales with varying degrees of randomness, acquiescence, and counter-acquiescence. *Psychological Assessment, 22*(1), 87–95. https://doi.org/10.1037/a0017061

Handel, R. W., Ben-Porath, Y. S., & Watt, M. (1999). Computerized adaptive assessment with the MMPI-2 in a clinical setting. *Psychological Assessment, 11*(3), 369–380. https://doi.org/10.1037/1040-3590.11.3.369

Hartmann, E., Sunde, T., Kristensen, W., & Martinussen, M. (2003). Psychological measures as predictors of military training performance. *Journal of Personality Assessment, 80*(1), 87–98. https://doi.org/10.1207/S15327752JPA8001_17

Hathaway, S. R., & McKinley, J. C. (1943). *The Minnesota Multiphasic Personality Inventory manual.* University of Minnesota Press.

Hawes, S. W., & Boccaccini, M. T. (2009). Detection of overreporting of psychopathology on the Personality Assessment Inventory: A meta-analytic review. *Psychological Assessment, 21*(1), 112–124. https://doi.org/10.1037/a0015036

Hilsenroth, M., Stein, M., & Pinsker, J. (2004). *Social Cognition and Object Relations Scale: Global Method (SCORS-G)* [Unpublished manuscript]. Derner Institute of Advanced Psychological Studies, Adelphi University.

Hopwood, C. J., Good, E. W., & Morey, L. C. (2018). Validity of the *DSM-5* Levels of Personality Functioning Scale–Self Report. *Journal of Personality Assessment, 100*(6), 650–659. https://doi.org/10.1080/00223891.2017.1420660

Hopwood, C. J., Morey, L. C., Ansell, E. B., Grilo, C. M., Sanislow, C. A., McGlashan, T. H., Markowitz, J. C., Gunderson, J. G., Yen, S., Shea, M. T., & Skodol, A. E. (2009). The convergent and discriminant validity of five-factor traits: Current and prospective social, work, and recreational dysfunction. *Journal of Personality Disorders, 23*(5), 466–476. https://doi.org/10.1521/pedi.2009.23.5.466

Hufford, M. R., Shields, A. L., Shiffman, S., Paty, J., & Balabanis, M. (2002). Reactivity to ecological momentary assessment: An example using undergraduate problem drinkers. *Psychology of Addictive Behaviors, 16*(3), 205–211. https://doi.org/10.1037/0893-164X.16.3.205

Hunsley, J., & Meyer, G. J. (2003). The incremental validity of psychological testing and assessment: Conceptual, methodological, and statistical issues. *Psychological Assessment, 15*(4), 446–455. https://doi.org/10.1037/1040-3590.15.4.446

Huprich, S. K. (2008). Necessary changes for the assessment of personality disorders. In I. V. Halvorsen & S. N. Olsen (Eds.), *New research on personality disorders* (pp. 27–53). Nova Science Publishers.

Huprich, S. K. (2011a). Contributions from personality- and psychodynamically oriented assessment to the development of the *DSM-5* personality disorders. *Journal of Personality Assessment, 93*(4), 354–361. https://doi.org/10.1080/00223891.2011.577473

Huprich, S. K. (2011b). Reclaiming the value of assessing unconscious and subjective psychological experience. *Journal of Personality Assessment, 93*(2), 151–160. https://doi.org/10.1080/00223891.2010.542531

Huprich, S. K., & Ganellen, R. J. (2006). The advantages of assessing personality disorders with the Rorschach. In S. K. Huprich (Ed.), *Rorschach assessment of the personality disorders* (pp. 27–53). Lawrence Erlbaum Associates.

Huprich, S. K., Nelson, S. M., Meehan, K. B., Siefert, C. J., Haggerty, G., Sexton, J., Dauphin, V. B., Macaluso, M., Jackson, J., Zackula, R., & Baade, L. (2018). Introduction of the *DSM-5* Levels of Personality Functioning Questionnaire. *Personality*

Disorders: Theory, Research, and Treatment, 9(6), 553–563. https://doi.org/10.1037/per0000264

Hutsebaut, J., Feenstra, D. J., & Kamphuis, J. H. (2016). Development and preliminary psychometric evaluation of a brief self-report questionnaire for the assessment of the *DSM-5* Level of Personality Functioning Scale: The LPFS Brief Form (LPFS-BF). *Personality Disorders: Theory, Research, and Treatment, 7*(2), 192–197. https://doi.org/10.1037/per0000159

Hyler, S. E., Rieder, R. O., Williams, J. B. W., Spitzer, R. L., Lyons, M., & Hendler, J. (1989). A comparison of clinical and self-report diagnoses of *DSM-III* personality disorders in 552 patients. *Comprehensive Psychiatry, 30*(2), 170–178. https://doi.org/10.1016/0010-440X(89)90070-9

Ickes, W., Snyder, M., & Garcia, S. (1997). Personality influences on the choice of situations. In R. Hogan, J. Johnson, & S. Briggs (Eds.), *Handbook of personality psychology* (pp. 165–195). Academic Press. https://doi.org/10.1016/B978-012134645-4/50008-1

John, O. P., & Robins, R. W. (1993). Determinants of interjudge agreement on personality traits: The Big Five domains, observability, evaluativeness, and the unique perspective of the self. *Journal of Personality, 61*(4), 521–551. https://doi.org/10.1111/j.1467-6494.1993.tb00781.x

Kampe, L., Zimmermann, J., Bender, D., Caligor, E., Borowski, A.-L., Ehrenthal, J. C., Benecke, C., & Hörz-Sagstetter, S. (2018). Comparison of the Structured *DSM-5* Clinical Interview for the Level of Personality Functioning Scale with the Structured Interview of Personality Organization. *Journal of Personality Assessment, 100*(6), 642–649. https://doi.org/10.1080/00223891.2018.1489257

Keeley, J. W., Webb, C., Peterson, D., Roussin, L., & Flanagan, E. H. (2016). Development of a response inconsistency scale for the Personality Inventory for *DSM-5*. *Journal of Personality Assessment, 98*(4), 351–359. https://doi.org/10.1080/00223891.2016.1158719

Kivisalu, T. M., Lewey, J. H., Shaffer, T. W., & Canfield, M. L. (2016). An investigation of interrater reliability for the Rorschach Performance Assessment System (R–PAS) in a nonpatient U.S. sample. *Journal of Personality Assessment, 98*(4), 382–390. https://doi.org/10.1080/00223891.2015.1118380

Klonsky, E. D., Oltmanns, T. F., & Turkheimer, E. (2002). Informant-reports of personality disorder: Relation to self-reports and future research directions. *Clinical Psychology: Science and Practice, 9*(3), 300–311. https://doi.org/10.1093/clipsy.9.3.300

Kolar, D. W., Funder, D. C., & Colvin, C. R. (1996). Comparing the accuracy of personality judgments by the self and knowledgeable others. *Journal of Personality, 64*(2), 311–337. https://doi.org/10.1111/j.1467-6494.1996.tb00513.x

Kostogianni, N. (2010). The Rorschach in planning treatment of alcohol addiction patients. *Rorschachiana, 31*(2), 192–222. https://doi.org/10.1027/1192-5604/a000011

Krall, V., Sachs, H., Lazar, B., Rayson, B., Growe, G., Novar, L., & O'Connell, L. (1983). Rorschach norms for inner city children. *Journal of Personality Assessment, 47*(2), 155–157. https://doi.org/10.1207/s15327752jpa4702_7

Krueger, R. F., Derringer, J., Markon, K. E., Watson, D., & Skodol, A. E. (2012). Initial construction of a maladaptive personality trait model and inventory for *DSM-5*. *Psychological Medicine, 42*(9), 1879–1890. https://doi.org/10.1017/S0033291711002674

Kurtz, J. E., & Sherker, J. L. (2003). Relationship quality, trait similarity, and self–other agreement on personality ratings in college roommates. *Journal of Personality, 71*(1), 21–48. https://doi.org/10.1111/1467-6494.t01-1-00005

Lawton, E. M., Shields, A. J., & Oltmanns, T. F. (2011). Five-factor model personality disorder prototypes in a community sample: Self- and informant-reports predicting interview-based *DSM* diagnoses. *Personality Disorders: Theory, Research, and Treatment, 2*(4), 279–292. https://doi.org/10.1037/a0022617

Lewis, K. C., Ridenour, J. M., Pitman, S., & Roche, M. (2021). Evaluating stable and situational expressions of passive-aggressive personality disorder: A multimethod experience sampling case study. *Journal of Personality Assessment, 103*(4), 558–570. https://doi.org/10.1080/00223891.2020.1818572

Lilienfeld, S. O., Wood, J. M., & Garb, H. N. (2000). The scientific status of projective techniques. *Psychological Science in the Public Interest, 1*(2), 27–66. https://doi.org/10.1111/1529-1006.002

Loevinger, J. (1954). The attenuation paradox in test theory. *Psychological Bulletin, 51*(5), 493–504. https://doi.org/10.1037/h0058543

Loevinger, J. (1957). Objective tests as instruments of psychological theory. *Psychological Reports, 3*(3), 635–694. https://doi.org/10.2466/pr0.1957.3.3.635

Maffei, C., Fossati, A., Agostoni, I., Barraco, A., Bagnato, M., Deborah, D., Namia, C., Novella, L., & Petrachi, M. (1997). Interrater reliability and internal consistency of the Structured Clinical Interview for *DSM-IV* Axis II personality disorders (SCID-II), Version 2.0. *Journal of Personality Disorders, 11*(3), 279–284. https://doi.org/10.1521/pedi.1997.11.3.279

Markon, K. E., Quilty, L. C., Bagby, R. M., & Krueger, R. F. (2013). The development and psychometric properties of an informant-report form of the Personality Inventory for *DSM-5* (PID-5). *Assessment, 20*(3), 370–383. https://doi.org/10.1177/1073191113486513

Mayer, J. D. (2005). A tale of two visions: Can a new view of personality help integrate psychology? *American Psychologist, 60*(4), 294–307. https://doi.org/10.1037/0003-066X.60.4.294

McCabe, G. A., & Widiger, T. A. (2020). A comprehensive comparison of the *ICD-11* and *DSM-5* Section III personality disorder models. *Psychological Assessment, 32*(1), 72–84. https://doi.org/10.1037/pas0000772

McCrae, R. R., Kurtz, J. E., Yamagata, S., & Terracciano, A. (2011). Internal consistency, retest reliability, and their implications for personality scale validity. *Personality and Social Psychology Review, 15*(1), 28–50. https://doi.org/10.1177/1088868310366253

McCredie, M. N., & Morey, L. C. (2019). Convergence between Thematic Apperception Test (TAT) and self-report: Another look at some old questions. *Journal of Clinical Psychology, 75*(10), 1838–1849. https://doi.org/10.1002/jclp.22826

Mellsop, G., Varghese, F., Joshua, S., & Hicks, A. (1982). The reliability of Axis II of *DSM-III*. *The American Journal of Psychiatry, 139*(10), 1360–1361. https://doi.org/10.1176/ajp.139.10.1360

Meloy, J. R., Acklin, M. W., Gacono, C. B., & Murray, J. F. (Eds.). (2013). *Contemporary Rorschach interpretation*. Routledge. https://doi.org/10.4324/9781315827377

Meyer, G. J. (1997). Assessing reliability: Critical corrections for a critical examination of the Rorschach Comprehensive System. *Psychological Assessment, 9*(4), 480–489. https://doi.org/10.1037/1040-3590.9.4.480

Meyer, G. J. (2000). On the science of Rorschach research. *Journal of Personality Assessment, 75*(1), 46–81. https://doi.org/10.1207/S15327752JPA7501_6

Meyer, G. J. (2002). Exploring possible ethnic differences and bias in the Rorschach Comprehensive System. *Journal of Personality Assessment, 78*(1), 104–129. https://doi.org/10.1207/S15327752JPA7801_07

Meyer, G. J., Finn, S. E., Eyde, L. D., Kay, G. G., Moreland, K. L., Dies, R. R., Eisman, E. J., Kubiszyn, T. W., & Reed, G. M. (2001). Psychological testing and psychological assessment: A review of evidence and issues. *American Psychologist, 56*(2), 128–165. https://doi.org/10.1037/0003-066X.56.2.128

Meyer, G. J., Hilsenroth, M. J., Baxter, D., Exner, J. E., Jr., Fowler, J. C., Piers, C. C., & Resnick, J. (2002). An examination of interrater reliability for scoring the Rorschach Comprehensive System in eight data sets. *Journal of Personality Assessment, 78*(2), 219–274. https://doi.org/10.1207/S15327752JPA7802_03

Meyer, G. J., Viglione, D. J., Mihura, J. L., Erard, R. E., & Erdberg, P. (2011). *Rorschach Performance Assessment System: Administration, coding, interpretation, and technical manual*. Rorschach Performance Assessment System.

Mihura, J. L., Dumitrascu, N., Roy, M., & Meyer, G. J. (2018). The centrality of the response process in construct validity: An illustration via the Rorschach space response. *Journal of Personality Assessment, 100*(3), 233–249. https://doi.org/10.1080/00223891.2017.1306781

Mihura, J. L., & Graceffo, R. A. (2014). Multimethod assessment and treatment planning. In C. J. Hopwood & R. F. Bornstein (Eds.), *Multimethod clinical assessment* (pp. 285–318). Guilford Press.

Mihura, J. L., Meyer, G. J., Dumitrascu, N., & Bombel, G. (2013). The validity of individual Rorschach variables: Systematic reviews and meta-analyses of the comprehensive system. *Psychological Bulletin, 139*(3), 548–605. https://doi.org/10.1037/a0029406

Millon, T., Davis, R., & Millon, C. (1997). *Millon Clinical Multiaxial Inventory-III* (2nd ed.). National Computer Systems.

Morey, L. C. (1991). *Personality Assessment Inventory*. Psychological Assessment Resources.

Morey, L. C. (2017). Development and initial evaluation of a self-report form of the *DSM-5* Level of Personality Functioning Scale. *Psychological Assessment, 29*(10), 1302–1308. https://doi.org/10.1037/pas0000450

Morey, L. C., & Lanier, V. W. (1998). Operating characteristics of six response distortion indicators for the Personality Assessment Inventory. *Assessment, 5*(3), 203–214. https://doi.org/10.1177/107319119800500301

Morey, L. C., & McCredie, M. N. (2019). Convergence between Rorschach and self-report: A new look at some old questions. *Journal of Clinical Psychology, 75*(1), 202–220. https://doi.org/10.1002/jclp.22701

Mueller, A. E., & Segal, D. L. (2014). Structured versus semistructured versus unstructured interviews. In R. L. Cautin & S. O. Lilienfeld (Eds.), *The encyclopedia of clinical psychology*. John Wiley & Sons.

Newcomb, M. E., Swann, G., Estabrook, R., Corden, M., Begale, M., Ashbeck, A., Mohr, D., & Mustanski, B. (2018). Patterns and predictors of compliance in a prospective diary study of substance use and sexual behavior in a sample of young men who have sex with men. *Assessment, 25*(4), 403–414. https://doi.org/10.1177/1073191116667584

O'Boyle, M., & Self, D. (1990). A comparison of two interviews for *DSM-III-R* personality disorders. *Psychiatry Research, 32*(1), 85–92. https://doi.org/10.1016/0165-1781(90)90138-U

Oh, I.-S., Wang, G., & Mount, M. K. (2011). Validity of observer ratings of the five-factor model of personality traits: A meta-analysis. *Journal of Applied Psychology, 96*(4), 762–773. https://doi.org/10.1037/a0021832

Olajide, K., Munjiza, J., Moran, P., O'Connell, L., Newton-Howes, G., Bassett, P., Akintomide, G., Ng, N., Tyrer, P., Mulder, R., & Crawford, M. J. (2018). Development and psychometric properties of the Standardized Assessment of Severity of Personality Disorder (SASPD). *Journal of Personality Disorders, 32*(1), 44–56. https://doi.org/10.1521/pedi_2017_31_285

Olino, T. M., & Klein, D. N. (2015). Psychometric comparison of self- and informant-reports of personality. *Assessment, 22*(6), 655–664. https://doi.org/10.1177/1073191114567942

Oltmanns, J. R., & Widiger, T. A. (2018). A self-report measure for the *ICD-11* dimensional trait model proposal: The Personality Inventory for *ICD-11. Psychological Assessment, 30*(2), 154–169. https://doi.org/10.1037/pas0000459

Oltmanns, J. R., & Widiger, T. A. (2021). The self- and informant-personality inventories for *ICD-11*: Agreement, structure, and relations with health, social, and satisfaction variables in older adults. *Psychological Assessment, 33*(4), 300–310. https://doi.org/10.1037/pas0000982

Paulhus, D. L., & Bruce, M. N. (1992). The effect of acquaintanceship on the validity of personality impressions: A longitudinal study. *Journal of Personality and Social Psychology, 63*(5), 816–824. https://doi.org/10.1037/0022-3514.63.5.816

Peebles-Kleiger, M. J. (2002). Elaboration of some sequence analysis strategies: Examples and guidelines for level of confidence. *Journal of Personality Assessment, 79*(1), 19–38. https://doi.org/10.1207/S15327752JPA7901_02

Peters, E. J., Hilsenroth, M. J., Eudell-Simmons, E. M., Blagys, M. D., & Handler, L. (2006). Reliability and validity of the Social Cognition and Object Relations Scale in clinical use. *Psychotherapy Research, 16*(5), 617–626. https://doi.org/10.1080/10503300600591288

Pianowski, G., Meyer, G. J., de Villemor-Amaral, A. E., Zuanazzi, A. C., & do Nascimento, R. S. G. F. (2021). Does the Rorschach Performance Assessment System (R-PAS) differ from the Comprehensive System (CS) on variables relevant to interpretation? *Journal of Personality Assessment, 103*(1), 132–147. https://doi.org/10.1080/00223891.2019.1677678

Pignolo, C., Giromini, L., Ando', A., Ghirardello, D., Di Girolamo, M., Ales, F., & Zennaro, A. (2017). An interrater reliability study of Rorschach Performance Assessment System (R–PAS) raw and complexity-adjusted scores. *Journal of Personality Assessment, 99*(6), 619–625. https://doi.org/10.1080/00223891.2017.1296844

Pilkonis, P. A., Heape, C. L., Proietti, J. M., Clark, S. W., McDavid, J. D., & Pitts, T. E. (1995). The reliability and validity of two structured diagnostic interviews for personality disorders. *Archives of General Psychiatry, 52*(12), 1025–1033. https://doi.org/10.1001/archpsyc.1995.03950240043009

Piotrowski, C. (2015). Projective techniques usage worldwide: A review of applied settings 1995–2015. *Journal of the Indian Academy of Applied Psychology, 41*(3), 9–19.

Porcerelli, J. H., Shahar, G., Blatt, S. J., Ford, R. Q., Mezza, J. A., & Greenlee, L. M. (2006). Social cognition and object relations scale: Convergent validity and changes following intensive inpatient treatment. *Personality and Individual Differences, 41*(3), 407–417. https://doi.org/10.1016/j.paid.2005.10.027

Poropat, A. E. (2009). A meta-analysis of the five-factor model of personality and academic performance. *Psychological Bulletin, 135*(2), 322–338. https://doi.org/10.1037/a0014996

Quirk, S. W., Christiansen, N. D., Wagner, S. H., & McNulty, J. L. (2003). On the usefulness of measures of normal personality for clinical assessment: Evidence of the incremental validity of the Revised NEO Personality Inventory. *Psychological Assessment, 15*(3), 311–325. https://doi.org/10.1037/1040-3590.15.3.311

Ram, N., Brinberg, M., Pincus, A. L., & Conroy, D. E. (2017). The questionable ecological validity of ecological momentary assessment: Considerations for design and analysis. *Research in Human Development, 14*(3), 253–270. https://doi.org/10.1080/15427609.2017.1340052

Ready, R. E., & Clark, L. A. (2002). Correspondence of psychiatric patient and informant ratings of personality traits, temperament, and interpersonal problems. *Psychological Assessment, 14*(1), 39–49. https://doi.org/10.1037/1040-3590.14.1.39

Reise, S. P., & Henson, J. M. (2000). Computerization and adaptive administration of the NEO PI-R. *Assessment, 7*(4), 347–364. https://doi.org/10.1177/107319110000700404

Reynolds, B. M., Robles, T. F., & Repetti, R. L. (2016). Measurement reactivity and fatigue effects in daily diary research with families. *Developmental Psychology, 52*(3), 442–456. https://doi.org/10.1037/dev0000081

Robins, R. W., Norem, J. K., & Cheek, J. M. (1999). Naturalizing the self. In L. A. Pervin & O. P. John (Eds.), *Handbook of personality: Theory and research* (pp. 443–477). Guilford Press.

Roche, M. J., Jacobson, N. C., & Phillips, J. J. (2018). Expanding the validity of the Level of Personality Functioning Scale observer report and self-report versions across psychodynamic and interpersonal paradigms. *Journal of Personality Assessment, 100*(6), 571–580. https://doi.org/10.1080/00223891.2018.1475394

Roche, M. J., Pincus, A. L., Rebar, A. L., Conroy, D. E., & Ram, N. (2014). Enriching psychological assessment using a person-specific analysis of interpersonal processes in daily life. *Assessment, 21*(5), 515–528. https://doi.org/10.1177/1073191114540320

Rodebaugh, T. L., Gianoli, M. O., Turkheimer, E., & Oltmanns, T. F. (2010). The interpersonal problems of the socially avoidant: Self and peer shared variance. *Journal of Abnormal Psychology, 119*(2), 331–340. https://doi.org/10.1037/a0019031

Rogers, R. (2001). *Handbook of diagnostic and structured interviewing*. Guilford Press.

Rogers, R., & Bender, S. D. (2003). Evaluation of malingering and deception. In A. M. Goldstein (Ed.), *Handbook of psychology: Forensic psychology* (Vol. 11, pp. 109–129). John Wiley & Sons.

Roper, B. L., Ben-Porath, Y. S., & Butcher, J. N. (1991). Comparability of computerized adaptive and conventional testing with the MMPI-2. *Journal of Personality Assessment, 57*(2), 278–290. https://doi.org/10.1207/s15327752jpa5702_7

Roper, B. L., Ben-Porath, Y. S., & Butcher, J. N. (1995). Comparability and validity of computerized adaptive testing with the MMPI-2. *Journal of Personality Assessment, 65*(2), 358–371. https://doi.org/10.1207/s15327752jpa6502_10

Rorschach, H. (1921). *Psychodiagnostik* [Psychodiagnostics]. Hans Huber.

Samuel, D. B., Sanislow, C. A., Hopwood, C. J., Shea, M. T., Skodol, A. E., Morey, L. C., Ansell, E. B., Markowitz, J. C., Zanarini, M. C., & Grilo, C. M. (2013). Convergent and incremental predictive validity of clinician, self-report, and structured interview diagnoses for personality disorders over 5 years. *Journal of Consulting and Clinical Psychology, 81*(4), 650–659. https://doi.org/10.1037/a0032813

Segal, D. L., & Coolidge, F. L. (2003). Structured interviewing and *DSM* classification. In M. Hersen & S. M. Turner (Eds.), *Adult psychopathology and diagnosis* (pp. 72–103). John Wiley & Sons.

Segal, D. L., Coolidge, F. L., O'Riley, A., & Heinz, B. A. (2006). Structured and semi-structured interviews. In M. Hersen (Ed.), *Clinician's handbook of adult behavioral assessment: Practical resources for the mental health professional* (pp. 121–144). Academic Press. https://doi.org/10.1016/B978-012343013-7/50007-0

Sellbom, M., Dhillon, S., & Bagby, R. M. (2018). Development and validation of an Overreporting Scale for the Personality Inventory for *DSM-5* (PID-5). *Psychological Assessment, 30*(5), 582–593. https://doi.org/10.1037/pas0000507

Shedler, J., Mayman, M., & Manis, M. (1993). The illusion of mental health. *American Psychologist, 48*(11), 1117–1131. https://doi.org/10.1037/0003-066X.48.11.1117

Shiffman, S., Stone, A. A., & Hufford, M. R. (2008). Ecological momentary assessment. *Annual Review of Clinical Psychology, 4,* 1–32. https://doi.org/10.1146/annurev. clinpsy.3.022806.091415

Siefert, C. J., Stein, M. B., Slavin-Mulford, J., Sinclair, S. J., Haggerty, G., & Blais, M. A. (2016). Estimating the effects of Thematic Apperception Test card content on SCORS–G ratings: Replication with a nonclinical sample. *Journal of Personality Assessment, 98*(6), 598–607. https://doi.org/10.1080/00223891.2016.1167696

Simms, L. J., & Clark, L. A. (2005). Validation of a computerized adaptive version of the Schedule for Nonadaptive and Adaptive Personality (SNAP). *Psychological Assessment, 17*(1), 28–43. https://doi.org/10.1037/1040-3590.17.1.28

Simms, L. J., Goldberg, L. R., Roberts, J. E., Watson, D., Welte, J., & Rotterman, J. H. (2011). Computerized adaptive assessment of personality disorder: Introducing the CAT-PD project. *Journal of Personality Assessment, 93*(4), 380–389. https://doi.org/10.1080/00223891.2011.577475

Skodol, A. E. (1991). Diagnostic of *DSM-III-R* personality disorders: A comparison of two structured interviews. *International Journal of Methods in Psychiatric Research, 1,* 13–26.

Slavin-Mulford, J., Sinclair, S. J., Stein, M., Malone, J., Bello, I., & Blais, M. A. (2012). External validity of the Personality Assessment Inventory (PAI) in a clinical sample. *Journal of Personality Assessment, 94*(6), 593–600. https://doi.org/10.1080/00223891. 2012.681817

Spain, J. S., Eaton, L. G., & Funder, D. C. (2000). Perspectives on personality: The relative accuracy of self versus others for the prediction of emotion and behavior. *Journal of Personality, 68*(5), 837–867. https://doi.org/10.1111/1467-6494.00118

Spitzer, R. L., Forman, J. B., & Nee, J. (1979). *DSM-III* field trials: I. Initial interrater diagnostic reliability. *The American Journal of Psychiatry, 136*(6), 815–817. https://doi.org/10.1176/ajp.136.6.815

Stein, M. B., Hilsenroth, M., Slavin-Mulford, J., & Pinsker, J. (2011). *Social Cognition and Object Relations Scale: Global Rating Method (SCORS–G; 4th ed.)* [Unpublished manuscript]. Massachusetts General Hospital and Harvard Medical School.

Stein, M. B., Slavin-Mulford, J., Siefert, C. J., Sinclair, S. J., Renna, M., Malone, J., Bello, I., & Blais, M. A. (2014). SCORS–G stimulus characteristics of select Thematic Apperception Test cards. *Journal of Personality Assessment, 96*(3), 339–349. https://doi.org/10.1080/00223891.2013.823440

Stein, M. B., Slavin-Mulford, J., Siefert, C. J., Sinclair, S. J., Smith, M., Chung, W.-J., Liebman, R., & Blais, M. A. (2015). External validity of SCORS-G ratings of Thematic Apperception Test narratives in a sample of outpatients and inpatients. *Rorschachiana, 36*(1), 58–81. https://doi.org/10.1027/1192-5604/a000057

Stein, M. B., Slavin-Mulford, J., Sinclair, S. J., Siefert, C. J., & Blais, M. A. (2012). Exploring the construct validity of the social cognition and object relations scale in a clinical sample. *Journal of Personality Assessment, 94*(5), 533–540. https://doi.org/10.1080/00223891.2012.668594

Stone, A. A., & Shiffman, S. (2002). Capturing momentary, self-report data: A proposal for reporting guidelines. *Annals of Behavioral Medicine, 24*(3), 236–243. https://doi.org/10.1207/S15324796ABM2403_09

Su, W.-S., Viglione, D. J., Green, E. E., Tam, W.-C. C., Su, J.-A., & Chang, Y.-T. (2015). Cultural and linguistic adaptability of the Rorschach Performance Assessment System as a measure of psychotic characteristics and severity of mental disturbance in Taiwan. *Psychological Assessment, 27*(4), 1273–1285. https://doi.org/10.1037/pas0000144

Suppiger, A., In-Albon, T., Hendriksen, S., Hermann, E., Margraf, J., & Schneider, S. (2009). Acceptance of structured diagnostic interviews for mental disorders in clinical practice and research settings. *Behavior Therapy, 40*(3), 272–279. https://doi.org/10.1016/j.beth.2008.07.002

Taylor, S. E., & Brown, J. D. (1988). Illusion and well-being: A social psychological perspective on mental health. *Psychological Bulletin, 103*(2), 193–210. https://doi.org/10.1037/0033-2909.103.2.193

van Os, J., Delespaul, P., Wigman, J., Myin-Germeys, I., & Wichers, M. (2013). Beyond *DSM* and *ICD*: Introducing "precision diagnosis" for psychiatry using momentary assessment technology. *World Psychiatry, 12*(2), 113–117. https://doi.org/10.1002/wps.20046

Vazire, S. (2006). Informant reports: A cheap, fast, and easy method for personality assessment. *Journal of Research in Personality, 40*(5), 472–481. https://doi.org/10.1016/j.jrp.2005.03.003

Vazire, S., & Gosling, S. D. (2004). e-Perceptions: Personality impressions based on personal websites. *Journal of Personality and Social Psychology, 87*(1), 123–132. https://doi.org/10.1037/0022-3514.87.1.123

Viglione, D., Giromini, L., Gustafson, M. L., & Meyer, G. J. (2014). Developing continuous variable composites for Rorschach measures of thought problems, vigilance, and suicide risk. *Assessment, 21*(1), 42–49. https://doi.org/10.1177/1073191112446963

Viglione, D. J., Blume-Marcovici, A. C., Miller, H. L., Giromini, L., & Meyer, G. (2012). An inter-rater reliability study for the Rorschach Performance Assessment System. *Journal of Personality Assessment, 94*(6), 607–612. https://doi.org/10.1080/00223891.2012.684118

Viglione, D. J., & Hilsenroth, M. J. (2001). The Rorschach: Facts, fictions, and future. *Psychological Assessment, 13*(4), 452–471. https://doi.org/10.1037/1040-3590.13.4.452

Waller, N. G., & Reise, S. P. (1989). Computerized adaptive personality assessment: An illustration with the Absorption scale. *Journal of Personality and Social Psychology, 57*(6), 1051–1058. https://doi.org/10.1037/0022-3514.57.6.1051

Watson, D., Hubbard, B., & Wiese, D. (2000). Self–other agreement in personality and affectivity: The role of acquaintanceship, trait visibility, and assumed similarity. *Journal of Personality and Social Psychology, 78*(3), 546–558. https://doi.org/10.1037/0022-3514.78.3.546

Waugh, M. H., Hopwood, C. J., Krueger, R. F., Morey, L. C., Pincus, A. L., & Wright, A. G. C. (2017). Psychological assessment with the *DSM-5* Alternative Model for Personality Disorders: Tradition and innovation. *Professional Psychology: Research and Practice, 48*(2), 79–89. https://doi.org/10.1037/pro0000071

Westen, D. (1997). Divergences between clinical and research methods for assessing personality disorders: Implications for research and the evolution of Axis II. *The American Journal of Psychiatry, 154*(7), 895–903. https://doi.org/10.1176/ajp.154.7.895

Westen, D., Lohr, N., Silk, K. R., Gold, L., & Kerber, K. (1990). Object relations and social cognition in borderlines, major depressives, and normals: A Thematic Appercep-tion Test analysis. *Psychological Assessment, 2*(4), 355–364. https://doi.org/10.1037/1040-3590.2.4.355

Widiger, T. A., & Coker, L. A. (2002). Assessing personality disorders. In J. N. Butcher (Ed.), *Clinical personality assessment: Practical approaches* (2nd ed., pp. 407–434). Oxford University Press.

Wiggins, J. S. (2003). *Paradigms of personality assessment.* Guilford Press.

World Health Organization. (2019). *International statistical classification of diseases and related health problems* (11th ed.). https://icd.who.int/

Wright, A. G. C., Calabrese, W. R., Rudick, M. M., Yam, W. H., Zelazny, K., Williams, T. F., Rotterman, J. H., & Simms, L. J. (2015). Stability of the *DSM-5* Section III pathological personality traits and their longitudinal associations with psychosocial functioning in personality disordered individuals. *Journal of Abnormal Psychology, 124*(1), 199–207. https://doi.org/10.1037/abn0000018

Wright, A. G. C., Hallquist, M. N., Stepp, S. D., Scott, L. N., Beeney, J. E., Lazarus, S. A., & Pilkonis, P. A. (2016). Modeling heterogeneity in momentary interpersonal and affective dynamic processes in borderline personality disorder. *Assessment, 23*(4), 484–495. https://doi.org/10.1177/1073191116653829

Wright, A. G. C., Hopwood, C. J., & Simms, L. J. (2015). Daily interpersonal and affective dynamics in personality disorder. *Journal of Personality Disorders, 29*(4), 503–525. https://doi.org/10.1521/pedi.2015.29.4.503

Zanarini, M. C., Frankenburg, F. R., Chauncey, D. L., & Gunderson, J. G. (1987). The Diag-nostic Interview for Personality Disorders: Interrater and test-retest reliability. *Compre-hensive Psychiatry, 28*(6), 467–480. https://doi.org/10.1016/0010-440X(87)90012-5

Zimmerman, M., & Mattia, J. I. (1999). Psychiatric diagnosis in clinical practice: Is comorbidity being missed? *Comprehensive Psychiatry, 40*(3), 182–191. https://doi.org/10.1016/S0010-440X(99)90001-9

Zimmerman, M., Pfohl, B., Coryell, W., Stangl, D., & Corenthal, C. (1988). Diagnosing personality disorder in depressed patients: A comparison of patient and informant interviews. *Archives of General Psychiatry, 45*(8), 733–737. https://doi.org/10.1001/archpsyc.1988.01800320045005

Zimmermann, J., Kerber, A., Rek, K., Hopwood, C. J., & Krueger, R. F. (2019). A brief but comprehensive review of research on the alternative *DSM-5* model for person-ality disorders. *Current Psychiatry Reports, 21*(9), Article 92. https://doi.org/10.1007/s11920-019-1079-z

Zimmermann, J., Woods, W. C., Ritter, S., Happel, M., Masuhr, O., Jaeger, U., Spitzer, C., & Wright, A. G. C. (2019). Integrating structure and dynamics in personality assess-ment: First steps toward the development and validation of a personality dynamics diary. *Psychological Assessment, 31*(4), 516–531. https://doi.org/10.1037/pas0000625

5

The Assessment of Personality Function in Adolescents

Carla Sharp, Kiana Cano, Sune Bo, and Joost Hutsebaut

We begin this chapter by presenting a case of a young man referred to an outpatient clinic by one of the authors. Names and sensitive information have been changed to ensure anonymity.

Henry is a 15-year-old White male who identifies as transgender. They live with their adopted mother, stepfather, and 5-year-old brother, who is biologically not related to Henry. Henry was referred for an evaluation after a recent suicide attempt. They were adopted at about 3 months of age. Henry's mother described them, as a baby, as often fussy and not easily soothed. She reported that as a toddler, they were very sensitive and had frequent tantrums. Henry's preschool teacher described them as active and energetic. Throughout elementary school, Henry began exhibiting symptoms of hyperactivity and anxiety and received a diagnosis of attention-deficit/hyperactivity disorder (ADHD) at age 6. Their teachers reported that Henry had difficulty staying in their seat, asked excessively to go to the bathroom, and would talk to other students during quiet time. During parent–teacher conferences, Henry's teachers reported that Henry had difficulty making friends and was often seen playing alone at recess. When they did make friends, Henry was very anxious to impress them, and Henry's feelings would get hurt easily if friends chose to play with someone else.

In third grade (age 9), Henry began exhibiting signs of school avoidance and reported somatic symptoms of anxiety, including stomachaches, headaches, and nausea. At this point, in addition to their ADHD diagnosis, they received a diagnosis of school refusal and generalized anxiety disorder. When they entered middle school in sixth grade (age 12), they became increasingly defiant and

https://doi.org/10.1037/0000310-006
Personality Disorders and Pathology: Integrating Clinical Assessment and Practice in the DSM-5 *and* ICD-11 *Era*, S. K. Huprich (Editor)
Copyright © 2022 by the American Psychological Association. All rights reserved.

began receiving detentions for tardiness and classroom misbehavior. They also reported increased stress related to schoolwork, developed a temper, and talked back to their parents on a daily basis. Henry's psychiatrist diagnosed Henry with oppositional defiant disorder (ODD). Their mother noted that they were often in a bad mood or irritable with the family nearly every day, but she thought that Henry was just going through a "teen phase." Henry reported that during that period, they felt sad much of the time and that the only thing that made them happy was playing video games.

After turning 13, Henry's feelings of sadness increased shortly after their only friend moved away. Henry reported cutting themself nine or 10 times on the arm with a knife during the eighth grade (age 14). They reported doing this for a variety of reasons (most notably [a] when being bullied by peers after Henry insisted on being called by the pronouns "they/them" and [b] when Henry's feelings were "dead" and Henry wanted to "turn them back on"). At this point, they were put on a mood stabilizer to try to manage the combined internalizing and externalizing symptoms.

Currently (age 15), Henry has reported having thoughts at least three times a week of death or dying. Their parents shared that Henry made an impulsive suicide attempt by taking pills from the parents' medicine cabinet the previous week, which led to an acute inpatient hospital stay. This happened after a breakup with Henry's girlfriend, who felt that she could not commit to them. Henry's parents also shared Henry having intense anger outbursts during admission to the hospital. Henry has said that such outbursts are the only times Henry feels emotions—that most of the time, Henry is emotionally dead or has no feelings inside. Henry has also reported that they have no friends and feel utterly alone. Their mother described them as a "follower" who succumbs to peer pressure yet does not fit in. Henry has further reported not feeling like they belong to any peer group at school and that they feel like the black sheep of their family because they ruin everything. During their inpatient stay, Henry was diagnosed with depression, general anxiety, insomnia, ODD, and ADHD, and their parents are now considering homeschooling.

Henry's case represents a developmental trajectory often found for young people who should be assessed for personality function early on but invariably fall through the cracks. This is because these young people are most often assessed and treated solely through the lens of common mental disorders (traditional Axis I syndromes). These children pose a diagnostic puzzle, due to patterns of heterotypic continuity manifesting in mixed internalizing-externalizing problems throughout their elementary-school-age years, with the onset of depression in adolescence and a continuation of impulsivity-related externalizing problems throughout young adulthood (self-harm, sexual risk taking, anger outbursts, and substance use problems). Parents tend to report contact with psychiatric services since an early age and often express frustration that none of the pharmacological or psychotherapeutic interventions offered to them over the years have been helpful (Goodman et al., 2011). By the time they have their first hospitalization for a suicide attempt in adolescence, these young people are taking multiple medications, including mood stabilizers, antidepressants, stimulants, and anxiolytics (Cailhol et al., 2013). For instance, in the Cailhol et al. (2013) study, 21% of the sample were on one medication, 45% were on two or three, and 10% were on four or more. The most commonly prescribed were antipsychotics (45%).

In this chapter, we discuss the importance of evaluating young people like Henry through the lens of personality function early on in development. We put forward the argument that the introduction of the Alternative *DSM-5* Model of Personality Disorders (AMPD) facilitates a clinical staging (CS) approach for the assessment of personality pathology in young people. As we will show, CS not only allows consideration of developmental aspects in terms of developmental epochs but also allows consideration of developmental aspects in terms of disease progression. We begin with an overview of traditional *DSM-5* Section II assessment of personality pathology, as this sets the stage for the AMPD and the CS approach to follow.

DSM-5 SECTION II ASSESSMENT OF PERSONALITY PATHOLOGY IN YOUTH

Up until about 10 to 15 years ago, myths and biases regarding the validity and reliability of personality disorder in adolescents have prohibited the assessment and treatment of personality challenges in young people. However, concerns over the reliability and validity of personality disorder in adolescence largely have been put to rest (Chanen, 2015; Chanen & Kaess, 2012; Sharp, 2017; Sharp & Fonagy, 2015; Sharp & Kalpakci, 2015). Based on strong and consistent research findings in support of personality disorder (PD) in youth, especially the construct of borderline personality disorder (BPD), *DSM-5* and *ICD-11* both allow for the diagnosis of PD in adolescence. Moreover, BPD in youth is now considered an important public health priority (Chanen et al., 2017).

First-generation studies of BPD in youth (1990–2005) relied on adult-interview and self-report measures of BPD that were downwardly extended to youth without any developmental adaptation. We will not review these here but refer readers to other reviews of the psychometric properties of these measures in youth samples (Sharp & Fonagy, 2015; Sharp & Romero, 2007). In more recent years, measures of personality pathology have been adapted or modified for use in adolescence. Typical adaptations include reducing the number of items, rephrasing some of the content to be more developmentally appropriate, and creating an informant-report companion measure for completion by parents. Some of these adapted measures include the most recent iteration of the Minnesota Multiphasic Personality Inventory for Adolescents, the Restructured Form (MMPI-A-RF; Archer et al., 2016), the adolescent version of the Shedler–Westen Assessment Procedure (SWAP-200-A; Westen et al., 2005; Westen & Muderrisoglu, 2003), the adolescent and parent-report version of the Borderline Personality Disorder Severity Index–IV (BPDSI-IV-ado/p; Schuppert et al., 2012), the Childhood Interview for *DSM-IV-TR* Borderline Personality Disorder (CI-BPD; Zanarini, 2003), the youth and parent-report variants of the Borderline Personality Features Scale for Children (BPFS-C; Crick et al., 2005; and BPFS-P; Chang et al., 2011), and the Personality Assessment Inventory–Adolescent (PAI-A; Morey, 2007). The MMPI-A-RF is a lengthy broadband measure of psychopathology that does not have directly corresponding PD subscales. The SWAP-200-A is a Q-sort procedure that is unlikely to be used in common everyday practice when alternative self-report or interview tools are available, and the BPDSI-IV adolescent and parent self-report measures have largely been evaluated in Dutch. Table 5.1 summarizes the measures most commonly used, due to their relative ease of administration and good psychometric properties across languages and settings (the CI-BPD, the BPFS battery, and the PAI-A).

DSM-5 SECTION III ASSESSMENT OF PERSONALITY PATHOLOGY IN YOUTH

The reasons for rejecting categorically defined PD constructs such as BPD have been well documented and are discussed elsewhere in this volume. The introduction of the AMPD has been particularly exciting for those with a developmental orientation because while not explicitly stated as such, the AMPD ushers in a new era where we may consider the assessment of maladaptive personality function not only in adolescents but also in children. First, the AMPD legitimizes a dimensional trait perspective (De Clercq et al., 2009; Rothbart & Bates, 2006; Shiner, 2009; Shiner & Tackett, 2014) operationalized in Criterion B of the AMPD. Because of the significant overlap in content and structure between temperamental traits, Big Five traits, and maladaptive Criterion B traits—and given the relative stability of these traits across development—the introduction of Criterion B allows for the assessment of personality function in children as young as preschool. Not only is there significant overlap in content and structure between temperamental traits, the Big Five traits, and maladaptive Criterion B traits, but this overlap extends to the internalizing-externalizing-psychotic spectra (Kotov et al., 2017). For instance, externalizing disorders are seen as extreme variants of the trait of Disinhibition, and depression and anxiety constitute the extreme variant of the trait of Negative Affectivity (Tackett, 2006; Tackett et al., 2016). As such, trait-defined personality is weaved into, or subserves, all manifestations of psychopathology and are understood within the same dimensional hierarchical framework across different age periods (Sharp et al., 2021).

Second, the AMPD legitimizes maladaptive self- and interpersonal function operationalized in Criterion A through the assessment of an individual's level of personality functioning (LPF). LPF is considered the common and core feature shared by all personality pathology regardless of Criterion B "flavor" (Bender et al., 2011). It was defined as a unidimensional severity criterion, conceptually independent of specific personality types or traits and representing a more general adaptive failure or delayed development of an intrapsychic system needed to fulfill adult life tasks (Livesley, 2003; Morey et al., 2011). A particular innovation of the LPF is that in describing the core components of

TABLE 5.1. Assessment Tools for *DSM* Section II Borderline Personality Disorder in Youth

Measure and description	Author and country/ language	Sample	Internal consistency	Reliability	Factor structure	Construct and criterion validity
CI-BPD Semistructured interview; nine *DSM-IV* criteria rated on 0 (*symptom absent*) to 2 (*symptom definitely present*) scale	Zanarini, 2003 (USA/English)		$\alpha = .81$	$\kappa = .65–.93$	Not reported	
	Sharp et al., 2012 (USA/English)	Inpatient sample: $N = 190$ ($M_{age} = 15.39$; range = 12–17; 60% F)	$\alpha = .80$	$\kappa = .89$	Unidimensional factor structure	Associated with PAI-A-BOR, clinician diagnosis, BPFS-C, BPFS-P, internalizing and externalizing problems $\kappa = .34$ with clinician diagnosis
BPFS-C & BPFS-P Self- and parent-report scales; adapted from the PAI-BOR; 24 items rated on 5-point Likert scale (1 = *not at all true*; 5 = *always true*)	Crick et al., 2005 (USA/English)	Community sample: $N = 400$ (54% F)	At all three timepoints $\alpha > .76$	Scores at all timepoints significantly correlated	Not reported	Associated with relational aggression, cognitive sensitivity, emotional sensitivity, friend exclusivity over time
	Chang et al., 2011 (USA/English)	Inpatient Sample: $N = 51$ ($M_{age} = 16$; 54.7% F)	Total score $\alpha = .89$ Subscale score $\alpha = .65–.86$	Not reported	Not reported	ROC identifying CI-BPD BPD: Child: Sensitivity .88; Specificity .84 Parent: Sensitivity .73; Specificity .72 Significant, large correlation between BPFS-C and BPFS-P

(continues)

TABLE 5.1. Assessment Tools for *DSM* Section II Borderline Personality Disorder in Youth (*Continued*)

Measure and description	Author and country/ language	Sample	Internal consistency	Reliability	Factor structure	Construct and criterion validity
BPFS-C-11 Shortened version of the BPFS-C; 11 items rated on 5-point Likert scale (1 = *not at all true*; 5 = *always true*)	Sharp, Steinberg, et al., 2014 (USA/English)	Community sample: N = 964 (age range = 14–19; 55.9% F) Clinical sample: N = 371 (age = 12–17)	α = .85	Not reported	Unidimensional structure	In clinical sample, significant mean difference between BPD and non-BPD (determined by the CI-BPD) ROC identifying CI-BPD BPD: Sensitivity .74 Specificity .71 Significantly correlated with emotion dysregulation (r = .67) and self-harm (r = .42)
PAI-A-BOR Self-report; 20 items from the PAI-A rated on 4-point scale; has four subscales (identity problems, affective instability, negative relationships, self-harm)	Morey, 2007 (USA/English) Venta et al., 2018 (USA/English)	Census-matched sample: N = 707 (age = 12–18) Clinical sample: N = 1,160 Clinical sample: N = 327 (M_{age} = 15.46; 61.8% female) Forensic sample: N = 151 (M_{age} = 15.26; 100% male)	Subscale α = .85–.87 Clinical sample: .88 Forensic sample: .82	 Not reported	Four-factor structure Poor fit of four-factor structure	Associated with range of other BPD relevant pathology Associated with presence of symptoms on the CI-BPD ROC identifying CI-BPD BPD: Sensitivity .77 Specificity .79

Note. BPD = borderline personality disorder; BPFS-C = Borderline Personality Features Scale for Children–self report; BPFS-C-11 = Borderline Personality Features Scale for Children–self report 11-item version; BPFS-P = Borderline Personality Features Scale for Children–parent report; CI-BPD = Childhood Interview for *DSM-IV* Borderline Personality Disorder; *DSM-IV = Diagnostic and Statistical Manual of Mental Disorders, Fourth Edition*; PAI-A = Personality Assessment Inventory for Adolescents; PAI-A-BOR = Personality Assessment Inventory–Adolescent version–borderline scale; PAI-BOR = Personality Assessment Inventory–Borderline; ROC = receiver operating characteristic curve.

LPF (identity, self-directedness, empathy, and intimacy), the intent was not to capture all distinct PD phenomena but, rather, to capture the central functions common to all PDs and, in fact, to all *people*—disordered or not (Morey et al., 2015). As such, the assessment of LPF allows a severity rating from 0 to 4 (5-point scale), ranging from 0 = *little or no impairment* to 4 = *extreme impairment*.

Taken together, both Criteria A and B provide, for the first time, a truly dimensional framework for assessing personality functioning in that it allows ratings of both healthy personality function (a rating of 0 = *little or no impairment* on Criterion A and low levels of maladaptive trait domain function on Criterion B) and unhealthy personality function (a rating > 2 on Criterion A and high levels of maladaptive trait function for Criterion B). It is this dimensionality that allows for the introduction of a CS model for the assessment of personality function not only across development but also across the different stages of disorder development. Put differently, dimensionality allows us to assess not only PD but personality function more generally. We consider this a significant advancement for the field, specifically for children and adolescents, because, as we will show, personality functioning can be assessed at earlier stages of development in terms of both chronological age and disease progression.

Based on reviews of the developmental literature, we have proposed a developmental model for personality pathology outlining the integrated developmental function of Criteria A and B (Sharp, 2020a; Sharp et al., 2018; Sharp & Wall, 2018). Developmental trait research shows that a child's position on any dispositional trait dimension (Criterion B/Big Five/internalizing-externalizing-psychotic spectra) can be readily identified and recognized already in infancy and has been found to remain relatively stable throughout development. However, while children may display extreme scores on temperamental measures indicative of maladaptive trait function, they are not diagnosed with PD before adolescence, because until adolescence, there is a limited requirement placed on children to acquire the new level of knowledge, skills, and cultural competence to successfully transition to an independent adult role (Dahl et al., 2018). Therefore, adolescence ushers in a qualitatively distinct maturational period where in order to take on adult rights, responsibilities, and social and occupational roles, certain functions—subserved by qualitative shifts in cognitive and neural maturation—must come "online" (Dahl et al., 2018; Sharp, 2020b). These functions of "work and love" are articulated in LPF, including identity, self-direction, empathy, and intimacy. While LPF domains can be assessed in preadolescence (e.g., empathy, theory of mind, self-concept, self-esteem, self-directedness), research in developmental personality psychology suggests that these components do not "bind together" until adolescence (McAdams, 2015; McAdams & Olson, 2010). Put differently, it is not until adolescence that LPF components coalesce into a unidimensional severity criterion (Sharp, 2020a; Sharp & Wall, 2021). During adolescence, the necessary developmental shifts in cognitive, emotional, and neural maturation occur that allow an individual, in Rogerian terms, to "become a person"—someone who can symbolize, perceive, and organize experience into some meaningful relation to the self (Sharp & Wall, 2021). Adolescence therefore offers a critical developmental juncture at which point we must evaluate whether personality is "binding" adequately. If not, we are able to conclude that personality disorder (personality diffusion) may ensue. To emphasize, high levels of maladaptive trait function are not enough to diagnose PD in youth, because its concepts fail to capture the emergence of the reflective self. Without the reflective self, mature personality function is not complete (Sharp, 2020b; Sharp & Wall, 2021).

Table 5.2 summarizes current validated measures for the assessment of Criteria A and B in youth, that were specifically developed with Section III in mind. These include the Assessment of Identity Development in Adolescence (AIDA; Goth et al., 2012), the Levels of Personality Functioning Questionnaire (LoPF-Q 12–18; Goth et al., 2018), and the Semistructured Interview for Personality Functioning *DSM-5* (STiP-5.1; Weekers et al., 2021). Other existing measures of constructs that predate the publication of the AMPD, including, for instance, the Severity Indices of Personality Problems (SIPP-118; Verheul et al., 2008), have also been evaluated in adolescent samples (Feenstra et al., 2011). For the assessment of Criterion B, the American Psychiatric Association published the 220-item Personality Inventory for *DSM-5* (PID-5; Krueger et al., 2012) and the 25-item Personality Inventory for *DSM-5*–Brief Form (PID-5-BF) derived from the full form. Alternative short forms of this measure have also been developed. Some variants of the PID-5 have been utilized in adolescent samples; however, they have not been adapted for youth (e.g., De Clercq, De Fruyt, et al., 2014; Fossati et al., 2017; Somma et al., 2017). Table 5.2 summarizes psychometric studies evaluating other existing measures of maladaptive personality traits, developed specifically for youth, which may be used to assess Criterion B traits. These include the Dimensional Assessment of Personality Pathology–Basic Questionnaire for Adolescents (DAPP-BQ-A) and corresponding parental report and short form (Tromp & Koot, 2008, 2010, 2015), the Dimensional Personality Symptom Item Pool (DIPSI; De Clercq et al., 2006; Decuyper et al., 2015), and the Schedule for Nonadaptive and Adaptive Personality–Youth Version (SNAP-Y; Linde et al., 2013).

CLINICAL STAGING AS FRAMEWORK FOR REFINING AND IMPROVING ASSESSMENT

While the assessment of Criteria A and B offers enormous potential for developmental considerations as discussed previously, they have not been formally integrated into a coherent developmental assessment framework. The mere use of an AMPD assessment tool with no regard for developmental stage or stage of disease progression fails to consider the heterotypic continuity of personality function and its interaction with the environment. Here, we build on the developmental model for personality pathology outlining the integrated developmental function of Criteria A and B described in the previous section, to offer a developmentally sensitive framework that considers heterotypic continuity, comorbidity, and developmental timing effects by proposing a CS assessment framework for personality function in young people.

TABLE 5.2. Assessment Tools for *DSM* Section III Criteria A and B in Youth

Measure and description	Author and country/ language	Sample	Internal consistency	Reliability	Factor structure	Criterion validity
AIDA Criterion A; 58 items rated on 5-point Likert scale (0 = *no*; 4 = *yes*)	Goth et al., 2012 (Switzerland and Germany)	Community sample: $N = 305$ ($M_{age} = 15$; range = 12–18; 51% female) PD sample: $N = 52$ ($M_{age} = 15.58$; range = 12–18; 67% female)	Scales $\alpha = .86–.94$ Subscales $\alpha = .73–.86$	Not reported	Unidimensional structure	Significant mean difference between school sample and PD subsample (determined by the SCID-II) on all scales and subscales ($d = 1.04–2.56$)
	Lind et al., 2019 (USA/English)	Inpatient sample: $N = 70$ ($M_{age} = 15.37$; range = 12–17; 80% female)	$\alpha = .95$	Not reported	Not reported	Identity diffusion ($r = .72$) and narrative coherence ($r = -.27$) correlated with BPFS-C Identity diffusion predictive of BPFS-C ($\beta = .68$)
LoPF-Q 12–18 Criterion A; 97 items rated on 5-point Likert scale (0 = *no*; 4 = *yes*); four subscales	Goth et al., 2018 (Switzerland/ German)	School sample: $N = 351$ ($M_{age} = 15.7$; range = 12–20; 59.8% male) Mixed clinical sample: $N = 415$ ($M_{age} = 15.4$; range = 11–19; 68.7% female)	Total scale $\alpha = .97$ Scales $\alpha = .88–.95$ Subscales $\alpha = .76–.91$	Not reported	Four-factor structure	Significant moderate correlations with BPFS-C ROC identifying SCID-II BPD: Sensitivity .81; Specificity .84 ROC identifying BPFS-C BPD: Sensitivity .81; Specificity .83 ROC identifying PD patients: Sensitivity: .75; Specificity: .59

(continues)

Measure and description	Author and country/ language	Sample	Internal consistency	Reliability	Factor structure	Criterion validity
STiP-5.1 Criterion A; semistructured interview; 28 open-ended questions assessing 12 facets of Criterion A— each rated on scale ranging from 0 (*little/no impairment*) to 4 (*extreme impairment*)	Weekers et al., 2021 (Netherlands/ Dutch)	Clinical sample: N = 84 (M_{age} = 15.60; range = 12–17; 89% female) Community sample: N = 12 (M_{age} = 15.08; range = 13–17; 75% female)	Total scale α = .96 Self-scale α = .94 Interpersonal scale α = .92	Total sample ICCs = .88–.99 Clinical sample ICCs = .47–.97	Not reported	Significant mean difference between clinical and community sample on STiP-5.1 scores (d = 4.68) but no significant difference on STiP-5.1 scores between clinical adolescents with and without a PD diagnosis STiP-5.1 total score significantly correlated with number of SCID-II BPD criteria, LPFS-BF 2.0 scores, SIPP-SF scores, and PID-5-BF scores
DAPP-BQ-A Criterion B; self- and parent-report scales; 290 items rated on 5-point Likert scale (1 = *very unlike me/ child*; 5 = *very like me/ child*); organized into 18 lower order scales and four higher order scales	Tromp & Koot, 2008 (Netherlands/ Dutch)	Referred sample: N = 170 (M_{age} = 15.9; range = 12–22; 65.9% female) Nonreferred sample: N = 1,628 (M_{age} = 14.6; range = 11–20; 51.4% male) Test–retest of referred and a community sample: N = 56 (age range = 13–23; 71% female)	Referred sample subscale α = .67–.97 Nonreferred sample subscale α = .73–.92	Subscale ICC = .07–.96	Four-factor structure	ROC analyses: several scales and subscales were significantly accurate in discriminating between referred, PD-referred, and nonreferred adolescents

Measure / Description	Study (country/language)	Sample	Internal consistency	Test–retest	Factor structure	Validity
DAPP-SF-A Shortened version of the DAPP-BQ-A; 144 items rated on 5-point Likert scale (1 = *very unlike child*; 5 = *very like child*); organized into 18 lower order scales and four higher order scales	Tromp & Koot, 2015 (Netherlands/ Dutch)	School sample: $N = 1{,}596$ ($M_{age} = 14.6$; range = 11–20; 51% male) Referred sample: $N = 166$ ($M_{age} = 15.9$; range = 12–22; 65% female) Test-retest of a referred and a community sample: $N = 58$ ($M_{age} = 18.7$; range = 13–23; 73% female)	School sample subscale $\alpha = .66$–.86 Referred sample subscale $\alpha = .78$–.93	Test-retest after a mean of 22 days ICC = .20–.93	Four-factor structure	ROC analyses: several scales and subscales were significantly accurate in discriminating between referred, PD-referred, and nonreferred adolescents
DIPSI Criterion B; self- and parent-report scales; 172 items rated on 5-point Likert scale (1 = *not characteristic*; 5 = *highly characteristic*); organized into 27 lower order scales and four higher order scales	De Clercq et al., 2006 (Belgium/ Dutch) Decuyper et al., 2015 (Canada/ English; Belgium/ Dutch)	Referred Sample: $N = 205$ ($M_{age} = 9.91$; range = 6–14; 58% male) Nonreferred sample: $N = 749$ ($M_{age} = 7.54$; range = 5–15; 51% male) Canadian sample: $N = 341$ ($M_{age} = 11.60$; range = 5–19; 55.1% female) Flemish sample: $N = 509$ ($M_{age} = 15.20$; range = 11–17; 68.2% female)	Facet $\alpha = .58$–.85 Maternal report domains $\alpha = .87$–.97 Self-report domains $\alpha = .88$–.97	Not reported Not reported	Four-factor higher order structure Four-factor higher order structure	Factors significantly correlated with relevant CBCL and HiPIC domains Factors significantly correlated with relevant CBCL domains Factor structure and covariation patterns replicated across informants

(continues)

TABLE 5.2. Assessment Tools for *DSM* Section III Criteria A and B in Youth (*Continued*)

Measure and description	Author and country/ language	Sample	Internal consistency	Reliability	Factor structure	Criterion validity
SNAP-Y Criterion B; self-report adaptation of the SNAP-2; 390 True/false items; organized into 15 lower order scales and three higher order scales	Linde et al., 2013 (USA/English)	Community sample: $N = 381$ ($M_{age} = 14.5$; 56% female) Outpatient sample: $N = 106$ ($M_{age} = 14.7$; 60% female)	Community sample trait scales $\alpha = .73–.89$; Clinical sample trait scales $\alpha = .65–.91$	Community sample dependability coefficient/ retest correlation = .79	Three-factor structure	Significantly associated with other dimensional measures of personality

Note. AIDA = Assessment of Identity Development in Adolescence; BPD = borderline personality disorder; BPFS-C = Borderline Personality Features Scale for Children–self report; CBCL = Child Behavior Checklist; DAPP-BQ-A = Dimensional Assessment of Personality Pathology–Basic Questionnaire for Adolescents; DAPP-SF-A = Dimensional Assessment of Personality Pathology–Short Form for Adolescents; DIPSI = Dimensional Personality Symptom Item Pool; HiPIC = Hierarchical Personality Inventory for Children; ICC = intraclass correlation coefficient; LoPF-Q 12–18 = Levels of Personality Functioning Questionnaire; LPFS-BF 2.0 = Level of Personality Functioning Scale–Brief Form 2.0; PD = personality disorder; PID-5-BF = Personality Inventory for *DSM-5*–Brief Form; ROC = receiver operating characteristic curve; SCID-II = Structured Clinical Interview for *DSM-IV* Axis II personality disorders; SIPP-SF = Severity Indices of Personality Problems–Short Form; SNAP-Y = Schedule for Nonadaptive and Adaptive Personality–Youth Version.

The same reasons that fueled the introduction of the AMPD also fueled the development of the CS approach, including (a) the documented high comorbidity in symptoms of PDs with each other and with other traditional Axis I disorders; (b) the artificial divisions between diagnosis and no diagnosis based on cross-sectional symptom sets that are confused with course-of-illness variables, especially in the developmental context; (c) the knowledge that clinical features are not differentiated from those that become apparent as a disorder persists; and (d) the understanding that diagnostic concepts are typically derived from adult samples of patients with chronic illness in tertiary care settings where the impression of stability and validity is enhanced (Chanen et al., 2016; McGorry, 2013). These issues are particularly problematic for youth whose mental disorders often do not present fully formed (Chanen et al., 2016; De Clercq et al., 2017). Rather, young people frequently present with nonspecific and evolving mixtures of symptoms that may or may not consolidate neatly into a categorically defined mental disorder. Diagnostic precision is frequently possible only in retrospect (Chanen et al., 2016). Nevertheless, even without categorically defined diagnosis, youth and families experience significant distress that disrupts developmental milestones with far-reaching consequences for education, family, and peer relationships (Chanen et al., 2007). For all these reasons, CS was proposed as a framework for intervention and assessment designed to assist young people to better navigate the transition to adulthood. CS and the notion of the "at risk mental state" was first applied to the identification of youth at ultra-high risk of developing psychosis (McGorry, 2010; McGorry et al., 2018) and has since been expanded to PD (Chanen et al., 2016; Hutsebaut et al., 2019, 2020). These adaptations of the CS model for personality pathology have offered a heuristic strategy to guide design and selection of appropriate treatment according to the stage of disease progression. However, these adaptations were focused on the categorically defined construct of BPD. Recently, we built on this prior work to develop an AMPD-informed CS model (Sharp et al., 2021). Here, we expand this model by adding stage-appropriate assessment tools. Not only would such an assessment approach improve fitness for purpose in the assessment of personality pathology in youth, but it would move the current focus on the assessment of late-stage disorders to a more preventive assessment strategy geared toward a more effective health management response to the needs associated with different stages of BPD throughout the life course.

Table 5.3 summarizes the AMPD-informed CS model. Stage 0 is defined as increased risk of disorder, but no current symptoms. However, young people might display high levels of Criterion B maladaptive trait scores. These children, who are temperamentally more reactive and sensitive, are the children who have been shown in longitudinal studies to be an increased risk for the development of later personality pathology (De Clercq, 2018; De Clercq et al., 2017; De Clercq, Decuyper, & De Caluwé, 2014). They are likely to have inherited maladaptive dispositional traits, or they might experience early adversity that negatively affects the development of typical stress responses to the environment—or an interaction of these factors. While the typical

TABLE 5.3. An AMPD-Informed Clinical Staging Model for Lifespan Personality Pathology

Stage	Stage definition	Target population	Clinical presentation	Assessment tools
0	Increased risk of disorder No current symptoms	For example, first-degree relatives Youth in adverse contexts Infancy, preschool, elementary school age, adolescence	Above-average scores on Criterion B maladaptive traits (or Big Five variants): negative affectivity (neuroticism), detachment (introversion), antagonism (low agreeableness), disinhibition (low conscientiousness) and psychoticism (openness). Subthreshold elevation on measures of internalizing and externalizing. No functional impairment.	Trait measures: HiPIC, DIPSI Temperament measures: BSQ, EAS, CBQ Internalizing-externalizing measures: CBCL, TRF, YSR, BASC-3, SDQ
1a	Mild or nonspecific symptoms Mild functional change or decline	Community screening Preschool, elementary school age, adolescence	Symptoms of both internalizing and externalizing disorder/high scores on Criterion B traits. Mild issues in social and school function that can be handled by parents or teachers. Some problems in empathy, theory of mind, and self-regulation.	Stage 0 measures Functioning measures: CBCL/YSR/TRF functioning scales; CAFAS or MAFS; BASC-3 self-regulation scales; ToM measures
1b	Ultra-high risk: moderate but subthreshold symptoms	Referrals from primary care Elementary school, adolescence, early adulthood	Confluence of internalizing and/or externalizing disorder/high scores on Criterion B traits. Escalation in social and educational challenges; may struggle in peer group. Significant problems in empathy, theory of mind, self-regulation, self-direction.	Stage 1a measures Additional trait measures: the PID-5
2	First episode of threshold disorder with moderate to severe symptoms and functional decline	Referrals from primary and specialist care Early, mid-, late adolescence; early adulthood; adulthood	High levels of Criterion A dysfunction: maladaptive self- and interpersonal function; significant problems in self-reflection and self-directedness, identity development, intimacy, empathy, and theory of mind. Internalizing and externalizing disorder/high levels of Criterion B traits maintained. Moderate to severe problems in social, educational, and/or work function; problems in maintaining mutually rewarding relationships.	Stage 1b measures Criterion A measures: AIDA, LoPF-Q 12–18, STiP-5.1 BPD measures: CI-BPD, BPFS-C-11, BPFS-P-11, PAI-A-BOR

3a	Recurrence of subthreshold symptoms	Referrals from primary and specialist care Early, mid-, late adolescence; early adulthood; adulthood	Recurrence of internalizing and/or externalizing disorder/high levels of Criterion B traits. Challenges in maladaptive self- and interpersonal functioning, social and educational settings return.	Stage 2 measures Additional severity measures: WHODAS 2.0, SASPD
3b	First threshold relapse of disorder	Referrals from primary and specialist care Early, mid-, late adolescence; early adulthood; adulthood	First threshold relapse of Criterion A dysfunction. Internalizing and externalizing disorder/high levels of Criterion B traits. Moderate to severe problems in social, educational, and/or work function; problems in maintaining mutually rewarding relationships.	Stage 2 measures Additional severity measures: WHODAS 2.0, SASPD
3c	Multiple relapses of disorder	Referrals from specialist care Early, mid-, late adolescence; early adulthood; adulthood	Multiple relapses of Criterion A function, as well as internalizing and externalizing disorder/high levels of Criterion B traits. Near-chronic levels of social, relationship, educational, and/or work impairment.	Stage 2 measures Additional severity measures: WHODAS 2.0, SASPD
4	Persistent, unremitting disorder	Referrals from specialist care Early, mid-, late adolescence; early adulthood; adulthood	Persistent, unremitting Criterion A dysfunction and comorbid internalizing and externalizing disorder/high levels of Criterion B traits. No or very limited participation in social and professional life.	Stage 2 measures Additional severity measures: WHODAS 2.0, SASPD

Note. AIDA = Assessment of Identity Development in Adolescence; AMPD = Alternative *DSM-5* Model of Personality Disorders; BASC-3 = Behavior Assessment System for Children, third edition; BPFS-C-11 = Borderline Personality Features Scale for Children–self report 11-item version; BPFS-P-11 = Borderline Personality Features Scale for Children–parent report 11-item version; BSQ = Behavioral Styles Questionnaire; CAFAS = Child and Adolescent Functional Assessment Scale; CBCL = Child Behavior Checklist; CBQ = Child Behavior Questionnaire; CI-BPD = Childhood Interview for *DSM-IV* Borderline Personality Disorder; DIPSI = Dimensional Personality Symptom Item Pool; EAS = EAS Temperament Survey; HiPIC = Hierarchical Personality Inventory for Children; LoPF-Q 12–18 = Levels of Personality Functioning Questionnaire; MAFS = Multidimensional Adolescent Functioning Scale; PAI-A-BOR = Personality Assessment Inventory–Adolescent version–borderline scale; PID-5 = Personality Inventory for *DSM-5*; SASPD = Standardized Assessment of Severity of Personality Disorder; SDQ = Strengths and Difficulties Questionnaire; STiP-5.1 = Semistructured Interview for Personality Functioning *DSM-5*; ToM = theory of mind; TRF = Teacher's Report Form; WHODAS 2.0 = World Health Organization Disability Assessment Schedule 2.0; YSR = Youth Self-Report.

trajectory for the development of BPD in particular has been described as one in which BPD is preceded by a reactive and sensitive temperament during infancy, and the preschool- and elementary-school-age years, it is also possible that high levels of maladaptive trait function (Criterion B) might present for the first time at puberty or thereafter. It is unusual, though, for elevated maladaptive traits to present for the first time in young adulthood. Therefore, for this stage of disorder, we suggest measures of personality traits that are appropriate for use in preschoolers (e.g., the Hierarchical Personality Inventory for Children [HiPIC]; Mervielde & De Fruyt, 2002) and elementary-school-age children (e.g., HiPIC, DIPSI), measures of temperament that are appropriate for preschoolers and elementary-school-age children (e.g., the Behavioral Styles Questionnaire [BSQ]; McDevitt & Carey, 1978; the EAS Temperament Survey [EAS]; Buss & Plomin, 1984; the Child Behavior Questionnaire [CBQ]; Putnam & Rothbart, 2006), and measures of preschool- and elementary-school-age internalizing and externalizing problems (e.g., preschool [ages 1.5–5] Child Behavior Checklist [CBCL; Achenbach & Rescorla, 2000], school age [ages 6–18] CBCL and Teacher's Report Form [TRF] and Youth Self-Report [YSR] for ages 11–18 [Achenbach & Rescorla, 2001], Behavior Assessment System for Children, third edition [BASC-3] measures [ages 2–21; Altmann et al., 2018], Strengths and Difficulties Questionnaire [SDQ] parent and teacher report [ages 3–16] and youth self-report [ages 11–16; Goodman, 1997]).

Risk for disorder progresses to Stage 1a if the necessary "scaffolding" was not provided for a sensitive and reactive temperament or if adverse events exacerbated sensitive temperament. Symptoms of anxiety, oppositionality, and irritability might emerge. Children or young people might be thought of as having pleomorphic problems, presenting with attenuated (or subthreshold) features of ADHD, mood disorder, or anxiety disorder. Parents and teachers begin to struggle to manage the young person but can do so without referral to specialist services. At this stage, similar measures as for Stage 0 are proposed, but now measures of function can be added (e.g., competence scale scores of the YSR and CBCL or adaptive functioning scales of the TRF; Child and Adolescent Functional Assessment Scale [CAFAS; Hodges, 1990]; Multidimensional Adolescent Functioning Scale [MAFS; Wardenaar et al., 2013]; indices of self-regulation, such as the attentional, behavioral, and emotional control scales of the BASC-3 system; measures of theory of mind for preschoolers or elementary-school-age children [Beaudoin et al., 2020; Ziatabar Ahmadi et al., 2015]).

In Stage 1b, traits and symptoms have consolidated into disorder, and a marked escalation in social and educational/vocational challenges is observed, often warranting a referral to more specialized services. Based on what we know of the development of BPD, Stage 1 might commonly map onto the prepubertal years, but it is also possible that the confluence of internalizing and externalizing problems might occur for the first time in the peripubertal or postpubertal period. However, as with Stage 0, it is very unlikely that the confluence of internalizing and externalizing disorder on the pathway to personality pathology would first emerge in young adulthood (acknowledging that late-onset PD does occur). Similar measures as suggested for Stage 1a are relevant for Stage 1b, including the PID-5, as it has been validated in adolescent samples. However, a trait measure such as the DIPSI, that can be administered earlier on, may be preferred for continuity.

Stage 2 is where we typically see the onset of traditionally defined (Section II) PD. In our model, this is when Criterion A (maladaptive self- and interpersonal function) comes online in its adult form—usually in the pubertal or post-pubertal period through to young adulthood. The failure of the reflective self to develop becomes apparent, and significant departure from healthy and integrated identity development can be observed. The young person struggles with peer relationships, and attempts at intimacy are thwarted. Aloneness and loneliness set in; alternatively, a promiscuous search for connection sets in. "Complex comorbidity" (i.e., a high burden of internalizing and externalizing psychopathology) is the norm (Chanen et al., 2007) and is associated with significant impairment in relationships and vocational functioning. It is not unusual that young people in this stage drop out of school, college, or work. Relationships are nonsatisfactory, and young people begin to fall behind on developmental milestones. At this juncture, it is critical to incorporate explicit measure of Criterion A function (e.g., the AIDA, LoPF-Q 12–18, or STiP-5.1). We also propose that at this stage, traditional measures of BPD may be useful. This is because, with others, we have argued that BPD features represent the generic markers of (severely) impaired personality development (Sharp et al., 2015, 2018; Sharp & Wall, 2018, 2021). These features are seen as the outcome of partly innate, partly developmentally determined dysregulations in self- and interpersonal functioning. To this end, any of the measures listed in Table 5.1 can be used to further assess personality function at this stage.

During Stage 3a, there is a relief or partial remission from the first episode of the disorder. Stage 3b is reached if subthreshold symptoms are maintained, with further relapse into full-blown disorder. Stage 3c is characterized by multiple relapses of Criterion A function. This is usually the phase of the disorder that clinicians will recognize as prototypical, characterized by multiple admissions and readmissions to the hospital; suicide attempts; and enduring levels of social, relationship, educational, and employment breakdown. This pattern might develop into a persistent, unremitting presentation of the disorder (Stage 4). Assessment approaches for Stages 3 and 4 are similar to Stage 2. However, additional indices of severity may be included (e.g., World Health Organization Disability Assessment Schedule 2.0 [WHODAS 2.0; Üstün et al., 2010], Standardized Assessment of Severity of Personality Disorder [SASPD; Olajide et al., 2018]).

Returning to the case of Henry (see also Table 5.3), we can see how assessment of Henry's personality function—and not just their internalizing and externalizing problems at earlier stages of disease progression—could have warranted personality-specific intervention approaches, if appropriately assessed. By the time Henry was hospitalized at age 15, there had been several missed opportunities for scaffolding Henry's personality function, and Henry had already reached Stage 2. Prevention and early intervention would have necessitated integrating personality explicitly into an assessment battery, case formulation, and treatment planning.

ADDITIONAL CLINICAL CONSIDERATIONS

In this section, we present a range of additional clinical considerations that should be considered to ensure a "good enough" assessment of personality function, depending on how services are set up—that is, not all services would allow for this level of service. These can be seen as the principles of best practice in assessment of personality function in youth. First, when suspicion is raised that a young person displays personality challenges, it is important to assess causal and interaction effects of failed social support. Thus, the interactive effects of current stress, that if addressed might relieve a more transient "state" condition, should be considered. If it turns out that by supporting the adolescent in their environment, immediate relief can be obtained from the problematic behavior or way of thinking, feeling, and relating to self and others, then further personality assessment may not be necessary.

We suggest a clinical PD assessment procedure containing seven elements:

1. When a young person is referred for personality assessment, a preliminary part of the assessment should be to exclude any potential somatic conditions as reasons for what we conceive as personality pathology. Hence, any personality assessment should be initiated with a somatic examination, including assessment of drug abuse, metabolic diseases, neurological disorders, and brain damage. A somatic investigation may reveal unhealthy lifestyle, which is not only a potential alternative explanation for symptoms but may in itself aggravate symptoms and thus constitute an additional risk factor for stage progression (e.g., reversed day–night rhythm or substance abuse may be, as well, a symptom of actual personality dysfunction as a cause for further stage progression). The somatic examination could also include medical imaging if considered necessary.

2. As outlined in the CS model, a personality assessment is conducted in the context of a general psychopathology evaluation to identify comorbid conditions. In addition, it is important to know whether the young person suffers from any developmental or neurological disorder such as autism or ADHD. Also, severe depression, anxiety, psychosis, and bipolar disorder should be assessed.

3. The assessment should also include a developmental history about the young person's early life (interviews both with the parents and the young person), including information about how they function in school and in leisure activities. It is important to collect information about self- and interpersonal functioning, potential traumas, and earlier contacts with the mental health system (including school psychologists). We suggest that even though very early life information is not part of the criteria for personality diagnostics, it is informative and says something about long-term personality patterns

and early temperamental issues. Early developmental history helps to generate a case formulation that may help to understand the observed impairments. Especially with these self-stigmatizing young people, it may be very helpful to normalize their impairments, given the life they have lived so far. Based on the general psychopathology assessment and the developmental interview, a timeline is drawn inserting potential important information such as (for example) first problematic behavior, first diagnoses, traumatic incidents, and so on. This timeline is central for the semistructured interview and aids the clinician and the young person in keeping track of when and in which contexts issues appeared.

4. An intellectual evaluation of the young person should be introduced if the clinician suspects impaired cognitive functioning, as issues related to self- and interpersonal functioning can also be anchored in intellectual impairment. Also, we consider intellectual assessment vital for later organization of the treatment (e.g., offering psychotherapy or pedagogical interventions [the former requiring some form of intellectual capacity]).

5. In a detailed personality assessment, it is fundamental to collect information from schoolteachers or other personnel who have knowledge about the young person from over a longer period. We suggest trying to collect the following information: (a) how the young person acts in social settings, whether they are capable of taking the perspective of the other, and how they express feelings and understand their own behavior; (b) whether the young person is impulsive or whether they are able to concentrate, focus on assignments, and abide by classroom rules; (c) how the young person gets along with other peers in general, including teachers; (d) what the young person's level of school performance (e.g., grades) is; (e) whether the young person is often absent from school—and if so, for what reasons; and (f) how collaboration is with the young person's parents.

6. A central part of PD assessment in adolescence is the clinical semistructured interview, using evidence-based standard PD evaluation interviews, summarized in Tables 5.1 and 5.2. We suggest conducting both an interview with the young person and an interview with their parents (or parents' substitutes). Including parents in the assessment adds an important perspective from sources who have a thorough understanding of the young person and are thereby able to help inform the clinician about whether the pathology is (a) persistent, inflexible, and pervasive or (b) more transient. When including parents, we recommend using the same structured interview as used for the young person but changing the wording in sentences. For example, the first item, for the young person, assessing Avoidant PD may be "Have you ever avoided jobs or tasks . . ." but we may reword it for the parents to "Has [young person's name] ever avoided jobs or tasks. . . ." We also suggest that the semistructured interview be supplemented with self-report questionnaires. It is essential for a precise and thorough personality assessment that different sources (e.g., the young person, the parents, the school) are

included, as well as different forms of collecting knowledge (e.g., interview based, self-report based). Particularly relevant here is to try to understand differences in opinions (e.g., if a parent perceives the young person as self-confident, while the young person feels very insecure about themself); it helps to understand what others see from the outside and how it mismatches with what is seen from the inside (often causing the interpersonal problems), and it helps to identify areas where self-reflection is lacking (e.g., understanding one's impact upon others).

7. As is good practice for any diagnostic evaluation, personality assessment should ideally be conducted while thinking critically about comorbid conditions. Recall that comorbidity is the rule rather than the exception in PD, and it is important to identify the impact of personality-related problems versus mood- or behavior-related problems. In Table 5.4, we have filled out the information for Henry, following the above principles.

TABLE 5.4. Clinical Considerations in PD Assessment of Adolescents

Clinical elements in PD assessment of adolescents	
1. Social investigation	• no somatic concerns, substance abuse, metabolic diseases, or history of neurological disorder or brain damage reported during semistructured interviews with Henry and parents
2. General psychopathological screening	• SCID-5, CBCL, and YSR administered to Henry and parents to identify current comorbid conditions (possible GAD, major depression, ADHD)
3. Clinical anamnestic interview	• clinical interview gathered information regarding Henry's
	– early life (e.g., adoption status, fussy and not easily soothed, history of description by teachers as hyperactive and disruptive)
	– school function and school history (e.g., history of classroom misbehavior pointing to long-term problems, teacher reports of having difficulty making friends)
	– mental health contacts and diagnostic history (e.g., diagnosed with ADHD at age 6, diagnosed with GAD at age 9, psychiatrist diagnosis of ODD at age 12, inpatient hospital stay week prior to assessment)
	– current presenting concerns (e.g., self-harm during the past year and recent suicide attempt)
	– environmental/other stressors (e.g., gender identity, experiences with bullying)
4. Intellectual testing	• no family or individual history of suspected intellectual disability or learning disorder, so no intellectual evaluation conducted
5. Data collection from external sources (school, leisure activities, etc.)	• TRF given to two current high school teachers to gather information about Henry's functioning at school and corroborating information for Step 2

TABLE 5.4. Clinical Considerations in PD Assessment of Adolescents (*Continued*)

6. Specific semistructured interviews and self-report questionnaires	• Henry completed self-report measures of Section II (the BPFS-C) and Section III personality disorder (PID-5-BF and LoPF-Q 12–18). Obtained corroborating sources of information through administration of the CI-BPD and having both parents complete the BPFS-P. Results indicated clinically significant symptoms of BPD.
7. Personality pathology decision	• BPD diagnosis given. Differential diagnosis consideration may include major depression. However, results of Step 6 suggest BPD better explains mood symptoms that occur simultaneously in the presence of feelings of chronic emptiness (e.g., feelings being dead and wanting to turn them back on, few feelings outside of anger). Additionally, self-harm and suicidality, also symptoms of depression, occur in the context of interpersonal rejection, are impulsive, or serve to regulate emotions—common functions of suicidal behavior in BPD.

Note. ADHD = attention-deficit/hyperactivity disorder; BPD = borderline personality disorder; BPFS-C = Borderline Personality Features Scale for Children–self report; BPFS-P = Borderline Personality Features Scale for Children–parent report; CBCL = Child Behavior Checklist; CI-BPD = Childhood Interview for *DSM-IV* Borderline Personality Disorder; GAD = generalized anxiety disorder; LoPF-Q 12–18 = Levels of Personality Functioning Questionnaire; ODD = oppositional defiant disorder; PID-5-BF = Personality Inventory for *DSM-5*-Brief Form; SCID-5 = Structured Clinical Interview for *DSM-5*; TRF = Teacher's Report Form; YSR = Youth Self-Report.

CONCLUSION

Our ultimate goal in this chapter was to help close the gap between research and clinical practice in the assessment of young people, which if unchanged will continue the deleterious effects—for individuals, their families, and society—of ignoring the assessment of personality function in young people. Vocal calls for closing this gap are expressed by those with lived experience (Baltzersen, 2021) and indicated by analyses of barriers to treatment (Wall et al., 2021). The surge of research on the prevention and early intervention in young people is heeding these calls but depends on the assessment of personality function early in development and early in disease progression. AMPD, especially when translated into a CS framework, allows a focus on personality function more broadly, which in turn opens up a developmental orientation in ways that Section II or traditional approaches to PD did not previously allow.

REFERENCES

Achenbach, T. M., & Rescorla, L. A. (2000). *Manual for the ASEBA preschool forms & profiles*. University of Vermont, Research Center for Children, Youth, & Families.

Achenbach, T. M., & Rescorla, L. A. (2001). *Manual for the ASEBA school-age forms & profiles*. University of Vermont, Research Center for Children, Youth, & Families.

Altmann, R. A., Reynolds, C. R., Kamphaus, R. W., & Vannest, K. J. (2018). BASC-3. In J. Kreutzer, J. DeLuca, & B. Caplan (Eds.), *Encyclopedia of clinical neuropsychology*. Springer. https://doi.org/10.1007/978-3-319-56782-2_1524-2

Archer, R. P., Handel, R. W., Ben-Porath, Y. S., & Tellegen, A. (2016). *Minnesota Multiphasic Personality Inventory-Adolescent-Restructured Form (MMPI-A-RF): Manual for administration, scoring, interpretation, and technical manual.* University of Minnesota Press.

Baltzersen, Å.-L. (2021). Moving forward: Closing the gap between research and practice for young people with BPD. *Current Opinion in Psychology, 37,* 77–81. https://doi.org/10.1016/j.copsyc.2020.08.008

Beaudoin, C., Leblanc, É., Gagner, C., & Beauchamp, M. H. (2020). Systematic review and inventory of theory of mind measures for young children. *Frontiers in Psychology, 10,* Article 2905. https://doi.org/10.3389/fpsyg.2019.02905

Bender, D. S., Morey, L. C., & Skodol, A. E. (2011). Toward a model for assessing level of personality functioning in *DSM-5,* Part I: A review of theory and methods. *Journal of Personality Assessment, 93*(4), 332–346. https://doi.org/10.1080/00223891.2011.583808

Buss, A. H., & Plomin, R. (1984). *Temperament: Early developing personality traits.* Lawrence Erlbaum Associates.

Cailhol, L., Jeannot, M., Rodgers, R., Guelfi, J. D., Perez-Diaz, F., Pham-Scottez, A., Corcos, M., & Speranza, M. (2013). Borderline personality disorder and mental healthcare service use among adolescents. *Journal of Personality Disorders, 27*(2), 252–259. https://doi.org/10.1521/pedi.2013.27.2.252

Chanen, A., Sharp, C., Hoffman, P., & the Global Alliance for Prevention and Early Intervention for Borderline Personality Disorder. (2017). Prevention and early intervention for borderline personality disorder: A novel public health priority. *World Psychiatry, 16*(2), 215–216. https://doi.org/10.1002/wps.20429

Chanen, A. M. (2015). Borderline personality disorder in young people: Are we there yet? *Journal of Clinical Psychology, 71*(8), 778–791. https://doi.org/10.1002/jclp.22205

Chanen, A. M., Berk, M., & Thompson, K. (2016). Integrating early intervention for borderline personality disorder and mood disorders. *Harvard Review of Psychiatry, 24*(5), 330–341. https://doi.org/10.1097/HRP.0000000000000105

Chanen, A. M., Jovev, M., & Jackson, H. J. (2007). Adaptive functioning and psychiatric symptoms in adolescents with borderline personality disorder. *The Journal of Clinical Psychiatry, 68*(2), 297–306. https://doi.org/10.4088/JCP.v68n0217

Chanen, A. M., & Kaess, M. (2012). Developmental pathways to borderline personality disorder. *Current Psychiatry Reports, 14*(1), 45–53. https://doi.org/10.1007/s11920-011-0242-y

Chang, B., Sharp, C., & Ha, C. (2011). The criterion validity of the Borderline Personality Features Scale for Children in an adolescent inpatient setting. *Journal of Personality Disorders, 25*(4), 492–503. https://doi.org/10.1521/pedi.2011.25.4.492

Crick, N. R., Murray-Close, D., & Woods, K. (2005). Borderline personality features in childhood: A short-term longitudinal study. *Development and Psychopathology, 17*(4), 1051–1070. https://doi.org/10.1017/S0954579405050492

Dahl, R. E., Allen, N. B., Wilbrecht, L., & Suleiman, A. B. (2018). Importance of investing in adolescence from a developmental science perspective. *Nature, 554*(7693), 441–450. https://doi.org/10.1038/nature25770

De Clercq, B. (2018). Integrating developmental aspects in current thinking about personality pathology. *Current Opinion in Psychology, 21,* 69–73. https://doi.org/10.1016/j.copsyc.2017.10.002

De Clercq, B., Decuyper, M., & De Caluwé, E. (2014). Developmental manifestations of borderline personality pathology from an age-specific dimensional personality disorder trait framework. In C. Sharp & J. L. Tackett (Eds.), *Handbook of borderline personality disorder in children and adolescents* (pp. 81–94). Springer. https://doi.org/10.1007/978-1-4939-0591-1_7

De Clercq, B., De Fruyt, F., De Bolle, M., Van Hiel, A., Markon, K. E., & Krueger, R. F. (2014). The hierarchical structure and construct validity of the PID-5 trait measure in adolescence. *Journal of Personality, 82*(2), 158–169. https://doi.org/10.1111/jopy.12042

De Clercq, B., De Fruyt, F., Van Leeuwen, K., & Mervielde, I. (2006). The structure of maladaptive personality traits in childhood: A step toward an integrative developmental perspective for *DSM-V. Journal of Abnormal Psychology, 115*(4), 639–657. https://doi.org/10.1037/0021-843X.115.4.639

De Clercq, B., De Fruyt, F., & Widiger, T. A. (2009). Integrating a developmental perspective in dimensional models of personality disorders. *Clinical Psychology Review, 29*(2), 154–162. https://doi.org/10.1016/j.cpr.2008.12.002

De Clercq, B., Hofmans, J., Vergauwe, J., De Fruyt, F., & Sharp, C. (2017). Developmental pathways of childhood dark traits. *Journal of Abnormal Psychology, 126*(7), 843–858. https://doi.org/10.1037/abn0000303

Decuyper, M., De Clercq, B., & Tackett, J. L. (2015). Assessing maladaptive traits in youth: An English-language version of the Dimensional Personality Symptom Itempool. *Personality Disorders: Theory, Research, and Treatment, 6*(3), 239–250. https://doi.org/10.1037/per0000114

Feenstra, D. J., Hutsebaut, J., Verheul, R., & Busschbach, J. J. V. (2011). Severity Indices of Personality Problems (SIPP-118) in adolescents: Reliability and validity. *Psychological Assessment, 23*(3), 646–655. https://doi.org/10.1037/a0022995

Fossati, A., Somma, A., Borroni, S., Markon, K. E., & Krueger, R. F. (2017). The Personality Inventory for *DSM-5* Brief Form: Evidence for reliability and construct validity in a sample of community-dwelling Italian adolescents. *Assessment, 24*(5), 615–631. https://doi.org/10.1177/1073191115621793

Goodman, M., Patil, U., Triebwasser, J., Hoffman, P., Weinstein, Z. A., & New, A. (2011). Parental burden associated with borderline personality disorder in female offspring. *Journal of Personality Disorders, 25*(1), 59–74. https://doi.org/10.1521/pedi.2011.25.1.59

Goodman, R. (1997). The Strengths and Difficulties Questionnaire: A research note. *The Journal of Child Psychology and Psychiatry, 38*(5), 581–586. https://doi.org/10.1111/j.1469-7610.1997.tb01545.x

Goth, K., Birkhölzer, M., & Schmeck, K. (2018). Assessment of personality functioning in adolescents with the LoPF–Q 12–18 Self-Report Questionnaire. *Journal of Personality Assessment, 100*(6), 680–690. https://doi.org/10.1080/00223891.2018.1489258

Goth, K., Foelsch, P., Schlüter-Müller, S., Birkhölzer, M., Jung, E., Pick, O., & Schmeck, K. (2012). Assessment of identity development and identity diffusion in adolescence—Theoretical basis and psychometric properties of the self-report questionnaire AIDA. *Child and Adolescent Psychiatry and Mental Health, 6*(1), Article 27. https://doi.org/10.1186/1753-2000-6-27

Hodges, K. (1990). *Child and Adolescent Functional Assessment Scale.* CAFAS.

Hutsebaut, J., Debbané, M., & Sharp, C. (2020). Designing a range of mentalizing interventions for young people using a clinical staging approach to borderline pathology. *Borderline Personality Disorder and Emotion Dysregulation, 7*(1), Article 6. https://doi.org/10.1186/s40479-020-0121-4

Hutsebaut, J., Videler, A. C., Verheul, R., & Van Alphen, S. P. J. (2019). Managing borderline personality disorder from a life course perspective: Clinical staging and health management. *Personality Disorders: Theory, Research, and Treatment, 10*(4), 309–316. https://doi.org/10.1037/per0000341

Kotov, R., Krueger, R. F., Watson, D., Achenbach, T. M., Althoff, R. R., Bagby, R. M., Brown, T. A., Carpenter, W. T., Caspi, A., Clark, L. A., Eaton, N. R., Forbes, M. K., Forbush, K. T., Goldberg, D., Hasin, D., Hyman, S. E., Ivanova, M. Y., Lynam, D. R., Markon, K., . . . Zimmerman, M. (2017). The Hierarchical Taxonomy of Psychopathology (HiTOP): A dimensional alternative to traditional nosologies. *Journal of Abnormal Psychology, 126*(4), 454–477. https://doi.org/10.1037/abn0000258

Krueger, R. F., Derringer, J., Markon, K. E., Watson, D., & Skodol, A. E. (2012). Initial construction of a maladaptive personality trait model and inventory for *DSM-5. Psychological Medicine, 42*(9), 1879–1890. https://doi.org/10.1017/S0033291711002674

Krueger, R. F., Derringer, J., Markon, K. E., Watson, D., & Skodol, A. E. (2013). *The Personality Inventory for* DSM-5—*Brief Form (PID-5-BF)* [Self-report]. https://www.psychiatry.org/psychiatrists/practice/dsm/educational-resources/assessment-measures

Lind, M., Vanwoerden, S., Penner, F., & Sharp, C. (2019). Inpatient adolescents with borderline personality disorder features: Identity diffusion and narrative incoherence. *Personality Disorders: Theory, Research, and Treatment, 10*(4), 389–393. https://doi.org/10.1037/per0000338

Linde, J. A., Stringer, D., Simms, L. J., & Clark, L. A. (2013). The Schedule for Nonadaptive and Adaptive Personality for Youth (SNAP-Y): A new measure for assessing adolescent personality and personality pathology. *Assessment, 20*(4), 387–404. https://doi.org/10.1177/1073191113489847

Livesley, W. J. (2003). *Practical management of personality disorder.* Guilford Press.

McAdams, D. P. (2015). *The art and science of personality development.* Guilford Press.

McAdams, D. P., & Olson, B. D. (2010). Personality development: Continuity and change over the life course. *Annual Review of Psychology, 61,* 517–542. https://doi.org/10.1146/annurev.psych.093008.100507

McDevitt, S. C., & Carey, W. B. (1978). The measurement of temperament in 3–7 year old children. *The Journal of Child Psychology and Psychiatry, 19*(3), 245–253. https://doi.org/10.1111/j.1469-7610.1978.tb00467.x

McGorry, P. D. (2010). Risk syndromes, clinical staging and *DSM V*: New diagnostic infrastructure for early intervention in psychiatry. *Schizophrenia Research, 120*(1-3), 49–53. https://doi.org/10.1016/j.schres.2010.03.016

McGorry, P. D. (2013). Early clinical phenotypes, clinical staging, and strategic biomarker research: Building blocks for personalized psychiatry. *Biological Psychiatry, 74*(6), 394–395. https://doi.org/10.1016/j.biopsych.2013.07.004

McGorry, P. D., Hartmann, J. A., Spooner, R., & Nelson, B. (2018). Beyond the "at risk mental state" concept: Transitioning to transdiagnostic psychiatry. *World Psychiatry, 17*(2), 133–142. https://doi.org/10.1002/wps.20514

Mervielde, I., & De Fruyt, F. (2002). Assessing children's traits with the Hierarchical Personality Inventory for Children. In B. de Raad & M. Perugini (Eds.), *Big Five assessment* (pp. 127–146). Hogrefe & Huber Publishers.

Morey, L. C. (2007). *Personality Assessment Inventory–Adolescent: Professional manual.* Psychological Assessment Resources.

Morey, L. C., Benson, K. T., Busch, A. J., & Skodol, A. E. (2015). Personality disorders in *DSM-5*: Emerging research on the alternative model. *Current Psychiatry Reports, 17*(4), Article 24. https://doi.org/10.1007/s11920-015-0558-0

Morey, L. C., Berghuis, H., Bender, D. S., Verheul, R., Krueger, R. F., & Skodol, A. E. (2011). Toward a model for assessing level of personality functioning in *DSM-5*, Part II: Empirical articulation of a core dimension of personality pathology. *Journal of Personality Assessment, 93*(4), 347–353. https://doi.org/10.1080/00223891.2011.577853

Olajide, K., Munjiza, J., Moran, P., O'Connell, L., Newton-Howes, G., Bassett, P., Akintomide, G., Ng, N., Tyrer, P., Mulder, R., & Crawford, M. J. (2018). Development and psychometric properties of the Standardized Assessment of Severity of Personality Disorder (SASPD). *Journal of Personality Disorders, 32*(1), 44–56. https://doi.org/10.1521/pedi_2017_31_285

Putnam, S. P., & Rothbart, M. K. (2006). Development of short and very short forms of the Children's Behavior Questionnaire. *Journal of Personality Assessment, 87*(1), 102–112. https://doi.org/10.1207/s15327752jpa8701_09

Rothbart, M. K., & Bates, J. E. (2006). Temperament. In W. Damon, R. Lerner, & N. Eisenberg (Eds.), *Handbook of child psychology: Vol. 3. Social, emotional, and personality development* (6th ed., pp. 99–166). Wiley. https://doi.org/10.1002/9780470147658.chpsy0303

Schuppert, H. M., Bloo, J., Minderaa, R. B., Emmelkamp, P. M. G., & Nauta, M. H. (2012). Psychometric evaluation of the Borderline Personality Disorder Severity

Index—IV—Adolescent Version and Parent Version. *Journal of Personality Disorders, 26*(4), 628–640. https://doi.org/10.1521/pedi.2012.26.4.628

Sharp, C. (2017). Bridging the gap: The assessment and treatment of adolescent personality disorder in routine clinical care. *Archives of Disease in Childhood, 102*(1), 103–108. https://doi.org/10.1136/archdischild-2015-310072

Sharp, C. (2020a). Adolescent personality pathology and the Alternative Model for Personality Disorders: Self development as nexus. *Psychopathology, 53*(3-4), 198–204. https://doi.org/10.1159/000507588

Sharp, C. (2020b). What's in a name? The importance of adolescent personality pathology for adaptive psychosocial function [Invited editorial]. *Journal of the American Academy for Child & Adolescent Psychiatry, 59*(10), 1130–1132.

Sharp, C., & Fonagy, P. (2015). Practitioner review: Borderline personality disorder in adolescence–recent conceptualization, intervention, and implications for clinical practice. *The Journal of Child Psychology and Psychiatry, 56*(12), 1266–1288. https://doi.org/10.1111/jcpp.12449

Sharp, C., Ha, C., Michonski, J., Venta, A., & Carbone, C. (2012). Borderline personality disorder in adolescents: Evidence in support of the Childhood Interview for *DSM-IV* Borderline Personality Disorder in a sample of adolescent inpatients. *Comprehensive Psychiatry, 53*(6), 765–774. https://doi.org/10.1016/j.comppsych.2011.12.003

Sharp, C., & Kalpakci, A. (2015). If it looks like a duck and quacks like a duck: Evaluating the validity of borderline personality disorder in adolescents. *Scandinavian Journal of Child and Adolescent Psychiatry and Psychology, 3*(1), 49–62. https://doi.org/10.21307/sjcapp-2015-005

Sharp, C., Kerr, S., & Chanen, A. M. (2021). Early identification and prevention of personality pathology: An AMPD-informed model of clinical staging. In A. E. Skodol & J. M. Oldham (Eds.), *The American Psychiatric Association Publishing textbook of personality disorders* (pp. 259–306). American Psychiatric Association Publishing.

Sharp, C., & Romero, C. (2007). Borderline personality disorder: A comparison between children and adults. *Bulletin of the Menninger Clinic, 71*(2), 85–114. https://doi.org/10.1521/bumc.2007.71.2.85

Sharp, C., Steinberg, L., Temple, J., & Newlin, E. (2014). An 11-item measure to assess borderline traits in adolescents: Refinement of the BPFSC using IRT. *Personality Disorders: Theory, Research, and Treatment, 5*(1), 70–78. https://doi.org/10.1037/per0000057

Sharp, C., Vanwoerden, S., & Wall, K. (2018). Adolescence as a sensitive period for the development of personality disorder. *Psychiatric Clinics of North America, 41*(4), 669–683. https://doi.org/10.1016/j.psc.2018.07.004

Sharp, C., & Wall, K. (2018). Personality pathology grows up: Adolescence as a sensitive period. *Current Opinion in Psychology, 21*, 111–116. https://doi.org/10.1016/j.copsyc.2017.11.010

Sharp, C., & Wall, K. (2021). *DSM-5* level of personality functioning: Refocusing personality disorder on what it means to be human. *Annual Review of Clinical Psychology, 17*(1), 313–337. https://doi.org/10.1146/annurev-clinpsy-081219-105402

Sharp, C., Wright, A. G. C., Fowler, J. C., Frueh, B. C., Allen, J. G., Oldham, J., & Clark, L. A. (2015). The structure of personality pathology: Both general ('g') and specific ('s') factors? *Journal of Abnormal Psychology, 124*(2), 387–398. https://doi.org/10.1037/abn0000033

Shiner, R. L. (2009). The development of personality disorders: Perspectives from normal personality development in childhood and adolescence. *Development and Psychopathology, 21*(3), 715–734. https://doi.org/10.1017/S0954579409000406

Shiner, R. L., & Tackett, J. L. (2014). Personality disorders in children and adolescents. In E. J. Mash & R. A. Barkley (Eds.), *Child psychopathology* (3rd ed., pp. 848–896). Guilford Press.

Somma, A., Borroni, S., Maffei, C., Giarolli, L. E., Markon, K. E., Krueger, R. F., & Fossati, A. (2017). Reliability, factor structure, and associations with measures of problem relationship and behavior of the Personality Inventory for *DSM-5* in a sample of Italian community-dwelling adolescents. *Journal of Personality Disorders, 31*(5), 624–646. https://doi.org/10.1521/pedi_2017_31_272

Tackett, J. L. (2006). Evaluating models of the personality–psychopathology relationship in children and adolescents. *Clinical Psychology Review, 26*(5), 584–599. https://doi.org/10.1016/j.cpr.2006.04.003

Tackett, J. L., Herzhoff, K., Balsis, S., & Cooper, L. (2016). Toward a unifying perspective on personality pathology across the life span. In D. Cicchetti (Ed.), *Developmental psychopathology: Vol. 3. Maladaptation and psychopathology* (pp. 1039–1078). John Wiley & Sons. https://doi.org/10.1002/9781119125556.devpsy323

Tromp, N. B., & Koot, H. M. (2008). Dimensions of personality pathology in adolescents: Psychometric properties of the DAPP-BQ-A. *Journal of Personality Disorders, 22*(6), 623–638. https://doi.org/10.1521/pedi.2008.22.6.623

Tromp, N. B., & Koot, H. M. (2010). Self- and parent report of adolescent personality pathology: Informant agreement and relations to dysfunction. *Journal of Personality Disorders, 24*(2), 151–170. https://doi.org/10.1521/pedi.2010.24.2.151

Tromp, N. B., & Koot, H. M. (2015). Psychometric qualities of the Dimensional Assessment of Personality Pathology—Short Form for Adolescents. *Scandinavian Journal of Child and Adolescent Psychiatry and Psychology, 3*(1), 71–79. https://tidsskrift.dk/sjcapp/article/view/17273

Üstün, T. B., Kostanjsek, N., Chatterji, S., & Rehm, J. (Eds.). (2010). *Measuring health and disability: Manual for WHO Disability Assessment Schedule (WHODAS 2.0)*. World Health Organization.

Venta, A., Magyar, M., Hossein, S., & Sharp, C. (2018). The psychometric properties of the Personality Assessment Inventory–Adolescent's Borderline Features Scale across two high-risk samples. *Psychological Assessment, 30*(6), 827–833. https://doi.org/10.1037/pas0000528

Verheul, R., Andrea, H., Berghout, C. C., Dolan, C., Busschbach, J. J. V., van der Kroft, P. J. A., Bateman, A. W., & Fonagy, P. (2008). Severity Indices of Personality Problems (SIPP-118): Development, factor structure, reliability, and validity. *Psychological Assessment, 20*(1), 23–34. https://doi.org/10.1037/1040-3590.20.1.23

Wall, K., Kerr, S., & Sharp, C. (2021). Barriers to care for adolescents with borderline personality disorder. *Current Opinion in Psychology, 37*, 54–60. https://doi.org/10.1016/j.copsyc.2020.07.028

Wardenaar, K. J., Wigman, J. T. W., Lin, A., Killackey, E., Collip, D., Wood, S. J., Ryan, J., Baksheev, G., Cosgrave, E., Nelson, B., & Yung, A. R. (2013). Development and validation of a new measure of everyday adolescent functioning: The Multidimensional Adolescent Functioning Scale. *Journal of Adolescent Health, 52*(2), 195–200. https://doi.org/10.1016/j.jadohealth.2012.06.021

Weekers, L. C., Verhoeff, S. C. E., Kamphuis, J. H., & Hutsebaut, J. (2021). Assessing Criterion A in adolescents using the Semistructured Interview for Personality Functioning *DSM-5*. *Personality Disorders: Theory, Research, and Treatment, 12*(4), 312–319. https://doi.org/10.1037/per0000454

Westen, D., Dutra, L., & Shedler, J. (2005). Assessing adolescent personality pathology. *The British Journal of Psychiatry, 186*(3), 227–238. https://doi.org/10.1192/bjp.186.3.227

Westen, D., & Muderrisoglu, S. (2003). Assessing personality disorders using a systematic clinical interview: Evaluation of an alternative to structured interviews. *Journal of Personality Disorders, 17*(4), 351–369. https://doi.org/10.1521/pedi.17.4.351.23967

Zanarini, M. C. (2003). Childhood Interview for *DSM-IV* borderline personality disorder (CI-BPD). *McLean Hospital and Harvard Medical School*.

Ziatabar Ahmadi, S. Z., Jalaie, S., & Ashayeri, H. (2015). Validity and reliability of published comprehensive theory of mind tests for normal preschool children: A systematic review. *Iranian Journal of Psychiatry, 10*(4), 214–224.

6

Principles of Treating Personality Pathology

Steven K. Huprich

Much has been written about the treatment of personality disorders (PDs), though fewer instructions have been offered as guiding principles for treatment—particularly now, with the advent of Section III of the *Diagnostic and Statistical Manual of Mental Disorders* (5th ed.; *DSM-5*; American Psychiatric Association, 2013) and the *International Statistical Classification of Diseases and Related Health Problems* (11th ed.; *ICD-11*; World Health Organization, 2019). Livesley and colleagues (Livesley, 2003; Livesley et al., 2015; Livesley & Larstone, 2018) perhaps have written the most broadly about treating PDs, although these texts were not written against the backdrop of the Alternative *DSM-5* Model of Personality Disorders (AMPD) or *ICD-11*. However, a recent book has offered some valuable and guiding ideas about the *DSM-5* model and how to integrate it into clinical practice (Hopwood et al., 2019). Now that the dimensional framework of diagnosing personality pathology is into the mainstream of psychiatric nomenclature, it is crucial to begin writing about personality pathology treatment within these perspectives.

In this chapter, I provide an overview of how the AMPD and *ICD-11*'s focus on severity of impairment can and should be utilized to guide clinicians in how to organize and conduct their treatment. I suggest that the severity framework offers a clinically useful way to understand every person's psychopathology and to integrate their personality functioning into their treatment, and that a

---

Case material presented herein is based on actual patients but has been masked to protect confidentiality.

https://doi.org/10.1037/0000310-007

Personality Disorders and Pathology: Integrating Clinical Assessment and Practice in the DSM-5 *and* ICD-11 *Era*, S. K. Huprich (Editor)

Copyright © 2022 by the American Psychological Association. All rights reserved.

consideration of these traits helps provide an expanded description of the patient's personality. I then introduce other clinically important considerations into this discussion as a means of highlighting their necessity in PD/pathology treatment; this includes a discussion of effective therapeutic action, defensive functioning, unconscious or implicit motivation, harm management, skill acquisition, and countertransferential reactions. I believe that in considering treatment from these broad perspectives, the clinician can be well-prepared to enter into the consulting room with clear guidelines of how to understand the patient and to effectively intervene.

SEVERITY OF FUNCTIONAL IMPAIRMENT AS AN ORGANIZING PRINCIPLE

According to *DSM-5*, a PD is most fundamentally composed of moderate or greater impairment in personality functioning. This is understood in terms of self-functioning (characterized by identity or self-directedness) and interpersonal functioning (characterized by empathy or intimacy). A *DSM-5* PD is also composed of one or more pathological personality traits and impairments that are relatively inflexible and pervasive across a broad range of personal and social situations (p. 761). *ICD-11* offers a similar description of PD:

> Personality disorder is characterised by problems in functioning of aspects of the self (e.g., identity, self-worth, accuracy of self-view, self-direction), and/or interpersonal dysfunction (e.g., ability to develop and maintain close and mutually satisfying relationships, ability to understand others' perspectives and to manage conflict in relationships) that have persisted over an extended period of time (e.g., 2 years or more). The disturbance is manifest in patterns of cognition, emotional experience, emotional expression, and behaviour that are maladaptive (e.g., inflexible or poorly regulated) and is manifest across a range of personal and social situations (i.e., is not limited to specific relationships or social roles). (https://icd. who.int/browse11/l-m/en#/http%3a%2f%2fid.who.int%2ficd%2fentity% 2f941859884)

It goes on to add the following:

> Trait domain qualifiers may be applied to Personality Disorders or Personality Difficulty to describe the characteristics of the individual's personality that are most prominent and that contribute to personality disturbance. . . . Trait domains are not diagnostic categories, but rather represent a set of dimensions that correspond to the underlying structure of personality. As many trait domain qualifiers may be applied as necessary to describe personality functioning. Individuals with more severe personality disturbance tend to have a greater number of prominent trait domains. (https://icd.who.int/browse11/l-m/en#/http%3a%2f%2fid. who.int%2ficd%2fentity%2f1128733473)

Notably in both models, the central features of PD are problems in how the self is experienced and how others are experienced and related to. Traits are available for descriptive purposes, though they are required for a diagnosis to be assigned per *DSM-5* guidelines. Both manuals articulate that there are levels of severity (*ICD-11*) or personality functioning (*DSM-5*) that need to be assessed.

Both manuals offer descriptions of what impairment looks like, with the explicit understanding that more severe personality pathology is related to greater problems in functioning. In *DSM-5*, a PD is diagnosed only when the patient has a moderate level of severity in functioning, while in *ICD-11*, the threshold is for a mild level of impairment. As Bach and Mulder describe in Chapter 2 earlier in this volume, the following comparisons can be made for minimum diagnostic thresholds across manuals:

ICD-11	*DSM-5*
Mild	Moderate
Moderate	Severe
Severe	Extreme

Such ideas about PD and functioning are not novel to these manuals. Psychoanalytic and psychodynamic frameworks have considered personality functioning in the context of object relations and other dimensions of personality (described later). Functioning is also assessed on a continuum that ranges as follows: normal—neurotic—high borderline—middle borderline—low borderline (e.g., Caligor et al., 2018), with some even considering a psychotic level of personality organization, such as in the *Psychodynamic Diagnostic Manual, Second Edition* (*PDM-2*; Lingiardi & McWilliams, 2017). According to Caligor et al. (2018), these levels of functioning are assessed across the domains of personality rigidity, identity, object relations, predominant defensive style, moral functioning, and reality testing.

Similarly, in *PDM-2*, 12 dimensions of functioning are assessed for personality organization and functioning, including capacities for regulation, attention, and learning; affective range; mentalization and reflective functioning; identity differentiation and integration; relationships and intimacy; self-esteem regulation and quality of internal experience; impulse control and regulation; defensive functioning; adaptation, resiliency, and strength; self-observation; use of internal standards and ideas; and meaning and purpose.

These ideas are not just found in psychoanalytic or psychodynamic models. For instance, in understanding personality pathology and treatment, Livesley and Larstone (2018) described the personality system, which is composed of four subsystems: self, interpersonal, regulatory and modulatory, and traits. They added that "at the highest level of description, PD is probably best characterized as a disorganization and lack of coherence in the personality system" (p. 649) and that functional impairment can occur in all but the trait subsystem, as "dysfunctional traits are largely manifested through the other domains" (p. 650). As more difficulty is observed throughout and across these domains, the individual is likely to develop more serious problems and struggle with solid adaptation to life's stressors. It should be noted, however, that these ideas differ somewhat from what is articulated in *DSM-5* and *ICD-11*, in that the traits being assessed are considered dysfunctional or pathological in and of themselves.

Because the concept of severity of personality problems has been a component in a number of systems of conceptualization and treatment, some clinicians may find the assessment of severity per *DSM-5* or *ICD-11* guidelines to be relatively straightforward. For others, however, these concepts might be novel and require some basic training. Fortunately, studies of clinical usability have been promising, including high reliability being established in novice raters, including young adults who have not been formally trained in psychiatric diagnosis (Zimmermann et al., 2014, 2019; see also Bach & Mulder, Chapter 8, this volume). Regardless of experience, in order to effectively treat PDs and personality pathology, it is critical that clinicians become familiar with how to differentiate patients by severity in order to effectively treat them.

TREATMENT GUIDELINES BASED ON LEVEL OF SEVERITY

Based on an assessment of severity with guidelines related to self- and interpersonal relationships, how might a clinician engage in treatment with such patients—and how might treatment be expected to proceed? I put forth several ideas and offer clinically relevant case examples. In doing so, I provide some descriptions of where previous categorical PDs might be placed, drawing frequently upon the ideas of Kernberg and his research team (Caligor et al., 2007, 2018). Arguably, these categorical labels might fall in other levels of functioning, something that McWilliams (2011) has suggested within the psychoanalytic framework. Additionally, as noted earlier, in *DSM-5*, a PD may only be diagnosed for patients with a moderate level of severity, while *ICD-11* allows for a diagnosis with mild levels of severity. Despite differing adjectives, both levels are comparable across manuals. Nevertheless, the reader should understand that these placements are not hard and fast within the newer systems but are offered only to assist the reader in thinking about previous categorical models within the new system.

Extreme (*DSM-5*)/Severe (*ICD-11*)

For those who have extreme levels of personality functioning impairment (*DSM-5*) or Severe PD (*ICD-11*), it is anticipated that clinicians will be hearing frequently about the disappointing, frightening, and enraging ways in which others affect the patient, or the frightening or troubling ways in which the patient interacts with others. Alternatively, others may be kept at arm's length, and the idea of becoming emotionally vulnerable to another person will be objectionable or of no interest. For other patients at the severe level, interpersonal relationships will be necessary in order for the patient to remain emotionally stable and functioning throughout the day. There will be little tolerance for frustration, and therapists will likely find these patients needing much from them or disengaging over most topics the therapists bring up. Depending upon the constellation of traits, the patient might be highly suspicious and withdraw from the therapist or else might become clinging, anxious, and entitled toward having the therapist's time and attention. Consequently, the therapist might find it difficult to establish a relationship in which the patient feels comfortable to speak openly with them, or the patient might treat the therapist as someone on whom they might "dump" all of the negative ideas, feelings, and frustrations that are inside of them. Patients at this level very often engage in self-destructive or other-destructive activities; it is not uncommon to see serious substance abuse, illegal activities, or engagement in behaviors that put themselves and/or others in jeopardy. Those with more psychopathic qualities take sadistic pleasure in hurting or manipulating others to get what they want. In contrast, those with serious deficits in intimacy and ability to relate to others might live in utter isolation and be very scared by those who show kindness or understanding, thus leading to drinking excessively on a daily basis—to the point of passing out several days per week.

Within a categorical framework, patients with Antisocial (or Psychopathic) personalities; certain manifestations of Borderline personality; and Paranoid, Schizoid, and Schizotypal personalities fall within this framework (Caligor et al., 2007). At the time the multiaxial system was developed in the *DSM* system, most of the severe PDs were represented by Cluster A (odd or eccentric types), with a strong association to psychotic and schizophrenia-spectrum disorders (Lenzenweger, 2015), with Antisocial (or Psychopathic) and Borderline being the exceptions. Cluster A and Antisocial patients rarely seek treatment; when they do, they often are extremely difficult. Therapists may feel intense anger or fear at their proclivity for aggression or their odd manner of speaking and may find themselves anxious when speaking with these patients, perhaps altering their own manner of communication to assuage the patient or to make sure the anger intensity does not become too extreme. Gabbard (2005) recommended that treatment for Antisocial personalities be very limited, given their inability to form an alliance with the therapist and their tendency to devalue or manipulate the therapist. McWilliams (2011) described her own experience of being deceived by one Antisocial patient with whom she thought an alliance had been formulated, only to find herself let down later. Those with paranoid or schizotypal features will present with hyper-scrutinized beliefs that resist logic and reason. The alliance will always be in jeopardy, as these patients will be highly reluctant to engage with the therapist and will be prone to suspecting the therapist will be unhelpful or even hurtful. Schizoid patients are rarely seen in therapy, and when they do come in, they might find the intensity of sitting in the room with a therapist to be too much. Consequently, they might shut down or require very careful support. One student therapist I supervised saw a patient who had to wear a hat pulled down to cover most of the top half of his face and who requested that the lights in the room be kept off. Only after a year in treatment did both the hat go away and the lights become allowed on.

Consider the case example of Ms. J, who was a 25-year-old Hispanic woman seeking treatment for borderline PD after having two previous hospitalizations for suicidal ideation and two failed attempts at dialectical behavior therapy (DBT; Linehan, 1993). She thought her treatments were not helpful, stating that she was rarely understood and was given techniques to use that did not work. She also found herself having repeated suicidal impulses and ideas, stating that she would sometimes go to her closet and get a rope, thinking about how to hang herself. On one occasion, she reported to the therapist that she put the rope around her neck and felt the tension for 10 minutes. Upon engaging with Ms. J, the therapist saw her to be highly suspicious of the therapist's activities but also desperately wanting help. Ms. J found empathic listening to be helpful, though she continued to present with suicidal ideation near the end of each session. Whenever hospitalization was presented, she balked and would eventually relinquish to self-care, only to sometimes state that between sessions, she had again thought about ways to kill herself (but without taking any steps toward acting on these thoughts).

As treatment progressed, the therapist recognized that Ms. J's identity was fused with that of her mother. Though not psychotic, Ms. J took on the belief system of her mother, who mistrusted health care professionals and American culture in general. Ms. J was more acculturated, though, and was able to adopt a lifestyle that did not cause the same anxiety as that of her mother; however, it was when Ms. J was distressed that she agreed with her mother's concerns and would treat the therapist with suspicion. Instead of being angry at her mother or her therapist, Ms. J found herself directing her anger toward herself, which intensified her suicidal ideation. She described herself as "empty," and indeed there were few qualities or interests that she could describe positively about herself. Additionally, her affect was chronically depressed—although it would change throughout the session, as she appreciated the validating and supportive comments of the therapist, who, too, observed the absence of Ms. J's identity and affirmed how hard it must be for Ms. J to know herself. Similarly, the therapist identified others as possessing considerable influence in Ms. J's life. Despite frustration with her mother, Ms. J became despondent after her mother left town for several weeks. Ms. J came to recognize her dependency on her mother for emotional support, even though she often hid from her mother and found times spent together to be almost unbearable due to her mother's dominating ideas and opinions about Ms. J's life.

Based upon this history, according to the definition provided in Table 6.1, Ms. J has an extreme level of impaired personality functioning and would be given a rating of 4 (*Extreme Impairment*) on the Levels of Personality Functioning Scale described in *DSM-5*. She also meets the *ICD-11* criteria for Severe PD. Ms. J possesses the traits of emotional lability, anxiousness, separation insecurity, depressivity, withdrawal, intimacy avoidance, suspiciousness, manipulativeness, and attention seeking. Treatment proceeded by way of first increasing Ms. J's separation and individuation from her mother, with the therapist emphasizing the patient's ideas, affects, goals, and wishes. The therapist often had to question Ms. J and even shared his own experience of how much he had to question her in order to enhance her self-awareness. Over time, Ms. J began to more spontaneously report her own ideas and feelings and eventually was able to move away from her mother. Ms. J found herself relying on the therapist less, though still contacting him periodically when feeling abandoned or separated from someone who cared for her. Ms. J's suicidal ideation decreased—and whenever it returned, she was able to recognize quickly how it was a manifestation of her anger at feeling alone or being frustrated with someone.

TABLE 6.1 *ICD-11* **Classification of PD Severity**

PD severity	PD description
Mild[a]	Disturbances affect some areas of personality functioning but not others (e.g., problems with self-direction in the absence of problems with stability and coherence of identity or self-worth) and may not be apparent in some contexts. There are problems in many interpersonal relationships and/or in performance of expected occupational and social roles, but some relationships are maintained and/or some roles are carried out. Specific manifestations of personality disturbances are generally of mild severity. Mild PD is typically not associated with substantial harm to self or others but may be associated with substantial distress or with impairment in personal, family, social, educational, occupational, or other important areas of functioning that is either limited to circumscribed areas (e.g., romantic relationships, employment) or present in more areas but milder.
Moderate	Disturbances affect multiple areas of personality functioning (e.g., identity or sense of self, ability to form intimate relationships, ability to control impulses and modulate behavior). However, some areas of personality functioning may be relatively less affected. There are marked problems in most interpersonal relationships, and the performance of most expected social and occupational roles are compromised to some degree. Relationships are likely to be characterized by conflict, avoidance, withdrawal, or extreme dependency (e.g., few friendships maintained, persistent conflict in work relationships and consequent occupational problems, romantic relationships characterized by serious disruption or inappropriate submissiveness). Specific manifestations of personality disturbance are generally of moderate severity. Moderate PD is sometimes associated with harm to self or others and is associated with marked impairment in personal, family, social, educational, occupational, or other important areas of functioning, although functioning in circumscribed areas may be maintained.
Severe	There are severe disturbances in functioning of the self (e.g., sense of self may be so unstable that individuals report not having a sense of who they are or so rigid that they refuse to participate in any but an extremely narrow range of situations, self-view may be characterized by self-contempt or be grandiose or highly eccentric). Problems in interpersonal functioning seriously affect virtually all relationships, and the ability and willingness to perform expected social and occupational roles is absent or severely compromised. Specific manifestations of personality disturbance are severe and affect most, if not all, areas of personality functioning. Severe PD is often associated with harm to self or others and is associated with severe impairment in all or nearly all areas of life, including personal, family, social, educational, occupational, and other important areas of functioning.

Note. ICD-11 = *International Statistical Classification of Diseases and Related Health Problems* (11th ed.); PD = personality disorder. From *International Statistical Classification of Diseases and Related Health Problems* (11th ed.), by the World Health Organization, 2019 (https://icd.who.int/). CC BY-ND 3.0 IGO.
[a]Minimum threshold for a PD diagnosis.

Severe (*DSM-5*)/Moderate (*ICD-11*)

For those with severe levels of functioning (*DSM-5*) or moderate severity (*ICD-11*), therapists should anticipate seeing patients who show marked discrepancies across all levels of personality functioning. These patients may appear to show some capacity of self-directedness and an ability to describe themselves—though such descriptions will change often or might be rather lean on content and experience. For instance, someone might describe herself as adventurous but then a few minutes later, in the same session, describe how she is very scared to try new things and likes predictability. Relationally, these patients often show interest in having intimate relationships and seem to have some ability to be empathic, though therapists might find some considerable deficits. For example, one patient who believes that he is a good spouse and partner will also believe that he must dominate and control his partner, out of fear for what that partner cannot do. He might expect sexual intimacy but remain oblivious to, or be unable to satisfy, the needs of his partner. Another patient might describe herself as being very "attuned" to what her children need yet dismiss them when they ask for some time to play together. That same patient might see herself as a loving wife who satisfies her husband every day but then devalues him as being unable to do anything helpful around the house. Certain traits may take on intense expressions, such as anhedonia, restricted affectivity, and suspiciousness, which lead the person to feel particularly limited in her ability to take decisive actions on moving her life forward or to trust the intentions of others in helping her. Alternatively, attention seeking, impulsivity, and callousness might lead the individual to act as the center of attention, which he must be in most situations in order for him to feel good about himself. By acting this way, that same person might dismiss the ideas of others and interrupt them, even when these other people are communicating something that has personal significance to him.

Within the traditional categorical framework, it has been suggested that Avoidant, Dependent, Histrionic, and Narcissistic personalities may be observed at this level (Caligor et al., 2007). Avoidant and Dependent personalities, though observed in Cluster C of the multiaxial *DSM* system, frequently experience considerable distress. Avoidant patients are withdrawn and desperately want connections to other people yet experience much emotional turmoil. One patient reported how lonely and depressed he could become; however, when a female acquaintance sent him a letter that had flowers on the stationery, he became anxious that she might be more romantically interested in him, causing great distress should he mention his interest in her and find, to his dismay, that he had misjudged her innocent expression. Bornstein (1995) described "active dependency" in patients with dependent personality disorder, who will go to great lengths to get support from others if a reliable other is not available. Though histrionic personality disorder is no longer within the *DSM* system, it was believed that these patients go to great lengths to get attention from others in ways that are overly dramatic and sexualized. Sadly, however, they are never able to maintain a long-term relationship, as they are unable to develop intimacy or engage with others in ways that are not entirely self-serving (Millon, 2011). Even with histrionic personality disorder's absence from the diagnostic system, clinicians might find a place for such patients within the trait structure, utilizing traits such as attention seeking, emotional lability, separation insecurity, and intimacy avoidance to describe them.

Narcissistic personalities frequently exist at this level, though it has been noted that their level of impairment can rise to the Extreme (*DSM-5*) or Severe (*ICD-11*) levels (Kernberg, 2009). Patients who present as more vulnerable (Ronningstam, 2020), having a more openly fragile self-esteem and a proclivity toward depression, are more likely to be seen as having a Moderate PD (*ICD-11*) or severe impairment in personality functioning (*DSM-5*), as their identity is frequently jeopardized by criticism, and their capacity for intimacy is threatened by their fears that others may judge them negatively. Patients with more grandiose presentations also present challenges for therapists, as these patients will frequently be comparing themselves to the therapists and others, looking for ways to demonstrate their strengths or accomplishments. Therapists might be put off by such presentations and find themselves needing to defend themselves or dreading their next meeting with the patient. Narcissistic patients are prone to using others for their own purposes, and therapists might find themselves feeling as though they are there solely to listen to the patients' comments.

A good description of severe (*DSM-5*) or moderate (*ICD-11*) PD is the case of Mr. E, who was a 30-year-old single White man seeking treatment for depression and general life unhappiness. He reported a breakup that occurred 2 years prior, from which he had not fully recovered (though he believed he had been depressed "on and off for years"). Relatively early in the treatment, the therapist identified the patient's relational pattern as being marked by having an idealized sense of self and devaluation of women; however, this pattern could quickly change when Mr. E felt threatened by another person's abilities or his own guilt, in which case he was more devalued and others were more competent or effective. When the therapist would offer an observation on this pattern, Mr. E would say, "That is really insightful," therein confirming the observation. Concomitantly, the therapist observed that Mr. E appeared to idealize the therapist and devalue himself, noting how Mr. E's inner world vacillated between idealization and devaluation. In fact, Mr. E would regularly compliment the therapist's accomplishments; yet, as the relationship unfolded, Mr. E wondered whether—and feared that—if he were to learn more about how psychotherapy worked, he might undermine the progress that was being made.

One time, after a brief romantic relationship did not end well, the patient smoked marijuana and contacted his former girlfriend. This led him to become very depressed, feeling suicidal, and then smoking even more marijuana and drinking too much alcohol. The therapist confronted Mr. E about the ways in which he was self-destructive. When presented with these issues, however, Mr. E avoided discussing his depression, though the therapist persisted. Mr. E believed he could never overcome his current state, which led to sadness as the session ended. While subsequent sessions would address these patterns, it was not at all uncommon for another problem to arise and be discussed.

Mr. E encountered a number of setbacks in his treatment. These included a job change that was very challenging (evoking feelings of inadequacy and envy of those who could work better than he could). This job change happened abruptly, after Mr. E recognized he would likely not get promoted, thus prompting him to leave the company in what amounted to a lateral move. His dog died also, which evoked a depressive episode and withdrawal for 10 days into a period of heavy alcohol consumption and pornography use. Though Mr. E was open to the therapist and entrusted deeply sensitive material to him, he could not sustain many other intimate relationships for more than a few weeks, and those relationships mostly centered on having brief sexual encounters. He reported concern for these women but quickly dismissed them upon consciously acknowledging his disgust with them (which was actually projected from his disgust with his own behavior).

Mr. E met criteria for a rating of 3 (Severe) on the *DSM-5* Levels of Personality Functioning Scale, as well as the criteria for Moderate PD per *ICD-11*. His trait mixture included emotional lability, anxiousness, hostility, depressivity, intimacy avoidance, manipulativeness, grandiosity, attention seeking, callousness, hostility, irresponsibility, impulsivity, and distractibility. Mr. E's treatment progressed slowly. His oscillation between grandiose and vulnerable states was indicative of a Narcissistic PD. Identification of these representations of himself and others was a frequent intervention the therapist made, and this led to Mr. E identifying early experiences with his father—who had left the family when Mr. E was in elementary school—in which he both idealized and devalued his father. His efforts to manage emotional pain and vulnerability relied on these psychological strategies, and considerable time and attention were needed to help Mr. E more fully acknowledge his distress and to abandon the idealized images of himself, his previous girlfriend, and the therapist. Medication was required in order to treat his ongoing depressive symptoms, though Mr. E was sporadic in taking this as prescribed.

Moderate (*DSM-5*)/Mild (*ICD-11*)

Patients with moderate levels of personality functioning (*DSM-5*) or a Mild PD (*ICD-11*) are often considered to be more easily treated than those with greater levels of difficulty. Clinicians are likely most at risk of missing the personality dynamics of these patients, whose ability to function is not as notably impaired or limited. These patients might be successful in their careers and have quality relationships with family and friends; however, there are problems in self and other functioning, as well as problematic trait manifestations, that might easily be missed with the symptoms being manifested from these constellations being the focus of attention. For instance, a depressive disorder might be incorrectly diagnosed in these patients, and the clinician without a personality focus might be interested only in reducing the symptoms. Biologically oriented psychiatry often is the first line of treatment, and medication might be helpful in a number of these patients' depressive or anxious symptoms. However, the patients will continue to remain dissatisfied with their lives and/or relationships. It is possible they seek out therapy at different points in their lives, with certain traits coming to the forefront on a regular basis: for example, rigid perfectionism. Without understanding the motivating forces for the perfectionism, as well as the ways in which self- and other functioning is regularly affected, treatment might provide some relief—although it is unlikely that the core reasons for such problems will ever be addressed.

Patients with Mild PD (*ICD-11*), or moderate impairment in levels of personality functioning (*DSM-5*), have traditionally been identified as having Depressive or Obsessive-Compulsive PDs (Caligor et al., 2007). Other personality styles are possible, however. These patients will have an established identity and sense of self-direction. While they might find themselves feeling depressed or anxious at times, their purpose and pathways in life are not too noticeably affected except when the depression or anxiety becomes more intense. These patients tend to have an interest in being with others and developing meaningful relationships; however, they might have trouble, at times, understanding others, because their own concerns overwhelm them. They also are likely to have intimate and fulfilling relationships, but the number of such relationships might be fewer than desired; or they might find themselves longing for greater closeness with others but might not know how to achieve it. As noted before, these patients regularly get diagnosed with depressive and anxiety disorders, which bring considerable distress in their lives. The depressive patient is likely to become more withdrawn or perhaps more perfectionistic, while the obsessive-compulsive patient might become more rigid in his or her expectations at work and/or at home.

A good example of a moderate impairment in levels of personality functioning (*DSM-5*) or Mild PD (*ICD-11*) is the case of Ms. W, a 36-year-old White woman who was a highly esteemed physician in her area of specialization. She sought treatment initially after becoming depressed in her previous position. Though she was highly regarded there, she disliked the office and some of the billing practices they utilized. In particular, she worried that billing codes were being misapplied, despite the fact that the level of activity she provided met the criteria for that given code. She also was expected to bill so many hours per month, which added to the pressure she felt. As therapy progressed, she revealed other ways in which she had high expectations of herself that were not being met, both as a professional and as a wife and mother. This led to periods of guilt and dysphoria, as she believed herself to be substandard in most areas of her life. Nonetheless, she described the bond with her children in ways that suggested they were closely attached to her and enjoyed a good relationship. Her marriage was good, though it was affected by her perfectionism. She often was tired and did not spend as much time with her husband as she wished, leading to intimacy problems between them. She also struggled to express her anger to her husband for not doing his fair share of chores around the house.

As treatment progressed, it became evident from her history that she had met the often reasonable expectations of her parents but had failed to be validated or recognized by them for this. She became more withdrawn throughout the middle and high school years, although she maintained a few close

146   *Steven K. Huprich*

friendships. While Ms. W was academically talented, her friends were not, which caused some tension between them and led her to feel like an outsider. Being studious, she excelled at the university level and then entered medical school, where she met her husband, who was studying in a graduate program at the same university. Throughout these times, she found her main support through him. During exams, she would become anxious and study "all the time," and when time came for the board exams, she found herself worrying about passing, despite having earned a well above average score. In the workplace, she could be direct and assertive, taking decisive measures as needed with both staff and patients. Internally, however, she felt inadequate at times, despite no evidence of actually exhibiting such inadequacy.

Ms. W met the *ICD-11* criteria for moderate impairment in levels of personality functioning and Mild PD. Her self-directedness and identity were well-established, but her strivings for perfectionism and her periodic lack of confidence threatened her self-esteem. She was empathic and could establish intimacy, though the latter suffered at times. Her *DSM-5* trait profile consisted of depressivity, anxiousness, withdrawal, and rigid perfectionism. Treatment focused on reducing her self-criticism and expectations of herself. She found it useful to contrast her sense of self at work—which was highly confident in many situations—to other times when her productivity was challenged or when she believed she was not being a good enough mother. This treatment technique led to the identification of those times when she was invalidated and in need of support and encouragement. She began a brief period of antidepressants early in treatment but later discontinued them and found herself functioning well without. Treatment proceeded well as she began recognizing her needs for validation and finding appropriate ways to have them met. Her self-directedness and agency improved, thus helping to further strengthen her identity and capacity for greater intimacy with others.

CLINICAL CONSIDERATIONS IN TREATING PERSONALITY PATHOLOGY

When treating patients with personality pathology, the clinician is well-advised to be familiar with a number of clinically relevant concepts and practices. Although PDs were once thought to be treatment resistant or almost too difficult to treat, recent advances have allowed clinicians to provide treatment that leads to meaningful change that enhances quality of life. Nonetheless, without knowledge of these relevant concepts and practices, the clinician is likely to struggle when treating these patients. Consequently, I provide an overview of these concepts and direct interested readers to receive additional training and supervision in order to maximize their skill sets and basic competencies with these patients. Furthermore, my aim in this section is not to speak to one particular PD category or construct in particular but instead to provide some guiding principles that are needed to maximize the therapeutic efforts across all patients.

Therapeutic Action

The sine qua non for any good therapeutic endeavor is the establishment of a solid therapeutic alliance with the patient. The alliance consists of a clear understanding of the nature of the relationship—that is, why the patient and therapist meet, what the purpose of the meeting is, what the parameters around which this work is established are, and what the anticipated outcome of the work is. The alliance instills within patients that their therapists are there to listen to and understand them, to accept their concerns without there needing to be any fear of criticism or negative judgments—and that a genuine and positive acceptance of the patient is part of the therapist's attitude toward the patient. Research has established that alliance helps predict outcome (Bender, 2005; Kramer et al., 2020; McMain et al., 2015) but does not guarantee it. With all the challenges that these patients bring to their understanding of themselves and others in the relationship, an accepting and caring attitude on the part of the therapist goes a long way when technique or words fail to effect therapeutic change.

Part of having effective therapeutic action is knowing what to listen for. Regardless of theoretical orientation or model, good therapy for patients with personality pathology always includes listening to the patient from multiple points of view. For instance, the patient may self-report in the session that he is angry with a spouse for not providing enough support. While this is an important clinical consideration to accept about the patient in his present situation, there is often more to why this affect produces such a significant reaction. These reactions often have other determinants. For instance, this concern might be a manifestation of how the patient is unkind and unloving toward himself; it might be an indictment of the therapist, displaced onto the spouse; it might be a learned pattern of responses to someone who fails to provide sensitive insight and specific types of validation and is not necessarily about the specific problem the patient experienced with the spouse; it might be a way of drawing attention to the self for other types of needs or concerns; or it might be a warning sign of more behavioral expressions of anger toward the spouse. The point is that what is driving this patient's concerns is often more than just what is on the surface. Self and other representations, and various personality traits, have origins that drive and guide behavior beyond what is present in the here and now. They often are the product of biological, temperamental, and early learned relational experiences that generate specific templates of ideas, affect, and behavior experiences (Kernberg, 2016; MacDonald et al., 2013; Panksepp et al., 2017). As such, the manifestations of the patient's personality are frequently multiply determined and must be appreciated this way.

Another component to effective therapeutic action is having an articulated approach on how to manage and work with the patient. Thus, training in one of the many psychotherapies for PDs (e.g., transference-focused, schema-focused, dialectical behavioral) can be considerably helpful in knowing how to direct the session and how to focus upon those things that are central to the patient's goals and development. Whether the patient is highly avoidant of affect or is highly impulsive, it can be very tempting for the therapist to act in ways that come from a place of reactivity to the behaviors and actions of the patient. This might send the therapist down a pathway that is not optimal, such as questioning the avoidant patient frequently or trying to win over their trust and liking by showing excessive empathy to their reluctance. Conversely, the therapist might find herself asking many questions when following the patient's discursive ideation, such that no clarity is gleaned from the patient about why it is that he suffers and what might be the cause. Stated differently, therapists must be able to (a) guide the session in ways that encourage the patient to be comfortable to speak freely but also (b) set parameters as needed on a patient who is unable to stay focused on the issues at hand.

Defensive Functioning

All people engage in adaptive mechanisms to prevent themselves from feeling, thinking, or experiencing things that are painful. With patients having personality pathology, these mechanisms are frequent and involve processes that are internal or external. For instance, from an external, or behavioral, perspective, it is easy to understand why an individual might avoid or leave situations that are upsetting or use drugs or alcohol to reduce the intensity of unwanted experiences. For others, excessive buying, gambling, or pornography become mechanisms by which an escape from pain is possible. For instance, one patient found himself becoming more and more distant from his wife, who was critical and emotionally uninterested in him. Upon switching jobs and finding himself working alone in an office suite most of the time, he found his time being spent looking at pornography. The specific scenes he viewed were of women being nurturing and loving toward men, often complimenting them for their strength and abilities. These were all qualities of the relationship with his wife that were missing. Upon learning of the motivation for his pornography use, he became kinder toward himself and found that he could think more constructively about his actions and how to move more purposefully and effectively toward getting his emotional needs met by his wife.

Defenses often involve actions or behaviors. Compulsive work might be a way in which the patient assures herself that she is qualified and capable to manage the position she has, or it might be a way by which she avoids having to face a child at home who has considerable psychological difficulties that evoke painful ideas about her ability to be a mother (such as might have been enacted by Ms. W). Nonsuicidal self-injury (NSSI) is another form of behavior that is meant to help a patient avoid or distract him- or herself from very painful emotion or affect.

Conversely, the absence of action or behavior is a defense as well. Missed appointments are common expressions of fear, anxiety, frustration, or anger toward the therapy or therapist. Failure to complete assigned homework from a DBT (Linehan, 1993) session, for instance, is another form of defense. Avoiding certain topics and/or switching topics (even to things that the patient says are "critical" or "more important") can be defensive. Therapists who work with personality pathology must be aware of how these actions or inactions manifest themselves in the treatment, as they are especially common in these patients.

Defenses are also commonly understood for the psychological processes that are enacted. Caligor et al. (2007) described mature, neurotic (repression-based), and image-distorting (splitting-based) defenses that tend to correspond with the level of severity of the patient's personality pathology, with more severe personality pathology utilizing more image-distorting defenses. Perry (1990) created the Defense Mechanism Rating Scale, a commonly used instrument that assesses seven levels of defense. Other commonly used defense mechanism scales and descriptions have been provided in *DSM-IV* (American Psychiatric Association, 1994), *DSM-IV-TR* (American Psychiatric Association, 2000), Vaillant (1992), and Cramer (2015), though other scales exist. Across systems, it is generally agreed that some defenses are healthier, while others move into the more pathological, including those that are psychotic. It should be noted that patients use a wide array of defenses and that many can be present at one time in a session.

Furthermore, these defenses might be intermixed and require "unpacking." For instance, Ms. J (described earlier) frequently presented with a denial of ideas or emotions, which was driven in part by the absence of a solidified sense of self. In some cases, these troubling emotions were related to ideas about her body image. As the therapist challenged and encouraged more expression of her ideas and affect, Ms. J would then project her negative feelings about herself onto the therapist, such that she believed the therapist would reject or find her feelings about her body image as irrelevant or silly. Across sessions, the patient would avoid the topic, particularly when it had been salient in the session before. However, throughout the subsequent session, the therapist would hear content related to the topic, about which he would inquire. The patient then acknowledged that she had thought about her body image between sessions, after beginning the session saying that she continued to feel "bad" and did not know where to begin—a common complaint that she would share. As these defenses became further understood and identified, the patient then would engage in intellectualization of her body image conflicts, thinking that they were important but should not consume her mental energy, as other topics were more important that day.

In one session, Ms. J was angry and dysphoric. After several sessions, the therapist learned that the patient had had a medical appointment the day earlier and was angry at what her physician had said to her regarding these issues related to her body. As the therapist learned more about these concerns and validated them as real and important, Ms. J began to speak more openly about them and share the distress she felt and how she was managing it. It was through this careful analysis of the patient's denial, followed by her projection, avoidance, and intellectualization, that the patient became more cognizant of her sense of self and corresponding body image. In doing so, Ms. J was able to hold ideas about herself as truly her own ideas, her own fears, and her own worries, as well as think about how to constructively manage these concerns without denial or substance abuse (something that happened periodically).

Unconscious and Implicit Motivation

Almost all patients enter therapy with some awareness that they do not know themselves well enough to solve some kind of problem they are experiencing. Some come into therapy thinking they need "tools" or "skills" to manage their problem, perhaps even having had some knowledge about DBT and it emphasis on skill acquisition and enhancing coping skills. Thus, a central component of all treatments involves helping patients have a new understanding or awareness of themselves in ways that they did not have previously. The extent to which this is the provision and acquisition of new knowledge, versus the degree to which the knowledge or information is already known and has an influence, is what differentiates a number of treatment approaches. DBT, for instance, focuses directly on instilling skills for affect and behavioral regulation, as well as on support seeking and alternate coping strategies besides self-injury or other impulsive actions. Integrated modular treatment (Livesley et al., 2015) also allows clinicians to strategically develop a treatment approach that can mix more relational-based and insight-oriented methods (which recognize that some unconscious information is able to be accessed within the mind) with skill acquisition that is specifically targeted toward the idiographic needs of the patient. Other methods, for instance, seek to bring greater insight and awareness of what is present within the mind but not yet readily known. These approaches happen with slightly differing frameworks, such as exploring what is enacted in the transference (Clarkin et al., 2018; Yeomans et al., 2002), bringing into awareness knowledge of one's mind and the ability to know and understand it as well as the minds of others (Bateman & Fonagy, 2004, 2010), and identifying and labeling core schemas that guide and shape individual and interpersonal functioning (Farrell et al., 2014; Young, 1994).

It is the identification of these underlying unconscious processes that becomes a key task throughout these psychotherapies, and failure to recognize these processes could lead to some treatment challenges, resistances, and complete breakdown of the therapeutic process. For instance, a young woman sought treatment for a history of extensive sexual trauma from a previous boyfriend. She seemed to have qualities of both an avoidant and dependent personality but also functioned at a level more consistent with a severe personality impairment (*DSM-5*) or Moderate PD (*ICD-11*). Her identity was fragmented in ways that did not allow her to know or access those parts of her mind that drew her to men who were unavailable or not helpful to her. She regularly struggled to describe her inner emotional states—though was very good at identifying the experiences of others, which made her effective at her work. Besides having dated the man who was abusive, she found herself currently in a relationship that was not optimal for her and quickly became part of the content of therapy process. In this case, her current boyfriend was described as outgoing, engaging, and adventure seeking, which was the opposite of herself.

The therapist learned that the abusive relationship happened shortly after the death of the patient's father, who had been a quiet and passive man. The boyfriend soon became sexually exploitative and forced sexual relations countless times throughout the relationship. He became physically abusive to the point that she feared for her life. Upon leaving the relationship after almost being killed by him, she found herself drawn to a man who was educated, professional, and kind. He, too, had experienced some trauma in his relationship history, and she found him to be empathic and one to whom she could be close. However, as time progressed, this man was not especially responsive to her emotional needs. She found him consumed by his own insecurities and eventually becoming unfaithful to their relationship.

Treatment allowed the patient to see that she was drawn to men who excited her, even though at the start of treatment she described both men as polar opposites of each other. She had enjoyed the initial attention from both and their early sexual relationships, but she soon found that their outgoing charm was a mask for vulnerability and more sadistic or neglectful desires toward her. Upon becoming more aware of the similarities between these two men and her attraction toward those whose charm was enticing but ultimately hurtful, she left the relationship and started to engage in more self-care, with less reliance and dependency on others to satisfy her needs.

Yet, as treatment progressed, the therapist found the patient withdrawing from an active, participatory stance to one that was more distant. He found her struggling with things to say, often sitting in long periods of silence. He would ask the patient specific questions at times, which allowed some material to come up—though only for one or two sessions. The therapist wondered about his role in her life—was he not exciting or stimulating enough? Was there sexual interest in him that she had not expressed? Did he seem too passive, too like her father? Did she fear loss of the therapist's support someday, much as she had lost her father? In actuality, the therapist knew that her father had his medical treatment stopped, but only later learned that she had actually been the one family member who agreed to take this action, as no one else in the family could make a decision. Consequently, the therapist thought more about guilt and the role it played—as well as perhaps some unconscious guilt she might have felt with other men, from whom she unconsciously sought punishment for her father's death.

Treatment ultimately came to an end, as the patient continued to struggle with what to say. She pleasantly tried to please the therapist by thinking of things to say, but she could not produce much. She decided to look for another therapist with a "different approach." In this case, the therapist was left wondering whether the patient's guilt about her father's death was too much to deal with. He continued to think about not being exciting or stimulating enough, like these other men, and wondered if her act of leaving was a way of punishing men who disappointed her. Though the patient's strong dependent and avoidant

Harm Management

If a therapist works with patients who have personality pathology, then that therapist must be prepared to be involved in managing potential harm patients bring to themselves or others. Suicide threats and attempts are common in those with personality pathology, with the risk of ideation and attempts being above what is commonly seen in clinical practice (Ansell et al., 2015). As Yeomans et al. (2002) wrote when discussing patients diagnosed with borderline PD, "it is important that therapists . . . accept the possibility that patients can kill themselves" (p. 92). NSSI (Andover & Gibb, 2010; Brown et al., 2002) is also one of the more common behaviors bringing harm to patients, sometimes causing damage which cannot be repaired (e.g., extensive scarring). However, drug and alcohol abuse are commonly observed (Grant et al., 2004; Trull et al., 2010), as is poor compliance with health care actions prescribed by primary care physicians (Sansone et al., 2011, 2015).

Specific treatments for PDs and pathology have clear directives for how to manage suicidality, which are addressed up front as part of the treatment. For instance, with regard to DBT, Linehan (1993, pp. 469–485) and colleagues (Linehan et al., 2012) discussed multiple steps on how to assess the degree of risk or lethality, understand the conditions leading up to the suicidal thinking, consider alternative responses, remove lethal items from the home, appreciate the negative effects of suicidal behavior, validate nonsuicidal behaviors and obtain a commitment from the patient not to act on their suicidal ideas, and validate the patient's pain. Between-session contact with the therapist is allowable under certain conditions, and skills to help with emotion and behavioral regulation are taught. By contrast, in transference-focused psychotherapy, Yeomans et al. (2002) wrote that

> while discussion of these feelings is welcome in the context of therapy, issues of suicidal intent or actions are not within the realm of psychotherapy but must be dealt with in the emergency services segment of the health care system . . . it can be argued that it is irresponsible for the therapist to pretend to provide a level of security and protection that is not realistically possible. (p. 91)

Yeomans et al. (2002) indicated that if a patient presents with clear intent to harm themselves, the therapist must take action to prevent harm; however, this can jeopardize the treatment continuing. In a similar vein, Linehan (1993) noted that after a suicide attempt, there is to be no contact between the patient and the therapist for 24 hours.

With regard to lethality, management becomes more challenging. The *Tarasoff* ruling (*Tarasoff v. Regents of the University of California et al.*, 1976) has mandated that mental health care providers must take reasonable efforts to inform unknowing parties about threats to their lives by the patient. This action is a clear violation of confidentiality and is likely to bring treatment to a close, particularly if the patient acts. It is recognized that patients with personality pathology do express lethality to therapists (Howard, 2015; Howard & Duggan, 2015). Furthermore, stalking, harassment, or threats of violence toward therapists are not that uncommon (Kivisto et al., 2015). Management of these situations is complex and beyond the scope of this chapter; however, therapists are advised to be aware that such problems can arise when working with patients with personality pathology and should consider actions and steps toward managing these patients while caring for themselves (an excellent resource for this can be found at https://www.kspope.com/stalking.php).

With regard to other issues of self-care, working with primary care physicians is highly recommended in order to understand the physical well-being of the patient. PD patients have significant health risks (Huprich, 2018), and one longitudinal study found patients with PDs to have a reduced life expectancy of 17.7 to 18.7 years (Fok et al., 2012). Clinicians who treat patients with personality pathology should expect some degree of physical impairment and problems in self-care, which very well could become a central issue in treatment. Similarly, alcohol and substance abuse regularly co-occur (Grant et al., 2004; Trull et al., 2010), and knowing guidelines and resources for dual diagnosis and treatment are critical when working with such patients.

Skill Acquisition

Many times in the course of treatment, patients with personality pathology seek to learn new ways of doing or saying things. For instance, a patient with narcissistic tendencies who has realized that he isolates people from his life because of his anger and perfectionism might ask the therapist about ways to communicate his concerns to individuals in ways that do not isolate them, or those who have avoidant personality traits might express a need for learning how to share their feelings toward others in ways that are clear and not so strongly influenced by anxiety. At a more extreme level, and what is written about the most, is how to help individuals develop affect and behavioral regulation strategies that are safer and less self-destructive. DBT (Linehan, 1993) has focused extensively on these skills, which have been extended to patients not diagnosed with a PD (see Nelson et al., Chapter 11, this volume). Livesley (2003) provided some behavioral guidance for suicidal crises, affective and impulsive dysregulation, and traumatic and dissociative behavior that is rooted in cognitive behavioral strategies, which have been extended more broadly into an integrated modular framework (Livesley et al., 2015).

It is difficult to imagine an ongoing and productive treatment for personality pathology in which some type of behavioral change or acquisition is not part of the treatment. Such work can be more directive, or in other cases more exploratory, as is found within insight-oriented approaches. For instance, through a collaborative process, the therapist could ask the patient to speculate what the patient might say and then consider what exactly it is that is to be communicated. Thus, for the narcissistic patient who can be angry or perfectionistic, an insight-oriented approach might ask the patient to consider what it is that he wants to communicate and what it is that must be heard in the mind of the other. However, it might be that such work may be futile unless the patient has developed enough of a capacity to recognize how his own needs and desires have been imposed upon others, thus generating a highly negative and aversive response. The patient would need to recognize what it is that the other person must feel and understand from his response that would allow the patient to do this work on his own. Those operating from a more directive approach might view direct instruction and guidance as having a more immediate effect on the patient's life at the moment and thus foster greater collaboration and participation. However, those opting for a more insight-oriented approach might have concerns about gratifying a man who has already been rather demanding, which would recreate, in some ways, the dynamics from which he suffers.

Countertransference

The use of countertransference in working with personality-disordered patients is critical for effective treatment. Kernberg (1975) wrote that countertransference is all of the therapist's emotional responses to the patient. These reactions are determined in at least four ways: (a) what transference the patient brings to the therapist, whether it be positive, negative, or neutral; (b) what life situation the patient experiences; (c) the therapist's transference to the patient; and (d) what life situation the therapist brings into the session with the patient (Caligor et al., 2007). Typically, the third component is what is understood as countertransference, though this is an incomplete picture. Utilizing countertransference can inform the therapist of the inner world of the patient. For instance, if the therapist feels mentally fatigued listening to the same content repeated over and over by a patient with an obsessive personality, the therapist might understand that the patient feels stuck and annoyed with being unable to solve his problem. In this situation, the therapist is experiencing a concordant countertransference, in that she is experiencing the same inner emotions as the patient. Alternatively, the therapist might find herself feeling angry at these obsessive ideas, which could be a manifestation of the patient's concerns that the therapist, and most likely an earlier parental figure, is not able to help him with problems he keeps mentioning. In this case, the countertransference is complementary. Countertransference reactions form the basis of empathy but also allow for the identification of unconscious material of which the patient may not be aware (Racker, 1968). However, sharing such material with the patient must be done with care and sensitivity. For instance, a patient who has a paranoid personality might be highly attuned to the subtlest reactivity by the therapist. In this case, acknowledging any feelings openly is important to affirm to the patient his subjective experience but also then utilize this as a means of understanding the fears and anxieties the patient has about the therapist (and others). Alternatively, a patient with a borderline personality might be highly fragile to the slightest hint of rejection or disappointment. Instead of acknowledging her disappointment with what the patient is saying, the therapist could use such feelings to explore whether the patient is feeling disappointed in some way or concerned about rejection. In both cases, countertransference is being used, but its expression is managed quite differently.

Many patients leave treatment because certain feelings they are experiencing have not been discussed or they believe the therapist is uninterested or annoyed with them. I have had patients share with me that their therapist "fired" them, as they were not making progress or complying. Clearly, there are times when a treatment must be ended by the therapist, such as when the patient is unable to resolve sexual feelings toward the therapist or starkly rejects the treatment frame or requirements. However, therapists who are not comfortable or familiar with working with countertransference would be well-advised to seek supervision and/or training in this content so to better understand the internal worlds of their patients and how those worlds are manifested.

CLOSING COMMENTS

The assessment and diagnosis of personality pathology is receiving a significant face-lift, one that has been needed for some time given all the limits of the categorical system. The dimensionalization of personality pathology allows one to identify patients based upon a level of severity in both *DSM-5* and *ICD-11*. Furthermore, patients are to be evaluated along five broad trait dimensions in each manual and can be further described more specifically with a constellation of 25 traits within *DSM-5*.

In this chapter, I have attempted to demonstrate how patients can be placed into this dimensionalized framework, along with showing how trait labels enhance one's description and working knowledge of the patient. I also have made brief comments about clinically relevant ideas that enhance the quality of treatment and are relevant regardless of the type of treatment approach being utilized. The treatment of specific trait constellations will likely take on more life in the future. However, some discussion of how to do this has already been published (Hopwood et al., 2019; see also Mulder & Bach, Chapter 8, this volume). Time and clinical use will demonstrate the clinical utility of these new frameworks.

REFERENCES

American Psychiatric Association. (1994). *Diagnostic and statistical manual of mental disorders* (4th ed.).

American Psychiatric Association. (2000). *Diagnostic and statistical manual of mental disorders* (4th ed., text rev.).

American Psychiatric Association. (2013). *Diagnostic and statistical manual of mental disorders* (5th ed.). https://doi.org/10.1176/appi.books.9780890425596

Andover, M. S., & Gibb, B. E. (2010). Non-suicidal self-injury, attempted suicide, and suicidal intent among psychiatric inpatients. *Psychiatry Research, 178*(1), 101–105. https://doi.org/10.1016/j.psychres.2010.03.019

Ansell, E. B., Wright, A. G. C., Markowitz, J. C., Sanislow, C. A., Hopwood, C. J., Zanarini, M. C., Yen, S., Pinto, A., McGlashan, T. H., & Grilo, C. M. (2015). Personality disorder risk factors for suicide attempts over 10 years of follow-up. *Personality Disorders: Theory, Research, and Treatment, 6*(2), 161–167. https://doi.org/10.1037/per0000089

Bateman, A., & Fonagy, P. (2004). *Psychotherapy for borderline personality disorder: Mentalization-based treatment.* Oxford University Press. https://doi.org/10.1093/med:psych/9780198527664.001.0001

Bateman, A., & Fonagy, P. (2010). Mentalization based treatment for borderline personality disorder. *World Psychiatry, 9*(1), 11–15. https://doi.org/10.1002/j.2051-5545.2010.tb00255.x

Bender, D. S. (2005). The therapeutic alliance in the treatment of personality disorders. *Journal of Psychiatric Practice, 11*(2), 73–87. https://doi.org/10.1097/00131746-200503000-00002

Bornstein, R. F. (1995). Active dependency. *The Journal of Nervous and Mental Disease, 183*(2), 64–77. https://doi.org/10.1097/00005053-199502000-00002

Brown, M. Z., Comtois, K. A., & Linehan, M. M. (2002). Reasons for suicide attempts and nonsuicidal self-injury in women with borderline personality disorder. *Journal of Abnormal Psychology, 111*(1), 198–202. https://doi.org/10.1037/0021-843X.111.1.198

Caligor, E., Kernberg, O. F., & Clarkin, J. F. (2007). *Handbook of dynamic psychotherapy for higher level personality pathology.* American Psychiatric Publishing.

Caligor, E., Kernberg, O. F., Clarkin, J. F., & Yeomans, F. E. (2018). *Psychodynamic therapy for personality pathology: Treating self and interpersonal functioning.* American Psychiatric Association Publishing.

Clarkin, J. F., Cain, N., Lenzenweger, M. F., & Levy, K. N. (2018). Transference-focused psychotherapy. In W. J. Livesley & R. Larstone (Eds.), *Handbook of personality disorders: Theory, research, and treatment* (pp. 571–585). Guilford Press.

Cramer, P. (2015). Defense mechanisms: 40 years of empirical research. *Journal of Personality Assessment, 97*(2), 114–122. https://doi.org/10.1080/00223891.2014.947997

Farrell, J. M., Reiss, N., & Shaw, I. A. (2014). *The schema therapy clinician's guide: A complete resource for building and delivering individual, group and integrated schema mode treatment programs.* John Wiley & Sons. https://doi.org/10.1002/9781118510018

Fok, M. L.-Y., Hayes, R. D., Chang, C.-K., Stewart, R., Callard, F. J., & Moran, P. (2012). Life expectancy at birth and all-cause mortality among people with personality disorder. *Journal of Psychosomatic Research, 73*(2), 104–107. https://doi.org/10.1016/j.jpsychores.2012.05.001

Gabbard, G. O. (2005). *Psychodynamic psychiatry in clinical practice* (4th ed.). American Psychiatric Publishing.

Grant, B. F., Hasin, D. S., Stinson, F. S., Dawson, D. A., Chou, S. P., Ruan, W. J., & Pickering, R. P. (2004). Prevalence, correlates, and disability of personality disorders in the United States: Results from the National Epidemiologic Survey on Alcohol and Related Conditions. *The Journal of Clinical Psychiatry, 65*(7), 948–958. https://doi.org/10.4088/JCP.v65n0711

Hopwood, C. J., Mulay, A. L., & Waugh, M. H. (Eds.). (2019). *The DSM-5 Alternative Model for Personality Disorders: Integrating multiple paradigms of personality assessment.* Routledge. https://doi.org/10.4324/9781315205076

Howard, R. (2015). Personality disorders and violence: What is the link? *Borderline Personality Disorder and Emotion Dysregulation, 2,* Article 12. https://doi.org/10.1186/s40479-015-0033-x

Howard, R. C., & Duggan, C. (2015). Personality disorders: Their relation to offending. In D. A. Crighton & G. J. Towl (Eds.), *Forensic psychology* (2nd ed., pp. 281–290). Wiley.

Huprich, S. K. (2018). Personality pathology in primary care: Ongoing needs for detection and intervention. *Journal of Clinical Psychology in Medical Settings, 25*(1), 43–54. https://doi.org/10.1007/s10880-017-9525-8

Kernberg, O. F. (1975). *Borderline conditions and pathological narcissism.* Jason Aronson.

Kernberg, O. F. (2009). Narcissistic personality disorders: Part 1 [Editorial]. *Psychiatric Annals, 39*(3), 105–107, 110, 164–166. https://doi.org/10.3928/00485713-20090301-04

Kernberg, O. F. (2016). What is personality? *Journal of Personality Disorders, 30*(2), 145–156. https://doi.org/10.1521/pedi.2106.30.2.145

Kivisto, A. J., Berman, A., Watson, M., Gruber, D., & Paul, H. (2015). North American psychologists' experiences of stalking, threatening, and harassing behavior: A survey of ABPP diplomates. *Professional Psychology: Research and Practice, 46*(4), 277–286. https://doi.org/10.1037/pro0000025

Kramer, U., Beuchat, H., Grandjean, L., & Pascual-Leone, A. (2020). How personality disorders change in psychotherapy: A concise review of process. *Current Psychiatry Reports, 22*(8), Article 41. https://doi.org/10.1007/s11920-020-01162-3

Lenzenweger, M. F. (2015). Schizotypic psychopathology: Theory, evidence, and future directions. In P. H. Blaney, T. Millon, & R. Krueger (Eds.), *Oxford textbook of psychopathology* (3rd ed., pp. 729–767). Oxford University Press.

Linehan, M. M. (1993). *Cognitive-behavioral treatment of borderline personality disorder.* Guilford Press.

Linehan, M. M., Comtois, K. A., & Ward-Ciesielski, E. F. (2012). Assessing and managing risk with suicidal individuals. *Cognitive and Behavioral Practice, 19*(2), 218–232. https://doi.org/10.1016/j.cbpra.2010.11.008

Lingiardi, V., & McWilliams, N. (Eds.). (2017). *Psychodynamic diagnostic manual: PDM-2* (2nd ed.). Guilford Press.

Livesley, W. J. (2003). *Practical management of personality disorder.* Guilford Press.

Livesley, W. J., Dimaggio, G., & Clarkin, J. F. (2015). *Integrated treatment for personality disorder: A modular approach.* Guilford Press.

Livesley, W. J., & Larstone, R. (Eds.). (2018). *Handbook of personality disorders: Theory, research, and treatment* (2nd ed.). Guilford Press.

MacDonald, K., Berlow, R., & Thomas, M. L. (2013). Attachment, affective temperament, and personality disorders: A study of their relationships in psychiatric outpatients. *Journal of Affective Disorders, 151*(3), 932–941. https://doi.org/10.1016/j.jad.2013.07.040

McMain, S. F., Boritz, T. Z., & Leybman, M. J. (2015). Common strategies for cultivating a positive therapy relationship in the treatment of borderline personality disorder. *Journal of Psychotherapy Integration, 25*(1), 20–29. https://doi.org/10.1037/a0038768

McWilliams, N. (2011). *Psychoanalytic diagnosis: Understanding personality structure in the clinical process* (2nd ed.). Guilford Press.

Millon, T. (2011). *Disorders of personality: Introducing a* DSM/ICD *spectrum from normal to abnormal* (3rd ed.). Wiley. https://doi.org/10.1002/9781118099254

Panksepp, J., Lane, R. D., Solms, M., & Smith, R. (2017). Reconciling cognitive and affective neuroscience perspectives on the brain basis of emotional experience. *Neuroscience & Biobehavioral Reviews, 76*(Part B), 187–215.

Perry, J. C. (1990). *The Defense Mechanism Rating Scales manual* (5th ed.).

Racker, H. (1968). *Transference and countertransference.* International Universities Press.

Ronningstam, E. (2020). Internal processing in patients with pathological narcissism or narcissistic personality disorder: Implications for alliance building and therapeutic strategies. *Journal of Personality Disorders, 34*(Suppl.), 80–103. https://doi.org/10.1521/pedi.2020.34.supp.80

Sansone, R. A., Bohinc, R. J., & Wiederman, M. W. (2015). Borderline personality symptomatology and compliance with general health care among internal medicine outpatients. *International Journal of Psychiatry in Clinical Practice, 19*(2), 132–136. https://doi.org/10.3109/13651501.2014.988269

Sansone, R. A., Farukhi, S., & Wiederman, M. W. (2011). Utilization of primary care physicians in borderline personality. *General Hospital Psychiatry, 33*(4), 343–346. https://doi.org/10.1016/j.genhosppsych.2011.04.006

Tarasoff v. Regents of the University of California et al., 551 P.2d 334 (Cal. S. Ct. 1976).

Trull, T. J., Jahng, S., Tomko, R. L., Wood, P. K., & Sher, K. J. (2010). Revised NESARC personality disorder diagnoses: Gender, prevalence, and comorbidity with substance dependence disorders. *Journal of Personality Disorders, 24*(4), 412–426. https://doi.org/10.1521/pedi.2010.24.4.412

Vaillant, G. E. (1992). *Ego mechanisms of defense: A guide for clinicians and researchers.* American Psychiatric Press.

World Health Organization. (2019). *International statistical classification of diseases and related health problems* (11th ed.). https://icd.who.int/

Yeomans, F. E., Clarkin, J. F., & Kernberg, O. F. (2002). *A primer of transference-focused psychotherapy for the borderline patient.* Jason Aronson.

Young, J. E. (1994). *Cognitive therapy for personality disorders: A schema-focused approach* (2nd ed.). Professional Resource Exchange.

Zimmermann, J., Benecke, C., Bender, D. S., Skodol, A. E., Schauenburg, H., Cierpka, M., & Leising, D. (2014). Assessing *DSM-5* level of personality functioning from video-taped clinical interviews: A pilot study with untrained and clinically inexperienced students. *Journal of Personality Assessment, 96*(4), 397–409. https://doi.org/10.1080/00223891.2013.852563

Zimmermann, J., Kerber, A., Rek, K., Hopwood, C. J., & Krueger, R. F. (2019). A brief but comprehensive review of research on the alternative *DSM-5* model for personality disorders. *Current Psychiatry Reports, 21*(9), Article 92. https://doi.org/10.1007/s11920-019-1079-z

7

The Alternative *DSM* Model for Personality Disorders in Psychological Assessment and Treatment

Mark H. Waugh, Jeremy M. Ridenour, and Katie C. Lewis

Evaluating and treating personality disorder (PD) begins with an understanding of personality. However, since the third edition of the *Diagnostic and Statistical Manual of Mental Disorders* (*DSM-III*; American Psychiatric Association, 1980), the modern editions of the *DSM* have defined PD syndromes by a symptom criterion-count method rather than by explicit focus on personality functioning. In contrast, the Alternative *DSM-5* Model for Personality Disorders (AMPD; 5th ed.; *DSM-5*; American Psychiatric Association, 2013) organizes features of personality into a hybrid categorical-dimensional framework for PD diagnosis. With the emphasis on personality, the complementary lenses of different paradigms of personality theory and personality science become inherent in AMPD diagnosis. But, we ask, what is personality?

Theorists from Allport (1937) to Kernberg (2016) have viewed *personality* as a dynamic (nonstatic) synthesis of aptitude, belief, temperament and trait, and implicit habit of mind that participate in expressing core life themes associated with personal history. Genetics and constitutional givens, experience and history, and personal agency are woven into a sense of self and identity. The personologist Dan McAdams (1995) asked, "What do we know when we know a person?" (p. 365). For McAdams (2015), the answer is plural, as he relies on the metaphors of *actor*, *agent*, and *author* to define qualities needed to know a person; these include (a) observable actions reflecting temperament and trait, (b) characteristic adaptations expressing internalized patterns or schemas of agentic coping and adapting, and (c) guiding self-reflexive themes

---

https://doi.org/10.1037/0000310-008
Personality Disorders and Pathology: Integrating Clinical Assessment and Practice in the DSM-5 *and* ICD-11 *Era*, S. K. Huprich (Editor)
Copyright © 2022 by the American Psychological Association. All rights reserved.

of the individual life story. These are the types of information the clinician integrates in the quest to "know a person."

A psychiatric nosology balances scientific construct validity (e.g., reliability, predictive validity) with the pragmatic goals of clinical utility. *Clinical utility* refers to the ease of use, communication value, and ability to advance treatment (Mullins-Sweatt & Widiger, 2009). Some of these aims stand in inverse relation to one another. Blashfield and Draguns (1976) pointed out that as diagnostic reliability increases (contributing to construct validity), breadth of coverage (clinical utility) of the nosology decreases. Furthermore, investigator, practitioner, and consumer communities often value different interests and concerns. No psychiatric nosology can achieve all things at once, and the AMPD is no exception. Nonetheless, the AMPD explicitly accommodates multiple theoretical points of view (Waugh et al., 2017; see also Hopwood et al., 2019), may be evaluated with various assessment methods, supports case formulation and treatment planning (Bach et al., 2015; Weekers et al., 2020), is buttressed by a rapidly expanding research base (Krueger & Hobbs, 2020; Zimmermann et al., 2019), and possesses clinical utility (Milinkovic & Tiliopoulos, 2020; Morey et al., 2014).

This chapter provides an overview of the *DSM-5* AMPD. The emphasis is on clinical applications, including the AMPD's connections to major traditions of personality science and clinical theory as well as its advantages relative to traditional categorical (syndrome) PD diagnoses. We emphasize ways in which the AMPD contributes to psychodiagnostic formulation beyond traditional psychiatric diagnosis. Representative assessment instruments and methods for the AMPD are noted, along with the clinical training-related benefits and challenges of learning to use the AMPD. The clinical utility of the approach is illustrated in a multimethod assessment of a clinical case.

DIAGNOSIS WITH THE AMPD

The AMPD is found in the *DSM-5*, Section III, "Emerging Measures and Models" (American Psychiatric Association, 2013). Despite its placement in Section III, the AMPD is already being used in clinical practice. AMPD diagnosis can be coded for third-party reimbursement (and other data tracking) using the diagnosis of Other Specified Personality Disorder (301.89 [F60.89]). Then, specification is accomplished with the AMPD scheme (see Waugh et al., 2017).

Formally, the AMPD is a hybrid categorical-dimensional nosology. This means categorical diagnoses are defined by two conjoint dimensions. They are *Criterion A*, which indexes level of impairment in personality functioning, and *Criterion B*, which depicts a profile of maladaptive personality traits. An individual's placement on the Criteria A and B dimensions determines if one (or more) of the six defined hybrid categorical-dimensional PD diagnoses apply. These are Antisocial, Avoidant, Borderline, Narcissistic, Obsessive-Compulsive, and Schizotypal PD. The diagnosis of PD-trait specified (PD-TS) is used to characterize the specific pattern of impaired functioning and maladaptive traits if none of the six defined PDs is matched or if trait specification provides the most apt characterization. This obviates the need for a term such as "PD-not otherwise specified," which was commonly used in previous editions of the *DSM* when PD features did not clearly fit a diagnostic category. PD-TS can also be used when a person's Criterion B traits yield more than one of the six defined PD configurations; it is possible to diagnose, for example, Avoidant PD with traits of Separation Insecurity and Suspiciousness. Of note, Clark et al. (2015) empirically investigated different ways to specify AMPD diagnosis. They showed that the maladaptive traits along with Criterion A in PD-TS were sufficient, offered diagnostic coverage, and rendered irrelevant comorbidity and within-diagnostic group heterogeneity concerns. Clark et al. argued that the term "PD-TS," rather than any of the typological characterizations, provides conceptual clarity, parsimony, and clinical utility.

Criterion A, Level of Personality Functioning (LPF), is operationalized in the Level of Personality Functioning Scale (LPFS; American Psychiatric Association, 2013; Bender et al., 2011). This dimensional scale for disturbance in self and interpersonal functioning uses a 5-point metric with a rating from 0 (*little or no impairment*) to 4 (*extreme impairment*). A global LPFS rating of 2 (*moderate*) or above indicates presence of PD. The LPFS subsumes impairment in self-functioning, characterized by the domains of Identity (ID) and Self-Direction (SD), and impairment in interpersonal functioning as seen in the domains of Empathy (EM) and Intimacy (IN). Each LPFS domain is evaluated on the 0-to-4 scale, and diagnosis of PD requires any two of the four domains to be rated at or above the moderate level of impairment.

Criterion B evaluates degrees of expression of a suite of maladaptive personality traits. The maladaptive traits are grouped into the five domains of Negative Affectivity, Detachment, Antagonism, Disinhibition, and Psychoticism. These trait domains are further differentiated into 25 pathological personality trait facets (i.e., Anhedonia to Withdrawal). For Criterion B, the clinician systematically surveys each of the five broad trait domains in performing PD diagnostic evaluation. AMPD diagnosis may be depicted at the broad trait domain level (e.g., Negative Affectivity) or by narrower trait facets (e.g., Anxiousness, Separation Insecurity). Notably, the *DSM-5* AMPD does not formally codify a threshold for clinical significance in the dimensional trait or facet rating. Rather, the clinician is advised to evaluate elevations with respect to population norms from psychometric tests or to use clinical judgment. In practice, a 0-to-3 scale is often used quantify trait level. This convention derives from the Personality Inventory for *DSM-5* (PID-5; Krueger et al., 2012). The trait or facet ratings are performed with a scale as follows: 0 (*very false or often false*), 1 (*sometimes or somewhat false*), 2 (*sometimes or somewhat true*), and 3 (*very true or often true*). Clinical significance is defined by a rating of 2 or greater (Samuel et al., 2013) or by 1.5 or greater (Clark et al., 2015). Once one or more maladaptive traits have been identified as clinically significant, they are reviewed with respect to the hybrid categorical-dimensional PD algorithms, or they are used to characterize PD by the PD-TS diagnosis.

LEARNING THE AMPD

It is not difficult to learn and apply the AMPD. Research has demonstrated that graduate students (Garcia et al., 2018), clinicians (Dereboy et al., 2018; Morey, 2019a; Zimmermann et al., 2014), and lay raters (Morey, 2018) can assign AMPD diagnoses with generally adequate inter-rater reliability, and the level of agreement is equal and at times superior to that with traditional categorical PD diagnoses. Satisfactory LPFS and pathological trait inter-rater reliability has been found in studies, with the rating targets ranging across short clinical vignettes, structured interviews, unstructured clinical interviews, and integration of multiple sources of clinical information in case conference format (see Zimmermann et al., 2019, for a review). Structured interview methods generally support greater agreement than more unstructured approaches to AMPD diagnosis, however (e.g., Hutsebaut et al., 2017).

Some have questioned the complexity of the model, particularly for Criterion A (e.g., Few et al., 2013). The apparent complexity of the AMPD may be illusory because clinicians are tacitly familiar with many of its elements as the model is founded on major clinical traditions and contemporary personality science (Waugh et al., 2017). In this way, the AMPD enjoys an inherent intuitive comprehensibility if the perceptual set of the traditional *DSM* criterion-count approach to diagnosis is set aside. Of note, although the 668-word count for Criterion B (see *DSM-5*; American Psychiatric Association, 2013, Table 3, pp. 779–781) is one third shorter than the 1,041 words of Criterion A (see *DSM-5*; American Psychiatric Association, 2013, Table 2, pp. 775–778), their Flesch–Kincaide readability index values are both at the 12th-grade level (Flesch, 1948). Like learning any new approach, training and practice with the AMPD improves performance (Garcia et al., 2018).

A further advantage of the conceptually rich AMPD is that it encourages students and clinicians to focus on diagnostically pertinent psychological constructs reflected in clinical material in contrast to diagnosis by counting predefined criteria. The AMPD is a literal alternative to the descriptive checklists of the modern editions of the *DSM*, which have quested for diagnostic reliability (with mixed success; Markon, 2013) and potentially sacrificed validity (Vaillant, 1984). Because the criterion-count approach has become virtually doctrinaire, it has contributed to reification, narrowing pluralistic conceptions of psychopathology to the descriptive realm, and an eclipse of the subjectivity of persons (Andreasen, 2007; Hyman, 2010). While the AMPD is conceptually complex in its reckoning across descriptive, characteristic adaptation, and narrative constructs to make a PD diagnosis, this does not mean it is too complicated for clinical use (see Adler & Clark, 2019; Garcia et al., 2018; Morey et al., 2014).

Exhibit 7.1 contains a sample clinical vignette used for training student clinicians (Garcia et al., 2018) and in rater agreement studies (e.g., Hopwood & Waugh, 2019). The reader is invited to study the vignette and make 0-to-4 LPFS and 0-to-3 trait facet ratings. These ratings may then be compared with Table 7.1.

EXHIBIT 7.1

Case A

A 28-year-old, male European American patient presents for psychotherapy. He is soft-spoken with halting speech, and he has an athletic build but a pale, sensitive face. He reports mild somatic symptoms, including sweaty palms, a feeling of fullness in his stomach, constipation alternating with diarrhea, social isolation, loneliness, feelings of shame, and sensitivity to slights.

Fragile self-esteem is observed in initial interviews. Interpersonally, he can be arrogant but is also vulnerable to hurt and self-esteem injury. Historically, he is an only child of an executive father and an artistically inclined mother with whom he reports a close relationship. He reports a "happy childhood" and that he was "the apple of his parents' eye," but he says his parents fought a lot, and they split up in his youth. He did well in school and is currently a graduate student. At age 11, he was befriended by a male teacher with whom he maintained a close relationship for several years. This relationship included hugging and other expressions of physical intimacy with two instances of full sexual activity.

Currently, he resides with his mother; his father died 4 years ago. He has no relationships with women; he has one close friend, a man, who also is socially isolated. For recreation, he attends movies alone or with his mother and his male friend, and he enjoys reading. In initial psychotherapy sessions, he reacted to therapist interpretations angrily and dismissively. He also reacted to a therapist's absence with fleeting suicidal ideation, hypochondriacal symptoms, and mild depression. He attends sessions as scheduled and fully participates in therapy.

Table 7.1 depicts the mean ratings made by 25 clinicians (mean age, 48 years; mean years of clinical experience, 19), with, for Case A (see Exhibit 7.1), 52% of the raters identifying as clinicians and 48% as academics. The two-way random effects model of absolute agreement mean intraclass correlation coefficient (ICC [2,25]) was .97, indicating excellent agreement across the clinicians' 0-to-4 ratings for LPFS and 0-to-3 ratings for the pathological traits. This AMPD profile (see Figure 7.1) establishes presence of PD with a moderate impairment global LPFS (2.44) and reveals severe impairment on the LPFS domain of IN (3.04). Trait facet elevations (rounded to whole number 2 or above) were found for Anhedonia, Anxiousness, Depressivity, Emotional Lability, Grandiosity, Hostility, Intimacy Avoidance, Restricted Affectivity, Separation Insecurity, and Withdrawal. Thus, this individual was viewed as warranting a diagnosis of PD marked by deficits in Identity and Intimacy functioning and displaying maladaptive trait domain elevations in Negative Affectivity and Detachment. The prominent problems in Emotional Lability, Grandiosity, and Separation Insecurity along with Restricted Affectivity and pronounced Withdrawal and Intimacy Avoidance suggest the covert or depleted/vulnerable syndrome of narcissistic disorders (Cain et al., 2008).

This case example (see Exhibit 7.1) was abstracted from Kohut's (1979) "The Two Analyses of Mr. Z," which describes a patient undergoing an (incomplete) orthodox psychoanalysis followed by a self-psychology psychoanalysis that reportedly was more successful. Historians have concluded that Mr. Z was Heinz Kohut writing about his own experiences in psychoanalysis (Strozier, 2001).

TABLE 7.1. Hunter's Assessment Data

Scale	Scores for Hunter	Scores for comparison group
	Raw (*T*)	*M* (*SD*)
LPFS-SR total score	284.50 (54)	244.94 (73.42)[a]
Identity	102.50 (59)	81.39 (23.91)
Self-Direction	54.00 (49)	55.95 (20.13)
Empathy	54.00 (59)	41.05 (14.09)
Intimacy	75.00 (54)	66.92 (22.27)
PID-5-BF total	1.48 (56)	1.12 (0.65)[b]
Negative Affectivity	1.60 (48)	1.75 (0.67)
Detachment	1.00 (46)	1.28 (0.63)
Antagonism	1.80 (68)	0.56 (0.59)
Disinhibition	1.00 (50)	1.00 (0.63)
Psychoticism	2.00 (64)	1.02 (0.71)
SCORS-G subscales		
Complexity of Representation of People (COM)	3.20 (49)	3.23 (0.58)[c]
Affective Quality of Representations (AFF)	2.70 (35)	3.39 (0.47)
Emotional Investment in Relationships (EIR)	2.45 (41)	2.83 (0.43)
Emotional Investment in Values and Moral Standards (EIM)	3.75 (53)	3.65 (0.33)
Understanding of Social Causality (SC)	3.25 (50)	3.23 (0.56)
Experience and Management of Aggressive Impulses (AGG)	3.10 (33)	3.63 (0.31)
Self-Esteem (SE)	3.35 (36)	3.69 (0.25)
Identity and Coherence of Self (ICS)	4.40 (55)	4.18 (0.44)
IIP-SC octants		
PA (Domineering/Controlling)	80 *T*	
BC (Vindictive/Self-Centered)	64 *T*	
DE (Cold/Distant)	83 *T*	
ISC octants		
HI (Sensitivity to Passivity)	67 *T*	
JK (Sensitive to Dependence)	65 *T*	

Note. The octants (e.g., PA, BC, DE) proceed in a counterclockwise direction around the circumplex; they are defined by their angular location, ranging from 0 degrees to 360 degrees. *T* = *T* score; LPFS-SR = Level of Personality Functioning Scale–Self-Report (Morey, 2017): Item score range 1 (*totally false, not at all true*) to 4 (*very true*); PID-5-BF = Personality Inventory for *DSM-5*–Brief Form (Krueger et al., 2013): Item scores range from 0 (*Very False or Often False*) to 3 (*Very True or Often True*); SCORS-G = Social Cognition and Object Relations Scale-Global Rating Method (Stein & Slavin-Mulford, 2017): Subscale ratings range from 1 (*more pathological*) to 7 (*more adaptive*); IIP-SC = Inventory of Interpersonal Problems–Short Circumplex (Hopwood et al., 2008); ISC = Interpersonal Sensitivities Circumplex (Hopwood et al., 2011).
[a]*T* scores are based on Hopwood, Good, and Morey (2018). [b]*T* scores are based on Bach et al. (2016). [c]*T* scores are based on local norms for the residential treatment center (K. Lewis & J. Ridenour of the Austen Riggs Center, personal communication, April 9, 2021).

FIGURE 7.1. Clinician Ratings of Case A ("Mr. Z")

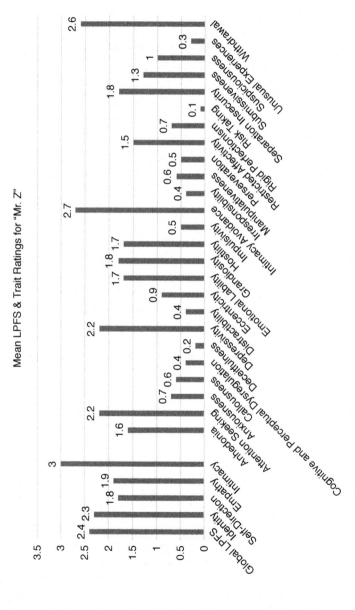

Note. LPFS = Level of Personality Functioning Scale (American Psychiatric Association, 2013; Bender et al., 2011): Rated on a 0-to-4 scale. Trait ratings are rated on a 0-to-3 scale.

DIMENSION AND PARADIGM IN AMPD DIAGNOSIS

The dimensionalization of Criterion A and Criterion B is an advance in PD nosology. The LPFS of Criterion A reflects closely related continua of severity of PD, impairment in functioning, and level of personality organization. These dimensions overlap but have different referents. *Severity* can be viewed as psychometric extremity benchmarked by the mean and/or median of a representative array of descriptive pathological trait ratings. *Impairment of functioning* refers to degrees of disturbance in symptoms (e.g., global assessment of functioning) or social and occupational impairment (e.g., Social and Occupational Functioning Scale [Goldman et al., 1992]). A third way of viewing the LPFS harkens to Kernberg's (1967) well-known *ordinal scaling* of personality organization into neurotic, borderline, and psychotic levels of personality organization. This is a theoretically substantive definition and is incorporated into the LPFS by way of its formulation from psychodynamic, interpersonal, and social-developmental personality theories and measures (Bender et al., 2011).

Criterion B resembles the familiar Big Five or five-factor model (FFM) prominent in contemporary multivariate personality trait research (Widiger & Costa, 2012). Accordingly, Criterion B trait domains and facets are schematized within the factor-analytic hierarchy of maladaptive personality traits. It should be emphasized that Criterion B does not assume factorial simple structure (i.e., absence of cross-loadings of variables on factors). Some Criterion B maladaptive personality traits are interstitial in that they cross-load on different constructs at the same level of the factor hierarchy (Krueger & Markon, 2014). For example, the trait facet Depressivity is a component of both Negative Affectivity and Detachment domains. Of note, some investigators have questioned the assignment of some facets within the current domain specification of Criterion B (Watters et al., 2019).

Criterion B is relatively more descriptive and less inferential than Criterion A, as demonstrated empirically by Mulay and colleagues (2018). Several Criterion B elements, such as Anhedonia and Disinhibition, for example, may map closely with psychobiological and neuroscience constructs (DeYoung, 2015). In this regard, Criterion B draws heavily on the dispositional trait constructs of McAdams and Pals (2006) and represents the general FFM psychometric trait tradition extended into personality psychopathology. Some traits, however, are subtended by various types of psychological and psychobiological constructs. For example, Separation Insecurity invokes developmental attachment psychology, psychodynamic and interpersonal theory, descriptive psychopathology, and cognitive behavior and schema conceptualizations.

There is built-in empirical overlap between measures of Criteria A and B, which is a source of controversy in the field. Some argue that AMPD elements should be respecified to reduce redundancy (e.g., McCabe et al., 2021; Williams et al., 2018). Others contend overlap is empirically unavoidable and that the existing specification has utility and adds conceptual heft (Meehan et al., 2019; Morey, 2019b). About these matters, the field will investigate and debate (see Garcia et al., 2021). For the present purposes, the important points are: (a) the

AMPD brings dimensionalization to diagnosis and (b) multiple paradigms of personality assessment and personality science are inherent within the scheme.

PSYCHODIAGNOSIS AND TREATMENT PLANNING

The AMPD contributes to clinical *psychodiagnosis* in addition to psychiatric diagnosis—that is, AMPD diagnosis is made by evaluating psychological constructs rather than symptom criterion counts. This goes beyond phenotypic symptom description and seeks inferential connections among symptoms; traits; vulnerabilities; adaptations; and situationally contingent patterns of thinking, responding, and relating. Empirical research on the AMPD has shown that the personological components of actor (traits), agent (characteristic adaptations), and author (narrative data) are represented in both Criterion A and B (Mulay et al., 2018). Capturing both the trait-descriptive and agentic aspects of PD functioning, Zimmermann et al. (2015) used the terms the "how" and the "what" of personality functioning, to characterize elements of the AMPD. In this view, Criterion A denotes the *how* and Criterion B the *what* of personality expression.

These ideas are illustrated in Ronningstam's (2014) discussion of the dynamic interplay of LPF (like LPFS) and diagnostic trait expression (like Criterion B). Maladaptive trait expression can be contingent on situational stresses interacting with level of LPF. For instance, a narcissistically vulnerable individual may behave one way when feeling secure, but maladaptive trait expression dramatically escalates when the self-system is challenged. Relatedly, Hopwood et al. (2011) showed that PD variance comprises dimensions of severity (LPF), statelike PD symptoms, and normative personality traits.

Understanding level of functioning (how) and specific patterns of maladaptive trait expression (what) has implications for psychiatric and psychotherapeutic treatment planning. Evaluation of LPF informs the clinician about needs for psychotherapeutic structure, external controls, and safeguarding of patient safety. As well, LPF speaks to the person's capacity for the self-reflection required in interpretive work (see Clarkin et al., 2015; Hopwood, 2018) and may also suggest need for psychopharmacological intervention (Silk, 2011). Criterion B describes stylistic patterns of maladaptive behavior. As such, evaluation of pathological personality traits can point to areas of vulnerability and guide the thematic focus of treatment. Certain problematic relationship patterns may be expressed in maladaptive personality trait functioning. For example, elevated Criterion B trait of Separation Insecurity speaks to issues of rejection sensitivity, and elevated Emotional Lability directs clinical attention to triggers of emotional dysregulation and the importance of more adaptive modes of coping with dysregulation. As Clarkin et al. (2020) pointed out, the traits per se may not be the target of treatment. Rather, becoming aware of, working through, and learning more adaptive responses to situations and triggers associated with maladaptive trait expression may be the treatment goal. Nonetheless, identification of personally salient maladaptive traits provides a map for psychotherapeutic focus.

The AMPD is ecumenical with regard to type of psychotherapy for PD. Empirically supported psychotherapies ranging from dialectical behavior therapy (Linehan, 2018) to mentalization-based treatment (MBT; Bateman & Fonagy, 2010), transference-focused psychotherapy (Clarkin et al., 2020), and schema therapy (Bach & Bernstein, 2019) are informed by evaluation of Criterion A and Criterion B. Criterion B concerns, such as Separation Insecurity or Grandiosity, can guide the therapist in developing treatment plans and strategy for these foci. The therapist alert to Criterion B themes can address the relevant cognitive-relational schema expressed in psychotherapeutic sessions. Being alert to momentary fluctuation in LPF within sessions orients the therapist to the need to adopt different therapeutic postures. For example, a dip in LPF may suggest the need to foster structure and slow the pace of exploration if a topic has become emotionally disorganizing.

ASSESSMENT METHODS

Numerous instruments and assessment approaches can inform AMPD diagnosis. Some instruments specifically are designed to assess the AMPD, whereas others evaluate related constructs and may be used to support diagnosis with the scheme. The assessment approaches span the multimethods of self-report, informant or observer report, interview methodologies, and performance-based assessment.

Self-Report

Self-report assessment of the AMPD began with the 220-item PID-5 (Krueger et al., 2012), designed to assess Criterion B traits. The PID-5 is generally regarded as a standard self-report benchmark and is also available in an intermediate length (100 items) short form (Maples et al., 2015), and a brief 25-item format, the PID-5–Brief form (PID-5-BF; Krueger et al., 2013). Importantly, other instruments demonstrate strong empirical correspondence with the PID-5. These include the Personality Psychopathology Five (Harkness et al., 1995) from the Minnesota Multiphasic Personality Inventory family of instruments (Anderson et al., 2013) and other broadband measures of maladaptive personality traits (Wright & Simms, 2014). Instruments not developed within the FFM tradition, such as the Personality Assessment Inventory (Morey, 2007), can also be used to predict PID-5 scores (Busch et al., 2017).

Recently, several self-report instruments for assessment of Criterion A have emerged. These include the 80-item Level of Personality Functioning Scale–Self Report (LPFS-SR; Morey, 2017); the 66-item *DSM-5* Levels of Personality Functioning Questionnaire (DLOPFQ; Huprich et al., 2018); the 24-item Self and Interpersonal Functioning Scale (Gamache et al., 2019); and the 12-item, brief self-report forms of the LPFS, the Level of Personality Functioning Scale–Brief Form (LPFS-BF; Hutsebaut et al., 2016; LPFS-BF-2.0; Weekers et al., 2020).

Waugh et al. (2020) analyzed the content characteristics of these and other self-report measures relevant to Criterion A (e.g., Inventory of Personality Organization [IPO; Lenzenweger et al., 2001], Severity Indices of Personality Problems [Verheul et al., 2008]). They found that although the contents were generally similar, they differed in relative coverage of component dimensions of the LPFS and severity of psychopathology reflected in items. For example, the item content of the IPO is generally more pathological than is the case with the LPFS-SR. Regarding the LPFS dimensions, the IPO and LPFS-BF capture more Identity content, and the DLOPFQ reflects relatively greater Empathy and Intimacy item content than the other instruments. This granular characterization of LPFS-related scales can aid the clinician and investigator in selecting instruments for particular purposes.

Informant Report

The PID-5 Informant Report Form (Markon et al., 2013) represents the most well-known informant report instrument for the AMPD. Investigators and clinicians generally have used clinician or observer ratings of the LPFS and of the Criterion B maladaptive traits as informant methods. This may be based on the *DSM-5* (American Psychiatric Association, 2013) text description or by less widely available formats, such as a rating scale from early work on the model (e.g., Personality Trait Rating Form; see Few et al., 2013) or the Clinician Rating Personality Disorder Level and Traits form (Waugh, 2014).

Interview Formats

Structured (e.g., First et al., 2017; Kampe et al., 2018) and semistructured (Hutsebaut et al., 2017) clinical interview formats are available for AMPD diagnosis, and practitioners may draw from free-form clinical interviews as well (Cruitt et al., 2019). In general, structured approaches show greater rater reliability than unstructured approaches (e.g., Buer Christensen et al., 2018), but the use of a formal structured interview is not always feasible in day-to-day practice. Structured clinical interviews developed by investigators to assess constructs kindred to Criterion A, for example, also are available and show close correspondence to the LPFS (Di Pierro et al., 2020).

Performance-Based Assessment

Performance-based assessment methods also inform AMPD diagnosis. The approach most closely resembling the AMPD may be the Social Cognition and Object Relations Scale-Global Rating Method (SCORS-G; Stein & Slavin-Mulford, 2017). With the SCORS-G, narrative data (e.g., early memories, Thematic Apperception Test [TAT] stories) and clinical observations can be rated on 8 dimensions. These dimensions include Complexity of Representation of People (COM), Affective Quality of Representations (AFF), Emotional Investment in Relationships (EIR), Emotional Investment in Values and Moral Standards (EIM), Understanding of Social Causality (SC), Experience and

Management of Aggressive Impulses (AGG), Self-Esteem (SE), and Identity and Coherence of Self (ICS). Garcia et al. (2021) showed that SCORS-G dimensions are highly correlated with the LPFS as well as several maladaptive traits (see also Stein et al., 2018). Performance-based assessment methods have been more often used in study of Criterion A rather than the Criterion B maladaptive traits (e.g., Beheydt et al., 2020; Zettl et al., 2020). However, empirically validated performance assessment indicators of constructs highly relevant to maladaptive traits, such as Anxiousness, Depressivity, Suspiciousness, Cognitive and Perceptual Dysfunction, and others (e.g., dependency), are available with the Rorschach Performance Assessment System (Meyer et al., 2011).

The mechanics, versatility, and scope of the AMPD in psychodiagnosis are illustrated in the following extended case example. The reader is also referred to excellent illustrations of clinical application of the AMPD by Bach et al. (2015) and Weekers et al. (2020).

CASE EXAMPLE

Hunter[1] was a 19-year-old, cisgender, gay, European American man who was in residential treatment because of ongoing struggles with anxiety, interpersonal difficulties, shame, and psychotic vulnerabilities. He entered residential treatment after experiencing psychotic symptoms on failing his first semester in college. He reported difficulty with class material and reacted by demeaning his professors if he was not awarded As on assignments. Being angry and hostile, he had trouble making friends and spent most of his free time alone in his dorm room. He was sensitive to rejection and felt disrespected by peers. Over time, he became convinced his professors were grading him harder than other students to humiliate him.

After completing final exams, he drank to intoxication and sent aggressive emails to professors, demanding that they give him As in recognition of his genius. When these actions were shared with college counseling staff, Hunter was given a psychological evaluation, which noted significant paranoia in addition to grandiosity and hostility. He was briefly hospitalized and then referred to longer term residential treatment to address his psychiatric instability, interpersonal difficulties, and disorganization. At this point, Hunter presented as flat, withdrawn, and annoyed. When the admitting psychiatrist posed questions, Hunter rolled his eyes and expressed irritation that he was being asked "basic" questions. During his treatment, he had trouble engaging with his psychotherapist and believed that if he simply transferred to a college with more "open-minded professors," his problems would go away.

As a part of routine psychological assessment conducted at residential treatment, Hunter was administered a standard battery of cognitive and personality-based measures, including the following: the LPFS-SR (Morey, 2017), PID-5-BF

---

[1]This is a pseudonym, and potentially identifying features have been altered in the case presentation.

The Alternative DSM Model for Personality Disorders in Psychological Assessment and Treatment 171

(Krueger et al., 2013), Inventory of Interpersonal Problems–Short Circumplex (IIP-SC; Hopwood et al., 2008), Interpersonal Sensitivities Circumplex (ISC; Hopwood et al., 2011), and TAT (coded with the SCORS-G; Stein & Slavin-Mulford, 2017). In the spirit of multimethod assessment approaches (Hopwood & Bornstein, 2014), here we focus on the integration of AMPD measures (LPFS-SR and the PID-5-BF) with data from other self-report and performance-based measures to illustrate the value of the AMPD for personality assessment and treatment planning.

For Criterion A, Hunter completed the LPFS-SR (Morey, 2017), an 80-item self-report measure that evaluates self- and interpersonal functioning. Respondents are asked to rate items along a 4-point Likert-type scale ranging from 1 (*totally false, not at all true*) to 4 (*very true*). Table 7.1 shows a comparison of Hunter's total score and his scores (raw and *T*) on the four subcomponents of the LPFS-SR with those scores obtained by a nonclinical population (Hopwood, Good, & Morey, 2018). Hunter's global score showed mild elevation. While his subcomponent score on Intimacy was also mildly elevated, his scores on the Identity and Empathy scales were approximately one standard deviation higher than the nonclinical population in the Hopwood, Good, and Morey (2018) study.

On the Identity subcomponent scale, Hunter endorsed several items using the most extreme item anchor option (*very true*). Examples included the following:

- "I tend to feel either really good or really bad about myself."
- "In many situations I feel quite differently than others seem to expect me to feel."
- "When feelings get too strong, I shut myself from them."

These items portray Hunter as someone whose self-esteem fluctuates between extremes: sometimes feeling great; other times, feeling terrible and very self-critical. This unstable self-experience might suggest potential narcissistic personality dynamics with vacillation between a grandiose and vulnerable sense of self. The other two extreme items on the Identity subcomponent scale suggest that Hunter's emotions often surprise other people and that he tries to push away strong feelings to maintain stability.

On the Self-Direction subcomponent scale, he endorsed as Very True an item asserting that "I set personal standards for myself that are very difficult to satisfy," providing further evidence that lofty ideals contributed to poor self-esteem.

On the Empathy subcomponent scale, Hunter's item endorsements suggested important dynamics relevant to his experience of closeness and engagement with others. On the one hand, he revealed a tendency to undervalue the extent to which his speech and behaviors have any effect on others ("Sometimes it is easy for me to overlook the impact that I'm having on others": Very True) as well as to overvalue others contingent on perceived self-interest ("I mainly pay attention to people based upon what they might do to me, or for me": Mainly True). On the other hand, he expressed feelings of confusion and limited mentalization capacities in regard to interpersonal relationships more generally

("I don't understand what motivates other people at all" and "Interacting with other people usually leaves me feeling confused": both Mainly True). Together, these items suggest that Hunter is largely focused on how people are influencing him, which might be driven by a focus on his self-esteem and his fluctuating self-appraisal. At the same time, he has substantial trouble understanding the motivations of others and might feel lost in social situations.

On the Intimacy subcomponent scale, Hunter's total score showed a mild elevation. However, three items were endorsed as Very True:

- "Although I value close relationships, sometimes strong emotions get in the way."
- "I can only get close to somebody who understands me very well."
- "Sometimes I am not very cooperative because other people don't live up to my standards."

Like the elevated Identity scores, these items suggest that Hunter experiences strong emotions as disrupting his capacity to engage in close relationships. Hunter also noted that he can only get close to somebody who understands him very well, tacitly implying the mental set of perfection and need for mirroring from others. We suspect Hunter's understanding of others is quite limited given his social confusion and self-preoccupation illustrated in endorsement of the Empathy items. These qualities are consistent with recent conceptualizations of narcissistic disorders that highlight deficits in emotional processing of self and other experiences (Ronningstam, 2020). Eventually, Hunter acknowledged he can be antagonistic when others disappoint him and fail to meet his standards.

For Criterion B, Hunter completed the PID5-BF, a 25-item self-report measure assessing pathological traits within the AMPD model. Respondents are asked to rate items along a 4-point Likert-type scale ranging from 0 (*very false or often false*) to 3 (*very true or often true*). Table 7.1 shows Hunter's total scores and his scores (raw and *T*) on the five maladaptive personality trait domains in comparison to a mixed clinical and nonclinical adult sample (see Bach et al., 2016).

On the Negative Affectivity subscale, Hunter endorsed the items "I fear being alone in life more than anything else" and "I get irritated easily by all sorts of things" as Very True or Often True. While not reporting significant problems with affective maladaptive traits at the mean subscale level, his endorsement of these items suggests that Hunter possesses a low threshold for irritation in everyday life and is concerned about being chronically alienated from others. Despite fears of being alone, his Antagonism mean score was two standard deviations above the mean, suggesting severe problems with oppositional interpersonal behavior that might be driven by an inflated sense of self-worth, expectation of special treatment, and callous disregard for others (American Psychiatric Association, 2013). Hunter acknowledged a desire to be noticed by others ("I crave attention": Very True or Often True) while simultaneously adopting a somewhat callous attitude toward the feelings of others ("It's not a big deal if I hurt other people's feelings" and "I use people to get what I want": both Sometimes or Somewhat True). His endorsement of these items suggests an inclination to manipulate others and to dismiss their feelings or needs. His elevated profile on Antagonism, but not Disinhibition, provides further support for Hunter's exhibiting a narcissistic personality organization.

The trait dimension of Psychoticism was also elevated in comparison to both Hunter's other trait domain scores and prior scores obtained by a mixed adult sample, suggesting that he has problems organizing his thoughts, perception, and experience of reality. His elevation on this scale was primarily driven by his higher endorsement of items such as "I have seen things that weren't really there" and "I often 'zone out' and then suddenly come to and realize that a lot of time has passed," which he rated as being Very True or Often True. Hunter's openness in endorsing items representing psychotic symptoms, such as hallucinations or dissociation, reveals an awareness of problems, suggesting an intact observing-ego capacity that may be a hopeful prognostic indicator for treatment.

Multimethod Assessment

With these results in mind, we briefly compare Hunter's AMPD data with other self-report and performance-based measures. On the IIP-SC (a measure of interpersonal problems; Hopwood et al., 2008), Hunter's results indicate he has problems with being excessively dominant, self-centered, and cold toward others, which keeps them at arm's length. This dominant and cold posture is consistent with his self-preoccupation and antagonistic manner of engaging others. On the ISC (a measure of interpersonal sensitivities; Hopwood et al., 2011), Hunter's results reveal a tendency to feel bothered by others who are passive, indecisive, conflict-avoidant, and dependent on him. His cold-dominant interpersonal posture leaves him feeling repelled when others act in warm and passive ways, making it difficult for him to establish trustful, reciprocal relationships.

Hunter's TAT stories were rated according to the SCORS-G (Stein & Slavin-Mulford, 2017), a coding system that includes eight subdimensions assessing cognitive and affective aspects of relational narratives and schemas. When comparing Hunter's mean raw and T scores (see Table 7.1) across these subdimensions to the residential treatment center local norms, his scores on AFF, AGG, and SE were more than one standard deviation below local norms, suggesting greater pathology compared to his peers. The lower mean score on AFF reflects Hunter's views that relationships are problematic and possibly harmful, evidenced by themes of physical violence, aggression, and murder across several of his interpersonal narratives. The lower mean AGG score indicates difficulty regulating his aggression, and he anticipates others might likewise be hostile and dangerous. The lower SE mean score flags Hunter's struggles with low self-worth and feelings of worthlessness beneath his overconfident and arrogant exterior.

The following is a narrative provided by Hunter in response to TAT Card 12M, which features a young man lying on a couch with his eyes closed and an elderly man standing over him with his hand stretched out (Murray, 1943):

> These are friends in boarding school. One has fallen asleep on a sofa in a common area, just taking a nap in between classes, and his friend walks by and sees that he's there, and he's going to poke his face and do weird things to him—maybe, like, hold his nose 'til he gasps for air, something not too malicious—just messing with him while he's asleep. But he's just trying to have fun, and the other one— the other one will be a little thrown off by it. Maybe he doesn't, maybe he's kind of sensitive to, he's freaked out by getting woken up in his sleep by someone doing something to him, but the other one was just trying to have fun. But the one who's sleeping does not admit that he didn't like it, like, socially, he doesn't think he can. They're not operating in an emotionally mature enough way that he can say to him, "Oh, I didn't like that you did that there, boys, in boarding school," so he just, like, shoves him off and, like, laughs or something, but he's a little bit shaken for the rest of the day from having been woken up suddenly.

In this narrative, Hunter presents a story of a sleeping (i.e., feeling vulnerable) student who is antagonized by his friend. The sleeping student is upset by his friend's behavior but does not feel that it is safe to express this directly because it would be socially awkward. Instead, the sleeping student pushes his friend off, although he continues to feel bothered by the intrusion and finds it hard to let it go as the day presses on. In this story, the vulnerable student is exploited by his friend, who shows remarkably little awareness or concern that his actions are bothersome and distressing. Hunter speaks in a devaluing manner about how the students are too immature to be direct about their upset in response to the interaction. From this story, we can infer that Hunter identifies with both sides of this relationship pair. On the one hand, he can be cold and dominant with little awareness that his aggressive behavior upsets others, and, on the other hand, he is sensitive to intrusion but does not feel comfortable sharing his feelings because it would expose him to ridicule and rejection. Expressing vulnerability is felt as risky because others may take advantage, a dynamic that drives Hunter to adopt a cold and dominant interpersonal stance to avoid being hurt and attacked.

Multimethod AMPD Formulation

On the two self-report AMPD measures, Hunter's profile was only mildly elevated, despite the significant problems that lead to his psychiatric hospitalization. Figure 7.2 shows the mean informant ratings on the AMPD made by two authors (M. H. W. and J. M. R.) using the full range of clinical material discussed earlier to depict an AMPD profile for Hunter (note that ICC [2,2] mean consistency agreement equals 0.85), diagnosing the presence of PD with a global LPFS rating of 3 (severe impairment).

Hunter's self-report AMPD profile indicates moderate problems with Identity and Empathy and more significant problems with Psychoticism and Antagonism in contrast to the more numerous AMPD elevations identified by the

The Alternative DSM Model for Personality Disorders in Psychological Assessment and Treatment 175

FIGURE 7.2. Clinician Ratings of Hunter

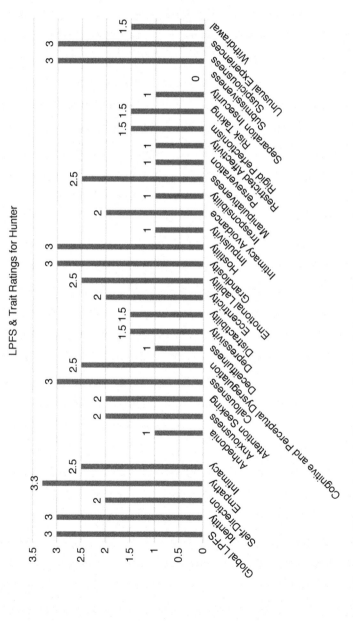

Note. LPFS = Level of Personality Functioning Scale (American Psychiatric Association, 2013; Bender et al., 2011): Rated on a 0-to-4 scale. Trait ratings are rated on a 0-to-3 scale.

two clinicians. This is understood as a reflection of Hunter's externalizing style of psychopathology interacting with self-report methodology. This probably contributed to the discrepancy between Hunter's own perception of his difficulties and those perceived by clinical observers. This style of limited self-insight (or at least limited self-disclosure of negative qualities) is common in narcissism (Cooper et al., 2012). Despite the likelihood that Hunter's self-report responses underrepresent his level of impairment, significant findings emerge when looking at individual subscales and elevated items. First, under the general umbrella category of problems related to the self, Hunter endorsed problems managing his sense of self-worth; this finding was evidenced across both AMPD measures and other multimethod assessment approaches. His self-appraisal appears to fluctuate dramatically, and he tries to regulate these painful self-states largely by focusing on how others affect him while discounting or minimizing how he impacts others. He struggles to bring his vulnerability forward given his expectations that people will respond negatively or aggressively and likely mistreat him. When he fails to achieve the high expectations he sets for himself, unrealistically assuming perfection and the receipt of academic accolades, he becomes deflated and falls into self-criticism. Longing for the admiring attention of others, he nonetheless is inclined to act in an exploitative and cold-dominant manner without feeling much remorse. Easily irritated, he is prone to become frustrated with people he perceives to be excessively dominant or passive.

Second, regarding relational functioning and social reasoning and logic more broadly, Hunter experiences interpersonal confusion, and his sense of reality is distorted; this impairs his capacity to mentalize and understand what others want from him. His impaired social awareness impedes his ability to read the intentions of others, potentially explaining his paranoid and suspicious attitude toward his professors. He might defensively direct his attention away from others and toward his own experiences given the fear and confusion that emerge when he cannot adequately mentalize the motivations of others. Furthermore, when others do not give him the admiration he craves, he lashes out with uncooperative, devaluing behavior to thwart the needs of others. From these findings, we infer Hunter is experiencing and expressing problems within the narcissistic PD spectrum. This narcissistic maladaptation is currently also imbued with psychotic tendencies (i.e., grandiosity, paranoia, hallucinations). The psychoticism probably reflects the destabilizing effect of profound self-esteem threat on his fragile self-system triggered by his poor adjustment to being away from home and at college. The interpersonal difficulties encountered at this time in his life, compounded by the high level of pressure to function as an independent and academically successful adult, apparently were too great for his level and style of personality organization to manage without fracturing. Formally, an apt AMPD diagnostic coding for Hunter is PD-TS with Antagonism and Psychoticism. As shown earlier, however, this diagnostic coding can be unpacked to reveal important personality qualities, vulnerabilities, and dynamics.

CONCLUSION

The AMPD is an exemplar of the contemporary dimensional paradigm in psychopathology (Hopwood, Kotov, et al., 2018). Moreover, the AMPD is conceptually rich and possesses clinical utility, and numerous assessment instruments may be used to apply the model in practice. We recommend clinicians in training and experienced practitioners alike try the approach.

The model pluralistically incorporates different classes of personality constructs reflecting McAdams's (2015) metaphors of actor, agent, and author; each clarifies our understanding of persons. We believe clinicians will find the model scientifically sound and reasonably experience-near while supporting psychodiagnosis of PD and the clinical care of persons suffering in these ways.

REFERENCES

Adler, J. M., & Clark, L. A. (2019). Incorporating narrative identity into structural approaches to personality and psychopathology. *Journal of Research in Personality, 82,* Article 103857. https://doi.org/10.1016/j.jrp.2019.103857

Allport, G. W. (1937). *Personality: A psychological interpretation.* Holt.

American Psychiatric Association. (1980). *Diagnostic and statistical manual of mental disorders* (3rd ed.).

American Psychiatric Association. (2013). *Diagnostic and statistical manual of mental disorders* (5th ed.). https://doi.org/10.1176/appi.books.9780890425596

Anderson, J. L., Sellbom, M., Bagby, R. M., Quilty, L. C., Veltri, C. O., Markon, K. E., & Krueger, R. F. (2013). On the convergence between PSY-5 domains and PID-5 domains and facets: Implications for assessment of *DSM-5* personality traits. *Assessment, 20*(3), 286–294. https://doi.org/10.1177/1073191112471141

Andreasen, N. C. (2007). *DSM* and the death of phenomenology in America: An example of unintended consequences. *Schizophrenia Bulletin, 33,* 108–112.

Bach, B., & Bernstein, D. P. (2019). Schema therapy conceptualization of personality functioning and traits in *ICD-11* and *DSM-5. Current Opinion in Psychiatry, 32*(1), 38–49. https://doi.org/10.1097/YCO.0000000000000464

Bach, B., Maples-Keller, J. L., Bo, S., & Simonsen, E. (2016). The alternative *DSM-5* personality disorder traits criterion: A comparative examination of three self-report forms in a Danish population. *Personality Disorders, 7*(2), 124–135. https://doi.org/10.1037/per0000162

Bach, B., Markon, K., Simonsen, E., & Krueger, R. F. (2015). Clinical utility of the *DSM-5* Alternative Model of Personality Disorders: Six cases from practice. *Journal of Psychiatric Practice, 21*(1), 3–25. https://doi.org/10.1097/01.pra.0000460618.02805.ef

Bateman, A., & Fonagy, P. (2010). Mentalization based treatment for borderline personality disorder. *World Psychiatry, 9*(1), 11–15. https://doi.org/10.1002/j.2051-5545.2010.tb00255.x

Beheydt, L., Schrijvers, D., Sabbe, B., Jansen, B., De Grave, C., & Luyten, P. (2020). *DSM-5* assessments of the level of personality functioning: Intrapersonal and interpersonal functioning. *Psychiatry, 83*(1), 84–93. https://doi.org/10.1080/00332747.2019.1650411

Bender, D. S., Morey, L. C., & Skodol, A. E. (2011). Toward a model for assessing level of personality functioning in *DSM-5*, part I: A review of theory and methods. *Journal of Personality Assessment, 93*(4), 332–346. https://doi.org/10.1080/00223891.2011.583808

Blashfield, R. K., & Draguns, J. G. (1976). Evaluative criteria for psychiatric classification. *Journal of Abnormal Psychology, 85*(2), 140–150. https://doi.org/10.1037/0021-843X.85.2.140

Buer Christensen, T., Paap, M. C. S., Arnesen, M., Koritzinsky, K., Nysaeter, T. E., Eikenaes, I., Germans Selvik, S., Walther, K., Torgersen, S., Bender, D. S., Skodol, A. E., Kvarstein, E., Pedersen, G., & Hummelen, B. (2018). Interrater reliability of the Structured Clinical Interview for the *DSM-5* Alternative Model of Personality Disorders module I: Level of Personality Functioning Scale. *Journal of Personality Assessment, 100*(6), 630–641. https://doi.org/10.1080/00223891.2018.1483377

Busch, A. J., Morey, L. C., & Hopwood, C. J. (2017). Exploring the assessment of the *DSM-5* Alternative Model for Personality Disorders with the Personality Assessment Inventory. *Journal of Personality Assessment, 99*(2), 211–218. https://doi.org/10.1080/00223891.2016.1217872

Cain, N. M., Pincus, A. L., & Ansell, E. B. (2008). Narcissism at the crossroads: Phenotypic description of pathological narcissism across clinical theory, social/personality psychology, and psychiatric diagnosis. *Clinical Psychology Review, 28*(4), 638–656. https://doi.org/10.1016/j.cpr.2007.09.006

Clark, L. A., Vanderbleek, E. N., Shapiro, J. L., Nuzum, H., Allen, X., Daly, E., Kingsbury, T. J., Oiler, M., & Ro, E. (2015). The brave new world of personality disorder-trait specified: Effects of additional definitions on coverage, prevalence, and comorbidity. *Psychopathology Review, 2*(1), 52–82. https://doi.org/10.5127/pr.036314

Clarkin, J. F., Cain, N., & Livesley, W. J. (2015). An integrated approach to treatment of patients with personality disorders. *Journal of Psychotherapy Integration, 25*(1), 3–12. https://doi.org/10.1037/a0038766

Clarkin, J. F., Caligor, E., & Sowislo, J. F. (2020). An object relations model perspective on the Alternative Model for Personality Disorders (*DSM-5*). *Psychopathology, 53*(3-4), 141–148. https://doi.org/10.1159/000508353

Cooper, L. D., Balsis, S., & Oltmanns, T. F. (2012). Self- and informant-reported perspectives on symptoms of narcissistic personality disorder. *Personality Disorders, 3*(2), 140–154. https://doi.org/10.1037/a0026576

Cruitt, P. J., Boudreaux, M. J., King, H. R., Oltmanns, J. R., & Oltmanns, T. F. (2019). Examining Criterion A: *DSM-5* level of personality functioning as assessed through life story interviews. *Personality Disorders, 10*(3), 224–234. https://doi.org/10.1037/per0000321

Dereboy, F., Dereboy, Ç., & Eskin, M. (2018). Validation of the *DSM-5* Alternative Model Personality Disorder diagnoses in Turkey, Part 1: LEAD validity and reliability of the personality functioning ratings. *Journal of Personality Assessment, 100*(6), 603–611. https://doi.org/10.1080/00223891.2018.1423989

DeYoung, C. G. (2015). Cybernetic Big Five theory. *Journal of Research in Personality, 56*, 33–58. https://doi.org/10.1016/j.jrp.2014.07.004

Di Pierro, R., Gargiulo, I., Poggi, A., Madeddu, F., & Preti, E. (2020). The Level of Personality Functioning Scale applied to clinical material From the Structured Interview of Personality Organization (STIPO): Utility in detecting personality pathology. *Journal of Personality Disorders, 34*(Suppl. C), 62–76. https://doi.org/10.1521/pedi_2020_34_472

Few, L. R., Miller, J. D., Rothbaum, A. O., Meller, S., Maples, J., Terry, D. P., Collins, B., & MacKillop, J. (2013). Examination of the Section III *DSM-5* diagnostic system for personality disorders in an outpatient clinical sample. *Journal of Abnormal Psychology, 122*(4), 1057–1069. https://doi.org/10.1037/a0034878

First, M. B., Skodol, A. E., Bender, D. S., & Oldham, J. M. (2017). *User's guide for the Structured Clinical Interview for the* DSM-5® *Alternative Model for Personality Disorders (SCID-5-AMPD)*. American Psychiatric Association Publishing.

Flesch, R. (1948). A new readability yardstick. *Journal of Applied Psychology, 32*(3), 221–233. https://doi.org/10.1037/h0057532

Gamache, D., Savard, C., Leclerc, P., & Côté, A. (2019). Introducing a short self-report for the assessment of *DSM-5* level of personality functioning for personality disorders: The Self and Interpersonal Functioning Scale. *Personality Disorders, 10*(5), 438–447. https://doi.org/10.1037/per0000335

Garcia, D. J., Skadberg, R. M., Schmidt, M., Bierma, S., Shorter, R. L., & Waugh, M. H. (2018). It's not that difficult: An interrater reliability study of the *DSM-5* Section III Alternative Model for Personality Disorders. *Journal of Personality Assessment, 100*(6), 612–620. https://doi.org/10.1080/00223891.2018.1428982

Garcia, D. J., Waugh, M. H., Skadberg, R. M., Crittenden, E. B., Finn, M. T. M., Schmidt, M. R., & Kurdziel-Adams, G. (2021). Deconstructing criterion a of the alternative model for personality disorders. *Personality Disorders: Theory, Research, and Treatment, 12*(4), 320–330. https://doi.org/10.1037/per0000431

Goldman, H. H., Skodol, A. E., & Lave, T. R. (1992). Revising axis V for *DSM-IV*: A review of measures of social functioning. *The American Journal of Psychiatry, 149*(9), 1148–1156. https://doi.org/10.1176/ajp.149.9.1148

Harkness, A. R., McNulty, J. L., & Ben-Porath, Y. S. (1995). The Personality Psychopathology Five (PSY-5): Constructs and MMPI-2 scales. *Psychological Assessment, 7*(1), 104–114. https://doi.org/10.1037/1040-3590.7.1.104

Hopwood, C. J. (2018). A framework for treating *DSM-5* Alternative Model for Personality Disorder features. *Personality and Mental Health, 12*(2), 107–125. https://doi.org/10.1002/pmh.1414

Hopwood, C. J., Ansell, E. B., Pincus, A. L., Wright, A. G., Lukowitsky, M. R., & Roche, M. J. (2011). The circumplex structure of interpersonal sensitivities. *Journal of Personality, 79*(4), 707–740. https://doi.org/10.1111/j.1467-6494.2011.00696.x

Hopwood, C. J., & Bornstein, R. F. (Eds.). (2014). *Multimethod clinical assessment.* The Guilford Press.

Hopwood, C. J., Good, E. W., & Morey, L. C. (2018). Validity of the *DSM-5* Levels of Personality Functioning Scale–Self Report. *Journal of Personality Assessment, 100*(6), 650–659. https://doi.org/10.1080/00223891.2017.1420660

Hopwood, C. J., Kotov, R., Krueger, R. F., Watson, D., Widiger, T. A., Althoff, R. R., Ansell, E. B., Bach, B., Michael Bagby, R., Blais, M. A., Bornovalova, M. A., Chmielewski, M., Cicero, D. C., Conway, C., De Clercq, B., De Fruyt, F., Docherty, A. R., Eaton, N. R., Edens, J. F., . . . Zimmermann, J. (2018). The time has come for dimensional personality disorder diagnosis. *Personality and Mental Health, 12*(1), 82–86. https://doi.org/10.1002/pmh.1408

Hopwood, C. J., Mulay, A. L., & Waugh, M. H. (Eds.). (2019). *The DSM-5 Alternative Model for Personality Disorders: Integrating multiple paradigms of personality assessment.* Routledge. https://doi.org/10.4324/9781315205076

Hopwood, C. J., Pincus, A. L., DeMoor, R. M., & Koonce, E. A. (2008). Psychometric characteristics of the Inventory of Interpersonal Problems–Short Circumplex (IIP-SC) with college students. *Journal of Personality Assessment, 90*(6), 615–618. https://doi.org/10.1080/00223890802388665

Hopwood, C. J., & Waugh, M. H. (Eds.). (2019). *Personality assessment paradigms and methods: A collaborative reassessment of Madeline G.* Routledge. https://doi.org/10.4324/9781315143620

Huprich, S. K., Nelson, S. M., Meehan, K. B., Siefert, C. J., Haggerty, G., Sexton, J., Dauphin, V. B., Macaluso, M., Jackson, J., Zackula, R., & Baade, L. (2018). Introduction of the *DSM-5* Levels of Personality Functioning Questionnaire. *Personality Disorders, 9*(6), 553–563. https://doi.org/10.1037/per0000264

Hutsebaut, J., Feenstra, D. J., & Kamphuis, J. H. (2016). Development and preliminary psychometric evaluation of a brief self-report questionnaire for the assessment of the *DSM-5* Level of Personality Functioning Scale: The LPFS Brief Form (LPFS-BF). *Personality Disorders, 7*(2), 192–197. https://doi.org/10.1037/per0000159

Hutsebaut, J., Kamphuis, J. H., Feenstra, D. J., Weekers, L. C., & De Saeger, H. (2017). Assessing *DSM-5*-oriented level of personality functioning: Development and psychometric evaluation of the Semi-Structured Interview for Personality Functioning *DSM-5* (STiP-5.1). *Personality Disorders, 8*(1), 94–101. https://doi.org/10.1037/per0000197

Hyman, S. E. (2010). The diagnosis of mental disorders: The problem of reification. *Annual Review of Clinical Psychology, 6*(1), 155–179. https://doi.org/10.1146/annurev.clinpsy.3.022806.091532

Kampe, L., Zimmermann, J., Bender, D., Caligor, E., Borowski, A. L., Ehrenthal, J. C., Benecke, C., & Hörz-Sagstetter, S. (2018). Comparison of the Structured *DSM-5* Clinical Interview for the Level of Personality Functioning Scale with the Structured Interview of Personality Organization. *Journal of Personality Assessment, 100*(6), 642–649. https://doi.org/10.1080/00223891.2018.1489257

Kernberg, O. (1967). Borderline personality organization. *Journal of the American Psychoanalytic Association, 15*(3), 641–685. https://doi.org/10.1177/000306516701500309

Kernberg, O. F. (2016). What is personality? *Journal of Personality Disorders, 30*(2), 145–156. https://doi.org/10.1521/pedi.2106.30.2.145

Kohut, H. (1979). The two analyses of Mr. Z. *The International Journal of Psycho-Analysis, 60*(1), 3–27.

Krueger, R. F., Derringer, J., Markon, K. E., Watson, D., & Skodol, A. E. (2012). Initial construction of a maladaptive personality trait model and inventory for *DSM-5*. *Psychological Medicine, 42*(9), 1879–1890. https://doi.org/10.1017/S0033291711002674

Krueger, R. F., Derringer, J., Markon, K. E., Watson, D., & Skodol, A. E. (2013). *The Personality Inventory for* DSM-5—*Brief form (PID-5-BF)–Adult*. American Psychiatric Association.

Krueger, R. F., & Hobbs, K. A. (2020). An overview of the *DSM-5* Alternative Model of Personality Disorders. *Psychopathology, 53*(3), 126–132. https://doi.org/10.1159/000508538

Krueger, R. F., & Markon, K. E. (2014). The role of the *DSM-5* personality trait model in moving toward a quantitative and empirically based approach to classifying personality and psychopathology. *Annual Review of Clinical Psychology, 10*(1), 477–501. https://doi.org/10.1146/annurev-clinpsy-032813-153732

Lenzenweger, M. F., Clarkin, J. F., Kernberg, O. F., & Foelsch, P. A. (2001). The Inventory of Personality Organization: Psychometric properties, factorial composition, and criterion relations with affect, aggressive dyscontrol, psychosis proneness, and self-domains in a nonclinical sample. *Psychological Assessment, 13*(4), 577–591. https://doi.org/10.1037/1040-3590.13.4.577

Linehan, M. M. (2018). *Cognitive–behavioral treatment of borderline personality disorder*. Guilford Press.

Maples, J. L., Carter, N. T., Few, L. R., Crego, C., Gore, W. L., Samuel, D. B., Williamson, R. L., Lynam, D. R., Widiger, T. A., Markon, K. E., Krueger, R. F., & Miller, J. D. (2015). Testing whether the *DSM-5* personality disorder trait model can be measured with a reduced set of items: An item response theory investigation of the Personality Inventory for *DSM-5*. *Psychological Assessment, 27*(4), 1195–1210. https://doi.org/10.1037/pas0000120

Markon, K. E. (2013). Epistemological pluralism and scientific development: An argument against authoritative nosologies. *Journal of Personality Disorders, 27*(5), 554–579. https://doi.org/10.1521/pedi.2013.27.5.554

Markon, K. E., Quilty, L. C., Bagby, R. M., & Krueger, R. F. (2013). The development and psychometric properties of an informant-report form of the Personality Inventory for *DSM-5* (PID-5). *Assessment, 20*(3), 370–383. https://doi.org/10.1177/1073191113486513

McAdams, D. P. (1995). What do we know when we know a person? *Journal of Personality, 63*(3), 365–396. https://doi.org/10.1111/j.1467-6494.1995.tb00500.x

McAdams, D. P. (2015). *The art and science of personality development*. The Guilford Press.

McAdams, D. P., & Pals, J. L. (2006). A new Big Five: Fundamental principles for an integrative science of personality. *American Psychologist, 61*(3), 204–217. https://doi.org/10.1037/0003-066X.61.3.204

McCabe, G. A., Oltmanns, J. R., & Widiger, T. A. (2021). Criterion A Scales: Convergent, discriminant, and structural relationships. *Assessment, 28*(3), 813–828. https://doi.org/10.1177/1073191120947160

Meehan, K. B., Siefert, C., Sexton, J., & Huprich, S. K. (2019). Expanding the role of levels of personality functioning in personality disorder taxonomy: Commentary on "Criterion A of the AMPD in HiTOP." *Journal of Personality Assessment, 101*(4), 367–373. https://doi.org/10.1080/00223891.2018.1551228

Meyer, G. J., Viglione, D. J., Mihura, J. L., Erard, R. E., & Erdberg, P. (2011). *Rorschach Performance Assessment System: Administration, coding, interpretation, and technical manual.* Author.

Milinkovic, M. S., & Tiliopoulos, N. (2020). A systematic review of the clinical utility of the *DSM-5* Section III Alternative Model of Personality Disorder. *Personality Disorders, 11*(6), 377–397. https://doi.org/10.1037/per0000408

Morey, L. C. (2007). *Personality Assessment Inventory (PAI): Professional manual.* Psychological Assessment Resources.

Morey, L. C. (2017). Development and initial evaluation of a self-report form of the *DSM-5* Level of Personality Functioning Scale. *Psychological Assessment, 29*(10), 1302–1308. https://doi.org/10.1037/pas0000450

Morey, L. C. (2018). Application of the *DSM-5* Level of Personality Functioning Scale by lay raters. *Journal of Personality Disorders, 32*(5), 709–720. https://doi.org/10.1521/pedi_2017_31_305

Morey, L. C. (2019a). Interdiagnostician reliability of the *DSM-5* Section II and Section III alternative model criteria for borderline personality disorder. *Journal of Personality Disorders, 33*(6), 721–735. https://doi.org/10.1521/pedi_2019_33_362

Morey, L. C. (2019b). Thoughts on the assessment of the *DSM-5* Alternative Model for Personality Disorders: Comment on Sleep et al. (2019). *Psychological Assessment, 31*(10), 1192–1199. https://doi.org/10.1037/pas0000710

Morey, L. C., Skodol, A. E., & Oldham, J. M. (2014). Clinician judgments of clinical utility: A comparison of *DSM-IV-TR* personality disorders and the Alternative Model for *DSM-5* Personality Disorders. *Journal of Abnormal Psychology, 123*(2), 398–405. https://doi.org/10.1037/a0036481

Mulay, A. L., Cain, N. M., Waugh, M. H., Hopwood, C. J., Adler, J. M., Garcia, D. J., Kurtz, J. E., Lenger, K. A., & Skadberg, R. (2018). Personality constructs and paradigms in the Alternative *DSM-5* Model of Personality Disorder. *Journal of Personality Assessment, 100*(6), 593–602. https://doi.org/10.1080/00223891.2018.1477787

Mullins-Sweatt, S. N., & Widiger, T. A. (2009). Clinical utility and *DSM-V. Psychological Assessment, 21*(3), 302–312. https://doi.org/10.1037/a0016607

Murray, H. A. (1943). *Thematic Apperception Test.* Harvard University Press.

Ronningstam, E. (2014). Beyond the diagnostic traits: A collaborative exploratory diagnostic process for dimensions and underpinnings of narcissistic personality disorder. *Personality Disorders, 5*(4), 434–438. https://doi.org/10.1037/per0000034

Ronningstam, E. (2020). Internal processing in patients with pathological narcissism or narcissistic personality disorder: Implications for alliance building and therapeutic strategies. *Journal of Personality Disorders, 34*(Suppl.), 80–103. https://doi.org/10.1521/pedi.2020.34.supp.80

Samuel, D. B., Hopwood, C. J., Krueger, R. F., Thomas, K. M., & Ruggero, C. J. (2013). Comparing methods for scoring personality disorder types using maladaptive traits in *DSM-5. Assessment, 20*(3), 353–361. https://doi.org/10.1177/1073191113486182

Silk, K. R. (2011). The process of managing medications in patients with borderline personality disorder. *Journal of Psychiatric Practice, 17*(5), 311–319. https://doi.org/10.1097/01.pra.0000405361.88257.4a

Stein, M. B., & Slavin-Mulford, J. (2017). *The Social Cognition and Object Relations Scale-Global Rating Method (SCORS-G): A comprehensive guide for clinicians and researchers.* Routledge. https://doi.org/10.4324/9781315207629

Stein, M. B., Slavin-Mulford, J., Sinclair, S. J., Chung, W.-J., Roche, M., Denckla, C., & Blais, M. A. (2018). Extending the use of the SCORS–G composite ratings in assessing level of personality organization. *Journal of Personality Assessment, 100*(2), 166–175. https://doi.org/10.1080/00223891.2016.1195394

Strozier, C. B. (2001). *Heinz Kohut: The making of a psychoanalyst*. Farrar, Straus and Giroux.

Vaillant, G. E. (1984). The disadvantages of *DSM-III* outweigh its advantages. *The American Journal of Psychiatry, 141*(4), 542–545. https://doi.org/10.1176/ajp.141.4.542

Verheul, R., Andrea, H., Berghout, C. C., Dolan, C., Busschbach, J. J. V., van der Kroft, P. J. A., Bateman, A. W., & Fonagy, P. (2008). Severity Indices of Personality Problems (SIPP-118): Development, factor structure, reliability, and validity. *Psychological Assessment, 20*(1), 23–34. https://doi.org/10.1037/1040-3590.20.1.23

Watters, C. A., Sellbom, M., Uliaszek, A. A., & Bagby, R. M. (2019). Clarifying the interstitial nature of facets from the Personality Inventory for *DSM-5* using the five factor model of personality. *Personality Disorders, 10*(4), 330–339. https://doi.org/10.1037/per0000327

Waugh, M. H. (2014). *Clinician Rating Personality Disorder Level and Traits* (PDLT-C) [Unpublished manuscript]. Department of Psychology, University of Tennessee.

Waugh, M. H., Hopwood, C. J., Krueger, R. F., Morey, L. C., Pincus, A. L., & Wright, A. G. C. (2017). Psychological assessment with the *DSM-5* Alternative Model for Personality Disorders: Tradition and innovation. *Professional Psychology: Research and Practice, 48*(2), 79–89. https://doi.org/10.1037/pro0000071

Waugh, M. H., McClain, C. M., Mariotti, E. C., Mulay, A. L., DeVore, E. N., Lenger, K. A., Russell, A. N., Florimbio, A. R., Lewis, K. C., Ridenour, J. M., & Beevers, L. G. (2020). Comparative content analysis of self-report scales for Level of Personality Functioning. *Journal of Personality Assessment*. Advance online publication. https://doi.org/10.1080/00223891.2019.1705464

Weekers, L. C., Hutsebaut, J., Bach, B., & Kamphuis, J. H. (2020). Scripting the *DSM-5* Alternative Model for Personality Disorders assessment procedure: A clinically feasible multi-informant multi-method approach. *Personality and Mental Health, 14*(3), 304–318. https://doi.org/10.1002/pmh.1481

Widiger, T. A., & Costa, P. T., Jr. (2012). Integrating normal and abnormal personality structure: The Five-Factor model. *Journal of Personality, 80*(6), 1471–1506. https://doi.org/10.1111/j.1467-6494.2012.00776.x

Williams, T. F., Scalco, M. D., & Simms, L. J. (2018). The construct validity of general and specific dimensions of personality pathology. *Psychological Medicine, 48*(5), 834–848. https://doi.org/10.1017/S0033291717002227

Wright, A. G. C., & Simms, L. J. (2014). On the structure of personality disorder traits: Conjoint analyses of the CAT-PD, PID-5, and NEO-PI-3 trait models. *Personality Disorders, 5*(1), 43–54. https://doi.org/10.1037/per0000037

Zettl, M., Volkert, J., Vögele, C., Herpertz, S. C., Kubera, K. M., & Taubner, S. (2020). Mentalization and criterion a of the Alternative Model for Personality Disorders: Results from a clinical and nonclinical sample. *Personality Disorders, 11*(3), 191–201. https://doi.org/10.1037/per0000356

Zimmermann, J., Benecke, C., Bender, D. S., Skodol, A. E., Schauenburg, H., Cierpka, M., & Leising, D. (2014). Assessing *DSM-5* level of personality functioning from videotaped clinical interviews: A pilot study with untrained and clinically inexperienced students. *Journal of Personality Assessment, 96*(4), 397–409. https://doi.org/10.1080/00223891.2013.852563

Zimmermann, J., Böhnke, J. R., Eschstruth, R., Mathews, A., Wenzel, K., & Leising, D. (2015). The latent structure of personality functioning: Investigating Criterion A from the alternative model for personality disorders in *DSM-5*. *Journal of Abnormal Psychology, 124*(3), 532–548. https://doi.org/10.1037/abn0000059

Zimmermann, J., Kerber, A., Rek, K., Hopwood, C. J., & Krueger, R. F. (2019). A brief but comprehensive review of research on the Alternative *DSM-5* Model for Personality Disorders. *Current Psychiatry Reports, 21*(9), Article 92. https://doi.org/10.1007/s11920-019-1079-z

8

Assessment and Treatment of Personality Disorders Within the *ICD-11* Framework

Roger Mulder and Bo Bach

The *International Statistical Classification of Diseases and Related Health Problems* (11th ed.; *ICD-11*; World Health Organization [WHO], 2019) introduced a radical change in the classification of personality disorders (PDs): Instead of traditional PD categories, clinicians first describe the severity of core personality dysfunction (i.e., mild, moderate or severe) when characterizing PDs (see Chapter 2, this volume, for highlights). They may then choose to describe the characteristics of patients using one or more of the five trait domain specifiers—Negative Affectivity, Detachment, Dissociality, Disinhibition, and Anankastia. In addition to coding a level of severity and one or more trait domain specifiers, the clinician is also allowed to specify a borderline pattern specifier, which the *ICD-11* has suggested serves as a familiar indicator for choosing psychotherapeutic treatment consistent with established treatment manuals.

This chapter examines how clinicians might use the *ICD-11* PD classification to assess their patients and how that classification may influence clinical management and treatment. A major purpose in changing the diagnostic classification is to assist clinicians in treating their patients. By improving the accuracy of clinical descriptions, the hope is that clinicians will be able to target interventions more effectively, leading to improved patient outcomes. Because the *ICD-11* is new and recently (January 2022) began to be used officially by WHO member states, there is limited specific evidence on how the *ICD-11* changes impact clinical practice. However, considerable indirect evidence is available and was used to inform this new classification, and some studies have examined face validity and clinical acceptance of the *ICD-11* PD classification. In addition, the Alternative

https://doi.org/10.1037/0000310-009
Personality Disorders and Pathology: Integrating Clinical Assessment and Practice in the DSM-5 *and* ICD-11 *Era*, S. K. Huprich (Editor)
Copyright © 2022 by the American Psychological Association. All rights reserved.

DSM-5 Model for Personality Disorders (AMPD) was introduced in 2013 as an emerging model (see *DSM-5*, the fifth edition of the *Diagnostic and Statistical Manual of Mental Disorders*; American Psychiatric Association, 2013). This model has been widely taken up by researchers and clinicians, and a great deal of the published literature on PDs since its introduction has used this model (Mulder & Tyrer, 2019). Fortunately, the *ICD-11* and AMPD are largely compatible, at least at the severity and domain trait levels (Bach & First, 2018; Bach et al., 2017).

PERSONALITY DISORDER SEVERITY

One of the few consistent themes in the PD literature is that severity of the disorder is important (Bender et al., 2011; Clark et al., 2018; Crawford et al., 2011). Therefore, *ICD-11* and the AMPD begin their assessment with identifying whether a PD is present and grading its severity as mild, moderate, or severe. Both procedures rely on the core capacities of self, interpersonal functioning, or both (see Exhibits 8.1 and 8.2).

The argument for the central role of severity in the assessment of PD is persuasive. Put simply, it enables clinicians to distinguish those who have the greatest level of personality disturbance from those who do not, thereby helping services target their interventions more effectively. It is also consistent with the evidence that severity, however it is assessed, is associated with higher levels of service contact, more impaired social functioning, and higher rates of unemployment (Crawford et al., 2011). Patients with *severe PD*—defined as a greater number of categories or clusters of PD—have a greater incidence of self-harm, and if they suffer from anxiety or depression, they are more likely to have a chronic course (Tyrer et al., 2004). More recently, evidence suggests that the general features of PD, the so-called p-factor (Sharp et al., 2015), may correspond to a global level of severity. This factor is associated with level of service use and suicidality (Clark et al., 1997; Conway et al., 2016) and is consistent with research reporting that a global measure of personality functioning outperformed the total categorical PD criteria in explaining psychosocial impairment (Buer Christensen et al., 2020; T. F. Oltmanns & Balsis, 2011).

ICD-11 PD severity may be assessed using the Personality Disorder Severity *ICD-11* scale (PDS-ICD-11; Bach, Brown, et al., 2021), which is currently being adapted to an interview format. Moreover, Bach and First (2018) suggested that established instruments developed for the AMPD framework of personality functioning and Kernberg's levels of personality organization may also be used to provide the necessary information for determining *ICD-11* PD severity.

CLINICAL UTILITY OF SEVERITY

As well as helping guide clinicians in deciding who to treat, a general dimension of PD severity may be a good target for intervention and monitoring efficacy. Most psychosocial interventions operate via common mechanisms

EXHIBIT 8.1

Aspects of Personality Functioning That Contribute to Severity Determination in Personality Disorder

Degree and pervasiveness of disturbances in functioning of aspects of the self

- stability and coherence of one's sense of identity (e.g., extent to which identity or sense of self is variable and inconsistent or overly rigid and fixed)
- ability to maintain an overall positive and stable sense of self-worth
- accuracy of one's view of one's characteristics, strengths, and limitations
- capacity for self-direction (ability to plan, choose, and implement appropriate goals)

Degree and pervasiveness of interpersonal dysfunction across various contexts and relationships (e.g., romantic relationships, school/work, parent–child, family, friendships, peer contexts)

- interest in engaging in relationships with others
- ability to understand and appreciate others' perspectives
- ability to develop and maintain close and mutually satisfying relationships
- ability to manage conflict in relationships

Pervasiveness, severity, and chronicity of emotional, cognitive, and behavioral manifestations of the personality dysfunction

Emotional manifestations:

- range and appropriateness of emotional experience and expression
- tendency to be emotionally over- or underreactive
- ability to recognize and acknowledge unwanted emotions (e.g., anger, sadness)

Cognitive manifestations:

- accuracy of situational and interpersonal appraisals, especially under stress
- ability to make appropriate decisions in situations of uncertainty
- appropriate stability and flexibility of belief systems

Behavioral manifestations:

- flexibility in controlling impulses and modulating behavior based on the situation and consideration of the consequences
- appropriateness of behavioral responses to intense emotions and stressful circumstances (e.g., propensity to self-harm or violence)

The extent to which the dysfunctions in the preceding areas are associated with distress or impairment in personal, family, social, educational, occupational, or other important areas of functioning

Note. Data from World Health Organization (2019).

(Mulder et al., 2017). Schema-focused therapy (SFT), for example, attempts to strengthen healthy adult functioning (a good sense of who one is, a stable sense of self-worth, and appropriate affect and impulse regulation) goals that are transdiagnostic for healthy personality functioning (Bach & Bernstein, 2019). Similarly, mentalization-based treatment (MBT)—in which the goal is more about mentalizing (the capacity to reflect on one's own and others' mental states)—is something all patients with PDs would benefit from (Bateman et al., 2018).

EXHIBIT 8.2

Abbreviated *ICD-11* Descriptions for Each Level of Severity

Personality Difficulty

Personality difficulty refers to pronounced personality characteristics that may affect treatment or health services but do not rise to the level of severity to merit a diagnosis of personality disorder (PD). Personality difficulty is characterized by long-standing difficulties (e.g., at least 2 years), in the individual's way of experiencing and thinking about the self, others, and the world. In contrast to PDs, these difficulties are manifested in cognitive and emotional experience and expression only intermittently (e.g., during times of stress) or at low intensity. The difficulties are associated with some problems in functioning, but these problems are insufficiently severe to cause notable disruption in social, occupational, and interpersonal relationships and may be limited to specific relationships or situations.

Mild Personality Disorder

All general diagnostic requirements for PD are met. Disturbances affect some areas of personality functioning but not others (e.g., problems with self-direction in the absence of problems with stability and coherence of identity or self-worth) and may not be apparent in some contexts. There are problems in many interpersonal relationships and/or in performance of expected occupational and social roles, but some relationships are maintained and/or some roles are carried out. Specific manifestations of personality disturbances are generally of mild severity. Mild Personality Disorder is typically not associated with substantial harm to self or others but may be associated with substantial distress or with impairment in personal, family, social, educational, occupational, or other important areas of functioning that is either limited to circumscribed areas (e.g., romantic relationships, employment) or present in more areas but is milder.

Moderate Personality Disorder

All general diagnostic requirements for PD are met. Disturbances affect multiple areas of personality functioning (e.g., identity or sense of self, ability to form intimate relationships, ability to control impulses and modulate behavior). However, some areas of personality functioning may be relatively less affected. There are marked problems in most interpersonal relationships, and the performance of most expected social and occupational roles are compromised to some degree. Relationships are likely to be characterized by conflict, avoidance, withdrawal, or extreme dependency (e.g., few friendships maintained, persistent conflict in work relationships and consequent occupational problems, romantic relationships characterized by serious disruption or inappropriate submissiveness). Specific manifestations of personality disturbance are generally of moderate severity. Moderate Personality Disorder is sometimes associated with harm to self or others and is associated with marked impairment in personal, family, social, educational, occupational, or other important areas of functioning, although functioning in circumscribed areas may be maintained.

Severe Personality Disorder

All general diagnostic requirements for PD are met. There are severe disturbances in functioning of the self (e.g., sense of self may be so unstable that individuals report not having a sense of who they are or so rigid that they refuse to participate in any but an extremely narrow range of situations; self-view may be characterized by self-contempt or be grandiose or highly eccentric). Problems in interpersonal functioning seriously affect virtually all relationships, and the ability and willingness to perform expected social and occupational roles are absent or severely compromised. Specific manifestations of personality disturbance are severe and affect most, if not all, areas of personality functioning. Severe Personality Disorder is often associated with harm to self or others and with severe impairment in all or nearly all areas of life, including personal, family, social, educational, occupational, and other important areas of functioning.

Note. PD = personality disorder; *ICD-11* = *International Statistical Classification of Diseases and Related Health Problems* (11th ed.). Data from World Health Organization (2019).

Because a general dimension of personality functioning is variable, it may be a better way of measuring progress than specific stylistic personality features that are more stable (Chanen & McCutcheon, 2013; National Institute for Health and Care Excellence [NICE], 2009; Stoffers et al., 2012). Treatment may improve patients from a severe to a moderate level of personality disturbance (Tyrer et al., 2011). A higher baseline level of personality functioning is generally associated with a better treatment outcome. However, patients with severe personality dysfunction may show larger pre-post-treatment effect in terms of improvement. Such patients have more to improve in personality functioning than those with milder personality problems (Bach & Simonsen, 2021).

The face value of the *ICD-11* PD severity model's clinical utility is supported by a survey of clinicians (Hansen et al., 2019). The survey indicated that clinicians generally find the *ICD-11* PD diagnosis, including classification of severity, more useful for treatment planning and communication with patients in comparison to familiar PD categories. This finding is consistent with a survey by Morey et al. (2014), which showed that clinicians consider levels of personality functioning to be most associated with prognosis and determination of optimal treatment intensity in comparison to PD categories (Hansen et al., 2019).

PD severity is associated with treatment alliance and risk of dropout. Perhaps unsurprisingly, those with more severe personality dysfunction have lower quality therapeutic relations and poorer treatment engagement (Kendall et al., 2010; Soloff, 1998). Clinicians also report that more severe personality pathology is associated with boundary confusion, increased negative countertransference, and increased need for supportive techniques (Gordon et al., 2019; Koelen et al., 2012). These findings underscore the importance of accurately assessing the severity of a patient's personality dysfunction and using this information in planning treatment. For example, severe PD may lead to a more supportive rather than interpretive framework in therapy (Tyrer & Davidson, 2000), or to "limited reparenting" in SFT. Table 8.1 provides a brief overview of tentative treatment strategies for the different levels of severity.

Severe PD should also alert clinicians to carefully monitor their own therapeutic processes because patients with severe PD are more likely to induce anger and reduce empathy. Managing this countertransference may be related to better outcomes (Silk & Feurino, 2012). The influence of therapist effects on treatment outcome may increase with the severity of the patient's pathology (American Psychiatric Association, 2001). Severe PD is associated with higher risk for dropout (Herpertz et al., 2007; Lieb et al., 2010), suggesting a more individualized approach to treatment may be necessary. For a more comprehensive overview of the implications of PD severity for clinical management and treatment, see Bach and Simonsen (2021).

PERSONALITY TRAIT DOMAINS

This section covers the assessment of trait domains and their use in enabling clinicians to focus their treatment. The general principles of treatment of trait domains, as well as *ICD-11* individual trait domains, are explored.

188 *Mulder and Bach*

TABLE 8.1. Tentative Treatment Strategies According to *ICD-11* Personality Disorder Severity

Treatment strategy	Mild PD	Moderate PD	Severe PD
General	Less structured and less intensive treatment settings are needed Little effort is needed for maintaining alliance and preventing irreparable ruptures Group therapy is usually sufficient without individual supporting sessions	Moderately structured treatment settings are needed Clinician needs to be more prepared for handling ruptures in alliance Risk of dropout is increased	Highly structured treatment settings and clear boundaries are needed Clinician must work consciously on building an alliance, repairing ruptures, and preventing dropout Priority needs to be given to suicidal and homicidal risks, self-harm and violence, and therapy-interfering behaviors
TFP	This level requires a predominantly interpretive and confrontative intervention rather than a supportive one	This level requires a balance of interpretative and supportive intervention in which interpretations are aimed at clarifying and uncovering meaning here and now, and are only gentle confrontative	A mostly supportive approach with a focus on the present (here and now) is required Patients at this level may show strong affect or aggression with extreme transference distortions that often lead to treatment disruption
DBT	The focus is on interpersonal problems and other quality-of-life issues Less comprehensive DBT may be considered (e.g., skills class plus consultation team)	The focus is on self-harm and suicidal behavior where present There is an increased focus on other destabilizing behaviors, including therapy-interfering ones	The primary focus is on reducing suicidal and self-harm behaviors, therapy-interfering behaviors, and other seriously destabilizing behaviors
MBT	Treatment must generally seek to support the existing capacity for mentalizing Patients at this level are usually less "hard to reach" and more open to new information because of relatively intact epistemic trust	Treatment must seek to restore mentalizing when lost by rebalancing the mentalizing poles: self–other, affect–cognition, and internal–external	Treatment must seek to increase epistemic trust and decrease epistemic hypervigilance by both seeing the world as the patient does and providing a useful alternative perspective

TABLE 8.1. Tentative Treatment Strategies According to *ICD-11* Personality Disorder Severity (*Continued*)

Treatment strategy	Mild PD	Moderate PD	Severe PD
SFT	Therapist must assist the patient's "healthy adult" part in meeting own emotional needs by means of empathic confrontation, cognitive behavior techniques, and experiential work (corrective emotional experiences)	Therapist must build up the patient's "healthy adult" to meet own emotional needs, while the clinician exhibits warmth, security, and acceptance to meet the needs that the patient is unable to meet—and help the patient integrate different self-modes	Therapist must compensate for lack of "healthy adult" functioning by intensive support and limited reparenting Therapist must combat or limit modes related to harming self or others Therapist needs to foster integration of dissociated self-modes through experiential work and therapeutic support

Note. The examples primarily apply to patients in general mental health care who are characterized by predominant internalizing problems. PD = personality disorder; TFP = transference focused therapy; DBT = dialectical behavior therapy; MBT = mentalization-based treatment; SFT = schema-focused therapy. Data from Bach and Simonsen (2021).

Assessment of Traits

There are a number of feasible methods for assessing trait domains but no sanctioned instruments to operationalize the *ICD-11* trait descriptions and guidelines. The 17-item Personality Assessment Questionnaire for *ICD-11* (Kim et al., 2020) is a brief measure that captures the five trait domains. The Personality Inventory for *ICD-11* (PiCD; J. R. Oltmanns & Widiger, 2018) captures the five *ICD-11* trait domains and can be administered as a self-report form and a clinician- or informant-report form (Bach, Christensen, et al., 2020). Moreover, the facet-level operationalization of the PiCD has been developed (i.e., the Five-Factor Inventory for *ICD-11*; J. R. Oltmanns & Widiger, 2020), which portrays the five domains, including 20 subfacets. The Personality Inventory for *DSM-5* (PID-5; Krueger et al., 2012), which has been around for a longer time, measures *DSM-5* trait domains but can be used to derive the *ICD-11* domains using a simple algorithm (Bach et al., 2017; Sellbom et al., 2020). The 36-item Personality Inventory for *DSM-5* and *ICD-11* Brief Form–Modified, developed and validated internationally, efficiently captures the combined six trait domains of both *DSM-5* and *ICD-11*, including 18 subfacet descriptors (Bach, Kerber, et al., 2020; Kerber et al., 2021). Chapter 2 provides a more extensive empirical overview of these measures. Perhaps of most relevance to nonresearch clinicians, the traits can simply be rated based on observations, unstructured questions, and other available clinical information (Bach, Christensen, et al., 2020; Hansen et al., 2019; Morey et al., 2013).

Use of Traits to Focus Treatment

The trait domains seem to be an obvious way to help focus treatment. For example, patients with Negative Affectivity as well as Disinhibition would usually be considered reactive. An important task for therapy, therefore, is to contain this behavior and attempt to reduce the patient's reactivity by teaching them to both tolerate and regulate it. In contrast, patients with Detachment are less emotionally responsive, and the therapeutic task is to increase emotional activity while also accepting their trait nature.

Treatment should focus on modulating trait expressions rather than seek to change the underlying trait. In addition, it should help the patient find more constructive or healthy ways to express or cope with the basic trait. The premise is that it is possible to change the expression of maladaptive traits by modifying the environment along with associated beliefs and coping patterns. Obvious examples are for patients to minimize stressful situations and relationships that evoke negative trait behaviors while also reducing the influence of maladaptive beliefs associated with the trait expressions (e.g., "I am worthless").

A patient with prominent Negative Affectivity may often be best helped by staying away from unhealthy relationships and situations that maintain the maladaptive trait expressions (e.g., shame, guilt) while seeking healthy relationships that are otherwise avoided as a result of mistrustfulness and poor self-confidence. In this process, the patient may also learn to apply healthy emotion regulation strategies (e.g., taking a walk or calling a friend instead of binge-eating chocolate) while challenging their own negative beliefs and coping patterns (e.g., being more authentic about their own feelings rather than faking that everything is fine). Likewise, patients with prominent features of Detachment may often be helped to seek out some interaction with other people that involves caring relationships and meaningful employment in a psychologically safe environment in which they can also open up and talk a little bit about their otherwise hidden feelings. From this perspective, the features of Detachment may be approached as a coping or defense mechanism against intimacy, and adapting a bit more extraverted behavior is necessary for the patient to find an intimate caring relationship. However, in many cases, patients with prominent features of Detachment may be best helped by encouraging them to create a way of living and a niche that is consistent with their basic stylistic traits and needs rather than attempt to become extraverted like many other people around them (Bach & Presnall-Shvorin, 2020).

Treatment of Maladaptive Trait Expressions

Traits need to be considered in terms of the personality disposition and their related functional impairment—an aspect that is strongly related to the severity of the personality difficulties. For example, a patient might have prominent features of Negative Affectivity that if mild, would lead to some distress in interpersonal relationships, but if severe, could lead to hatred, self-harm, and possible dissociation.

The basic clinical principle is that traits tend to be resistant to change, but the level of impairment and adaptions to the traits are less so. It is argued that treatment should target the characteristic adaption of the patient rather than the traits themselves (Bach & Presnall-Shvorin, 2020). The patient is encouraged to find new adaptive ways of coping with their personality traits. Therapy should therefore focus attention on understanding the traits while attempting to change their consequences. These ideas are not new. Wachtel (1973) suggested that psychotherapeutic interventions should be targeted toward the choices of current environmental stimuli rather than toward the underlying dispositions. Lasting therapeutic change often depends on modulating the impact of the traits rather than getting rid of them.

Use of Patient Traits in the Therapeutic Process

Using traits encourages a collaborative therapeutic approach that may help promote self-knowledge and insight (Fischer & Finn, 2008). An example is helping patients to identify their own traits and how they are demonstrated in everyday life, and then helping them accept that traits are part of their (probably biological) heritage—something that they must own—while conveying the idea that traits can be changed into something more adaptive. Livesley (2003) suggested presenting the information by discussing the probable adaptive advantages of common traits. This model proposes that the traits themselves are not maladaptive but may become so when individuals have learned to express them in ways that cause dysfunction or that lack flexibility. The focus is not on changing a core part of their trait features; rather, it is on specific aspects of their trait expressions, including overall severity.

Acknowledging the adaptive significance of traits when the context is considered may be important. An obvious example is that emotional lability may lead to creativity and artistic excellence. Because traits are context dependent, they may be valuable in some situations but not in others. For example, the Detachment trait domain may be problematic in social situations but useful when cool-headed, self-absorbed behavior is called for (e.g., an academic researcher, a truck driver). Traits are not an all-or-none prospect; rather, they are dimensional in nature.

SPECIFIC *ICD-11* TRAIT DOMAINS

Currently, very little evidence exists about the usefulness of specific domains guiding treatment. Both the *ICD-11* and *DSM-5* domains are relatively new. Although they are related to the five-factor model (FFM) and even though that model is more than 50 years old, there is virtually no evidence on how FFM traits specifically guide treatment and prognosis. Most FFM studies are confined to normal populations. One of the major problems in the field has been this disconnection between PD categories and personality traits. Nevertheless, we can provide some ideas around the treatment of *ICD-11* domains

Negative Affectivity

This domain is similar to high neuroticism. Negative Affectivity is important in that it is strongly associated with treatment-seeking and may lead to behaviors, such as emotional crises and suicidality, that are likely to bring the patient into contact with mental health services. Negative Affectivity is associated with increased emotional suffering shared with a wide range of mental disorders as well as physical problems. Because emotional distress is associated with treatment-seeking, virtually all models of therapy target Negative Affectivity to some degree (Widiger & Trull, 1992). For example, dialectical behavior therapy (DBT) targets emotional dysregulation (Linehan & Dexter-Mazza, 2008), whereas acceptance and commitment therapy focuses on acceptance of negative affect (Hayes, 2004), and MBT attempts to increase emotional regulation with improved mentalizing capacity (Bateman & Fonagy, 2016).

As we have noted previously (Bach & Presnall-Shvorin, 2020), the aim of treatment is not to transform a person with high Negative Affectivity into a carefree and confident individual. Usually, the best that can be hoped for is that the patient can better identify and manage negative automatic appraisals in a healthier manner. Learning better emotional regulation and stress management skills will not convert a patient with high Negative Affectivity to one with low Negative Affectivity. But it may significantly improve their tolerance to emotions, thereby helping their mood and anxiety.

A range of emotional disorders share the underlying trait of Negative Affectivity, and specific, albeit transdiagnostic, approaches have been developed to help. The Unified Protocol for Transdiagnostic Treatment of Emotional Disorders (UP; Barlow, Ellard, et al., 2011; Barlow, Farchione, et al., 2011) is a cognitive behavior approach to mood and anxiety disorders as well as avoidant PD and borderline PD (BPD; Barlow, Farchione, et al., 2011; Sauer-Zavala et al., 2016). The approach targets Negative Affectivity by reducing stress in response to the experience of strong emotions. The underlying rationale is that reduction of adverse reactions to emotions by improving tolerance leads to less reliance on maladaptive, avoidant emotion-regulating strategies that exacerbate symptoms, thereby reducing negative emotions.

Mindfulness-based treatments have also been identified as having value for helping those with Negative Affectivity cope with challenging life situations (Drake et al., 2017). In practice, patients are encouraged not to judge aspects of Negative Affectivity as negative but, instead, to take a gentle, inquisitive attitude, which reduces rumination, worry, and racing thoughts. Mindfulness is therefore a skill that may reduce the distress associated with Negative Affectivity. It is part of other psychotherapies, including DBT (Linehan & Dexter-Mazza, 2008) and the UP (Barlow, Ellard, et al., 2011; Barlow, Farchione, et al., 2011).

Negative Affectivity is also substantially related to most maladaptive schemas of emotional disorders as outlined in schema therapy. For example, separation insecurity aligns with the schema of abandonment, whereas submissiveness aligns with the schema of subjugation (Bach & Bernstein, 2019). Patients with high Negative Affectivity may benefit from schema therapy, such as enhancement of the patient's healthy adult functions, that protect and soothe the vulnerable part of the patient (Bach & Presnall-Shvorin, 2020).

Detachment

This domain is associated with low extraversion, and patients are usually described as a "loner," are shy, and display intimacy avoidance. They are unlikely to seek treatment but may feel that they are missing out on life. Sometimes concerned friends or relatives will bring them to therapy. Behavioral therapy skills training, including such approaches as behavioral activation, might be useful (Lejuez et al., 2011). Possibly more important is to have realistic expectations around what change is possible, which involves understanding the patient and helping them understand and appreciate themselves (Fischer & Finn, 2008). It is important not to become discouraged by the patient's lack of apparent interest in the therapy; patients with Detachment are unlikely to give much positive feedback. The therapist should understand that the low level of positive affectivity is not the same as the patient's being shut down or repressed (Bach & Presnall-Shvorin, 2020). Sometimes changing the environment may be more helpful, consistent with nidotherapy (Tyrer, 2002). *Nidotherapy* attempts to systematically manipulate the physical and social environments to help achieve a better fit for a person.

Dissociality

This domain is associated with low agreeableness and includes features like callousness, manipulativeness, hostility, and grandiosity. Patients with Dissociality tend to be resistant to the therapist's efforts to establish rapport; thus, they may be dishonest and will often see other people as the cause of their problems. They may be referred through the justice system or their employer.

Some researchers have suggested that therapists considering treating patients with high levels of Dissociality should reflect on their own ability to confront unpleasant behaviors without moral judgment or defensiveness (Harkness & McNulty, 2006). The therapist should avoid engaging in power struggles or responding defensively when challenged with explicit attempts to share control. Some insight and sensitivity to the patient's worldview may be an advantage.

Treatment goals should be moderate and realistic. Some evidence suggests that despite resistance to interventions, treatment goals are possible (Behary & Dieckmann, 2012; Ronningstam, 2010). A reasonable goal for therapy can be structured around the patient's developing an awareness of the costs of using such an antagonistic/dissocial strategy (Harkness & McNulty, 2006; Livesley, 2003). If a reasonable alliance is established, there is some evidence of gains using MBT (Bateman & Fonagy, 2016), SFT (Bernstein et al., 2007), or transference-focused therapy (Stern et al., 2017).

Disinhibition

This domain is associated with low conscientiousness. Patients are typically characterized by impulsivity, risk-taking, lack of persistence, and irresponsibility. Patients with Disinhibition are often brought to treatment by concerned family members or friends. The underlying principles of treatment remain similar. The goal is to help the patient live with a disinhibited personality—not to transform them into inhibition or Anankastia (Harkness & McNulty, 2006). Behavioral therapy is an obvious treatment, but there are no randomized clinical trials (RCTs). As well as attempting to modify behavior, the therapist should assist the patient in changing their environment to create an effective reward and punishment system that is naturally maintained in the environment (Bach & Presnall-Shvorin, 2020).

Some researchers have suggested that in clinical settings, Disinhibition may be equated with attention-deficit/hyperactivity disorder (ADHD), which is consistent with evidence that facets of Disinhibition, notably distractibility and impulsivity, capture much of ADHD (Sellbom et al., 2018; Smith & Samuel, 2017). Treatment involves helping the patient find safer and healthier activities that still fit with their need for excitement and novelty. Moreover, the sociogenomic trait intervention model (Roberts et al., 2017) has been adapted to a specific treatment approach for problems related to low levels of conscientiousness corresponding to features of Disinhibition.

Anankastia

This domain is associated with high conscientiousness, which results in the patient's having features of perfectionism, emotional and behavioral constraints, a preoccupation with following rules and meeting obligations, stubbornness, and orderliness. Again, patients with Anankastia are unlikely to present for treatment because they see the world as particularly disorderly, untidy, and morally dissolute.

There are no evidence-based treatments, possibly related to the lack of treatment-seeking in anankastic individuals. Again, a logical goal would be to help the patient find more adaptive expressions of their underlying traits without expectation that the traits themselves would change (Lynch et al., 2015). Anankastic patients may respond better with specific goals and an active therapist who provides direction, guidance, and reasonable advice. It might be helpful if the therapist is on time and consistently refers to a plan within a structured session (Bach & Presnall-Shvorin, 2020).

Compassion-focused therapy (Gilbert, 2014) that focuses on exchanging self-criticisms (e.g., internalized critical/demanding authority) with self-compassion (e.g., acceptance and compassion from an internalized, "good" authority) may be useful (Bach & Presnall-Shvorin, 2020). In addition, a modified version of DBT for obsessive-compulsive PD features and disorder of emotional overcontrol targets the inhibited emotional expression, rigidity, and stubbornness characterizing the Anankastia domain (Lynch et al., 2015; Miller & Kraus, 2007).

PHARMACOTHERAPY

In some ways, the rationale for using drugs in the treatment of PDs anticipates the *ICD-11* classification. Researchers have largely ignored individual PDs and have tried to focus on dimensions of personality pathology. The algorithm generally used to study drug effects was proposed by Siever and Davis (1991) and further developed by Soloff (1998). It proposes four dimensions— affective instability, anxiety/inhibition, cognitive-perceptual disturbances, and impulsivity/aggression—that cut across all PD categories; furthermore, it suggests that drug treatment effects on these dimensions, rather than the individual PDs, should be studied.

There are two problems. First, although the validity of the dimensions is heuristically appealing, little evidence exists to support it. The four dimensions have never been tested in hypothesis-driven studies. Second, although the algorithm was designed to study behaviors across all PD categories, more than 70% of all field trials involve patients with BPD. In addition, most trials are underpowered; one review reported a mean of 22.4 participants in one treatment group and 19.3 in the control group (Duggan et al., 2008).

Perhaps unsurprisingly, recommendations about drug treatment are confusing and, at times, contradictory. The treatment guidelines all focus on BPD. Because samples of individuals with BPD are likely to be heterogeneous, results are inconsistent. Some guidelines advocate symptom-targeted pharmacotherapy based on Siever and Davis's (1991) dimensions, whereas others state drug treatment should generally be avoided in patients with BPD (Stoffers-Winterling et al., 2018).

The American Psychiatric Association's (2001) guideline states that symptom-targeted pharmacotherapy is an important adjunct treatment. It suggests that affective instability is treated with selective serotonin reuptake inhibitors (SSRIs) or monoamine oxidase inhibitors, impulsive aggression with SSRIs or mood stabilizers, and cognitive-perceptual disturbances treated with low-dose antipsychotics. The World Federation of Societies of Biological Psychiatry's guidelines (Herpertz et al., 2007) state that moderate evidence exists that antipsychotic drugs are effective for cognitive-perceptual and impulsive-aggressive symptoms, that some evidence exists that SSRIs are effective for emotional dysregulation, and that evidence exists suggesting that mood stabilizers are effective for emotional dysregulation and impulsive-aggressive symptoms. The most recent Cochrane systematic review (Stoffers-Winterling et al., 2018) partially contradicted these guidelines: It reported no evidence for the efficacy of SSRIs; however, it did report that mood stabilizers could diminish affective dysregulation and impulsive-aggressive symptoms in patients with BPD and that antipsychotics could improve cognitive-perceptual symptoms and affective dysregulation.

In contrast, the United Kingdom's NICE (2009) guidelines state that drug treatment should generally be avoided, except in a crisis, and then given for no longer than 1 week. The more recent guidelines for treatment of BPD from the Australian National Health and Medical Research Council (NHMRC; 2012) again reviewed the literature, including conducting a series of meta-analyses. The NHMRC's conclusion is that pharmacotherapy does not appear to be effective in altering the nature and course of BPD.

These apparently contradictory recommendations may reflect the weight given to risks as well as benefits of drug treatment. Both the NICE and NHMRC committees acknowledged that evidence existed that some second-generation antipsychotics (notably, aripiprazole and olanzapine) and mood stabilizers (notably, topiramate, lamotrigine, and valproate) may reduce BPD symptoms over the short term. They concluded that the substantial long-term risks did not justify recommending these drugs when alternative psychosocial interventions do not carry such risks.

A pragmatic compromise may be to acknowledge the real concerns about using drugs in this population and be guided toward using them with at least some evidence of efficacy and using them sparingly and for short periods. The current evidence (Abraham & Calabrese, 2008) would suggest use of atypical antipsychotics and mood stabilizers rather than SSRIs tricyclic antidepressants and benzodiazepines. A recent and large RCT, however, reported that the mood stabilizer lamotrigine is ineffective in treating BPD (Crawford et al., 2018). A more radical view, articulated in the NICE (2009) guidelines, is that if patients have no comorbid illness, efforts should be made to reduce or stop pharmacotherapy.

The *ICD-11* domain structure would, on the face of it, appear a more promising model than the *ICD-10* (tenth edition of the *International Statistical Classification of Diseases and Related Health Problems*; WHO, 1990) or *DSM-5* models to test the effects of drugs on PDs. The domains may, at least theoretically, be related to drug effects. The Disinhibition domain might benefit from atypical antipsychotics or possibly mood stabilizers. Increased Negative Affectivity might respond, at least partially, to antidepressant and antianxiety drugs. It is possible that agents with antiobsessive properties, such as serotonergic antidepressants, might help reduce maladaptive features of Anankastia. It seems unlikely that medication would have much effect on Dissociality given the lack of evidence that medication has any effect on antisocial PD (Duggan et al., 2008; Khalifa et al., 2010). There have been no drug studies on patients with detached or schizoid personality traits. Whether drugs ever justify their long-term risk in patients with PDs remains contentious. However, the *ICD-11* model offers a more plausible and coherent model to test out their efficacy in the short and long term.

BLENDS OF TRAITS IN PATIENTS

While we have focused on treatment and single personality domains, this is a simplistic approach. Most patients will have more than one prominent trait domain, particularly if they have moderate or severe PD. A more finely detailed formulation is appropriate for these patients. Consider, for example, two patients for whom Negative Affectivity constitutes the most prominent feature, but one has a secondary domain of Disinhibition and the other has a secondary domain of Detachment. In the first patient, the behavior exhibited is externalizing anger or overcompensating grandiosity related to dysregulated emotion. The second patient presents with internalizing features of withdrawal, depressivity, and anxiety. Obviously, the consideration of such trait blends has substantial consequences for treatment planning and targets.

Traditional PD categories often comprise different constellations of overlapping trait domains. For example, a constellation of Dissociality and Disinhibition captures much of Antisocial PD (Bateman & Fonagy, 2016), whereas Negative Affectivity and Detachment capture much of Avoidant PD. While pure Anankastia is similar to Obsessive-Compulsive PD (Simon, 2015), when associated with Negative Affectivity, it may be treated as a conscientious and worried type, whereas when associated with Dissociality, it may be treated as a bureaucratic, overcontrolling, and narcissistic type (Bach & Presnall-Shvorin, 2020). Likewise, BPD is the most heterogeneous and complex PD type and usually comprises several domains. Milder cases may largely be characterized primarily by Negative Affectivity (i.e., anxiousness, separation anxiety, and emotional lability), whereas more severe cases may have Negative Affectivity accompanied by Disinhibition (e.g., impulsivity) and Dissociality (e.g., hostility). Such differences have probable implications for treatment planning and may help explain the inconsistent results of treatment RCTs in those with BPD.

Although the multiple trait model is heuristically appealing and has face validity, there is only limited evidence of its applicability and usefulness in individuals with PDs. The UP is an evidence-based approach that has been specifically adapted to treatment of emotional disorders, including emotionally undercontrolled PDs, focusing on Negative Affectivity as a transdiagnostic and underlying trait disposition (Sauer-Zavala et al., 2016). Likewise, radically open-DBT is an evidence-based approach that has been adapted to treatment of emotionally overcontrolled PDs, focusing on Anankastia-related issues and Anankastia (Lynch et al., 2015). Diagnostic issues need to be carefully thought about or we may reduce patients to simple, if different, rigid categories, thus leading to the stalemate we are in now. The domains are dimensions, not categorical diagnoses, and need to be treated as such. While this adds complexity, it provides a way to more specifically target treatments to the patient.

BORDERLINE PATTERN SPECIFIER

After clinicians have determined PD severity and the most prominent trait domains, the *ICD-11* PD classification allows them to specify a borderline pattern specifier that essentially relies on the nine *DSM-IV* (4th ed.; American Psychiatric Association, 1994) diagnostic features (see Exhibit 8.3). The option of coding a borderline pattern specifier was officially included in *ICD-11* as a pragmatic solution to enhance clinical utility by facilitating the identification of individuals who may respond to well-established psychotherapeutic treatments aimed at this historically important construct (Reed, 2018). The vast majority of studies on PD treatment focus on individuals labeled as having BPD (Storebø et al., 2020). Thus, practitioners are understandably worried that the lack of an explicit reference to this syndrome within the *ICD-11* would be problematic to its continued clinical research, funding, and national guidelines (Herpertz et al., 2017). In this respect, the inclusion of a borderline pattern specifier would appear to be a reasonable compromise to gain acceptance of the revision. Nevertheless, the essential severity and trait model was originally considered by the *ICD-11* Working Group to fully account for the borderline pattern (Tyrer et al., 2019). According to Reed (2018), research will eventually tell us whether the borderline pattern provides information that is nonredundant with or distinct from that provided by the trait domains.

In response to this call, J. R. Oltmanns and Widiger (2019) developed the 12-item Borderline Pattern Scale to assess the nine features as presented in the *ICD-11* diagnostic guidelines. They found the *ICD-11* PD severity, as well as the trait dimensions, to substantially account for the total symptom score in individuals who were currently or had been in mental health treatment. This finding has been corroborated in another clinical study using the same operationalization (McCabe & Widiger, 2020). Likewise, a clinical study by Mulder et al. (2020), based on structured clinical diagnoses PD diagnoses, concluded that the addition of a borderline pattern specifier is essentially captured by PD severity as well as trait domains of Negative Affectivity, Disinhibition, and Dissociality, and that the BPD pattern therefore does not add much to the *ICD-11* PD classification. This assumption was also supported by Bach, Brown, et al. (2021), who found the PDS-ICD-11 operationalization of PD severity to substantially account for a BPD symptom score. Moreover, emerging research generally indicates that both *DSM-5* and *ICD-11* trait domains adequately and largely account for BPD features (Bach, Kerber, et al., 2020; Bach & Sellbom, 2016; Bach et al., 2018; Sellbom et al., 2014).

The aforementioned findings are consistent with research showing that BPD symptoms load strongly on a general index ("g-factor") similar to a global

EXHIBIT 8.3

Borderline Pattern Specifier

The borderline pattern specifier may be applied to individuals whose pattern of personality disturbance is characterized by a pervasive pattern of instability of interpersonal relationships, self-image, and affects, as well as marked impulsivity as indicated by five (or more) of the following:

- frantic efforts to avoid real or imagined abandonment

- a pattern of unstable and intense interpersonal relationships, typically characterized by alternating between extremes of idealization and devaluation

- identity disturbance manifested in markedly and persistently unstable self-image or sense of self

- impulsivity manifested in potentially self-damaging behaviors (e.g., risky sexual behavior, reckless driving, excessive alcohol or substance use, binge eating)

- recurrent episodes of self-harm (e.g., suicide attempts or gestures, self-mutilation)

- emotional instability as the result of marked reactivity of mood; fluctuations of mood may be triggered either internally (e.g., by one's own thoughts) or by external events; consequently, the individual experiences intense dysphoric mood states that typically last for a few hours but may last for up to several days

- chronic feelings of emptiness

- inappropriate intense anger or difficulty controlling anger manifested in frequent displays of temper (e.g., yelling or screaming, throwing or breaking things, getting into physical fights)

- transient dissociative symptoms or psychoticlike features (e.g., brief hallucinations, paranoia) in situations of high affective arousal

Other manifestations of borderline pattern, not all of which may be present in a given individual at a given time, include the following:

- a view of the self as inadequate, bad, guilty, disgusting, and contemptible

- an experience of the self as profoundly different and isolated from other people as well as a painful sense of alienation and pervasive loneliness

- proneness to rejection hypersensitivity, problems in establishing and maintaining consistent and appropriate levels of trust in interpersonal relationships, frequent misinterpretation of social signals

Note. Data from World Health Organization (2019).

severity dimension rather than a homogenous BPD factor (Sharp et al., 2015). A common interpretation of this finding has been that BPD features generally define what is central to all PDs (Sharp et al., 2015), which reflects impaired capacities of self- and interpersonal functioning (Wright et al., 2016). Therefore, when treating BPD, we may be dealing with a heterogeneous field of "borderlineness," which typically involves functional impairments in sense of identity, self-directedness, and reality testing along with traits of Negative

Affectivity (e.g., poor emotion regulation), Disinhibition (e.g., impulsivity, recklessness), and Dissociality (e.g., aggressiveness, anger).

Against this background, it seems reasonable that more meaningful treatment would focus on the overall impairment of personality functioning along with prominent maladaptive trait expressions rather than focus on a heterogeneous category of problems. In other words, clinicians may benefit from focusing on the more specific problems portrayed by the severity and trait features (e.g., impaired capacity for emotion regulation, traits of Negative Affectivity and Disinhibition) rather than the heterogeneous borderline pattern (Bach & Presnall-Shvorin, 2020). In this way, individuals traditionally characterized by the BPD category may be portrayed and treated in a more individualized manner.

CLINICAL CASE ILLUSTRATION: MR. Z

We now briefly illustrate the application of the *ICD-11* PD classification, including pretreatment considerations and posttreatment reevaluation.

Mr. Z[1] is a sensitive and intelligent 35-year-old man with a history of panic attacks, social anxiety, and recurrent depressive episodes. He was referred to mental health care by his family physician because he had dropped out of college as a result of the aforementioned symptomatology. Mr. Z had grew up in a family characterized by emotional neglect and abuse; the mother was dominant and abusive, and the father was a nervous and absentminded man who suffered from severe depressive episodes and alcoholism. His older siblings moved away from home as soon as they were able, and they did not maintain connection to any family members.

As an adolescent, Mr. Z had suffered from excessive insecurity, poor self-worth, loneliness, and self-defeating behaviors, such as letting peers abuse or make fun of him. Consequently, he tended to act as an underdog or a people-pleaser. This pattern had followed him into adulthood in terms of inhibitedness, avoidance, and social withdrawal to avoid feeling criticized, ashamed, or rejected. He once had a girlfriend, who had a drug problem. She was dominant, took advantage of him, and controlled him by means of physical and verbal aggression. Mr. Z had always enjoyed playing the guitar, and he managed to give guitar lessons to children 2 hours a week.

The intake evaluation concluded that Mr. Z's clinical presentation of persistent difficulties fulfilled the *ICD-11* diagnostic requirements for a Moderate Personality Disorder based on impairments in self- and interpersonal functioning, manifestations, and global impairment.[2] Accordingly, Mr. Z had a negative sense of self-worth associated with shame and a negative view of his own characteristics in which he overestimated his perceived weaknesses and harshly underestimated his strengths. His capacity for self-direction was

---

[1]Details have been disguised to protect patient confidentiality.
[2]The pattern corresponded to the traditional *ICD-10* typological descriptions for F60.6 Avoidant Personality Disorder and a secondary F60.7 Dependent Personality Disorder.

compromised in terms of reluctance to engage in activities involving interpersonal contact, and he always overestimated the potential risk of failure in social situations, which particularly caused him to be goal inhibited and resign from many social situations. He was interested in other people but was too inhibited to express it. His ability to understand others' perspectives was compromised by a distorted inference of others' perspectives as being negative, which caused him to be disengaged with other people and overly sensitive to perceived criticism. He was afraid of taking the first step when meeting new people, which prevented him from developing and maintaining friendships. In the few relationships he had been able to maintain, he usually played the submissive and overcompliant role when facing conflicts. From other people's perspective, he was a friendly, empathic, and humble guy—yet shy and inhibited.

Mr. Z was not classified as having a Severe Personality Disorder because he was able to maintain functioning in certain areas, such as keeping contact with a few people, pursuing his interest in playing the guitar, and performing certain expected occupational roles (e.g., teaching kids to play the guitar). With respect to stylistic trait specifiers, Mr. Z's personality style was characterized by prominent features of Negative Affectivity (e.g., anxiousness, shame, submissiveness, low self-esteem) and Detachment (e.g., inhibition, avoidance, social withdrawal). Based on the aforementioned diagnostic information, it was considered that Mr. Z would benefit from working with his inner models of self (i.e., "I am inadequate and defective") and others (i.e., "Other people will expose or humiliate me") along with his overcompliant way of coping with the associated anxiousness (i.e., "I must avoid conflicts with others at any cost").

After 8 months of weekly group psychotherapy, Mr. Z improved to such a degree that he was able to maintain a stable job teaching kids several days a week and started a couple of new friendships (see Table 8.2). His self-worth was still characterized by shame and a sense of inferiority but now mostly in situations of stress. He was also able to acknowledge that he has certain strengths, such as being skilled at playing the guitar. His capacity for self-direction was still compromised by some reluctance to engage in activities involving interpersonal contact. He was now able to express an interest in hanging out with some of his musician colleagues, which paved the way for developing and maintaining some relationships, although he continued to be compliant in his approach. However, he remained very sensitive to perceived criticism, which therefore

TABLE 8.2. Mr. Z's Level of Severity and Trait Domains Before and After Treatment

At intake assessment	After 8 months of weekly therapy
Mr. Z virtually has no friends except for a few relationships, and those people tend to take advantage of him. He avoids most occupational roles except for a part-time job teaching children to play the guitar.	Mr. Z is now able to maintain a job; he teaches guitar several days a week and has a few stable and healthy relationships with new friends who play the guitar.
Moderate Personality Disorder	Mild Personality Disorder
Negative Affectivity	Negative Affectivity
Detachment	Detachment

compromised his capacity for understanding others' perspectives. Because of this clinical presentation, his difficulties were now classified as only Mild Personality Disorder but with the same stylistic tendencies reflected in his enduring but now less maladaptive pattern of Negative Affectivity and Detachment (see Table 8.2).

CONCLUSION

Assessment and treatment of PDs using *ICD-10* and *DSM-5* classification models with eight to 10 categories have had limited success. Nearly all of the effort has focused on BPD, with a little trickling down to antisocial PD, essentially demonstrating that all structured therapies (including structured clinical care without any theoretical model) are moderately and equally effective (Cristea et al., 2017). Drug treatments have fared even worse with inconsistent and conflicting recommendations, including nonrecommendations of any drug. There has been no real progress in 20 years (Newton-Howes & Mulder, 2020).

ICD-11 provides a new way of examining personality pathology. It is based on severity that seems the most relevant variable in deciding who to treat, how to treat, and how to measure outcome. The trait domains that are congruent with normally distributed personality traits allow further formulation of individual patients. This moderately sophisticated diagnostic system may allow treatment to be tailored to individual patients. It moves away from a simplistic focus on BPD symptoms and encourages more consideration of the wide range of personality pathology found in some of our patients. The combination of mild, moderate, and severe PD along with personality difficulty and the five trait domains can produce nearly 500 different diagnostic outcomes.

The *ICD-11* model offers a way forward. Although its success—or not—will be apparent only after a period of evaluation and data gathering, it provides an approach for assessment and treatment much closer to the evidence than the one we have left behind.

REFERENCES

Abraham, P. F., & Calabrese, J. R. (2008). Evidence-based pharmacologic treatment of borderline personality disorder: A shift from SSRIs to anticonvulsants and atypical antipsychotics? *Journal of Affective Disorders, 111*(1), 21–30. https://doi.org/10.1016/j.jad.2008.01.024

American Psychiatric Association. (1994). *Diagnostic and statistical manual of mental disorders* (4th ed.).

American Psychiatric Association. (2001). Practice guideline for the treatment of patients with borderline personality disorder. *The American Journal of Psychiatry, 158*(10, Suppl.), 1–52.

American Psychiatric Association. (2013). *Diagnostic and statistical manual of mental disorders* (5th ed.). https://doi.org/10.1176/appi.books.9780890425596

Bach, B., & Bernstein, D. P. (2019). Schema therapy conceptualization of personality functioning and traits in *ICD-11* and *DSM-5*. *Current Opinion in Psychiatry, 32*(1), 38–49. https://doi.org/10.1097/YCO.0000000000000464

Bach, B., Brown, T. A., Mulder, R. T., Newton-Howes, G., Simonsen, E., & Sellbom, M. (2021). Development and initial evaluation of the *ICD-11* Personality Disorder Severity Scale: PDS-ICD-11. *Personality and Mental Health, 15*(3), 223–236. https://doi.org/10.1002/pmh.1510

Bach, B., Christensen, S., Kongerslev, M. T., Sellbom, M., & Simonsen, E. (2020). Structure of clinician-reported *ICD-11* personality disorder trait qualifiers. *Psychological Assessment, 32*(1), 50–59. https://doi.org/10.1037/pas0000747

Bach, B., & First, M. B. (2018). Application of the ICD-11 classification of personality disorders. *BMC Psychiatry, 18*(1), Article 351. https://doi.org/10.1186/s12888-018-1908-3

Bach, B., Kerber, A., Aluja, A., Bastiaens, T., Keeley, J. W., Claes, L., Fossati, A., Gutierrez, F., Oliveira, S. E. S., Pires, R., Riegel, K. D., Rolland, J. P., Roskam, I., Sellbom, M., Somma, A., Spanemberg, L., Strus, W., Thimm, J. C., Wright, A. G. C., & Zimmermann, J. (2020). International assessment of *DSM-5* and *ICD-11* Personality disorder traits: Toward a common nosology in *DSM-5.1. Psychopathology, 53*(3-4), 179–188. https://doi.org/10.1159/000507589

Bach, B., & Presnall-Shvorin, J. (2020). Using *DSM-5* and *ICD-11* personality traits in clinical treatment. In C. Lejuez & K. Gratz (Eds.), *The Cambridge handbook of personality disorders* (pp. 450–467). Cambridge University Press. https://doi.org/10.1017/9781108333931.079

Bach, B., & Sellbom, M. (2016). Continuity between *DSM-5* categorical criteria and traits criteria for borderline personality disorder. *The Canadian Journal of Psychiatry, 61*(8), 489–494. https://doi.org/10.1177/0706743716640756

Bach, B., Sellbom, M., Kongerslev, M., Simonsen, E., Krueger, R. F., & Mulder, R. (2017). Deriving *ICD-11* personality disorder domains from *DSM-5* traits: Initial attempt to harmonize two diagnostic systems. *Acta Psychiatrica Scandinavica, 136*(1), 108–117. https://doi.org/10.1111/acps.12748

Bach, B., Sellbom, M., Skjernov, M., & Simonsen, E. (2018). *ICD-11* and *DSM-5* personality trait domains capture categorical personality disorders: Finding a common ground. *The Australian & New Zealand Journal of Psychiatry, 52*(5), 425–434. https://doi.org/10.1177/0004867417727867

Bach, B., & Simonsen, S. (2021). How does level of personality functioning inform clinical management and treatment? Implications for *ICD-11* classification of personality disorder severity. *Current Opinion in Psychiatry, 34*(1), 54–63. https://doi.org/10.1097/YCO.0000000000000658

Barlow, D. H., Ellard, K. K., Fairholme, C. P., Farchione, T. J., Boisseau, C. L., Allen, L. B., & Ehrenreich-May, J. (2011). *The Unified Protocol for Transdiagnostic Treatment of Emotional Disorders: Client workbook.* Oxford University Press.

Barlow, D. H., Farchione, T. J., Fairholme, C. P., Ellard, K. K., Boisseau, C. L., Allen, L. B., & Ehrenreich-May, J. T. (2011). *Unified Protocol for Transdiagnostic Treatment of Emotional Disorders: Therapist guide.* Oxford University Press.

Bateman, A., Campbell, C., Luyten, P., & Fonagy, P. (2018). A mentalization-based approach to common factors in the treatment of borderline personality disorder. *Current Opinion in Psychology, 21*, 44–49. https://doi.org/10.1016/j.copsyc.2017.09.005

Bateman, A., & Fonagy, P. (2016). *Mentalization-based treatment for personality disorders: A practical guide.* Oxford University Press. https://doi.org/10.1093/med:psych/9780199680375.001.0001

Behary, W. T., & Dieckmann, E. (2012). Schema therapy for narcissism: The art of empathic confrontation, limit-setting, and leverage. In W. K. Campbell & J. D. Miller (Eds.), *The handbook of narcissism and narcissistic personality disorder: Theoretical approaches, empirical findings, and treatments* (pp. 445–456). John Wiley & Sons. https://doi.org/10.1002/9781118093108.ch40

Bender, D. S., Morey, L. C., & Skodol, A. E. (2011). Toward a model for assessing level of personality functioning in *DSM-5*, Part I: A review of theory and methods. *Journal of Personality Assessment, 93*(4), 332–346. https://doi.org/10.1080/00223891.2011.583808

Bernstein, D. P., Arntz, A., & de Vos, M. (2007). Schema focused therapy in forensic settings: Theoretical model and recommendations for best clinical practice. *International Journal of Forensic Mental Health*, *6*(2), 169–183. https://doi.org/10.1080/14999013.2007.10471261

Buer Christensen, T., Eikenaes, I., Hummelen, B., Pedersen, G., Nysæter, T.-E., Bender, D. S., Skodol, A. E., & Selvik, S. G. (2020). Level of personality functioning as a predictor of psychosocial functioning—Concurrent validity of Criterion A. *Personality Disorders: Theory, Research, and Treatment*, *11*(2), 79–90. https://doi.org/10.1037/per0000352

Chanen, A. M., & McCutcheon, L. (2013). Prevention and early intervention for borderline personality disorder: Current status and recent evidence. *The British Journal of Psychiatry*, *202*(S54), S24–S29. https://doi.org/10.1192/bjp.bp.112.119180

Clark, L. A., Livesley, W. J., & Morey, L. (1997). Special feature: Personality disorder assessment: The challenge of construct validity. *Journal of Personality Disorders*, *11*(3), 205–231. https://doi.org/10.1521/pedi.1997.11.3.205

Clark, L. A., Nuzum, H., & Ro, E. (2018). Manifestations of personality impairment severity: Comorbidity, course/prognosis, psychosocial dysfunction, and "borderline" personality features. *Current Opinion in Psychology*, *21*, 117–121. https://doi.org/10.1016/j.copsyc.2017.12.004

Conway, C. C., Hammen, C., & Brennan, P. A. (2016). Optimizing prediction of psychosocial and clinical outcomes with a transdiagnostic model of personality disorder. *Journal of Personality Disorders*, *30*(4), 545–566. https://doi.org/10.1521/pedi_2015_29_218

Crawford, M. J., Koldobsky, N., Mulder, R., & Tyrer, P. (2011). Classifying personality disorder according to severity. *Journal of Personality Disorders*, *25*(3), 321–330. https://doi.org/10.1521/pedi.2011.25.3.321

Crawford, M. J., Sanatinia, R., Barrett, B., Cunningham, G., Dale, O., Ganguli, P., Lawrence-Smith, G., Leeson, V., Lemonsky, F., Lykomitrou, G., Montgomery, A. A., Morriss, R., Munjiza, J., Paton, C., Skorodzien, I., Singh, V., Tan, W., Tyrer, P., Reilly, J. G., & the LABILE Study Team. (2018). The clinical effectiveness and cost-effectiveness of lamotrigine in borderline personality disorder: A randomized placebo-controlled trial. *The American Journal of Psychiatry*, *175*(8), 756–764. https://doi.org/10.1176/appi.ajp.2018.17091006

Cristea, I. A., Gentili, C., Cotet, C. D., Palomba, D., Barbui, C., & Cuijpers, P. (2017). Efficacy of psychotherapies for borderline personality disorder: A systematic review and meta-analysis. *JAMA Psychiatry*, *74*(4), 319–328. https://doi.org/10.1001/jamapsychiatry.2016.4287

Drake, M. M., Morris, M., & Davis, T. J. (2017). Neuroticism's susceptibility to distress: Moderated with mindfulness. *Personality and Individual Differences*, *106*, 248–252. https://doi.org/10.1016/j.paid.2016.10.060

Duggan, C., Huband, N., Smailagic, N., Ferriter, M., & Adams, C. (2008). The use of pharmacological treatments for people with personality disorder: A systematic review of randomized controlled trials. *Personality and Mental Health*, *2*(3), 119–170. https://doi.org/10.1002/pmh.41

Fischer, C. T., & Finn, S. E. (2008). Developing the life meaning of psychological test data: Collaborative and therapeutic approaches. In R. P. Archer & S. R. Smith (Eds.), *Personality assessment* (pp. 379–404). Routledge.

Gilbert, P. (2014). The origins and nature of compassion focused therapy. *The British Journal of Clinical Psychology*, *53*(1), 6–41. https://doi.org/10.1111/bjc.12043

Gordon, R. M., Spektor, V., & Luu, L. (2019). Personality organization traits and expected countertransference and treatment interventions. *International Journal of Psychology and Psychoanalysis*, *5*(1), Article 39. https://doi.org/10.23937/2572-4037.1510039

Hansen, S. J., Christensen, S., Kongerslev, M. T., First, M. B., Widiger, T. A., Simonsen, E., & Bach, B. (2019). Mental health professionals' perceived clinical utility of the *ICD-10* vs. *ICD-11* classification of personality disorders. *Personality and Mental Health*, *13*(2), 84–95. https://doi.org/10.1002/pmh.1442

Harkness, A. R., & McNulty, J. L. (2006). An overview of personality: The MMPI-2 Personality Psychopathology Five (PSY-5) Scales. In J. N. Butcher (Ed.), *MMPI-2: A practitioner's guide* (pp. 73–97). American Psychological Association. https://doi.org/10.1037/11287-004

Hayes, S. C. (2004). Acceptance and commitment therapy and the new behavior therapies: Mindfulness, acceptance, and relationship. In S. C. Hayes, V. M. Follette, & M. M. Linehan (Eds.), *Mindfulness and acceptance: Expanding the cognitive-behavioral tradition* (pp. 1–29). The Guilford Press.

Herpertz, S. C., Huprich, S. K., Bohus, M., Chanen, A., Goodman, M., Mehlum, L., Moran, P., Newton-Howes, G., Scott, L., & Sharp, C. (2017). The challenge of transforming the diagnostic system of personality disorders. *Journal of Personality Disorders, 31*(5), 577–589. https://doi.org/10.1521/pedi_2017_31_338

Herpertz, S. C., Zanarini, M., Schulz, C. S., Siever, L., Lieb, K., Möller, H. J., Herpertz, S. C., Zanarini, M., Schulz, C. S., Siever, L., Lieb, K., Möller, H.-J., the WFSBP Task Force on Personality Disorders, & the World Federation of Societies of Biological Psychiatry. (2007). World Federation of Societies of Biological Psychiatry (WFSBP) guidelines for biological treatment of personality disorders. *The World Journal of Biological Psychiatry, 8*(4), 212–244. https://doi.org/10.1080/15622970701685224

Kendall, T., Burbeck, R., & Bateman, A. (2010). Pharmacotherapy for borderline personality disorder: NICE guideline. *The British Journal of Psychiatry, 196*(2), 158–159. https://doi.org/10.1192/bjp.196.2.158

Kerber, A., Schultze, M., Müller, S., Rühling, R. M., Wright, A. G. C., Spitzer, C., Krueger, R. F., Knaevelsrud, C., & Zimmermann, J. (2021). Development of a short and *ICD-11* compatible measure for *DSM-5* maladaptive personality traits using ant colony optimization algorithms. *Psychological Assessment.* https://doi.org/10.1177/1073191120971848

Khalifa, N., Duggan, C., Stoffers, J., Huband, N., Völlm, B. A., Ferriter, M., & Lieb, K. (2010). Pharmacological interventions for antisocial personality disorder. *Cochrane Database of Systematic Reviews.* https://doi.org/10.1002/14651858.CD007667.pub2

Kim, Y.-R., Tyrer, P., & Hwang, S.-T. (2020). Personality Assessment Questionnaire for *ICD-11* personality trait domains: Development and testing. *Personality and Mental Health.* Advance online publication. https://doi.org/10.1002/pmh.1493

Koelen, J. A., Luyten, P., Eurelings-Bontekoe, L. H. M., Diguer, L., Vermote, R., Lowyck, B., & Bühring, M. E. F. (2012). The impact of level of personality organization on treatment response: A systematic review. *Psychiatry: Interpersonal and Biological Processes, 75*(4), 355–374. https://doi.org/10.1521/psyc.2012.75.4.355

Krueger, R. F., Derringer, J., Markon, K. E., Watson, D., & Skodol, A. E. (2012). Initial construction of a maladaptive personality trait model and inventory for *DSM-5. Psychological Medicine, 42*(9), 1879–1890. https://doi.org/10.1017/S0033291711002674

Lejuez, C. W., Hopko, D. R., Acierno, R., Daughters, S. B., & Pagoto, S. L. (2011). Ten year revision of the Brief Behavioral Activation Treatment for Depression: Revised treatment manual. *Behavior Modification, 35*(2), 111–161. https://doi.org/10.1177/0145445510390929

Lieb, K., Völlm, B., Rücker, G., Timmer, A., & Stoffers, J. M. (2010). Pharmacotherapy for borderline personality disorder: Cochrane Systematic Review of randomised trials. *The British Journal of Psychiatry, 196*(1), 4–12. https://doi.org/10.1192/bjp.bp.108.062984

Linehan, M. M., & Dexter-Mazza, E. T. (2008). Dialectical behavior therapy for borderline personality disorder. In D. H. Barlow (Ed.), *Clinical handbook of psychological disorders: A step-by-step treatment manual* (4th ed., pp. 365–420). Guilford Press.

Livesley, W. J. (2003). *Practical management of personality disorder.* Guilford Press.

Lynch, T. R., Hempel, R. J., & Dunkley, C. (2015). Radically open-dialectical behavior therapy for disorders of over-control: Signaling matters. *American Journal of Psychotherapy, 69*(2), 141–162. https://doi.org/10.1176/appi.psychotherapy.2015.69.2.141

McCabe, G. A., & Widiger, T. A. (2020). A comprehensive comparison of the *ICD-11* and *DSM-5* section III personality disorder models. *Psychological Assessment, 32*(1), 72–84. https://doi.org/10.1037/pas0000772

Miller, T. W., & Kraus, R. F. (2007). Modified dialectical behavior therapy and problem solving for obsessive-compulsive personality disorder. *Journal of Contemporary Psychotherapy, 37*(2), 79–85. https://doi.org/10.1007/s10879-006-9039-4

Morey, L. C., Krueger, R. F., & Skodol, A. E. (2013). The hierarchical structure of clinician ratings of proposed *DSM-5* pathological personality traits. *Journal of Abnormal Psychology, 122*(3), 836–841. https://doi.org/10.1037/a0034003

Morey, L. C., Skodol, A. E., & Oldham, J. M. (2014). Clinician judgments of clinical utility: A comparison of *DSM-IV-TR* personality disorders and the alternative model for *DSM-5* personality disorders. *Journal of Abnormal Psychology, 123*(2), 398–405. https://doi.org/10.1037/a0036481

Mulder, R., Murray, G., & Rucklidge, J. (2017). Common versus specific factors in psychotherapy: Opening the black box. *The Lancet Psychiatry, 4*(12), 953–962. https://doi.org/10.1016/S2215-0366(17)30100-1

Mulder, R., & Tyrer, P. (2019). Diagnosis and classification of personality disorders: Novel approaches. *Current Opinion in Psychiatry, 32*(1), 27–31. https://doi.org/10.1097/YCO.0000000000000461

Mulder, R. T., Horwood, L. J., & Tyrer, P. (2020). The borderline pattern descriptor in the *International Classification of Diseases, 11th Revision*: A redundant addition to classification. *The Australian and New Zealand Journal of Psychiatry, 54*(11), 1095–1100. https://doi.org/10.1177/0004867420951608

National Health and Medical Research Council. (2012). *Clinical practice guideline for the management of borderline personality disorder.*

National Institute for Health and Care Excellence. (2009). *Borderline personality disorder: Recognition and management* (Clinical Guideline CG78). https://www.nice.org.uk/guidance/cg78

Newton-Howes, G., & Mulder, R. (2020). Treatment and management of personality disorder. In J. R. Geddes, N. C. Andreasen, & G. M. Goodwin (Eds.), *New Oxford textbook of psychiatry* (3rd ed., pp. 1257–1264). Oxford University Press.

Oltmanns, J. R., & Widiger, T. A. (2018). A self-report measure for the *ICD-11* dimensional trait model proposal: The Personality Inventory for *ICD-11*. *Psychological Assessment, 30*(2), 154–169. https://doi.org/10.1037/pas0000459

Oltmanns, J. R., & Widiger, T. A. (2019). Evaluating the assessment of the *ICD-11* personality disorder diagnostic system. *Psychological Assessment, 31*(5), 674–684. https://doi.org/10.1037/pas0000693

Oltmanns, J. R., & Widiger, T. A. (2020). The Five-Factor Personality Inventory for *ICD-11*: A facet-level assessment of the *ICD-11* trait model. *Psychological Assessment, 32*(1), 60–71. https://doi.org/10.1037/pas0000763

Oltmanns, T. F., & Balsis, S. (2011). Personality disorders in later life: Questions about the measurement, course, and impact of disorders. *Annual Review of Clinical Psychology, 7*(1), 321–349. https://doi.org/10.1146/annurev-clinpsy-090310-120435

Reed, G. M. (2018). Progress in developing a classification of personality disorders for *ICD-11*. *World Psychiatry, 17*(2), 227–229. https://doi.org/10.1002%2Fwps.20533

Roberts, B. W., Hill, P. L., & Davis, J. P. (2017). How to change conscientiousness: The sociogenomic trait intervention model. *Personality Disorders: Theory, Research, and Treatment, 8*(3), 199–205. https://doi.org/10.1037/per0000242

Ronningstam, E. (2010). Narcissistic personality disorder: A current review. *Current Psychiatry Reports, 12*(1), 68–75. https://doi.org/10.1007/s11920-009-0084-z

Sauer-Zavala, S., Bentley, K. H., & Wilner, J. G. (2016). Transdiagnostic treatment of borderline personality disorder and comorbid disorders: A clinical replication series. *Journal of Personality Disorders, 30*(1), 35–51. https://doi.org/10.1521/pedi_2015_29_179

Sellbom, M., Bach, B., & Huxley, E. (2018). Related personality disorders located within an elaborated externalizing psychopathology spectrum. In J. E. Lochman & W. Matthys (Eds.), *The Wiley handbook of disruptive and impulse-control disorders* (pp. 103–124). John Wiley & Sons.

Sellbom, M., Sansone, R. A., Songer, D. A., & Anderson, J. L. (2014). Convergence between *DSM-5* Section II and Section III diagnostic criteria for borderline personality disorder. *The Australian and New Zealand Journal of Psychiatry, 48*(4), 325–332. https://doi.org/10.1177/0004867413511997

Sellbom, M., Solomon-Krakus, S., Bach, B., & Bagby, R. M. (2020). Validation of Personality Inventory for *DSM-5* (PID-5) algorithms to assess *ICD-11* personality trait domains in a psychiatric sample. *Psychological Assessment, 32*(1), 40–49. https://doi.org/10.1037/pas0000746

Sharp, C., Wright, A. G. C., Fowler, J. C., Frueh, B. C., Allen, J. G., Oldham, J., & Clark, L. A. (2015). The structure of personality pathology: Both general ('g') and specific ('s') factors? *Journal of Abnormal Psychology, 124*(2), 387–398. https://doi.org/10.1037/abn0000033

Siever, L. J., & Davis, K. L. (1991). A psychobiological perspective on the personality disorders. *The American Journal of Psychiatry, 148*(12), 1647–1658. https://doi.org/10.1176/ajp.148.12.1647

Silk, K. R., & Feurino, L., III. (2012). Psychopharmacology of personality disorders. In T. A. Widiger (Ed.), *The Oxford handbook of personality disorders* (pp. 713–726). Oxford University Press.

Simon, K. M. (2015). Obsessive–compulsive personality disorder. In A. T. Beck, D. D. Davis, & A. Freeman (Eds.), *Cognitive therapy of personality disorders* (3rd ed., pp. 203–222). The Guilford Press.

Smith, T. E., & Samuel, D. B. (2017). A multi-method examination of the links between ADHD and personality disorder. *Journal of Personality Disorders, 31*(1), 26–48. https://doi.org/10.1521/pedi_2016_30_236

Soloff, P. H. (1998). Algorithms for pharmacological treatment of personality dimensions: Symptom-specific treatments for cognitive-perceptual, affective, and impulsive-behavioral dysregulation. *Bulletin of the Menninger Clinic, 62*(2), 195–214.

Stern, B. L., Diamond, D., & Yeomans, F. E. (2017). Transference-focused psychotherapy (TFP) for narcissistic personality: Engaging patients in the early treatment process. *Psychoanalytic Psychology, 34*(4), 381–396. https://doi.org/10.1037/pap0000145

Stoffers, J. M., Völlm, B. A., Rücker, G., Timmer, A., Huband, N., & Lieb, K. (2012). Psychological therapies for people with borderline personality disorder. *Cochrane Database of Systematic Reviews.* https://doi.org/10.1002/14651858.CD005652.pub2

Stoffers-Winterling, J. M., Storebø, O. J., Völlm, B. A., Mattivi, J. T., Nielsen, S. S., Kielsholm, M. L., Faltinsen, E. G., Simonsen, E., & Lieb, K. (2018). Pharmacological interventions for people with borderline personality disorder. *Cochrane Database of Systematic Reviews.* https://doi.org/10.1002/14651858.CD012956

Storebø, O. J., Stoffers-Winterling, J. M., Völlm, B. A., Kongerslev, M. T., Mattivi, J. T., Jørgensen, M. S., Faltinsen, E., Todorovac, A., Sales, C. P., Callesen, H. E., Lieb, K., & Simonsen, E. (2020). Psychological therapies for people with borderline personality disorder [Review]. *Cochrane Database of Systematic Reviews.* https://doi.org/10.1002/14651858.CD012955.pub2

Tyrer, P. (2002). Nidotherapy: A new approach to the treatment of personality disorder. *Acta Psychiatrica Scandinavica, 105*(6), 469–471. https://doi.org/10.1034/j.1600-0447.2002.01362.x

Tyrer, P., Crawford, M., Mulder, R. T., Blashfield, R., Farnam, A., Fossati, A., Kim, Y.-R., Koldobsky, N., Lecic-Tosevski, D., Ndetei, D., Swales, M., Clark, L. A., & Reed, G. M. (2011). The rationale for the reclassification of personality disorder in the 11th revision of the *International Classification of Diseases* (*ICD-11*). *Personality and Mental Health, 5*(4), 246–259. https://doi.org/10.1002/pmh.190

Tyrer, P., & Davidson, K. (2000). Cognitive therapy for personality disorders. In J. G. Gunderson & G. O. Gabbard (Eds.), *Psychotherapy for personality disorders* (Vol. 19, pp. 131–149). American Psychiatric Press.

Tyrer, P., Mulder, R., Kim, Y.-R., & Crawford, M. J. (2019). The development of the *ICD-11* classification of personality disorders: An amalgam of science, pragmatism, and politics. *Annual Review of Clinical Psychology, 15*(1), 481–502. https://doi.org/10.1146/annurev-clinpsy-050718-095736

Tyrer, P., Seivewright, H., & Johnson, T. (2004). The Nottingham Study of Neurotic Disorder: Predictors of 12-year outcome of dysthymic, panic and generalized anxiety disorder. *Psychological Medicine, 34*(8), 1385–1394. https://doi.org/10.1017/S0033291704002569

Wachtel, P. L. (1973). Psychodynamics, behavior therapy, and the implacable experimenter: An inquiry into the consistency of personality. *Journal of Abnormal Psychology, 82*(2), 324–334. https://doi.org/10.1037/h0035132

Widiger, T. A., & Trull, T. J. (1992). Personality and psychopathology: An application of the five-factor model. *Journal of Personality, 60*(2), 363–393. https://doi.org/10.1111/j.1467-6494.1992.tb00977.x

World Health Organization. (1990). *International statistical classification of diseases and related health problems* (10th ed.). https://icd.who.int/browse10/2010/en

World Health Organization. (2019). *International statistical classification of diseases and related health problems* (11th ed.). https://icd.who.int/

Wright, A. G. C., Hopwood, C. J., Skodol, A. E., & Morey, L. C. (2016). Longitudinal validation of general and specific structural features of personality pathology. *Journal of Abnormal Psychology, 125*(8), 1120–1134. https://doi.org/10.1037/abn0000165

III

COMMON FRAMEWORKS TREATING PERSONALITY PATHOLOGY

Transference-Focused Psychotherapy

Kenneth N. Levy, Frank E. Yeomans, and Daniel S. Spina

Transference-focused psychotherapy (TFP) is an evidence-based modified psychodynamic psychotherapy designed for use with patients suffering from severe personality disorders (PDs), most prototypically borderline and narcissistic PDs (Yeomans et al., 2015). TFP is based on Otto Kernberg's object relations model that integrates object relations theory with psychoanalytic ego psychology and aspects of Sigmund Freud's drive theory (O. F. Kernberg, 1984). Kernberg articulated his theory of PDs based, in part, on his experiences with the Menninger Foundation's Psychotherapy Research Project (O. F. Kernberg et al., 1972). Drawing on his clinical observations and data coming from the project, he began modifying standard psychodynamic psychotherapy. Kernberg initially described this treatment as exploratory or expressive psychotherapy, distinguishing it from psychodynamic psychotherapies that had a more explicitly supportive dimension and that were beginning to be articulated (Wallerstein, 1986; Wallerstein et al., 1956). Kernberg's (1967) articulation of the developmental psychopathology underlying severe PDs as well as his clinical experience treating those with severe personality pathology served as the basis of this novel treatment. TFP was still further elaborated in a series of treatment manuals written by Kernberg and his colleagues at the Personality Disorders Institute of Cornell University (in chronological

---

Portions of this chapter are based on "Transference-Focused Psychotherapy (TFP)," by K. N. Levy, N. Draijer, Y. Kivity, F. E. Yeomans, and L. K. Rosenstein, 2019, *Current Treatment Options in Psychiatry*, 6, pp. 312–324 (https://doi.org/10.1007/s40501-019-00193-9). Copyright 2019 by Springer. Adapted with permission.

https://doi.org/10.1037/0000310-010
Personality Disorders and Pathology: Integrating Clinical Assessment and Practice in the DSM-5 *and* ICD-11 *Era*, S. K. Huprich (Editor)
Copyright © 2022 by the American Psychological Association. All rights reserved.

order: O. F. Kernberg et al., 1989; Yeomans et al., 1992; Clarkin et al., 1999; Koenigsberg et al., 2000; Clarkin et al., 2006; Yeomans et al., 2015; Diamond et al., 2021).

As the name implies, TFP focuses on the transference, with the *transference* conceptualized as "a tendency in which representational aspects of important and formative relationships (such as with parents and siblings) can be both consciously experienced and/or unconsciously ascribed to other relationships" (Levy & Scala, 2012, p. 392; see also Levy, 2009). Transference can occur in an array of relationships, including in the relationship between therapists and patients, particularly with patients with PDs. Although patients with PDs may perceive aspects of their therapist in realistic ways, transference is the product of the patient's distortions, in varying degrees, within their interpersonal schemas. These distortions are based on the impact of the patient's internal mental representations of other that stand in the way of an accurate perception of others. Thus, transference may be more or less amenable to reality testing by the therapist, as the patient's awareness of these distorted representations of others fluctuates, varying at different times and with different emotional states.

Transference may also overlap or coexist with real elements of others. Real aspects of an individual's presentation may "pull" for certain transferences (e.g., older men may pull for father transferences). Even in such cases, it is important to remember that the internal images are not literal representations of the past but larger than life images that have been influenced by unconscious fantasies, fears, and desires. At other times, though, patients may subtly provoke others to behave in ways that are congruent with their transferential expectations (e.g., finding a way to provoke anger that seems to confirm the expectation of another's harsh criticism of them). An important feature of transference is that some aspects are unconscious and related to conflicts and defensive processes. In neurotic individuals, irrelevant or distorted representations are quickly modified based on new experience, or what Gelso (2014) called the *real relationship*. However, in those with borderline personality disorder (BPD), this process is slower and less guaranteed. In the therapy, therapists focus on the patient's affective experience for identifying and explicating their dominant relational patterns as they are experienced and expressed in the here and now of the relationship with the therapists (conceptualized as the transference relationship). The therapist's timely, clear, and tactful interpretations of the dominant, affect-laden themes and patient enactments in the here and now of the relationship between the two are hypothesized to lead to the resolution of the tendency toward rigid and distorted transference.

Several studies have revealed that TFP leads to both symptom and personality change within controlled trials and in comparison to community experts treating BPD. Recent meta-analyses and Cochrane Collaboration reviews have found that TFP and other empirically supported treatments are likely equally effective and equally efficacious in general (Cristea et al., 2017). Given the efficacy and effectiveness of TFP in these studies, several prominent treatment guidelines, including the Society of Clinical Psychology Committee on Science and Practice, the United Kingdom's National Institute for Health and

Care Excellence guidelines, the German Society for Psychiatry, Psychotherapy, and Psychosomatics's (2009) *Treatment Guidelines for Personality Disorders*, Australia's National Health and Medical Research Council Clinical Practice Guidelines, the Swiss Association for Psychiatry and Psychotherapy, and the Netherlands' Multidisciplinary Directive for Personality Disorders, recognize TFP as an empirically supported treatment. TFP is recognized as one among the "big four" specialized therapies for treating BPD, alongside dialectical behavior therapy (DBT), mentalization-based treatment, and schema-focused therapy (SFT).

In this chapter, we describe the underlying theoretical framework for TFP; the goals, structure, and techniques of the treatment; and its indications. We also summarize the existing body of empirical studies on symptom and personality change in TFP as well as recent innovations and novel clinical uses for TFP. We conclude the chapter with a discussion conceptual and empirical relationships between the Alternative *DSM-5* Model of Personality Disorders (AMPD) in Section III of the fifth edition of the *Diagnostic and Statistical Manual of Mental Disorders* (*DSM-5*; American Psychiatric Association, 2013) and the object relations model of personality pathology central to TFP.

GOALS OF THE TREATMENT

The overarching goals for patients undergoing TFP are—in helping an individual move from a fragmented sense of self to an integrated one—to build a greater capacity for self-control; to have less impulsive behaviors; to better process and regulate intense emotions; and to foster a greater capacity for closeness, pleasure and intimacy in relationships. In addition, TFP aims to help patients achieve a greater level of functioning such that appropriate life goals that patients desire can be met. In regard to symptom domains as well as domains of functioning that are more specific to BPD, patients' suicidal and parasuicidal behaviors, angry outbursts, and impulsive behaviors are targets for improvement in the treatment. From the perspective of TFP, change in these specific difficulties leads to less hospitalization, fewer emergency services, and fewer difficulties in relationships. In the TFP model, the integration of disparate, contradictory, and incoherent internal mental representations of self and others leads to these significant improvements in BPD symptoms. Otto Kernberg (O. F. Kernberg, 1984) referred to this as the *resolution of identity diffusion* or, conversely, *the achievement of identity consolidation*.

Identity, or one's sense of self, is defined as one's represented experience of themselves as well as one's represented experience of others; it includes both one's representation of oneself in interaction with others and the affect that characterizes these representations of self and others. Although the content and valance of these representations of self and other are important, more relevant are the structural aspects of these representations. By *structural aspects*, we are referring to the degree of differentiation, integration, and hierarchical organization of representations. This way of thinking about representations of self and others is central to many psychodynamic thinkers going back to Sigmund Freud but is also consistent with developmental psychologists like Piaget, Vygotsky, and Werner. By *degree of differentiation*, Otto Kernberg was referring to the number of discrete aspects of representations as well as the representational integrity or boundary of these aspects. By *degree of integration*, Kernberg was referring to the connections between discrete representations so that there is contextualization through the relation of these aspects to one another. By *hierarchical organization*, Kernberg, like Werner's (1957) elaboration of the orthogenetic principle, suggested that as development proceeds, representations of self and others move from global and integrated states to more hierarchically integrated ones in which more important specific information is nested in superordinate structures. This organization allows for more relevant information to be accessed when needed. Impairments in these structural aspects of self and other representations and defenses against integration are seen as central and as underlying the difficulties experienced by those with severe PDs. In more typical and healthy development, the individual is supported in and learns to integrate disparate, contradictory, and incoherent internal mental representations of self and others.

The object relations model underlying TFP posits that BPD derives from a failure to develop internal representations of self and others that are complex, realistic, and characteristic of adaptive psychological functioning. Complex representations of self and others facilitate a person's capacity to reflect on interactions with others. While these representations support one's understanding of one's own thought processes and beliefs, and ultimately allow one to behave in a thoughtful and purposeful manner, those with more fragmented or unintegrated representations may struggle in these domains. Patients with fragmented representations experience difficulties seeing others in complex ways that account for contradictory aspects, such as considering mental states that integrate positive and negative elements. Thus, they experience themselves in incongruent ways—for example, punishing and gratifying, or frustrating and satisfying, or fragile and exploiting aspects of others are dynamically held apart in conscious experience such that only one aspect of these representations is present in awareness at one time. Becoming momentarily aware of both aspects in one person or in oneself, what is typically required for accurate and meaningful reflection on someone's mental states, may initially leave those without complex representations confused rather than in a state of clarity.

In addition, without integrated representations of self and others, and the capacity for complexity that comes with them, extreme positive emotions can quickly shift into negative ones, further impeding an individual's perception of day-to-day interactions. Within a cognitive behavior framework, Beck referred to this process as *black and white thinking* (Beck & Freeman, 1990), and from an SFT perspective, Young referred to this as *schema flipping* (Kellogg & Young, 2006). In the TFP model, the inconsistent sense of self and others and the vacillation or oscillations between these mental states are together referred to as "identity diffusion," which is analogous to identity disturbance defined in *DSM-III* (3rd ed.; American Psychiatric Association, 1980) and is captured nicely in the *DSM-5*, Section III, AMPD Criterion A description of self-functioning. In addition, this formulation is consistent with the psychological processes regarding identity formation described by Blatt (1974; Blatt & Blass, 1990), Erikson (1950), Marcia (1966), and McAdams (2001), among others.

In the TFP model, difficulty regulating emotions derives directly from identity diffusion. The treatment therefore attempts to bring together diffuse aspects of the patient's representations of self and other as well as the affect that links them. This integration is hypothesized to generate new and more nuanced ways of experiencing emotions and the world. Bringing together and clarifying these disparate representations allows patients to think more flexibly about the therapist, significant others, and themselves. Therefore, making patients aware of their contradictory experiences of self and others, and particularly of the therapist, is the main method by which internal representations become integrated (Levy et al., 2006).

INDICATIONS

Conceptually, TFP is indicated for the outpatient treatment of severe PDs, including borderline, histrionic, narcissistic, and antisocial PDs as described in Section II of *DSM-5*. From the perspective of the *DSM-5* AMPD, TFP is indicated for severities above 0 (*little or no impairment*) from Level 1 (*some impairment*) to Level 4 (*extreme impairment*) with Borderline, Narcissistic, Antisocial, Schizotypal, and Avoidant PD types. When using the World Health Organization's (WHO; 2019) *International Statistical Classification of Diseases and Related Health Problems* (11th ed.; *ICD-11*), TFP is suitable for those with moderate or severe PDs, particularly when the borderline pattern specifier is specified. In addition, when using the Psychodynamic Diagnostic Manual–Version 2 (PDM-2; Lingiardi & McWilliams, 2017), TFP is suitable for those in the borderline level of personality organization and with personality syndromes of borderline, narcissistic, psychopathic, and histrionic. Common to all of these disorders is what Otto Kernberg referred to as a *borderline organization of personality structure*, a structure characterized by identity disturbance; intact reality testing that can become impaired with severe levels of stress; and the use of maladaptive defenses to cope with strong emotions, especially the use of splitting. An adapted form of TFP, called TFP–Extended (TFP-E; Caligor et al., 2007, 2018) has recently been articulated and is more suitable for individuals with less severe personality pathology, such as obsessive-compulsive (Section II and III, *DSM-5*; American Psychiatric Association, 2013; and PDM-2; Lingiardi & McWilliams, 2017), dependent (Section II, PDM-2), or avoidant PDs (Section II, PDM-2). Likewise, recent modifications have been suggested when treating

PDs characterized by narcissism; these modifications are described later in the section "Recent Clinical and Theoretical Developments and Advances."

THEORY UNDERLYING TFP

In the object relations framework of TFP, BPD is understood to be based in incomplete, incoherent, and distorted psychological or representational structures, in particular narrow, extreme, and disconnected internal mental representations of self and others. As such, those with BPD have difficulty evoking internal representations of one's self and others that are complex, integrated, and realistic. Without complex representations, patients suffer from impaired psychological functioning, particularly under times of stress or during ambiguous interpersonal situations. O. F. Kernberg (1984) referred to this undifferentiated and unintegrated representational state as *identity diffusion*. Patients struggling with identity diffusion vacillate between exclusively negative or exclusively positive representations of themselves and others, and these quick shifts are hypothesized to undergird extreme negative and extreme positive emotional reactions characteristic of BPD. These reactions tend to distort everyday interactions with others, leading to severe interpersonal difficulties.

In TFP, the therapist tries to work through and integrate the patient's incoherent representations of others by both clarifying the patient's experience and maintaining a reflective position despite the patient's affectively charged representation of the therapist. Within this reflective stance, the patient's contradictory representations are repeatedly brought into awareness within the holding environment of the session, and identity diffusion eventually resolves or reduces. Following successful treatment and the reduction of identity diffusion, the patient will approach others and the self with flexibility and openness, experiencing others as generally more benign and with multiple aspects. This greater complexity and realistic perception of others fosters relationships that are significantly more fulfilling and that are based in more stable and enduring feelings that can now coexist and integrate with disappointments and irritations. Following the reduction of identity diffusion, the patient will likely have a greater capacity to temper self-destructive impulses and have a greater ability to function autonomously in work and life in general.

STRUCTURE AND TECHNIQUES OF TFP TREATMENT

In its original and typical form, TFP is a twice-weekly, individual, face-to-face, outpatient psychotherapy. Similar to other therapies for PDs, TFP is a long-term treatment that lasts at least 12 to 18 months. Experienced therapists, trained and certified by the International Society for Transference-Focused Therapy (ISTFP; https://istfp.org/) or who are in training and under supervision by an approved ISTFP supervisor (ISTFP, n.d.), are permitted to deliver TFP.

TFP has four treatment phases: (a) assessment, (b) the establishment of the treatment frame or contract, (c) the active treatment phase, and (d) termination.

Assessment

TFP begins with a thorough assessment to establish a clear diagnosis and to better understand the patient's difficulties and life structure. The assessment phase tends to last between one to three sessions, each session running about 1 hour, and may require collateral information from previous treatments and family members. This assessment is used to help the therapist establish a diagnostic understanding and develop a case formulation (Levy et al., 2019).

This understanding and formulation are shared with the patient to provide them with an understanding of their difficulties and include not only diagnostic feedback but an explanation of the differential diagnosis and the patient's interpersonal dynamics related to perception of self and others. The provision of such feedback requires transparency and tact and must be done collaboratively rather than seen as an imposition to the patient. Once the therapist and patient agree on the conceptualization of the patient's difficulties, this information can be used to collaboratively establish the treatment goals and set the treatment frame, including explicating the roles and responsibilities of both the patient and therapist in the treatment.

Establishment of a Treatment Frame

The treatment contract, or "treatment frame," as it is called in TFP, establishes the conditions or frame of the therapy in a way that emphasizes the experiencing of emotions and curbs the expression of emotions in the form of impulsive behavior, such as cutting, abusing substance, or having risky sex. This contract or treatment frame, in the case of inactive or socially isolated individuals, also encourages individuals to become involved with other people through a structured activity, such as employment or volunteer work. The treatment frame articulates the expectations and responsibilities for both patient and therapist. The patient's responsibilities typically include attending session, working toward the treatment goals, and reducing impulsivity and self-harm behaviors. The treatment frame also includes expressing oneself without censoring or screening and reflecting on thoughts and feelings as well as the therapist's comments. The sharing of thoughts and feelings without censorship is modified from the classical sense in psychoanalysis and is more focused on the problems that bring the patient to therapy. Therapist responsibilities typically include logistical responsibilities, such as scheduling appointments; monitoring the time; articulating policies about absences, rescheduling, vacations, missed sessions; and clarifying boundaries and the limits of the therapist's involvement. Most importantly, the therapist is responsible for attending to the patient's communications and making every effort to understand and, when useful, to comment to the patient.

Active Phase of Treatment, or the Implantation of the Treatment

Following the assessment, the patient and therapist jointly discuss the therapist's diagnostic impressions, and the frame is collaboratively set and agreed on; the active phase of therapy begins. The patient begins the treatment, as outlined in the treatment contract, with what is on their mind, and this prompt reminds the patient to bring to the foreground of the session the most relevant issues and thoughts that characterize their most recent and pressing difficulties. Three primary directives guide the patient toward the most relevant therapeutic tasks in session: (a) maintaining the integrity of the treatment and discussing life-threatening difficulties, such as suicide, homicide, or behaviors that compromise the patient's or therapist's safety; (b) making every effort to apprehend the patient's inner representations as they are elaborated in the patient's experience of the therapist (the "transference" of internal mental material to the external situation); and (c) discussing the patient's experience of others and day-to-day difficulties that occur outside session.

Within session, repetitive relational themes are brought into the patient's awareness, especially as they pertain to the patient's transference. The therapist closely follows the patient's emotions and helps articulate their experience, especially unconscious and unintegrated aspects of their experience. Over the course of one or more sessions, the therapist first helps to clarify and reflect the patient's subjective experience (Caligor et al., 2009). The therapist then tactfully makes the patient aware of discrepancies between what the patient is saying, doing, or communicating nonverbally, and encourages the patient to reflect on those discrepancies. In TFP and many psychodynamic therapies, this is called a *confrontation*. Obviously, this kind of confrontation does not feel "in your face" or abrupt. Rather, this approach sheds light on information that is being disavowed or dissociated, makes the patient more aware of maladaptive defensive maneuvers intended to keep difficult content out of awareness, and allows for exploration and integration. Confrontation should be done with tact so as to make the unintegrated information more palatable.

Once these discrepancies in the patient's experience are noted, a broader process of interpretation of relational patterns with the therapist and outside treatment begins. Interpretations should be delivered in a timely, clear, and tactful way and address the patient's continued representations of others in polarized or incoherent ways Interpretations may involve pointing out that a patient strongly wants to separate positive aspects of themselves and others in their life from ones that are negative in an effort to protect the good aspects from the bad. Interpretations may introduce aspects of a patient's experience that are disavowed and that feel threatening, and therefore appropriate timing within the here and now immediate moment of the patient's experience must be balanced with tact, finesse, and empathic understanding. Interpretations should therefore build over time, should feel relatively palatable to the patient, and should contain material that is already close to the patient's present awareness. This maximizes the emotional impact of the interpretation and the likelihood that it might be received by the patient. In addition, while they are always hypotheses that are responsive to feedback and correction, interpretations should be delivered with some conviction and without unnecessary trepidation. Such a process promotes improved reflective ability, richer and more positive perceptions of self and others, and improvement in intimate relationships. In this way, interpretations are not so much an isolated intervention but part of a broader hermeneutical endeavor that seeks to capture and reflect the full nuance of the client's experience of themselves and others, a process that equally includes clarification and confrontation.

Advanced Phase of Treatment, Evolution of the Therapy, and Planned Termination

As the treatment progresses and the patient improves, either the patient or therapist, or both, may begin thinking about the termination of the therapy. This process may begin as early of 6 months into the treatment, or it could take years. Poor prognosis indicators, such as antisocial, paranoid, and narcissistic features, may result in longer time frames. Regardless, the process is often not linear and may proceed in starts and stops, and there may be regressions to earlier levels of functioning after steady improvements. With improvement, two things can happen. First, the patient's better functioning leads them to participate in life in a way that often results in challenges. A patient who was previously unable to date emotionally available partners now is required to delve into deeper intimacy. Likewise, a patient who was previously unable to work at positions consistent with their intellect and capacities may find themselves in a job that requires more responsibility and commitment. These kinds of situations can be challenging and may require additional therapeutic work to meet the demands of increased commitments in the patient's life. Second, as patients become more integrated, they often realize their own role in their difficulties. The reduction in externalizing defenses and in splitting lead them to be aware of difficulties within themselves, and with more realistic views of self and others comes the challenge of dealing with having to integrate contradictory views and feelings.

Several markers indicate that the patient may be ready for the therapy to end or to transform into a therapy more typical of neurotic process. As the therapy progresses, the patient begins to experience events less concretely and at a more abstract or representational level. More frequently, they recognize the self and other representational dyads, can observe their vacillation, and tolerate these interchanges, including with the therapist. The transference moves from more primitive and paranoid ones to more depressive ones that resemble the kinds of transference seen in neurotic patients. Paranoid transferences become transient, resolve quickly, and can be discussed more easily. Enactments have decreased and even disappeared, although they may resurface during the termination phase. However, the patient can more readily reflect on these enactments and see them as part of the termination process. As this happens, the relationship with the therapist is deepened and becomes more reality based, with increased gratitude. The patient is more autonomous in session and is increasingly able to use free association and present coherent narratives that can be reflected on.

The patient's reaction to discussions of termination is an indicator of readiness for ending the therapy. Patients may experience intense anxiety and fear of abandonment during the termination phase. These feelings, along with experiencing the therapist's absence as an attack, complete with reactive rage toward the therapist, can be expressed overtly but may also include missing sessions, which limits the discussion of terminations. These may be indicators that there is more work to be done. However, the capacity to tolerate, reflect, discuss, and resolve these events may suggest that termination is warranted. The narcissistic patient may decide unilaterally to end therapy abruptly, like ripping a bandage off a scab. The patient may declare themselves better. In doing so, they may deny the importance of the therapy and the therapist. This reaction is often called a "flight into health," which is thought to be defensive and brittle. A skilled therapist will sense this possibility in a narcissistic patient, predict that the patient may feel this urge, and emphasize the value of additional work in such a situation. Healthier reactions to termination, including contained sadness, awareness of loss, and overt mourning, as well as the capacity for gratitude, are clear indicators of readiness for termination.

EMPIRICAL SUPPORT

A growing body of literature has elucidated the efficacy and effectiveness of TFP, including its underlying mechanisms of change as well as personality changes that are unique to TFP and that map onto associated brain regions. In this section, we review the current empirical literature on TFP and recent modifications to the frame of treatment that make it indicated for a range of personality disorders that can be conceptualized with the AMPD.

Evidence for the Underlying Theoretical Assumptions of TFP

From a TFP perspective, identity diffusion is the central mechanism that underlies BPD and therefore underlies the core symptoms and traits typical in BPD, including emotional dysregulation and suicidality. A burgeoning literature currently is examining the importance of identity in the characteristic difficulties of those with BPD.

In a series of complementary studies, Levy and colleagues have attempted to better understand identity and representations of oneself and others (Beeney et al., 2016; Ellison et al., 2020; Levy et al., 2010; Levy, Steiner, et al., 2022; Scala et al., 2018; Steiner et al., 2021). Levy et al. (2010) found that vacillations in mental states about the self and others (including the therapist) predicted the quality of the observer-rated therapeutic alliance in a subset of patient–therapist dyads from the Clarkin et al. (2007) randomized clinical trial (RCT). Beeney et al. (2016) found anomalies in the neural basis of self and other processing for those with BPD. Greater activation in the precuneus and posterior cingulate was found for those with BPD within both self-reflection at baseline and other-reflection at baseline contrasts, whereas the control group evidenced greater activation in the self–other contrast in the angular gyrus (all results $p < .005$, $k = 24$, equivalent to family-wise error correction, $p < .05$).

Behaviorally, BPD patients showed more fragmented, unintegrated, fluctuating, and negative self-concept on a self-concept card sorting task completed twice over a 3-hour period. In Scala et al. (2018), those with BPD were compared to patients with anxiety disorders in an intensive repeated measurement design collecting both random and event contingent data via smartphones over 21 days. Patients recorded data 12 times per day on average. The authors found that affect regulation deficits, operationalized as a repeated experience of negative affect during the day, predicted suicidal urges. However, this association was only significant when patients were in identity diffuse mental states. Although BPD patients scored significantly higher and experienced more identity disturbance, negative affect, and suicidal urges than those with anxiety disorders, consistent with a transdiagnostic approach, the process worked similarly across both groups.

In an unpublished study, Levy, Steiner, et al. (2022) examined the capacity of those with BPD traits to form accurate visual self-images. In a series of 300 presentations, participants were tasked with choosing between two faces as to which one looked more similar to themselves. Two images were generated using a reverse correlation method: one based on all the images selected as more similar to the participant and the other, the rejected image. The self-relevant generated image was then computer compared to the participant's actual image, and a similarity score was generated. BPD traits were negatively related to the accuracy of the generated self-image. The greater the number of BPD traits and symptoms, the more diffuse the self-image ($b = -.29$, $p < .02$). In contrast, Steiner et al. (2021) found that although narcissistic traits, similar to BPD traits, also predicted less accurate self-images, those higher in narcissism generated images of the self that were significantly more likely to be rated by independent assessors as more attractive than the participant's actual photograph. Thus, those participants with greater BPD traits tended to create more diffuse self-images, whereas those with greater narcissistic traits and symptoms tended to create more enhanced self-images.

Treatment Effectiveness and Efficacy

TFP's effectiveness and efficacy have been demonstrated in multiple pre–post studies (Clarkin et al., 2001; Clarkin & Levy, 2003; Cuevas et al., 2000; Perez et al., 2016), a quasi-experimental study (Levy, Clarkin, et al., 2022), and three RCTs completed by separate research teams across four countries (Clarkin et al., 2007; see also Doering et al., 2010; Giesen-Bloo et al., 2006; Levy et al., 2006).

In the first RCT, Clarkin et al. (2006) compared TFP, DBT, and supportive psychodynamic therapy. All of these treatments led to improvements in depression, anxiety, functioning, and adjustment; however, those in the TFP arm of treatment also improved in a broader number of domains, particularly anger and aggression. In another study, TFP was compared to treatment in the community by therapists experienced in treating BPD (Doering et al., 2010). In that study, the authors found that those in the TFP arm of treatment experienced a reduction in suicide attempts, fewer admissions to a psychiatric department, and fewer patients unexpectedly leaving treatment. The TFP arm also had significantly fewer borderline symptoms, significantly better psychosocial functioning, and healthier personality organization when compared to the other arm of treatment at termination. Patients treated in either group showed similar improvements in depression and anxiety. Arnoud Arntz and colleagues' RCT compared schema therapy (ST) with TFP conceptualized as a control group (Giesen-Bloo et al., 2006). Both treatments were effective, producing large effect sizes. Although ST showed better results in the intent-to-treat analyses, the completer analyses showed no differences between the treatments (Giesen-Bloo et al., 2006; Levy, Wasserman, et al., 2009; Levy et al., 2012). Differences in nonrandom dropout between treatment arms explain the discrepancy between ST and TFP. There were also various indications that the randomization had failed in the trial. For example, patients in the TFP group scored higher on measures of self-destructiveness than patients in the ST group and thus had more severe difficulties than the ST group. This greater severity has been shown to be related to worse outcome in treatment for BPD. It is also important to realize that despite these issues and others (see Yeomans, 2007), differences between groups did not emerge until Year 3.

Meta-Analytic Studies

A number of meta-analytic reviews have examined TFP in relation to other treatments (Binks et al., 2006; Cristea et al., 2017; Kliem et al., 2010; Oud et al., 2018; Stoffers-Winterling et al., 2012). These studies have consistently found that there are no reliable differences in overall effect sizes between psychodynamic treatments, including TFP and other treatments, when compared with DBT. This finding is consistent with the effect sizes found in individual studies and those that directly compare DBT with TFP (Clarkin et al., 2007) and with other treatments (Doering et al., 2010; Giesen-Bloo et al., 2006).

Changes in Personality

Although symptom change is important, and especially for BPD, given that the consequences of untreated BPD symptoms are grave, TFP aspires for structural change within a patient's personality, a more extensive and ambitious outcome. Changes in deep personality structures have therefore been a main interest within psychotherapy research on TFP. Although these changes are especially important for personality pathology given that personality difficulties are hypothesized as being rooted in personality proper, current research on these more ambitious outcomes in specialized treatment for BPD has been neglected. However, within RCTs of TFP, structural changes have been assessed, and TFP has reliably demonstrated specific benefits in this domain. In two RCTs and a pre–post study on TFP, patients in these studies demonstrated unique and significant increases in attachment security and mentalizing (the ability to make sense of one's and others' mental states) when compared with non-TFP control groups (Buchheim et al., 2017; Fischer-Kern et al., 2015; Levy, Diamond, et al., 2022; Levy et al., 2006). Levy et al. (2006) found that almost a third (29%) of patients in the TFP condition adopted secure attachment styles following a year of TFP. By comparison, none of the patients in the control treatments was securely attached by the end of treatment. Similarly, Buchheim and colleagues (2017) found that 12 of the 38 (31%) patients in the TFP arm of the Doering et al. (2010) study showed improved scores in terms of attachment security, whereas no participant in the control group showed significant improvements in attachment security. Levy, Diamond, et al. (2022) also found significant changes in attachment security following 1 year of treatment, particularly that 30% of the patients treated in TFP became securely attached.

With regard to mentalizing abilities in patients following treatment, the pre–post effect size in all three studies (Fischer-Kern et al., 2015; Levy, Diamond, et al., 2022; Levy et al., 2006) demonstrated similar improvement even though the studies were conducted on two separate continents; at three separate cohort times; and with a set of different therapists, interviewers, and coders. These findings suggest improved relationships, greater awareness of one's own motivations, and more accurate inference about other people's intentions and behaviors as well as the potential for more satisfying interpersonal relationships. These unique findings for TFP are central to research on BPD treatment; from the perspective of TFP, patients sustainedly cope better with internal conflict, relationships, and major life events as a result of these unique changes in personality.

Changes in Brain Functioning

Perez et al. (2016) conducted a pilot study on neural correlates of improved emotion regulation and improved impulsivity after TFP treatment. Using a within-subjects design, they examined pre–post treatment neural changes using functional magnetic resonance imaging (fMRI) scans in 10 women reliably diagnosed with BPD who were treated in 1 year of TFP by trained, supervised, and adherent therapists. During the scans, a BPD-specific, emotional-linguistic, go/no-go task was used to assess the relation between negative emotional processing and inhibitory control. Perez et al. found fMRI measured brain changes that were associated with variation in outcome. They found that brain changes were significantly related to symptom changes from TFP treatment. Specifically, there was relative increased dorsal prefrontal (dorsal anterior cingulate, dorsolateral prefrontal, and frontopolar cortices) activation and relative decreased ventrolateral prefrontal cortex and hippocampal activations following treatment. Clinical improvement in constraint was positively associated with relative increased left anterior-dorsal anterior cingulate cortex activation. Clinical improvement in affective lability was positively associated with left posterior-medial orbitofrontal cortex/ventral striatum activation, and negatively with right amygdala parahippocampal activation.

RECENT CLINICAL AND THEORETICAL DEVELOPMENTS AND ADVANCES

In the mid-1960s, Otto Kernberg began describing his treatment approach for patients with borderline personality organization (BPO) based on his work at the Menninger psychotherapy project (O. F. Kernberg et al., 1972). Following that early articulation, Kernberg and colleagues have continually clarified and elaborated the theory and techniques in TFP. In 1989, the first TFP manual was published (O. F. Kernberg et al., 1989) and followed up by updates in 1999 (Clarkin et al., 1999), 2006 (Clarkin et al., 2006) and 2015 (Yeomans et al., 2015). Along the way, important supplements were published on contracting (Yeomans et al., 1994) and on dealing with difficult patients and clinical situations (Koenigsberg et al., 2000), and a primer was published (Yeomans et al., 2002).

Although these manuals outlined a treatment intended primarily for patients with BPD, Kernberg always envisioned that the ideas underlying the TFP model had broader relevance. In Kernberg's view, all manifestations of a more general category of pathology that he identified as BPO might benefit from TFP principles. The concept of BPO was articulated before the narrower definition of BPD adopted by *DSM-III* (American Psychiatric Association, 1980), *DSM-IV* (4th ed.; American Psychiatric Association, 1994), and *DSM-5* (American Psychiatric Association, 2013), and has a similar focus as the AMPD, particularly an emphasis on levels of self- and interpersonal functioning. The concept of BPO includes BPD but also several other personality styles or disorders, including narcissistic PD. Consonant with this broader perspective on personality organization and pathology, Kernberg had interests in narcissism coexisting with his broader interest in borderline pathology (O. F. Kernberg, 1975/1985, 2004, 2007), and, as mentioned previously, some preliminary evidence supports TFP as a uniquely efficacious treatment for NPD when compared with DBT and a supportive psychotherapy (Levy, Kivity, et al., 2022). Nevertheless, Kernberg and a number of clinical researchers have recently written about a modified TFP treatment frame for patients experiencing significant narcissistic pathology primarily to address differences in the way personality style in NPD and BPD impact treatment process (Caligor et al., 2015; Diamond & Yeomans, 2008; Diamond et al., 2011, 2021; O. F. Kernberg, 2014; Levy, 2012; Levy, Chauhan, et al., 2009; Stern et al., 2013, 2017; Yeomans et al., 1994, 2013).

TFP was originally conceptualized within a developmental psychopathology framework based in identify diffusion and polarized representations of others and the self that cut across PD categories, and authors have therefore noted that other styles and levels of severity of personality pathology may benefit from TFP principles (Caligor et al., 2007, 2018). The application of TFP principles have now been described for working with college students (Hersh, 2013), prescribing psychiatric medication (Hersh, 2015), treating patients in acute clinical care settings (Hersh et al., 2017; Zerbo et al., 2013), working with traumatized patients (Draijer & Van Zon, 2013), treating complex depression

(Clarkin et al., 2019), and training psychiatric residents (Bernstein et al., 2015). Integrating TFP with other treatments has also been explored: Good psychiatric management (McCommon & Hersh, 2021), supportive psychotherapy (O. F. Kernberg, 2022), behavioral activation (Levy & Scala, 2015; Yeomans et al., 2017), and modular treatments (Clarkin et al., 2015) have all been considered as potential modalities for integration.

TFP principles have also been considered within child and adolescent treatments (Biberdzic et al., 2018; Ensink et al., 2015; Normandin et al., 2014, 2015, 2021), and these modifications were largely inspired by Paulina Kernberg's work (P. Kernberg et al., 2000).

TFP APPLIED TO *DSM-5* AMPD AND *ICD-11*

Several authors stress that Otto Kernberg's conceptualization of personality organization, with its focus on linking self and other representations to self- and interpersonal functioning and the overall severity of personality pathology not only predated the AMPD but was influential in its architecture (Bender et al., 2011; Clarkin et al., 2020; Natoli, 2021; Waugh et al., 2017; Yalch, 2020). Bender et al. (2011) noted that Kernberg's object relations model, the concept of personality organization that is the basis for the TFP model, was one of the first to articulate a model of personality types arrayed along a continuum of severity. First articulated in the late 1960s, Kernberg proposed a model for understanding a range of PDs along two dimensions: severity and internalizing versus externalizing (O. F. Kernberg, 1967; O. F. Kernberg & Caligor, 2005). Various PDs could be arrayed along this two-dimensional space. Consistent with recent research (Sharp et al., 2015; Wright et al., 2016), Kernberg conceptualized the severity dimension in terms of level of borderline functioning. The progression from lower levels of severity in personality pathology to higher levels of severity is tied to more impaired and maladaptive self—other representations and functioning. Thus, in Kernberg's model, the central BPD symptoms—abandonment fears, unstable relationships that alternate between idealization and devaluation, affect instability, identity disturbance, paranoid ideation, chronic feelings of emptiness, and angry outbursts—arise from an individual's impaired and distorted internal images of self and other, what Kernberg called identity diffusion. The data from Sharp et al. (2015) and Wright et al. (2016) are consistent with this idea. This conceptualization is also consistent with the AMPD in Section III of *DSM-5* (American Psychiatric Association, 2013) in that borderline pathology is of central heuristic value for representing what is common to all personality pathology (Criterion A) and the severity model in the PDM-2 (Lingiardi & McWilliams, 2017).

Kernberg's model led to several dimensional rating scales of self-functioning and interpersonal functioning in measures, such as the *DSM-5* Level of Personality Functioning Scale (Bender et al., 2011), Level of Personality Functioning Scale–Self-Report (Morey, 2017), the Self and Interpersonal Functioning Scale

(Gamache et al., 2019), *DSM-5* Levels of Personality Functioning Questionnaire (Huprich et al., 2018), and Inventory of Personality Organization (Lenzenweger et al., 2001).

Kernberg's concept of personality organization provides a broad and comprehensive framework for an understanding of both typical or normal personality development and personality pathology that is consistent and interdigitates closely with the models proposed in the dimensional aspects of the AMPD and the *ICD-11* (WHO, 2019) as well as the PDM-2 (Lingiardi & McWilliams, 2017), HiTOP (the Hierarchical Taxonomy of Psychopathology; Kotov et al., 2017), and cognitive affective personality system (CAPS) framework (Mischel & Shoda, 1995). The concept of personality organization is based on several underlying dimensional constructs, such as identity, defense mechanisms used, and capacity for social reality testing.

Identity refers to one's representations of self and others and their degree of differentiation and integration. For Kernberg, similar to Anna Freud (1966) and Vaillant (1992), defenses can be conceptualized along a developmental continuum from more healthy and mature defenses through neurotic defenses; to more immature or primitive borderline defenses, such as splitting, projective identification, and omnipotent control; to psychotic or pathological level defenses. Reality testing can vary from generally intact to subtle and transient deficits in social reality testing, to frank deficits in physical reality testing (e.g., hallucinations). One's level of personality organization is based on the degree of identity consolidation or diffusion, the maturity or immaturity of defenses used, and the capacity for social reality testing that, taken together, can be arrayed along a dimension from relatively healthy or neurotic levels through high and low borderline levels to psychotic levels of personality organization. Those at a neurotic level of personality organization show mild impairments in self- and interpersonal functioning. Their identity is characterized by a consistent sense of self and others, is consolidated, and is thus resilient in the face of challenges. They generally rely on mature defenses, even when stressed, and their reality testing is intact. Those organized at a borderline level show more severity and impairment in self- and interpersonal functioning, with indications of identity diffusion as characterized by unintegrated and fragmented sense of self and others as well as use of immature or primitive defenses. Although reality testing is generally intact, these individuals can show deficits in social reality testing, particularly when under stress. Those at a psychotic level experience the most severe impairments in self- and interpersonal functioning.

In the TFP model, this concept of level personality organization or functioning runs orthogonal to the dimension of introversion versus extraversion, which is similar to Blatt's (1974) concepts of introjective (self, agency) versus anaclitic (dependent, relatedness, communion) focus but also clearly maps well onto trait theories with their focus on introversion and extraversion. In addition, in TFP, there are several personality styles or types, many of which are consistent with Section II and III personality types and that can be arrayed along these two dimensions. Sharp and colleagues (2015) conducted an exploratory bifactor analysis of the diagnostic criteria for six PDs. They found a general factor for personality pathology (*g*-PD) emerged with the BPD criteria loading solely on the *g*-PD factor. Specific factors (s-factors) also emerged with strong average loadings for three PD types: Antisocial, Schizotypal, and Narcissistic PDs. Sharp and colleagues proposed that the *g*-PD factor was a strong representation of the *DSM-5*, Section III, AMPD Criterion A. Wright and colleagues (2016) similarly found the evidence for a *g*-PD factor in a bifactor analysis of 10 PDs, noting that these findings were consistent with O. F. Kernberg's (1984) concept of BPO.

Interestingly, although Widiger (Widiger & McCabe, 2020; see also Sleep et al., 2021) has suggested that Criterion B can account for Criterion A of the AMPD, the TFP model more elegantly encompasses the main aspects of both Criterion A and Criterion B in an integrative and seamless manner. Criterion B represents maladaptive personality traits assessed through five broad trait domains of Negative Affectivity, Detachment, Antagonism, Disinhibition, and Psychoticism that are further differentiated into 25 underlying facets. Although not readily apparent because these trait domains emphasize the maladaptive extremes, they also map onto the five-factor model (FFM) such that negative affectivity is conceptually similar to neuroticism, detachment to introversion, antagonism to low agreeableness, and disinhibition to low conscientiousness. Although psychoticism's relation to the FFM conception is more tenuous, Miller et al. (2018) suggested that it is related to openness, but the correlation is the lowest of such comparisons, it fits well with alternative trait models like Eysenck's (1987) that has found a psychoticism dimension. Obviously, the introversion–extroversion dimension maps to the same named dimension in the FFM and the detachment dimension of the AMPD.

In regard to the personality organization dimension, neurotic level of organization relates to moderate levels negative affectivity, and borderline level of organization relates to high levels of negative affectivity. High levels of disinhibition can be found in the impulsive PDs, typically at the borderline level of personality organization. Similarly, high levels of Antagonism would be found more typically at the borderline level of personality organization, while the psychotic level of personality functioning would be characterized by high levels of psychoticism in the AMPD. Thus, all five of the maladaptive trait dimensions are accounted for in a model that allows for differences in personality styles or types that are consistent with conceptualizations and empirical findings from various models. The TFP frame allows for responsivity to Criteria A and B by using recent adaptations. Consider, for example, that the presence of narcissism, either based on Criterion B traits or the diagnosis proper, may require modifications to the TFP frame and transference-based interventions as described in several papers (Caligor et al., 2015; Diamond et al., 2021; Levy, 2012). In contrast, impairments more characteristic of higher level functioning PDs may require modifications consistent with TFP-E (Caligor et al., 2007; Caligor et al., 2018).

With regard to the *ICD-11*, although not necessarily acknowledging its consistency with the TFP model, its dimensional focus, along with its focus on severity of impairment in the areas of self- and interpersonal functioning and the retaining of borderline pattern descriptor, parallels aspects of the AMPD and is consistent with the most prominent aspects of the TFP model. Although the narrow focus on a general PD, the abandonment of other types of PDs, and the failure to consider defensive functioning is inconsistent with the TFP model, the *ICD-11* (WHO, 2019) inclusion of reality testing as a key dimension for assessing the severity of PD is conceptually closer to an important aspect of the TFP model than the AMPD's focus on psychoticism.

CONCLUSION

TFP is a specialized psychodynamic psychotherapy for individuals with PDs that has been empirically demonstrated as effective for BPD. TFP aims to integrate diffuse identity, increase emotion regulation, and improve relationships, and is therefore ambitious in its intended goals of structural change. From the perspective of TFP, these changes allow patients the potential for intimate and satisfying love relationships as well as the development of sustained interests, commitments, and the capacity for investments requisite for a successful work life. Observation of and reflection on the relationship with the TFP therapist is the primary conduit of change, the foundation for exploring and integrating the patient's split and fragmented representations of self and others within the here-and-now moment of the patient's experience. Increased awareness and understanding of unintegrated experiences, emotions, and representations often result from this specialized treatment process. Multiple studies from separate countries and patient cohorts support the claim that TFP leads to improvements in both BPD symptoms as well as more structural changes in personality, such as security of attachment and capacity for reflecting on mental states in oneself and others.

We contend that the TFP model converges with the findings of a general psychopathology or "p" factor (Caspi & Moffitt, 2018), the AMPD, the recent findings within assessment of personality pathology about general ('g') and specific ('s') factors (Sharp et al., 2015; Wright et al., 2016), the main structure of the WHO (2019) *ICD-11* (Blüml & Doering, 2021; Tyrer et al., 2019), and the CAPS model (Mischel & Shoda, 1995; for reviews, see Clarkin et al., 2010, and Huprich & Nelson, 2015). These convergences show the TFP model is not only theoretically and clinically useful but has been absorbed into the main models in use today (Levy, 2020).

REFERENCES

American Psychiatric Association. (1980). *Diagnostic and statistical manual of mental disorders* (3rd ed.).

American Psychiatric Association. (1994). *Diagnostic and statistical manual of mental disorders* (4th ed.).

American Psychiatric Association. (2013). *Diagnostic and statistical manual of mental disorders* (5th ed.). https://doi.org/10.1176/appi.books.9780890425596

Beck, A. T., & Freeman, A. M. (1990). *Cognitive therapy of personality disorders*. Guilford Press.

Beeney, J. E., Hallquist, M. N., Ellison, W. D., & Levy, K. N. (2016). Self–other disturbance in borderline personality disorder: Neural, self-report, and performance-based evidence. *Personality Disorders, 7*(1), 28–39. https://doi.org/10.1037/per0000127

Bender, D. S., Morey, L. C., & Skodol, A. E. (2011). Toward a model for assessing level of personality functioning in *DSM-5*, Part I: A review of theory and methods. *Journal of Personality Assessment, 93*(4), 332–346. https://doi.org/10.1080/00223891.2011.583808

Bernstein, J., Zimmerman, M., & Auchincloss, E. L. (2015). Transference-focused psychotherapy training during residency: An aide to learning psychodynamic psychotherapy. *Psychodynamic Psychiatry, 43*(2), 201–221. https://doi.org/10.1521/pdps.2015.43.2.201

Biberdzic, M., Ensink, K., Normandin, L., & Clarkin, J. F. (2018). Empirical typology of adolescent personality organization. *Journal of Adolescence, 66*, 31–48. https://doi.org/10.1016/j.adolescence.2018.04.004

Binks, C. A., Fenton, M., McCarthy, L., Lee, T., Adams, C. E., & Duggan, C. (2006). Psychological therapies for people with borderline personality disorder. *Cochrane Database of Systematic Reviews*. https://doi.org/10.1002/14651858.CD005652

Blatt, S. J. (1974). Levels of object representation in anaclitic and introjective depression. *The Psychoanalytic Study of the Child, 29*(1), 107–157. https://doi.org/10.1080/00797308.1974.11822616

Blatt, S. J., & Blass, R. B. (1990). Attachment and separateness. A dialectic model of the products and processes of development throughout the life cycle. *The Psychoanalytic Study of the Child, 45*(1), 107–127. https://doi.org/10.1080/00797308.1990.11823513

Blüml, V., & Doering, S. (2021). *ICD-11* personality disorders: A psychodynamic perspective on personality functioning. *Frontiers in Psychiatry*, Article 654026. https://doi.org/10.3389/fpsyt.2021.654026

Buchheim, A., Hörz-Sagstetter, S., Doering, S., Rentrop, M., Schuster, P., Buchheim, P., Pokorny, D., & Fischer-Kern, M. (2017). Change of unresolved attachment in borderline personality disorder: RCT study of transference-focused psychotherapy. *Psychotherapy and Psychosomatics, 86*(5), 314–316. https://doi.org/10.1159/000460257

Caligor, E., Diamond, D., Yeomans, F. E., & Kernberg, O. F. (2009). The interpretive process in the psychoanalytic psychotherapy of borderline personality pathology. *Journal of the American Psychoanalytic Association, 57*(2), 271–301. https://doi.org/10.1177/0003065109336183

Caligor, E., Kernberg, O. F., & Clarkin, J. F. (2007). *Handbook of dynamic psychotherapy for higher level personality pathology*. American Psychiatric Publishing.

Caligor, E., Kernberg, O. F., Clarkin, J. F., & Yeomans, F. E. (2018). *Psychodynamic therapy for personality pathology: Treating self and interpersonal functioning*. American Psychological Association.

Caligor, E., Levy, K. N., & Yeomans, F. E. (2015). Narcissistic personality disorder: Diagnostic and clinical challenges. *The American Journal of Psychiatry, 172*(5), 415–422. https://doi.org/10.1176/appi.ajp.2014.14060723

Caspi, A., & Moffitt, T. E. (2018). All for one and one for all: Mental disorders in one dimension. *The American Journal of Psychiatry, 175*(9), 831–844. https://doi.org/10.1176/appi.ajp.2018.17121383

Clarkin, J. F., Cain, N., & Livesley, W. J. (2015). An integrated approach to treatment of patients with personality disorders. *Journal of Psychotherapy Integration, 25*(1), 3–12. https://doi.org/10.1037/a0038766

Clarkin, J. F., Caligor, E., & Sowislo, J. F. (2020). An object relations model perspective on the Alternative Model for Personality Disorders (*DSM-5*). *Psychopathology, 53*(3-4), 141–148. https://doi.org/10.1159/000508353

Clarkin, J. F., Foelsch, P. A., Levy, K. N., Hull, J. W., Delaney, J. C., & Kernberg, O. F. (2001). The development of a psychodynamic treatment for patients with borderline personality disorder: A preliminary study of behavioral change. *Journal of Personality Disorders, 15*(6), 487–495. https://doi.org/10.1521/pedi.15.6.487.19190

Clarkin, J. F., & Levy, K. N. (2003). A psychodynamic treatment for severe personality disorders: Issues in treatment development. *Psychoanalytic Inquiry, 23*(2), 248–267. https://doi.org/10.1080/07351692309349033

Clarkin, J. F., Levy, K. N., & Ellison, W. D. (2010). Personality disorders. In L. M. Horowitz & S. Strack (Eds.), *Handbook of interpersonal psychology: Theory, research, assessment, and therapeutic interventions* (pp. 383–403). John Wiley & Sons.

Clarkin, J. F., Levy, K. N., Lenzenweger, M. F., & Kernberg, O. F. (2007). Evaluating three treatments for borderline personality disorder: A multiwave study. *The American Journal of Psychiatry, 164*(6), 922–928. https://doi.org/10.1176/ajp.2007.164.6.922

Clarkin, J. F., Petrini, M., & Diamond, D. (2019). Complex depression: The treatment of major depression and severe personality pathology. *Journal of Clinical Psychology, 75*(5), 824–833. https://doi.org/10.1002/jclp.22759

Clarkin, J. F., Yeomans, F. E., & Kernberg, O. F. (1999). *Psychotherapy for borderline personality.* John Wiley & Sons.

Clarkin, J. F., Yeomans, F. E., & Kernberg, O. F. (2006). *Psychotherapy for borderline personality: Focusing on object relations.* American Psychiatric Publishing.

Cristea, I. A., Gentili, C., Cotet, C. D., Palomba, D., Barbui, C., & Cuijpers, P. (2017). Efficacy of psychotherapies for borderline personality disorder: A systematic review and meta-analysis. *JAMA Psychiatry, 74*(4), 319–328. https://doi.org/10.1001/jamapsychiatry.2016.4287

Cuevas, P., Camacho, J., Mejía, R., Rosario, I., Parres, R., Mendoza, J., & López, D. (2000). Cambios en la psicopatología del trastorno limítrofe de la personalidad, en los pacientes trtados con lapsicoterapia psicodinámica [Changes in the psychopathology of borderline personality disorder in patients treated with psychodynamic psychotherapy]. *Salud Mental, 23*(6), 1–11.

Deutsche Gesellschaft für Psychiatrie und Psychotherapie, Psychosomatik und Nervenheilkunde [German Association for Psychiatry, Psychotherapy, and Psychosomatics]. (2009). *Band 1: Treatment guideline personality disorders.* Steinkopff Verlag.

Diamond, D., & Yeomans, F. (2008). Psychopathologies narcissiques et psychothérapie focalisée sur le transfert (PFT) [Narcissism, its disorders, and the role of TFP]. *Sante Mentale au Quebec, 33*(1), 115–139. https://doi.org/10.7202/018475ar

Diamond, D., Yeomans, F. E., & Levy, K. N. (2011). Psychodynamic psychotherapy for narcissistic personality. In W. K. Campbell & J. D. Miller (Eds.), *The handbook of narcissism and narcissistic personality disorder: Theoretical approaches, empirical findings, and treatments* (pp. 423–433). John Wiley & Sons.

Diamond, D., Yeomans, F. E., & Stern, B. L. (2021). *Treating pathological narcissism with transference-focused psychotherapy.* The Guilford Press.

Doering, S., Hörz, S., Rentrop, M., Fischer-Kern, M., Schuster, P., Benecke, C., Buchheim, A., Martius, P., & Buchheim, P. (2010). Transference-focused psychotherapy v. treatment by community psychotherapists for borderline personality disorder: Randomised controlled trial. *The British Journal of Psychiatry, 196*(5), 389–395. https://doi.org/10.1192/bjp.bp.109.070177

Draijer, N., & Van Zon, P. (2013). Transference-focused psychotherapy with former child soldiers: Meeting the murderous self. *Journal of Trauma & Dissociation, 14*(2), 170–183. https://doi.org/10.1080/15299732.2013.724339

Ellison, W. D., Levy, K. N., Newman, M. G., Pincus, A. L., Wilson, S. J., & Molenaar, P. C. M. (2020). Dynamics among borderline personality and anxiety features in psychotherapy outpatients: An exploration of nomothetic and idiographic patterns. *Personality Disorders, 11*(2), 131–140. https://doi.org/10.1037/per0000363

Ensink, K., Biberdzic, M., Normandin, L., & Clarkin, J. F. (2015). A developmental psychopathology model of borderline personality disorder in adolescence. *Journal of*

Infant, Child, and Adolescent Psychotherapy, 14(1), 46–69. https://doi.org/10.1080/15289168.2015.1007715

Erikson, E. H. (1950). *Childhood and society*. W. W. Norton.

Eysenck, H. J. (1987). The definition of personality disorders and the criteria appropriate for their description. *Journal of Personality Disorders, 1*(3), 211–219. https://doi.org/10.1521/pedi.1987.1.3.211

Fischer-Kern, M., Doering, S., Taubner, S., Hörz, S., Zimmermann, J., Rentrop, M., Schuster, P., Buchheim, P., & Buchheim, A. (2015). Transference-focused psychotherapy for borderline personality disorder: Change in reflective function. *The British Journal of Psychiatry, 207*(2), 173–174. https://doi.org/10.1192/bjp.bp.113.143842

Freud, A. (1966). *The ego and the mechanisms of defense* (rev. ed.). International Universities Press.

Gamache, D., Savard, C., Leclerc, P., & Côté, A. (2019). Introducing a short self-report for the assessment of *DSM-5* level of personality functioning for personality disorders: The Self and Interpersonal Functioning Scale. *Personality Disorders, 10*(5), 438–447. https://doi.org/10.1037/per0000335

Gelso, C. (2014). A tripartite model of the therapeutic relationship: Theory, research, and practice. *Psychotherapy Research, 24*(2), 117–131. https://doi.org/10.1080/10503307.2013.845920

Giesen-Bloo, J., van Dyck, R., Spinhoven, P., van Tilburg, W., Dirksen, C., van Asselt, T., Kremers, I., Nadort, M., & Arntz, A. (2006). Outpatient psychotherapy for borderline personality disorder: Randomized trial of schema-focused therapy vs transference-focused psychotherapy. *Archives of General Psychiatry, 63*(6), 649–658. https://doi.org/10.1001/archpsyc.63.6.649

Hersh, R. G. (2013). The assessment and treatment of borderline personality disorder in the college and university population. *Journal of College Student Psychotherapy, 27*(4), 304–322. https://doi.org/10.1080/87568225.2013.824326

Hersh, R. G. (2015). Using transference-focused psychotherapy principles in the pharmacotherapy of patients with severe personality disorders. *Psychodynamic Psychiatry, 43*(2), 181–199. https://doi.org/10.1521/pdps.2015.43.2.181

Hersh, R. G., Caligor, E., & Yeomans, F. E. (2017). *Fundamental of transference-focused psychotherapy: Applications in psychiatric and medical settings*. Springer.

Huprich, S. K., & Nelson, S. M. (2015). Advancing the assessment of personality pathology with the cognitive-affective processing system. *Journal of Personality Assessment, 97*(5), 467–477. https://doi.org/10.1080/00223891.2015.1058806

Huprich, S. K., Nelson, S. M., Meehan, K. B., Siefert, C. J., Haggerty, G., Sexton, J., Dauphin, V. B., Macaluso, M., Jackson, J., Zackula, R., & Baade, L. (2018). Introduction of the *DSM-5* Levels of Personality Functioning Questionnaire. *Personality Disorders, 9*(6), 553–563. https://doi.org/10.1037/per0000264

International Society of Transference-Focused Therapy. (n.d.). *Certified TFP teachers and supervisors*. https://istfp.org/training/certified-tfp-teachers-and-supervisors/

Kellogg, S. H., & Young, J. E. (2006). Schema therapy for borderline personality disorder. *Journal of Clinical Psychology, 62*(4), 445–458. https://doi.org/10.1002/jclp.20240

Kernberg, O. (1967). Borderline personality organization. *Journal of the American Psychoanalytic Association, 15*(3), 641–685. https://doi.org/10.1177/000306516701500309

Kernberg, O., Burstein, E. D., Coyne, L., Appelbaum, A., Horwitz, L., & Voth, H. (1972). Psychotherapy and psychoanalysis: The final report of the Menninger Foundation's Psychotherapy Project. *Bulletin of the Menninger Clinic, 36*, 1–275.

Kernberg, O. F. (1984). *Severe personality disorders: Psychotherapeutic strategies*. Yale University Press.

Kernberg, O. F. (1985). *Borderline conditions and pathological narcissism*. Jason Aronson. (Original work published 1975)

Kernberg, O. F. (2004). *Aggressivity, narcissism, and self-destructiveness in the psychotherapeutic relationship: New developments in the psychopathology and psychotherapy of* severe personality disorders. Yale University Press. https://doi.org/10.12987/yale/9780300101805.001.0001

Kernberg, O. F. (2007). The almost untreatable narcissistic patient. *Journal of the American Psychoanalytic Association, 55*(2), 503–539. https://doi.org/10.1177/00030651070550020701

Kernberg, O. F. (2014). An overview of the treatment of severe narcissistic pathology. *The International Journal of Psycho-Analysis, 95*(5), 865–888. https://doi.org/10.1111/1745-8315.12204

Kernberg, O. F. (2022). *Supportive psychotherapy based on TFP principles: SPT* [Unpublished manuscript]. Department of Psychiatry, Weill Cornell Medical College.

Kernberg, O. F., & Caligor, E. (2005). A psychoanalytic theory of personality disorders. In M. Lenzenweger & J. F. Clarkin (Eds.), *Major theories of personality disorder* (2nd ed., pp. 114–156). The Guilford Press.

Kernberg, O. F., Selzer, M. A., Koenigsberg, H. W., Carr, A. C., & Appelbaum, A. H. (1989). *Psychodynamic psychotherapy of borderline patients*. Basic Books.

Kernberg, P., Weiner, A. S., & Bardenstein, K. K. (2000). *Personality disorders in children and adolescents*. Basic Books.

Kliem, S., Kröger, C., & Kosfelder, J. (2010). Dialectical behavior therapy for borderline personality disorder: A meta-analysis using mixed-effects modeling. *Journal of Consulting and Clinical Psychology, 78*(6), 936–951. https://doi.org/10.1037/a0021015

Koenigsberg, H. W., Kernberg, O. F., Stone, M. H., Appelbaum, A. H., Yeomans, F. E., & Diamond, D. (2000). *Borderline patients: Extending the limits of treatability*. Basic Books.

Kotov, R., Krueger, R. F., Watson, D., Achenbach, T. M., Althoff, R. R., Bagby, R. M., Brown, T. A., Carpenter, W. T., Caspi, A., Clark, L. A., Eaton, N. R., Forbes, M. K., Forbush, K. T., Goldberg, D., Hasin, D., Hyman, S. E., Ivanova, M. Y., Lynam, D. R., Markon, K., . . . Zimmerman, M. (2017). The Hierarchical Taxonomy of Psychopathology (HiTOP): A dimensional alternative to traditional nosologies. *Journal of Abnormal Psychology, 126*(4), 454–477. https://doi.org/10.1037/abn0000258

Lenzenweger, M. F., Clarkin, J. F., Kernberg, O. F., & Foelsch, P. A. (2001). The Inventory of Personality Organization: Psychometric properties, factorial composition, and criterion relations with affect, aggressive dyscontrol, psychosis proneness, and self-domains in a nonclinical sample. *Psychological Assessment, 13*(4), 577–591. https://doi.org/10.1037/1040-3590.13.4.577

Levy, K. N. (2009). Psychodynamic and psychoanalytic psychotherapy. In D. C. S. Richard & S. Huprich (Eds.), *Clinical psychology: Assessment, treatment, and research* (pp. 181–214). Elsevier Academic Press.

Levy, K. N. (2012). Subtypes, dimensions, levels, and mental states in narcissism and narcissistic personality disorder. *Journal of Clinical Psychology, 68*(8), 886–897. https://doi.org/10.1002/jclp.21893

Levy, K. N. (2020). Contemporary psychodynamic treatments: Commentary on psychoanalytic/psychodynamic approaches to personality disorders. In C. W. Lejuez & K. L. Gratz (Eds.), *The Cambridge handbook of personality disorders* (pp. 440–443). Cambridge University Press. https://doi.org/10.1017/9781108333931.076

Levy, K. N., Beeney, J. E., Wasserman, R. H., & Clarkin, J. F. (2010). Conflict begets conflict: Executive control, mental state vacillations, and the therapeutic alliance in treatment of borderline personality disorder. *Psychotherapy Research, 20*(4), 413–422. https://doi.org/10.1080/10503301003636696

Levy, K. N., Chauhan, P., Clarkin, J. F., Wasserman, R. H., & Reynoso, J. S. (2009). Narcissistic pathology: Empirical approaches. *Psychiatric Annals, 39*(4), 203–213. https://doi.org/10.3928/00485713-20090401-03

Levy, K. N., Clarkin, J. F., Foelsch, P. S., & Kernberg, O. F. (2022). *Outpatient treatment with transference-focused psychotherapy for patients diagnosed with borderline personality disorder: An ecologically valid quasi-experimental comparison with a treatment-as-usual cohort* [Unpublished manuscript]. Department of Psychiatry, Weill Cornell Medical College.

Levy, K. N., Diamond, D., Clarkin, J. F., & Kernberg, O. F. (2022). *Changes in attachment, reflective function, and object representation in transference focused psychotherapy for borderline personality disorder* [Unpublished manuscript]. Department of Psychology, The Pennsylvania State University.

Levy, K. N., Kivity, Y., Diamond, D., Kernberg, O. F., & Clarkin, J. F. (2022). *The impact of narcissism on the evidence-based treatment of borderline personality disorder* [Unpublished manuscript]. Department of Psychology, The Pennsylvania State University.

Levy, K. N., Kivity, Y., & Yeomans, F. E. (2019). Transference-focused psychotherapy: Structural diagnosis as the basis for case formulation. In U. Kramer (Ed.), *Case formulation for personality disorders: Tailoring psychotherapy to the individual client* (pp. 19–40). Academic Press. https://doi.org/10.1016/B978-0-12-813521-1.00002-3

Levy, K. N., Meehan, K. B., Kelly, K. M., Reynoso, J. S., Weber, M., Clarkin, J. F., & Kernberg, O. F. (2006). Change in attachment patterns and reflective function in a randomized control trial of transference-focused psychotherapy for borderline personality disorder. *Journal of Consulting and Clinical Psychology, 74*(6), 1027–1040. https://doi.org/10.1037/0022-006X.74.6.1027

Levy, K. N., Meehan, K. B., & Yeomans, F. E. (2012). An update and overview of the empirical evidence for transference-focused psychotherapy and other psychotherapies for borderline personality disorder. In R. A. Levy, J. S. Ablon, & H. Kächele (Eds.), *Psychodynamic psychotherapy research* (pp. 139–167). Springer.

Levy, K. N., & Scala, J. W. (2012). Transference, transference interpretations, and transference-focused psychotherapies. *Psychotherapy, 49*(3), 391–403. https://doi.org/10.1037/a0029371

Levy, K. N., & Scala, J. W. (2015). Psychotherapy integration for personality disorders: A commentary. *Journal of Psychotherapy Integration, 25*(1), 49–57. https://doi.org/10.1037/a0038771

Levy, K. N., Steiner, T. G., Brandenburg, J., & Adams, R. B. (2022). *The elusive self: The role of borderline personality disorder traits in the inability to represent the self* [Unpublished manuscript]. Department of Psychology, The Pennsylvania State University.

Levy, K. N., Wasserman, R. H., Scott, L. N., & Yeomans, F. E. (2009). Empirical evidence for transference-focused psychotherapy and other psychodynamic psychotherapies for borderline personality disorder. In R. Levy & J. S. Ablon (Eds.), *Handbook of evidence-based psychodynamic psychotherapy: Bridging the gap between science and practice* (pp. 93–119). Humana.

Lingiardi, V., & McWilliams, N. (Eds.). (2017). *Psychodynamic Diagnostic Manual—PDM-2* (2nd ed.). Guilford Press.

Marcia, J. E. (1966). Development and validation of ego-identity status. *Journal of Personality and Social Psychology, 3*(5), 551–558. https://doi.org/10.1037/h0023281

McAdams, D. P. (2001). The psychology of life stories. *Review of General Psychology, 5*(2), 100–122. https://doi.org/10.1037/1089-2680.5.2.100

McCommon, B., & Hersh, R. (2021). Good psychiatric management and transference-focused psychotherapy for borderline personality disorder: A spectrum of psychodynamically informed treatments. *Psychodynamic Psychiatry, 49*(2), 296–321. https://doi.org/10.1521/pdps.2021.49.2.296

Miller, J. D., Sleep, C., & Lynam, D. R. (2018). *DSM-5* alternative model of personality disorder: Testing the trait perspective captured in Criterion B. *Current Opinion in Psychology, 21*, 50–54. https://doi.org/10.1016/j.copsyc.2017.09.012

Mischel, W., & Shoda, Y. (1995). A cognitive-affective system theory of personality: Reconceptualizing situations, dispositions, dynamics, and invariance in personality structure. *Psychological Review, 102*(2), 246–268. https://doi.org/10.1037/0033-295X.102.2.246

Morey, L. C. (2017). Development and initial evaluation of a self-report form of the *DSM-5* Level of Personality Functioning Scale. *Psychological Assessment, 29*(10), 1302–1308. https://doi.org/10.1037/pas0000450

Natoli, A. P. (2021). Integrating the assessment of implicit personality factors into clinical practice. *Journal of Personality Assessment, 103*(3), 427–428. https://doi.org/10.1080/00223891.2021.1903909

Normandin, L., Ensink, K., & Kernberg, O. F. (2015). Transference-focused psychotherapy for borderline adolescents: A neurobiologically informed psychodynamic psychotherapy. *Journal of Infant, Child, and Adolescent Psychotherapy, 14*(1), 98–110. https://doi.org/10.1080/15289168.2015.1006008

Normandin, L., Ensink, K., Weiner, A., & Kernberg, O. F. (2021). *Transference-focused psychotherapy for adolescents with severe personality disorders*. American Psychiatric Association Publishing.

Normandin, L., Ensink, K., Yeomans, F. E., & Kernberg, O. F. (2014). Transference-focused psychotherapy for personality disorders in adolescence. In C. Sharp & J. Tackett (Eds.), *Handbook of borderline personality disorder in children and adolescents* (pp. 333–359). Springer. https://doi.org/10.1007/978-1-4939-0591-1_22

Oud, M., Arntz, A., Hermens, M. L., Verhoef, R., & Kendall, T. (2018). Specialized psychotherapies for adults with borderline personality disorder: A systematic review and meta-analysis. *The Australian and New Zealand Journal of Psychiatry, 52*(10), 949–961. https://doi.org/10.1177/0004867418791257

Perez, D. L., Vago, D. R., Pan, H., Root, J., Tuescher, O., Fuchs, B. H., Leung, L., Epstein, J., Cain, N. M., Clarkin, J. F., Lenzenweger, M. F., Kernberg, O. F., Levy, K. N., Silbersweig, D. A., & Stern, E. (2016). Frontolimbic neural circuit changes in emotional processing and inhibitory control associated with clinical improvement following transference-focused psychotherapy in borderline personality disorder. *Psychiatry and Clinical Neurosciences, 70*(1), 51–61. https://doi.org/10.1111/pcn.12357

Scala, J. W., Levy, K. N., Johnson, B. N., Kivity, Y., Ellison, W. D., Pincus, A. L., Newman, M. G., & Wilson, S. J. (2018). The role of negative affect and self-concept clarity in predicting self-injurious urges in borderline personality disorder using ecological momentary assessment. *Journal of Personality Disorders, 32*(Suppl.), 36–57. https://doi.org/10.1521/pedi.2018.32.supp.36

Sharp, C., Wright, A. G. C., Fowler, J. C., Frueh, B. C., Allen, J. G., Oldham, J., & Clark, L. A. (2015). The structure of personality pathology: Both general ('g') and specific ('s') factors? *Journal of Abnormal Psychology, 124*(2), 387–398. https://doi.org/10.1037/abn0000033

Sleep, C., Lynam, D. R., & Miller, J. D. (2021). Personality impairment in the *DSM-5* and *ICD-11*: Current standing and limitations. *Current Opinion in Psychiatry, 34*(1), 39–43. https://doi.org/10.1097/YCO.0000000000000657

Steiner, T. G., Levy, K. N., Brandenburg, J. C., & Adams, R. B., Jr. (2021). In the mind of the beholder: Narcissism relates to a distorted and enhanced self-image. *Personality and Individual Differences, 173*, Article 110608. https://doi.org/10.1016/j.paid.2020.110608

Stern, B. L., Diamond, D., & Yeomans, F. E. (2017). Transference-focused psychotherapy (TFP) for narcissistic personality: Engaging patients in the early treatment process. *Psychoanalytic Psychology, 34*(4), 381–396. https://doi.org/10.1037/pap0000145

Stern, B. L., Yeomans, F. E., Diamond, D., & Kernberg, O. F. (2013). Transference-focused psychotherapy for narcissistic personality. In J. S. Ogrodniczuk (Ed.), *Understanding and treating pathological narcissism* (pp. 235–252). American Psychological Association. https://doi.org/10.1037/14041-014

Stoffers-Winterling, J. M., Völlm, B. A., Rücker, G., Timmer, A., Huband, N., & Lieb, K. (2012). Psychological therapies for people with borderline personality disorder. *The Cochrane Database of Systematic Reviews*. https://doi.org/10.1002/14651858.CD005652.pub2

Tyrer, P., Mulder, R., Kim, Y. R., & Crawford, M. J. (2019). The development of the *ICD-11* classification of personality disorders: An amalgam of science, pragmatism, and politics. *Annual Review of Clinical Psychology, 15*(1), 481–502. https://doi.org/10.1146/annurev-clinpsy-050718-095736

Vaillant, G. E. (1992). *Ego mechanisms of defense: A guide for clinicians and researchers.* American Psychiatric Press.

Wallerstein, R. S. (1986). *Forty-two lives in treatment: A study of psychoanalysis and psychotherapy.* Guilford Press.

Wallerstein, R. S., Robbins, L. L., Sargent, H. D., & Luborsky, L. (1956). The Psychotherapy Research Project of the Menninger Foundation: Rationale, method and sample use. *Bulletin of the Menninger Clinic, 20*(5), 221–278.

Waugh, M. H., Hopwood, C. J., Krueger, R. F., Morey, L. C., Pincus, A. L., & Wright, A. G. C. (2017). Psychological Assessment with the *DSM-5* Alternative Model for Personality Disorders: Tradition and innovation. *Professional Psychology: Research and Practice, 48*(2), 79–89. https://doi.org/10.1037/pro0000071

Werner, H. (1957). The concept of development from a comparative and organismic point of view. In D. B. Harris (Ed.), *The concept of development* (pp. 125–148). University of Minnesota Press.

Widiger, T. A., & McCabe, G. A. (2020). The Alternative Model of Personality Disorders (AMPD) from the perspective of the five-factor model. *Psychopathology, 53*(3-4), 149–156. https://doi.org/10.1159/000507378

World Health Organization. (2019). *International statistical classification of diseases and related health problems* (11th ed.). https://icd.who.int/

Wright, A. G. C., Hopwood, C. J., Skodol, A. E., & Morey, L. C. (2016). Longitudinal validation of general and specific structural features of personality pathology. *Journal of Abnormal Psychology, 125*(8), 1120–1134. https://doi.org/10.1037/abn0000165

Yalch, M. M. (2020). Psychodynamic underpinnings of the *DSM-5* Alternative Model for Personality Disorder. *Psychoanalytic Psychology, 37*(3), 219–231. https://doi.org/10.1037/pap0000262

Yeomans, F. (2007). Questions concerning the randomized trial of schema-focused therapy vs transference-focused psychotherapy. *Archives of General Psychiatry, 64*(5), 609–610. https://doi.org/10.1001/archpsyc.64.5.609-c

Yeomans, F. E., Clarkin, J. F., & Kernberg, O. F. (2002). *A primer of transference-focused psychotherapy for the borderline patient.* Jason Aronson.

Yeomans, F. E., Clarkin, J. F., & Kernberg, O. F. (2015). *Transference-focused psychotherapy for borderline personality disorder: A clinical guide.* American Psychiatric Publishing.

Yeomans, F. E., Delaney, J. C., & Levy, K. N. (2017). Behavioral activation in TFP: The role of the treatment contract in transference-focused psychotherapy. *Psychotherapy, 54*(3), 260–266. https://doi.org/10.1037/pst0000118

Yeomans, F. E., Gutfreund, J., Selzer, M. A., Clarkin, J. F., Hull, J. W., & Smith, T. E. (1994). Factors related to drop-outs by borderline patients: Treatment contract and therapeutic alliance. *The Journal of Psychotherapy Practice and Research, 3*(1), 16–24.

Yeomans, F. E., Levy, K. N., & Caligor, E. (2013). Transference-focused psychotherapy. *Psychotherapy, 50*(3), 449–453. https://doi.org/10.1037/a0033417

Yeomans, F. E., Selzer, M. A., & Clarkin, J. F. (1992). *Treating the borderline patient: A contract-based approach.* Basic Books.

Zerbo, E., Cohen, S., Bielska, W., & Caligor, E. (2013). Transference-focused psychotherapy in the general psychiatry residency: A useful and applicable model for residents in acute clinical settings. *Psychodynamic Psychiatry, 41*(1), 163–181. https://doi.org/10.1521/pdps.2013.41.1.163

10

Mentalization-Based Treatment

Anthony W. Bateman

Psychosocial interventions known to create change in people with personality disorders (PDs) share a number of qualities often subsumed under the "four Cs": *consistency, coherence, continuity,* and *communication*. These overlapping qualities of different treatments may partly explain why such a range of treatments, diverse in content and interventional process, are equally effective (Storebø et al., 2020). The four Cs create a context in which metacognitive reorganization becomes possible, allowing new and more effective mental processes to be stimulated and embedded. This is exampled by borderline personality disorder (BPD), which is characterized by metacognitive disorganization and instability of self-experience (Fonagy et al., 2017), and creating conditions to address these problems may be the crucial component for positive change. Thus, any coordinated group of interventions within a framework that is understandable to the patient, which are consistently delivered over time, may be key to effective treatments. This implies that people with PD may be best defined as individuals with a level of metacognitive disorganization that leads them to experience considerable personal distress rather than as a category defined by a bundle of descriptive characteristics, and that metacognitive disorganization is a key domain process of all the PDs currently categorized in the psychiatric classification systems.

Despite the similarities in people with PDs, the classification systems continue with a categorical approach. Section II of the *Diagnostic and Statistical Manual of Mental Disorders* (5th ed.; *DSM-5*; American Psychiatric Association, 2013) provides 10 discrete diagnostic categories of PD, despite the evidence

---

https://doi.org/10.1037/0000310-011
Personality Disorders and Pathology: Integrating Clinical Assessment and Practice in the DSM-5 *and* ICD-11 *Era*, S. K. Huprich (Editor)
Copyright © 2022 by the American Psychological Association. All rights reserved.

that BPD and other named PDs are heterogenous groups within which there are widely differing levels of severity and symptomatology and that there are no well-defined boundaries between normal and pathological descriptive characteristics (Skodol et al., 2011).

The reliance on categories has important ramifications. The current evidence base for effective treatments is therefore flawed to the extent that studies are based on a supposedly homogeneous group of patients who are anything but that. This may explain why current treatments are effective overall, but within groups, some patients respond spectacularly well and others do not. Treatments may not, in fact, be equally applicable to all subtypes of BPD.

To counter this problem and future-proof research, a hybrid dimensional–categorical model was included in *DSM-5* Section III. This model calls for evaluation of impairments in personality functioning, specifically defined as "how an individual typically experiences himself or herself as well as others," rather than reliance on a discrete category of diagnosis. This is a move to a more dimensional approach to PD, with one central domain being subjective experience of self and others. The inadequacies of the categorical approach to PD and the recognition of the importance of the dimensional aspects of personality functioning for treatment was also why the *International Statistical Classification of Diseases and Related Health Problems* (11th ed.; *ICD-11*; World Health Organization, 2019) proposed breaking away from categorization using the alternative concept of trait domains (Tyrer et al., 2011) and has indeed done so (World Health Organization, 2019). While not proposing mentalizing as the named core dimension, the proposal of the domain of self and other experience as central to personality function allows an understanding and assessment of the individual according to a range of underlying cognitive and affective processes that make up their overall mentalizing ability.

For the purposes of this chapter on mentalization-based treatment (MBT), it is important to note that the mental processes enabling a person to access and integrate their subjective self-states—how they experience themselves—and others' own self-states, as proposed in *DSM-5*, are mental processes subsumed by the term "mentalizing"; thus, MBT is fully aligned with this suggested dimensional system of understanding PD. Poor ability and persistent instability in the domain of mentalizing indicate severe personality problems. Effective mentalizing protects against metacognitive disorganization, integrating a range of mental experience into a coherent processing system allowing effective social communication, which is at the heart of personality function. Targeting this process in treatment may therefore provide a route to more stable self-experience and improved social cognitive function, thereby reducing the harmful personal and societal effects of PD.

The focus on mentalizing in treatment of people with PD is therefore warranted, and MBT was developed to do just that (Bateman & Fonagy, 2004, 2006, 2016). This chapter further defines mentalization and the effects of poor mentalizing and provides clinical details of MBT, which aims to stabilize an individual's mentalizing capacity as the primary target of treatment.

Interventions tailored to stabilize and increase mentalizing ability will be illustrated with a clinical vignette.

DEFINING MENTALIZATION

Mentalizing can be defined as thinking about one's own and others' actions in terms of thoughts and feelings and using this knowledge of mental states to master life challenges. Mentalizing allows us to integrate information from internal and external sources and make sense of ourselves in the world. For example, it allows us to have thoughts that we recognize are not necessarily reality and helps us to reflect on them to establish their meaning to us. As mentioned, deficits in mentalizing are a conspicuous feature of all PDs, suggesting that it is a necessary dimension or domain of PD to assess and to focus on in treatment. For example, BPD is characterized by emotion dysregulation, impulsivity, and social-interpersonal dysfunction, all of which can be considered as resulting from an inability to use higher executive mental control and higher order cognitive processes, namely, mentalizing processes, to control and modulate experiences of self. As a higher order mental processing system extending across PDs, focusing on it may partly explain why MBT and other types of treatment may be effective with a range of PDs and other disorders (Bateman & Fonagy, 2009, 2016).

Mentalizing is not a single entity or aptitude, and four different components, or *dimensions*, to mentalizing—which reflect different social-cognitive processes—have been defined. It is helpful to distinguish the dimensions during clinical assessment of mentalizing, as they have significant clinical ramifications for treatment. They are

1. mentalizing the self versus mentalizing others,
2. automatic versus controlled mentalizing,
3. mentalizing with regard to internal versus external features, and
4. cognitive versus affective mentalizing.

The dimensions of mentalizing and their clinical application are described in detail elsewhere (Fonagy & Luyten, 2009). The capacity to mentalize one's own state—the *self* (including one's own physical experiences)—and the state of others and to differentiate them is a necessary ability to experience a sense of agency and independence of thought, which can be very unstable in people with BPD or too rigid in people with Antisocial and Narcissistic PDs. The two capacities are closely connected, and an imbalance in one signals vulnerability in the other. Individuals with mentalizing difficulties are likely to preferentially focus on one end of the spectrum, although they may be impaired at both. Any individual whose disorder is characterized by severe impairments in feelings of self-identity will also show problems in reflecting on and responding to others' mental states but may even give priority to others' experience of them to fill the void—and in doing so, become what others want them to be.

An individual who shows excessive use of self-processing with grandiosity and overinflated self-esteem may be preferentially sensitive to seeking confirmation of their self-experience from others' experience of them and be unable to identify with, empathize with, and react to others' personal experiences about themselves.

MENTALIZATION-BASED TREATMENT

The MBT clinician's first task is assessment and formulation (discussed later) of the patient's personality functioning, in terms of how the individual typically experiences himself or herself as well as others. This appraisal of the self–other dimension is fully in keeping with the *DSM* criteria for PD. But the MBT assessment goes beyond this and also concerns the relational attachment strategies of the individual that are activated during interpersonal stress and which lead to the repetitive pattern of relational distortions so evident in PD. This wider aspect of relational assessment includes an appraisal of the patient's ability to represent an "us-ness" or "we-ness," which is more than simply a self-and-other representation. This is a mental capacity to take a perspective that transcends what occurs within the separate selves of "you" and "me" to represent what is occurring for the relational unit of "us" (Gallotti & Frith, 2013; O'Madagain & Tomasello, 2019; Tomasello, 2016). Thus, it represents a higher level of mentalizing, enabling people to go beyond individuality—a mental process that can be problematic for people with PD and that is strikingly reduced in Narcissistic PD. Effective social interaction is partly dependent on groups of individuals seeing their actions as collaboratively directed in pursuit of a shared goal (as a "we") and, in doing so, creating another mind that is neither me nor you nor any of us. It is this collective mode of cognition, the we-mode of MBT, that is targeted in the group work.

We-ness in the clinical interaction is distinct from either patient or clinician individual self/other perspectives. In principle, the MBT approach requires the clinician to help the patient build ever increasing levels of mentalizing, from simplicity to complexity, that integrate experiences that are stable, flexible, and constructive in propelling social and intimate interaction forward. As an inherently relational representation, we-ness is a state actively developed and promoted in MBT, starting out with a collaboratively developed formulation and a personal mentalizing profile agreed on with the patient, followed by working explicitly not only with the mind states of the patient but also with those of the clinician scrutinizing the reciprocity of their interaction.

MBT clinicians openly present their mind states and their counterrelational responses to the patient, clarifying that neither person in the therapy interaction has a monopoly on valid views of reality, and both must accept that each side experiences interpersonal interactions only impressionistically. The patient is asked to mentalize the clinician just as the clinician has to mentalize the patient. A sense of we-ness emerges as all participants in either individual or group therapy are beholden to the shared task of mentalizing others as well as themselves. In MBT groups, a sense of we-ness is additionally generated by participants defining "our" group values at the outset and then revisiting and reformulating the group functioning around those values at regular intervals (Bateman, Campbell, & Fonagy, 2021).

In BPD, there are specific distortions or imbalances in mentalizing that typically manifest in situations of interpersonal stress or challenge; these are identified in the assessment and formulation phase of MBT. At these moments, patients' mental functioning becomes fixed in ineffective mentalizing modes that crystallize into three main types: psychic equivalence mode, teleological mode, and pretend mode (Fonagy & Bateman, 2008). MBT clinicians and their patients become alert to the deployment of these modes, paying special attention to what triggers them in the patient's daily life and even exploring interpersonal interaction that activates them in sessions. The MBT clinician is cautious about focusing too much on the adverse consequences of using the modes—that is, the outcomes of failure to understand the social world accurately, as these are the end product of low mentalizing rather than the area of vulnerability and sensitivity; too great an emphasis on the outcomes of mentalizing failures can often fuel negative self-esteem and be demotivating. It is best to catch oneself falling into low mentalizing, rather than try to address the pain of the consequences.

INEFFECTIVE MENTALIZING MODES

In the introductory phase of MBT, patients are inducted into the model. Identifying the use of ineffective mentalizing is an essential component of this process and becomes a significant element of the patient–clinician formulation. The rather clumsy and unappealing technical jargonistic terms for the ineffective mentalizing modes are often discussed with patients using more serviceable terms; for example, psychic equivalence mode becomes "boom brain" mode, teleological mode becomes "doing time" mode or "action man/person" mode, and pretend mode becomes "fake news" mode, "bullshit" mode, "bubble" mode, or "talk the talk but not walk the walk" mode. It is necessary to identify patient-specific contexts and sensitivities that trigger the modes, so that the formulation becomes personal and is exampled by the circumstances of the patient's life and mental function.

In psychic equivalence mode ("boom brain" mode), thoughts and feelings become "too real" to a point where it is extremely difficult for the individual to entertain possible alternative perspectives. Thoughts are facts and are lived in the moment as a reality, and there is no doubt or reflection on them. In phenomenological terms, this is akin to "concrete thinking." It is particularly present in complex trauma, BPD, and other PDs when an image or fragmented memory from the past is experienced as active in the current moment, leading to a very real, immediate intensity of feeling and bodily experience and a need for action. There is an imbalance in the cognitive-affective dimension, with thoughts and experience being processed according to emotional reality, giving an overriding sense of certainty about subjective experience ("She absolutely hates me"). Such a state of mind can be extremely frightening and gives justification for extreme reaction that is often incomprehensible to others. The reification of mental experience can lead to quasipsychotic symptoms, with thoughts and images becoming fleeting delusional and hallucinatory experiences, respectively. From a mentalizing perspective, the severity of BPD is "measured" not simply by the range of co-occurring conditions that accompany the diagnosis but by how persistent and extensive the use of ineffective mentalizing modes is, how easily they are triggered, and how problematic it is to reinstate effective mentalizing.

In teleological mode ("doing time" mode or "action man/person" mode), states of mind are given credibility according to only what happens in the physical world (e.g., "I am what I do and not what I think," "You are what you do and not what you say"). What happens tells an individual about the underlying motive (e.g., "You looked at your watch, so you are bored and want to leave"). Actions speak louder than words, so a patient who feels the clinician does not take them seriously and who feels their mental pain is not understood may have to express their state by physical action (e.g., the patient leaves a session and cuts themself in the waiting room's toilet). Inevitably, this triggers action on the part of the clinician, who may implement more sessions to manage the risk. This was not a manipulation, though: It was a desperate attempt to manage an intensely painful internal self-state of others failing to understand them and leaving them alone in their pain. In terms of the dimensions of mentalizing, the patient is stuck in the external pole, relying on how people behave and how they themselves behave to tell them what is going on in others' and their own mind.

In pretend mode (e.g., "fake news" mode, "bullshit" mode), thoughts and feelings become disconnected from reality. In the extreme, this leads to out-of-body experience, dissociation, and dissociative identities. Patients in pretend mode can discuss experiences extensively without rooting them within any reality and with even failing to recognize contradictions. They are in an "as if" world, and they recruit cognitive processing preferentially leading to "hypermentalization," a state akin to overthinking in which they talk endlessly about states of mind but with little depth in terms of retrieving memories and connecting ideas to feeling (Sharp & Vanwoerden, 2015). They attribute mental states and motives to themselves and others, giving their understanding an increasing complexity without any grounding in reality. Circumstantiality and excessive detail characterize the narrative. The problem is that the therapist may initially give credibility to pretend mode, joining with it and elaborating it further and further so that therapy becomes interminable with little change. Patients recognize this mental state when they are introduced to it in the psychoeducational phase of MBT. For example, those who spend considerable time trying to decide if their partner loves them are aware that their mind can run riot and never reach a conclusion—or if it does, that conclusion is rapidly questioned again and again.

These ineffective or "nonmentalizing" modes (or, termed in childhood, "pre-mentalizing" modes) are generated by imbalances within the dimensions of mentalizing. It is important to remember that the use of nonmentalizing modes is normal in early years and in adults when under stress, which is a time when earlier modes of mental function come forward for everyone. This is reassuring to patients, as they feel that their experiences are less abnormal (albeit extremely painful). There is a predominance of prementalizing/nonmentalizing in the early years of life when, for example, affect-focused mental-state thinking antedates more cognitive mentalizing (Harris et al., 2016), and psychic equivalence and pretend mode are part of the life of a child aged 3 to 5 years. It is the reliance on low mentalizing that characterizes people with PD, and the rapidity with which they fall into nonmentalizing and the difficulty they have in retrieving mentalizing that are the problems.

The three ineffective mentalizing modes are particularly important to identify with patients in their formulation right at the start of MBT, as they are often accompanied by a pressure to externalize unmentalized aspects of the self which are experienced as painful and disruptive. Externalizing may be demonstrated in attempts to dominate the mind of others or in self-harm and other types of behavior that, in the teleological mode, are expected to relieve tension and arousal, a characteristic feature of BPD.

CLINICAL IMPLEMENTATION OF MBT

Armed with this understanding of mentalizing and personality functioning, the MBT clinician works with the patient to generate a mentalizing formulation while following other principles related to the importance of the four Cs with which this chapter began. On the basis of the equivalence of outcomes between a range of different treatments and the lack of clarity about mechanisms of change, it is important to ensure that implementation of MBT respects coherence, consistency, continuity, and communication channels between patient and clinician throughout treatment. These are underpinned in treatment by systematic personalization of treatment through formulation, socialization of the patient to the model, and collaborative and democratic implementation with an emphasis on validation of the patient's sense of agency, effected through stimulating mentalizing processes robust enough for patients to use between sessions within their everyday life. From this perspective, what happens beyond therapy in the patient's social environment brings about change, although the instigator of this change process—mentalizing—is generated within the therapy.

Robust mentalizing generated through therapy allows the patient to recognize felicitous circumstances and take advantage of life chances that present in their daily situations. They are able to recognize and respond to opportunities that in the past, they would either not have recognized or would have been overly suspicious about. Other studies suggest that this process of change is the case. When session-by-session monitoring is implemented, it is the patient–clinician alliance in a given session that predicts change in the next (Falkenström et al., 2013). This suggests that a beneficial cycle is set up with the stimulation of mentalizing in sessions triggering changes in attitudes, which then allow more flexible reading of social and personal situations in the patient's life—and these, in turn, increase the likelihood of further learning in therapy to be reapplied in life (and so on). Thus, part of the focus for MBT is to bridge to the patient's general life the elaboration of mental processes undertaken in sessions, and then for the patient to feed them back into treatment. This process starts in the assessment and formulation, which is reviewed regularly and carried forward in treatment. An outline for clinicians to follow in making their MBT formulation is provided in Exhibit 10.1.

Assessment and Formulation

The assessment process results in a written formulation jointly agreed on between the clinician and the patient. As previously mentioned, it includes a personal *mentalizing profile*, which summarizes the patient's effective and ineffective use of the dimensions of mentalizing, illustrated from the patient's interpersonal and behavioral actions and reactions in life and linked to the social sensitivities that lead to the onset of their ineffective mentalizing modes. The formulation is generally free from any jargon. Exhibit 10.2 summarizes some clinical information from a prototypical patient, Jennifer, and Exhibit 10.3 shows the formulation extracted from the available information and from the clinical assessment, which would then have to be agreed on with Jennifer.

Patients with severe PD who show poor metacognitive integration will not be able to see themselves within, or take meaning from, a complex psychological treatise about their mental function—not because of any issue about their intelligence, but more because of difficulties in forming a coherent narrative of themselves and placing themselves in a current and historical context. Therefore, it is necessary to write the formulation in keeping with their capacity for reflection.

The formulation includes initial foci for intervention, which are extracted by the clinician and patient from the foremost difficulties—especially those that are likely to disrupt engagement in treatment, such as disorganized attachment processes, or those that endanger life, such as suicidal behavior. To some extent, the management of disorganized attachment takes priority: A patient who cannot engage in treatment cannot be helped to reduce and manage their impulsivity. Linking elements of the formulation to treatment processes forms the final part of the formulation. For example (see Exhibit 10.3), Jennifer's anxious-ambivalent strategies are linked to a possibility that she might become worried about being liked by others in the group or become overly concerned about displeasing the therapists. Her "doing" state of mind might lead to constant phone calls or emails to the clinicians as she becomes increasingly concerned that she has done something wrong and as her self-esteem falls. Under these circumstances, the clinician will consider linking the formulation to a contract with the patient around the level of contact between sessions.

EXHIBIT 10.1

Formulation Outline for Clinicians

Achievements and Problems

- Developmental summary/family background/traumatic or difficult consequences (three to four sentences)
- Triggering situations for loss of mentalizing (one sentence)
  - In what situations do your interpersonal difficulties occur?
  - What situations do you most struggle with?
- View of self at the time (one sentence)
  - How do you see yourself in this moment?
- Experience of other at the time/adult relational pattern (one sentence)
  - What do you think is in the mind of the other and how does that affect you?
- Dominant affect/most difficult emotions (one sentence)
  - What feelings are present in that moment?
  - Ways of coping/reaction/including self-harm and destructive behavior (one sentence)
  - These are likely to fit with nonmentalizing
- Strengths (one sentence)
  - Despite these difficulties, what have you managed to achieve?

Mentalizing Vulnerabilities

- Summary of mentalizing profile/key mentalizing vulnerabilities
- Needs to be written in ordinary language
- Be relevant to key nonmentalizing modes
  - psychic equivalence mode
  - teleological mode
  - pretend mode
- Have relevance to mentalizing dimensions and indicate when there is imbalance between
  - automatic/controlled mentalizing
  - self/other
  - internal/external
  - affect/cognition

Agreed Treatment Goals

Given the above understanding, we agreed on the following goals for psychological treatment:

- regarding yourself and ways in which you act
- regarding your relationships with other people
- regarding making changes in your life and changing or increasing activities

These goals will relate to the examples that you may bring into group, and it would be useful to consider how other people's examples link with the areas you would like help with.

246   *Anthony W. Bateman*

EXHIBIT 10.2

Clinical Information About Jennifer

Jennifer is 28 years old. She has had problems with drug addiction. She used cocaine and cannabis for a number of years, but she has now been clear of all drugs for over 6 months. Her current complaint is that she cannot bear to be alone. She separated from a long-term partner around 1 year ago. They had a son who is now age 5. She has joint custody with her partner. She feels "normal" when she is looking after her son, but when she is on her own in her flat, she becomes anxious and needs to see people. Consequently, she goes out frequently, because—in her own words—"I am desperate to be with other people."

There is some indication of relationship problems, to the extent that her previous partner was controlling and at times would be violent. She does not believe that she was in danger and so continued the relationship until 1 year ago, when he left her. She now has another relationship with a man she thinks is devoted to her. She recognizes that she causes problems in this relationship by constantly asking for reassurance. She constantly asks him if he loves her and frequently asks about his previous girlfriends and how they compare to her.

She shows some mood fluctuations and has, in the past, engaged in self-harm. She is not currently at risk in terms of suicidal impulses, but she took an overdose of drugs 2 years ago, wanting to die.

When I saw her, she presented as someone who is able to talk about herself, and she seems a likeable person. She has rapidly shifting mood states, and these seem to be dependent on environmental triggers. She feels good when she is with other people and bad when she is alone.

EXHIBIT 10.3

Jennifer: Putting Our Discussions Together

We have talked about a lot of things, and I will summarize those aspects that we have identified as really important for you to focus on in MBT.

Strengths
First, we need to say how much strength you have shown in very difficult circumstances over a long time—right from the start, things were really frightening in your childhood, and you had to grow up too quickly and look after yourself. You wobbled at times when you were a teenager—like anyone would—and drugs were the only way to take away some of the pain. But later, you managed to stop misusing them and began to rely more on your own strengths, just as you did when you stopped cutting yourself (even though that is still tempting). In treatment, we need to work out what progressions, understandings, and skills helped you do this—build on recognizing the need for and utilizing those just as you did when you managed to not go back to Dylan's father, despite being tempted by him. You stood your ground and are rightfully pleased with yourself about that. We need to identify those times that you decide what is best for you, compared with those times when you decide on things because someone else wants you to.

Who Am I, and What Do I Want?
We worked out that you often have problems sorting out what you think and what you feel. This is really difficult when you are on your own—and also when you are with your boyfriend. You have feelings that are intense and take you over, but you couldn't easily say what they were as we talked. We agreed that this needs looking at really carefully, as those feelings lead to "action mind." Sometimes—mostly when you feel bad about yourself—you try to work out what is going on in other people's minds and be whatever they want you to be (like with Dylan's dad). It makes you feel better, but then you start resenting them.

Mentalization-Based Treatment 247

EXHIBIT 10.3

Jennifer: Putting Our Discussions Together (*Continued*)

"Action Mind"

You have to go out and be with someone at times. You cannot see any other way of looking after yourself. When you are like this, you become desperate and want to be told or shown that you are liked and wanted. This is such a problem for you that it has led to you putting yourself at risk of harm. For that reason, looking at "action mind" is one of the first things to think about in therapy.

"Boom Brain"

Sometimes you become convinced that your boyfriend no longer loves you, and you end up irritating him by asking him more and more about it. We thought that, at these times, your mind had gone "boom" and you could not get the thought out of your mind—even when you sometimes begin to realize that you have no idea why you think it. It makes you more "needy," and "doing" becomes necessary—like seeing him straightaway. You want to protect this relationship, as you think he is good for you, you feel strongly for him, and he gets on well with Dylan.

"Boom brain" can come on when you feel criticized or diminished. You are often alert to such attitudes toward you when with other people. We need to watch out for how sensitive you can be and check it out when it happens in therapy (perhaps most easily in the individual sessions we talked about but also in the group, too).

Relationships

With your current boyfriend, we worked out that (a) you want him to look after you and (b) you often try to please him. With Dylan's father, you were mostly worried that you were not pleasing him enough and also worried that you were always doing something wrong. You said you were "clingy." I thought that was a bit rude about yourself and mentioned that this was a pattern that links with not knowing who you are and with being anxious, so it will be important to look at it in the group therapy when you are with other people, in order to see if you have the same pattern with others *there*—will you try to be liked, for example, and thereby find it hard to stand up for yourself?

The good relationship you have with Dylan is important, and you "know you are a good mother." Sometimes your interaction with his father creates difficulties for you, so the interaction between you all should be talked about in order to make sure you feel his care is safe and supportive.

MBT

Keep all of this in your mind, and we will ask the therapists to keep it all in mind, too. Then you can both focus on these areas to start with.

You might even worry that you won't do well enough in therapy or that you might have displeased your therapist and will want to see them quickly if you panic—so we need to work out what happens if you worry too much between sessions and get "action mind."

Aims at the Beginning

Work on being alone and what happens.

Consider your relationship with your boyfriend to try to protect it and allow it to continue.

Keep considering "you and Dylan" and how things are for you as a mum and how he is getting on.

Watch out for "action mind" and "boom brain," and work out what happens to bring them on.

If we do all of these things over time in individual and group sessions, we aim to help you answer "Who am I?" and "What do I want?" as well as support your relationships. We still have to decide how to measure whether that is happening.

Developing the formulation not only allows the therapist to convey to the patient that there is a coherent model that can be used to understand their mind and their distress but also helps the patient develop an image of themselves as being understood by another person who sees things from their perspective, which so often for people with PD is something that has been singularly lacking in their lives. Seeing themselves within the description may in itself create a therapeutic alliance and lower the patient's levels of distrust—the patient begins to imagine a clinician who understands them accurately, which is the key to them opening themselves up to learning from others.

Introductory Group

Following the agreement of the formulation, the patient attends a 10- to 12-session introductory group with other patients with PD, during which more detail is added to the framework of therapy. The aims are to promote group interaction, to reduce levels of epistemic vigilance and distrust, and to rekindle curiosity in the social and interpersonal environment (Fonagy et al., 2017). This adds an additional C to the core components of all therapies for PD mentioned earlier, namely, generating *curiosity*. Without this and the other Cs, the individual cannot learn. The evolutionary purpose of epistemic trust is to allow the individual to learn from the social environment. Learning requires us to be open to others' perspectives. This mechanism for opening the channel to social learning exists because individuals are self-protective and have to be vigilant toward others until it is clear that they are friend and not foe, at which point the individuals can open themselves up. The channel cannot be left open by default, as it leaves the person too vulnerable (Recanati, 1997; Sperber et al., 2010).

The biggest threats to the development of socially and personally effective epistemic mistrust/trust processes are environmental adversity, genetic propensity, or an interaction between the two. Once there is a breakdown in the capacity for affiliative and soothing interaction with others within a trusting environment, the individual is vulnerable to emotional dysregulation, impulsivity, and social dysfunction, all of which characterize individuals with severe mental health difficulties—and particularly those with BPD and other PDs. Hence, group intervention is an important part of MBT. Mentalizing oneself with others in an MBT group is the practice ground for allowing trust in the social world, which is necessary if learning and changing over the long term is to be stimulated.

MBT Individual and Group Psychotherapy

MBT was originally implemented as a combined group and individual treatment offered over 18 months. Clinical services have modified this combination and may offer MBT as either individual or group therapy alone. This clinical dismantling of the original research-based intervention is without empirical evidence for its benefits, equivalences, or detriments to patient outcomes—so the question as to whether MBT requires the combination of group and individual components for its effectiveness remains unanswered. MBT is also often offered for 1 year, as a time-limited intervention, which has some credibility. Research trials show that improvements start at around 6 months of treatment, and there is little, if any, reemergence of earlier symptoms later in treatment, with most gains being achieved by 1 year. Follow-up of patients treated with MBT shows that gains made at 18 months are maintained over at least 5 years (Bateman, Constantinou, et al., 2021; Bateman & Fonagy, 2008), but it remains unclear if these long-term rehabilitative effects of treatment are in process after only 1 year of treatment.

A structured intervention pathway is used in individual and group treatment to focus on mentalizing. A clinician's initial work in a session is to identify current problems and to explore issues in enough detail to empathically validate the patient's mental experience. The clinician responds to the patient with marked and contingent statements that demonstrate that they are seeing things from the patient affective perspective and that this understanding is without judgement or cognitive reinterpretation—the clinician shows that they see the issues through the eyes of the patient. In a group, the initial aims of the MBT clinician are to identify current problems that the members of the group wish to address, decide which problems are to be addressed, and then ensure that the group members empathically validate the identified patient's experience before it is explored in detail. While this process sounds like a simple and universal therapeutic intervention, it is hard to implement effectively. Patients with BPD are sensitive and hypervigilant and place considerable emphasis on information garnered from their external mentalizing focus. As a consequence, they are alert to tone of voice, facial expression, and indicators of rejection or disagreement. Patients with BPD bring preconceived schemas or working models to any relational interaction and interact accordingly, being overly influenced by the assumptions of automatic mentalizing. It is easy for the clinician to become defensive in these circumstances, which is unhelpful; so the clinician needs to avoid reciprocal reactivity and, to do so, to be in a state of mind known as the "not-knowing stance" throughout the exploratory phase of an MBT session.

Not-Knowing Stance

The *not-knowing stance* is a state of mind in which the clinician is open to seeing things from others' perspective without bringing in their own preconceptions and assumptions. The not-knowing is about mental states; it is not about knowledge and information, of which the clinician may have plenty.

The ongoing stance of curiosity and openness about patient experience, and the move to empathic validation, is made harder in the face of frightening or disturbing material that the patients bring—whether this is about their own suicidality or about their actions, such as violence towards others, and about which the clinician and indeed society may disapprove. The patient may describe situations that are not familiar to the lives of the clinicians; for example, in MBT treatment of patients with Antisocial PD, clients often allude to a value system that they have encoded and violent behavior that is alien to the clinician. But clinicians must remain curious about how these beliefs and feelings arise and what they are based on. Rather than assuming that they know what the person is feeling and why, it is essential that the clinician helps the client to reflect on themself; to do so, they model being authentically curious about, interested in, and empathic to the client's beliefs and states of mind. Once this joint platform between clinician and patient is established, it becomes possible to move on to the next phase of exploration, which is seeking to increase the mentalizing process by instilling doubt and complexity into a narrative that is so often being portrayed and experienced by the patient in a rigid, fixed, and singular way.

Exploratory Phase of MBT Session Related to the Mentalizing Model

The focus of exploration of the patient's narrative is affectively and relationally based. The mentalizing model of BPD purports that the patients have a need for social contact and even a willingness to discuss their feelings but struggle to benefit from and build upon constructive social relations in a sustainable manner because the social learning that this requires is not accessible to them. Their mentalizing vulnerabilities prevent constructive use of their personal interactions and interfere with their abilities to describe, contextualize, and effectively manage their emotional experiences. All of this has significant implications. The patient and clinician work systematically on defining inner experience affectively and cognitively; integrating the understanding with context, both current and past; and building a comprehensive and coherent "story" of inner experience and understanding of the personal–social world over time. In doing so, the relational interactions of the patient with others in their lives and with the clinician become a subject for scrutiny in terms of the assumptions that are made and how the attachment processes that undermine mentalizing are activated.

BPD is a condition that is often characterized by intense interpersonal distress and feelings of social isolation; helping individuals to develop more balanced mentalizing provides the fundamental social building blocks that make possible the construction of more benign and cooperative relationships with people in the wider social environment. As a result, the MBT clinician focuses on the patient's social and personal interactions and, in doing so, "stresses and exercises" the patient's mentalizing "muscle." This can be fraught with danger, as it may trigger uncontrolled affective and relational experience that destabilizes mentalizing, so it is essential that the clinician monitors levels of anxiety sensitively. But there is little point in the clinician doing all the mentalizing about events and giving answers to difficulties—this will not stimulate the patient's mentalizing process—so the clinician, using the not-knowing stance, asks the patient to scrutinize and to reconsider affectively salient relational events, to place them in their temporal context, and to consider their experience at the time while reflecting back on them from a mentalizing present. It is essential, therefore, that the clinician actively supports mentalizing in the session itself; otherwise, the patient will continue to be dominated by poorly regulated affect, which becomes increasingly painful if it is mired in psychic equivalence. So painful had such an experience become for Jennifer (discussed earlier) that she had become desperate and, unusually for her, told her boyfriend to leave.

JENNIFER: My boyfriend has done it now [*said angrily*]. He came home in the middle of the night and had been drinking with his friends. He doesn't love me. I know that now. So I told him to move out last night.

CLINICIAN: Tell me a bit more about it and how things stand between you now? [*Asking to develop an affectively salient theme, which initially appears to be described through a low mentalizing lens*]

JENNIFER: We had a row, and he slept on the sofa—and when he left this morning, I told him not to come back.

CLINICIAN: Oh. How are you in yourself about all this? [*Trying to establish the patient's current feeling state and self-representation*]

JENNIFER: I feel good. Finished with him. If he loved me, he would have at least told me he was not coming home, and he would not have left when I told him to. [*Teleological understanding of boyfriend's states of mind*]

CLINICIAN: It is such a painful thing to be with someone who shows he does not love you like that, leaving you with wanting to end the whole relationship. [*Empathically responding to the patient's emotional experience and its effect on her*] Your mind really went into blow-up time. [*Patient and clinician have already established, in the formulation and in the introductory phase, the psychic equivalent mind that the patient often falls into—so they can name it and note it.*]

CLINICIAN: How had things been going between you before this happened?

At this point, the clinician is concerned that Jennifer is currently in low mentalizing mode, so the primary task is to rekindle mentalizing in the session before further exploration can fruitfully take place. Here, the clinician engages in a "linked diversion" away from the immediate incident by asking Jennifer to reflect on her relationship with the boyfriend over a longer time frame rather than maintaining focus on the content and affect triggered by the event itself. The aim of this diversion is to stimulate wider reflection by getting her to stand alongside the incident and place it in a broader context and even gradually move to a metarepresentational we-ness level of her relationship with her boyfriend. This push and prod to increase the stability of mentalizing, and particularly its stability around the relationship with the boyfriend, is necessary if Jennifer and clinician are to revisit the incident itself and explore what happened through a mentalizing lens. Indeed, once this was done, the clinician was able to work around Jennifer's relationship with the boyfriend in terms of her anxious-ambivalent attachment strategies.

JENNIFER: Do you think I should go and apologize to him? I suppose I must have overreacted. Oh, shit. It's my fault that I have ruined it. He won't want me back.

CLINICIAN: Whoa. Let's back up from there and work out what you want in the relationship before you decide it was your fault. [*The clinician is suggesting more work on what has happened and also on her revision of the event, which might be more related to current activation of her "people pleasing" mode and submission in the relationship than to reflective appraisal.*]

JENNIFER: Do you think it was my fault?

CLINICIAN: I think that we need to consider that you reacted and then acted, and now you are backtracking and putting yourself down. Let's think about you being assertive like this and if that is worrying you.

As already outlined, balanced mentalizing is the fundamental tool for social learning and benefiting from social communication. New learning about the social world and how to operate within it is achievable only if the social environment is accurately interpreted; being able to understand the mental states of others' actions and reactions—that is, adequate mentalizing—is critical to this. In session, the patient is asked to relearn from revisiting their personal and social environment and then to consider how to implement their new understanding over time. In this incident with the boyfriend, Jennifer has to work out if his actions do confirm a preexisting concern about the reality of their relationship or whether her explosive reaction is based on her own reactivity and sensitivity which is leading to "action" mode. Of course, the patient's perspective taking may become increasingly complicated and nuanced as exploration continues, and in this session, the patient began to describe her sense that she was too dependent on her boyfriend. His lateness had led to escalating feelings of helplessness, to which she reacted by taking back control and by dismissing him. In the end, the patient uses the reflection about her reality and the meaning of the incident to take ownership of the experience. Only then will she be able to change her relationship with her boyfriend, for example, by discussing with him how his behaviors and responses to her play on her sensitivities—or alternatively, by insisting on separation. This work of transforming an unmentalized narrative into a mentalized narrative in therapy is a "rehearsal," to some extent, for daily life. It is possible to reap the benefits of future constructive social experiences only through the ongoing mentalizing maintenance of improved relationships, emotion regulation, and good behavioral control; improved mentalizing within the experiences is essential for these benefits, and this is facilitated by continual exploration of both the poorly and expertly mentalized experiences in treatment.

Clinicians have a natural tendency to focus on problematic or negative affects and experiences of patients, perhaps because patients with BPD often bring narratives of adverse experience to sessions. Rarely do patients bring good news stories. Nevertheless, the clinician should never forget that working on the patient's positive emotional experiences and on their mentalizing successes exercises the mentalizing muscle and may promote mentalizing resilience just as much as does a focus on learning to manage negative affects and to reappraise experiences initially filtered through ineffective mentalizing; it is the process of stimulating and using mentalizing that is important, rather than its content. Patients with BPD show a negative association between experience of positive affect levels and overall BPD severity, implying that rebalancing the dominance of negative affects by increasing the ability to focus on positive affects may increase mentalizing resilience. In a pilot study in which MBT clinicians were instructed to focus more on developing and maintaining positive affect and to lessen their focus on negative affect (Harpøth et al., 2020), there was a significant decrease in mean level of BPD severity compared to standard MBT in which both negative and positive affects were focused on equally (Harpøth et al., 2020). Focusing on positive affect in MBT was also effective in maintaining a good working alliance. In the case of Jennifer, the clinician did not fall into the trap of focusing on her guilt and self-blame, which are a consequence of—rather than the cause of—her initial assertiveness and then explosiveness.

Finally, the clinician began to work with Jennifer on her relationship patterns and attachment strategies that are activated by stressful interaction, looking at the relational sensitivities of the patient and the interaction between their misunderstandings in relationships, the activation of default attachment strategies, and the adverse effects on their emotional states and personal life. To some extent, the relationship with the clinician becomes the prototype for this exploration, which has led to the question about whether MBT "uses the transference" following principles of psychodynamic therapy or whether it is more allied with cognitive psychotherapies. MBT is an integrative therapy, in that treatment combines techniques into coherent strategies that are likely to enhance mentalizing irrespective of their origins in cognitive or dynamic therapy. An MBT clinician will "microslice" mental states leading up to self-harm in a "mentalizing functional analysis" in much the same way as a radical behaviorist will insist on a chain/functional behavioral analysis to seek escape routes for a patient from an uncontrolled cascade into self-destructive behavior. In a similar vein, the MBT clinician uses a focus on the attachment and relational strategies set up with the clinician in order to understand the interpersonal problems of the patient. However, there is a distinct difference from psychoanalytic transference-focused intervention in the aim of this work. It is not to understand the childhood origins or to give insight into such behaviors and ways of relating by using genetic or causal interpretation of the process; rather, it is to increase the patient's awareness of the complexity of their interactions and to free them from becoming stuck in a single reality. The relationship in MBT is explored in detail to generate an alternative perspective to interactions that were or are dominated by a single perspective processed in nonmentalizing mode to achieve a sense that "what is happening or happened is not quite how I initially saw it; now I can see more." It is not so much the insight, but the process of undertaking the task, that is essential. This is the time when the not-knowing stance, modeled by the clinician, can become rooted in the reflections of the patient. An ability for the patient to maintain their reflective capacity even under relational stress is necessary not only to effect dynamic reciprocity in daily relationships and find constructive solutions to problems but also to achieve a trusting intimacy and partnership with others.

OUTCOME RESEARCH

Recently, there have been a number of meta-analyses and reviews of treatments for BPD, and some have focused specifically on MBT. All meta-analyses conclude that MBT is an empirically supported intervention, particularly for BPD. Malda-Castillo and colleagues (2019) reviewed 23 studies that included nine randomized controlled trials (RCTs) and concluded that most of the studies showed positive clinical outcomes on most measures for people with BPD. Some of the research papers also attested to the suggestion, outlined earlier in this chapter, that a focus on mentalizing as a generic psychological process is likely to benefit those with a range of disorders. These include adolescents who self-harm, at-risk mothers in substance abuse treatment, and people diagnosed with Antisocial PD in an RCT (Bateman et al., 2016). These are all patient groups who are known to be difficult to treat with psychological intervention.

In a further review of MBT for BPD, Vogt and Norman (2019) included 14 papers—11 original studies and three follow-up papers. MBT was found to achieve either superior or equal reductions in psychiatric symptoms when compared with other well-organized treatments such as supportive group therapy, structured clinical management, and specialized clinical management. The authors concluded that MBT can achieve significant reductions in BPD symptom severity and the severity of comorbid disorders, as well as improve quality of life, when compared with targeted and methodically delivered intervention. This undermines the earlier suggestion of the four Cs being the effective components of any intervention, as the comparator treatments were organized with these in mind. It seems that a focus on mentalizing might add an additional element. Perhaps the generation of robust mentalizing increases the patient's ability to open the channel of epistemic trust/distrust more effectively. This is the subject of current research.

A Cochrane systematic review of all psychological treatments for BPD (Storebø et al., 2020) found that MBT and DBT had the highest number of primary trials and MBT the longest follow-up of outcome of treatment with a comparison group. MBT follow-up shows that gains made at the end of treatment are maintained for at least 5 years (Bateman, Constantinou, et al., 2021;

Bateman & Fonagy, 2008). Overall, the review concluded that MBT reduced self-harm and suicide at end of treatment and at long-term follow-up, with MBT having the highest effect size ($g = 1.032$) on suicidality of any treatment. MBT also improved psychosocial function and reduced depression at end of treatment and follow-up. Intriguingly, MBT reduced interpersonal problems at end of treatment but not at follow-up.

Adaptations of the core model of MBT for BPD have been investigated, in RCTs, for the treatment of other complex mental health disorders such as Antisocial PD (Bateman et al., 2016), eating disorders (Robinson et al., 2016), drug addiction (Philips et al., 2018), and depression (Jakobsen et al., 2014); applied to different age groups with specific problems, such as self-harming adolescents (Rossouw & Fonagy, 2012); and implemented in different settings, such as a day hospital (Bales et al., 2012; Bateman & Fonagy, 1999), inpatient units, prisons (Bateman & Fonagy, 2019), and schools (Fonagy et al., 2009).

MBT is currently being studied as an intervention for people with psychosis. A rationale for the intervention has been developed (Debbané et al., 2016), and mentalizing problems associated with psychotic mental functioning are well described (Frith, 2004; Frith & Frith, 2006). A multicenter RCT comparing MBT with treatment as usual (TAU; Weijers et al., 2020) showed promising results in the predeclared primary outcome of social functioning. Patients treated with MBT plus TAU showed more robust improvements in social functioning at follow-up. Patients in the MBT group also performed better on measures of mentalizing ability.

CONCLUSION

MBT has joined a range of empirically supported treatments for BPD and is proving to be an effective intervention for other groups of patients. Part of the explanation for the broad application may be the diligent focus on mentalizing, which, as a transdiagnostic mental process, is implicated as a contributing factor in a range of disorders. However, the principled following of the three Cs in treatment—and the addition of a focus on a fourth C of communication in social and interpersonal relationships—is probably equally important if long-term outcomes are to be improved further.

Additionally, MBT is well placed in terms of the current focus on understanding personality and defining PD from a dimensional, rather than a categorical, perspective. Mentalizing is a higher order multidimensional mental process, and this level of psychological processing forms a substantial component of *DSM-5* Section III Criterion A definition of levels of personality functioning. PD is considered as a failure to develop a sense of self-identity and a socially adaptive capacity for interpersonal functioning, suggested, for example, by poorly integrated representations of others; so (a) a disordered sense of self and (b) dysfunctional interpersonal relationships driven by problems in mentalizing become central components to personality function itself, with relevance well beyond the restricted domain of BPD or other former categories of PD. Mentalizing allows us to experience ourselves as unique and differentiated from others, and it also gives us accurate self-appraisal, stable self-esteem, and ability to regulate a range of emotional experience—all of which are part of the self component of the new dimensional definitions of personality function; it allows us to understand and appreciate others' experiences and therefore to be empathic and intimate and understand the effects of our behaviors on others, both of which are included in the interpersonal components. In *ICD-11*, the severity criteria require assessment of self-dysfunction and interpersonal dysfunction along with ability to manage emotional states and a rating of trait domain specifiers. The latter form as a result of an imbalance in the domains of mentalizing; for example, dissociality arises from problems at the "other" pole of the self–other dimension, with some overuse of self-mentalizing. In MBT, patients are assessed according to their abilities to use mentalizing in a range of circumstances across their personal and social relationships, which are at the heart of this definition of personality (dys)function. The formulation agreed on with patients focuses on the dimension of mentalizing and how that interferes with self-identity and ability to understand others in interpersonal contexts. Treatment targets are not a series of descriptive characteristics but the mental processes that drive our personalities. Therefore, as the field moves away from categories and toward dimensions of personality function, a focus on mentalizing, as a target for psychotherapy for people with PD, increases in relevance for clinicians and researchers alike.

REFERENCES

American Psychiatric Association. (2013). *Diagnostic and statistical manual of mental disorders* (5th ed.). https://doi.org/10.1176/appi.books.9780890425596

Bales, D., van Beek, N., Smits, M., Willemsen, S., Busschbach, J. J., Verheul, R., & Andrea, H. (2012). Treatment outcome of 18-month, day hospital mentalization-based treatment (MBT) in patients with severe borderline personality disorder in the Netherlands. *Journal of Personality Disorders, 26*(4), 568–582. https://doi.org/10.1521/pedi.2012.26.4.568

Bateman, A., Campbell, C., & Fonagy, P. (2021). Rupture and repair in mentalization-based group psychotherapy. *International Journal of Group Psychotherapy, 71*(2), 371–392. https://doi.org/10.1080/00207284.2020.1847655

Bateman, A., Constantinou, M. P., Fonagy, P., & Holzer, S. (2021). Eight-year prospective follow-up of mentalization-based treatment versus structured clinical management for people with borderline personality disorder. *Personality Disorders: Theory, Research, and Treatment, 12*(4), 291–299. https://doi.org/10.1037/per0000422

Bateman, A., & Fonagy, P. (1999). Effectiveness of partial hospitalization in the treatment of borderline personality disorder: A randomized controlled trial. *The American Journal of Psychiatry, 156*(10), 1563–1569. https://doi.org/10.1176/ajp.156.10.1563

Bateman, A., & Fonagy, P. (2004). *Psychotherapy for borderline personality disorder: Mentalization-based treatment.* Oxford University Press. https://doi.org/10.1093/med:psych/9780198527664.001.0001

Bateman, A., & Fonagy, P. (2006). Mentalizing and borderline personality disorder. In J. G. Allen & P. Fonagy (Eds.), *The handbook of mentalization-based treatment* (pp. 185–200). John Wiley & Sons. https://doi.org/10.1002/9780470712986.ch9

Bateman, A., & Fonagy, P. (2008). 8-year follow-up of patients treated for borderline personality disorder: Mentalization-based treatment versus treatment as usual. *The American Journal of Psychiatry, 165*(5), 631–638. https://doi.org/10.1176/appi.ajp.2007.07040636

Bateman, A., & Fonagy, P. (2009). Randomized controlled trial of outpatient mentalization-based treatment versus structured clinical management for borderline personality disorder. *The American Journal of Psychiatry, 166*(12), 1355–1364. https://doi.org/10.1176/appi.ajp.2009.09040539

Bateman, A., & Fonagy, P. (2016). *Mentalization-based treatment for personality disorders: A practical guide.* Oxford University Press. https://doi.org/10.1093/med:psych/9780199680375.001.0001

Bateman, A., & Fonagy, P. (Eds.). (2019). *Handbook of mentalizing in mental health practice* (2nd ed.). American Psychiatric Association Publishing.

Bateman, A., O'Connell, J., Lorenzini, N., Gardner, T., & Fonagy, P. (2016). A randomised controlled trial of mentalization-based treatment versus structured clinical management for patients with comorbid borderline personality disorder and antisocial personality disorder. *BMC Psychiatry, 16*(1), Article 304. https://doi.org/10.1186/s12888-016-1000-9

Debbané, M., Benmiloud, J., Salaminios, G., Solida-Tozzi, A., Armando, M., Fonagy, P., & Bateman, A. (2016). Mentalization-based treatment in clinical high-risk for psychosis: A rationale and clinical illustration. *Journal of Contemporary Psychotherapy, 46*(4), 217–225. https://doi.org/10.1007/s10879-016-9337-4

Falkenström, F., Granström, F., & Holmqvist, R. (2013). Therapeutic alliance predicts symptomatic improvement session by session. *Journal of Counseling Psychology, 60*(3), 317–328. https://doi.org/10.1037/a0032258

Fonagy, P., & Bateman, A. (2008). The development of borderline personality disorder—A mentalizing model. *Journal of Personality Disorders, 22*(1), 4–21. https://doi.org/10.1521/pedi.2008.22.1.4

Fonagy, P., & Luyten, P. (2009). A developmental, mentalization-based approach to the understanding and treatment of borderline personality disorder. *Development and Psychopathology, 21*(4), 1355–1381. https://doi.org/10.1017/S0954579409990198

Fonagy, P., Luyten, P., Allison, E., & Campbell, C. (2017). What we have changed our minds about: Part 1. Borderline personality disorder as a limitation of resilience. *Borderline Personality Disorder and Emotion Dysregulation, 4*(1), Article 11. https://doi.org/10.1186/s40479-017-0061-9

Fonagy, P., Twemlow, S. W., Vernberg, E. M., Nelson, J. M., Dill, E. J., Little, T. D., & Sargent, J. A. (2009). A cluster randomized controlled trial of child-focused psychiatric consultation and a school systems-focused intervention to reduce aggression. *Journal of Child Psychology and Psychiatry, 50*(5), 607–616. https://doi.org/10.1111/j.1469-7610.2008.02025.x

Frith, C. D. (2004). Schizophrenia and theory of mind. *Psychological Medicine, 34*(3), 385–389. https://doi.org/10.1017/S0033291703001326

Frith, C. D., & Frith, U. (2006). The neural basis of mentalizing. *Neuron, 50*(4), 531–534. https://doi.org/10.1016/j.neuron.2006.05.001

Gallotti, M., & Frith, C. D. (2013). Social cognition in the we-mode. *Trends in Cognitive Sciences, 17*(4), 160–165. https://doi.org/10.1016/j.tics.2013.02.002

Harpøth, T. S. D., Kongerslev, M. T., Moeyaert, M., Bo, S., Bateman, A. W., & Simonsen, E. (2020). Evaluating "mentalizing positive affect" as an intervention for enhancing positive affectivity in borderline personality disorder using a single-case multiple-baseline design. *Psychotherapy, 57*(4), 580–586. https://doi.org/10.1037/pst0000251

Harris, P. L., de Rosnay, M., & Pons, F. (2016). *Understanding emotion.* In L. Feldman Barrett, M. Lewis, & J. M. Haviland-Jones (Eds.), *Handbook of emotions* (4th ed.). Guilford Press.

Jakobsen, J. C., Gluud, C., Kongerslev, M., Larsen, K. A., Sørensen, P., Winkel, P., Lange, T., Søgaard, U., & Simonsen, E. (2014). Third-wave cognitive therapy versus mentalisation-based treatment for major depressive disorder: A randomised clinical trial. *BMJ Open, 4*(8), Article e004903. https://doi.org/10.1136/bmjopen-2014-004903

Malda-Castillo, J., Browne, C., & Perez-Algorta, G. (2019). Mentalization-based treatment and its evidence-base status: A systematic literature review. *Psychology and Psychotherapy: Theory, Research and Practice, 92*(4), 465–498. https://doi.org/10.1111/papt.12195

O'Madagain, C., & Tomasello, M. (2019). Joint attention to mental content and the social origin of reasoning. *Synthese, 198,* 4057–4078. https://doi.org/10.1007/s11229-019-02327-1

Philips, B., Wennberg, P., Konradsson, P., & Franck, J. (2018). Mentalization-based treatment for concurrent borderline personality disorder and substance use disorder: A randomized controlled feasibility study. *European Addiction Research, 24*(1), 1–8. https://doi.org/10.1159/000485564

Recanati, F. (1997). Can we believe what we do not understand? *Mind & Language, 12*(1), 84–100. https://doi.org/10.1111/1468-0017.00037

Robinson, P., Hellier, J., Barrett, B., Barzdaitiene, D., Bateman, A., Bogaardt, A., Clare, A., Somers, N., O'Callaghan, A., Goldsmith, K., Kern, N., Schmidt, U., Morando, S., Ouellet-Courtois, C., Roberts, A., Skårderud, F., & Fonagy, P. (2016). The NOURISHED randomised controlled trial comparing mentalisation-based treatment for eating disorders (MBT-ED) with specialist supportive clinical management (SSCM-ED) for patients with eating disorders and symptoms of borderline personality disorder. *Trials, 17*(1), Article 549. https://doi.org/10.1186/s13063-016-1606-8

Rossouw, T. I., & Fonagy, P. (2012). Mentalization-based treatment for self-harm in adolescents: A randomized controlled trial. *Journal of the American Academy of Child & Adolescent Psychiatry, 51*(12), 1304–1313.e3. https://doi.org/10.1016/j.jaac.2012.09.018

Sharp, C., & Vanwoerden, S. (2015). Hypermentalizing in borderline personality disorder: A model and data. *Journal of Infant, Child, and Adolescent Psychotherapy, 14*(1), 33–45. https://doi.org/10.1080/15289168.2015.1004890

Skodol, A. E., Clark, L. A., Bender, D. S., Krueger, R. F., Morey, L. C., Verheul, R., Alarcon, R. D., Bell, C. C., Siever, L. J., & Oldham, J. M. (2011). Proposed changes in personality and personality disorder assessment and diagnosis for *DSM-5* Part I: Description and rationale. *Personality Disorders: Theory, Research, and Treatment, 2*(1), 4–22. https://doi.org/10.1037/a0021891

Sperber, D., Clement, F., Heintz, C., Mascaro, O., Mercier, H., Origgi, G., & Wilson, D. (2010). Epistemic vigilance. *Mind & Language, 25*(4), 359–393. https://doi.org/10.1111/j.1468-0017.2010.01394.x

Storebø, O. J., Stoffers-Winterling, J. M., Völlm, B. A., Kongerslev, M. T., Mattivi, J. T., Jørgensen, M. S., Faltinsen, E., Todorovac, A., Sales, C. P., Callesen, H. E., Lieb, K., & Simonsen, E. (2020). Psychological therapies for people with borderline personality disorder. *Cochrane Database of Systematic Reviews.* https://doi.org/10.1002/14651858.cd012955.pub2

Tomasello, M. (2016). *A natural history of human morality.* Harvard University Press. https://doi.org/10.4159/9780674915855

Tyrer, P., Crawford, M., Mulder, R., Blashfield, R., Farnam, A., Fossati, A., Kim, Y.-R., Koldobsky, N., Lecic-Tosevski, D., Ndetei, D., Swales, M., Clark, L. A., & Reed, G. M. (2011). The rationale for the reclassification of personality disorder in the 11th revision of the *International Classification of Diseases (ICD-11). Personality and Mental Health, 5*(4), 246–259. https://doi.org/10.1002/pmh.190

Vogt, K. S., & Norman, P. (2019). Is mentalization-based therapy effective in treating the symptoms of borderline personality disorder? A systematic review. *Psychology and Psychotherapy: Theory, Research, and Practice, 92*(4), 441–464. https://doi.org/10.1111/papt.12194

Weijers, J., Ten Kate, C., Viechtbauer, W., Rampaart, L. J. A., Eurelings, E. H. M., & Selten, J. P. (2020). Mentalization-based treatment for psychotic disorder: A rater-blinded, multi-center, randomized controlled trial. *Psychological Medicine, 51*(16), 2846–2855. https://doi.org/10.1017/s0033291720001506

World Health Organization. (2018). *ICD-11 for mortality and morbidity statistics (ICD-11 MMS).*

11

Dialectical Behavior Psychotherapy

Sharon M. Nelson, Chelsea D. Cawood, Takakuni Suzuki, Elizabeth Chapman, and Rebecca Lusk

Ms. A was a 52-year-old White female veteran with a long history of childhood and adulthood trauma exposure, including childhood sexual abuse by her mother and a priest and military sexual trauma in which she was raped by a commanding officer.[1] She had been dealing with chronic suicidal ideation and self-harm (cutting and burning herself) since childhood, though her mood and symptoms had significantly worsened after the death of her ex-wife (whom the client calls her "sister"). Ms. A had an extensive treatment history, beginning as a teenager when she was hospitalized on the recommendation of her mother following an episode of self-harm. She engaged in supportive counseling for many years in the private sector until she established care at her local VA hospital. Soon after beginning care at the VA hospital, she was again hospitalized for increased suicidal ideation. She had participated previously in dialectical behavior therapy (DBT) but did not complete a full course of treatment, as her previous therapist resigned. In addition, she had participated briefly in prolonged exposure therapy but withdrew from the treatment due to increased emotional distress.

Ms. A described experiencing significant invalidation from others, beginning at an early age. Her mother not only sexually abused her but also reprimanded her when she expressed negative emotions. Her problems were often oversimplified, and her mother frequently verbally punished her when she sought nonsexual

---

[1]All clinical cases discussed in this chapter have had minor details changed in order to blind them and have been reviewed by a privacy officer prior to publication.

https://doi.org/10.1037/0000310-012

Personality Disorders and Pathology: Integrating Clinical Assessment and Practice in the DSM-5 *and* ICD-11 *Era*, S. K. Huprich (Editor)

Copyright © 2022 by the American Psychological Association. All rights reserved.

attention. When she began cutting herself at age 6, however, her mother would then give her extra attention and reassurance, thus reinforcing this maladaptive behavior. Ms. A described regularly experiencing very intense, reactive emotions. She was particularly vulnerable to anxiety, noting that she often incorrectly assumed people were angry with her, and as a result, would ruminate for days.

Prior to the development of DBT, individuals like Ms. A, who were chronically suicidal, might have been treated in a traditional cognitive or behavioral model, with minimal success. Marsha Linehan observed that when chronically suicidal individuals—later focusing on individuals with borderline personality disorder (BPD)—were treated within cognitive or behavioral therapies not designed for the severity of their symptoms, several recurring issues emerged, including (a) the focus only on change was experienced as invalidating and led to early therapy withdrawal; (b) it was too difficult to work on developing new skills while also focusing on decreasing suicidal behaviors within an individual therapy framework; and (c) the client unknowingly reinforced iatrogenic therapy patterns, while punishing the therapist for effective treatment (Dimeff & Linehan, 2001).

From these observations, Linehan developed DBT using a traditional cognitive behavioral base and incorporating theories such as the idea of "transference" (from a psychodynamic perspective) and the need to balance acceptance and change, from Zen practices (Koerner, 2011; Linehan, 1993a). Since it was first developed, DBT has had a remarkable impact, with over 40,000 clinicians across 30 countries having received training in providing DBT (Behavioral Tech, 2020). This chapter describes the theoretical etiology of BPD from a DBT perspective, the role of assessment throughout DBT, and the structure and techniques that DBT utilizes, and briefly summarizes some of the empirical work evaluating DBT. In addition, we end with a look toward the future of DBT, including the broadening application and the way in which newer models for understanding personality disorders (such as the Alternative *DSM-5* Model for Personality Disorders [AMPD] in the *Diagnostic and Statistical Manual of Mental Disorders* [5th ed.; *DSM-5*; American Psychiatric Association, 2013]) might be readily applied to a DBT framework.

THEORETICAL ETIOLOGY OF BPD FROM A DBT PERSPECTIVE: BIOSOCIAL THEORY

In conceptualizing the development of BPD from a DBT perspective, Linehan (1993a, 2015) described a biosocial theory of personality development. This theory puts a strong emphasis both on the role of neurobiology and on how others have responded to the individual (Linehan, 2015) and posits that the core dysfunction for individuals with BPD is found in the emotion regulation system, which stems from biology but is perpetuated through learning (Linehan, 1993a). This emotional dysregulation leads individuals to be more *sensitive* (responding to lower levels of emotional stimuli more quickly), demonstrate more *reactivity* (both feeling and expressing emotion more intensely), and have longer lasting emotional arousal (Koerner, 2011; Linehan, 1993a).

Biological Vulnerability to Develop Difficulty Regulating Emotions

According to the biosocial model, the emotional dysregulation that causes greater emotional sensitivity, reactivity, and arousal is related to a biological vulnerability (Koerner, 2011). This greater emotional reactivity is evidenced in Ms. A, as she describes experiencing emotions more intensely and more suddenly than others. One study seeking to assess this phenomenon asked individuals with and without BPD to complete multiple survey prompts throughout the day, finding that individuals with BPD demonstrated more frequent, more intense, and more rapidly increasing states of distress (Stiglmayr et al., 2005), similar to previous findings (Stiglmayr et al., 2001). More recently, Southward et al. (2020) found similar levels of frequency and intensity of emotional experiences in individuals with BPD, using hourly measures of emotions across 2 days, and observed differences in emotion regulation strategies based on emotion experienced. The evidence for emotion dysregulation among individuals with BPD has also been assessed through network analysis of BPD symptoms; one study using a large sample ($N = 4,386$) of participants with BPD found intense moods to be one of the most central features in BPD (Southward & Cheavens, 2018).

The Role of Repeated Invalidation in Developing Difficulty Regulating Emotion

In addition to a theorized biological predisposition leading toward difficulty regulating emotions, Linehan's (1993a, 1993b) biosocial theory assumes that poorness of fit with the environment (Thomas & Chess, 1986) combines with biological predispositions to result in dysfunctional emotion regulation systems. This poor fit, where the environmental demands are not in line with the individual's abilities or needs (Linehan, 1993a, 1993b), is theorized to lead to a chronic invalidation of the individual, further leading to the development of BPD. Invalidation takes place when the inner experience, thoughts, or emotions of an individual are implied to be wrong, are punished, or are disregarded as unimportant (Linehan, 1993b, 2015)—such as when Ms. A was punished for experiencing negative emotions. When this happens repeatedly, it serves to cause an individual to learn that they are incapable of accurately interpreting their own experiences or emotions and that their inner experiences are not acceptable and are representative of negative characteristics (Linehan, 1993a, 2015; Swenson, 2016). For individuals with BPD, this repeated invalidation leads to a learned process of ever-escalating behavior (such as Ms. A's increase in self-harm) and affect in order to attempt to be understood by others (Koerner, 2011), as invalidation can increase emotional arousal and feelings of loss of control (Shenk & Fruzzetti, 2011). It is these conditions combined—the presence of a biologic vulnerability and a chronically invalidating environment—that cause a learned pattern of thought, emotion, and behavior, in the biosocial theory, to lead to the development of BPD.

Ms. A was referred to the DBT program at a large Midwestern VA hospital and completed several assessments as part of the intake process. She was diagnosed with PTSD, bipolar disorder, and BPD. She presented to the DBT program with symptoms that included mood lability, "abandonment issues," irritability, periods of mania (characterized by hyposomnia and engagement in impulsive, risky behavior), avoidance of situations that involved men, and guilt.

THE ROLE OF ASSESSMENT IN DBT

Linehan (1993a) stated that "behavior must be subject to assessment, not assumptions" (p. 92), meaning that the careful assessment of behavior is an essential component of DBT and informs ongoing treatment planning and conceptualization. This point is especially important when working with individuals with BPD, who often struggle to accurately convey their thoughts or feelings or whose dysregulation can make accurate self-report difficult (Solhan et al., 2009). Outcome monitoring throughout treatment is important to track progress toward patients' individual goals and may include identifying patterns across diary cards, chain analysis, self-report measures, and client check-in conversations (Rizvi & Sayrs, 2020).

Diary Cards

Diary cards were developed to assist in guiding therapy week to week, and clients use the cards to track changes in problem behaviors, moods, self-efficacy, DBT skills use, and whether the client feels that those skills are helping him or her (Koerner, 2011; Linehan, 2015). Several versions of diary cards are freely available; however, most include an area for clients to record daily suicidal ideation, self-harm urges or actions, substance use, and mood ratings (e.g., misery, joy). There is usually a section to record a weekly behavioral goal and the number of days they worked on that goal. In addition, there is a list of the skills taught in DBT, and clients are instructed to mark which days they worked on them and how effective the skills use was. These weekly assessments are reviewed and discussed at the beginning of each therapy session, and the information provided guides that session (Linehan, 2015).

Behavioral Chain Analysis/Functional Analysis

Though considered by some a therapeutic technique, *behavioral chain analysis* or *functional analysis* is a form of assessment used repeatedly as needed, throughout treatment, to determine which behaviors need to be changed (Linehan, 2015). Based on the original work by Skinner (1957), chain analysis has been referred to as the "primary assessment tool" in DBT (Rizvi & Ritschel, 2014, p. 335) and is theorized to be a mechanism of change within DBT (Lynch et al., 2006; Rizvi, 2019). Chain analysis is typically conducted when the client engages in problem behavior (Koerner, 2011; Linehan, 2015), such as self-harm or not attending therapy. This chain analysis is designed to help clinician and client assess what steps led to the client engaging in the problematic behavior and identify steps for behavioral change (Linehan, 2015; Rizvi & Ritschel, 2014; Rizvi & Sayrs, 2020). Chain analysis is unique in its therapeutic benefit, as the assessment process itself is therapeutic, helping the client to gain insight into their patterns of behavior and be able to better assess their own problematic behaviors in the future (Koerner, 2011; Rizvi, 2019). DBT therapists then tailor DBT skills based on the chain analysis—a process called *solution analysis* (Rizvi & Sayrs, 2020).

Recommended Self-Report Measures for Outcome Measurement

In addition to the use of behavioral chain analysis and diary card review, it is helpful to include self-report measures as part of measurement-based care within DBT. Self-report measures should be readministered throughout treatment, used in conjunction with diary cards, chain analysis, and conversations with patients. The goal of self-report measures is to aid in identifying patterns in progress that can be used to inform treatment (Rizvi & Sayrs, 2020). The following measures have been frequently utilized for these purposes.

Linehan Risk Assessment & Management Protocol

The Linehan Risk Assessment and Management Protocol (LRAMP; Linehan, 2009) is a semistructured assessment checklist developed to allow standardization for research, provide clinicians with a systematic way to assess and manage suicide risk, and promote good clinical practice (Linehan et al., 2012). The LRAMP is meant to be completed by clinicians at the start of treatment and then again if the client attempts suicide, threatens suicide, notes an increase in suicidal ideation, or engages in self-harm (Linehan et al., 2012).

Dialectical Behavior Therapy Ways of Coping Checklist

In order to have a reliable and valid way to assess client skills use in DBT, the Dialectical Behavior Therapy Ways of Coping Checklist was created (DBT-WCCL; Neacsiu et al., 2010). In DBT, BPD symptomatology is conceptualized as arising, in large part, from a lack of effective skills. Thus, increasing effective skills use is a theorized mechanism of change, making it an important construct to adequately assess throughout the course of treatment (Stein et al., 2016).

Borderline Symptom List

The Borderline Symptom List (BSL; Bohus et al., 2007) is a self-report developed to assess for BPD symptomatology, basing items on the BPD conceptualization in *DSM-IV* and *DSM-5* and on the Diagnostic Interview for BPD, as well as consulting both clients with BPD and expert clinicians. The BSL has been found to be able to differentiate between diagnostic groups and capture change in symptom severity (Bohus et al., 2007).

Difficulties in Emotion Regulation Scale

The Difficulties in Emotion Regulation Scale (DERS; Gratz & Roemer, 2004) was developed to comprehensively assess (a) emotion regulation difficulties and (b) theorized dimensions of emotion regulation, including awareness and understanding of emotions, acceptance of emotions, ability to engage in goal-directed behavior (rather than impulsive behavior) when in distress, and ability to utilize effective emotion regulation strategies (Gratz & Roemer, 2004).

Ms. A's diary card was customized to track self-harm behavior and monitor her urges to seek reassurance from others. Chain analysis was used when either self-harm or reassurance-seeking behaviors were noted. When chaining Ms. A's cutting and burning behaviors, it was highlighted that those behaviors served to regulate intense emotions as well as to increase support from others. Her chain analyses for urges to seek reassurance indicated that this behavior functioned as a way to avoid strong feelings of abandonment, and she did not have skillful means to effectively ask for support.

STAGES AND TECHNIQUES OF DBT

The DBT therapist is continually creating, shaping, and reshaping microtreatment plans that are based upon the client's goals and the stage of treatment. These microtreatment plans are fluid, flexible, living guides that both anchor the DBT therapist where they are with the client and help the therapist with direction finding for which DBT techniques to try. The stage of treatment and microtreatment plan help influence the therapist in what skills and techniques are needed to help change the client's behavior to build a life worth living.

DBT Therapist Training

DBT is conducted by therapists who have been trained in two 5-day workshops (including a 5-day foundational workshop), though additional board certification is recommended to ensure that the therapist is skilled in DBT and adherent to the model (Landes & Linehan, 2012). In the field of DBT, the most credible source of board certification is provided by the DBT-Linehan Board of Certification (DBT-LBC; 2021), which offers both program-level certification for DBT treatment programs and individual-level certification for individual licensed independent mental health providers. The process of DBT-LBC certification is rigorous and involves several steps, including submission of an application, verification of education, passing a written examination, submission of a written case conceptualization, and submission of video samples of recorded DBT sessions with a real-life DBT client. Program certification requires an additional step: a program site visit by a rater appointed by the DBT-LBC board (2021).

Basic Treatment Structure

While in DBT, clients attend 1 hour of individual therapy and 1.5 to 2 hours of group therapy a week, for an average of 1 year. During this time, clients are taught skills from four broad modules (Mindfulness, Distress Tolerance, Emotion Regulation, and Interpersonal Effectiveness). Clients have access to skills coaching via telephone 24 hours a day (Ben-Porath, 2004, 2011; Chapman, 2019; Choi-Kain et al., 2016; Koons, 2011). In addition, clinicians attend a weekly DBT team consultation meeting (Chapman, 2006; Choi-Kain et al., 2016; Sayrs & Linehan, 2019).

Stages of Treatment

The first stage of DBT, following diagnostic assessment, is pretreatment. During this stage, the therapist and client collaboratively establish a mutual under-standing of the work they will do, including agreement on behavioral targets and commitment to treatment (Koerner, 2011; Swales et al., 2000; Swenson, 2016). Pretreatment has been shown to be important in decreasing premature dropout by the client (Linehan, 1993a; Parloff et al., 1978), an especially high risk for individuals diagnosed with BPD. During this phase, the clinician also provides psychoeducation on the diagnosis of BPD and on DBT as a treatment (Koerner, 2011; Linehan, 2015).

Stage 1 of DBT follows pretreatment and addresses the client's behaviors based on the following hierarchy: life-threatening behavior (e.g., suicidal or nonsuicidal self-injury), therapy-interfering behavior (e.g., not attending regularly), then behavior that impacts the client's quality of life (such as sub-stance abuse and verbal outbursts; Koerner, 2011; Linehan, 1993a; Swenson, 2016). To establish this hierarchy, the clinician and client work together to establish (a) a behavioral definition of the problematic behaviors and (b) goals toward building a life worth living (Swales et al., 2000; Swenson, 2016). Stage 1 is the longest section of treatment, with more severe clients taking a year or longer to gain some control of the first two steps on the hierarchy (life-threatening and therapy-interfering behavior; Linehan, 1993a). During Stage 2, the focus of treatment turns toward addressing stress resulting from previous trauma, as well as other comorbid disorders. Stage 2 is started only when the client has demonstrated control over previously described targets on the hierarchy, as it is believed that prior to developing that control, the client may struggle to handle the discussions revolving around their trauma(s) (Linehan, 1993a). In Stage 3, the client works toward improving self-respect and problems in living, with the overarching goal of managing ordinary hap-piness and unhappiness. In the final stage, Stage 4, skills and abilities learned in the first stages are integrated to assist the client in moving toward trusting their own opinions and ability to validate themself independent of the thera-pist (Linehan, 1993a; Swenson, 2016).

During Ms. A's pretreatment phase, she collaboratively identified her primary goals for treatment as (a) to build a sense of self-validation by finding healthy and effective ways to cope with challenging emotions and (b) to improve her relationships. When Ms. A began DBT, she was in Stage 1 of treatment, as she was regularly engaging in life-threatening behavior, cutting or burning herself approximately once a week.

Therapeutic Techniques Used Throughout Treatment

Techniques in DBT are too numerous to detail here; however, several key techniques are thought to be most essential to the work of DBT, including the following.

Skills Training

One of the main assumptions of DBT is that clients want to do better but lack the skills to (Linehan, 1993a, 2015), so group and individual sessions teach clients skills from four overarching modules. The first module, on which much of DBT is built, is Mindfulness. Clients learn skills, adapted from Zen techniques (Linehan, 1993b), to help them move toward "wise mind"—conceptualized as the space between one's "emotional mind" (which operates on urges) and one's "reasonable mind" (which operates on what is logical, disregarding emotions; Linehan, 1993b, 2015). Wise mind refers to a state of mind wherein both emotion and logic can be integrated.

The next module is Distress Tolerance, which involves a set of skills designed to assist clients in accepting feelings of emotional pain and suffering without engaging in behaviors that may prolong their suffering or make their situation worse (Linehan, 2015; Swales et al., 2000). Skills in this module are best used when emotions run high and clients are at their skills breakdown point. The Distress Tolerance skills may be implemented to help the clients access more effective coping skills, as opposed to making the situation worse. For example, if a client learns that their spouse is leaving them, they may feel intense abandonment and believe that the relationship can be saved if only they express their need to remain connected. In this case, the client may express this by repeatedly calling and texting their spouse, begging their spouse not to leave them, and following their spouse when their spouse is traveling away from home. The spouse responds by further trying to distance themselves from the client and even considers a restraining order for stalking. The client is overwhelmed by their feelings of abandonment and with making their problems worse by engaging in these behaviors, which are accomplishing the exact opposite of their intended goal of preserving the relationship. In this example, Distress Tolerance skills may be used (a) to help reduce the client's emotional suffering so that they do not make the situation worse and (b) to down regulate their emotional intensity so that they can effectively access other coping skills to accept and cope with reality.

Emotion Regulation is the next module, with a group of skills designed to help clients understand their emotions, reduce vulnerability to mood swings, and increase positive moods (Linehan, 2015; Swales et al., 2000). Finally, the Interpersonal Effectiveness module is a group of skills that are aimed to help clients manage interpersonal relationships, including (a) communicating effectively and (b) evaluating their objectives in a relationship and making decisions accordingly (Linehan, 2015; Swales et al., 2000).

Dialectics

Dialectical theory states that identity is defined relationally (Linehan & Schmidt, 1995; Swales et al., 2000), meaning that two individuals influence each other.

Dialectics encourages clients to take a complex view of the world—rather than only extremes—in which one can hold seemingly opposing views at the same time (such as acceptance and change; Koerner, 2011; Linehan, 1993a, 1993b). In session, clinicians discuss or observe these viewpoints with or to the client as needed, helping the client to gain the ability to take an integrated viewpoint on their own.

Validation

Validation is not just empathy for another person but also the communication that, in some way, their thoughts or emotions are valid (Koerner, 2011; Swales et al., 2000). Skillful utilization of validation is thought to be an important tool in helping clients move toward change (Koerner, 2011; Linehan, 1993a; Swenson, 2016). In therapy, this can be done through (a) active listening to the client, accurate reflection of what the client is communicating, observing nonverbal communication, and communicating to the client how their current symptoms make sense based on their past and current experiences and (b) the DBT therapist remaining their genuine self—a concept called "radical genuineness" (Linehan, 1993a, 1997; Swales et al., 2000; Swenson, 2016).

In line with Ms. A's goal of finding healthy and effective ways to cope with intense emotions, she and her therapist used her diary card to track her self-harm behaviors and used chain analysis when those behaviors occurred. This allowed them to note several patterns, including that when Ms. A was unable to get reassurance from others, she would often cut or burn herself, leading to increased feelings of guilt and shame. To address this problematic behavior, her therapist worked to increase Ms. A's knowledge and practice of behavioral skills, including emotion regulation and distress tolerance. In particular, problem solving techniques were highlighted to assist Ms. A in identifying more effective ways to manage her feelings while breaking her previous pattern of behavior. Negative consequences of self-harm behavior were highlighted, and skillful behavior was consistently linked to her goals. In addition, positive reinforcement was provided when skillful behavior was practiced.

To address Ms. A's goal of improving her relationships, the therapist and Ms. A collaboratively worked to identify areas where she struggled with interpersonal relationships. Ms. A had a pattern of excessively contacting providers, leading to burnout or frustration. For example, when she felt that her medical providers might be angry with her, she would call frequently throughout the day, leaving messages that were increasingly tearful and ruminative. She would sometimes call her therapist up to seven times a day. She would leave messages stating that she needed reassurance and that she would cut herself if she did not receive it, or she would accuse her therapist of not caring for her. Ms. A's habit of leaving messages insisting that providers return her messages immediately was highlighted as being counterproductive to her goal of increasing relationships.

Her frequent phone calls to her therapist were highlighted—as therapy-interfering behavior, due to the risk of burnout—as was her behavior of calling others when she was distressed, which was something potentially damaging to those other relationships. As a result, interpersonal effectiveness skills were frequently practiced in session, and the therapist reinforced this by increasing validation and responsiveness when Ms. A communicated her needs using these skills.

EMPIRICAL SUPPORT FOR DBT FOR TREATMENT OF BPD

DBT is the most widely studied treatment for BPD, with empirical support found across numerous randomized controlled trials (RCTs) to date, both within and outside of the United States. Based on criteria about determining evidence-based treatments set by the American Psychological Association Task Force on Promotion and Dissemination of Psychological Procedures (Tolin et al., 2015), DBT is considered a "well-established" treatment for BPD. Across seven RCTs comparing DBT with treatment as usual (TAU), DBT was more helpful than TAU in reducing suicidal ideation, self-harm/self-mutilation, suicide attempts, and hospitalizations for suicidal ideation (Feigenbaum et al., 2012; Koons et al., 2001; Linehan et al., 1991; Linehan, Comtois, Brown, et al., 2006; Pistorello et al., 2012; Priebe et al., 2012; Verheul et al., 2003). Given that DBT was designed to address suicidal and self-harming behaviors, these findings are especially promising. However, DBT has also been found to be an effective treatment for other outcomes, with RCTs of DBT demonstrating improvements in impulsive behaviors (Verheul et al., 2003), anger (Koons et al., 2001; Linehan et al., 1994), global functioning (Linehan et al., 1994), and social adjustment (Linehan et al., 1994), when compared with TAU. Follow-up studies have been conducted with some of Linehan's earlier RCT samples, finding that treatment gains from the 1991 RCT were sustained at 6-month and 1-year follow-ups (Linehan et al., 1994).

Research on DBT has additionally included RCTs comparing DBT with treatment by experts. In 2006, Linehan, Comtois, Murray, et al. assessed differences in 12 months of DBT and treatment by non-DBT expert therapists in the community. The participants were 101 women diagnosed with BPD. Results indicated that the DBT group had significantly lower rates of dropout, suicide attempts, and hospitalizations/crisis service utilization than the control group. Both groups saw decreases in nonsuicidal self-harm. Harned et al. (2008) examined changes in co-occurring Axis I disorders using participants in Linehan, Comtois, Murray, et al.'s (2006) RCT of DBT versus therapy by community experts. After 1 year of treatment, the DBT group had significantly higher rates of full remission from substance dependence disorders than the control group (87% and 33%, respectively; this effect was large, Cohen's w effect size = 0.55). The groups did not differ in rates of remission for any other co-occurring Axis I disorders.

More recently, the literature on DBT has begun demonstrating a shift from a focus on effectiveness to efficacy in naturalistic clinical settings. Pilot studies in community mental health settings have been promising (Ben-Porath et al., 2004; Blennerhassett et al., 2009; Comtois et al., 2007), although lacking controls and randomization. Flynn et al. (2020) recently conducted a multisite study examining DBT across nine community mental health sites in Ireland. Results indicated a significant reduction in suicidal and self-harm behaviors from initial assessment to the end of treatment. Santamarina-Perez et al. (2020) conducted an RCT of DBT for adolescents in a community clinic, finding that the DBT group had greater reductions in nonsuicidal self-injury than the control group. Recent research has also focused on adaptations of DBT, finding efficacious outcomes with stand-alone skills training groups (Zeifman et al., 2020) and forensic populations (Bianchini et al., 2019). Although further RCTs in real-world clinical settings are needed, these results demonstrate that DBT is not only an effective treatment for BPD in clinical trials but is applicable in naturalistic treatment settings.

Ms. A regularly and consistently participated in the DBT program. She attended weekly individual therapy, where diary cards and chain analysis set the framework for increasing behavioral changes. Ms. A also participated in the weekly skills group and used phone coaching in order to generalize the skills to her environment. She completed a full year of DBT, which consisted of two 6-month cycles of skills acquisition. Ms. A was effective in meeting her treatment goals. During the course of treatment, she stopped cutting—with the exception of occasional episodes—and reported a reduction in suicidal ideation. When she did engage in self-harm behavior, she was able to implement her use of chain analysis to identify controlling variables and find more effective behavior. Her use of skills allowed her to tolerate painful emotions without engaging in problematic behavior, which ultimately reduced her feelings of shame and guilt.

Overall, Ms. A reported an improvement in her ability to validate herself and was able to resist urges to seek reassurance from others. Her phone calls to her therapist were drastically reduced, and when she did reach out, it was for very targeted skills coaching. While she still struggled with anxiety and worries of abandonment, she was able to act opposite of her urges for reassurance, which ultimately improved her relationships and gave her a sense of mastery and self-validation.

EMPIRICAL SUPPORT FOR DBT WITH NON-BPD SAMPLES

Several studies have demonstrated the effectiveness of DBT for comorbid conditions such as substance abuse, eating disorders, and PTSD. RCTs have found DBT effective for reducing substance use in both opiate (Linehan et al., 2002; Rezaie et al., 2021) and alcohol use (Harned et al., 2008; Linehan et al., 1999) disorders when compared with control groups. Harned et al. (2014) conducted an RCT of DBT plus prolonged exposure therapy (DBT PE) to traditional DBT for participants with comorbid PTSD and BPD. The DBT PE group had 80% remission from PTSD, compared with 40% of the DBT group. The DBT PE group was also 2.4 times less likely to make a suicide attempt and 1.5 times less likely to self-injure than those in traditional DBT. Safer et al. (2001) tested the efficacy of DBT for bulimia nervosa compared with a wait-list control group.

After 20 weeks of treatment, the DBT group had significantly lower rates of binge eating and purging than the control group, with 28.6% of the DBT group, compared with none of the control group, demonstrating abstinence from binging and purging. Telch et al. (2001) conducted an RCT, comparing the efficacy of a modified DBT skills training group with a wait-list control group, among 44 women with binge-eating disorder. After the 20-week skills group, participants who attended the group significantly decreased frequency of binge eating compared with controls (abstinence rates were 89% and 12.5%, respectively; $p < .001$).

Comparatively little research has been done on the application of DBT to personality disorders beyond BPD. Despite that, several people have proposed adaptations to DBT that may allow it to be effectively utilized with a wider range of clients with PDs. One notable example of this is the discussion around radically open dialectical behavior therapy (RO-DBT; Drago et al., 2016; Gilmartin & Valladares, 2019; Lynch et al., 2006; Lynch & Cheavens, 2008). Different from BPD's emotional lability and impulsivity, several PDs are characterized by being overly in control of oneself, emotionally restricted, perfectionistic, and cognitively rigid (Lynch & Cheavens, 2008), including Paranoid, Obsessive-Compulsive, and Avoidant PDs. RO-DBT emphasizes becoming more open and flexible, and less rigid, in thinking and behavior (different from DBT's usual emphasis on managing extreme emotions and reducing impulsive behavior). One of the largest adaptations for this group is the removal of the distress tolerance skills (except as needed) and instead including a Radical Openness module (Lynch & Cheavens, 2008). Lynch and colleagues (2006) found that RO-DBT led to significant improvement in personality dysfunction, compared with control groups among those with Obsessive-Compulsive, Paranoid, and Avoidant PDs.

There have also been several efforts to adapt DBT to other Cluster B disorders (Histrionic, Narcissistic, Antisocial, Borderline PDs). McCann et al. (2000) described their efforts to adapt DBT for an inpatient forensic population: They elicited the help of both patients diagnosed with Antisocial PD and therapists to review the DBT manual and identify areas that were not as applicable to those with Antisocial PD (versus BPD). The group decided to add skills in the Emotion Regulation module, including adding goals of increasing emotional attachment and increasing mindfulness of consequences to others. A DBT graduate group was also developed for individuals who completed two rounds of basic DBT skills, which was focused on increasing victim empathy and preventing a relapse of violence. McCann and colleagues (2000) noted several other differences to keep in mind while applying DBT to this population, including that there will need to be more of a focus on other-harm versus self-harm behaviors. Several people have proposed adaptations to DBT for working with individuals with Narcissistic PD (NPD; Marra, 2005; Reed-Knight & Fischer, 2011). Suggestions for adapting DBT for NPD have included (a) attending to how clinicians provide the diagnosis in pretreatment, (b) operationalizing narcissistic characteristics as discrete thoughts/behaviors to target during treatment, (c) tracking symptoms by use of adapted diary cards, and

(d) utilizing NPD-specific measures. In addition, there will likely be less of an emphasis on assertiveness skills and more on nonjudgmental observation. Reed-Knight and Fischer (2011) described a client with NPD who was treated with adapted DBT, noting that by the end of treatment, the client demonstrated decreases in both grandiose and vulnerable narcissism.

MR. B

Mr. B is a 34-year-old Caucasian Hispanic man engaging in DBT due to a history of chronic suicidal ideation and threats, with comorbid diagnoses of NPD, BPD, and recurrent major depressive disorder. Mr. B was prompted to seek treatment after being asked to take a leave of absence from his MBA program because of frequent verbal altercations with his peers and professors, while declining offers for mediation due to believing his behaviors were justified (for reasons of incompetency on the part of the program). Mr. B's goals are to have a lucrative career in business, get married, and purchase a home. His primary behavioral treatment targets are suicidal threats, yelling, criticizing others, making disparaging comments, and isolation.

During Mr. B's first 3 months of treatment, he engaged in several therapy-interfering behaviors; these included making sexist comments in the skills training group and criticism and interruption of his individual therapist during sessions. Additionally, Mr. B often asked his therapist personal questions about her dating history and commented on her physical appearance. When she addressed these issues and requested that he not make these comments or ask these questions, Mr. B increased behaviors of criticizing, interrupting, and speaking over her.

To address interpersonal behavioral targets, Mr. B's diary card was customized to include tracking behaviors of yelling and criticizing others. The therapy began with chain analysis of these behaviors and highlighting that these behaviors appeared to function as a method for avoiding the emotion of shame. Mindfulness skills in observing and describing emotions were frequently taught and practiced in session with the client to assist in the generalization of this skill, which was helpful in reducing these behaviors. Mr. B's therapy-interfering behaviors were addressed in several ways: His individual therapist used the DBT team consultation meetings for assistance with her own skills use, as well as for feedback on interventions. She recognized that Mr. B's questions pushed her limits, and this led her to feel judgmental and nonempathetic toward him. She worked to maintain a nonpejorative understanding of his behaviors and began framing to Mr. B that respecting her limits and not asking personal questions could be used as practice for his interactions with colleagues and to help him meet his goals. She also validated that his asking questions about dating were appropriate with peers, in certain contexts. After making sexist and disparaging comments during the skills training group, he was asked to engage in a therapy-interfering behavior protocol. This included taking a vacation from the skills training group while he completed a chain analysis and a solution analysis with his individual therapist. He then presented his chain analysis and solution analysis to the group and made a *repair*, which in DBT is an action that assists to rectify the situation and typically involves an apology and corrective behavior. In this instance, Mr. B struggled to apologize, although he recognized the need to be accountable for his behavior. For his repair, he stated to the group, "I recognize that what I said was unprofessional and hurtful, and I strive to be a professional and treat you all respectfully in the future." He also agreed to be in the observer role the following 2 weeks of group and to practice gently acknowledging anytime he or his peers made a judgmental comment. Group members provided feedback to him about how his comments impacted them, and he agreed to listen to this feedback. In individual therapy, he was able to identify that although he did not agree with all of the feedback, he could see how his comments created challenges in his relationships and his ability to meet his goals. Mr. B expressed feeling good about the way he acknowledged his behaviors, and he saw that he might be able to use these skills to rectify future interpersonal situations as they might come up in his school or work lives.

Although Mr. B's relationships with his therapy team and skills training group improved, he continued to struggle with his family relationships. On his diary card, he would admit to making critical and disparaging comments to family members; however, during chain analysis of these behaviors, he struggled to recognize how his comments were problematic. For example, he admitted to saying to his uncle, "You don't know shit about anything! Why should I listen to someone with a community college education?" When his therapist probed further in session, he expressed, "It's true, so why not say it? I value honesty, and if he can't deal with that, f*** him." His therapist found success in practicing generalizing mindfulness, observing, and describing skills by saying, "If we watched that argument back like a scene in a movie, what observations could we make about your behavior? Your uncle's? Which character would we be rooting for after we watched the scene?" Mr. B began to express that his statements came from feeling invalidated: "My uncle never lets me finish a sentence; he tells me therapy is for wussies and to get over it." Mr. B began to convey willingness to identify what he wanted in his interactions and to learn how to ask for his objectives effectively, as well as how to tolerate and heal from invalidation. This led to improvements in his ability to acknowledge the feelings of others and to be more tolerable when feeling slighted by others' behavior.

DBT AND DIMENSIONAL MODELS

As described in other chapters of this volume, the conceptualization and assessment of personality disorders are moving away from the traditional categorical model (e.g., BPD) and toward transdiagnostic dimensional models. Here, the potential ways in which DBT might be adapted or utilized within a dimensional model are briefly discussed. Two diagnostic dimensional models for understanding personality pathology that have emerged are the *DSM-5* AMPD and the *International Statistical Classification of Diseases and Related Health Problems* (11th ed.; *ICD-11*; World Health Organization, 2019) model. Although the models differ slightly, the overall structure of the degree of impairment in self- and/or interpersonal functioning, and the five broad domains to assess the transdiagnostic traits, are the same. Further, four of the five domains of the two models are very similar to each other and share similarities with the five-factor model of personality (e.g., Oltmanns & Widiger, 2018). However, to date, there has been a lack of research investigating the effects of DBT on functional impairments and traits of the *DSM-5* or *ICD-11* models, and integration of DBT with five-factor model traits is also very scarce (e.g., Davenport et al., 2010; Stepp et al., 2013). At the same time, clinicians tend to find dimensional models to be more clinically useful than categorical models (e.g., Morey et al., 2014; Nelson et al., 2017; Samuel & Widiger, 2006), and there is substantial promise in using dimensional models for case conceptualization and treatment planning in clinical practice (e.g., Bucher et al., 2019). Therefore, this section focuses on demonstrating some potential conceptual use of dimensional models to inform DBT-based treatment. Given the richer literature and more descriptions of the five dimensional traits (Criterion B) and the level of functioning (Criterion A), terminology from the *DSM-5* model will be used.

Negative Affectivity is a trait characterized by the tendency to experience emotions that include depression, anxiety, and emotional instability. This broad trait is included in virtually all dimensional models (e.g., Oltmanns & Widiger, 2018) and is a prominent trait in a prototypical BPD profile, as well as in many other forms of PDs. For those high on this Negative Affectivity trait, DBT skills from Mindfulness (e.g., assuming a nonjudgmental view of experiencing these emotions), Emotion Regulation (e.g., managing vulnerability to intense emotions, and maladaptive behaviors due to those emotions, such as through Opposite Action [where one behaves in a way that is counter to how they feel like behaving]), and Distress Tolerance (given the high chance of clients experiencing intense negative emotions) may be particularly helpful.

Antagonism is another prominent trait, which is characterized by low sociability and tendency to put higher priority on self than on others, that could cause interpersonal problems. For example, prototypical profiles of individuals with Antisocial and Narcissistic PDs are high on Antagonism. For Antagonism, Interpersonal Effectiveness (skills such as understanding factors in determining how long to persist, or how intense to be, in one's communication) and mindfulness (e.g., nonjudgmental validation of the other person's and the client's feelings) may be particularly helpful.

Disinhibition is a trait characterized by lack of planning and the tendency to "act in the moment." The prototypical profile of Antisocial PD is also high on this trait. Individuals high on Disinhibition could especially benefit from Mindfulness (such as the wise mind framework), and teaching and extended practice of this module may be of high priority early in the treatment.

In addition to the five traits (Criterion B), there are four areas of possible personality functioning impairment (Criterion A) in the *DSM-5* model, though comparatively few studies have investigated this criterion itself (Zimmermann et al., 2019). However, these impairments can also likely serve as treatment targets using DBT. For example, Criterion A includes two domains under "Self": Identity and Self-Direction. Self-Direction is characterized by functioning associated with pursuing various goals. DBT has several skills designed to help with impairment in motivation or difficulty in reaching personal goals. For example, a client with impairment in the Self-Direction domain might benefit from spending additional treatment time elaborating on the Build Mastery skills. As part of the Emotion Regulation module, Build Mastery emphasizes increasing one's sense of self-efficacy and accomplishment through planning on doing at least one task a day, planning for success, mindfully increasing the task difficulty over time, and looking for something that provides some challenge (Linehan, 2015).

The Interpersonal domain of Criterion A includes both Empathy and Intimacy. Deficits in this domain indicate that spending additional time on skills in the Interpersonal Effectiveness module of DBT (Linehan, 2015) would be helpful. For example, a client who has difficulty initiating intimacy may benefit from Interpersonal Effectiveness skills meant to help start and grow a relationship, whereas if they are someone who is overly high on intimacy, they may benefit from skills designed to help gain greater independence as well as set boundaries and maintain or improve current relationships.

For a client that is low on Empathy, it may be helpful to emphasize Interpersonal Effectiveness skills, such as "GIVE" (communicating in a gentle, interested, validating, and easy manner; Linehan, 2015), as well as focus on a dialectical approach and validation of both the other person's and the client's feelings; whereas when a client is overly high on Empathy, it may be more effective to focus on Interpersonal Effectiveness (Linehan, 2015) skills that help with setting boundaries, saying no, and not being overly apologetic, or focusing on Emotion Regulation skills around understanding and recognizing one's emotions (to gain insight into how the emotions of others may be impacting oneself).

These examples are not exhaustive but hopefully can provide readers with a general sense of how dimensional conceptualization of PDs might inform treatment using DBT. Because everyone lies somewhere on all of the dimensions, these models could allow for adapting and generalizing DBT to clients (a) struggling with symptoms but who are below threshold for a traditional BPD diagnosis, (b) suffering from PDs that are not commonly studied (e.g., Schizoid, Dependent), and (c) with unspecified PD diagnoses. Further, once the effects of specific DBT components on each trait have been evaluated, this line of research could also provide further empirical support for individualized treatment utilizing DBT. Finally, dimensional models are being applied to other, non-PD forms of psychopathology as well—for example, the National Institute of Mental Health's (2020) Research Domain Criteria and the Hierarchical Taxonomy of Psychopathology (Kotov et al., 2017). Clearly, more research investigating the effects of DBT on the dimensional traits is needed. However, the potential for integrating dimensional models and DBT to aid clinicians and researchers in providing this mode of care to a broad population is an exciting prospect.

CONCLUSION

Since it was first developed as a cognitive behaviorally based integrative treatment for chronically suicidal clients, DBT has become the most researched and widely utilized BPD-specific treatment. Multiple RCTs have demonstrated its (a) effectiveness in reducing suicidal or self-harming behavior and (b) improvement in multiple outcomes related to BPD symptoms. In addition to demonstrating efficacy for treating BPD, a steadily growing number of studies have demonstrated the benefit of applying DBT to disorders other than BPD. This is especially important for non-BPD PDs, as little attention has been paid to developing empirically supported treatments for PDs besides BPD. In addition to discussions of adapting DBT for other categorical PDs, DBT's framework theoretically allows for utilization within a dimensional model. Though further research is needed, there is clearly a great deal of potential in the application of aspects of DBT to not only BPD and PDs but also a wide range of disorders that previously lacked solid treatment options. With the development, refinement, and exponential growth of DBT, clients like Ms. A (and, with adaptations, Mr. B) have access to therapy designed to address their intense symptoms. As research on DBT—and PDs in general—continues to grow, clinicians will be able to offer greater evidence-based hope for an ever-broadening population of previously underserved clients.

REFERENCES

American Psychiatric Association. (1994). *Diagnostic and statistical manual of mental disorders* (4th ed.).

American Psychiatric Association. (2013). *Diagnostic and statistical manual of mental disorders* (5th ed.). https://doi.org/10.1176/appi.books.9780890425596

Behavioral Tech. (2020). *The reach of DBT.* https://behavioraltech.org/about-us/our-impact/

Ben-Porath, D. D. (2004). Intersession telephone contact with individuals diagnosed with borderline personality disorder: Lessons from dialectical behavior therapy. *Cognitive and Behavioral Practice, 11*(2), 222–230. https://doi.org/10.1016/S1077-7229(04)80033-6

Ben-Porath, D. D. (2011). Special series introduction. *Cognitive and Behavioral Practice, 18*(2), 165–167. https://doi.org/10.1016/j.cbpra.2010.06.001

Ben-Porath, D. D., Peterson, G. A., & Smee, J. (2004). Treatment of individuals with borderline personality disorder using dialectical behavior therapy in a community mental health setting: Clinical application and a preliminary investigation. *Cognitive and Behavioral Practice, 11*(4), 424–434. https://doi.org/10.1016/S1077-7229(04)80059-2

Bianchini, V., Cofini, V., Curto, M., Lagrotteria, B., Manzi, A., Navari, S., Ortenzi, R., Paoletti, G., Pompili, E., Pompili, P. M., Silvestrini, C., & Nicolò, G. (2019). Dialectical behaviour therapy (DBT) for forensic psychiatric patients: An Italian pilot study. *Criminal Behaviour and Mental Health, 29*(2), 122–130. https://doi.org/10.1002/cbm.2102

Blennerhassett, R., Bamford, L., Whelan, A., Jamieson, S., & Wilson O'Raghaillaigh, J. (2009). Dialectical behaviour therapy in an Irish community mental health setting. *Irish Journal of Psychological Medicine, 26*(2), 59–63. https://doi.org/10.1017/S0790966700000227

Bohus, M., Limberger, M. F., Frank, U., Chapman, A. L., Kühler, T., & Stieglitz, R.-D. (2007). Psychometric properties of the borderline symptom list (BSL). *Psychopathology, 40*(2), 126–132. https://doi.org/10.1159/000098493

Bucher, M. A., Suzuki, T., & Samuel, D. B. (2019). A meta-analytic review of personality traits and their associations with mental health treatment outcomes. *Clinical Psychology Review, 70*, 51–63. https://doi.org/10.1016/j.cpr.2019.04.002

Chapman, A. L. (2006). Dialectical behavior therapy: Current indications and unique elements. *Psychiatry, 3*(9), 62–68.

Chapman, A. L. (2019). *Phone coaching in dialectical behavior therapy*. Guilford Press.

Choi-Kain, L. W., Albert, E. B., & Gunderson, J. G. (2016). Evidence-based treatments for borderline personality disorder: Implementation, integration, and stepped care. *Harvard Review of Psychiatry, 24*(5), 342–356. https://doi.org/10.1097/HRP.0000000000000113

Comtois, K. A., Elwood, L., Holdcraft, L. C., Smith, W. R., & Simpson, T. L. (2007). Effectiveness of dialectical behavior therapy in a community mental health center. *Cognitive and Behavioral Practice, 14*(4), 406–414. https://doi.org/10.1016/j.cbpra.2006.04.023

Davenport, J., Bore, M., & Campbell, J. (2010). Changes in personality in pre- and post-dialectical behaviour therapy borderline personality disorder groups: A question of self-control. *Australian Psychologist, 45*(1), 59–66. https://doi.org/10.1080/00050060903280512

DBT-Linehan Board of Certification. (2021). *Why and how to get certified*. https://dbt-lbc.org/index.php?page=101138

Dimeff, L., & Linehan, M. M. (2001). Dialectical behavior therapy in a nutshell. *The California Psychologist, 34*(3), 10–13.

Drago, A., Marogna, C., & Søgaard, H. J. (2016). A review of characteristics and treatments of the avoidant personality disorder. Could the DBT be an option? *International Journal of Psychology and Psychoanalysis, 2*(1), 13. https://doi.org/10.23937/2572-4037.1510013

Feigenbaum, J. D., Fonagy, P., Pilling, S., Jones, A., Wildgoose, A., & Bebbington, P. E. (2012). A real-world study of the effectiveness of DBT in the UK National Health Service. *British Journal of Clinical Psychology, 51*(2), 121–141. https://doi.org/10.1111/j.2044-8260.2011.02017.x

Flynn, D., Kells, M., Joyce, M., Corcoran, P., Hurley, J., Gillespie, C., Suarez, C., Swales, M., & Arensman, E. (2020). Multisite implementation and evaluation of 12-month standard dialectical behavior therapy in a public community setting. *Journal of Personality Disorders, 34*(3), 377–393. https://doi.org/10.1521/pedi_2018_32_402

Gilmartin, T., & Valladares, D. (2019). Introducing Radically Open-DBT (RO-DBT) as a treatment for maladaptive over-control. *Australian Clinical Psychologist, 2*, 1–4. https://acp.scholasticahq.com/article/6864-introducing-radically-open-dbt-ro-dbt-as-a-treatment-for-maladaptive-over-control

Gratz, K. L., & Roemer, L. (2004). Multidimensional assessment of emotion regulation and dysregulation: Development, factor structure, and initial validation of the difficulties in emotion regulation scale. *Journal of Psychopathology and Behavioral Assessment, 26*(1), 41–54. https://doi.org/10.1023/B:JOBA.0000007455.08539.94

Harned, M. S., Chapman, A. L., Dexter-Mazza, E. T., Murray, A., Comtois, K. A., & Linehan, M. M. (2008). Treating co-occurring Axis I disorders in recurrently suicidal women with borderline personality disorder: A 2-year randomized trial of dialectical behavior therapy versus community treatment by experts. *Journal of Consulting and Clinical Psychology, 76*(6), 1068–1075. https://doi.org/10.1037/a0014044

Harned, M. S., Korslund, K. E., & Linehan, M. M. (2014). A pilot randomized controlled trial of dialectical behavior therapy with and without the dialectical behavior therapy prolonged exposure protocol for suicidal and self-injuring women with borderline personality disorder and PTSD. *Behaviour Research and Therapy, 55*, 7–17. https://doi.org/10.1016/j.brat.2014.01.008

Koerner, K. (2011). *Doing dialectical behavior therapy: A practical guide*. Guilford Press.

Koons, C. R. (2011). The role of the team in managing telephone consultation in dialectical behavior therapy: Three case examples. *Cognitive and Behavioral Practice, 18*(2), 168–177. https://doi.org/10.1016/j.cbpra.2009.10.008

Koons, C. R., Robins, C. J., Tweed, J. L., Lynch, T. R., Gonzalez, A. M., Morse, J. Q., Bishop, G. K., Butterfield, M. I., & Bastian, L. A. (2001). Efficacy of dialectical behavior therapy in women veterans with borderline personality disorder. *Behavior Therapy, 32*(2), 371–390. https://doi.org/10.1016/S0005-7894(01)80009-5

Kotov, R., Krueger, R. F., Watson, D., Achenbach, T. M., Althoff, R. R., Bagby, R. M., Brown, T. A., Carpenter, W. T., Caspi, A., Clark, L. A., Eaton, N. R., Forbes, M. K., Forbush, K. T., Goldberg, D., Hasin, D., Hyman, S. E., Ivanova, M. Y., Lynam, D. R., Markon, K., . . . Zimmerman, M. (2017). The Hierarchical Taxonomy of Psychopathology (HiTOP): A dimensional alternative to traditional nosologies. *Journal of Abnormal Psychology, 126*(4), 454–477. https://doi.org/10.1037/abn0000258

Landes, S. J., & Linehan, M. M. (2012). Dissemination and implementation of dialectical behavior therapy: An intensive training model. In R. K. McHugh & D. H. Barlow (Eds.), *Dissemination and implementation of evidence-based psychological interventions* (pp. 187–208). Oxford University Press.

Linehan, M. M. (1993a). *Cognitive-behavioral treatment of borderline personality disorder*. Guilford Press.

Linehan, M. M. (1993b). *Skills training manual for treating borderline personality disorder*. Guilford Press.

Linehan, M. M. (1997). Validation and psychotherapy. In A. C. Bohart & L. S. Greenberg (Eds.), *Empathy reconsidered: New directions in psychotherapy* (pp. 353–392). American Psychological Association. https://doi.org/10.1037/10226-016

Linehan, M. M. (2009). *University of Washington Risk Assessment Action Protocol: UWRAMP* [Unpublished work]. University of Washington.

Linehan, M. M. (2015). *DBT skills training manual*. Guilford Press.

Linehan, M. M., Armstrong, H. E., Suarez, A., Allmon, D., & Heard, H. L. (1991). Cognitive-behavioral treatment of chronically parasuicidal borderline patients. *Archives of General Psychiatry, 48*(12), 1060–1064. https://doi.org/10.1001/archpsyc.1991.01810360024003

Linehan, M. M., Comtois, K. A., Brown, M. Z., Heard, H. L., & Wagner, A. (2006). Suicide Attempt Self-Injury Interview (SASII): Development, reliability, and validity of a scale to assess suicide attempts and intentional self-injury. *Psychological Assessment, 18*(3), 303–312. https://doi.org/10.1037/1040-3590.18.3.303

Linehan, M. M., Comtois, K. A., Murray, A. M., Brown, M. Z., Gallop, R. J., Heard, H. L., Korslund, K. E., Tutek, D. A., Reynolds, S. K., & Lindenboim, N. (2006). Two-year randomized controlled trial and follow-up of dialectical behavior therapy vs therapy by experts for suicidal behaviors and borderline personality disorder. *Archives of General Psychiatry, 63*(7), 757–766. https://doi.org/10.1001/archpsyc.63.7.757

Linehan, M. M., Comtois, K. A., & Ward-Ciesielski, E. F. (2012). Assessing and managing risk with suicidal individuals. *Cognitive and Behavioral Practice, 19*(2), 218–232. https://doi.org/10.1016/j.cbpra.2010.11.008

Linehan, M. M., Dimeff, L. A., Reynolds, S. K., Comtois, K. A., Welch, S. S., Heagerty, P., & Kivlahan, D. R. (2002). Dialectical behavior therapy versus comprehensive validation therapy plus 12-step for the treatment of opioid dependent women meeting criteria for borderline personality disorder. *Drug and Alcohol Dependence, 67*(1), 13–26. https://doi.org/10.1016/S0376-8716(02)00011-X

Linehan, M. M., Heard, H. L., & Wagner, A. W. (1994). *Parasuicide history interview: Comprehensive assessment of parasuicidal behavior* [Unpublished manuscript]. University of Washington.

Linehan, M. M., & Schmidt, H., III. (1995). The dialectics of effective treatment of borderline personality disorder. In W. T. O'Donohue & L. Krasner (Eds.), *Theories of behavior therapy: Exploring behavior change* (pp. 553–584). American Psychological Association. https://doi.org/10.1037/10169-020

Linehan, M. M., Schmidt, H., III, Dimeff, L. A., Craft, J. C., Kanter, J., & Comtois, K. A. (1999). Dialectical behavior therapy for patients with borderline personality disorder and drug-dependence. *The American Journal on Addictions, 8*(4), 279–292. https://doi.org/10.1080/105504999305686

Lynch, T. R., Chapman, A. L., Rosenthal, M. Z., Kuo, J. R., & Linehan, M. M. (2006). Mechanisms of change in dialectical behavior therapy: Theoretical and empirical observations. *Journal of Clinical Psychology, 62*(4), 459–480. https://doi.org/10.1002/jclp.20243

Lynch, T. R., & Cheavens, J. S. (2008). Dialectical behavior therapy for comorbid personality disorders. *Journal of Clinical Psychology, 64*(2), 154–167. https://doi.org/10.1002/jclp.20449

Marra, T. (2005). *Dialectical behavioral therapy in private practice: A practical and comprehensive guide*. New Harbinger.

McCann, R. A., Ball, E. M., & Ivanoff, A. (2000). DBT with an inpatient forensic population: The CMHIP forensic model. *Cognitive and Behavioral Practice, 7*(4), 447–456. https://doi.org/10.1016/S1077-7229(00)80056-5

Morey, L. C., Skodol, A. E., & Oldham, J. M. (2014). Clinician judgments of clinical utility: A comparison of *DSM-IV-TR* personality disorders and the alternative model for *DSM-5* personality disorders. *Journal of Abnormal Psychology, 123*(2), 398–405. https://doi.org/10.1037/a0036481

National Institute of Mental Health. (2020). *Research domain criteria (RDoC)*. https://www.nimh.nih.gov/research/research-funded-by-nimh/rdoc/index.shtml

Neacsiu, A. D., Rizvi, S. L., Vitaliano, P. P., Lynch, T. R., & Linehan, M. M. (2010). The dialectical behavior therapy ways of coping checklist: Development and psychometric properties. *Journal of Clinical Psychology, 66*(6), 563–582. https://doi.org/10.1002/jclp.20685

Nelson, S. M., Huprich, S. K., Shankar, S., Sohnleitner, A., & Paggeot, A. V. (2017). A quantitative and qualitative evaluation of trainee opinions of four methods of personality disorder diagnosis. *Personality Disorders: Theory, Research, and Treatment, 8*(3), 217–227. https://doi.org/10.1037/per0000227

Oltmanns, J. R., & Widiger, T. A. (2018). A self-report measure for the *ICD-11* dimensional trait model proposal: The personality inventory for *ICD-11*. *Psychological Assessment, 30*(2), 154–169. https://doi.org/10.1037/pas0000459

Parloff, M. B., Waskow, I. E., & Wolfe, B. E. (1978). Research on client variables in psychotherapy. In A. E. Bergin & S. L. Garfield (Eds.), *Handbook of psychotherapy and behavior change* (pp. 233–282). Wiley.

Pistorello, J., Fruzzetti, A. E., Maclane, C., Gallop, R., & Iverson, K. M. (2012). Dialectical behavior therapy (DBT) applied to college students: A randomized clinical trial. *Journal of Consulting and Clinical Psychology, 80*(6), 982–994. https://doi.org/10.1037/a0029096

Priebe, S., Bhatti, N., Barnicot, K., Bremner, S., Gaglia, A., Katsakou, C., Molosankwe, I., McCrone, P., & Zinkler, M. (2012). Effectiveness and cost-effectiveness of dialectical behaviour therapy for self-harming patients with personality disorder: A pragmatic randomised controlled trial. *Psychotherapy and Psychosomatics, 81*(6), 356–365. https://doi.org/10.1159/000338897

Reed-Knight, B., & Fischer, S. (2011). Treatment of narcissistic personality disorder symptoms in a dialectical behavior therapy framework: A discussion and case example. In W. K. Campbell & J. D. Miller (Eds.), *The handbook of narcissism and narcissistic personality disorder: Theoretical approaches, empirical findings, and treatments* (pp. 466–475). Wiley. https://doi.org/10.1002/9781118093108.ch42

Rezaie, Z., Afshari, B., & Balagabri, Z. (2021). Effects of dialectical behavior therapy on emotion regulation, distress tolerance, craving, and depression in patients with opioid dependence disorder. *Journal of Contemporary Psychotherapy*. Advance online publication. https://doi.org/10.1007/s10879-020-09487-z

Rizvi, S. L. (2019). *Chain analysis in dialectical behavior therapy*. Guilford Press.

Rizvi, S. L., & Ritschel, L. A. (2014). Mastering the art of chain analysis in dialectical behavior therapy. *Cognitive and Behavioral Practice, 21*(3), 335–349. https://doi.org/10.1016/j.cbpra.2013.09.002

Rizvi, S. L., & Sayrs, J. H. R. (2020). Assessment-driven case formulation and treatment planning in dialectical behavior therapy: Using principles to guide effective treatment. *Cognitive and Behavioral Practice, 27*(1), 4–17. https://doi.org/10.1016/j.cbpra.2017.06.002

Safer, D. L., Telch, C. F., & Agras, W. S. (2001). Dialectical behavior therapy for bulimia nervosa. *The American Journal of Psychiatry, 158*(4), 632–634. https://doi.org/10.1176/appi.ajp.158.4.632

Samuel, D. B., & Widiger, T. A. (2006). Clinicians' judgments of clinical utility: A comparison of the *DSM-IV* and five-factor models. *Journal of Abnormal Psychology, 115*(2), 298–308. https://doi.org/10.1037/0021-843X.115.2.298

Santamarina-Perez, P., Mendez, I., Singh, M. K., Berk, M., Picado, M., Font, E., Moreno, E., Martínez, E., Morer, A., Borràs, R., Cosi, A., & Romero, S. (2020). Adapted dialectical behavior therapy for adolescents with a high risk of suicide in a community clinic: A pragmatic randomized controlled trial. *Suicide and Life-Threatening Behavior, 50*(3), 652–667. https://doi.org/10.1111/sltb.12612

Sayrs, J. H. R., & Linehan, M. M. (2019). *DBT teams: Development and practice*. Guilford Press.

Shenk, C. E., & Fruzzetti, A. E. (2011). The impact of validating and invalidating responses on emotional reactivity. *Journal of Social and Clinical Psychology, 30*(2), 163–183. https://doi.org/10.1521/jscp.2011.30.2.163

Skinner, B. F. (1957). The experimental analysis of behavior. *American Scientist, 45*(4), 343–371. https://www.americanscientist.org/article/the-experimental-analysis-of-behavior

Solhan, M. B., Trull, T. J., Jahng, S., & Wood, P. K. (2009). Clinical assessment of affective instability: Comparing EMA indices, questionnaire reports, and retrospective recall. *Psychological Assessment, 21*(3), 425–436. https://doi.org/10.1037/a0016869

Southward, M. W., & Cheavens, J. S. (2018). Identifying core deficits in a dimensional model of borderline personality disorder features: A network analysis. *Clinical Psychological Science, 6*(5), 685–703. https://doi.org/10.1177/2167702618769560

Southward, M. W., Semcho, S. A., Stumpp, N. E., MacLean, D. L., & Sauer-Zavala, S. (2020). A day in the life of borderline personality disorder: A preliminary analysis of within-day emotion generation and regulation. *Journal of Psychopathology and Behavioral Assessment, 42*(4), 702–713. https://doi.org/10.1007/s10862-020-09836-1

Stein, A. T., Hearon, B. A., Beard, C., Hsu, K. J., & Björgvinsson, T. (2016). Properties of the dialectical behavior therapy ways of coping checklist in a diagnostically diverse partial hospital sample. *Journal of Clinical Psychology, 72*(1), 49–57. https://doi.org/10.1002/jclp.22226

Stepp, S. D., Whalen, D. J., & Smith, T. D. (2013). Dialectical behavior therapy from the perspective of the five-factor model of personality. In T. A. Widiger & P. T. Costa, Jr. (Eds.), *Personality disorders and the five-factor model of personality* (pp. 395–407). American Psychological Association. https://doi.org/10.1037/13939-024

Stiglmayr, C. E., Grathwol, T., Linehan, M. M., Ihorst, G., Fahrenberg, J., & Bohus, M. (2005). Aversive tension in patients with borderline personality disorder: A computer-based controlled field study. *Acta Psychiatrica Scandinavica, 111*(5), 372–379. https://doi.org/10.1111/j.1600-0447.2004.00466.x

Stiglmayr, C. E., Shapiro, D. A., Stieglitz, R. D., Limberger, M. F., & Bohus, M. (2001). Experience of aversive tension and dissociation in female patients with borderline personality disorder—A controlled study. *Journal of Psychiatric Research, 35*(2), 111–118. https://doi.org/10.1016/S0022-3956(01)00012-7

Swales, M., Heard, H. L., & Williams, J. M. G. (2000). Linehan's dialectical behaviour therapy (DBT) for borderline personality disorder: Overview and adaptation. *Journal of Mental Health, 9*(1), 7–23. https://doi.org/10.1080/09638230016921

Swenson, C. R. (2016). *DBT principles in action: Acceptance, change, and dialectics.* Guilford Press.

Task Force on Promotion and Dissemination of Psychological Procedures. (1995). Training and dissemination of empirically validated psychosocial treatments: Report and recommendations. *Clinical Psychologist, 48*(1), 3–23.

Telch, C. F., Agras, W. S., & Linehan, M. M. (2001). Dialectical behavior therapy for binge eating disorder. *Journal of Consulting and Clinical Psychology, 69*(6), 1061–1065. https://doi.org/10.1037/0022-006X.69.6.1061

Thomas, A., & Chess, S. (1986). The New York Longitudinal Study: From infancy to early adult life. In R. Plomin & J. Dunn (Eds.), *The study of temperament: Changes, continuities and challenges* (pp. 39–52). Erlbaum.

Tolin, D. F., McKay, D., Forman, E. M., Klonsky, E. D., & Thombs, B. D. (2015). Empirically supported treatment: Recommendations for a new model. *Clinical Psychology: Science and Practice, 22*(4), 317–338. https://doi.org/10.1037/h0101729

Verheul, R., Van Den Bosch, L. M. C., Koeter, M. W. J., De Ridder, M. A. J., Stijnen, T., & Van Den Brink, W. (2003). Dialectical behaviour therapy for women with borderline personality disorder: 12-month, randomised clinical trial in the Netherlands. *The British Journal of Psychiatry, 182*(2), 135–140. https://doi.org/10.1192/bjp.182.2.135

World Health Organization. (2019). *International statistical classification of diseases and related health problems* (11th ed.). https://icd.who.int/

Zeifman, R. J., Boritz, T., Barnhart, R., Labrish, C., & McMain, S. F. (2020). The independent roles of mindfulness and distress tolerance in treatment outcomes in dialectical behavior therapy skills training. *Personality Disorders: Theory, Research, and Treatment, 11*(3), 181–190. https://doi.org/10.1037/per0000368

Zimmermann, J., Kerber, A., Rek, K., Hopwood, C. J., & Krueger, R. F. (2019). A brief but comprehensive review of research on the alternative *DSM-5* model for personality disorders. *Current Psychiatry Reports, 21*(9), Article 92. https://doi.org/10.1007/s11920-019-1079-z

12

Schema Therapy

Conceptualization and Treatment of Personality Disorders

Joan Farrell and Ida A. Shaw

This chapter provides an overview of the conceptualization, empirical evidence, and clinical application of the schema therapy (ST) mode model to treat personality disorders (PDs). ST grew out of the efforts of Jeffrey Young and others to more effectively treat clients with PDs (Behary, 2021; Farrell et al., 2014; Farrell & Shaw, 1994, 2012; Roediger et al., 2018; Young, 1990; Young et al., 2003). The ST model proposes that the etiology of PDs lies in the extent to which the core developmental needs of childhood are met combined with the child's temperament (see Figure 12.1). When these needs are chronically not adequately met, early maladaptive schemas (EMSs) develop. This theory is consistent with attachment theory, developmental psychology, and interpersonal neurobiology (Young et al., 2003). The interaction between the child's biological temperament and early toxic environments (e.g., parental neglect and abuse) is hypothesized to cause elevated vulnerability and emotional neediness in adult life (Flanagan, 2010; Young et al., 2003). A study by Bach et al. (2018) provided empirical validation for the hypothesized associations between Young's 18 EMSs and need-thwarting parental experiences in childhood.

This chapter first describes the core concepts of ST, the models of PD etiology and function, and the empirical evidence supporting these models. Next, the treatment of PD in the ST model is discussed, including the interventions used, the stages and goals of treatment, and the evidence for the effectiveness of the treatment. A case example of a patient with borderline PD (BPD) treated by the authors with individual and group ST is presented. The chapter concludes with

https://doi.org/10.1037/0000310-013

Personality Disorders and Pathology: Integrating Clinical Assessment and Practice in the DSM-5 *and* ICD-11 *Era*, S. K. Huprich (Editor)

Copyright © 2022 by the American Psychological Association. All rights reserved.

282 Farrell and Shaw

comments about the compatibility of the ST model for conceptualizing PD with the most recent classification approaches of both the *Diagnostic and Statistical Manual of Mental Disorders* (5th ed.; *DSM-5*; American Psychiatric Association, 2013) and the *International Statistical Classification of Diseases* (11th ed.; *ICD-11*; World Health Organization, 2019).

CORE CONCEPTS: SCHEMAS AND MODES

EMSs are psychological constructs that include unconditional and maladaptive beliefs about oneself, the world, and other people. The ST definition of EMS includes memories, bodily sensations, emotions, and cognitions that are thought to originate in childhood and adolescence that are elaborated through a person's lifetime. Eighteen schemas have been identified and validated with confirmatory factor analysis. These EMSs correspond with unmet core childhood needs identified by Bowlby (Young et al., 2003). Table 12.1 presents the hypothesized relationship between unmet core needs and the development of early maladaptive schemas. Schemas are assessed with the Young Schema Questionnaire (YSQ; Young & Brown, 1990), a self-report inventory that evaluates intensity rated on a 6-point scale (from *completely untrue of me* to *describes me perfectly*). The original 205-item version of the YSQ was adapted to a short form for research purposes (90 items) and is in its third version, the YSQ-S3 (Young, 2005). Evaluations in several countries indicate that the YSQ-S3 is a psychometrically sound instrument for measuring schemas, including factorial validity, test–retest stability, and convergent and discriminant validity (summarized in Bach et al., 2016). Schemas are stable over time, suggesting overall trait-like features (Riso et al., 2006). The presence of EMSs hypothesized for the various PDs measured by the YSQ and their relative absence in nonpatient controls has been investigated empirically (summarized in Bach et al., 2016; Kunst et al., 2020). Kunst et al. (2020) found that borderline, avoidant, dependent, and obsessive–compulsive PD traits positively relate to a wide range of EMSs. This finding supports a dimensional conceptualization of PDs because the content of some EMSs seems to underlie more general PD pathology. However, they also found several distinctive patterns: vulnerability to harm for BPD, emotional deprivation for avoidant PD, self-sacrifice for dependent PD, and unrelenting standards for obsessive-compulsive PD traits. The authors suggest that these findings support a hybrid model of PDs and EMSs, which is informative for clinicians because various EMSs per PD may be targeted in therapy.

Schema modes are defined as the intense emotional, cognitive, behavioral, and neurobiological states that a person experiences when EMSs are activated (Young et al., 2003). They reflect aspects of self that are not entirely integrated. The mode categories developed by Young are described in Table 12.2 (Young et al., 2003).

The Schema Mode Inventory (SMI) is a 118-item self-report inventory profiling 14 modes; long and short forms are available (Lobbestael et al., 2010). Modes are assessed on the basis of their frequency. Each item is rated on a

TABLE 12.1. Relationship Between Early Maladaptive Schemas and Unmet Core Childhood Needs

Early maladaptive schema	Unmet core childhood need
Disconnection and rejection • Abandonment/instability • Mistrust/abuse • Emotional deprivation • Defectiveness/shame • Social isolation/alienation	Secure attachment: care, acceptance, protection, safety, love, validation
Impaired autonomy and performance • Dependence/incompetence • Vulnerability to harm/illness • Enmeshment/undeveloped self • Failure	Support for autonomy, competence, sense of identity
Impaired limits • Entitlement/grandiosity • Insufficient self-control/self-discipline	Realistic limits, self-control
Other-directedness • Self-sacrifice • Subjugation • Approval-seeking/recognition-seeking	Free expression of needs and emotions
Overvigilance and inhibition • Negativity/pessimism • Emotional inhibition • Unrelenting standards • Punitiveness	Spontaneity, playfulness

TABLE 12.2. Young's Schema Mode Categories

Innate Child modes	Vulnerable, angry, impulsive or undisciplined child
Innate Child modes	Innate responses to unmet needs from childhood that are triggered in adulthood when schemas are activated. Primarily emotion.
Dysfunctional Critic modes (aka Parent modes)	Punitive Critic, Demanding Critic The selective internalization of negative aspects of childhood caregivers (parent, nanny, teacher, etc.; adolescent peer group). Punitive Critic is harsh and punishing, Demanding Critic sets unreachable standards and expectations. Primarily thoughts.
Maladaptive Coping modes	Overused survival responses to unmet needs and trauma—variations of flight (Avoidance), fight (Overcompensation), and freeze (Surrender) triggered when schema(s) are activated Avoidant protector—detached protector, detached self-soother or stimulator Overcompensator: perfectionistic overcontroller, self-aggrandizer, bully-attack, approval/attention seeker Compliant Surrenderer—surrender to a schema(s); the person acts as if the early maladaptive schema is true; primarily behavior.
Healthy modes	Happy Child, Healthy Adult Modes in which adaptive functioning occurs, which is accompanied by a sense of well-being and fulfillment

6-point scale (from *never or almost never* to *all of the time*). The SMI has been evaluated in many countries with consistent results supporting its factorial validity, internal consistency, construct validity, and ability to discriminate between subgroups (summarized in Bach et al., 2016). Several studies have explored the relationship between schemas and modes and other PD measures (Bach et al., 2018; Kunst et al., 2020) and the concept of defense mechanisms (Jacobs et al., 2019).

UNDERSTANDING PDs IN MODE TERMS

Figure 12.1 summarizes the etiology of PDs in ST concepts. The schema mode approach is one of the major developments in the treatment of PDs. It is transdiagnostic because it approaches treatment by targeting maladaptive schemas and schema modes rather than specific symptoms or disorders. A number of disorder-specific models for PDs have been hypothesized and empirically investigated. However, an individual case conceptualization that specifies a patient's unique structure of schemas and modes (not a psychiatric diagnosis) is what guides ST treatment. The mode model explains to a patient, in user-friendly terms, their symptoms and problems in the context of pathogenic early experiences. It provides a highly structured frame, which allows a meta-understanding of even complex problems like those common to BPD.

FIGURE 12.1. The Schema Therapy Etiology of Personality Disorders

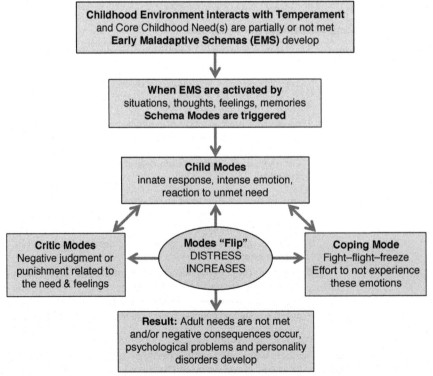

The BPD mode model was the first ST model to be developed and the most investigated (Sempértegui et al., 2013). Young and colleagues (2003) hypothesized that patients with BPD tend to flip from one of eight maladaptive schema modes to another. The modes hypothesized for BPD correlate well with the *DSM-5* Alternative *DSM-5* Model of Personality Disorders (*DSM-5*-AMPD) BPD traits (Bach & Farrell, 2018). Table 12.3 identifies the schema mode equivalent of the *DSM-5* traits of BPD.

Evidence in many studies using the SMI support the presence of the hypothesized modes of Young's BPD model, but these same modes are also found in other PDs. Validation for the hypothesized mode models for other PDs comes from two large-scale studies (Bamelis et al., 2011; Lobbestael et al., 2008). The main findings of these studies are summarized in Table 12.4.

It is noteworthy that borderline, avoidant, and dependent PDs were all negatively correlated with scores on the Healthy Adult mode, with BPD patients having the lowest scores. Bach and Bernstein (2018) proposed that the content of the Healthy Adult mode is comparable to the transdiagnostic measure of healthy personality functioning operationalized in the *ICD-11*-PD and *DSM-5*-AMPD classifications of PDs. SMI scores on the Healthy Adult mode correspond to the severity of personality dysfunction in these classifications. Arntz et al. (2005) tested the hypothesis that the Detached Protector mode is employed by BPD patients in situations of negative emotion. They compared BPD and avoidant PD and normal control groups' mode scores after viewing a BPD-specific stress induction film. Negative emotion was induced in all groups, but the BPD group was unique in having Detached Protector mode scores increase significantly.

TREATMENT OF PDs USING THE MODE MODEL

The mode model has high clinical utility (summarized in Jacob & Arntz, 2013). Modes provide user-friendly, understandable language for clients and provide the foci for psychotherapeutic intervention for therapists. Mode language focuses more on learning and less on psychopathology, giving clients hope

TABLE 12.3. *DSM-5* Borderline Personality Disorder (BPD) Traits Explained by Schema Modes

DSM-5-AMPD BPD trait	Schema mode explanation
Emotional lability	Mode flipping, Impulsive or Undisciplined Child
Anxiousness	Anxious Vulnerable Child, Punitive or Demanding Critic
Separation insecurity	Abandoned Vulnerable Child
Depressivity	Punitive Critic, Sad Vulnerable Child
Hostility	Angry Child, Bully–Attack, Angry Protector
Risk-taking	Impulsive or Undisciplined Child
Impulsivity	Impulsive or Undisciplined Child
Suspiciousness (tentative)	Abused Vulnerable Child

Note. AMPD = Alternative *DSM-5* Model of Personality Disorders; BPD = borderline personality disorder; *DSM-5* = Diagnostic and Statistical Manual of Mental Disorders (5th ed.).

286 *Farrell and Shaw*

TABLE 12.4. Mode Profiles Found in Personality Disorders

Personality disorder	Child modes	Coping modes	Critic modes	Healthy modes
Borderline	Abandoned, Angry	Detached Protector, Bully–Attack	Punitive	Negative correlation
Narcissistic	Lonely, Enraged	Self-Aggrandizer, Detached Self-Soother	Demanding	Healthy Adult (endorsed)
Antisocial	Abused, Abandoned, Enraged	Bully–Attack, Conning, or Predator versions	Punitive	Healthy Adult (endorsed)
Avoidant	*Lonely*, Abandoned, Abused, *Undisciplined*	Avoidant Protector, Detached Self-soother, *Surrender*, *Suspicious Overcontroller*, *Attention Seeker* (negative)	Punitive	Negative correlation
Dependent	Dependent, Abandoned, Abused, *Undisciplined*	Compliant Surrender	Punitive	Negative correlation
Histrionic	Dependent			
Obsessive Compulsive	*Lonely*	Perfectionistic Overcontroller, *Self-Aggrandizer*, *Detached Self-Soother*	Demanding *Punitive*	Medium score
Paranoid	Humiliated, Abused	Suspicious, Overcontroller	Punitive	Negative correlation
Psychotherapist Low scores on all	Sad, Anxious or Lonely Child	Perfectionistic Overcontroller, Detached Protector or Detached Self-Soother	Demanding	High score

Note. Data from Lobbestael et al. (2008) and Bamelis et al. (2011). Italics indicate finding was from only one study.

regarding change. A thorough and individualized ST case conceptualization is developed, which is transparent and highly collaborative. It describes the joint understanding of the therapist and client of how the current problems developed, the schemas and modes maintaining them, and specifies the plan for treatment. It includes current major problems and life patterns, developmental origins, core childhood memories or images, core unmet needs, most relevant schemas, current schema triggers, schema modes, temperamental factors, and core cognitive distortions. It includes a description of the therapy relationship, the impact of schemas and modes on in-session behavior, and the therapist's personal reaction to the client. Conceptualization begins early in treatment and, if needed, can easily be adapted to add information that arises later. It is a working document, which identifies the goals of treatment and describes the specific interventions needed at any moment in time. The full case conceptualization form with an example and full instructions can be found on the website of the International Society of Schema Therapy (https://schematherapysociety.org/). A shorter plan for the main presenting problems describes how the four main types of modes are involved in the problem and what the steps of change are by mode (Farrell et al., 2014; Farrell & Shaw, 2012). An example of this problem analysis form is given in the case example of this chapter.

The Goals of ST in Mode Terms

The schema mode model has high clinical utility, as modes guide the treatment interventions of ST. The overall goal of ST is to develop the Healthy Adult mode so that a person can maintain a fulfilling life, including work, obligations, commitments, satisfying relationships, healthy sex life, hobbies, recreation, and fun. This is accomplished by developing awareness of the triggering of maladaptive modes and the person being able to access their Healthy Adult mode to perform the following needed functions:

- **Care for the Vulnerable Child mode.** This requires developing an internal "good parent" who can comfort or act to meet the underlying need present in the various Child modes with their intense feelings of fear, sadness, or loneliness are triggered.

- **Replace the Maladaptive Coping modes** with adaptive coping behavior that has little or no negative consequence. For example, be able to experience emotions when they arise, connect with others, and express one's needs. Active choices are made that meet needs in the adult situational reality rather than defaulting to primitive fight, flight, or freeze Coping mode responses.

- **Replace the Angry or Impulsive or Undisciplined Child mode** behavior with appropriate and effective ways to express emotions and needs—for example, the ability to express needs and anger in an assertive adult manner rather than as tantrum.

- **Reduce the power and control of the Dysfunctional Critic modes**; replace the punitive or demanding internalized critic with the ability to motivate oneself in a healthy, positive manner; accept one's mistakes; make necessary retribution; and have realistic expectations and standards.

- **Free the Happy Child mode** to pursue activities that provide joy in life and allow for play.

- The specifics of mode goals are individualized.

An example of the goals by mode approach is given in the case example. Progress with ST goals is measured by decreases in the YSQ and SMI and in standard PD measures. (e.g., the Borderline Severity Index).

ST Interventions Based on Modes

ST is integrative in its full use of experiential, cognitive, and behavioral pattern-breaking interventions to accomplish treatment goals. It balances experiential or emotion-focused interventions, the cognitive processing of new awareness and insights from corrective emotional experiences, and behavioral pattern-breaking. ST's interventions address the emotional, cognitive, and behavioral levels of experience and can be divided into four main components: limited reparenting, mode awareness, mode management, and mode healing (Farrell & Shaw, 2018).

Limited Reparenting

Limited reparenting is both a therapist style and an intervention. It is thought to be one of the active ingredients of mode change work. It provides corrective emotional experiences for the Child modes' unmet needs, models healthy action to meet needs to replace Maladaptive Coping mode behavior and challenges the Dysfunctional Critic modes' negative internalizations. The schema therapist's behaviors during limited reparenting can be summed up as "doing what a good parent would" in meeting the client's needs within the bounds of a professional therapy relationship. This means providing protection, validation, and comfort for the Vulnerable Child mode; the opportunity to express one's unpleasant feelings and be heard for the Angry Child, and empathic confrontation and limit setting for the Impulsive or Undisciplined Child mode.

The goal of limited reparenting is to establish an active, supportive, and genuine relationship with the client that provides a safe environment for the client to be vulnerable and express emotions and needs. Limited reparenting attempts to fill critical gaps in emotional learning via secure attachment and accurate mirroring, which leads to the client feeling valued and worthy, often for the first time. It attempts to compensate for the deficits in how childhood needs for support in competence and development of identity and healthy limits were met. The schema therapist initially assesses these needs and the strength of a client's Healthy Adult mode to choose an appropriate reparenting approach.

The reparenting style is adjusted accordingly for healthier clients who have infrequent triggering of the Vulnerable Child mode and a much stronger Healthy Adult mode. Over time, the experience of the therapy relationship fosters clients learning to care for their needs effectively and eventually to attain autonomy and healthy interpersonal functioning. This approach to needs is in sharp contrast to most other therapy models, which we see as focusing too early on clients meeting their own needs when they have never had the experience of them being met.

Mode Awareness

Mode awareness interventions are primarily cognitive, with some emotion-focused aspects. The goal is that patients become able to identify their mode experiences, the triggering schemas, and the underlying need. Identifying the different aspects of experience—feeling, physical sensations, and memories—helps them become aware of the mode that is present. Connecting the current situation to childhood memories allows them to understand the roots of their schemas and modes. After a patient is aware of the mode they are currently in, they can make a conscious decision whether to stay in this mode or access their Healthy Adult mode.

Mode Management

Mode management refers to the plan of action developed to pause the maladaptive mode triggered and access their Healthy Adult mode to meet the underlying need present. Mode Management Plans are primarily the behavioral pattern-breaking component of ST, which ensures that therapeutic changes generalize to behavior outside of the therapy setting. In this component, any barriers to change, such as cognitive distortions, beliefs, or actions that maintain maladaptive mode behavior, are identified and challenged.

Mode Healing

Mode healing includes visual imagery, imagery rescripting, mode dialogues, mode role-plays, corrective emotional experiences in the therapy relationship, and creative work to symbolize positive experiences. To change modes at the emotional level, the therapist develops "experiential antidotes" with clients. For example, patients often say they "*know* in my head that I am not defective or abandoned, but I *feel* defective and abandoned." This indicates the need to target the emotional level of modes, the implicational level of experience, to affect deeper level change. Knowing that one is not defective or a failure does not eliminate the feeling that one is defective and a failure. Feelings like these (implicit knowledge) with their accompanying shame, self-hatred, and fears of rejection are what keep clients miserable, unhappy, and functioning below their abilities even when they have learned cognitive and behavioral skills. Creative and symbolizing work in the mode healing sessions includes using art or written material that can facilitate recall of and the emotional reexperiencing of schema contradicting events (Farrell & Shaw, 2012; Farrell et al., 2014).

Stages and Goals of ST

Table 12.5 summarizes the stages of ST and the goals associated with each stage. Length and frequency of ST for PDs are individualized. However, general guidelines and protocols for various PDs are available (Farrell et al., 2014; van Vreeswijk et al., 2012). ST, however, cannot be completely manualized. A critical part of limited reparenting is providing the corrective emotional experience of attunement to the patient's needs and mode in the present moment. Plans from protocols are put to the side when it is possible to seize an "experiential moment" in a session and an opportunity for Vulnerable Child mode work (described in Farrell & Shaw, 2012).

EVIDENCE FOR THE TREATMENT EFFECTIVENESS OF ST FOR PDs

The effectiveness of ST for BPD has been validated empirically in several large-scale randomized controlled trials (RCTs) of individual ST (Giesen-Bloo et al., 2006; Nadort et al., 2009), in one trial of Group ST (Farrell et al., 2009), and in one of combined individual and group ST compared with treatment by experts with 495 BPD patients (Arntz et al., 2022). ST has demonstrated effectiveness in a large multisite trial for avoidant, dependent, and obsessive–compulsive PDs (Bamelis et al., 2014) and for forensic patients

TABLE 12.5. Stages and Goals of Schema Therapy

Stage	Goals
Bonding and emotional regulation	Assessment, education, understanding presenting problems in schema therapy concepts
	Connecting with the Vulnerable Child (safety)
	Getting around or through the Maladaptive Coping modes
	Affect regulation and coping skills (if needed)
Schema mode change	Replacing Maladaptive Coping modes with adaptive choices
	Combating and challenging the Dysfunctional Critic modes
	Helping the Vulnerable Child mode heal through limited reparenting and corrective emotional experiences such as imagery rescripting
	Rechanneling the Angry and Impulsive Child into Healthy Adult action
Autonomy	Development of the Healthy Adult Mode and Happy Child Mode and reliable access to these modes
	Individuation: following natural inclinations, pursuing activities that are pleasurable and fulfilling, accepting the responsibilities of adult roles
	Developing healthy relationships
	Gradual termination of psychotherapy with the option of future contact

with PDs (Keulen-de Vos et al., 2017). The effectiveness of ST reported in these studies included patients having improved function and quality of life, reductions in PD symptoms, global severity of psychopathology, and remission in PD for a majority of patients. Such findings have led to the growing use of ST as well as pilot studies and additional RCTs underway worldwide to evaluate its effectiveness with other disorders (avoidant PD and social phobia; Baljé et al., 2016), mixed PD groups (Simpson et al., 2015), complex trauma (Younan et al., 2017), depression (Renner et al., 2016), geriatric clients with PDs (Videler et al., 2014) and dissociative identity disorder (Huntjens et al., 2019). ST can be adapted to varying lengths of treatment. Three years of individual sessions demonstrated effectiveness in reducing BPD symptoms and improving quality of life (Giesen-Bloo et al., 2006), but so did 30 sessions of group ST added to nonspecialized individual treatment as usual (Farrell et al., 2009). The ST treatment being evaluated in the studies underway varies in length from 20 sessions to a tapering schedule over 2 years, is conducted at a variety of levels of care (inpatient, day hospitals, outpatient) and in treatment settings (public and private hospitals and outpatient clinics, as well as forensic settings), and includes individual ST alone or combined with group ST. ST is an approach that is rated positively by clients and therapists (de Klerk et al., 2016; Spinhoven et al., 2006). In addition, ST has growing evidence for its cost-effectiveness for the individual modality (van Asselt et al., 2008).

AN ST CASE EXAMPLE OF BPD

In the following case, we describe a patient whom one of us (JF) treated individually and both of us treated in group ST. We provide an ST conceptualization and description of how we engaged the patient so that she could move toward a better life and relational functioning.

Main diagnosis: Borderline personality disorder

Level of functioning: Sally's[1] symptoms interfere with keeping a job, having a healthy marriage, and taking adequate care of her young son. She left college after one semester and is estranged from her husband, parents, and brother. She is intolerant of time alone but has no close friends.

Major life problems and symptoms: Impulsivity—self-injury by cutting and impulsive suicide attempts by prescription drug overdose, separation insecurity, depression, anxiety, hostility, emotional lability, instability of self.

Childhood and adolescent origins of problems: Sally was adopted at 3 years old with her 1-year-old brother. Her parents told her that after 6 months, they felt she was "too much for them," and they "tried to give me back" but were unable to do so. Sally reported that her parents described her

---

[1]Although the case example in this chapter is based on the authors' real experiences, the identity of the individual has been properly disguised to protect her confidentiality.

as "too sensitive" and "too needy." She described her parents as "emotionally cold, strict, and critical." They had many rules for Sally but only a few for her brother. They belonged to a fundamentalist Christian church, which was strict about the need for punishment and not "spoiling" children. Sometimes Sally was beaten, and other times she was locked in the cold, unfinished basement of the house for 24 hours as a punishment. Her history is full of physical and emotional abuse and emotional deprivation. She had some difficulty in school with paying attention and keeping quiet during classes. She was bullied throughout middle school for her conservative, homemade clothing. As an older teen, boys became interested in Sally, who was slim and pretty. She was pleased by this but also frightened. At 15, she was not allowed to date but found ways to sneak out to meet boys. On one of these "dates," she was raped by a boy she met and his friend. In that situation, she froze in response to the first sexual move, which was taken as consent. When she returned home that night in a disheveled state, her parents were furious, blamed her, and refused to report it to the police. She was kicked out of home for 3 days. The parents saw this as another example of her "poor morals." The next 2 years were a "blur" to her, and during this time, she began cutting her arms. She said that this was both "punishment" and her way to make the "inside pain outside." At 17, she left home and moved in with a group of adolescents who supported themselves with odd jobs, handouts, and sex work. She viewed herself as "only good for sex," and sex was the only way she had to get approval or closeness. She managed to begin community college at 20 with the help of a social worker. She met a man there, whom she married at age 22. She describes her husband as cold and not emotionally expressive. He was 8 years older and steadily employed. Sally saw him as her route to a "normal life." She describes their first few years together as good, but after a child's birth when she was 25, their relationship changed. Sally thought he was more attentive to their son than to her and felt increasingly left out and unhappy. She identified parallels in this situation to her family of origin, in which her parents favored her brother. She resumed cutting her arms, and when her son was 2 years old, she made a serious suicide attempt by overdose while she was caring for him. Her husband was furious and not at all sympathetic. He threatened divorce and taking custody of their son if she did not "shape up." Her parents supported the husband and told Sally that she was an unfit mother.

Specific early unmet core needs: Her secure attachment needs were not met by parents, who really did not want her and let her know this. She felt unloved—a worthless bother. She was not encouraged to express her needs or feelings and was told that she was too needy. She did not have healthy limits but rather harsh ones enforced by punishment. She was given many rules but no support for her competence or her development of a positive sense of identity. Spontaneity and fun were discouraged in her family, and her early environment was without love or nurture. Sally's childhood did not provide her with the necessary experiences to learn that her needs were normal or that she deserved love and validation.

Possible temperamental factors: Sally was described as sensitive and emotionally labile by her parents. The accuracy of their assessment is unclear.

Possible cultural, ethnic, and religious factors: Sally had a strict fundamentalist religious upbringing emphasizing the threat of hell.

Translating Sally's Presenting Problems Into ST Concepts

Table 12.6 presents a flowchart of the emotional distress and problematic actions that occur when Sally's early maladaptive schemas are activated, triggering specific dysfunctional modes. It is important for patients to develop awareness of the early signs that a schema has been activated, and consequently the beginning of mode behavior or thoughts, to make the deliberate choice of a more effective action.

Exhibit 12.1 is an example of the shortened explanation of how schemas and modes explain the patient's presenting problems. This analysis in ST concepts and the patient's own words provides face validity for the focus on modes in treatment. Exhibit 12.2 shows the second part of this form. It lists treatment goals for each of the modes—both the dysfunctional modes, which need to be decreased in frequency or intensity, and the healthy modes, which need to be strengthened. The first steps for the patient to take and the results of those steps are also listed here.

Interventions by ST Component and Mode

Limited Reparenting Work

The therapy relationship gave Sally the experience of safe connection and that being vulnerable can lead to understanding and support, not criticism or punishment; opportunities for receiving nurturing and caring; and the experience that others can find her lovable—you "matter." Limited reparenting provided many corrective emotional experiences to counter her parents' rejection. Sally's mistrust/abuse schema was initially an obstacle to our connection because she was emotionally reactive in early sessions. On one occasion, she rushed to the corner of my office and curled up in a fetal position saying, "Don't hit me." Her Abused Child mode had been triggered in response to my wrinkling my forehead. In childhood, this behavior from her mother was the only warning she had that a physical beating was coming, so she became hypervigilant to this sign. I wrinkle my brow when I am thinking, so this occurred frequently in sessions. With my support, Sally was able to signal me when this happened, and I could reassure her.

Her Angry Child mode needed to express negative affect safely and for me to hear her. It was equally important for me to set healthy limits when needed and empathically confront her Bully–Attack mode. This overcompensating coping mode was one of the ways that Sally survived the pain and unmet needs of her childhood. However, as an adult, this behavior was a main source of her problems with her husband and others. Empathic confrontation pointed out the problem behavior and the evidence that it did not get her

294 *Farrell and Shaw*

TABLE 12.6. Sally's Pattern of Schema Activation and Mode Triggering

External event	Schema activated	Internal event	Mode triggered	External action
Husband acts removed	Abandonment, emotional deprivation, defectiveness/ shame	Feels worthless, unwanted, memories of parent's rejection "flight" coping is triggered	Abandoned Child ↓ Angry Child ↓ Detached Protector	Rages at husband, he withdraws further Forgets to feed 2-year-old son
Parents criticize her mothering, threaten CPS	Defectiveness/ shame, mistrust/ abuse	Feels frightened, shamed and then angry at perceived unfairness	Abused Child ↓ Angry Child ↓	
	Defectiveness/ shame	Hears schema maintaining negative messages	Punitive Critic	Cuts her arm as punishment.
Husband threatens her with hospitalization; says she is "crazy," unfit mother	Defectiveness/ shame	Feels hurt and frightened Fight coping style is triggered	Abandoned/ Abused ↓ Angry Child Bully–Attack ↓	Cries Rages at him, tries to hurt him to not feel her pain
Husband leaves the house, taking their son	Abandonment Emotional deprivation Defectiveness/ shame	Feels worthless, despondent, critic intensifies these feelings	Abandoned/ Abused Child ↓ Punitive Critic ↓	Cries, rocks
		Flight coping takes over At first she is numb	Detached Protector ↓	
	Defectiveness/ shame, abandonment	Feelings off despair and hopelessness break through	Vulnerable Child ↓	
		Action urge is intense	Impulsive Child	Overdose to end feelings

Note. CPS = child protective services.

EXHIBIT 12.1

Sally's Problem Analysis

1. My identified problem	Self-injury, suicide attempts, may lose husband and son due to impulsivity, "I feel unstable, empty, and think I am crazy."
2. Schema(s) involved	Defectiveness/shame, abandonment/insecurity, mistrust/abuse, emotional deprivation
3. Activating situations	Husband is not attentive, leaves her alone, threatens divorce and taking son; parents say she is an unfit mother
4. What is her underlying need?	Safety, security, love, understanding, acceptance
5. How is the Vulnerable Child mode involved?	Sally feels shame, worthlessness, despair, fear, hopelessness
6. Is another Child mode involved? How?	Angry Child: Sometimes Sally explodes with the unfairness of it all and that no one listens to her
7. Is a Critic mode involved? How?	Sally hears the things her parents said to her about being a bad kid, unwanted, stupid, worthless: "I have memories of punishment. This is what leads me to cutting myself or taking overdoses to end it all."
8. Is a Maladaptive Coping mode involved? How?	"I detach sometimes. Other times I attack my husband verbally to make him feel the pain I do."
9. What is the result?	"He withdraws more and stays away from home, takes my son with him. My parents call and threaten me when they hear what I have done."
10. Is your underlying need met?	"No. I make the whole situation worse, so I start over with the self-criticism and the vicious circle you described starts over."

needs met in the present and caused interpersonal problems while acknowledging its childhood survival origins. Acting as a good parent, I challenged her Critic mode voices and replaced it with a "good parent" voice. We worked to build Sally's Healthy Adult mode's strength and skills and her ability to access it when other modes were triggered. We also evoked her Happy Child mode: to encourage play, fun, and pleasurable experiences. This is another underdeveloped mode in BPD. Access to the Happy Child mode can be a powerful motivator for the patient to continue the at times difficult work of ST (Shaw, 2020).

Mode Awareness Work

Sally used a circle monitoring form (Farrell & Shaw, 2018) to collect information about the triggering situation, thought, feeling, physical sensation, schema, mode, need, usual action, and outcome. Her awareness work is summarized in Table 12.7.

EXHIBIT 12.2

Sally's Schema Therapy Treatment Goals

Sally: My goals by mode

Maladaptive Coping mode (behavior)	"I need to notice when the pain goes up and then I start to feel really angry and will lash back at whoever is there. I need to train myself to take a break, then use my schema flashcards, and go into the backyard to swing."
	"When I start to feel spacey, I need to do a soothing thing like smelling lavender oil."
Dysfunctional Critic mode (thoughts)	"I need to tell the critic to shut up. I need to get the list of good parent messages we made in therapy and read it over. I need to remember that I was just a normal little girl and it was my parents' problem that they did not have enough love for me."
Vulnerable Child (emotions)	"I need to keep working on compassion for little me. I can look at my son and see myself in him. I would never hurt him the way I was hurt. I need to remember that I deserved love too—I was not a bad kid; I was treated badly."
Angry/Impulsive or Undisciplined Child mode (emotions/ behavior)	"I need to work on hearing my Angry Child. She speaks for little Sally's needs but is too extreme. When she says something is not OK I need to say 'no' assertively instead of having a tantrum."
Healthy Adult mode	"I need to work on accessing this part of me when another mode is triggered. I can use the 'swing' imagery to connect with adult Sally or hold the bead that represents healthy me that the schema therapy group gave me."
Happy Child mode	"I need to do fun things with my son that little me likes—blowing bubbles, flying a kite, even taking a walk with our dog. I need to do things regularly just for fun to balance the pain of my life."
First steps	"My first step will be to be as kind and gentle to myself when my Abandoned or frightened child is triggered as I am when I comfort my son when he is sad or scared. I have the skills I just need to use them for me."
Results	"I am cutting less, and I feel less desperate and abandoned. I am starting to feel like I can be there for me—I am not completely alone."

TABLE 12.7. Sally's Mode Awareness and Mode Management Plan

Mode awareness	Mode management
Whenever I think that I have made a mistake, <u>my internal critic voice starts in on me</u> (PC)—she tells me that I am a loser, the black sheep of the family and I will never be happy. The voice sounds like my mother. <u>I feel really sad and helpless (AbC) then angry</u>—it is so unfair. My AC is triggered, then I sometimes flip into BA mode and <u>yell at my husband trying to hurt him.</u> He withdraws, and <u>my PC comes in again</u> to criticize me. That is when I <u>decide that I deserve some punishment</u> (PC) like the beatings my mom gave me, and I self-injure. This confirms my mother's message that I am a "loser," I am "worthless." Then I feel even worse and mode flip a lot—my AbC is usually affected by the PC, then I quickly flip to a Coping mode like DP. If I still feel the emotional pain, I become desperate and my IC mode is triggered. That is when I have taken overdoses to end all of the pain.	1. My suicide attempts start with the PC mode. I need to recognize the voice as my mother and remind myself that she was not able to love me not because I was bad but because of her problems. When the PC voice starts I need to fight it from my HA mode by listening to the Good Parent recording from therapy. If I cannot shake the voice, I need to call a friend from group to talk about what we are learning there. If it continues, I can use my emergency plan and the numbers I have to call.

2. I need to build up my Good Parent part of my HA by using the recording and the soothing image of my grandma, who loved me. I need to use the self-soothing plan of rocking and wrapping the fleece blanket around me. |
| My Vulnerable Child's needs | Step I can take this week: |
| 1. Connection

2. Validation

3. A hug

4. Safety from SIB | Stay safe by noticing the PC voice and using my plan for Little Sally. I can put my picture of Grandma holding me where I will see it. Her messages are antidotes to the Critic messages. This should prevent a flip to PC that leads to SIB. I can also ask for help to stay safe while I do this. |

Note. AbC = Abandoned/Abused Child mode; AC = Angry Child mode; BA = Bully–Attack mode; DP = Detached Protector mode; HA = Healthy Adult mode; IC = Impulsive Child; PC = Punitive Critic mode; SIB = self-injury behavior.

Mode Management Work

After Sally's awareness of modes being triggered increased, we worked on a plan of healthy action to meet the need involved. These plans are written and made easily accessible to support the new behavior until it becomes more automatic. An example of one of Sally's later Mode Management Plans is shown in the right column of Table 12.7. These plans list specific steps to take to replace maladaptive mode behavior or thoughts.

Mode Healing Work

In addition to limited reparenting, other experiential interventions are employed as corrective emotional experiences. The "Good Parent Script" (Farrell et al., 2014) referred to in Sally's goals by mode is a recording in the therapist's voice that lists all of the individualized schema-challenging positive messages that the patient should have heard in childhood; for example, "You are lovable just the way you are." Sally listened to this recording regularly until it became an internalized "good parent" voice against her Punitive Critic mode.

Imagery rescripting is used to develop specific corrective emotional experiences for schema origin memories (Arntz, 2011). We rescripted Sally's main experiences of neglect and abuse from her parents and the rape trauma. For example, we identified memories of harsh punishment after a minor transgression such as forgetting to make her brother's after school snack. In imagery, Sally connected with the memory and described the point just before the traumatic event, which provided adequate emotional activation for the rescript to have an emotional impact. Before the imagery work began, we developed a new ending for the memory, which met Sally's need for understanding, validation, and nurturance to take the place of her mother's unreasonable expectation and beating. In this rescripting, I entered Sally's image to protect her and explain to first her and then her mother that it was not reasonable to expect a 6-year-old to faultlessly remember to make her brother's snack, particularly when it had to be heated. In fact, we discussed whether a 6-year-old should be left home alone for 2 hours before her mother came home from work. In imagery, I took Sally off to a playground leaving her brother to be cared for by their mother. In ST rescripting, we ask the patient if "anything else is needed" before we end. In this rescripting, Sally said that she wanted to be given a snack like her brother was. After the imagery, we identified the new message Sally could form from this corrective experience. These were "A child of 6 deserves to be taken care of" and "I was not a bad kid; I was too young to be expected to babysit my brother"; "I deserved to be taken care of." Later rescripting had Sally in the Healthy Adult mode go into the scene and model my actions protecting and caring for Little Sally. Imagery rescripting work for Sally included rescue from her punishment in the basement, rescue from bullying, and counter her parents' story of trying to give her back to the adoption agency and the date rape. The same process was used for the rape in that we identified the point before anything traumatic happened and then rescripted what should have happened to protect her and prevent the rape. In that rescripting, I took her away from the meeting with the boys to the safety of my home and talked to her about understanding that she wanted to have dates but that this was not a safe way. I reassured her that she was not bad for wanting to date and talked to her about ways to stay safe in these situations. The goal of rescripting is to provide a corrective experience that meets the patient's need in the scene. In this case, the need was safety and protection, to be rescued, and reassurance that she was "not bad." Sally's original message from the rape was "I am bad and alone. The world and other people are dangerous. No one cares about me." The new message she chose was "I deserve protection and safety. I am valuable, and I matter, I have worth." This message was a cognitive antidote to her defectiveness/shame schema. Through cognitive reattribution, Sally no longer saw the abuse she received in childhood when in need of emotional reassurance to her inherent worthlessness but to the psychological problems of her parents in dealing with emotions and attaching to any child. Sally came to state this directly as "the abuse is not my fault; it did not happen because I was a 'bad' kid." She changed the message from her parents "I am a kid no one wants" to "my parents were inadequate in not loving and valuing me."

It is important to note that Sally did not have enough Healthy Adult mode to be the protagonist in the imagery rescripting at the beginning of this work. She first needed to experience an adult (the therapist) caring for and rescuing her to internalize a healthy caregiver and develop good parent skills. In the ST treatment of BPD, we assume that the patient has little Healthy Adult mode available to them and needs to experience us acting as a "good parent" to develop this component. Patients need this corrective experience at an emotional level to counter schemas such as defectiveness/shame. Mode healing experiences reduce the strength of the Critic modes and build the good parent part of the Healthy Adult mode. Other ST interventions with the Critic mode for Sally included making a cloth effigy of the Critic mode with her negative messages, which could be the target of mode dialogues with her Healthy Adult mode coached by me and for her Angry Child mode to vent anger at. Mode dialogues allow patients to feel fully and understand the experience of a dysfunctional mode and then move to their Healthy Adult mode to respond to, manage, or contain the unhealthy mode.

Summary of Progress

Sally spent 3 months in our inpatient ST combined individual and group program. She continued individual and primarily group outpatient ST for a year. She attended an ST advanced support group, which met monthly for an additional year for a total of 2 years of treatment. She and her husband went to couples counseling in which they were able to improve communication and understanding of each other's needs and modes. Her husband came to understand the relationship between Sally's childhood experiences and her current reactions. He was able to respond effectively when Sally communicated her needs directly, which reduced the frequency of her dissociation and bully–attack behavior. Sally understood the triggering effect of her son and was able to be a good parent to him and little Sally. She resumed college. When she left active treatment, her scores on the SMI had reduced in all dysfunctional modes, and her Healthy Adult mode had increased considerably. She no longer met criteria for a BPD diagnosis on the BPD Severity Index (Arntz & Giesen-Bloo, 1999).

CONCLUDING REMARKS: ST AND THE TRANSITION TO *DSM-5*-AMPD AND *ICD-11*

This chapter described the ST mode model for the treatment of PDs and summarized the empirical status of the model's theoretical background and its effectiveness. ST is a promising treatment for PDs, with several large RCTs demonstrating its effectiveness in reducing EMSs, modes, PD symptoms, improving quality of life, and achieving remission. Studies also demonstrate cost-effectiveness, implementability, and the positive evaluation of the treatment by patients and therapists. The mode model provides a clear structure for planning interventions and setting treatment goals. The case example of the chapter illustrates this, providing a case conceptualization, goals, and interventions in schema and mode terms.

The ST model for conceptualizing PD is compatible with the most recent classification approaches of both the *DSM-5* and the *ICD-11*-PD. These systems combine a dimensional approach that measures severity combined with the presence of a number of traits (*DSM-5*-AMPD) or what is identified as a BPD pattern specifier (*ICD-11*-PD). The overall YSQ scores and the number of EMS endorsed at clinically significant levels provides an impairment rating, while the specific EMS or domains with elevated scores serve the function of traits (*DSM-5*) or patterns (*ICD-11*-PD). The ST approach to PD attempts to deal with the heterogeneity within various traditional diagnoses and the high rate of comorbidity in PD by focusing in treatment on their specific and individual combination of EMS and modes. Because of this, ST is sometimes characterized as transdiagnostic.

Several recent publications discuss the compatibility of the ST approach to PD conceptualization with recent developments in *DSM-5*-AMPD and *ICD-11* PD (Bach & Lobbestael, 2018). In ST, the distinction between disorder and normal limits is determined by the frequency and intensity of schema activation and mode triggering, which is a dimensional approach. This is compatible with current views suggesting that the personality traits associated with a particular PD are best understood as extreme variants of ordinary personality traits that differ by degree, rather than being a difference in type. Correlational research has identified many relationships between EMSs and the different PDs (summarized in Kunst et al., 2020). This finding supports a more dimensional rather than categorical conceptualization of PDs. The content of some EMSs seems to underpin more general PD pathology. There were, however, also several distinctive patterns, with vulnerability to harm for BPD, emotional deprivation for avoidant PD, self-sacrifice for dependent PD, and unrelenting standards for obsessive–compulsive PD. This suggests that PDs may be best reflected by a hybrid model of EMSs, with some EMSs that seem to reflect a broader vulnerability factor for PDs, whereas others are particularly relevant for specific PDs.

Research suggests that certain PD features are best captured by schemas, whereas others features are best captured by modes (Bach & Farrell, 2018; Bach et al., 2016). Accordingly, certain PD features are mostly schema-like (e.g., poor self-worth), whereas other PD features are mostly mode-like (e.g., self-harm). For example, *DSM-5* Section III traits of impulsivity and hostility are mostly related to dynamic modes, whereas traits of separation insecurity and suspiciousness are mostly related to schemas (Bach et al., 2016). Thus, it is possible to distinguish between stable traits and more dynamic mode-like traits when working with PDs. The forthcoming *ICD-11* model explicitly takes into account that traits may be manifested in different ways based on the presence of other traits. This is similar to the way ST identifies how the activation of combinations of EMS can trigger a variety of dysfunctional modes. The effect on maladaptive coping modes of the specific schemas a person scores high on parallels the manner in which the *ICD-11*-PD frames how specific traits contribute to the manner in which personality dysfunction is expressed. ST examines how combinations of EMS function in the here and now through the modes they trigger just as the *ICD-11*-PD approach takes into account that traits may be manifest in different ways due to the presence of additional traits. The same EMS mistrust and abuse may trigger an avoidant or overcompensating response depending on the activation of other EMS and the situations in which EMS activation occurs. In ST, EMS (trait-like structures) are assessed, but the clinician is most concerned with how EMS triggers modes—the current moment experience and behavior—as this is what we target in therapy as the case example amply demonstrates. ST conceptualized PD in terms of EMS combined with the states (i.e., modes) that they trigger in activating situations rather than PD symptoms. It is recognized that some EMSs are more likely to be present in a particular PD and that other EMS reflect global dysfunction. The ST conceptualization is compatible with PD diagnoses based on the criteria of *DSM-5*-AMPD and *ICD-11*-PD, but the most useful conceptualization to guide treatment remains a client's schema and mode profile. An example is provided in the case description for Sally in this chapter.

REFERENCES

American Psychiatric Association. (2013). *Diagnostic and statistical manual of mental disorders* (5th ed.). https://doi.org/10.1176/appi.books.9780890425596

Arntz, A. (2011). Imagery rescripting for personality disorders. *Cognitive and Behavioral Practice, 18*(4), 466–481. https://doi.org/10.1016/j.cbpra.2011.04.006

Arntz, A., & Giesen-Bloo, J. (1999). *Borederline personality disorder severity index, 4th version.* Department of Medical, Clinical and Experimental Psychology, University Maastricht.

Arntz, A., Jacob, G. A., Lee, C. W., Brand-de Wilde, O. M., Fassbinder, E., Harper, R. P., Lavender, A., Lockwood, G., Malogiannis, I. A., Ruths, F. A., Schweiger, U., Shaw, I. A., Zarbock, G., & Farrell, J. M. (2022). Effectiveness of predominantly group schema therapy and combined individual and group schema therapy for borderline personality disorder: A randomized clinical trial. *JAMA Psychiatry, 79*(4), 287–299. https://doi.org/10.1001/jamapsychiatry.2022.0010

Arntz, A., Klokman, J., & Sieswerda, S. (2005). An experimental test of the schema mode model of borderline personality disorder. *Journal of Behavior Therapy and Experimental Psychiatry, 36*(3), 226–239. https://doi.org/10.1016/j.jbtep.2005.05.005

Bach, B., & Bernstein, D. P. (2018). Schema therapy conceptualization of personality functioning and traits in *ICD-11* and *DSM-5*. *Current Opinion in Psychiatry, 32*(1), 38–49.

Bach, B., & Farrell, J. M. (2018). Schemas and modes in borderline personality disorder: The mistrustful, shameful, angry, impulsive, and unhappy child. *Psychiatry Research, 259*, 323–329. https://doi.org/10.1016/j.psychres.2017.10.039

Bach, B., Lee, C., Mortensen, E. L., & Simonsen, E. (2016). How do *DSM-5* personality traits align with schema therapy constructs? *Journal of Personality Disorders, 30*(4), 502–529. https://doi.org/10.1521/pedi_2015_29_212

Bach, B., & Lobbestael, J. (2018). Elucidating *DSM-5* and *ICD-11* diagnostic features of borderline personality disorder using schemas and modes. *Psychopathology, 51*(6), 400–407. https://doi.org/10.1159/000495845

Bach, B., Lockwood, G., & Young, J. E. (2018). A new look at the schema therapy model: Organization and role of early maladaptive schemas. *Cognitive Behaviour Therapy*, 47(4), 328–349. https://doi.org/10.1080/16506073.2017.1410566

Bach, B., Simonsen, E., Christoffersen, P., & Kriston, L. (2017). The Young Schema Questionnaire3-Short Form (YSQ-S3): Psychometric properties and association with personality disorders. *European Journal of Psychological Assessment*, 33(2), 134–143. https://doi.org/10.1027/1015-5759/a000272

Baljé, A., Greeven, A., van Giezen, A., Korrelboom, K., Arntz, A., & Spinhoven, P. (2016). Group schema therapy versus group cognitive behavioral therapy for social anxiety disorder with comorbid avoidant personality disorder: Study protocol for a randomized controlled trial. *Trials*, 17(1), 487. https://doi.org/10.1186/s13063-016-1605-9

Bamelis, L. L., Evers, S. M., Spinhoven, P., & Arntz, A. (2014). Results of a multicenter randomized controlled trial of the clinical effectiveness of schema therapy for personality disorders. *The American Journal of Psychiatry*, 171(3), 305–322. https://doi.org/10.1176/appi.ajp.2013.12040518

Bamelis, L. L. M., Renner, F., Heidkamp, D., & Arntz, A. (2011). Extended Schema Mode conceptualizations for specific personality disorders: An empirical study. *Journal of Personality Disorders*, 25(1), 41–58. https://doi.org/10.1521/pedi.2011.25.1.41

Behary, W. (2021). *Disarming the narcissist* (3rd ed.). New Harbinger Publications.

de Klerk, N., Abma, T., Bamelis, L., & Arntz, A. (2016). Schema therapy for personality disorders: A qualitative study of patients' and therapists' perspectives. *Behavioural and Cognitive Psychotherapy*, 45(1), 31–45.

Farrell, J. M., Reiss, N., & Shaw, I. A. (2014). *The schema therapy clinician's guide: A complete resource for building and delivering individual, group and integrated schema mode treatment programs*. Wiley. https://doi.org/10.1002/9781118510018

Farrell, J. M., & Shaw, I. A. (1994). Emotional awareness training: A prerequisite to effective cognitive-behavioral treatment of borderline personality disorder. *Cognitive and Behavioral Practice*, 1(1), 71–91. https://doi.org/10.1016/S1077-7229(05)80087-2

Farrell, J. M., & Shaw, I. A. (2012). *Group schema therapy for borderline personality disorder: A step-by-step treatment manual with patient workbook*. Wiley-Blackwell. https://doi.org/10.1002/9781119943167

Farrell, J. M., & Shaw, I. A. (2018). *Experiencing schema therapy from the inside out: A self-practice/self-reflection workbook for therapists*. Guilford Press.

Farrell, J. M., Shaw, I. A., & Webber, M. A. (2009). A schema-focused approach to group psychotherapy for outpatients with borderline personality disorder: A randomized controlled trial. *Journal of Behavior Therapy and Experimental Psychiatry*, 40(2), 317–328. https://doi.org/10.1016/j.jbtep.2009.01.002

Flanagan, C. M. (2010). The case for needs in psychotherapy. *Journal of Psychotherapy Integration*, 20(1), 1–36. https://doi.org/10.1037/a0018815

Giesen-Bloo, J., van Dyck, R., Spinhoven, P., van Tilburg, W., Dirksen, C., van Asselt, T., Kremers, I., Nadort, M., & Arntz, A. (2006). Outpatient psychotherapy for borderline personality disorder: Randomized trial of schema-focused therapy vs transference-focused psychotherapy. *Archives of General Psychiatry*, 63(6), 649–658. https://doi.org/10.1001/archpsyc.63.6.649

Huntjens, R. J. C., Rijkeboer, M. M., & Arntz, A. (2019). Schema therapy for dissociative identity disorder (DID): Rationale and study protocol. *European Journal of Psychotraumatology*, 10(1), 1571377. https://doi.org/10.1080/20008198.2019.1571377

Jacob, G. A., & Arntz, A. (2013). Schema therapy for personality disorders: A review. *International Journal of Cognitive Therapy*, 6(2), 171–185. https://doi.org/10.1521/ijct.2013.6.2.171

Jacobs, I., Lenz, L., Dörner, S., & Wegener, B. (2019). How do schema modes and mode factors align with defense styles and personality disorder symptoms? *Personality Disorders*, 10(5), 427–437. Advance online publication. https://doi.org/10.1037/per0000329

Keulen-de Vos, M., Bernstein, D. P., Clark, L. A., Vogel, V., Bogaerts, S., Slaats, M., & Arntz, A. (2017). Validation of the schema mode concept in personality disordered offenders. *Legal and Criminological Psychology, 22*(2), 420–441. https://doi.org/10.1111/lcrp.12109

Kunst, H., Lobbestael, J., Candel, I., & Batink, T. (2020). Early maladaptive schemas and their relation to personality disorders: A correlational examination in a clinical population. *Clinical Psychology & Psychotherapy, 27*(6), 837–846. https://doi.org/10.1002/cpp.2467

Lobbestael, J., van Vreeswijk, M., Spinhoven, P., Schouten, E., & Arntz, A. (2010). Reliability and validity of the short Schema Mode Inventory (SMI). *Behavioural and Cognitive Psychotherapy, 38*(4), 437–458. https://doi.org/10.1017/S1352465810000226

Lobbestael, J., van Vreeswijk, M. F., & Arntz, A. (2008). An empirical test of schema mode conceptualizations in personality disorders. *Behaviour Research and Therapy, 46*(7), 854–860. https://doi.org/10.1016/j.brat.2008.03.006

Nadort, M., Arntz, A., Smit, J. H., Giesen-Bloo, J., Eikelenboom, M., Spinhoven, P., van Asselt, T., Wensing, M., & van Dyck, R. (2009). Implementation of outpatient schema therapy for borderline personality disorder: Study design. *BMC Psychiatry, 9*, 64.

Renner, F., Arntz, A., Peeters, F., Lobbestael, J., & Huibers, M. (2016). Schema therapy for chronic depression: Results of a multiple single case series. *Journal of Behavior Therapy and Experimental Psychiatry, 51*(6), 66–73.

Riso, L. P., Froman, S. E., Raouf, M., Gable, P., Maddux, R. E., Turini-Santorelli, N., & Cherry, M. (2006). The long-term stability of early maladaptive schemas. *Cognitive Therapy and Research, 30*(4), 515–529. https://doi.org/10.1007/s10608-006-9015-z

Roediger, E., Stevens, B. A., & Brockman, R. (2018). *Contextual schema therapy*. New Harbinger Publications.

Sempértegui, G. A., Karreman, A., Arntz, A., & Bekker, M. H. (2013). Schema therapy for borderline personality disorder: A comprehensive review of its empirical foundations, effectiveness and implementation possibilities. *Clinical Psychology Review, 33*(3), 426–447. https://doi.org/10.1016/j.cpr.2012.11.006

Shaw, I. (2020). Spontaneity and play in schema therapy. In G. Heath & H. Startup (Eds.), *Creative methods in schema therapy* (pp. 167–178). Routledge.

Simpson, S. G., Skewes, S. A., van Vreeswijk, M., & Samson, R. (2015). Commentary: Short-term group schema therapy for mixed personality disorders: An introduction to the treatment protocol. *Frontiers in Psychology, 6*, Article 609. https://doi.org/10.3389/fpsyg.2015.00609

Spinhoven, P. Giesen-Bloo, J., van Dyck, R., Koolman, K., & Arntz, A. (2006). The therapeutic alliance in schema-focused therapy and transference-focused psychotherapy for borderline personality disorder. *Journal of Consulting and Clinical Psychology, 75*(1), 104–115.

van Asselt, A. D., Dirksen, C. D., Arntz, A., Giesen-Bloo, J. H., van Dyck, R., Spinhoven, P., van Tilburg, W., Kremers, I. P., Nadort, M., & Severens, J. L. (2008). Out-patient psychotherapy for borderline personality disorder: Cost-effectiveness of schema-focused therapy v. transference-focused psychotherapy. *The British Journal of Psychiatry, 192*(6), 450–457. https://doi.org/10.1192/bjp.bp.106.033597

van Vreeswijk, M., Nadort, M., & Broeresen, J. (Eds.). (2012). *The Wiley-Blackwell handbook of schema therapy: Theory, research, and practice*. John Wiley & Sons.

Videler, A. C., Rossi, G., Schoevaars, M., van der Feltz-Cornelis, C. M., van Alphen, S. P. J. (2014). Effects of schema group therapy in older outpatients: A proof of concept study. *International Psychogeriatrics, 26*(10), 1709–1717. https://doi.org/10.1017/S1041610214001264

World Health Organization. (2019). *International statistical classification of diseases and related health problems* (11th ed.). https://icd.who.int/

Younan, R., Farrell, J. M., & May, T. (2017). "Teaching me to parent myself": The feasibility of an in-patient group schema therapy programme for complex trauma. *Behavioural and Cognitive Psychotherapy, 46*(4), 1–16.

Young, J. E. (1990). *Cognitive therapy for personality disorders: A schema-focused approach.* Professional Resource Press.

Young, J. E. (2005). *Young Schema Questionnaire—Short Form 3 (YSQ-S3).* Cognitive Therapy Center.

Young, J. E., & Brown, G. (1990). *Young Schema Questionnaire.* Cognitive Therapy Center of New York.

Young, J. E., Klosko, J., & Weishaar, M. E. (2003). *Schema therapy: A practitioner's guide.* Guilford Press.

13

Pharmacotherapy for Personality Disorders

Lea K. Marin, Celia Foster, and Marianne Goodman

Personality disorders (PDs) are frequently encountered in outpatient and inpatient psychiatric settings, with estimates of up to 14% of the U.S. population carrying a PD diagnosis (Grant et al., 2004). PDs are associated with significant impairments in social and occupational functioning, as well as high utilization of health services (Powers & Oltmanns, 2012). Psychotherapy is often considered first-line treatment for PDs because there is limited evidence supporting the use of medications. Currently, no medications are approved by the U.S. Food and Drug Administration (FDA) for the treatment of any PD, and all medication use is off-label. The best utility for medications in individuals with PDs may be for the treatment of comorbid mood, anxiety, psychotic, or trauma-related psychiatric illnesses or for the treatment of symptom domains, rather than specific PD diagnoses. For example, current practice targets domains of impulsive aggression, affective instability, and cognitive disorganization that correlate with the growing understanding of the neurobiological basis of PDs.

Although the evidence is sometimes limited, with pharmacologic trials best studied in schizotypal PD (SPD), borderline PD (BPD), and antisocial PD (ASPD), this chapter reviews the research that does exist for the use of various medication classes for each PD.

---

https://doi.org/10.1037/0000310-014
Personality Disorders and Pathology: Integrating Clinical Assessment and Practice in the DSM-5 *and* ICD-11 *Era,* S. K. Huprich (Editor)
Copyright © 2022 by the American Psychological Association. All rights reserved.

CLUSTER A

Paranoid PD

Paranoid PD (PPD) has a prevalence between 1.21% and 4.4% in the general population and is often comorbid with other PDs, such as BPD, avoidant PD (AvPD), and narcissistic PD (NPD; Lee, 2017). It is characterized by suspiciousness, mistrust of others, and a belief that others' motives are malevolent (American Psychiatric Association, 2013). PPD causes significant disability and can be associated with aggressive behavior (Lee, 2017). Despite the impact that this disorder has on its patients, there is minimal research on pharmacologic management of PPD. The authors were able to identify only one retrospective case series examining the naturalistic course of 15 hospitalized patients with PPD over 6 weeks. Of the 10 patients who received medication, several received unnamed antidepressants, and the effects of their use were not delineated in the article. The four patients who received antipsychotics (flupentixol, promazine, and bromperidol) and presented to the 6-week follow-up appeared to have improvements in mean scores on Clinical Global Impression Scales (Birkeland, 2013). However, the small number of patients who received treatment, the use of older antipsychotics that are rarely used in the United States, and the retrospective nature of this study suggest that these conclusions are preliminary, and additional research is needed to evaluate the role of pharmacologic treatment in PPD. It would be helpful for future studies to investigate the use of more commonly used antipsychotics to target the symptom domain of cognitive disorganization with paranoia in PPD.

Schizoid PD

Schizoid PD (ScPD) is commonly comorbid with persistent depressive disorder, bipolar disorder, and anxiety disorders (Triebwasser et al., 2012). ScPD is characterized by reclusive behavior with detachment from social relationships and a restricted range of affect (American Psychiatric Association, 2013). Although ScPD can be devastating to patients and is associated with low levels of achievement and limited interpersonal relations (Cramer et al., 2006), the authors could identify no studies examining the role of medications in targeting this illness. This may be related to the fact that ScPD is rare, with an estimated prevalence of less than 1% (Esterberg et al., 2010) and that patients' inherent reclusiveness can limit their seeking mental health care (Tyrer et al., 2003). The research that does exist evaluates the impact of ScPD in the treatment of comorbid psychiatric illnesses. Mulder and colleagues (2006) evaluated 175 patients with major depressive disorder (MDD) treated prospectively with the antidepressants nortriptyline and fluoxetine. Although 101 patients (58%) achieved recovery and remained well, the presence of schizoid traits was associated with worse treatment outcomes. Thus, providers should be aware that the presence of comorbid ScPD traits might hinder pharmacologic treatment of other psychiatric disorders for which patients may be more likely to seek care.

Schizotypal PD

SPD is characterized by cognitive impairments, perceptual and psychotic disturbances, eccentric behavior, and discomfort in close relationships (American Psychiatric Association, 2013). Prevalence is estimated to be between 0.6% and 4.6% of the general population. SPD shares many features with schizophrenia, and both family and adoptive studies suggest a greater prevalence of SPD in relatives of individuals with schizophrenia than in the general population (Pulay et al., 2009). Studies have also found that conversion rates from SPD to schizophrenia are between 20% and 40% (Debbané et al., 2015; Raine, 2006).

As a schizophrenia spectrum disorder, research primarily supports the use of antipsychotics for the treatment of SPD. Early investigations evaluated thiothixene, an older antipsychotic less commonly used today, in two cohorts of patients with comorbid SPD and BPD. These studies found that thiothixene reduced symptoms of SPD and BPD, particularly illusions, ideas of reference, and paranoia (Goldberg et al., 1986; Serban & Siegel, 1984). Treatment with haloperidol, another antipsychotic, has also been shown to reduce symptoms of SPD, including hostility and psychotic symptoms (Hymowitz et al., 1986; Soloff et al., 1986, 1989, 1993). Studies have also investigated the use of the antipsychotics olanzapine and risperidone. Specifically, Keshavan and colleagues (2004) conducted a 26-week open-label study administering olanzapine in 11 participants with SPD. They found significant improvements in overall functioning as well as in symptoms of psychosis and depression. Koenigsberg and colleagues (2003) evaluated the effects of low-dose risperidone on 25 patients with SPD in a randomized, double-blind, placebo-controlled study. This study found a statistically significant improvement on the Positive and Negative Symptoms Scale among individuals treated with risperidone compared with those who received placebo (Koenigsberg et al., 2003). Although antipsychotics can be helpful for positive psychotic symptoms and even some negative symptoms, they have limited effects on cognition (Koychev et al., 2012; McClure et al., 2009).

Similar to schizophrenia, SPD can cause cognitive deficits. Investigations into pharmacologic management of cognitive symptoms have revealed some benefit from the attention-deficit/hyperactivity disorder medications D-amphetamine (Siegel et al., 1996) and guanfacine (McClure et al., 2007). For example, McClure and colleagues (2007) found improvement in cognitive processing with selective α2A-adrenergic-receptor-agonist guanfacine in a randomized, double-blind, placebo-controlled trial with 29 participants. Guanfacine resulted in improved cognitive processing in patients with SPD. Studies have also shown some improvement in cognition via treatment with dopamine agonists, dihydrexidine, and pergolide, medications more commonly used to treat Parkinson's disease (McClure et al., 2010; Rosell et al., 2015).

Overall, antipsychotics can be considered for the treatment of psychotic symptoms, and there is some support for the use of ADHD and Parkinson's medications for the treatment of cognitive symptoms in SPD.

CLUSTER B

Antisocial PD

ASPD has a prevalence of 2% to 3% in the general population and 50% to 80% of the prison population. ASPD is often comorbid with substance use disorders (SUDs) and anxiety disorders; ASPD is also associated with higher rates of unemployment, homelessness, impaired relationships, criminality, and premature mortality (Angstman & Rasmussen, 2011; Brazil et al., 2018; Levy et al., 2010; Volkert et al., 2018). This diagnosis is characterized by unlawfulness, deceitfulness, aggressiveness, and a disregard for the rights of others (American Psychiatric Association, 2013).

For the most part, there is insufficient evidence for psychopharmacologic treatment of ASPD, and in many cases, medications are mostly recommended to target comorbid conditions. Khalifa and colleagues conducted a Cochrane Database Systematic Review for pharmacologic interventions in ASPD in 2010, which was recently updated in September 2020. This meta-analysis evaluated the use of antiepileptic (phenytoin), antidepressant (desipramine and amitriptyline), and dopamine agonist (bromocriptine and amantadine) medications in 11 studies, which included 416 participants. Because the evidence supporting pharmacotherapy relied on unreplicated studies with methodological concerns as well as the use of older classes of medications, it was concluded that evidence is insufficient to draw any conclusions regarding the aforementioned pharmacologic treatments for ASPD (Khalifa et al., 2020).

Medications have also been evaluated for their efficacy in targeting specific symptom domains found in ASPD—specifically, mood stabilizers and antiepileptics for the treatment of impulsivity and aggression. Huband and colleagues (2010) conducted a Cochrane Systematic Review evaluating the roll of mood stabilizers and antiepileptics (valproic acid, carbamazepine, oxcarbazepine, and phenytoin) for aggression and impulsivity in 14 studies including 672 participants. Although there was some evidence to support the use of these medications, other studies in the review did not find any advantage in their utilization. Therefore, the authors concluded there was insufficient evidence to support the use of antiepileptics for aggression and impulsivity in ASPD.

In conclusion, more research is needed to inform medication management in ASPD, given that two large-scale Cochrane Reviews have found inconclusive evidence to strongly support medication for ASPD or symptoms of impulsivity and aggression. Future studies should focus on the neurobiological aspects of this illness and targeting associated symptom domains of impulsive aggression and affective instability.

Histrionic PD

Histrionic PD (HPD), characterized by a pattern of extreme emotionality and attention-seeking behavior, has a U.S. prevalence of approximately 2% and is more common in women (Grant et al., 2004). The limited research supporting psychopharmacologic interventions for HPD is often more than 30 years old and therefore focuses on older generations of psychiatric medications that are not used as frequently today. The studies that have been written, however, discuss some benefit with the use of the monoamine oxidase inhibitory antidepressant phenelzine for the treatment of "hysteroid dysphoria," described as hysterical characteristics in individuals with comorbid MDD (Kayser et al., 1985; Liebowitz et al., 1988, 1984). The applicability of these findings to HPD treatment should be met with caution. The dearth of literature on this disorder is consistent with Roger Blashfield et al.'s (2012) belief that HPD is a "dying disorder" because it can be perceived as a misogynistic diagnosis, aligns with outdated psychoanalytic principles, is not a unique syndrome, and is not consistent with the changing diagnostic framework supporting more empirical and neurobiological models of personality disorders.

Narcissistic PD

NPD has a prevalence of up to 6% in the general population and is often comorbid with other psychiatric disorders: SUDs, anxiety disorders, major depressive disorder (MDD), bipolar disorder, and other PDs (Caligor et al., 2015; Ronningstam, 2009). NPD can cause significant impairment due to its characteristic grandiosity, need for admiration, lack of empathy, and exploitation of relationships (American Psychiatric Association, 2013). Despite the impact of this disease, research is limited (and what is available is often in anecdotal reports and case series) to support pharmacotherapy for NPD in the absence of other comorbid conditions that may benefit from medication management (Roepke et al., 2008).

Borderline PD

BPD is a complex neuropsychiatric disorder characterized by a pervasive pattern of instability in emotional regulation, interpersonal relationships, self-image, and impulse control. Estimated to occur in 1% to 2% of the population, BPD is the most common PD in clinical settings, affecting 10% of psychiatric outpatients and 20% of inpatients. BPD is associated with significant resource utilization, functional impairment, morbidity, and mortality (American Psychiatric Association, 2013). Despite BPD's prevalence and impact, there is no definitive psychopharmacologic treatment, no FDA-approved medication, and the various clinical guidelines and systematic reviews that do exist offer differing opinions on the role for medication management.

There is a fair amount of research, including several randomized, double-blind, placebo-controlled trials with large numbers of participants evaluating the role of pharmacotherapy for BPD. Building on these studies, the American Psychiatric Association proposed guidelines in 2001 that recommended symptom-based pharmacotherapy via an algorithmic approach treating domains of affective dysregulation, behavioral dyscontrol, and perceptual disturbance. Although the goal of targeting neurobiological symptom domains was promising, the American Psychiatric Association's recommendations mistakenly supported the use of selective serotonin reuptake inhibitors (SSRIs) over mood stabilizers and atypical antipsychotic agents, which have received more support in subsequent trials. In 2009, the National Institute for Health and Clinical Excellence (NICE) reviewed 27 medication trials and released its own guidelines, which recommended against the use of any medication in BPD other than for the treatment of comorbid psychiatric illnesses (Levy et al., 2010). In 2010, the Cochrane Database released a systematic review of 28 trials evaluating the use of antipsychotics, mood stabilizers, antidepressants, and dietary supplements in 1,742 participants. The authors concluded that atypical antipsychotics, mood stabilizers, and omega-3-fatty-acids have more support in the treatment of BPD than antidepressants, which they recommend should only be used for comorbid conditions. The authors caution that more research is needed as these conclusions were often based on small trials of short duration and with mixed outcomes (Stoffers et al., 2010).

These conflicting guidelines, combined with the acute treatment need for severe BPD symptoms, have contributed to rampant polypharmacy for BPD (Marin et al., 2018). Bridler and colleagues (2015) found that 90% of patients with BPD are prescribed at least one psychiatric medication, 80% are prescribed two or more medications, and 54% are prescribed at least three medications concurrently. The most prescribed medications are antidepressants (70%), antipsychotics (69%), mood stabilizers/antiepileptics (32%), and benzodiazepine/hypnotics (30%).

Antidepressants, particularly SSRIs and selective norepinephrine (SNRIs), are some of the most widely used medicines in BPD, despite a lack of consistent evidence supporting their use. As mentioned earlier, both the 2010 Cochrane Database Systematic Review and the 2009 NICE guidelines recommend using antidepressants only for comorbid psychiatric conditions in individuals with BPD (Levy et al., 2010; Stoffers et al., 2010). Supporting this, one study by Jariani and colleagues (2010) compared the efficacy of sertraline to olanzapine in a sample of 120 BPD patients with opiate dependence on methadone maintenance therapy. The authors concluded that sertraline was better than olanzapine in treating depressive symptoms, whereas olanzapine was superior for treating BPD symptoms of interpersonal difficulties and anger. However, given that patients receiving methadone maintenance therapy constitute a minority of the BPD population, the results are not generalizable. Another open-label, 12-week, unblinded pilot study found that duloxetine might be helpful not only for depressive and anxious symptoms but also for impulsivity, anger, and affective instability (Bellino et al., 2010). Ultimately, because no randomized, placebo-controlled trials evaluating antidepressant use in BPD have been published in the years since the 2010 Cochrane Review and 2009 NICE guidelines, current treatment should continue to follow their guidance and only use antidepressants for comorbid conditions, rather than for the treatment of BPD symptoms.

Antipsychotics are prescribed nearly as frequently as antidepressants for BPD but carry a bit more support for their use. Olanzapine may be the most studied of the antipsychotics, and does appear to have good effect on affective instability, anger, and psychotic symptoms in BPD, although with some mixed results (Stoffers et al., 2010). Bogenschutz and Nurnberg (2004) found olanzapine to be superior to placebo for improvement on the Clinical Global Impressions Scale modified for BPD in 40 patients who participated in a randomized, double-blind, placebo-controlled trial (Bogenschutz & Nurnberg, 2004). Schulz and colleagues (2008) conducted a 12-week, randomized, double-blind, placebo-controlled trial with 314 patients and found no significant difference in response between placebo and olanzapine. Zanarini and colleagues (2011) conducted an open-label extension for 12 weeks after an initial 2011 study and Schulz's and colleagues (2008) initial 12-week study, evaluating the effects of olanzapine in 440 patients, and found a modest but significant decrease in mean BPD symptom severity scores on the Zanarini Rating Scale for BPD (Zanarini et al., 2012). Olanzapine's effect in BPD has also been compared with other antipsychotics that appear to have beneficial effects in BPD. In 2010, Shafti and Shahveisi conducted a parallel, randomized, double-blind trial comparing olanzapine to haloperidol over 8 weeks in 28 female inpatients with BPD. Both medications were similarly effective for anger, hostility, psychosis, anxiety, depression, and overall functioning, with no statistically significant differences between groups. In another comparison study, Bozzatello and colleagues (2017) compared olanzapine with asenapine in a 12-week, open-label, randomized controlled trial in 51 outpatients with BPD. Although the study had no placebo group, the medications appeared to have similar overall efficacy, with olanzapine being superior for dissociation and paranoid ideation and asenapine better for affective instability (Bozzatello et al., 2017). Other antipsychotics have also been studied in BPD. For instance, aripiprazole showed significant improvement compared with placebo in symptoms related to anger, aggressiveness, hostility, and paranoid ideation (Nickel et al., 2006). More recently, quetiapine was studied in a randomized, placebo-controlled trial evaluating the use of low-dose (150 mg) and moderate-dose (300 mg) quetiapine in 95 participants with BPD. The study found that 82% of participants in the low-dose group "responded" (defined as 50% reduction of BPD symptom severity on the Zanarini Rating Scale for BPD) to treatment, 74% in the moderate-dose group responded, and 48% in the placebo group responded. Individuals in the moderate-dose group were more likely to experience side effects, particularly sedation, and only 58% of that group completed the study (Black et al., 2014). Although antipsychotics, particularly olanzapine, appear to have benefit in BPD, larger scale trials of longer durations are needed to confirm their utility.

Mood stabilizers and antiepileptic drugs are also widely prescribed in BPD, and valproate appears to be the most promising choice in this medication class. Hollander and colleagues (2005) conducted a randomized, double-blind, placebo-controlled trial evaluating the effects of valproate in 54 participants with BPD; they found that the treatment group had significantly improved rates of impulsive aggression compared with the placebo group. Another notable double-blind, placebo-controlled trial was conducted by Frankenburg and Zanarini (2002). This 24-week study found that valproate significantly decreased interpersonal sensitivity, anger, and aggression in a cohort of 30 women with BPD and bipolar disorder (Frankenburg & Zanarini, 2002). It appears that valproate may be more effective when combined with omega-3-fatty-acids. Bellino and colleagues (2014) conducted a 12-week randomized trial in 43 BPD outpatients comparing valproate monotherapy to valproate combined with omega-3-fatty-acids. Combination therapy was better than monotherapy in the treatment of anger outbursts, impulse dyscontrol, and self-harm (Bellino et al., 2014). In 2018, the authors published a 24-week follow-up study in 34 of the original patients, concluding that there were long-lasting effects in the control of anger outbursts, even after omega-3-fatty-acids were discontinued (Bozzatello et al., 2018). Other mood stabilizers, including topiramate and lamotrigine, have also been studied. Topiramate appears to be of potential benefit for irritability, anger, and interpersonal sensitivity (Loew et al., 2006; Loew & Nickel, 2008; Nickel et al., 2004; Nickel & Loew, 2008). Lamotrigine was recently evaluated in a large, randomized, double-blind, placebo-controlled trial of 276 participants. The authors found no significant differences between treatment and placebo groups over a significant trial length of 12 months (Crawford et al., 2018). Although the negative results were found in the well-designed Crawford lamotrigine trial, mood stabilizers (particularly valproate) appear to have benefit in BPD. However, valproate and other mood stabilizers should be used with caution in women of child-bearing age—a core group seeking treatment for BPD—because of their known potential for teratogenic side effects.

In conclusion, although medications are frequently used in the management of BPD, the evidence supporting this practice is mixed, and first-line treatment should focus on the use of evidence-based psychotherapies (including dialectical behavioral therapy, mentalization-based therapy, and transference focused psychotherapy; Storebø et al., 2020). If medications are to be used, research supports the use of antipsychotics and mood stabilizers, particularly olanzapine and valproate; and antidepressants should be reserved for the treatment of comorbid diagnoses rather than for the treatment of BPD.

CLUSTER C

Dependent PD

Dependent PD (DPD) has a prevalence of less than 1% in the general population (Sansone & Sansone, 2011) and is characterized by submissiveness, an excessive need to be taken care of, and clingy behavior (American Psychiatric Association, 2013). Patients with DPD are likely to have comorbid MDD, AvPD, bipolar disorder, and separation anxiety disorder (Loranger, 1996; Mroczkowski et al., 2016). Limited research has been conducted on pharmacologic treatment of DPD. One study assessed 308 patients with MDD, 61 of whom had comorbid DPD, in a 24-week, double-blind treatment study with the SSRI antidepressants sertraline and citalopram. Results showed a significant reduction in the frequency of DPD diagnosis after antidepressant treatment, suggesting that SSRIs may have a role in the treatment patients with comorbid MDD and DPD (Ekselius & von Knorring, 1998).

Avoidant PD

AvPD is characterized by social inhibition, hypersensitivity to criticism, and feelings of inadequacy. AvPD has an estimated prevalence of 1.5% to 2.5% in the general population and is often comorbid with DPD, social anxiety disorder, MDD, and SUD (Friborg et al., 2013; Lampe & Malhi, 2018). There is minimal research on AvPD, and clinical recommendations largely support the treatment of comorbid social anxiety disorder with antidepressants—particularly SSRI and SNRIs antidepressants—and other antianxiety medications, including gabapentin (Herpertz et al., 2007; Ripoll et al., 2011). Additional research is needed to better understand the effects of medications on specific symptoms of AvPD.

Obsessive-Compulsive PD

Obsessive-compulsive PD (OCPD) is characterized by a need for perfectionism, preoccupation with details, desire for control, and inflexibility (American Psychiatric Association, 2013). Its prevalence is estimated at 2.1% to 7.9% of the U.S. population, and it is often comorbid with obsessive-compulsive disorder, MDD, anxiety disorders, and eating disorders (American Psychiatric Association, 2013). There is limited research for treatment with SSRIs and mood stabilizers. Most recently, a 2002 case study found a decrease in OCPD traits over 8 months with the mood stabilizer carbamazepine (Greve & Adams, 2002). Another earlier randomized controlled trial examined the antidepressants sertraline and citalopram in 308 patients with comorbid MDD, OCPD, and OCD. This study found a decrease in OCPD traits on the Structured Clinical Interview for *Diagnostic and Statistical Manual of Mental Disorders* (*DSM*) Disorders with both medications and in OCPD diagnosis with citalopram (Ekselius & von Knorring, 1998). Antidepressants can be considered in individuals with comorbid MDD an OCPD because they may improve OCPD symptoms in addition to treating MDD. Future studies could also investigate the role of mood stabilizers such as carbamazepine.

EVOLVING MODELS FOR PD CLASSIFICATION

The future of PD pharmacotherapy is evolving to mirror a growing understanding of the underlying neurobiology and associated symptoms of these disorders. Similarly, there has been a shift from traditional "cluster-based" classification of PDs to newly proposed empirically based dimensional models for PDs (Trull & Widiger, 2013).

One such model can be found in Section III of the *DSM-5*. The Alternative *DSM-5* Model for PDs (AMPD) characterizes PDs by impaired personality functioning and pathological personality traits. Impaired personality functioning includes disturbances in "self" ("identity" and "self-direction") as well as "interpersonal" ("empathy" and "intimacy") disturbances, whereas impaired personality traits include disturbances in "negative affectivity," "detachment," "antagonism," "disinhibition," and "psychoticism." The new model includes modified criteria for antisocial, avoidant, borderline, narcissistic, obsessive-compulsive, and schizotypal PDs, as well as a new diagnosis of "personality disorder—trait specified" (American Psychiatric Association, 2013; Zimmermann et al., 2019).

Another model for PD classification is planned to be incorporated into the *International Statistical Classification of Diseases and Related Health Problems* (11th ed.; *ICD-11*), which went into effect in January 2022. This model identifies impaired interpersonal functioning and its associated degree of severity (i.e., mild, moderate, severe). Additionally, the code can include a "borderline pattern" specifier or identification of the following personality trait domains: negative affectivity, detachment, disinhibition, dissociality, and anankastia (Bach & First, 2018; Zimmermann et al., 2019).

Finally, the Hierarchical Taxonomy of Psychopathology (HiTOP) system (Kotov et al., 2017) proposes an evidence-based framework to address limitations of current *DSM-5* and *ICD-10* terminology, including the frequent comorbidity and lack of differentiation between disorders, within-diagnosis heterogeneity, and the murky borders between pathology and variations of normality. Using structural modeling, HiTOP reconceptualizes psychopathologies as a set of dimensions that includes super spectra, spectra, subfactors, syndromes/disorders, components, and symptoms. The hierarchical structure of transdiagnostic dimensions lends itself to neurobiological study including genetic, animal, and neuroimaging investigations, some of which are currently underway.

Ultimately, the AMPD, *ICD-11*, and HiTOP models all provide novel empirical reconceptualization of PDs that may pave the way for future pharmacotherapeutic targets.

CONCLUSION

Despite frequent medication prescriptions for patients with PDs, there is not robust evidence to support this practice. Psychopharmacologic research is limited in PDs, and the majority of studies include patients with SPD, BPD, and ASPD. For SPD, antipsychotics can be used to target psychotic symptoms. Atypical antipsychotics (especially olanzapine) and mood stabilizers (especially valproate) have utility in targeting affective instability, impulsivity, anger and psychotic symptoms in BPD, while antidepressants should be used only for comorbid conditions. Medications are not currently recommended for the treatment of ASPD.

A growing body of research suggests that neurotransmitters and other biological factors contribute to the symptoms of these disorders. Researchers have found evidence for the brain networks involved in impulsivity and aggression, symptom clusters present in several PDs (Soloff et al., 2017). This may suggest that instead of researching medication effects on a specific PD, further studies should look at their effects on specific symptom domains, mirroring the evolving models for PD classification found in the *DSM-5* AMPD, *ICD-11*, and HiTOP systems. For example, affective dysregulation can be targeted with mood stabilizers and low-dose antipsychotics; cognitive and perceptual disturbances should be treated with antipsychotics; and impulsivity and behavioral dyscontrol can be managed with mood stabilizers (Ingenhoven et al., 2010; Ripoll, 2013; Ripoll et al., 2011). In conclusion, the high prevalence of PDs combined with their significant morbidity and mortality, as well as the limited access to psychotherapists trained in evidence-based modalities, makes psychopharmacologic treatment of PDs an attractive option. Unfortunately, other than supporting the treatment of comorbid psychiatric illnesses, the evidence base supporting the use of psychopharmacology is limited for most PDs. Clinicians therefore should actively involve the patient in decision-making around medications, and discussion with the patient should include reviewing the effectiveness of the drug, side effects, and relative safety.

REFERENCES

American Psychiatric Association. (2001). Practice guideline for the treatment of patients with borderline personality disorder. *The American Journal of Psychiatry, 158*(10, Suppl.), 1–52.

American Psychiatric Association. (2013). *Diagnostic and statistical manual of mental disorders* (5th ed.).

Angstman, K. B., & Rasmussen, N. H. (2011). Personality disorders: Review and clinical application in daily practice. *American Family Physician, 84*(11), 1253–1260.

Bach, B., & First, M. B. (2018). Application of the *ICD-11* classification of personality disorders. *BMC Psychiatry, 18*(1), 351. https://doi.org/10.1186/s12888-018-1908-3

Bellino, S., Bozzatello, P., Rocca, G., & Bogetto, F. (2014). Efficacy of omega-3 fatty acids in the treatment of borderline personality disorder: A study of the association with valproic acid. *Journal of Psychopharmacology, 28*(2), 125–132. https://doi.org/10.1177/0269881113510072

Bellino, S., Paradiso, E., Bozzatello, P., & Bogetto, F. (2010). Efficacy and tolerability of duloxetine in the treatment of patients with borderline personality disorder: A pilot study. *Journal of Psychopharmacology, 24*(3), 333–339. https://doi.org/10.1177/0269881108095715

Birkeland, S. F. (2013). Psychopharmacological treatment and course in paranoid personality disorder: A case series. *International Clinical Psychopharmacology, 28*(5), 283–285. https://doi.org/10.1097/YIC.0b013e328363f676

Black, D. W., Zanarini, M. C., Romine, A., Shaw, M., Allen, J., & Schulz, S. C. (2014). Comparison of low and moderate dosages of extended-release quetiapine in borderline personality disorder: A randomized, double-blind, placebo-controlled trial. *The American Journal of Psychiatry, 171*(11), 1174–1182. https://doi.org/10.1176/appi.ajp.2014.13101348

Blashfield, R. K., Reynolds, S. M., & Stennett, B. (2012). The death of histrionic personality disorder. In T. A. Widiger (Ed.), *The Oxford handbook of personality disorders* (pp. 603–627). Oxford University Press. https://doi.org/10.1093/oxfordhb/9780199735013.013.0028

Bogenschutz, M. P., & Nurnberg, H. G. (2004). Olanzapine versus placebo in the treatment of borderline personality disorder. *The Journal of Clinical Psychiatry, 65*(1), 104–109. https://doi.org/10.4088/JCP.v65n0118

Bozzatello, P., Rocca, P., & Bellino, S. (2018). Combination of omega-3 fatty acids and valproic acid in treatment of borderline personality disorder: A follow-up study. *Clinical Drug Investigation, 38*(4), 367–372. https://doi.org/10.1007/s40261-017-0617-x

Bozzatello, P., Rocca, P., Uscinska, M., & Bellino, S. (2017). Efficacy and tolerability of asenapine compared with olanzapine in borderline personality disorder: An open-label randomized controlled trial. *CNS Drugs, 31*(9), 809–819. https://doi.org/10.1007/s40263-017-0458-4

Brazil, I. A., van Dongen, J. D. M., Maes, J. H. R., Mars, R. B., & Baskin-Sommers, A. R. (2018). Classification and treatment of antisocial individuals: From behavior to biocognition. *Neuroscience and Biobehavioral Reviews, 91*, 259–277. https://doi.org/10.1016/j.neubiorev.2016.10.010

Bridler, R., Häberle, A., Müller, S. T., Cattapan, K., Grohmann, R., Toto, S., Kasper, S., & Greil, W. (2015). Psychopharmacological treatment of 2195 in-patients with borderline personality disorder: A comparison with other psychiatric disorders. *European Neuropsychopharmacology, 25*(6), 763–772. https://doi.org/10.1016/j.euroneuro.2015.03.017

Caligor, E., Levy, K. N., & Yeomans, F. E. (2015). Narcissistic personality disorder: Diagnostic and clinical challenges. *The American Journal of Psychiatry, 172*(5), 415–422. https://doi.org/10.1176/appi.ajp.2014.14060723

Cramer, V., Torgersen, S., & Kringlen, E. (2006). Personality disorders and quality of life. A population study. *Comprehensive Psychiatry, 47*(3), 178–184. https://doi.org/10.1016/j.comppsych.2005.06.002

Crawford, M. J., Sanatinia, R., Barrett, B., Cunningham, G., Dale, O., Ganguli, P., Lawrence-Smith, G., Leeson, V. C., Lemonsky, F., Lykomitrou-Matthews, G., Montgomery, A., Morriss, R., Munjiza, J., Paton, C., Skorodzien, I., Singh, V., Tan, W., Tyrer, P., & Reilly, J. G. (2018). Lamotrigine for people with borderline personality disorder: A RCT. *Health Technology Assessment, 22*(17), 1–68. https://doi.org/10.3310/hta22170

Debbané, M., Eliez, S., Badoud, D., Conus, P., Flückiger, R., & Schultze-Lutter, F. (2015). Developing psychosis and its risk states through the lens of schizotypy. *Schizophrenia Bulletin, 41*(Suppl. 2), S396–S407. https://doi.org/10.1093/schbul/sbu176

Ekselius, L., & von Knorring, L. (1998). Personality disorder comorbidity with major depression and response to treatment with sertraline or citalopram. *International Clinical Psychopharmacology, 13*(5), 205–212. https://doi.org/10.1097/00004850-199809000-00003

Esterberg, M. L., Goulding, S. M., & Walker, E. F. (2010). Cluster A personality disorders: Schizotypal, schizoid and paranoid personality disorders in childhood and adolescence. *Journal of Psychopathology and Behavioral Assessment, 32*(4), 515–528. https://doi.org/10.1007/s10862-010-9183-8

Frankenburg, F. R., & Zanarini, M. C. (2002). Divalproex sodium treatment of women with borderline personality disorder and bipolar II disorder: A double-blind placebo-controlled pilot study. *The Journal of Clinical Psychiatry, 63*(5), 442–446. https://doi.org/10.4088/JCP.v63n0511

Friborg, O., Martinussen, M., Kaiser, S., Overgård, K. T., & Rosenvinge, J. H. (2013). Comorbidity of personality disorders in anxiety disorders: A meta-analysis of 30 years of research. *Journal of Affective Disorders, 145*(2), 143–155. https://doi.org/10.1016/j.jad.2012.07.004

Goldberg, S. C., Schulz, S. C., Schulz, P. M., Resnick, R. J., Hamer, R. M., & Friedel, R. O. (1986). Borderline and schizotypal personality disorders treated with low-dose thiothixene vs placebo. *Archives of General Psychiatry, 43*(7), 680–686. https://doi.org/10.1001/archpsyc.1986.01800070070009

Grant, B. F., Hasin, D. S., Stinson, F. S., Dawson, D. A., Chou, S. P., Ruan, W. J., & Pickering, R. P. (2004). Prevalence, correlates, and disability of personality disorders in the United States: Results from the national epidemiologic survey on alcohol and related conditions. *The Journal of Clinical Psychiatry, 65*(7), 948–958. https://doi.org/10.4088/JCP.v65n0711

Greve, K. W., & Adams, D. (2002). Treatment of features of obsessive-compulsive personality disorder using carbamazepine. *Psychiatry and Clinical Neurosciences, 56*(2), 207–208. https://doi.org/10.1046/j.1440-1819.2002.00946.x

Herpertz, S. C., Zanarini, M., Schulz, C. S., Siever, L., Lieb, K., Möller, H. J., Herpertz, S. C., Zanarini, M., Schulz, C. S., Siever, L., Lieb, K., Möller, H.-J., the WFSBP Task Force on Personality Disorders, & the World Federation of Societies of Biological Psychiatry (WFSBP). (2007). World Federation of Societies of Biological Psychiatry (WFSBP) guidelines for biological treatment of personality disorders. *The World Journal of Biological Psychiatry, 8*(4), 212–244. https://doi.org/10.1080/15622970701685224

Hollander, E., Swann, A. C., Coccaro, E. F., Jiang, P., & Smith, T. B. (2005). Impact of trait impulsivity and state aggression on divalproex versus placebo response in borderline personality disorder. *The American Journal of Psychiatry, 162*(3), 621–624. https://doi.org/10.1176/appi.ajp.162.3.621

Huband, N., Ferriter, M., Nathan, R., & Jones, H. (2010). Antiepileptics for aggression and associated impulsivity. *Cochrane Database of Systematic Reviews, 2010*(2), CD003499. https://doi.org/10.1002/14651858.CD003499.pub3

Hymowitz, P., Frances, A., Jacobsberg, L. B., Sickles, M., & Hoyt, R. (1986). Neuroleptic treatment of schizotypal personality disorders. *Comprehensive Psychiatry, 27*(4), 267–271. https://doi.org/10.1016/0010-440X(86)90001-5

Ingenhoven, T., Lafay, P., Rinne, T., Passchier, J., & Duivenvoorden, H. (2010). Effectiveness of pharmacotherapy for severe personality disorders: Meta-analyses of randomized controlled trials. *The Journal of Clinical Psychiatry, 71*(1), 14–25. https://doi.org/10.4088/JCP.08r04526gre

Jariani, M., Saaki, M., Nazari, H., & Birjandi, M. (2010). The effect of olanzapine and sertraline on personality disorder in patients with methadone maintenance therapy. *Psychiatria Danubina, 22*(4), 544–547.

Kayser, A., Robinson, D. S., Nies, A., & Howard, D. (1985). Response to phenelzine among depressed patients with features of hysteroid dysphoria. *The American Journal of Psychiatry, 142*(4), 486–488. https://doi.org/10.1176/ajp.142.4.486

Keshavan, M., Shad, M., Soloff, P., & Schooler, N. (2004). Efficacy and tolerability of olanzapine in the treatment of schizotypal personality disorder. *Schizophrenia Research, 71*(1), 97–101. https://doi.org/10.1016/j.schres.2003.12.008

Khalifa, N. R., Gibbon, S., Völlm, B. A., Cheung, N. H., & McCarthy, L. (2020). Pharmacological interventions for antisocial personality disorder. *Cochrane Database of Systematic Reviews, 9*, CD007667. https://doi.org/10.1002/14651858.CD007667.pub3

Koenigsberg, H. W., Reynolds, D., Goodman, M., New, A. S., Mitropoulou, V., Trestman, R. L., Silverman, J., & Siever, L. J. (2003). Risperidone in the treatment of schizotypal personality disorder. *The Journal of Clinical Psychiatry, 64*(6), 628–634. https://doi.org/10.4088/JCP.v64n0602

Kotov, R., Krueger, R. F., Watson, D., Achenbach, T. M., Althoff, R. R., Bagby, R. M., Brown, T. A., Carpenter, W. T., Caspi, A., Clark, L. A., Eaton, N. R., Forbes, M. K., Forbush, K. T., Goldberg, D., Hasin, D., Hyman, S. E., Ivanova, M. Y., Lynam, D. R., Markon, K., . . . Zimmerman, M. (2017). The Hierarchical Taxonomy of Psychopathology (HiTOP): A dimensional alternative to traditional nosologies. *Journal of Abnormal Psychology, 126*(4), 454–477. https://doi.org/10.1037/abn0000258

Koychev, I., McMullen, K., Lees, J., Dadhiwala, R., Grayson, L., Perry, C., Schmechtig, A., Walters, J., Craig, K. J., Dawson, G. R., Dourish, C. T., Ettinger, U., Wilkinson, L., Williams, S., Deakin, J. F., & Barkus, E. (2012). A validation of cognitive biomarkers for the early identification of cognitive enhancing agents in schizotypy: A three-center double-blind placebo-controlled study. *European Neuropsychopharmacology, 22*(7), 469–481. https://doi.org/10.1016/j.euroneuro.2011.10.005

Lampe, L., & Malhi, G. S. (2018). Avoidant personality disorder: Current insights. *Psychology Research and Behavior Management, 11*, 55–66. https://doi.org/10.2147/PRBM.S121073

Lee, R. (2017). Mistrustful and misunderstood: A review of paranoid personality disorder. *Current Behavioral Neuroscience Reports, 4*(2), 151–165. https://doi.org/10.1007/s40473-017-0116-7

Levy, K. N., Yeomans, F. E., Denning, F., & Fertuck, E. A. (2010). UK national institute for clinical excellence guidelines for the treatment of borderline personality disorder. *Personality and Mental Health, 4*(1), 54–58. https://doi.org/10.1002/pmh.119

Liebowitz, M. R., Quitkin, F. M., Stewart, J. W., McGrath, P. J., Harrison, W., Rabkin, J., Tricamo, E., Markowitz, J. S., & Klein, D. F. (1984). Phenelzine v imipramine in atypical depression. A preliminary report. *Archives of General Psychiatry, 41*(7), 669–677. https://doi.org/10.1001/archpsyc.1984.01790180039005

Liebowitz, M. R., Quitkin, F. M., Stewart, J. W., McGrath, P. J., Harrison, W. M., Markowitz, J. S., Rabkin, J. G., Tricamo, E., Goetz, D. M., & Klein, D. F. (1988). Antidepressant specificity in atypical depression. *Archives of General Psychiatry, 45*(2), 129–137. https://doi.org/10.1001/archpsyc.1988.01800260037004

Loew, T. H., & Nickel, M. K. (2008). Topiramate treatment of women with borderline personality disorder, part II: An open 18-month follow-up. *Journal of Clinical Psychopharmacology, 28*(3), 355–357. https://doi.org/10.1097/JCP.0b013e318173a8fb

Loew, T. H., Nickel, M. K., Muehlbacher, M., Kaplan, P., Nickel, C., Kettler, C., Fartacek, R., Lahmann, C., Buschmann, W., Tritt, K., Bachler, E., Mitterlehner, F., Pedrosa Gil, F., Leiberich, P., Rother, W. K., & Egger, C. (2006). Topiramate treatment for women with borderline personality disorder: A double-blind, placebo-controlled study. *Journal of Clinical Psychopharmacology, 26*(1), 61–66. https://doi.org/10.1097/01.jcp.0000195113.61291.48

Loranger, A. W. (1996). Dependent personality disorder: Age, sex, and axis I comorbidity. *Journal of Nervous and Mental Disease, 184*(1), 17–21. https://doi.org/10.1097/00005053-199601000-00004

Marin, L. K., Kapil-Pair, K. N., Harris, R. E., & Goodman, M. (2018). Combination treatments in borderline personality disorder: Bridging the gap between clinical practice and empirical data. *Current Treatment Options in Psychiatry, 5*(1), 141–161. https://doi.org/10.1007/s40501-017-0124-y

McClure, M. M., Barch, D. M., Romero, M. J., Minzenberg, M. J., Triebwasser, J., Harvey, P. D., & Siever, L. J. (2007). The effects of guanfacine on context processing abnormalities in schizotypal personality disorder. *Biological Psychiatry, 61*(10), 1157–1160. https://doi.org/10.1016/j.biopsych.2006.06.034

McClure, M. M., Harvey, P. D., Goodman, M., Triebwasser, J., New, A., Koenigsberg, H. W., Sprung, L. J., Flory, J. D., & Siever, L. J. (2010). Pergolide treatment of cognitive deficits associated with schizotypal personality disorder: Continued evidence of the importance of the dopamine system in the schizophrenia spectrum. *Neuropsychopharmacology, 35*(6), 1356–1362. https://doi.org/10.1038/npp.2010.5

McClure, M. M., Koenigsberg, H. W., Reynolds, D., Goodman, M., New, A., Trestman, R., Silverman, J., Harvey, P. D., & Siever, L. J. (2009). The effects of risperidone on the cognitive performance of individuals with schizotypal personality disorder. *Journal of Clinical Psychopharmacology, 29*(4), 396–398. https://doi.org/10.1097/JCP.0b013e3181accfd9

Mroczkowski, M. M., Goes, F. S., Riddle, M. A., Grados, M. A., Bienvenu, O. J., Greenberg, B. D., Fyer, A. J., McCracken, J. T., Rauch, S. L., Murphy, D. L., Knowles, J. A., Piacentini, J., Cullen, B., Rasmussen, S. A., Pauls, D. L., Nestadt, G., & Samuels, J. (2016). Dependent personality, separation anxiety disorder and other anxiety disorders in OCD. *Personality and Mental Health*, *10*(1), 22–28. https://doi.org/10.1002/pmh.1321

Mulder, R. T., Joyce, P. R., Frampton, C. M., Luty, S. E., & Sullivan, P. F. (2006). Six months of treatment for depression: Outcome and predictors of the course of illness. *The American Journal of Psychiatry*, *163*(1), 95–100. https://doi.org/10.1176/appi.ajp.163.1.95

Nickel, M. K., & Loew, T. H. (2008). Treatment of aggression with topiramate in male borderline patients, Part II: 18-month follow-up. *European Psychiatry*, *23*(2), 115–117. https://doi.org/10.1016/j.eurpsy.2007.09.004

Nickel, M. K., Muehlbacher, M., Nickel, C., Kettler, C., Pedrosa Gil, F., Bachler, E., Buschmann, W., Rother, N., Fartacek, R., Egger, C., Anvar, J., Rother, W. K., Loew, T. H., & Kaplan, P. (2006). Aripiprazole in the treatment of patients with borderline personality disorder: A double-blind, placebo-controlled study. *The American Journal of Psychiatry*, *163*(5), 833–838. https://doi.org/10.1176/ajp.2006.163.5.833

Nickel, M. K., Nickel, C., Mitterlehner, F. O., Tritt, K., Lahmann, C., Leiberich, P. K., Rother, W. K., & Loew, T. H. (2004). Topiramate treatment of aggression in female borderline personality disorder patients: A double-blind, placebo-controlled study. *The Journal of Clinical Psychiatry*, *65*(11), 1515–1519. https://doi.org/10.4088/JCP.v65n1112

Powers, A. D., & Oltmanns, T. F. (2012). Personality disorders and physical health: A longitudinal examination of physical functioning, healthcare utilization, and health-related behaviors in middle-aged adults. *Journal of Personality Disorders*, *26*(4), 524–538. https://doi.org/10.1521/pedi.2012.26.4.524

Pulay, A. J., Stinson, F. S., Dawson, D. A., Goldstein, R. B., Chou, S. P., Huang, B., Saha, T. D., Smith, S. M., Pickering, R. P., Ruan, W. J., Hasin, D. S., & Grant, B. F. (2009). Prevalence, correlates, disability, and comorbidity of *DSM-IV* schizotypal personality disorder: Results from the Wave 2 national epidemiologic survey on alcohol and related conditions. *Primary Care Companion to the Journal of Clinical Psychiatry*, *11*(2), 53–67. https://doi.org/10.4088/PCC.08m00679

Raine, A. (2006). Schizotypal personality: Neurodevelopmental and psychosocial trajectories. *Annual Review of Clinical Psychology*, *2*(1), 291–326. https://doi.org/10.1146/annurev.clinpsy.2.022305.095318

Ripoll, L. H. (2013). Psychopharmacologic treatment of borderline personality disorder. *Dialogues in Clinical Neuroscience*, *15*(2), 213–224. https://doi.org/10.31887/DCNS.2013.15.2/lripoll

Ripoll, L. H., Triebwasser, J., & Siever, L. J. (2011). Evidence-based pharmacotherapy for personality disorders. *The International Journal of Neuropsychopharmacology*, *14*(9), 1257–1288. https://doi.org/10.1017/S1461145711000071

Roepke, S., Merkl, A., Dams, A., Ziegenhorn, A., Anghelescu, I. G., Heuser, I., & Lammers, C. H. (2008). Preliminary evidence of improvement of depressive symptoms but not impulsivity in Cluster B personality disorder patients treated with quetiapine: An open label trial. *Pharmacopsychiatry*, *41*(5), 176–181. https://doi.org/10.1055/s-2008-1076730

Ronningstam, E. (2009). Narcissistic personality disorder: Facing *DSM-V*. *Psychiatric Annals*, *39*(3), 111–121. https://doi.org/10.3928/00485713-20090301-09

Rosell, D. R., Zaluda, L. C., McClure, M. M., Perez-Rodriguez, M. M., Strike, K. S., Barch, D. M., Harvey, P. D., Girgis, R. R., Hazlett, E. A., Mailman, R. B., Abi-Dargham, A., Lieberman, J. A., & Siever, L. J. (2015). Effects of the D1 dopamine receptor agonist dihydrexidine (DAR-0100A) on working memory in schizotypal personality disorder. *Neuropsychopharmacology*, *40*(2), 446–453. https://doi.org/10.1038/npp.2014.192

Sansone, R. A., & Sansone, L. A. (2011). Personality disorders: A nation-based perspective on prevalence. *Innovations in Clinical Neuroscience*, *8*(4), 13–18.

Schulz, S. C., Zanarini, M. C., Bateman, A., Bohus, M., Detke, H. C., Trzaskoma, Q., Tanaka, Y., Lin, D., Deberdt, W., & Corya, S. (2008). Olanzapine for the treatment of borderline personality disorder: Variable dose 12-week randomised double-blind placebo-controlled study. *The British Journal of Psychiatry*, *193*(6), 485–492. https://doi.org/10.1192/bjp.bp.107.037903

Serban, G., & Siegel, S. (1984). Response of borderline and schizotypal patients to small doses of thiothixene and haloperidol. *The American Journal of Psychiatry*, *141*(11), 1455–1458. https://doi.org/10.1176/ajp.141.11.1455

Shafti, S. S., & Shahveisi, B. (2010). Olanzapine versus haloperidol in the management of borderline personality disorder: A randomized double-blind trial. *Journal of Clinical Psychopharmacology*, *30*(1), 44–47. https://doi.org/10.1097/JCP.0b013e3181c826ff

Siegel, B. V., Jr., Trestman, R. L., O'Flaithbheartaigh, S., Mitropoulou, V., Amin, F., Kirrane, R., Silverman, J., Schmeidler, J., Keefe, R. S., & Siever, L. J. (1996). D-amphetamine challenge effects on Wisconsin Card Sort Test. Performance in schizotypal personality disorder. *Schizophrenia Research*, *20*(1-2), 29–32. https://doi.org/10.1016/0920-9964(95)00002-X

Soloff, P. H., Abraham, K., Burgess, A., Ramaseshan, K., Chowdury, A., & Diwadkar, V. A. (2017). Impulsivity and aggression mediate regional brain responses in borderline personality disorder: An fMRI study. *Psychiatry Research: Neuroimaging*, *260*, 76–85. https://doi.org/10.1016/j.pscychresns.2016.12.009

Soloff, P. H., Cornelius, J., George, A., Nathan, S., Perel, J. M., & Ulrich, R. F. (1993). Efficacy of phenelzine and haloperidol in borderline personality disorder. *Archives of General Psychiatry*, *50*(5), 377–385. https://doi.org/10.1001/archpsyc.1993.01820170055007

Soloff, P. H., George, A., Nathan, R. S., Schulz, P. M., Ulrich, R. F., & Perel, J. M. (1986). Progress in pharmacotherapy of borderline disorders. A double-blind study of amitriptyline, haloperidol, and placebo. *Archives of General Psychiatry*, *43*(7), 691–697. https://doi.org/10.1001/archpsyc.1986.01800070081010

Soloff, P. H., George, A., Nathan, S., Schulz, P. M., Cornelius, J. R., Herring, J., & Perel, J. M. (1989). Amitriptyline versus haloperidol in borderlines: Final outcomes and predictors of response. *Journal of Clinical Psychopharmacology*, *9*(4), 238–246. https://doi.org/10.1097/00004714-198908000-00002

Stoffers, J., Völlm, B. A., Rücker, G., Timmer, A., Huband, N., & Lieb, K. (2010). Pharmacological interventions for borderline personality disorder. *Cochrane Database of Systematic Reviews*, *6*, CD005653. https://doi.org/10.1002/14651858.CD005653.pub2

Storebø, O. J., Stoffers-Winterling, J. M., Völlm, B. A., Kongerslev, M. T., Mattivi, J. T., Jørgensen, M. S., Faltinsen, E., Todorovac, A., Sales, C. P., Callesen, H. E., Lieb, K., & Simonsen, E. (2020). Psychological therapies for people with borderline personality disorder. *Cochrane Database of Systematic Reviews*, *5*(5), CD012955. https://doi.org/10.1002/14651858.CD012955.pub2

Triebwasser, J., Chemerinski, E., Roussos, P., & Siever, L. J. (2012). Schizoid personality disorder. *Journal of Personality Disorders*, *26*(6), 919–926. https://doi.org/10.1521/pedi.2012.26.6.919

Trull, T. J., & Widiger, T. A. (2013). Dimensional models of personality: The five-factor model and the *DSM-5*. *Dialogues in Clinical Neuroscience*, *15*(2), 135–146. https://doi.org/10.31887/DCNS.2013.15.2/ttrull

Tyrer, P., Mitchard, S., Methuen, C., & Ranger, M. (2003). Treatment rejecting and treatment seeking personality disorders: Type R and Type S. *Journal of Personality Disorders*, *17*(3), 263–268. https://doi.org/10.1521/pedi.17.3.263.22152

Volkert, J., Gablonski, T. C., & Rabung, S. (2018). Prevalence of personality disorders in the general adult population in Western countries: Systematic review and meta-analysis. *The British Journal of Psychiatry, 213*(6), 709–715. https://doi.org/10.1192/bjp.2018.202

Zanarini, M. C., Schulz, S. C., Detke, H., Zhao, F., Lin, D., Pritchard, M., Deberdt, W., Fitzmaurice, G., & Corya, S. (2012). Open-label treatment with olanzapine for patients with borderline personality disorder. *Journal of Clinical Psychopharmacology, 32*(3), 398–402. https://doi.org/10.1097/JCP.0b013e3182524293

Zanarini, M. C., Schulz, S. C., Detke, H. C., Tanaka, Y., Zhao, F., Lin, D., Deberdt, W., Kryzhanovskaya, L., & Corya, S. (2011). A dose comparison of olanzapine for the treatment of borderline personality disorder: A 12-week randomized, double-blind, placebo-controlled study. *The Journal of Clinical Psychiatry, 72*(10), 1353–1362. https://doi.org/10.4088/JCP.08m04138yel

Zimmermann, J., Kerber, A., Rek, K., Hopwood, C. J., & Krueger, R. F. (2019). A brief but comprehensive review of research on the Alternative *DSM-5* Model for Personality Disorders. *Current Psychiatry Reports, 21*(9), 92. https://doi.org/10.1007/s11920-019-1079-z

14

Neuroscience and Personality Disorders

Sabine C. Herpertz and Katja Bertsch

The past decade has brought forward tremendous changes in the conceptualization and understanding of personality disorders (PDs) with new dimensional concepts in the *Diagnostic and Statistical Manual of Mental Disorders* (5th ed.; *DSM-5*; American Psychiatric Association, 2013) Alternative *DSM-5* Model of Personality Disorders (AMPD) and the *International Statistical Classification of Diseases and Related Health Problems* (11th ed.; *ICD-11*; World Health Organization, 2019, 2022) section on PDs. These dimensional approaches are consistent with neurobiological findings that neither support categorical entities nor provide specific biological landmarks for particular disorders, but rather reflect complex processes that support key capacities that we need to function and to integrate and adapt to new information about ourselves and our social surrounding.

Dimensional approaches also allow the integration of different levels of information—ranging from genetics and brain function and structure to behavior and self-reports—into a more detailed and richer picture (see the National Institute of Mental Health Research Domain Criteria; Insel et al., 2010), which may allow us to better capture individual differences and targeted mechanistic treatments. Nevertheless, almost all of the available results from neuroscientific studies on personality and PDs are based on the "old" categorical thinking. Most of these studies included one specific PD and compared patients fulfilling the diagnostic criteria of this disorder with a healthy control group, or at most one other patient group, with regard to brain structure or activity patterns (or both), in the whole brain or certain predefined brain areas at rest

https://doi.org/10.1037/0000310-015
Personality Disorders and Pathology: Integrating Clinical Assessment and Practice in the DSM-5 *and* ICD-11 *Era*, S. K. Huprich (Editor)
Copyright © 2022 by the American Psychological Association. All rights reserved.

or while performing specific tasks. In the latter case, these tasks most often involve a capacity that has been supposed to be of particular relevance for the studied patient group, which is why these studies provide important information on neural correlates of central facets of PDs and possible neural mechanisms. The shortcomings of such an approach are apparent because the majority of individuals meeting the criteria of one PD also fulfill criteria of a second, and there is vast comorbidity with other mental disorders. Furthermore, the specificity of alterations for a certain disorder reported in such studies remain unclear as to the question of whether they should be regarded as biological vulnerability factors or consequences of the disorder. Taking these limits into account, we recently tried to apply existing neuroscientific findings to the new concepts of PDs (Herpertz et al., 2018).

The current chapter includes an updated and extended version of this review. Following *DSM-5*-AMPD and *ICD-11*, we first describe how central facets of self and interpersonal functioning are represented in the brain and then present the most recent neuroscientific findings from studies on PDs for both domains and their relation to emotional, cognitive, and behavioral manifestations of personality dysfunction. We discuss how neurobiological alterations or impairments in these domains correspond to those underlying facets of self- and other-processing. It should be noted that most of the available publications focus on the categories borderline (BPD) and antisocial (ASPD) PDs or the psychopathic subtype of ASPD, whereas little is known about narcissistic (NPD) and other specific PDs.

Most of the presented findings were discovered in magnetic resonance imaging (MRI) studies. This noninvasive method provides information on alterations in brain structure, such as in volume, gyrification, or cortical surface and in brain activation and connectivity at rest (resting state [rs]MRI) or in response to certain stimuli or instructions (functional [f]MRI). In addition, results from electroencephalographic (EEG) studies provide details on the timing of different processes. Other methods, such as positron emotion tomography or magnetic encephalography, have played only a minor role in this domain of research and are included where available. It is critical to note that neuroscientific results always represent an average across a certain population of participants or the comparison of averages between two or more participant groups. Furthermore, the (low) reproducibility of neuroscientific results has earned some critical attention and needs to be considered when interpreting results from single studies with limited and selected samples.

Consistent with Criterion A of the *DSM-5*-AMPD and the *ICD-11*, we differentiate between processes related to self and interpersonal functioning despite significant overlaps in involved brain regions (Beer & Ochsner, 2006). These overlaps are not surprising taking into account the plasticity of brain mechanisms and the high social dependence of human nature. Early interpersonal interactions, such as those between children and their caregivers, influence the development of self-states (Fonagy et al., 2007) and other people's feedback affects self-referential learning (e.g., Müller-Pinzler et al., 2019), while, vice versa, interpersonal functioning is associated with our awareness of and ability to regulate our emotions, thoughts, and behaviors (Thompson et al., 2019).

The most common brain areas of self- and other-referential processing include regions in the frontal lobes, particularly the orbitofrontal cortex (OFC), medial prefrontal cortex (mPFC), anterior cingulate cortex (ACC), the precuneus/posterior cingulate cortex (PCC), regions in the temporal lobes, both cortical parts and subcortical parts including the amygdala, as well as somatosensory cortices (Beer & Ochsner, 2006). As part of the frontolimbic and the frontoparietal networks, the frontal lobes orchestrate executive control of cognitive, emotional, and social processes and behaviors influenced by motivational biases (Amodio & Frith, 2006), whereas the temporal lobes assess the (emotional) salience of stimuli (Phan et al., 2003).

NEUROSCIENCE AND SELF-FUNCTIONING

Self-functioning spans from identity to self-direction or self-regulation. It includes the stability and coherence of one's sense of identity, the ability to maintain a positive and stable sense of self-worth, self-awareness, and the accuracy of one's view of one's characteristics, strengths, and limitations, including the capability to reflect on and mentalize one's own motives and emotions, as well as the capacity for self-direction including planning, choosing, and implementing appropriate goals.

Neurobiological studies have mainly addressed aspects of self-awareness, self-referential processing, and self-control, which includes the regulation of emotions and behaviors. *Self-awareness*, starting at the very basic level of sensing signals from one's body and their integration into higher order attentional, emotional, and cognitive processes, has been regarded as an essential part of the minimal self. It involves a cascade of brain regions from the brainstem and thalamus up to cortical regions including the anterior insula and dorsal ACC, where the integration of signals from the own body with those from the external world and motivational and emotional states takes place. Furthermore, *self-referential processing* plays a crucial role in planning, decision making, and behavioral control, as well as self-reflection and metacognitive processes, and is supported by cortical midline structures, such as the mPFC and the PCC. These regions are part of the default mode network (DMN), which subsumes brain regions that show sustained functional activity during rest and relative deactivation in tasks demanding attention directed to the external world. Together with cortical reappraisal regions that modify initial emotional responses of the amygdala and ventral striatum, these cortical midline structures are also neural underpinnings of *self-control*, the cognitive ability to regulate thoughts, emotions, and behaviors against temptations and impulses. This chapter focuses on cognitive control of emotions and behavioral impulses, rather than on automatic, implicit emotion reactivity and delay discounting in line with the conceptualization of self-functioning in the *DSM-5*-AMPD and *ICD-11*.

Interestingly, results of some recent studies allow the drawing of associations between alterations in these processes and behavioral manifestations, such as suicidal or aggressive acts, or between the plasticity of these processes and the success of psychotherapy in improving PD symptomatology.

Impairments in Self-Awareness

Being aware of oneself requires a cascade of processes that allow the sensing of signals from the own body, their interpretation with regard to motivational and emotional experiences, and their integration (Khalsa et al., 2018). Because many of these processes take place unconsciously or at the border of awareness, the ability to become aware of them requires attentional and cognitive processes (Khalsa et al., 2018). The processing of bodily signals takes place at a subcortical level, including regions of the brainstem and the thalamus, but their integration into higher order cognitive, attentional, motivational, and emotional processes is located in the anterior insula and dorsal ACC (Vaitl, 1996). Deficits in the processing of bodily feelings or signals (Müller et al., 2015; Schmitz et al., 2020) and the awareness of one's body ownership (Kleindienst et al., 2014, 2020; Löffler et al., 2020) have been reported in patients with BPD. These deficits have been related to emotional numbness, dissociation, and emotion dysregulation as well as early-life maltreatment (Kleindienst et al., 2020; Müller et al., 2015). Reduced self-awareness has therefore been recently discussed as a possible mediator in the interplay between early adversity and emotion dysregulation as key feature of BPD (Löffler et al., 2018). According to this idea, early maltreatment may hinder a child's learning to be aware of, integrate, and update bodily signals, which may eventually lose their predictive value. The emotional states and well-being of patients with BPD consistently rely heavily on external, situational cues, leading to a high level of instability and feelings of a lack of control.

Heartbeat-evoked potentials in the EEG are used as a marker for the cortical representation of cardiac signals (Schandry & Montoya, 1996). Their generators are located in the anterior insula and dorsal anterior cingulate cortex (Pollatos et al., 2005)—and thus, in regions important for the integration and awareness of bodily signals (Critchley et al., 2004). Two independent studies have reported reduced resting-state heartbeat-evoked potentials in patients with BPD compared with healthy volunteers (Müller et al., 2015; Schmitz et al., 2020), in line with the reduced self-reported body awareness (Schmitz et al., 2021). Interestingly, no significant difference in the amplitude of heartbeat-evoked potentials could be found between patients with a former diagnosis of BPD and healthy volunteers (Müller et al., 2015), which may suggest plasticity in self-awareness related to symptom amelioration. Furthermore, patients with BPD showed decreased activation in the dorsal mPFC compared with healthy volunteers during mindful introspection of emotions and bodily feelings versus cognitive self-reflection (Scherpiet et al., 2015). In line with the aforementioned elevated external focus, earlier reports of problems in self–other differentiation, and a tendency toward hypermentalization (i.e., to overattribute intentions and emotions about the self and others in a complex and abstract way), patients with BPD were found to show elevated activation in regions of the mentalization network (discussed subsequently), such as the mPFC and, at the same time, poorer behavioral performance in a self–other representation task. Few studies have experimentally induced dissociation, which may be regarded as a state of minimal self-awareness. Winter and colleagues (2015) found decreased neural activity in fusiform gyrus and parietal cortices and increased activation in the dorsolateral and inferior frontal gyri during an emotional Stroop task in patients who underwent dissociation induction. In another study, Krause-Utz et al. (2018) reported reduced amygdala and lingual gyri, cuneus, and PCC activation when performing an emotional working memory task after dissociation induction. These results may suggest influences of different states of self-awareness on brain regions involved in the processing of emotions. Although increasing self-awareness is one of the major goals of dialectic behavioral therapy for BPD (Linehan, 1995), associated changes in brain mechanisms remain an open question. According to a systematic review, the most consistent longitudinal effect of mindfulness-based interventions was increased insular cortex activity following the interventions suggesting modulations in a core brain region for self-awareness (Young et al., 2018).

Impairments in Self-Referential Processing

Self-referential processing concerns the processing of information that is experienced as strongly related to one's own person and is common to the distinct concepts of self in different domains (Northoff et al., 2006). An increased self-focus, often persistent, ruminative, and self-critical in nature, is found in many psychiatric disorders, including PDs. The processing of self-referential information has been associated with activations in and connectivity within the DMN (Yoon et al., 2019). Yet only a few neuroscientific studies have tried to capture alterations in neural correlates of self-referential processing in individuals with PDs.

Extensive self-referential processing is one of the core symptoms of obsessive-compulsive PD (OCPD). Preliminary results suggest increased resting-state functional connectivity within the DMN and particularly the precuneus in OCPD patients (Coutinho et al., 2016). The precuneus is a posterior node of the DMN, which is known for its involvement in the retrieval manipulation of past event and careful planning. In a recent study, patients with OCPD showed increased spontaneous neural activity in the precuneus compared with healthy control participants, and activity in this region was positively related to OCPD symptom severity (Lei et al., 2020). In OCPD, an elevated and rigid self-focus is combined with excessive self-control and high moral norms, whereas careless and irresponsible behavior and high levels of egocentricity and lack of empathy are characteristic of individuals with ASPD, particularly those with high psychopathic traits. Prisoners with high psychopathic traits failed to deactivate the posterior medial cortical region of the DMN in an attention-demanding task (Freeman et al., 2015). The same regions are also involved in a wide range of other cognitive processes, including the representation of others' mental state; thus, this result is of particular interest. In another study, midline brain activation of psychopathic prisoners was not correlated with psychopathy Factor 1 (egocentricity and lack of empathy) while judging personality traits about themselves versus familiar others (Deming et al., 2018). However, Factor 2 traits (impulsivity and irresponsibility) were associated with reduced activity to self-judgments in the bilateral PCC and right temporoparietal junction, which may suggest tight relations between altered self-referential processing and interpersonal dysfunctions found in individuals with high psychopathic traits. Furthermore, rumination—repetitive, passive, unconstructive thinking about negative emotions and problems—is known to intensify negative affect and reduce problem-solving ability (Nolen-Hoeksema et al., 2008). In patients with BPD, studies have found increased anger rumination, in which individuals focus on anger and previous provocations (Peters et al., 2017). Anger rumination has been shown to increase interpersonal dysfunctions, such as aggression in BPD. First preliminary results suggest that individuals with BPD show increased activation in the dorsomedial prefrontal cortex as well as in the nucleus accumbens, a part of the brain's reward network, during provocation-focused rumination (Peters et al., 2018), which may suggest a rewarding, self-affirmative component of excessive self-referential processing of anger-related situations in BPD. Yet studies investigating neural mechanisms of disturbed self–other differentiation as seen in individual with severe PDs, such as BPD, are missing.

Impairments in Self-Control

Self-control subsumes different cognitive processes that support an individual's ability to pursue goal-directed behavior—most importantly, inhibitory control and emotion regulation. Whereas inhibitory or behavior control implies the inhibition of fast, premature, uncontrolled behavioral responses (Insel et al., 2010), emotion regulation or emotion control is defined as the ability to down-regulate negative emotions or suppress emotional responses that may interfere with goal-related behaviors (McRae & Gross, 2020). Cognitive self-control is mediated by a broad frontal–parietal–insular network of brain regions implicated in monitoring, selecting, modulating, and evaluating behavioral and emotional responses—namely, the dorsomedial prefrontal cortex/dorsal ACC/presupplementary motor area, bilateral anterior insula reaching into the inferior frontal gyrus and ventrolateral prefrontal cortex, the dorsolateral prefrontal cortex, and the inferior parietal lobules (Langner et al., 2018).

Deficits in cognitive self-control are prominent characteristics of individuals with ASPD and BPD. Using tasks that require the inhibition of behavioral responses to irrelevant (emotional) distractors, individuals with BPD showed increased amygdala activation as a neural bias of negative affect interference with cognitive processes, which fits with their slower behavioral responses (Krause-Utz et al., 2014). Furthermore, increased functional coupling of dorsal ACC with PCC, insula, and frontoparietal regions during emotion distraction may indicate stronger attention for task-irrelevant emotional information in individuals with BPD. Such interference of negative affect with cognitive processes in BPD may be associated with hyperactivity in the superior parietal/precuneus during attention-driven tasks or hypoactivity of the hippocampus in stimulus-driven tasks (Soloff et al., 2015).

Difficulties in overriding fast emotional action tendencies, which is needed when instructed to avoid happy and approach angry faces instead of approaching happy and avoiding angry faces, have been found to be associated with reduced activations in the ventrolateral (vlPFC) and dorsolateral prefrontal cortex (dlPFC) and a reduced lateral prefrontal–amygdala connectivity in individuals with BPD (Bertsch et al., 2019; Bertsch, Roelofs, et al., 2018) and prisoners with high psychopathy traits (Volman et al., 2016); this was related to elevated anger and aggression (Bertsch et al., 2019). Similarly, reduced dlPFC activity in response to emotional stimuli has been reported across studies and, together with elevated amygdala activity, may reflect deficient emotion regulation in BPD (Schulze et al., 2016). In fact, several studies have found altered prefrontal activations in patients with BPD during explicit emotion regulation (van Zutphen et al., 2018), as well as weaker posttask increase in resting state connectivity between the amygdala and the medial, dorsolateral, and ventrolateral prefrontal cortex, and thus regions implicated in effortful emotion regulation (Baczkowski et al., 2017). Interestingly, findings from a study that included not only individuals with BPD but also a sample of individuals with Cluster C PDs support a dimensional rather than dichotomous differentiation with regard to altered neural correlates of emotion regulation (van Zutphen et al., 2018). In this study, healthy controls showed greater activity in the dorsal ACC, dlPFC, middle temporal gyrus, and bilateral inferior parietal lobule than individuals with PDs.

These functional neuroimaging results are supplemented by data from structural MRI studies that, across the studies, demonstrate an association between impulsivity (i.e., reduced inhibitory control) and reduced gray-matter volume in frontal brain structures in BPD (Davies et al., 2020). Reduced gray-matter volume in insular cortex and inferior frontal gyrus were also reported in self-injuring adolescents (Beauchaine et al., 2019), and this was negatively related to self-reported emotion- and self-regulation in line with dimensional approaches. Finally, lower white-matter integrity was found in the cingulum, corpus callosum, and inferior and superior longitudinal fasciculus in individuals with BPD compared with healthy participants, indicating that a large-scale emotional brain network might be affected in this disorder (Vandekerckhove et al., 2020), a finding consistent with previously reported associations between reduced white-matter integrity in the cingulum and fornix and anger and affective instability in individuals with BPD (Whalley et al., 2015).

In ASPD, deficits in impulse control were related to reduced cortical thickness and increased surface area in the frontal and temporal lobes as well as in the insula (Jiang et al., 2016). In addition, reduced white-matter integrity of the frontal-parietal control network and the frontal-temporal network were found in ASPD (Jiang et al., 2017; Wolf et al., 2015). However, prefrontal volumes and intraprefrontal connectivity were positively related to impulsive and antisocial traits in prisoners with high psychopathy traits (Korponay et al., 2017).

There is also some evidence for structural alterations of cognitive control networks in individuals with NPD. Although one study found reduced prefrontal white-matter integrity in individuals with NPD, another reported structural abnormalities in frontoparalimbic brain regions. Consistently, self-reported narcissism correlated negatively with cortical thickness and volume in the right dlPFC, cortical volume in the right postcentral gyrus and medial prefrontal cortex, and cortical thickness in the right inferior frontal cortex in a large population-based sample (Mao et al., 2016).

Several studies have shown effects of psychotherapy on neural activation and connectivity of regions subserving self-control in individuals with BPD (Niedtfeld et al., 2017; Schmitt et al., 2016; for a review, see Marceau et al., 2018). Furthermore, hypoactivity in prefrontal and cingulate regions predicted treatment response (for a review, see Marceau et al., 2018). Using machine learning, Schmitgen et al. (2019) analyzed predictors for response to an inpatient dialectical behavior therapy using demographic and clinical as well as functional and structural MRI pretreatment data of individuals with BPD. Amygdala and parahippocampus activation during a cognitive reappraisal task along with severity measures of BPD psychopathology and gray-matter volume of the amygdala provided the best predictive power with neuronal hyper-reactivities in nonresponders.

NEUROSCIENCE AND INTERPERSONAL FUNCTIONING

Interpersonal functioning captures an individual's capacity to form and maintain relationships in various contexts, such as within a romantic relationship; between parent and child; in the family; and with friends, colleagues, schoolmates, or peers. In *DSM-5*-AMPD and *ICD-11* interpersonal functioning contains the components empathy and intimacy. High interpersonal functioning is seen as being interested in interpersonal engagement and having the ability to understand and appreciate other people's perspectives, to develop and maintain close and mutually satisfying relationships, and to manage conflict in relationships. Deficits in the capacity to form and maintain relationships in an empathic, cooperative way are common in individuals with BPD and ASPD, particularly in the psychopathic subtype, and NPD. Apparently, the nature of interpersonal dysfunctioning among these disorders is rather heterogenous. Recent progress in social neuroscience has contributed to understanding the differential brain mechanisms mediating specific patterns of interpersonal dysfunctioning and shed light on emotional, cognitive, and motivational facets of empathy.

On a neural level, interpersonal functioning draws on multiple interacting brain networks that implement different combinations of psychological component processes (Hooker, 2015). Previous literature has factorized interpersonal processes in a wide range of components, from broad networks for identification, interpretation, and reaction (Hermans et al., 2019) to highly specific processes separating multiple domains, including affiliation, agent identification, emotion processing, empathy, individual's information store, social hierarchy mapping, social policing, ingroup–outgroup categorization, for example (Happé & Frith, 2014). Up to now, studies on interpersonal functioning in PDs have been widely restricted to some fundamental impairments related to *facial emotion recognition*, *empathy*, and *theory of mind* (ToM), and there are some additional studies dedicated to aspects associated with the capacity to *develop and maintain intimacy in relationships*. Interestingly, empathetic processing recruits the same brain regions that are involved in the processing of own emotional or painful experiences, such as amygdala, anterior insula, dorsal ACC, and somatosensory cortex.

The recognition of interpersonal cues, particularly *facial emotion recognition*, is often mentioned as a primary fundamental process and prerequisite for interpersonal functioning. As such, Capozzi and Ristic (2018) deemed it a key mechanism for dynamic interplay between perceptual, interpretive, and evaluative processes. The capacity to adequately recognize facial emotions is based on an intact interplay among the amygdala, the posterior superior temporal sulcus, the fusiform face area, and lateral occipital areas. At a higher level, interpersonal functioning involves the sharing of other people's emotions, or *empathy*, as well as the understanding of other's mental states including beliefs, thoughts, and emotions, also known as ToM or mentalizing. Most recently, a meta-analysis of neuroimaging data resulted in the differentiation of predominantly cognitive processes engaged in ToM or mentalizing that require self-generated cognitions. These are represented in the cortical midline and temporoparietal areas (similar to self-referential processing or mentalizing one's own emotional or motivational states, respectively) and are predominantly affective processes involved in the recognition of emotions in others based on shared emotions or motor and somatosensory representations, localized in the frontal cortex and extending to the insula and the temporal pole, as well as to somatosensory areas and the supramarginal gyrus (Schurz, Radua, et al., 2020). Furthermore, combined processes were identified that simultaneously engage cognitive and affective functions. ToM or mentalizing are constructs closely related to *cognitive empathy*, which refers to inferring and reasoning about others' mental states, including beliefs, thoughts (cognitive ToM), and emotions (affective ToM). These constructs subsume processes related to the abstract representation of mental states and have been associated with the superior temporal cortex in addition to midline structures, such as the temporoparietal junction, mPFC, and precuneus. *Empathy*, or affective sharing, denotes the sharing of other people's emotions and involves activations of the same neural networks engaged in the firsthand experience of that emotion—for instance, the anterior insula and dorsal ACC, in addition to the amygdala and somatosensory cortices for negative emotional states. Studies on the neuronal processing of empathy are often based on paradigms related to the processing and recognition of facial emotions and to other people's pain. Despite the automatic simulation of affective and sensorimotor states, *emotional empathy* includes the knowledge that the source of the emotion is another individual and not oneself and thus differs from emotional contagion in which one's emotions and the emotions of others conflate.

Impairments in Facial Emotion Recognition

As noted earlier, the correct recognition of facial emotions is discussed as a core and basic psychological mechanism enabling social interaction. Facial emotion recognition can be disturbed in many ways. Individuals can have difficulties recognizing facial emotions in general, which means that they respond slower or make more errors in emotion classification experiments no matter what facial emotion is presented. Moreover, specific alterations, such as a proneness for identifying certain emotions in facial expressions or responding faster or slower when a particular emotion is presented have also been noted and related to interpersonal dysfunctions. On a neural level, such alterations may be associated with response patterns in the circuit supporting facial emotion recognition. This includes primary and secondary visual cortices, the fusiform face area and posterior superior temporal sulcus involved in the processing of facial structures, and the amygdala as part of the salience system. It should be mentioned that facial emotion recognition fell into the domain of affective processes in the aforementioned meta-analysis (Schurz, Radua, et al., 2020) and may be more closely related to empathy than ToM.

Numerous studies are available that indicate a negativity bias in facial emotion recognition as a core psychological mechanism underlying the perception of interpersonal threat and rejection hypersensitivity in BPD. In particular, patients with BPD exhibit a negative response bias to neutral and ambiguous facial expressions in patients (for reviews, see Bertsch, Hillmann, et al., 2018; Daros et al., 2014; Mitchell et al., 2014). Furthermore, they show reduced thresholds for anger detection in predominantly happy faces, and this bias is found to be associated with higher occipital P100 amplitudes reflecting abnormal initial visual processes, whereas lower amplitudes in later phases of facial processing indicate deficits in structural (N170) and categorical (P300) facial processing (Izurieta Hidalgo et al., 2016). Also consistent with the notion of threat hypersensitivity, analyses of eye gaze indicate faster saccades toward the eyes of briefly presented neutral and angry faces and slower saccades away from fearful and angry eyes compared with healthy volunteers (Bertsch et al., 2013, 2017). It has been discussed that threat hypersensitivity could reflect a biological vulnerability factor or a consequence of adverse early experiences (Teicher & Samson, 2013). As discussed earlier, such experiences might result in an external focus and a habitual hypervigilance for potential interpersonal threats. The latter is supported by first results showing positive correlations between self-reported childhood maltreatment and misclassifications of emotional and neutral faces as angry in BPD (Seitz et al., 2021). Interestingly, in patients with remitted BPD (Schneider et al., 2018), a normalization of behavior is found in terms of valence responses and reaction times and the EEG response pattern toward healthy controls. Compared with patients with current BPD, remitted patients evaluate ambiguous faces more positively, exhibit faster reaction times when classifying predominantly happy faces, and show a normalization of P100 amplitudes. However, BPD-like impairments are still present in later cognitive processing of ambiguous faces (P300; Schneider et al., 2018). Due to the cross-sectional nature of this study, it remains unclear whether a "normalization" of early visual processes is a prerequisite for or a consequence of symptom amelioration. Nevertheless, they suggest a higher plasticity of early stages of facial emotion processing, whereas later, more cognitively controlled processes might be more stable, consistent with findings of a faster amelioration of stress-related symptoms in BPD (Temes & Zanarini, 2018).

Early sensory biases for interpersonal threat signals might be driven by the amygdala, given that enhanced amygdala activation to threat-related faces is reported from BPD together with hyperactivation in prefrontal regions involved in emotion regulation (Cullen et al., 2016). Consistent with this, more and faster eye movements toward the eyes of angry faces were associated with elevated amygdala responses in patients with BPD (Bertsch et al., 2013). Further findings suggest that patients with BPD try to control emotions—albeit unsuccessfully, probably because of a deficient in functional interplay within the prefrontal–amygdala circuit (Herpertz et al., 2017). Following the hypothesis that frontolimbic connectivity is disrupted in BPD, a magnetoencephalography study pointed to an underconnected network of areas including the bilateral amygdalae and anterior cingulate cortex during implicit angry (but not happy) face perception in a passive viewing task in adolescents high in BPD traits (Safar et al., 2019). Recent work suggests that enhanced amygdala activation to threat-related faces may reflect deficient habituation to repeatedly presented negative stimuli; notably, decreased habituation correlated with BPD symptom severity as well as with adverse childhood experiences (Bilek et al., 2019). As mentioned previously, patients with BPD appear to be faster in approaching than avoiding angry faces, which may point to deficits in emotional action control; this was related to a reduced negative coupling between the dlPFC and amygdala in BPD (Bertsch, Roelofs, et al., 2018).

Psychopaths have difficulties recognizing fearful—and, to a lesser extent, sad and happy faces (for a review, see Dawel et al., 2012). Poor performance in recognizing fearful faces is linked to trait callousness and is associated with reduced N170 amplitudes over the fusiform face area (Brislin et al., 2018). However, deficient face recognition appears not be restricted to fearful faces. Decreased activations in the fusiform face area as well as in the superior temporal sulcus to dynamic presentations of fearful, but also sad, happy, and painful facial expressions are found in psychopathic criminal offenders (Decety et al., 2014) suggesting a pervasive deficit in facial emotion processing beyond fear.

Interestingly, first reports indicate that oxytocin may be an agent that compensates for impairment in facial processing in ASPD (Timmermann et al.,

Impairments in Empathy

Empathy, or the sharing of emotions, which includes the processing and recognition of facial emotions as well as other people's pain, has recently been devoted to the "affective path" of social cognition (Schurz, Radua, et al., 2020). Empathetic processing recruits the same brain regions that are involved in the processing of one's own emotional or painful experiences, such as amygdala, anterior insula, dorsal ACC, and somatosensory cortex. Impairments in empathy are prominent features of PDs and have recently been devoted to the "affective path" of social cognition (Schurz, Radua, et al., 2020). When patients with BPD are asked to think of their own emotions while watching other people suffering, thus challenging their empathic capacity, they exhibited higher activity in the right middle insular cortex and showed enhanced skin conductance response, a peripheral measure of emotional arousal (Dziobek et al., 2011). Patients with BPD who were exposed to stylized scenes of mourning individuals affected by loss or separation exhibited higher activation of the mirror neuron system—namely, in the sensorimotor areas, the middle cingulate cortex, and the posterior insula (Sosic-Vasic et al., 2019). Patients with BPD also showed enhanced activation of the right supramarginal gyrus while viewing pained facial expressions when other people's hands were exposed to painful stimuli (Flasbeck et al., 2019).

Deficient emotional empathy is a central feature of psychopathy and has been reported in adolescents with callous-unemotional traits (Blair et al., 2014). Reduced activity to fearful facial expressions (Viding et al., 2012) may not only result from deficient recognition of fear but may also reflect deficient sharing of others' emotions. During the Reading-the-Mind-in-the-Eyes Task individuals with ASPD were found to exhibit decreased left amygdala activation but enhanced activations in ToM regions, such as the left superior temporal sulcus, the temporoparietal junction, the precuneus, the mPFC, and vlPFC (Schiffer et al., 2017). Notably, amygdala activation was negatively correlated with the psychopathy Factor 1 scores reflecting interpersonal and affective traits. Furthermore, higher psychopathy scores were related to lower activity in the anterior insula, the dorsal ACC, the amygdala, and the inferior frontal gyrus when subjects were asked to score their subjective emotional responses to emotional faces, thus provoking emotional empathetic processes (Seara-Cardoso et al., 2016). This fits to results observed in the "watching others in pain" paradigm, during which participants with high psychopathy scores showed lower activations in the emotional empathy circuit (i.e., the anterior insula, the inferior frontal gyrus, and the midcingulate cortex; Seara-Cardoso et al., 2015). Results from a large-scale study of a forensic sample of nearly 1,000 participants support the theory of aberrant connectivity in the paralimbic system (comprising the endorhinal and parahippocampal cortex, the medial surface of the temporal lobe, and the cingulate cortex) as a central characteristic of psychopathy, which is associated with the psychopathy Factor 1. Particularly strong reductions in connectivity were found in the salience network comprising the insula, anterior cingulate cortex, and amygdala as well as between the amygdala and cuneus, whereby the latter is linked to the DMN involved in self-referential thinking (Espinoza et al., 2018; also discussed earlier in this chapter). Another study points to a more efficiently organized dorsal attention network in inmates scoring high on psychopathy which suggests a strong top-down allocation of selective attention during goal-pursuit and cost–benefit calculations (Tillem et al., 2019). These data correspond with the attentional bottleneck hypothesis of psychopathy referring to the interference between goal-pursuit and processing of contextual information—namely, the timely processing of affective and interpersonal cues (Baskin-Sommers & Newman, 2014). Correspondingly, in a recently finalized study, individuals high in psychopathology showed increased activations in parietal regions, associated with the accumulation of cost–benefit signals in decision making, when processing social signals of others requesting for altruistic help (Ueltzhöffer et al., unpublished data). Furthermore, the results of two fMRI studies (Decety et al., 2013; Meffert et al., 2013) indicate that subjects with psychopathology do not differ from control participants in the activation of the emotional empathy circuit (e.g., the anterior insula) when instructed to pay attention to social cues depicting others in pain, but rather in the ventromedial prefrontal cortex mediating empathic concern and moral decision making. In a large group of criminal offenders, individuals scoring high on psychopathy showed reduced activities in the superior temporal sulcus/temporoparietal junction, the ACC, and the dorsomedial prefrontal cortex when passively watching a harmful as opposed to a supportive social interaction (Decety et al., 2015). However, when instructed to infer the emotional state of the victim versus the perpetrator, they showed increased activity in the same brain areas. In a large-scale diffusion tensor imaging study of several thousand incarcerated criminal offenders, the severity of psychopathy was found to be linked to the microstructural integrity of major white-matter tracts in the brain—namely, reduced fractional anisotropy in the right uncinate fasciculus connecting ventral frontal and anterior temporal cortices and underlying a host of social functions such as empathy, value representation, and moral judgment. Moreover, the right uncinate fasciculus finding is specifically related to the interpersonal features of psychopathy, probably indicating a neural marker for interpersonal dysfunction in psychopathic symptomatology (Wolf et al., 2015).

Deficits in empathy are also common in individuals with NPD. However, there are no functional neuroimaging studies, and there is only one report about reduced gray-matter volume in the left anterior insula in individuals with NPD (Ritter et al., 2011). In this study, anterior insula volume correlated with self-reported empathy suggesting an association between reduced insular volume and empathetic deficits in NPD (Schulze et al., 2013).

Interestingly, a recent study found beneficial effects of an intranasal oxytocin administration on affective empathy and social approach motivation in patients with BPD adapting their level of interpersonal functioning to healthy volunteers

(Domes et al., 2019). Yet, no improvements were found for cognitive empathy, and studies on oxytocinergic effects in other PDs are missing.

Impairments in ToM

ToM or *mentalizing* refers to the recognition of other people's thoughts, beliefs, and emotions. The latter has been termed "affective ToM," whereas thinking about other's thought and beliefs is known as "cognitive ToM" or, more recently, the "cognitive route" of social cognition. Affective ToM seems to recruit both cognitive and affective processes and might be closely related to cognitive empathy. ToM involves the superior temporal cortex and the temporoparietal junction associated to perspective taking as well as midline structures, such as the mPFC and the precuneus. Interestingly, prominent overlaps between ToM and the DMN have recently been documented (Schurz, Maliske, et al., 2020).

In BPD deficits in ToM are rather profound ranging from the decoding of and the reasoning about others' mental states up to drawing conclusions (Németh et al., 2018). In false-belief situations, patients made more errors in the cognitive ToM condition compared with healthy control participants and reported worse affective states more often in and after false-belief situations (Hillmann et al., 2021). Using the Movie for the Assessment of Social Cognition Task, which involves watching a short video and answering questions referring to the actors' mental states (Dziobek et al., 2006), patients with BPD showed excessive ToM or hypermentalization, compared with healthy volunteers and patients with other PDs (Normann-Eide et al., 2020). According to the results of this study, hypermentalization is likely not to be specifically associated with a BPD diagnosis per se but with the severity of psychopathology in general and interpersonal difficulties in particular.

In fMRI tasks requiring affective ToM, patients with BPD or young adults with high BPD traits exhibit decreased activity in the superior temporal sulcus, and partially in the temporoparietal junction (Dziobek et al., 2011; Haas & Miller, 2015; Mier et al., 2013). Furthermore, reduced resting-state connectivity between the structures responsible for emotion regulation (ACC and amygdala) and those responsible for social cognitive responses (medial prefrontal areas and middle temporal gyrus) are found in BPD (Duque-Alarcón et al., 2019), consistent with the finding that emotion dysregulation and ToM impairments negatively interact with one another. Correspondingly, another resting-state study, in which patients with BPD were compared with healthy control participants indicated decreased functional connectivity between the ACC and three brain areas involved in ToM processes: the left superior temporal lobe, the right supramarginal and inferior parietal lobes, and the right middle cingulate cortex (O'Neill et al., 2015). These fMRI data are complemented by structural alterations in brain circuits involved in social cognition and emotion processing including the temporal lobes and the fusiform face area, as well as the orbitofrontal cortex, the ACC, and the PCC (Rossi et al., 2015).

Challenging affective ToM, criminal psychopathic offenders showed reduced activations in the amygdala, the fusiform face area, the superior temporal sulcus, and the inferior prefrontal cortex with lower functional connectivity between the amygdala and the superior temporal sulcus (Mier et al., 2014). Recently, affective ToM was induced in a large sample of inmates when instructed to select the opposite emotional face that best matched the emotion of an actor with an obscured face in social senses depicting five emotion categories (anger, fear, happiness, sadness, and neutral), thus taking the perspective of the target individual in the scene (Deming et al., 2020). Psychopathy (Psychopathology Checklist—Revised total score) was found to be related to reduced neural activity in the left anterior insula only during fear trials, suggesting a distinct impairment in affective ToM when viewing others in fearful, threatening states.

Tailored interventions that focus on improving mentalizing capacity are an interesting target for treatment development in ASPD in the future. Most recently, the protocol of a multisite randomized controlled trial (RCT) was published that was designed to test the effectiveness and cost-effectiveness of mentalization-based therapy (MBT) for reducing aggression and other symptoms of ASPD in adult male offenders such as poor mentalizing capacity (Fonagy et al., 2020). Some years ago this group reported a decrement of ASPD-associated behaviors following MBT, such as the reduction of anger and hostility and the improvement of social adjustment in patients with BPD and a comorbid condition of ASPD (Bateman et al., 2016). Notably, combining RCTs on efficacy and effectiveness with neuroimaging could elucidate whether the expected mechanisms of change in fact are related to improving ToM capacity and social functioning, in general.

Impairments in Intimacy and Mutually Satisfying Relationships

Interpersonal functioning subsumes several facets that affect how satisfying and mutual social interactions are experienced. The ability to form and sustain intimate relationships has to do with how salient and rewarding relationships are experienced, whether individuals dare to engage in trustful relationships, and how sensitive individuals respond to frustration of affiliative needs or assumed social rejection. Regarding the inclination of individuals with PDs— namely, BPD and ASPD—to frequently run into conflicts with others, another focus of research aims to detect which brain mechanisms may underlie their difficulties to deescalate conflicts.

Close relationships of individuals with BPD are characterized by mistrust, neediness, and anxious preoccupation with assumed rejection and abandonment (Gunderson et al., 2018). Nevertheless, despite the significant role these features play in the social life of BPD, there have only been a limited number of studies dedicated to the understanding of the brain mechanisms underlying mistrust and impaired intimacy. Individuals with BPD are highly oriented toward the social world and suffer from the feeling of being alone or abandonment. They tend to engage in intense intimate relationships that are vulnerable to misunderstandings, distortions, and sudden breakups. Consistent with these characteristics of behavior, compared with healthy individuals, they exhibit increased activity in the superior temporal gyrus when anticipating social compared with nonsocial cues (Doell et al., 2020). Because, as described earlier, the superior temporal gyrus is part of the ToM network, these data may point to intense social cognitive processes inspired by the anticipation of social cues, which were followed by positive or negative social feedback. Despite intense longing for relationship and attachment, individuals with BPD have difficulties in synchronizing and harmonizing mental processes in social exchange. In a hyperscanning context when performing the Joint Attention Task, patients with BPD showed reduced cross-brain neural coupling between temporoparietal junction networks compared with dyads of healthy individuals (Bilek et al., 2017). Social exchange in BPD is further prone to disruptions as a consequence of rejection hypersensitivity. The paradigm used most often in this context is the Cyberball Paradigm, which is a virtual ball-tossing game in which participants are excluded, included, or participate in a control condition. Individuals with BPD reported more perceived ostracism in the inclusion condition when they were indeed included equally to game partners in social exchange (Weinbrecht et al., 2018). On the neural level, they showed higher activation of the dorsal ACC in all conditions (exclusion and inclusion), indicating a higher sensitivity to a neural threat signal associated with social pain even in situations in which exclusion is absent. In another fMRI study using the Cyberball Paradigm, patients with BPD showed an increment of activations in the dorsomedial prefrontal cortex and the PCC during the inclusion condition compared with healthy control participants and patients with major depression whereby these increased activations were correlated with higher BPD symptom severity (Malejko et al., 2018). Similar findings have been reported from adolescents with BPD (Brown et al., 2017). Because, as described earlier, these regions are involved in emotional conflict monitoring and self-referential mentalizing, data are consistent with hypermentalizing in social scenario in BPD that allude to feelings of belonging or not belonging. The highly prevalent phenomenon of distrust may also be related to rejection hypersensitivity. When appraising trustworthiness of facial stimuli, individuals with BPD judged stimuli as less trustworthy compared with healthy control participants, and this was associated with decreased activities in the lateral prefrontal cortex and the insula (Fertuck et al., 2019), probably pointing to less cognitive/evaluative processing of trustworthiness.

In patients with NPD, elevated activation in several regions of the social pain network, including the anterior insula, dorsal ACC, and subgenual ACC, were found during social exclusion in a Cyberball Paradigm. The hypersensitivity to exclusion in narcissists may be a function of hypersensitivity in brain systems associated with distress (Cascio et al., 2015).

As a diagnostic criterion in the *DSM* and *ICD* classification systems, proneness to anger, aggression, conflict proneness, and domestic violence in BPD patients has been intensively studied (for a review, see Bertsch et al., 2020). In BPD, reactive aggressive behavior is closely related to social threat hypersensitivity and dysfunction of the brain's threat circuitry subsuming the amygdala, hypothalamus, and periaqueductal gray (PAG) and their connectivity with the ventromedial prefrontal cortex. Accordingly, individuals with BPD showed higher amygdala activity to angry faces, and, most interestingly, amygdala hyperactivity was associated with faster behavioral threat responses, such as faster saccades to the eyes of angry faces compared with healthy controls (described earlier; for a review, see Bertsch et al., 2020). The brain's threat response is also involved in aggressive behavior in response to provocation, as suggested by data collected in clinical groups of adolescents with disruptive behavior disorders, a frequent adolescent antecedent of BPD and ASPD. Here, activities in the amygdala and PAG, as well as reduced connectivity between amygdala and ventromedial prefrontal cortex in response to provocation, were associated with retaliatory behavior as well as trait measures of aggression in the Ultimatum Game, which creates provocation by unfair offers (White et al., 2016). Furthermore, violent psychopathic criminal offenders exhibited increased amygdala activity to provocation in the Point Subtraction Aggression Paradigm, in which aggression is provoked by a fictitious opponent stealing points from the participant's account (da Cunha-Bang et al., 2017). Provocation-induced aggression is strongly associated with anger and deficits in cognitive control, including emotion regulation and inhibitory control. For example, highly anger-prone patients with BPD responded with lower activity in the vlPFC and dlPFC, two regions known to be involved in inhibitory control when instructed to inhibit fast-action tendencies to avoid angry (Bertsch et al., 2019; Bertsch, Roelofs, et al., 2018; also described earlier in this chapter).

Up to now, improving functioning in intimate relationships in individuals with PDs has not been a specific focus in psychotherapy, although this is a focus of most psychotherapies. Recently, a manualized group psychotherapy aiming to reduce reactive aggression was found to be successful (Herpertz et al., 2020), and reduction of aggression was associated with a decrement of amygdalar activity in a face-matching paradigm (Neukel et al., 2021). Before broadly implementing this approach in mental health care services of BPD patients, this finding has to be replicated in a large-scale study.

SUMMARY AND CONCLUSION

PDs are complex mental disorders with often-severe impairments in personal and interpersonal functioning. Results from neuroscientific studies may help to better understand the underlying mechanisms of these dysfunctions, thereby elucidating novel therapeutic pathways. New approaches to classifying PDs challenge the existing ways of studying brain alterations in PDs, providing new opportunities for more mechanistic, transdiagnostic thinking; this may enable a better translation from neuroscience to clinical practice and vice versa. Thus far, studies have revealed alterations in brain circuits involved in self-awareness, self-referential processing, and self-control, as well as in facial emotion recognition, empathy, theory of mind, and response to challenging interpersonal situations. Due to the complexity of these processes, it is not surprising that impairments in self and other functioning are not the result of structural or functional alterations in single brain regions, but rather of alterations in large circuits, including the brain's midline structures; the frontolimbic network, including regions activated in response to salient and emotional stimuli; those related to cognitive control, supporting behavior and emotion regulation; and those supporting social cognition and behavior.

REFERENCES

American Psychiatric Association. (2013). *Diagnostic and statistical manual of mental disorders* (5th ed.). https://doi.org/10.1176/appi.books.9780890425596

Amodio, D. M., & Frith, C. D. (2006, April). Meeting of minds: The medial frontal cortex and social cognition. *Nature Reviews Neuroscience, 7*(4), 268–277. https://doi.org/10.1038/nrn1884

Baczkowski, B. M., van Zutphen, L., Siep, N., Jacob, G. A., Domes, G., Maier, S., Sprenger, A., Senft, A., Willenborg, B., Tüscher, O., Arntz, A., & van de Ven, V. (2017, September). Deficient amygdala-prefrontal intrinsic connectivity after effortful emotion regulation in borderline personality disorder. *European Archives of Psychiatry and Clinical Neuroscience, 267*(6), 551–565. https://doi.org/10.1007/s00406-016-0760-z

Baskin-Sommers, A. R., & Newman, J. P. (2014, October). Psychopathic and externalizing offenders display dissociable dysfunctions when responding to facial affect. *Personality Disorders, 5*(4), 369–379. https://doi.org/10.1037/per0000077

Bateman, A., O'Connell, J., Lorenzini, N., Gardner, T., & Fonagy, P. (2016, August 30). A randomised controlled trial of mentalization-based treatment versus structured clinical management for patients with comorbid borderline personality disorder and antisocial personality disorder. *BMC Psychiatry, 16*(1), 304. https://doi.org/10.1186/s12888-016-1000-9

Beauchaine, T. P., Sauder, C. L., Derbidge, C. M., & Uyeji, L. L. (2019, October). Self-injuring adolescent girls exhibit insular cortex volumetric abnormalities that are similar to those seen in adults with borderline personality disorder. *Development and Psychopathology, 31*(4), 1203–1212. https://doi.org/10.1017/S0954579418000822

Beer, J. S., & Ochsner, K. N. (2006, March 24). Social cognition: A multi level analysis. *Brain Research, 1079*(1), 98–105. https://doi.org/10.1016/j.brainres.2006.01.002

Bertsch, K., Florange, J., & Herpertz, S. C. (2020, November 12). Understanding brain mechanisms of reactive aggression. *Current Psychiatry Reports, 22*(12), 81. https://doi.org/10.1007/s11920-020-01208-6

Bertsch, K., Gamer, M., Schmidt, B., Schmidinger, I., Walther, S., Kästel, T., Schnell, K., Büchel, C., Domes, G., & Herpertz, S. C. (2013, October). Oxytocin and reduction of social threat hypersensitivity in women with borderline personality disorder. *The American Journal of Psychiatry, 170*(10), 1169–1177. https://doi.org/10.1176/appi.ajp.2013.13020263

Bertsch, K., Hillmann, K., & Herpertz, S. C. (2018). Behavioral and neurobiological correlates of disturbed emotion processing in borderline personality disorder. *Psychopathology, 51*(2), 76–82. https://doi.org/10.1159/000487363

Bertsch, K., Krauch, M., Roelofs, K., Cackowski, S., Herpertz, S. C., & Volman, I. (2019, September 15). Out of control? Acting out anger is associated with deficient prefrontal emotional action control in male patients with borderline personality disorder. *Neuropharmacology, 156*, 107463. https://doi.org/10.1016/j.neuropharm.2018.12.010

Bertsch, K., Krauch, M., Stopfer, K., Haeussler, K., Herpertz, S. C., & Gamer, M. (2017, October). Interpersonal threat sensitivity in borderline personality disorder: An eye-tracking study. *Journal of Personality Disorders, 31*(5), 647–670. https://doi.org/10.1521/pedi_2017_31_273

Bertsch, K., Roelofs, K., Roch, P. J., Ma, B., Hensel, S., Herpertz, S. C., & Volman, I. (2018, May). Neural correlates of emotional action control in anger-prone women with borderline personality disorder. *Journal of Psychiatry & Neuroscience, 43*(3), 161–170. https://www.ncbi.nlm.nih.gov/pubmed/29688872. https://doi.org/10.1503/jpn.170102

Bilek, E., Itz, M. L., Stößel, G., Ma, R., Berhe, O., Clement, L., Zang, Z., Robnik, L., Plichta, M. M., Neukel, C., Schmahl, C., Kirsch, P., Meyer-Lindenberg, A., & Tost, H. (2019, December 15). Deficient amygdala habituation to threatening stimuli in borderline personality disorder relates to adverse childhood experiences. *Biological Psychiatry, 86*(12), 930–938. https://doi.org/10.1016/j.biopsych.2019.06.008

Bilek, E., Stößel, G., Schäfer, A., Clement, L., Ruf, M., Robnik, L., Neukel, C., Tost, H., Kirsch, P., & Meyer-Lindenberg, A. (2017, September 1). State-dependent cross-brain information flow in borderline personality disorder. *JAMA Psychiatry, 74*(9), 949–957. https://doi.org/10.1001/jamapsychiatry.2017.1682

Blair, R. J., Leibenluft, E., & Pine, D. S. (2014, December 4). Conduct disorder and callous-unemotional traits in youth. *The New England Journal of Medicine, 371*(23), 2207–2216. https://doi.org/10.1056/NEJMra1315612

Brislin, S. J., Yancey, J. R., Perkins, E. R., Palumbo, I. M., Drislane, L. E., Salekin, R. T., Fanti, K. A., Kimonis, E. R., Frick, P. J., Blair, R. J. R., & Patrick, C. J. (2018, March). Callousness and affective face processing in adults: Behavioral and brain-potential indicators. *Personality Disorders, 9*(2), 122–132. https://doi.org/10.1037/per0000235

Brown, R. C., Plener, P. L., Groen, G., Neff, D., Bonenberger, M., & Abler, B. (2017). Differential neural processing of social exclusion and inclusion in adolescents with non-suicidal self-injury and young adults with borderline personality disorder. *Frontiers in Psychiatry, 8*, 267. https://doi.org/10.3389/fpsyt.2017.00267

Capozzi, F., & Ristic, J. (2018, May 25). How attention gates social interactions. *Annals of the New York Academy of Sciences, 1426*(1), 179–198. https://doi.org/10.1111/nyas.13854

Cascio, C. N., Konrath, S. H., & Falk, E. B. (2015, March). Narcissists' social pain seen only in the brain. *Social Cognitive and Affective Neuroscience, 10*(3), 335–341. https://doi.org/10.1093/scan/nsu072

Coutinho, J., Goncalves, O. F., Soares, J. M., Marques, P., & Sampaio, A. (2016, October 30). Alterations of the default mode network connectivity in obsessive-compulsive personality disorder: A pilot study. *Psychiatry Research: Neuroimaging, 256*, 1–7. https://doi.org/10.1016/j.pscychresns.2016.08.007

Critchley, H. D., Wiens, S., Rotshtein, P., Ohman, A., & Dolan, R. J. (2004, February). Neural systems supporting interoceptive awareness. *Nature Neuroscience, 7*(2), 189–195. https://doi.org/10.1038/nn1176

Cullen, K. R., LaRiviere, L. L., Vizueta, N., Thomas, K. M., Hunt, R. H., Miller, M. J., Lim, K. O., & Schulz, S. C. (2016, June). Brain activation in response to overt and covert fear and happy faces in women with borderline personality disorder. *Brain Imaging and Behavior, 10*(2), 319–331. https://doi.org/10.1007/s11682-015-9406-4

da Cunha-Bang, S., Fisher, P. M., Hjordt, L. V., Perfalk, E., Persson Skibsted, A., Bock, C., Ohlhues Baandrup, A., Deen, M., Thomsen, C., Sestoft, D. M., & Knudsen, G. M. (2017). Violent offenders respond to provocations with high amygdala and striatal reactivity. *Social Cognitive and Affective Neuroscience, 12*(5), 802–810. https://doi.org/10.1093/scan/nsx006

Daros, A. R., Uliaszek, A. A., & Ruocco, A. C. (2014, January). Perceptual biases in facial emotion recognition in borderline personality disorder. *Personality Disorders, 5*(1), 79–87. https://doi.org/10.1037/per0000056

Davies, G., Hayward, M., Evans, S., & Mason, O. (2020, February 13). A systematic review of structural MRI investigations within borderline personality disorder: Identification of key psychological variables of interest going forward. *Psychiatry Research, 286*, 112864. https://doi.org/10.1016/j.psychres.2020.112864

Dawel, A., O'Kearney, R., McKone, E., & Palermo, R. (2012, November). Not just fear and sadness: Meta-analytic evidence of pervasive emotion recognition deficits for facial and vocal expressions in psychopathy. *Neuroscience and Biobehavioral Reviews*, *36*(10), 2288–2304. https://doi.org/10.1016/j.neubiorev.2012.08.006

Decety, J., Chen, C., Harenski, C. L., & Kiehl, K. A. (2015, June). Socioemotional processing of morally-laden behavior and their consequences on others in forensic psychopaths. *Human Brain Mapping, 36*(6), 2015–2026. https://doi.org/10.1002/hbm.22752

Decety, J., Skelly, L., Yoder, K. J., & Kiehl, K. A. (2014, February). Neural processing of dynamic emotional facial expressions in psychopaths. *Social Neuroscience, 9*(1), 36–49. https://doi.org/10.1080/17470919.2013.866905

Decety, J., Skelly, L. R., & Kiehl, K. A. (2013, June). Brain response to empathy-eliciting scenarios involving pain in incarcerated individuals with psychopathy. *JAMA Psychiatry, 70*(6), 638–645. https://doi.org/10.1001/jamapsychiatry.2013.27

Deming, P., Dargis, M., Haas, B. W., Brook, M., Decety, J., Harenski, C., Kiehl, K. A., Koenigs, M., & Kosson, D. S. (2020, December). Psychopathy is associated with fear-specific reductions in neural activity during affective perspective-taking. *NeuroImage, 223*, 117342. https://doi.org/10.1016/j.neuroimage.2020.117342

Deming, P., Philippi, C. L., Wolf, R. C., Dargis, M., Kiehl, K. A., & Koenigs, M. (2018). Psychopathic traits linked to alterations in neural activity during personality judgments of self and others. *NeuroImage: Clinical, 18*, 575–581. https://doi.org/10.1016/j.nicl.2018.02.029

Doell, K. C., Olié, E., Courtet, P., Corradi-Dell'Acqua, C., Perroud, N., & Schwartz, S. (2020). Atypical processing of social anticipation and feedback in borderline personality disorder. *NeuroImage: Clinical, 25*, 102126. https://doi.org/10.1016/j.nicl.2019.102126

Domes, G., Ower, N., von Dawans, B., Spengler, F. B., Dziobek, I., Bohus, M., Matthies, S., Philipsen, A., & Heinrichs, M. (2019, December 4). Effects of intranasal oxytocin administration on empathy and approach motivation in women with borderline personality disorder: A randomized controlled trial. *Translational Psychiatry, 9*(1), 328. https://doi.org/10.1038/s41398-019-0658-4

Duque-Alarcón, X., Alcalá-Lozano, R., González-Olvera, J. J., Garza-Villarreal, E. A., & Pellicer, F. (2019). Effects of childhood maltreatment on social cognition and brain functional connectivity in borderline personality disorder patients. *Frontiers in Psychiatry, 10*, 156. https://doi.org/10.3389/fpsyt.2019.00156

Dziobek, I., Fleck, S., Kalbe, E., Rogers, K., Hassenstab, J., Brand, M., Kessler, J., Woike, J. K., Wolf, O. T., & Convit, A. (2006, July). Introducing MASC: A movie for the assessment of social cognition. *Journal of Autism and Developmental Disorders, 36*(5), 623–636. https://doi.org/10.1007/s10803-006-0107-0

Dziobek, I., Preissler, S., Grozdanovic, Z., Heuser, I., Heekeren, H. R., & Roepke, S. (2011, July 15). Neuronal correlates of altered empathy and social cognition in borderline personality disorder. *NeuroImage, 57*(2), 539–548. https://doi.org/10.1016/j.neuroimage.2011.05.005

Espinoza, F. A., Vergara, V. M., Reyes, D., Anderson, N. E., Harenski, C. L., Decety, J., Rachakonda, S., Damaraju, E., Rashid, B., Miller, R. L., Koenigs, M., Kosson, D. S., Harenski, K., Kiehl, K. A., & Calhoun, V. D. (2018, June). Aberrant functional network connectivity in psychopathy from a large ($N = 985$) forensic sample. *Human Brain Mapping, 39*(6), 2624–2634. https://doi.org/10.1002/hbm.24028

Fertuck, E. A., Grinband, J., Mann, J. J., Hirsch, J., Ochsner, K., Pilkonis, P., Erbe, J., & Stanley, B. (2019). Trustworthiness appraisal deficits in borderline personality disorder are associated with prefrontal cortex, not amygdala, impairment. *NeuroImage: Clinical, 21*, 101616. https://doi.org/10.1016/j.nicl.2018.101616

Flasbeck, V., Enzi, B., & Brüne, M. (2019). Enhanced processing of painful emotions in patients with borderline personality disorder: A functional magnetic resonance imaging study. *Frontiers in Psychiatry, 10*, 357. https://doi.org/10.3389/fpsyt.2019.00357

Fonagy, P., Gergely, G., & Target, M. (2007, March–April). The parent–infant dyad and the construction of the subjective self. *Journal of Child Psychology and Psychiatry, and Allied Disciplines, 48*(3-4), 288–328. https://doi.org/10.1111/j.1469-7610.2007.01727.x

Fonagy, P., Yakeley, J., Gardner, T., Simes, E., McMurran, M., Moran, P., Crawford, M., Frater, A., Barrett, B., Cameron, A., Wason, J., Pilling, S., Butler, S., & Bateman, A. (2020, December 7). Mentalization for Offending Adult Males (MOAM): Study protocol for a randomized controlled trial to evaluate mentalization-based treatment for antisocial personality disorder in male offenders on community probation. *Trials, 21*(1), 1001. https://doi.org/10.1186/s13063-020-04896-w

Freeman, S. M., Clewett, D. V., Bennett, C. M., Kiehl, K. A., Gazzaniga, M. S., & Miller, M. B. (2015, May). The posteromedial region of the default mode network shows attenuated task-induced deactivation in psychopathic prisoners. *Neuropsychology, 29*(3), 493–500. https://doi.org/10.1037/neu0000118

Gunderson, J. G., Herpertz, S. C., Skodol, A. E., Torgersen, S., & Zanarini, M. C. (2018, May 24). Borderline personality disorder. *Nature Reviews: Disease Primers, 4*(1), 18029. https://doi.org/10.1038/nrdp.2018.29

Haas, B. W., & Miller, J. D. (2015, October). Borderline personality traits and brain activity during emotional perspective taking. *Personality Disorders, 6*(4), 315–320. https://doi.org/10.1037/per0000130

Happé, F., & Frith, U. (2014, June). Annual research review: Towards a developmental neuroscience of atypical social cognition. *Journal of Child Psychology and Psychiatry, and Allied Disciplines, 55*(6), 553–557. https://doi.org/10.1111/jcpp.12162

Hermans, K., Achterhof, R., Myin-Germeys, I., Kasanova, Z., Kirtley, O., & Schneider, M. (2019). Improving ecological validity in research on social cognition. *Social Cognition in Psychosis*, 249–268. https://doi.org/10.1016/B978-0-12-815315-4.00010-0

Herpertz, S. C., Bertsch, K., & Jeung, H. (2018, June). Neurobiology of Criterion A: Self and interpersonal personality functioning. *Current Opinion in Psychology, 21*, 23–27. https://doi.org/10.1016/j.copsyc.2017.08.032

Herpertz, S. C., Matzke, B., Hillmann, K., Neukel, C., Mancke, F., Jaentsch, B., Schwenger, U., Honecker, H., Bullenkamp, R., Steinmann, S., Krauch, M., Bauer, S., Borzikowsky, C., Bertsch, K., & Dempfle, A. (2020, December 14). A mechanism-based group-psychotherapy approach to aggressive behaviour in borderline personality disorder: Findings from a cluster-randomised controlled trial. *BJPsych Open, 7*(1), e17. https://doi.org/10.1192/bjo.2020.131

Herpertz, S. C., Nagy, K., Ueltzhöffer, K., Schmitt, R., Mancke, F., Schmahl, C., & Bertsch, K. (2017, August 15). Brain mechanisms underlying reactive aggression in borderline personality disorder—Sex matters. *Biological Psychiatry, 82*(4), 257–266. https://doi.org/10.1016/j.biopsych.2017.02.1175

Hillmann, K., Neukel, C., Krauch, M., Spohn, A., Schnell, K., Herpertz, S. C., & Bertsch, K. (2021). Cognitive and affective theory of mind in female patients with borderline personality disorder. *Journal of Personality Disorders, 35*(5), 672–690. https://doi.org/10.1521/pedi_2020_34_490

Hooker, C. I. (2015). Social neuroscience and psychopathology: Identifying the relationship between neural function, social cognition, and social behavior. In R. K. Schutt, L. J. Seidman, & M. S. Keshavan (Eds.), *Social neuroscience: Mind, brain, and society* (pp. 123–145). Harvard University Press.

Insel, T., Cuthbert, B., Garvey, M., Heinssen, R., Pine, D. S., Quinn, K., Sanislow, C., & Wang, P. (2010, July). Research domain criteria (RDoC): Toward a new classification framework for research on mental disorders. *The American Journal of Psychiatry, 167*(7), 748–751. https://doi.org/10.1176/appi.ajp.2010.09091379

Izurieta Hidalgo, N. A., Oelkers-Ax, R., Nagy, K., Mancke, F., Bohus, M., Herpertz, S. C., & Bertsch, K. (2016, January). Time course of facial emotion processing in women with borderline personality disorder: An ERP study. *Journal of Psychiatry & Neuroscience, 41*(1), 16–26. https://doi.org/10.1503/jpn.140215

Jiang, W., Li, G., Liu, H., Shi, F., Wang, T., Shen, C., Shen, H., Lee, S. W., Hu, D., Wang, W., & Shen, D. (2016, November 19). Reduced cortical thickness and increased surface area in antisocial personality disorder. *Neuroscience, 337,* 143–152. https://doi.org/10.1016/j.neuroscience.2016.08.052

Jiang, W., Shi, F., Liu, H., Li, G., Ding, Z., Shen, H., Shen, C., Lee, S. W., Hu, D., Wang, W., & Shen, D. (2017, February 22). Reduced white matter integrity in antisocial personality disorder: A diffusion tensor imaging study. *Scientific Reports, 7*(1), 43002. https://doi.org/10.1038/srep43002

Khalsa, S. S., Adolphs, R., Cameron, O. G., Critchley, H. D., Davenport, P. W., Feinstein, J. S., Feusner, J. D., Garfinkel, S. N., Lane, R. D., Mehling, W. E., Meuret, A. E., Nemeroff, C. B., Oppenheimer, S., Petzschner, F. H., Pollatos, O., Rhudy, J. L., Schramm, L. P., Simmons, W. K., Stein, M. B., . . . the Interoception Summit 2016 participants. (2018, June). Interoception and mental health: A roadmap. *Biological Psychiatry: Cognitive Neuroscience and Neuroimaging, 3*(6), 501–513. https://doi.org/10.1016/j.bpsc.2017.12.004

Kleindienst, N., Löffler, A., Herzig, M., Bertsch, K., & Bekrater-Bodmann, R. (2020, June 25). Evaluation of the own body in women with current and remitted borderline personality disorder: Evidence for long-lasting effects of childhood sexual abuse. *European Journal of Psychotraumatology, 11*(1), 1764707. https://doi.org/10.1080/20008198.2020.1764707

Kleindienst, N., Priebe, K., Borgmann, E., Cornelisse, S., Krüger, A., Ebner-Priemer, U., & Dyer, A. (2014). Body self-evaluation and physical scars in patients with borderline personality disorder: An observational study. *Borderline Personality Disorder and Emotion Dysregulation, 1*(1), 2. https://doi.org/10.1186/2051-6673-1-2

Korponay, C., Pujara, M., Deming, P., Philippi, C., Decety, J., Kosson, D. S., Kiehl, K. A., & Koenigs, M. (2017, July 1). Impulsive-antisocial psychopathic traits linked to increased volume and functional connectivity within prefrontal cortex. *Social Cognitive and Affective Neuroscience, 12*(7), 1169–1178. https://doi.org/10.1093/scan/nsx042

Krause-Utz, A., Elzinga, B. M., Oei, N. Y., Paret, C., Niedtfeld, I., Spinhoven, P., Bohus, M., & Schmahl, C. (2014). Amygdala and dorsal anterior cingulate connectivity during an emotional working memory task in borderline personality disorder patients with interpersonal trauma history. *Frontiers in Human Neuroscience, 8,* 848. https://doi.org/10.3389/fnhum.2014.00848

Krause-Utz, A., Winter, D., Schriner, F., Chiu, C. D., Lis, S., Spinhoven, P., Bohus, M., Schmahl, C., & Elzinga, B. M. (2018, June). Reduced amygdala reactivity and impaired working memory during dissociation in borderline personality disorder. *European Archives of Psychiatry and Clinical Neuroscience, 268*(4), 401–415. https://doi.org/10.1007/s00406-017-0806-x

Langner, R., Leiberg, S., Hoffstaedter, F., & Eickhoff, S. B. (2018, July). Towards a human self-regulation system: Common and distinct neural signatures of emotional and behavioural control. *Neuroscience and Biobehavioral Reviews, 90,* 400–410. https://doi.org/10.1016/j.neubiorev.2018.04.022

Lei, H., Huang, L., Li, J., Liu, W., Fan, J., Zhang, X., Xia, J., Zhao, K., Zhu, X., & Rao, H. (2020, January). Altered spontaneous brain activity in obsessive-compulsive personality disorder. *Comprehensive Psychiatry, 96,* 152144. https://doi.org/10.1016/j.comppsych.2019.152144

Linehan, M. M. (1995). *Understanding borderline personality disorder.* Guilford Press.

Löffler, A., Foell, J., & Bekrater-Bodmann, R. (2018, March 28). Interoception and its interaction with self, other, and emotion processing: Implications for the understanding of psychosocial deficits in borderline personality disorder. *Current Psychiatry Reports, 20*(4), 28. https://doi.org/10.1007/s11920-018-0890-2

Löffler, A., Kleindienst, N., Cackowski, S., Schmidinger, I., & Bekrater-Bodmann, R. (2020, March–April). Reductions in whole-body ownership in borderline personality disorder—A phenomenological manifestation of dissociation. *Journal of Trauma & Dissociation, 21*(2), 264–277. https://doi.org/10.1080/15299732.2019.1678213

Malejko, K., Neff, D., Brown, R., Plener, P. L., Bonenberger, M., Abler, B., & Graf, H. (2018). Neural correlates of social inclusion in borderline personality disorder. *Frontiers in Psychiatry, 9*, 653. https://doi.org/10.3389/fpsyt.2018.00653

Mao, Y., Sang, N., Wang, Y., Hou, X., Huang, H., Wei, D., Zhang, J., & Qiu, J. (2016, July 22). Reduced frontal cortex thickness and cortical volume associated with pathological narcissism. *Neuroscience, 328*, 50–57. https://doi.org/10.1016/j.neuroscience.2016.04.025

Marceau, E. M., Meuldijk, D., Townsend, M. L., Solowij, N., & Grenyer, B. F. S. (2018, November). Biomarker correlates of psychotherapy outcomes in borderline personality disorder: A systematic review. *Neuroscience and Biobehavioral Reviews, 94*, 166–178. https://doi.org/10.1016/j.neubiorev.2018.09.001

McRae, K., & Gross, J. J. (2020, February). Emotion regulation. *Emotion, 20*(1), 1–9. https://doi.org/10.1037/emo0000703

Meffert, H., Gazzola, V., den Boer, J. A., Bartels, A. A., & Keysers, C. (2013, August). Reduced spontaneous but relatively normal deliberate vicarious representations in psychopathy. *Brain: A Journal of Neurology, 136*(Pt. 8), 2550–2562. https://doi.org/10.1093/brain/awt190

Mier, D., Haddad, L., Diers, K., Dressing, H., Meyer-Lindenberg, A., & Kirsch, P. (2014, August). Reduced embodied simulation in psychopathy. *The World Journal of Biological Psychiatry, 15*(6), 479–487. https://doi.org/10.3109/15622975.2014.902541

Mier, D., Lis, S., Esslinger, C., Sauer, C., Hagenhoff, M., Ulferts, J., Gallhofer, B., & Kirsch, P. (2013, June). Neuronal correlates of social cognition in borderline personality disorder. *Social Cognitive and Affective Neuroscience, 8*(5), 531–537. https://doi.org/10.1093/scan/nss028

Mitchell, A. E., Dickens, G. L., & Picchioni, M. M. (2014, June). Facial emotion processing in borderline personality disorder: A systematic review and meta-analysis. *Neuropsychology Review, 24*(2), 166–184. https://doi.org/10.1007/s11065-014-9254-9

Müller, L. E., Schulz, A., Andermann, M., Gäbel, A., Gescher, D. M., Spohn, A., Herpertz, S. C., & Bertsch, K. (2015, November). Cortical representation of afferent bodily signals in borderline personality disorder: Neural correlates and relationship to emotional dysregulation. *JAMA Psychiatry, 72*(11), 1077–1086. https://doi.org/10.1001/jamapsychiatry.2015.1252

Müller-Pinzler, L., Czekalla, N., Mayer, A. V., Stolz, D. S., Gazzola, V., Keysers, C., Paulus, F. M., & Krach, S. (2019, October 8). Negativity-bias in forming beliefs about own abilities. *Scientific Reports, 9*(1), 14416. https://doi.org/10.1038/s41598-019-50821-w

Németh, N., Mátrai, P., Hegyi, P., Czéh, B., Czopf, L., Hussain, A., Pammer, J., Szabó, I., Solymár, M., Kiss, L., Hartmann, P., Szilágyi, A. L., Kiss, Z., & Simon, M. (2018, December). Theory of mind disturbances in borderline personality disorder: A meta-analysis. *Psychiatry Research, 270*, 143–153. https://doi.org/10.1016/j.psychres.2018.08.049

Neukel, C., Bertsch, K., Wenigmann, M., Spieß, K., Steinmann, S., & Herpertz, S. C. (2021). A mechanistic approach to an anti-aggression psychotherapy in borderline personality disorder: group treatment effects amygdala activation and connectivity. *Brain Sciences, 11*(12), 1627. https://doi.org/10.3390/brainsci11121627

Niedtfeld, I., Schmitt, R., Winter, D., Bohus, M., Schmahl, C., & Herpertz, S. C. (2017, May 1). Pain-mediated affect regulation is reduced after dialectical behavior therapy in borderline personality disorder: A longitudinal fMRI study. *Social Cognitive and Affective Neuroscience, 12*(5), 739–747. https://doi.org/10.1093/scan/nsw183

Nolen-Hoeksema, S., Wisco, B. E., & Lyubomirsky, S. (2008, September). Rethinking rumination. *Perspectives on Psychological Science, 3*(5), 400–424. https://doi.org/10.1111/j.1745-6924.2008.00088.x

Normann-Eide, E., Antonsen, B. R. T., Kvarstein, E. H., Pedersen, G., Vaskinn, A., & Wilberg, T. (2020, December). Are impairments in theory of mind specific to borderline personality disorder? *Journal of Personality Disorders, 34*(6), 827–841. https://doi.org/10.1521/pedi_2019_33_417

Northoff, G., Heinzel, A., de Greck, M., Bermpohl, F., Dobrowolny, H., & Panksepp, J. (2006, May 15). Self-referential processing in our brain—A meta-analysis of imaging studies on the self. *NeuroImage, 31*(1), 440–457. https://doi.org/10.1016/j.neuroimage.2005.12.002

O'Neill, A., D'Souza, A., Samson, A. C., Carballedo, A., Kerskens, C., & Frodl, T. (2015, January 30). Dysregulation between emotion and theory of mind networks in borderline personality disorder. *Psychiatry Research, 231*(1), 25–32. https://doi.org/10.1016/j.pscychresns.2014.11.002

Peters, J. R., Chester, D. S., Walsh, E. C., DeWall, C. N., & Baer, R. A. (2018). The rewarding nature of provocation-focused rumination in women with borderline personality disorder: A preliminary fMRI investigation. *Borderline Personality Disorder and Emotion Dysregulation, 5*(1), 1. https://doi.org/10.1186/s40479-018-0079-7

Peters, J. R., Eisenlohr-Moul, T. A., Upton, B. T., Talavera, N. A., Folsom, J. J., & Baer, R. A. (2017, September). Characteristics of repetitive thought associated with borderline personality features: A multimodal investigation of ruminative content and style. *Journal of Psychopathology and Behavioral Assessment, 39*(3), 456–466. https://doi.org/10.1007/s10862-017-9594-x

Phan, K. L., Taylor, S. F., Welsh, R. C., Decker, L. R., Noll, D. C., Nichols, T. E., Britton, J. C., & Liberzon, I. (2003, February 1). Activation of the medial prefrontal cortex and extended amygdala by individual ratings of emotional arousal: A fMRI study. *Biological Psychiatry, 53*(3), 211–215. https://doi.org/10.1016/S0006-3223(02)01485-3

Pollatos, O., Kirsch, W., & Schandry, R. (2005, September). Brain structures involved in interoceptive awareness and cardioafferent signal processing: A dipole source localization study. *Human Brain Mapping, 26*(1), 54–64. https://doi.org/10.1002/hbm.20121

Ritter, K., Dziobek, I., Preissler, S., Rüter, A., Vater, A., Fydrich, T., Lammers, C. H., Heekeren, H. R., & Roepke, S. (2011, May 15). Lack of empathy in patients with narcissistic personality disorder. *Psychiatry Research, 187*(1-2), 241–247. https://doi.org/10.1016/j.psychres.2010.09.013

Rossi, R., Lanfredi, M., Pievani, M., Boccardi, M., Rasser, P. E., Thompson, P. M., Cavedo, E., Cotelli, M., Rosini, S., Beneduce, R., Bignotti, S., Magni, L. R., Rillosi, L., Magnaldi, S., Cobelli, M., Rossi, G., & Frisoni, G. B. (2015, February). Abnormalities in cortical gray matter density in borderline personality disorder. *European Psychiatry, 30*(2), 221–227. https://doi.org/10.1016/j.eurpsy.2014.11.009

Safar, K., Sato, J., Ruocco, A. C., Korenblum, M. S., O'Halpin, H., & Dunkley, B. T. (2019, May 14). Disrupted emotional neural circuitry in adolescents with borderline personality traits. *Neuroscience Letters, 701*, 112–118. https://doi.org/10.1016/j.neulet.2019.02.021

Schandry, R., & Montoya, P. (1996, January 5). Event-related brain potentials and the processing of cardiac activity. *Biological Psychology, 42*(1-2), 75–85. https://doi.org/10.1016/0301-0511(95)05147-3

Scherpiet, S., Herwig, U., Opialla, S., Scheerer, H., Habermeyer, V., Jäncke, L., & Brühl, A. B. (2015, September 30). Reduced neural differentiation between self-referential cognitive and emotional processes in women with borderline personality disorder. *Psychiatry Research, 233*(3), 314–323. https://doi.org/10.1016/j.pscychresns.2015.05.008

Schiffer, B., Pawliczek, C., Müller, B. W., Wiltfang, J., Brüne, M., Forsting, M., Gizewski, E. R., Leygraf, N., & Hodgins, S. (2017, October 21). Neural mechanisms underlying affective theory of mind in violent antisocial personality disorder and/or schizophrenia. *Schizophrenia Bulletin, 43*(6), 1229–1239. https://doi.org/10.1093/schbul/sbx012

Schmitgen, M. M., Niedtfeld, I., Schmitt, R., Mancke, F., Winter, D., Schmahl, C., & Herpertz, S. C. (2019, September). Individualized treatment response prediction of dialectical behavior therapy for borderline personality disorder using multimodal magnetic resonance imaging. *Brain and Behavior, 9*(9), e01384. https://doi.org/10.1002/brb3.1384

Schmitt, R., Winter, D., Niedtfeld, I., Herpertz, S. C., & Schmahl, C. (2016, November). Effects of psychotherapy on neuronal correlates of reappraisal in female patients with borderline personality disorder. *Biological Psychiatry: Cognitive Neuroscience and Neuroimaging, 1*(6), 548–557. 10.1016/j.bpsc.2016.07.003

Schmitz, M., Bertsch, K., Löffler, A., Steimann, S., Herpertz, S. C., & Bekrater-Bodmann, R. (2021). Mind–body connection mediates the relationship between adverse childhood experiences and impaired emotion regulation in borderline personality disorder. *Borderline Personality Disorder and Emotion Dysregulation, 8*(1), 17. https://doi.org/10.1186/s40479-021-00157-7

Schmitz, M., Müller, L. E., Schulz, A., Kleindienst, N., Herpertz, S. C., & Bertsch, K. (2020, March 1). Heart and brain: Cortical representation of cardiac signals is disturbed in borderline personality disorder, but unaffected by oxytocin administration. *Journal of Affective Disorders, 264*, 24–28. https://doi.org/10.1016/j.jad.2019.11.139

Schneider, I., Bertsch, K., Izurieta Hidalgo, N. A., Müller, L. E., Schmahl, C., & Herpertz, S. C. (2018, June). Remnants and changes in facial emotion processing in women with remitted borderline personality disorder: An EEG study. *European Archives of Psychiatry and Clinical Neuroscience, 268*(4), 429–439. https://doi.org/10.1007/s00406-017-0841-7

Schneider, I., Boll, S., Volman, I., Roelofs, K., Spohn, A., Herpertz, S. C., & Bertsch, K. (2020). Oxytocin normalizes approach-avoidance behavior in women with borderline personality disorder. *Frontiers in Psychiatry, 11*, 120. https://doi.org/10.3389/fpsyt.2020.00120

Schulze, L., Dziobek, I., Vater, A., Heekeren, H. R., Bajbouj, M., Renneberg, B., Heuser, I., & Roepke, S. (2013, October). Gray matter abnormalities in patients with narcissistic personality disorder. *Journal of Psychiatric Research, 47*(10), 1363–1369. https://doi.org/10.1016/j.jpsychires.2013.05.017

Schulze, L., Schmahl, C., & Niedtfeld, I. (2016, January 15). Neural correlates of disturbed emotion processing in borderline personality disorder: A multimodal meta-analysis. *Biological Psychiatry, 79*(2), 97–106. https://doi.org/10.1016/j.biopsych.2015.03.027

Schurz, M., Maliske, L., & Kanske, P. (2020, September). Cross-network interactions in social cognition: A review of findings on task related brain activation and connectivity. *Cortex, 130*, 142–157. https://doi.org/10.1016/j.cortex.2020.05.006

Schurz, M., Radua, J., Tholen, M. G., Maliske, L., Margulies, D. S., Mars, R. B., Sallet, J., & Kanske, P. (2020, November 5). Toward a hierarchical model of social cognition: A neuroimaging meta-analysis and integrative review of empathy and theory of mind. *Psychological Bulletin, 147*(3), 293–327. 10.1037/bul0000303

Seara-Cardoso, A., Sebastian, C. L., Viding, E., & Roiser, J. P. (2016). Affective resonance in response to others' emotional faces varies with affective ratings and psychopathic traits in amygdala and anterior insula. *Social Neuroscience, 11*(2), 140–152. https://doi.org/10.1080/17470919.2015.1044672

Seara-Cardoso, A., Viding, E., Lickley, R. A., & Sebastian, C. L. (2015). Neural responses to others' pain vary with psychopathic traits in healthy adult males. *Cognitve, Affective & Behavioral Neuroscience, 15*(3), 578–88. https://doi.org/10.3758/s13415-015-0346-7

Seitz, K., Leitenstorfer, J., Krauch, M., Hillmann, K., Boll, S., Uethoeffer, K., Neukel, C., Herpertz, S. C., & Bertsch, K. (2021). Threat sensitivity and adverse childhood experiences in borderline personality disorder: an eye-tracking study. *Borderline Personality Disorder and Emotion Dysregulation, 8*(1). https://doi.org/10.1186/s40479-020-00141-7

Soloff, P. H., White, R., Omari, A., Ramaseshan, K., & Diwadkar, V. A. (2015, July 30). Affective context interferes with brain responses during cognitive processing in borderline personality disorder: fMRI evidence. *Psychiatry Research, 233*(1), 23–35. https://doi.org/10.1016/j.pscychresns.2015.04.006

Sosic-Vasic, Z., Eberhardt, J., Bosch, J. E., Dommes, L., Labek, K., Buchheim, A., & Viviani, R. (2019). Mirror neuron activations in encoding of psychic pain in borderline personality disorder. *NeuroImage: Clinical, 22,* 101737. https://doi.org/10.1016/j.nicl.2019.101737

Teicher, M. H., & Samson, J. A. (2013, October). Childhood maltreatment and psychopathology: A case for ecophenotypic variants as clinically and neurobiologically distinct subtypes. *The American Journal of Psychiatry, 170*(10), 1114–1133. https://doi.org/10.1176/appi.ajp.2013.12070957

Temes, C. M., & Zanarini, M. C. (2018, December). The longitudinal course of borderline personality disorder. *The Psychiatric Clinics of North America, 41*(4), 685–694. https://doi.org/10.1016/j.psc.2018.07.002

Thompson, N. M., Uusberg, A., Gross, J. J., & Chakrabarti, B. (2019). Empathy and emotion regulation: An integrative account. *Progress in Brain Research, 247,* 273–304. https://doi.org/10.1016/bs.pbr.2019.03.024

Tillem, S., Harenski, K., Harenski, C., Decety, J., Kosson, D., Kiehl, K. A., & Baskin-Sommers, A. (2019). Psychopathy is associated with shifts in the organization of neural networks in a large incarcerated male sample. *NeuroImage: Clinical, 24,* 102083. https://doi.org/10.1016/j.nicl.2019.102083

Timmermann, M., Jeung, H., Schmitt, R., Boll, S., Freitag, C. M., Bertsch, K., & Herpertz, S. C. (2017, November). Oxytocin improves facial emotion recognition in young adults with antisocial personality disorder. *Psychoneuroendocrinology, 85,* 158–164. https://doi.org/10.1016/j.psyneuen.2017.07.483

Vaitl, D. (1996, January 5). Interoception. *Biological Psychology, 42*(1-2), 1–27. https://doi.org/10.1016/0301-0511(95)05144-9

Vandekerckhove, M., Berens, A., Wang, Y. L., Quirin, M., & De Mey, J. (2020, February). Alterations in the fronto-limbic network and corpus callosum in borderline-personality disorder. *Brain and Cognition, 138,* 103596. https://doi.org/10.1016/j.bandc.2019.103596

van Zutphen, L., Siep, N., Jacob, G. A., Domes, G., Sprenger, A., Willenborg, B., Goebel, R., & Arntz, A. (2018, January). Always on guard: Emotion regulation in women with borderline personality disorder compared to nonpatient controls and patients with cluster-C personality disorder. *Journal of Psychiatry & Neuroscience, 43*(1), 37–47. https://doi.org/10.1503/jpn.170008

Viding, E., Sebastian, C. L., Dadds, M. R., Lockwood, P. L., Cecil, C. A., De Brito, S. A., & McCrory, E. J. (2012, October). Amygdala response to preattentive masked fear in children with conduct problems: The role of callous-unemotional traits. *The American Journal of Psychiatry, 169*(10), 1109–1116. https://doi.org/10.1176/appi.ajp.2012.12020191

Volman, I., von Borries, A. K., Bulten, B. H., Verkes, R. J., Toni, I., & Roelofs, K. (2016, February). Testosterone modulates altered prefrontal control of emotional actions in psychopathic offenders. *eNeuro, 3*(1), ENEURO.0107-15.2016. https://doi.org/10.1523/ENEURO.0107-15.2016

Weinbrecht, A., Niedeggen, M., Roepke, S., & Renneberg, B. (2018). Feeling excluded no matter what? Bias in the processing of social participation in borderline personality disorder. *NeuroImage: Clinical, 19,* 343–350. https://doi.org/10.1016/j.nicl.2018.04.031

Whalley, H. C., Dimitrova, R., Sprooten, E., Dauvermann, M. R., Romaniuk, L., Duff, B., Watson, A. R., Moorhead, B., Bastin, M., Semple, S. I., Giles, S., Hall, J., Thomson, P., Roberts, N., Hughes, Z. A., Brandon, N. J., Dunlop, J., Whitcher, B., Blackwood, D. H., . . . Lawrie, S. M. (2015). Effects of a balanced translocation between chromosomes 1 and 11 disrupting the DISC1 locus on white matter integrity. *PLOS ONE, 10*(6), e0130900. https://doi.org/10.1371/journal.pone.0130900

White, S. F., VanTieghem, M., Brislin, S. J., Sypher, I., Sinclair, S., Pine, D. S., Hwang, S., & Blair, R. J. (2016, March 1). Neural correlates of the propensity for retaliatory behavior in youths with disruptive behavior disorders. *The American Journal of Psychiatry, 173*(3), 282–290. https://doi.org/10.1176/appi.ajp.2015.15020250

Winter, D., Krause-Utz, A., Lis, S., Chiu, C. D., Lanius, R. A., Schriner, F., Bohus, M., & Schmahl, C. (2015, September 30). Dissociation in borderline personality disorder: Disturbed cognitive and emotional inhibition and its neural correlates. *Psychiatry Research, 233*(3), 339–351. https://doi.org/10.1016/j.pscychresns.2015.05.018

Wolf, R. C., Pujara, M. S., Motzkin, J. C., Newman, J. P., Kiehl, K. A., Decety, J., Kosson, D. S., & Koenigs, M. (2015, October). Interpersonal traits of psychopathy linked to reduced integrity of the uncinate fasciculus. *Human Brain Mapping, 36*(10), 4202–4209. https://doi.org/10.1002/hbm.22911

World Health Organization. (2019). *International statistical classification of diseases and related health problems* (11th ed.). https://icd.who.int/

World Health Organization. (2022). ICD-11 *clinical descriptions and diagnostic guidelines for mental and behavioural disorders.* https://gcp.network/en/private/icd-11-guidelines

Yoon, H. J., Seo, E. H., Kim, J. J., & Choo, I. H. (2019, February 28). Neural correlates of self-referential processing and their clinical implications in social anxiety disorder. *Clinical Psychopharmacology and Neuroscience, 17*(1), 12–24. https://doi.org/10.9758/cpn.2019.17.1.12

Young, K. S., van der Velden, A. M., Craske, M. G., Pallesen, K. J., Fjorback, L., Roepstorff, A., & Parsons, C. E. (2018, January). The impact of mindfulness-based interventions on brain activity: A systematic review of functional magnetic resonance imaging studies. *Neuroscience and Biobehavioral Reviews, 84,* 424–433. https://doi.org/10.1016/j.neubiorev.2017.08.003

IV

TREATMENT FOR SPECIFIC PERSONALITY DISORDERS

15

Borderline Personality Disorder

Kenneth N. Levy, Johannes C. Ehrenthal, and Jacob A. Martin

In this chapter, we provide an overview of borderline personality disorder (BPD), its clinical presentation, and the treatment approaches available in the context of *Diagnostic and Statistical Manual of Mental Disorders* (5th ed.; *DSM-5*; American Psychiatric Association, 2013) and the *International Statistical Classification of Diseases and Related Health Problems* (11th ed.; *ICD-11*; World Health Organization, 2019). Almost all definitions of BPD emphasize that it is characterized by broad instability in one's sense of self (or identity), interpersonal relationships, and mood. This instability is expressed or manifests itself in uncertainty about oneself, one's values, and one's life goals; emotional lability and dysregulation; chaotic, dysfunctional, and unstable interpersonal relationships; impulsive behaviors, angry outbursts, suicidality; and perhaps the most perplexing symptom, nonsuicidal self-injury (NSSI). The most widely used definition in the United States is that based on the *DSM*, whereas Europe and much of the world have been using definitions developed by the World Health Organization in the *ICD*, now in its upcoming 11th edition.

Portions of this chapter are based on "Borderline Personality Disorder," by J. Pantelides and K. N. Levy, in B. J. Carducci, C. S. Nave, J. S. Mio, and R. E. Riggio (Eds.), *The Wiley Encyclopedia of Personality and Individual Differences* (Vol. 4, pp. 89–95), 2020, John Wiley & Sons, Inc. Copyright 2020 by John Wiley & Sons, Inc. Adapted with permission.

https://doi.org/10.1037/0000310-016

Personality Disorders and Pathology: Integrating Clinical Assessment and Practice in the DSM-5 *and* ICD-11 *Era*, S. K. Huprich (Editor)

Copyright © 2022 by the American Psychological Association. All rights reserved.

BRIEF HISTORY

Patients with characteristics consistent with what we now call BPD were described as far back as 1884 (Hughes, 1884; Rosse, 1890). These authors, as well as several other clinical writers in the early 20th century, wrote about patients who presented at the borderline between neurotic and psychotic disorders (Clark, 1919; Jones, 1918). However, it is Stern (1938) who is credited with first coining the term *borderline*[1] in describing a group of patients who appeared neurotic during the initial evaluation for therapy but during treatment tended to oscillate between devaluation and idealization of the therapist, displayed difficulty in controlling emotions, and would even "regress" into mild, transient psychotic states during treatment. However, unlike psychotic patients, these borderline personalities quickly returned to intact reality testing. Stern also noted that these patients evoked strong countertransferential reactions in clinicians. Later work by Zilboorg (1941), Deutsch (1942), Rapaport et al. (1946/1968), Schmideberg (1947), and Hoch and Polatin (1949) helped the concept coalesce, although several of these writers did not use the term *borderline* and saw the disorder as more strongly related to psychosis than neurosis or as in between the two. It was the writings of Knight (1953) discussing borderline states that popularized the term *borderline*, although the *DSM-II* (American Psychiatric Association, 1968) later reverted to the term *latent schizophrenia* to describe such difficulties.

BPD began to gain traction through the writings of Otto Kernberg (1967, 1975/1985, 1984), who in an unusual mix of "Kraepelin-like" descriptive psychiatry and an integration of writings from classical drive theory, ego psychology, and object relations theory articulated an explicit description of clinical characteristics and the bases for the diagnosis based on readily observable behavior. He distinguished what he called borderline personality organization (BPO) from neurotic and psychotic levels of organization using clear, clinically relevant descriptions that resonated with clinicians and stimulated increased interest in the concept. However, despite his crisp descriptive approach and the use of vivid clinical examples, many of the concepts and etiological explanations remained abstract. Particularly difficult to grasp and execute was the clinical interview, which he called the structural interview, to assess the intrapsychic psychological structure for determining BPO. Around the same time, Grinker and colleagues (1968) published the first empirically based criterion set based on research that distinguished subtypes and recognized the heterogeneity of the disorder. Subsequently, Gunderson and colleagues (Gunderson & Kolb, 1978; Gunderson & Singer, 1975), building on Kernberg and Grinker, provided diagnostic criteria for BPD and later, in contrast to Kernberg's clinical interview, Gunderson and colleagues developed a structured interview called the Diagnostic Interview for Borderlines (DIB; Gunderson et al., 1981). The DIB was easier to understand, train in, and conduct, which further helped to increase awareness in BPD.

---

[1] Actually, Stern (1938) used the term *Border Line* as in *Border Line Neurosis*.

The writings of Kernberg, Grinker, and Gunderson, along with Millon (1981), provided the basis for the diagnosis of BPD in the *DSM-III* diagnostic system (American Psychiatric Association, 1980), which was the first official nomenclature to adopt the term. Consistent with the general polythetic approach taken by Spitzer in the *DSM-III*, the eight criteria were based on a combination of observable behaviors, symptoms, and traits that required little inference. To receive a diagnosis of BPD, an individual has to meet at least five of the eight criteria as characteristic of an individual's current and long-term functioning: (a) impulsivity or unpredictability in at least two areas that are potentially self-damaging; (b) a pattern of unstable and intense interpersonal relationships; (c) inappropriate, intense anger or lack of control of anger; (d) identity disturbance; (e) affective instability; (f) intolerance of being alone; (g) physically self-damaging acts; and (h) chronic feelings of emptiness or boredom.

In the *DSM-III* (American Psychiatric Association, 1980) Spitzer and the personality disorder workgroup decided to differentiate BPD characterized by more interpersonal and affective instability from schizotypal personality disorder characterized by psychotic-like symptoms. This decision was based largely on Stone's (1977) family pedigree study of borderline patients, which found that blood relatives of BPD patients were at increased risk for an affective disorder rather than a schizophrenic spectrum disorder and Danish adoptive studies by Kety et al. (1968), which found nonpsychotic relatives of those with schizophrenia were at increased risk for "borderline schizophrenia." Both studies were consistent with the descriptions by Kernberg, Grinker, and Gunderson; however, subsequent research by Gunderson resulted in the *DSM-III-R* incorporating the ninth criterion of the experience of stress related transient psychotic and dissociative symptoms.

The publication of the *DSM-III* in 1980 led to a more than 30-year relative consistency in the criteria for BPD. After the addition of the ninth criterion in 1987, only minor adjustments to the wording of the description and criteria occurred until the publication of the *DSM-5* in 2013.

CURRENT DIAGNOSTIC CRITERIA

DSM-5 Section II

The *DSM-5* describes personality disorders in two sections: Section II—Diagnostic Criteria and Codes and Section III. Section II is for the diagnostic criteria and codes for all included disorders, personality or otherwise, whereas Section III contains an alternative model for conceptualizing personality disorders. The current approach to personality disorders appears in Section II and was retained from *DSM-IV* to provide continuity with current clinical practice.

DSM-5 Section III Alternative Model of Personality Disorders

The Alternative *DSM-5* Model for Personality Disorders (AMPD) was included in Section III to introduce a new approach that aims to address numerous shortcomings of the current approach to personality disorders (e.g., comorbidity) and was included to stimulate research into this new approach. The AMPD employs two main measures to make a diagnosis of a PD. Criterion A assesses impairments in personality functioning through two domains: Impairment in self-functioning and impairment in interpersonal functioning. Self-functioning includes both identity and self-direction, and interpersonal functioning includes both the capacity for empathy and the capacity for intimacy (Sharp & Wall, 2021). Criterion B assesses maladaptive personality traits through five broad trait domains of Negative Affectivity (vs. Emotional Stability), Detachment (vs. Extraversion), Antagonism (vs. Agreeableness), Disinhibition (vs. Conscientiousness), and Psychoticism (vs. Lucidity). These dimensions map onto the five domains in the five-factor model (FFM; Costa & McCrae, 1992) but are conceptualized from the pathological personality end of these traits. These five trait domains are further differentiated into 25 underlying facets. These trait domains labels emphasize maladaptive extremes and map onto the FFM such that negative affective is conceptually similar to neuroticism, detachment to introversion, antagonism to low agreeableness, and disinhibition to low conscientiousness (Widiger & McCabe, 2020).

BPD in the AMPD requires meeting both Criterion A (moderate or greater impairment in self- and interpersonal functioning) and Criterion B (pathological personality traits). For criterion B, at least four of seven pathological traits must be present for the diagnosis. The traits fall under the domains of negative affectivity, disinhibition, and antagonism. At least one trait under disinhibition (either impulsivity or risk-taking) or antagonism (i.e., hostility) must be met, along with any of the four traits related to negative affectivity (emotional lability, anxiousness, separation insecurity, depressivity). Reliability of the BPD diagnosis using the AMPD was equal to that of the categorical model in a study of clinicians making diagnoses from case vignettes (Morey, 2019). In the *DSM-5* Section III, there are six identified personality disorders: antisocial, avoidant, borderline, narcissistic, obsessive-compulsive, and schizotypal. The inclusion of most of these is consistent with factor analytic work by Sharp et al. (2015) and Wright et al. (2016), who found both g (general) factor and several s (specific) factors in two large independent broad clinical samples, where the g factor is consistent with the borderline conceptualization, with higher scores suggesting more "borderlineness" and low scores less. These findings have also been interpreted as consistent with the AMPD and Kernberg's model of borderline personality organization (Sharp et al., 2015; Wright et al., 2016) but have also raised questions about the categorical nature of BPD (see Clark, 2007).

ICD-11

The *ICD-11* represents a radical departure from the *ICD-10* and its predecessors by jettisoning categorical diagnoses to emphasize dimensional approach. Paralleling the AMPD, the *ICD-11* focuses on severity of impairment in the areas of self-functioning and interpersonal functioning and retained the borderline pattern descriptor but abandoned the other types of personality disorders (Tyrer et al., 2011, 2019).

Although there is currently substantial research on a variety of dimensional approaches to studying personality disorders beyond *DSM* and *ICD* (e.g., Ehrenthal & Benecke, 2019; Widiger et al., 2019), a full consideration of strengths and weaknesses concerning the assessment and conceptualization of BPD is beyond the scope of the chapter. Because most of the existing data, especially concerning treatment models, have been collected from a *DSM-IV–*oriented perspective, we for now contend that BPD can be considered a categorical diagnostic construct.

EPIDEMIOLOGY

Epidemiological and clinical studies have found prevalence rates of BPD between 1% and 5.9% in the general population, 15% and 20% in outpatients, and up to 40% in inpatient samples. These rates indicate that BPD is more common than bipolar disorder, autism, and schizophrenia combined (when comparing low and high rates of each disorder). Within outpatient departments, women account for as much as 75% of the cases of BPD; however, high rates of BPD among men are found in substance use, mandated treatment programs, and forensic samples. Thus, the differences in prevalence rates between men and women may be due to setting, symptom presentation (women may show symptoms that are perceived as more dramatic such as self-injury, but men exhibit symptoms perceived as impulsive, or related to substance abuse), treatment-seeking (again with women seeking treatment for self-injury and other BPD symptoms, whereas men are more often seen in mandated treatment or substance abuse programs) than because of gender bias. However, recent epidemiological data provide little evidence for substantial differences in BPD prevalence rates between women and men.

COMORBIDITY OF BPD WITH OTHER PSYCHOLOGICAL DISORDERS

BPD, as measured by the *DSM-III* through *DSM-5* Section II criteria set, has been found to be frequently comorbid with several other psychiatric and psychological disorders such as major depressive disorder, persistent depressive disorder (formerly dysthymia), bipolar disorder, a range of anxiety disorders (e.g., panic disorder), substance abuse disorders (SUD), eating disorders, and posttraumatic stress disorder (PTSD). Recent evidence has also found significant comorbidity with attention-deficit disorder (e.g., Matthies & Philipsen, 2014). Mary Zanarini referred to this pattern of comorbidity as *complex comorbidity* because of the number of comorbid diagnoses and the co-occurrence of both internalizing and externalizing disorders, which are otherwise thought to be orthogonal (Zanarini et al., 1998). The comorbidity observed in BPD is of particular significance because comorbid BPD has a negative effect on course and efficacy of treatment. For anxiety disorders, bipolar II disorder, and depression, this effect is likely to be unidirectional, meaning that comorbid BPD negatively influences course and outcome of depressive, anxious, and manic symptoms. By contrast, a number of large longitudinal studies that in total included thousands of patients found that these disorders have negligible effects on the course and outcome of BPD.[2] For instance, those with bipolar disorder and comorbid BPD are at increased likelihood for higher rates of substance abuse including alcohol, higher medication use and higher levels of unemployment; showed poorer treatment response and had significantly worse functioning between illness episodes. However, comorbid bipolar disorder did not affect the course or outcome for BPD patients. Similarly, several large follow-up studies found that improvement in depressive disorder was preceded by improvements in BPD but that improvements in MDD were not followed by improvements in BPD (Grilo et al., 2010; Gunderson et al., 2004, 2014; Morey et al., 2010).

DIFFERENTIAL DIAGNOSIS

An important consideration in assessing for BPD is the differential diagnosis between BPD and similar disorders. Differential diagnosis consists of choosing between similar diagnostic criteria sets to determine the diagnosis that best conceptually represents the reported symptoms and dynamics. Common differential diagnosis for BPD includes mood disorders (e.g., bipolar disorder, major depression, and dysthymia), PTSD, anxiety disorders, and attention-deficit/hyperactivity disorder, and other personality disorders. Eating disorders and substance use disorders are common as well. These disorders, even when not comorbid with BPD, can appear in ways that are similar to BPD. The similarities in presentation can be confusing and require attention to nuance to accurately distinguish BPD from other forms of psychopathology. Determining whether BPD is present is extremely important for ensuring proper treatment; several studies have found that the time between first psychiatric contact and receiving an adequate BPD diagnosis can be up to 6 to 10 years (Meyerson, 2009; Zanarini, Frankenburg, Dubo, et al., 1998). During this time, patients are not typically triaged to proper treatment and may also be prescribed medication and psychotherapies that are not useful or titrated to their difficulties.

Depressive Disorders

Perhaps the most frequent differential diagnosis with BPD is depressive disorders. The differential diagnosis with mood disorders is particularly difficult because those with BPD, similar to those with other disorders, often experience

---

[2]Although the negative effects between BPD and these disorders can be reciprocal, particularly for SUD and PTSD.

depressed mood, and the individual's phenomenological experience is that they frequently feel "depressed." Consistent with this, research has found that those with BPD often score as elevated or greater on depression measures than even those with MDD (Köhling et al., 2015; Levy et al., 2007). Distinguishing between these disorders requires a thorough evaluation of the depressive symptoms in terms of both quality and course. In contrast to MDD where depressed mood occurs episodically, in BPD depressed mood is most typically chronic (Zanarini et al., 1998) and tends to be characterized by more mood lability, with vacillations between anger/irritability and depressed mood (as opposed to shifts between normal mood and depression or depression and expansive mood in bipolar disorder). Also, BPD patients may perceive more mood reactivity than would be typical for those suffering just from a depressive episode. For example, it is common for a suicidal and, on the face of it, depressed patient with BPD upon admission to an inpatient hospital unit to suddenly show a shift in mood where they become rather relieved, quite social with other patients, and cavalier. Additionally, BPD patients frequently do not show or report neurovegetative symptoms that are common in those with major depression proper. When they do, BPD patients tend to report inconsistent and atypical neurovegetative signs, such as increased appetite and excessive sleeping. When neurovegetative signs are reported, it is important to get a detailed history. Regarding loss of interest in sex, it is important to distinguish between loss of interest in sexual relationships from lack of interest in current partners, inhibitions due to body concerns or related to traumatic experiences, lack of opportunity for sexual behavior, and relatively transient states of loss interest rather than loss of libido. A key consideration when parsing apart BPD from MDD is identity disturbance. People with MDD generally do not present with identity disturbance, whereas it is a core feature in BPD.

Bipolar Disorders

Another particularly important, frequent, and difficult differential diagnosis is between BPD and bipolar disorder, especially bipolar II disorder. BPD comorbidity rates with bipolar disorder are similar to the comorbidity rates with substance use disorders (Compton et al., 2007) and PTSD (Pietrzak et al., 2011). Thus, those with BPD are at no increased risk of meeting criteria for bipolar disorder; however, there is a large robust literature indicating that many patients with BPD are at increased risk of having been or being misdiagnosed with bipolar disorder (Zimmerman et al., 2010, 2019).

Pragmatically, perhaps the main confusion in distinguishing BPD from bipolar disorder relates to emotional lability and affective instability. Affective instability is a core symptom of both bipolar disorder and BPD, and thus its occurrence in the context of BPD is frequently confused as a marker of bipolar disorder. However, affective instability in BPD is qualitatively different from affective instability in bipolar disorder. In bipolar disorder, affective instability occurs spontaneously and progresses over several days and weeks and can go on for even longer when not treated with mood stabilizing medications

(American Psychiatric Association, 2013), whereas in BPD the affective instability is often precipitated by external events or internal thought processes and tends to vacillate more quickly, over a few days, hours, and even minutes. Moreover, mood changes in bipolar disorder typically are between feeling depressed and elated, expansive, and grandiose. In BPD, the emotional lability is often in reaction to the experience of external, interpersonal events or internal processes and tends to be much shorter in duration, and displays frequent vacillations. Those vacillations are typically observed between states of depression and anger, hostility, and irritability (Reisch et al., 2008). Importantly, the affective instability seen in BPD patients, compared with bipolar patients, tends to be more frequently occurring and intense, with shifts between depression and anxiety on the one hand and irritability and anger on the other (Henry et al., 2001). Additionally, rather than occurring episodically as in bipolar disorder, affective instability is one of the most stable characteristics of patients with BPD (Paris, 2003), and as would be predicted by etiological theories of BPD, affective instability in BPD is related to identity disturbance (Koenigsberg et al., 2001) and a history of emotional abuse (Goodman et al., 2003).

There is further confusion in distinguishing impulsivity and irritability in patients with BPD versus bipolar disorder. Impulsivity and irritability, much like depressed mood, is more chronic in BPD. To be counted toward a bipolar disorder diagnosis, such symptoms must be confined to a manic or hypomanic episode. Individuals with BPD will frequently display transient psychotic symptoms as a reaction to stressors, whereas those with bipolar disorder will display more pervasive and longer lasting losses of reality testing, often with hallucinations and delusions (particularly of grandeur). The loss of reality testing in BPD is much subtler and can be characterized as loss of social reality testing or brief transient psychotic-like symptoms rather than frank psychotic symptoms that are more typical of bipolar disorder.

PTSD

Differentiating BPD from PTSD can be relatively easy when the PTSD symptoms are part of an acute reaction to a clearly identified traumatic event. In such cases, identity disturbance, chronic impulsivity, and irritability points toward BPD rather than PTSD. This is most obvious when BPD symptoms are found to have onset before the traumatic event because in noncomplex PTSD, premorbid functioning is often good.

It is significantly more challenging to distinguish the two disorders when early and chronic trauma are present because this can have important implications on personality development. Several theorists have proposed reconceptualizing BPD as a form of complex PTSD (C-PTSD; Herman, 1993; Kroll, 1993). Opposing evidence has found that although 30% to 70% of BPD patients have reported experiencing a traumatic event (e.g., Zanarini & Frankenburg, 1997), an equal 30% to 70% of those with BPD have not. Importantly research findings from studies of consecutive admissions indicate that 30% to 45% of those with BPD report a history of abuse, a finding that does not significantly differ from other psychiatric disorders (e.g., Chapman et al., 2004; Paris et al., 1994), although some studies clearly show differences in trauma exposure between BPD patients and other diagnostic groups (e.g., Herman et al., 1989). Whether trauma is more frequent in those with BPD, the rates of trauma in BPD samples suggest that trauma cannot conceptually be a necessary etiological factor in BPD. Certainly, there are multiple pathways to BPD, and trauma could be one; however, Levy (2005) suggested that the relative ratio between constitutional factors and environmental ones (including trauma) may interact to leave a person susceptible to the development of a personality disorder. The higher the genetic loading, the less negative environmental input is needed for the development of the disorder. This view may better explain the potential contribution of trauma to the development of BPD.

In a study of women with PTSD who experienced early childhood abuse, Heffernan and Cloitre (2000) found that a comorbid BPD diagnosis did not adversely affect PTSD symptoms, including frequency and severity of intrusive, avoidance, and arousal symptoms. Thus, it appears that BPD and PTSD can be effectively discriminated by their symptom profiles, casting doubt on complex PTSD as a construct that would subsume BPD. In the context of trauma and PTSD, intense anger, interpersonal difficulties, anxiety, and dissociation should signal a possible comorbid diagnosis of BPD and thus the need to assess for it. Perhaps the most informative study of the relationship between BPD and PTSD comes from Cloitre et al. (2014). They examined data from a randomized control trial (RCT) of treatment for women with PTSD related to childhood abuse. Using latent class analysis, they found four classes among those presenting for treatment: The first class, "low symptom" (20% of the participants), scored low on symptoms of PTSD, complex PTSD, and BPD. The second class, "PTSD" (25.7% of the participants), scored high on PTSD symptoms but low on CPTSD and BPD symptoms. The third class, "CPTSD," scored high on PTSD and CPTSD symptoms but low on BPD symptoms. Finally, the fourth class scored high on PTSD, CPTSD, and BPD symptoms. Diagnostically, in the low-symptom group, 88% met criteria for no diagnosis (12% for BPD). In the PTSD group, 68% met criteria for PTSD (11% no diagnosis and 19% complex PTSD). In the CPTSD group 78% met criteria for CPTSD (80% for concurrent PTSD, but only 8% for BPD), and in the BPD group 92% met criteria for BPD (44% met for CPTSD, and 54% for PTSD). This finding suggests that a significant subset of patients with childhood trauma are comorbid for PTSD and BPD. In examining the groups further, Cloitre et al. found that the groups could be differentiated by BPD symptoms such that the experience of BPD was low among PTSD patients (emptiness being the highest at 22% and identity disturbance the lowest at 2%). Among the CPTSD patients, emptiness was the most commonly met criteria (82%), followed by mood lability (42%), unstable relationships (34%), and paranoia/dissociation (33%), but the remaining symptoms were 20% or lower. For both the PTSD and CPTSD groups suicidality and self-harm were at about 15%. However, for the BPD group, suicidality and self-harm was endorsed by 49% and identity disturbance by 68%. BPD patients scored higher than the PTSD and CPTSD patients on every criterion except emptiness: Both

BPD and CPTSD scored higher than those in the PTSD class. Cloitre et al. found that the relationship difficulties in those with CPTSD tended to consist of avoiding relationships much like those with internalizing anxiety disorders; BPD patients also can be scared of getting close to others, but this tends to vacillate with dependency, fears of abandonment, and chaotic relationships. With regard to identity, those with BPD tend to have vacillating self-concepts (often blaming self vs. blaming others), those with CPTSD have stable negative self-concepts, and those with PTSD proper tend not to have negative self-concepts. With regard to affect regulation, there is much less impulsivity, anger, and mood lability in CPTSD and PTSD than in BPD. Importantly, self-harm and suicidality are important predictors of BPD and much less common among those with CPTSD and PTSD.

Consistent with these findings, although several studies suggest that suicidality is present in those with PTSD, Gratz and Tull (2012) found that the relationship between PTSD and deliberate self-harm was moderated by personality disorder symptoms. Further, in a meta-analysis by Klonsky and Moyer (2008), there was no relationship between childhood sexual abuse and self-injury. These findings are consistent with those of Goodman et al. (2003) and Bornovalova et al. (2013), who have found that childhood trauma does not have a direct causal role in the development of BPD.

Attention-Deficit Disorder and Attention-Deficit/Hyperactivity Disorder

The comorbidity and differential diagnosis between BPD and attention-deficit/hyperactivity disorder (ADHD) in both adolescent and adult patients is increasingly being recognized (Kernberg & Yeomans, 2013). Frequently patients with BPD seek assessments and testing to establish or confirm the presence of ADHD. Identity disturbance in BPD, which can manifest as problems in self-direction, can result in difficulty maintaining the focus needed to complete relatively boring and tedious tasks, such as planning, reading for coursework, and studying for exams, especially in the context of competing pulls such as leisure, recreation, and spending time with friends. Because of the identity disturbance, the individual is unable to subvert immediate interests for longer term goals and muster the effortful control needed to focus and attend to the task at hand. This inability to attend and concentrate is often experienced by the patient with BPD as an attentional problem rather than an identity one. This idea is often compounded for the patient due to school or work failures, such as not having completed assignments or sufficiently studying for exams or work tasks. Although ADHD and BPD can be comorbid, the risk of misdiagnosis is high. The diagnosis of ADHD should be confirmed by parents or school records from early childhood and accompanied by learning difficulties.

Suicidality

Without argument the most consequential characteristic of BPD is the high rate of suicidality. In BPD, suicidality includes suicidal urges, suicidal ideation, threats of suicide and self-harm, NSSI, and suicidal intent. Studies have found that more than 80% of BPD patients report some history of suicidal behavior, with an average of 3.4 lifetime attempts. Completed suicide rates among those with BPD is also high. In a meta-analytic study, Pompili et al. (2005) found that 8% of more than 1,100 patients completed suicide (although a slightly lower rate of 6% was found in two prospective studies; Gunderson et al., 2011; Temes et al., 2019). Regardless, the rate of completed suicide in BPD is much higher than both the general population and for other psychiatric disorders. For instance, meta-analytic studies found a suicide rate of 2.3% among 1,500 plus patients with anorexia nervosa and 1.3% for unmedicated bipolar disorder. Predictors of suicidality include history of parasuicidality, hospitalizations, younger age, hostility, and impulsivity.

Nonsuicidal Self-Injury

The most perplexing symptom of BPD is perhaps NSSI, with 70% to 75% of individuals diagnosed with BPD having engaged in acts of cutting, burning, and overdosing, for example. Studies have also found that those with BPD report varied of reasons for engaging in NSSI. There have been suggestions that individuals diagnosed with BPD are less receptive to pain (Russ et al., 1992; Schmahl et al., 2006). However, the evidence is mixed; for instance, other research has found that BPD is associated with pain sensitivity, particularly with regard to chronic pain syndromes (Carpenter & Trull, 2015). In addition to possible insensitivity to pain, several other precipitants have been reported for engaging in NSSI. These reasons include fighting off and distracting from dissociation and psychological pain with physical pain, punishing the self, trying to reexperience control over one's will, releasing bottled-up feelings of anger and shame, hostility, guilt, general stress, and a means to communicate internal states to others. Zanarini, Frankenburg, Ridolfi, et al. (2006) and others found that roughly a third of individuals with BPD with NSSI start before age 13, a third begin engaging in NSSI during adolescence, and most others in young adulthood (Levy & Clarkin, 2003). In these studies, it was found that it was unusual for those with BPD to begin cutting after their 30s. Importantly, accidental death during NSSI is a risk, as it heightens the risk for intended suicide attempts, but also death as a result of these actions without suicidal ideation.

ASSESSMENT, DIAGNOSIS, AND MISDIAGNOSIS

Despite the obvious clinical utility of knowing whether a patient meets criteria for BPD, research findings indicate that clinicians in ordinary clinical practice often fail to recognize and diagnose personality disorders. As already pointed out earlier, in some studies it has taken up to 10 years to receive a correct BPD diagnosis for nearly three quarters of an affected sample. When directly comparing diagnosis in routine practice to prevalence rates assessed with structured interviews in almost 500 patients, clinicians diagnosed BPD in just 0.4%, whereas structured interviews found 14.4% in the same sample (Zimmerman & Mattia, 1999). At the same time, clinicians seemed to value the clinical utility of structured interviews, as when they were provided with to option to use this information because it was then used two thirds of the time, increasing percentage of diagnosis from 0.4% to 9.5%.

In sum, without formal or structured assessment, clinicians are likely to miss many cases of BPD, which can have negative consequences for case conceptualization and result in insufficient treatment. Although simultaneous interventions for comorbid conditions such as depression may be needed in patients with BPD, the evidence strongly suggests that BPD will not remit when those symptoms get less burdensome but requires specialized treatment. Therefore, the use of formal assessment methods for detecting BPD is recommended for routine practice. This is particularly important for patients meeting criteria for disorders commonly comorbid with BPD, complex comorbidity in general, or a history of diagnoses of a variety of mental disorders.

TREATMENT

Historically, BPD has been considered difficult to treat. Clinical writers have noted that those with BPD often do not adhere to treatment recommendations, use services chaotically, and frequently drop out of treatment. Not surprisingly clinicians are intimidated by those with BPD and thus often expect a negative course of treatment. In addition, therapist burnout, enactments, and even engagement in iatrogenic behavior are more prominent in individuals treating BPD patents. However, contrary to popular—yet outdated—belief, BPD is indeed a treatable disorder.

Psychotherapy

Practitioners and patients have a range of evidence-based treatment options across a number of orientations available to them. Although most of the available treatments were derived from a psychodynamic or cognitive behavioral tradition, they usually tend to be either explicitly or implicitly integrative. In addition to psychodynamic (e.g., transference-focused psychotherapy [Clarkin et al., 2007; Levy et al., 2006]), mentalization-based (Bateman & Fonagy, 2006), and cognitive behavioral treatments (e.g., dialectic behavioral therapy [DBT]; Linehan, 1993), there is a short-term psychoeducational, skills-based group, frequently referenced with the acronym STEPPS (Blum et al., 2002), that was found to be effective as an adjunct with other psychosocial treatments. Furthermore, the American Psychiatric Association practice guidelines name general psychiatric management (Gunderson & Links, 2008) in conjunction with psychodynamic psychotherapy specifically designed for BPD as an efficacious treatment option. Evidence from direct comparisons and meta-analyses shows clearly that there is no advantage provided by DBT compared with these other approaches (e.g., Cristea et al., 2017), although DBT has been tested in more RCTs than other approaches. In other words, there are several equally good treatments available with no credible or reliable evidence that any one treatment is significantly better than any other, which is also important for patient preferences and choice.

Treatment Length

BPD develops over many years and tends to be chronic disorder; thus, it is not surprising that it most likely requires a longer term treatment in which patients and therapists meet at least weekly, often twice weekly, or in a combination of individual and group treatment. To date, all efficacious treatments for BPD have been conceptualized as a multiyear process, although most research endeavors have only examined efficacy after 1 year of treatment; several studies have shown that for intense treatments, effects are often detectable by 6 months, particularly with regard to symptoms (as opposed to personality).

Expected Outcomes

In addition to patient choice preferences, it is important to have different treatment options; given the heterogeneity of BPD, it is unlikely that any one treatment will be equally effective for all patients. Findings from RCTs suggest that approximately 50% to 60% of patients make symptomatic improvements within a year of treatment, with many of those showing change even in the first half of that time. Approximately 49% to 71% achieve remission in longer follow-up studies (Álvarez-Tomás et al., 2019). At the same time, about 50% of patients do not respond to treatments (Woodbridge et al., 2021) and still experience significant impairments. From a clinical perspective, even though effective interventions are available for BPD, a significant portion of patients are not improving from a given treatment, again pointing toward the relevance of having a variety of different therapies available.

Therapist Training

A key part of successful treatments for BPD is their modification and adaptation from standard approaches commonly practiced in the community. In fact, there is little evidence that unmodified psychodynamic, cognitive behavioral, humanistic, and other approaches are beneficial for individuals suffering from BPD (Cristea et al., 2017). Examples of modifications include the explication of a coherent model of the problem and treatment, a clear focus and priorities, an increased attention to explicit frame issues, vigilance for indications of colluding with the patient, acting out or iatrogenic behaviors on the therapist's part, provision of supervision or intervision, and integration with other services, among other aspects. These modifications require specific skills, and therefore clinicians who treat individuals with BPD should have training in one or more of the empirically supported treatments (but see Levy & Ellison, 2021), and employ evidence-based principles deriving from these treatments.

Medications

Medications are a useful adjunct in the overall treatment of BPD but are generally not considered to be sufficient in themselves. To date, there is no medication that is efficacious in the treatment of BPD. Instead, a medication approach targeting specific symptom domains has evolved. Historically, the symptom domains of impulses, affect and mood, and cognitive-perceptual processes were frequent targets. Over time, this approach fell out of favor because it led to increased medication rates and polypharmacological complications, which have been associated with several unwanted and adverse events, iatrogenic symptoms, and being a risk factor for negative health outcomes, such as obesity and diabetes. In fact, even compared with a family history of obesity or a physically inactive lifestyle, being on three or more psychotropic medications results in a greater risk factor for obesity. Further, prescribed medications are all too frequently used in drug overdoses. Moreover, there is evidence that monopharmacotherapy is superior to polypharmacology Thus, the recommendation is for selecting medications, if needed, on the bases of safety and tolerability rather than specific symptom picture. In line with this recommendation, several RCTs have convincingly shown that during successful psychotherapy, medication use can be substantially reduced.

CONCLUSION

We argue that the diagnosis of BPD is an important clinical concept that has important clinical utility. Factor analytic studies show that its symptoms are regularly associated with each other to form a coherent construct (Hallquist & Pilkonis, 2012; Johnson & Levy, 2020; Sharp et al., 2015; Wright et al., 2016). Current data from the AMPD and the main structure of the *ICD-11* (Bluml & Doering, 2021; Tyrer et al., 2019) converge with the findings of a general psychopathology or "p" factor (Caspi & Moffitt, 2018), and the recent findings within assessment of personality pathology about general ('g') and specific ('s') factors (Sharp et al., 2015; Wright et al., 2016; see also Levy, 2018). Additionally, epidemiological studies show that BPD is quite prevalent (Grant et al., 2008) and a serious psychiatric and psychological problem. Suicidality and NSSI are among the most serious symptoms of BPD, with 60% to 85% of patients attempting suicide at least once, and with completed suicide found in 8% of patients in one meta-analysis, a rate higher than the general population and then other psychiatric disorders. The good news is that a burgeoning number of RCTs showing efficacy in the treatment of BPD with specialized psychotherapies deriving from both cognitive behavioral and psychodynamic traditions (Cristea et al., 2017). Efficacious therapies include DBT (Linehan, 1993), mentalization-based treatment (Bateman & Fonagy, 2006), schema therapy (Young et al., 2003), transference-focused psychotherapy (Yeomans et al., 2015), and dynamic deconstructive psychotherapy (Gregory & Remen, 2008). In addition, there is some evidence that a generalist approach, known as general psychiatric management (Gunderson & Links, 2008), that includes an individual therapy component, is effective. Finally, several adjunctive therapies may be useful as add-ons to individual specialized treatments. These include systems training for emotional predictability and problem-solving (Blum et al., 2002), emotion regulation group therapy (Gratz & Gunderson, 2006), DBT skills groups (Linehan et al., 2015), and motive-oriented therapeutic relationship (Kramer et al., 2014), although it would be premature and not supported by research to rely exclusively on such approaches. Efforts to disseminate treatments more widely are needed.

REFERENCES

Álvarez-Tomás, I., Ruiz, J., Guilera, G., & Bados, A. (2019). Long-term clinical and functional course of borderline personality disorder: A meta-analysis of prospective studies. *European Psychiatry, 56*, 75–83. https://doi.org/10.1016/j.eurpsy.2018.10.010

American Psychiatric Association. (1980). *Diagnostic and statistical manual of mental disorders* (3rd ed.).

American Psychiatric Association. (2013). *Diagnostic and statistical manual of mental disorders* (5th ed.).

American Psychiatric Association, Committee on Nomenclature and Statistics. (1968). *Diagnostic and statistical manual of mental disorders* (2nd ed.).

Bateman, A. W., & Fonagy, P. (2006). *Mentalization-based treatment for borderline personality disorder: A practical guide.* Oxford University Press. https://doi.org/10.1093/med/9780198570905.001.0001

Beck, A. T., & Freeman, A. M. (1990). *Cognitive therapy of personality disorders.* Guilford Press.

Biberdzic, M., Ensink, K., Normandin, L., & Clarkin, J. F. (2018). Empirical typology of adolescent personality organization. *Journal of Adolescence, 66*, 31–48.

Blum, N., Pfohl, B., John, D. S., Monahan, P., & Black, D. W. (2002). STEPPS: A cognitive-behavioral systems-based group treatment for outpatients with borderline personality disorder—A preliminary report. *Comprehensive Psychiatry, 43*(4), 301–310.

Bluml, V., & Doering, S. (2021). *ICD-11* personality disorders: A psychodynamic perspective on personality functioning. *Frontier in Psychiatry, 12*, 654026. https://doi.org/10.3389/fpsyt.2021.654026

Bornovalova, M. A., Hicks, B. M., Iacono, W. G., & McGue, M. (2013). Longitudinal twin study of borderline personality disorder traits and substance use in adolescence: Developmental change, reciprocal effects, and genetic and environmental influences. *Personality Disorders, 4*(1), 23–32. https://doi.org/10.1037/a0027178

Carpenter, R. W., & Trull, T. J. (2015). The pain paradox: Borderline personality disorder features, self-harm history, and the experience of pain. *Personality Disorders: Theory, Research, and Treatment, 6*(2), 141–151.

Caspi, A., & Moffitt, T. E. (2018). All for one and one for all: Mental disorders in one dimension. *American Journal of Psychiatry, 175*(9), 831–844.

Chapman, D. P., Whitfield, C. L., Felitti, V. J., Dube, S. R., Edwards, V. J., & Anda, R. F. (2004). Adverse childhood experiences and the risk of depressive disorders in adulthood. *Journal of Affective Disorders, 82*(2), 217–225. https://doi.org/10.1016/j.jad.2003.12.013

Clark, L. A. (2007). Assessment and diagnosis of personality disorder: Perennial issues and an emerging reconceptualization. *Annual Review of Psychology, 58*(1), 227–257. https://doi.org/10.1146/annurev.psych.57.102904.190200

Clark, P. (1919). Some practical remarks about the use of modified psychoanalysis in the treatment of borderland neurosis and psychoses. *Psychoanalytic Review, 6*, 3066308.

Clarkin, J. F., Levy, K. N., & Ellison, W. D. (2010). Personality disorders. In L. M. Horowitz & S. Strack (Eds.), *Handbook of interpersonal psychology: Theory, research, assessment, and therapeutic interventions* (pp. 383–403). John Wiley & Sons.

Clarkin, J. F., Levy, K. N., Lenzenweger, M. F., & Kernberg, O. F. (2007). Evaluating three treatments for borderline personality disorder: A multiwave study. *The American Journal of Psychiatry, 164*(6), 922–928. https://doi.org/10.1176/ajp.2007.164.6.922

Cloitre, M., Garvert, D. W., Weiss, B., Carlson, E. B., & Bryant, R. A. (2014). Distinguishing PTSD, complex PTSD, and borderline personality disorder: A latent class analysis. *European Journal of Psychotraumatology, 5*(1), 25097. https://doi.org/10.3402/ejpt.v5.25097

Compton, W. M., Thomas, Y. F., Stinson, F. S., & Grant, B. F. (2007). Prevalence, correlates, disability, and comorbidity of *DSM-IV* drug abuse and dependence in the United States: Results from the national epidemiologic survey on alcohol and related conditions. *Archives of General Psychiatry, 64*(5), 566–576. https://doi.org/10.1001/archpsyc.64.5.566

Costa, P. T., & McCrae, R. R. (1992). Normal personality assessment in clinical practice: The NEO Personality Inventory. *Psychological Assessment, 4*(1), 5–13. https://doi.org/10.1037/1040-3590.4.1.5

Cristea, I. A., Gentili, C., Cotet, C. D., Palomba, D., Barbui, C., & Cuijpers, P. (2017). Efficacy of psychotherapies for borderline personality disorder: A systematic review and meta-analysis. *JAMA Psychiatry, 74*(4), 319–328. https://doi.org/10.1001/jamapsychiatry.2016.4287

Deutsch, H. (1942). Some forms of emotional disturbance and their relationship to schizophrenia. *Psychoanalytic Quarterly, 11*, 301–321.

Diamond, D., Yeomans, F. E., & Levy, K. N. (2011). Psychodynamic psychotherapy for narcissistic personality. In W. K. Campbell & J. D. Miller (Eds.), *The handbook of narcissism and narcissistic personality disorder: Theoretical approaches, empirical findings, and treatments* (pp. 423–433). John Wiley & Sons.

Ehrenthal, J. C., & Benecke, C. (2019). Tailored treatment planning for individuals with personality disorders: The OPD approach. In U. Kramer (Ed.), *Case formulation for personality disorders: Tailoring psychotherapy to the individual client* (pp. 291–314). Elsevier. https://doi.org/10.1016/B978-0-12-813521-1.00015-1

Goodman, M., Weiss, D. S., Koenigsberg, H., Kotlyarevsky, V., New, A. S., Mitropoulou, V., Silverman, J. M., O'Flynn, K., & Siever, L. J. (2003). The role of childhood trauma in differences in affective instability in those with personality disorders. *CNS Spectrums, 8*(10), 763–770. https://doi.org/10.1017/S1092852900019131

Grant, B. F., Chou, S. P., Goldstein, R. B., Huang, B., Stinson, F. S., Saha, T. D., Smith, S. M., Dawson, D. A., Pulay, A. J., Pickering, R. P., & Ruan, W. J. (2008). Prevalence, correlates, disability, and comorbidity of *DSM-IV* borderline personality disorder: Results from the Wave 2 National Epidemiologic Survey on Alcohol and Related Conditions. *Journal of Clinical Psychiatry, 69*(4), 533–545. https://doi.org/10.4088/jcp.v69n0404

Gratz, K. L., & Gunderson, J. G. (2006). Preliminary data on an acceptance-based emotion regulation group intervention for deliberate self-harm among women with borderline personality disorder. *Behavior Therapy, 37*(1), 25–35. https://doi.org/10.1016/j.beth.2005.03.002

Gratz, K. L., & Tull, M. T. (2012). Exploring the relationship between posttraumatic stress disorder and deliberate self-harm: The moderating roles of borderline and avoidant personality disorders. *Psychiatry Research, 199*(1), 19–23. https://doi.org/10.1016/j.psychres.2012.03.025

Gregory, R. J., & Remen, A. L. (2008). A manual-based psychodynamic therapy for treatment-resistant borderline personality disorder. *Psychotherapy: Theory, Research, Practice, Training, 45*(1), 15–27.

Grilo, C. M., Stout, R. L., Markowitz, J. C., Sanislow, C. A., Ansell, E. B., Skodol, A. E., Bender, D. S., Pinto, A., Shea, M. T., Yen, S., Gunderson, J. G., Morey, L. C.,

Hopwood, C. J., & McGlashan, T. H. (2010). Personality disorders predict relapse after remission from an episode of major depressive disorder: A 6-year prospective study. *The Journal of Clinical Psychiatry, 71*(12), 1629–1635. https://doi.org/10.4088/JCP.08m04200gre

Grinker, R., Werble, B., & Drye, R. (1968). *The borderline syndrome: A behavioral study of ego functions*. Basic Books.

Gunderson, J. G., & Kolb, J. E. (1978). Discriminating features of borderline patients. *The American Journal of Psychiatry, 135*(7), 792–796. https://doi.org/10.1176/ajp.135.7.792

Gunderson, J. G., Kolb, J. E., & Austin, V. (1981). The diagnostic interview for borderline patients. *The American Journal of Psychiatry, 138*(7), 896–903. https://doi.org/10.1176/ajp.138.7.896

Gunderson, J. G., & Links, P. (2008). *Borderline personality disorder: A clinical guide* (2nd ed.). American Psychiatric Press.

Gunderson, J. G., Morey, L. C., Stout, R. L., Skodol, A. E., Shea, M. T., McGlashan, T. H., Zanarini, M. C., Grilo, C. M., Sanislow, C. A., Yen, S., Daversa, M. T., & Bender, D. S. (2004). Major depressive disorder and borderline personality disorder revisited: Longitudinal interactions. *The Journal of Clinical Psychiatry, 65*(8), 1049–1056. https://doi.org/10.4088/JCP.v65n0804

Gunderson, J. G., & Singer, M. T. (1975). Defining borderline patients: An overview. *The American Journal of Psychiatry, 132*(1), 1–10. https://doi.org/10.1176/ajp.132.1.1

Gunderson, J. G., Stout, R. L., McGlashan, T. H., Shea, M. T., Morey, L. C., Grilo, C. M., Zanarini, M. C., Yen, S., Markowitz, J. C., Sanislow, C., Ansell, E., Pinto, A., & Skodol, A. E. (2011). Ten-year course of borderline personality disorder: Psychopathology and function from the Collaborative Longitudinal Personality Disorders study. *Archives of General Psychiatry, 68*(8), 827–837.

Gunderson, J. G., Stout, R. L., Shea, M. T., Grilo, C. M., Markowitz, J. C., Morey, L. C., Sanislow, C., Yen, S., Zanarini, M. C., & Keuroghlian, A. S. (2014). Interactions of borderline personality disorder and mood disorders over 10 years. *The Journal of Clinical Psychiatry, 75*(8), 829–834. https://doi.org/10.4088/JCP.13m08972

Gunderson, J. G., Weinberg, I., Daversa, M., Kueppenbender, K., Zanarini, M., Shea, M., Skodol, A. E., Sanislow, C. A., Yen, S., Morey, L. C., Grilo, C. M., McGlashan, T. H., Stout, R. L., & Dyck, I. (2006). Descriptive and longitudinal observations on the relationship of borderline personality disorder and bipolar disorder. *American Journal of Psychiatry, 163*(7), 1173–1178.

Hallquist, M. N., & Pilkonis, P. A. (2012). Refining the phenotype of borderline personality disorder: Diagnostic criteria and beyond. *Personality Disorders, 3*(3), 228–246. https://doi.org/10.1037/a002795

Heffernan, K., & Cloitre, M. (2000). A comparison of posttraumatic stress disorder with and without borderline personality disorder among women with a history of childhood sexual abuse: Etiological and clinical characteristics. *The Journal of Nervous and Mental Disease, 188*(9), 589–595. https://doi.org/10.1097/00005053-200009000-00005

Henry, C., Mitropoulou, V., New, A. S., Koenigsberg, H. W., Silverman, J., & Siever, L. J. (2001). Affective instability and impulsivity in borderline personality and bipolar II disorders: Similarities and differences. *Journal of Psychiatric Research, 35*(6), 307–312. https://doi.org/10.1016/S0022-3956(01)00038-3

Herman, J. L. (1993). Sequelae of prolonged and repeated trauma: Evidence for a complex posttraumatic syndrome (DESNOS). In J. R. T. Davidson & E. B. Foa (Eds.), *Posttraumatic stress disorder: DSM-IV and beyond* (pp. 213–228). American Psychiatric Press.

Herman, J. L., Perry, J. C., & van der Kolk, B. A. (1989). Childhood trauma in borderline personality disorder. *The American Journal of Psychiatry, 146*(4), 490–495. https://doi.org/10.1176/ajp.146.4.490

Hoch, P., & Polatin, P. (1949). Pseudoneurotic forms of schizophrenia. *Psychiatric Quarterly, 23*(2), 248–276. https://doi.org/10.1007/BF01563119

Hughes, C. (1884). Borderline psychiatric records-prodromal symptoms of physical impairments. *The Alienist and Neurologist, 5*, 85–90.

Johnson, B. N., & Levy, K. N. (2020). Identifying unstable and empty phenotypes of borderline personality through factor mixture modeling in a large nonclinical sample. *Personality Disorders: Theory, Research, and Treatment, 11*(2), 141–150. https://doi.org/10.1037/per0000360

Jones, E. (1918). Anal erotic character traits. In E. Jones (Ed.), *Papers on psychoanalysis* (pp. 261–284). Bailhere, Tindall & Cox. https://doi.org/10.1037/h0075758

Kernberg, O. F. (1967). Borderline personality organization. *Journal of the American Psychoanalytic Association, 15*(3), 641–685. https://doi.org/10.1177/000306516701500309

Kernberg, O. F. (1975/1985). *Borderline conditions and pathological narcissism.* Jason Aronson. (Original work published 1985)

Kernberg, O. F. (1984). *Severe personality disorders: Psychotherapeutic strategies.* Yale University Press.

Kernberg, O. F., & Yeomans, F. E. (2013). Borderline personality disorder, bipolar disorder, depression, attention deficit/hyperactivity disorder, and narcissistic personality disorder: Practical differential diagnosis. *Bulletin of the Menninger Clinic, 77*(1), 1–22. https://doi.org/10.1521/bumc.2013.77.1.1

Kernberg, P. F., Weiner, A. S., & Bardenstein, K. K. (2000). *Personality disorders in children and adolescents.* Basic Books.

Kety, S. S., Rosenthal, D., Wender, P. H., & Schulsinger, F. (1968). The types and prevalence of mental illness in the biological and adoptive families of adopted schizophrenics. *Journal of Psychiatric Research, 6*, 345–362. https://doi.org/10.1016/0022-3956(68)90026-5

Klonsky, E. D., & Moyer, A. (2008). Childhood sexual abuse and non-suicidal self-injury: Meta-analysis. *The British Journal of Psychiatry, 192*(3), 166–170. https://doi.org/10.1192/bjp.bp.106.030650

Knight, R. (1953). Borderline states. In R. Knight & C. Friedman (Eds.), *Psychoanalytic psychiatry & psychology* (pp. 110–122). International Universities Press. https://doi.org/10.1037/10633-012

Koenigsberg, H. W., Harvey, P. D., Mitropoulou, V., New, A. S., Goodman, M., Silverman, J., Serby, M., Schopick, F., & Siever, L. J. (2001). Are the interpersonal and identity disturbances in the borderline personality disorder criteria linked to the traits of affective instability and impulsivity? *Journal of Personality Disorders, 15*(4), 358–370. https://doi.org/10.1521/pedi.15.4.358.19181

Köhling, J., Ehrenthal, J. C., Levy, K. N., Schauenburg, H., & Dinger, U. (2015). Quality and severity of depression in borderline personality disorder: A systematic review and meta-analysis. *Clinical Psychology Review, 37*, 13–25. https://doi.org/10.1016/j.cpr.2015.02.002

Kramer, U., Kolly, S., Berthoud, L., Keller, S., Preisig, M., Caspar, F., Berger, T., de Roten, Y., Marquet, P., & Despland, J. N. (2014). Effects of motive-oriented therapeutic relationship in a ten-session general psychiatric treatment of borderline personality disorder: A randomized controlled trial. *Psychotherapy and Psychosomatics, 83*(3), 176–186. https://doi.org/10.1159/000358528

Kroll, J. (1993). *PTSD/borderlines in therapy: Finding the balance.* W.W. Norton & Company.

Levy, K. N. (2005). The implications of attachment theory and research for understanding borderline personality disorder. *Development and Psychopathology, 17*(4), 959–986. https://doi.org/10.1017/s0954579405050455

Levy, K. N. (2018). Contemporary psychodynamic treatments: Commentary on psychoanalytic/psychodynamic approaches to personality disorders. In C. Lejuez & K. L. Gratz (Eds.), *The handbook on personality disorders* (pp. 440–443). Cambridge University Press.

Levy, K. N., & Clarkin, J. F. (2003). [Unpublished data]. Joan and Sanford I. Weill Medical College of Cornell University.

Levy, K. N., Clarkin, J. F., Foelsch, P. A., & Kernberg, O. F. (2022). *Outpatient treatment with transference-focused psychotherapy for patients diagnosed with borderline personality disorder:*

An ecologically valid, quasi-experimental comparison with a treatment-as-usual cohort [Unpublished manuscript]. Department of Psychology, The Pennsylvania State University.

Levy, K. N., Diamond, D., Clarkin, J. F., & Kernberg, O. F. (in press). Changes in attachment, reflective function, and object representation in transference focused psychotherapy for borderline personality disorder. *Psychoanalytic Psychology*.

Levy, K. N., & Ellison, W. D. (2021). The availability of training opportunities in personality disorders in American Psychological Association- and Psychological Clinical Science Accreditation System-accredited clinical and counseling psychology doctoral programs. *Training and Education in Professional Psychology*. Advance online publication. https://doi.org/10.1037/tep0000376

Levy, K. N., & Johnson, B. N. (2016). Personality disorders. In J. C. Norcross, G. R. VandenBos, D. K. Freedheim, & N. Pole (Eds.), *APA handbook of clinical psychology: Psychopathology and health* (pp. 173–207). American Psychological Association. https://doi.org/10.1037/14862-006

Levy, K. N., Kivity, Y., & Yeomans, F. E. (2019). Case formulation in transference-focused psychotherapy. In U. Kramer (Ed.), *Case formulation for personality disorders: Tailoring psychotherapy to the individual client*. Elsevier.

Levy, K. N., Meehan, K. B., Kelly, K. M., Reynoso, J. S., Weber, M., Clarkin, J. F., & Kernberg, O. F. (2006). Change in attachment patterns and reflective function in a randomized control trial of transference-focused psychotherapy for borderline personality disorder. *Journal of Consulting and Clinical Psychology, 74*(6), 1027–1040.

Levy, K. N., Reynoso, J. S., Wasserman, R. W., & Clarkin, J. F. (2007). Narcissistic personality disorder. In W. O'Donohue, K. A. Fowler, & S. O. Lilienfeld (Eds.), *Personality disorders: Toward the DSM-V* (pp. 233–277). Sage Publications. https://doi.org/10.4135/9781483328980.n9

Linehan, M. M. (1993). *Cognitive-behavioral treatment of borderline personality disorder*. Guilford Press.

Linehan, M. M., Korslund, K. E., Harned, M. S., Gallop, R. J., Lungu, A., Neacsiu, A. D., McDavid, J., Comtois, K. A., & Murray-Gregory, A. M. (2015). Dialectical behavior therapy for high suicide risk in individuals with borderline personality disorder: A randomized clinical trial and component analysis. *JAMA Psychiatry, 72*(5), 475–482. https://doi.org/10.1001/jamapsychiatry.2014.3039

Matthies, S. D., & Philipsen, A. (2014). Common ground in attention deficit hyperactivity disorder (ADHD) and borderline personality disorder (BPD)—Review of recent findings. *Borderline Personality Disorder and Emotion Dysregulation, 1*(1), 3. https://doi.org/10.1186/2051-6673-1-3

Meyerson, D. (2009, May). *Is borderline personality disorder underdiagnosed?* [Paper presentation]. 162nd Annual Convention of the American Psychiatric Association, San Francisco, CA, United States.

Millon, T. (1981). *Disorders of personality: DSM-III, Axis II*. John Wiley & Sons.

Morey, L. C. (2019). Interdiagnostician reliability of the *DSM-5* Section II and Section III Alternative Model criteria for borderline personality disorder. *Journal of Personality Disorders, 33*(6), 721–S18. https://doi.org/10.1521/pedi_2019_33_362

Morey, L. C., Shea, M. T., Markowitz, J. C., Stout, R. L., Hopwood, C. J., Gunderson, J. G., Grilo, C. M., McGlashan, T. H., Yen, S., Sanislow, C. A., & Skodol, A. E. (2010). State effects of major depression on the assessment of personality and personality disorder. *The American Journal of Psychiatry, 167*(5), 528–535. https://doi.org/10.1176/appi.ajp.2009.09071023

Paris, J. (2003). Personality disorders over time: Precursors, course and outcome. *Journal of Personality Disorders, 17*(6), 479–488. https://doi.org/10.1521/pedi.17.6.479.25360

Paris, J., Zweig-Frank, H., & Guzder, J. (1994). Psychological risk factors for borderline personality disorder in female patients. *Comprehensive Psychiatry, 35*(4), 301–305. https://doi.org/10.1016/0010-440X(94)90023-X

Pietrzak, R. H., Goldstein, R. B., Southwick, S. M., & Grant, B. F. (2011). Prevalence and Axis I comorbidity of full and partial posttraumatic stress disorder in the United

States: Results from Wave 2 of the National Epidemiologic Survey on Alcohol and Related Conditions. *Journal of Anxiety Disorders, 25*(3), 456–465. https://doi.org/10.1016/j.janxdis.2010.11.010

Pompili, M., Girardi, P., Ruberto, A., & Tatarelli, R. (2005). Suicide in borderline personality disorder: A meta-analysis. *Nordic Journal of Psychiatry, 59*(5), 319–324. https://doi.org/10.1080/08039480500320025

Rapaport, D., Gill, M. M., & Schafer, R. (1968). *Diagnostic psychological testing*. International Universities Press. (Original work published 1946)

Reisch, T., Ebner-Priemer, U. W., Tschacher, W., Bohus, M., & Linehan, M. M. (2008). Sequences of emotions in patients with borderline personality disorder. *Acta Psychiatrica Scandinavica, 118*(1), 42–48. https://doi.org/10.1111/j.1600-0447.2008.01222.x

Rosse, J. (1890). Clinical evidence of borderline insanity. *Journal of Nervous and Mental Disease, 15*(10), 669–683. https://doi.org/10.1097/00005053-189010000-00004

Russ, M. J., Roth, S. D., Lerman, A., Kakuma, T., Harrison, K., Shindledecker, R. D., Hull, J., & Mattis, S. (1992). Pain perception in self-injurious patients with borderline personality disorder. *Biological Psychiatry, 32*(6), 501–511.

Schmahl, C., Bohus, M., Esposito, F., Treede, R. D., Di Salle, F., Greffrath, W., Laudaescher, P., Lieb, K., Scheffler, K., Hennig, J., & Seifritz, E. (2006). Neural correlates of anti-nociception in borderline personality disorder. *Archives of General Psychiatry, 63*(6), 659–666.

Schmideberg, M. (1947). The treatment of psychopaths and borderline patients. *American Journal of Psychotherapy, 1*(1), 45–70. https://doi.org/10.1176/appi.psychotherapy.1947.1.1.45

Sharp, C., & Wall, K. (2021). *DSM-5* level of personality functioning: Refocusing personality disorder on what it means to be human. *Annual Review of Clinical Psychology, 17*(1), 313–337. https://doi.org/10.1146/annurev-clinpsy-081219-105402

Sharp, C., Wright, A. G. C., Fowler, J. C., Frueh, B. C., Allen, J. G., Oldham, J., & Clark, L. A. (2015). The structure of personality pathology: Both general ('g') and specific ('s') factors? *Journal of Abnormal Psychology, 124*(2), 387–398. https://doi.org/10.1037/abn0000033

Stern, A. (1938). Psychoanalytic investigation of therapy in the borderline neuroses. *The Psychoanalytic Quarterly, 7*(4), 467–489. https://doi.org/10.1080/21674086.1938.11925367

Stern, B. L., Diamond, D., & Yeomans, F. E. (2017, October). Transference-focused psychotherapy (TFP) for narcissistic personality: Engaging patients in the early treatment process. *Psychoanalytic Psychology, 34*(4), 381–396. https://doi.org/10.1037/pap0000145

Stone, M. H. (1977). The borderline syndrome: Evolution of the term, genetic aspects, and prognosis. *American Journal of Psychotherapy, 31*(3), 345–365. https://doi.org/10.1176/appi.psychotherapy.1977.31.3.345

Temes, C. M., Frankenburg, F. R., Fitzmaurice, G. M., & Zanarini, M. C. (2019). Deaths by suicide and other causes among patients with borderline personality disorder and personality-disordered comparison subjects over 24 years of prospective follow-up. *Journal of Clinical Psychiatry, 80*(1), 18m12436. https://doi.org/10.4088/jcp.18m12436

Tyrer, P., Crawford, M., Mulder, R., Blashfield, R., Farnam, A., Fossati, A., Kim, Y.-R., Koldobsky, N., Lecic-Tosevski, D., Ndetei, D., Swales, M., Clark, L. A., & Reed, G. M. (2011). The rationale for the reclassification of personality disorder in the 11th revision of the *International Classification of Diseases (ICD-11)*. *Personality and Mental Health, 5*(4), 246–259. https://doi.org/10.1002/pmh.190

Tyrer, P., Mulder, R., Kim, Y. R., & Crawford, M. J. (2019). The development of the *ICD-11* classification of personality disorders: An amalgam of science, pragmatism, and politics. *Annual Review of Clinical Psychology, 15*(1), 481–502. https://doi.org/10.1146/annurev-clinpsy-050718-095736

Widiger, T. A., Bach, B., Chmielewski, M., Clark, L. A., DeYoung, C., Hopwood, C. J., Kotov, R., Krueger, R. F., Miller, J. D., Morey, L. C., Mullins-Sweatt, S. N., Patrick, C. J., Pincus, A. L., Samuel, D. B., Sellbom, M., South, S. C., Tackett, J. L., Watson, D., Waugh, M. H., . . . Thomas, K. M. (2019). Criterion A of the AMPD in HiTOP. *Journal of Personality Assessment, 101*(4), 345–355. https://doi.org/10.1080/00223891.2018.1465431

Widiger, T. A., & McCabe, G. A. (2020). The Alternative Model of Personality Disorders (AMPD) from the perspective of the five-factor model. *Psychopathology, 53*(3-4), 149–156. https://doi.org/10.1159/000507378

Woodbridge, J., Townsend, M., Reis, S., Singh, S., & Grenyer, B. F. (2021). Non-response to psychotherapy for borderline personality disorder: A systematic review. *The Australian and New Zealand Journal of Psychiatry*, 48674211046893. Advance online publication. https://doi.org/10.1177/00048674211046893

World Health Organization. (2019). *International statistical classification of diseases and related health problems* (11th ed.). https://icd.who.int/

Wright, A. G., Hopwood, C. J., Skodol, A. E., & Morey, L. C. (2016). Longitudinal validation of general and specific structural features of personality pathology. *Journal of Abnormal Psychology, 125*(8), 1120–1134. https://doi.org/10.1037/abn0000165

Yeomans, F. E., Clarkin, J. F., & Kernberg, O. F. (2015). *Transference-focused psychotherapy for borderline personality disorder: A clinical guide.* American Psychiatric Publishing.

Young, J. E., Weishaar, M. E., Klosko, J. S. (2003). *Schema therapy: A practitioner's guide.* Guilford Press.

Zanarini, M. C., & Frankenburg, F. R. (1997). Pathways to the development of borderline personality disorder. *Journal of Personality Disorders, 11*(1), 93–104. https://doi.org/10.1521/pedi.1997.11.1.93

Zanarini, M. C., Frankenburg, F. R., Dubo, E. D., Sickel, A. E., Trikha, A., Levin, A., & Reynolds, V. (1998). Axis I comorbidity of borderline personality disorder. *The American Journal of Psychiatry, 155*(12), 1733–1739. https://doi.org/10.1176/ajp.155.12.1733

Zanarini, M. C., Frankenburg, F. R., Hennen, J., Reich, D. B., & Silk, K. R. (2006). Prediction of the 10-year course of borderline personality disorder. *The American Journal of Psychiatry, 163*(5), 827–832. https://doi.org/10.1176/ajp.2006.163.5.827

Zanarini, M. C., Frankenburg, F. R., Ridolfi, M. E., Jager-Hyman, S., Hennen, J., & Gunderson, J. G. (2006). Reported childhood onset of self-mutilation among borderline patients. *Journal of Personality Disorders, 20*(1), 9–15. https://doi.org/10.1521/pedi.2006.20.1.9

Zilboorg, G. (1941). Ambulatory schizophrenia. *Psychiatry, 4*(2), 149–155. https://doi.org/10.1080/00332747.1941.11022329

Zimmerman, M., Chelminski, I., Dalrymple, K., & Martin, J. (2019). Screening for bipolar disorder and finding borderline personality disorder: A replication and extension. *Journal of Personality Disorders, 33*(4), 533–543. https://doi.org/10.1521/pedi_2018_32_357

Zimmerman, M., Galione, J. N., Ruggero, C. J., Chelminski, I., Young, D., Dalrymple, K., & McGlinchey, J. B. (2010). Screening for bipolar disorder and finding borderline personality disorder. *The Journal of Clinical Psychiatry, 71*(9), 1212–1217. https://doi.org/10.4088/JCP.09m05161yel

Zimmerman, M., & Mattia, J. I. (1999). Differences between clinical and research practices in diagnosing borderline personality disorder. *The American Journal of Psychiatry, 156*(10), 1570–1574. https://doi.org/10.1176/ajp.156.10.1570

16

Narcissistic Personality Disorder

Elsa Ronningstam

Narcissism, pathological narcissism (PN), and narcissistic personality disorder (NPD) have been defined differently in social and clinical psychology, as well as in psychiatry and psychoanalysis. This has contributed to confusion and opposing assessments of individuals struggling with these conditions, and efforts to reach consistency or clarity have often been unsuccessful. However, the recent introduction of a dimensional diagnostic approach to personality disorders has paved the way for connection and integration of a broader range of definitions and identifying facets of narcissistic personality functioning. The decision to preserve NPD and include it as a diagnosis in the Alternative *DSM-5* Model for Personality Disorders (AMPD) in Section III of the *Diagnostic and Statistical Manual of Mental Disorders* (5th ed.; *DSM-5*; American Psychiatric Association, 2013; see Exhibit 16.1) is an important step forward in providing an integrated and clinically comprehensive conceptualization of narcissistic pathology and the NPD diagnosis. Similarly, the recently published *International Statistical Classification of Diseases and Related Health Problems* (11th ed.; *ICD-11*; World Health Organization, 2019) classification of personality disorders, with its focus on core personality dysfunction and levels of severity with trait domain specifiers, opens the possibility for internationally coordinated diagnostic assessments of NPD. This is also of significant importance given that NPD was not included in previous editions of the *ICD*.

There are major similarities between AMPD and *ICD-11*; for example, both incorporate personality functioning and trait domains in the diagnosis of personality disorders. *ICD-11* includes in its diagnostic criteria self-functioning;

https://doi.org/10.1037/0000310-017
Personality Disorders and Pathology: Integrating Clinical Assessment and Practice in the DSM-5 *and* ICD-11 *Era*, S. K. Huprich (Editor)
Copyright © 2022 by the American Psychological Association. All rights reserved.

EXHIBIT 16.1

Narcissistic Personality Disorder in *DSM-5*, Section III: The Alternative Hybrid Model Dimensions and Traits

Moderate or greater impairment in personality functioning, manifested by characteristic difficulties in two\or more of the following areas:

1. **Identity:** Excessive reference to others for self-definition and self-esteem regulation; exaggerated self-appraisal may be inflated or deflated, or vacillate between extremes; emotional regulation mirrors fluctuations in self-esteem

2. **Self-direction:** Goal-setting is based on gaining approval from others; personal standards are unreasonably high in order to see oneself as exceptional, or too low based on a sense of entitlement; often unaware of own motivations

3. **Empathy:** Impaired ability to recognize or identify with the feelings and needs of others; excessively attuned to reactions of others, but only if perceived as relevant to self; over- or underestimates own effect on others

4. **Intimacy:** Relationships are largely superficial and exist to serve self-esteem regulation; mutuality is constrained by little genuine interest in others' experiences and predominance of a need for personal gain

Narcissistic Personality Disorder Traits

1. **Grandiosity** (an aspect of Antagonism):
   - feelings of entitlement, either overt or covert;
   - self-centeredness;
   - firmly holding to the belief that one is better than others; condescending toward others.

2. **Attention seeking** (an aspect of Antagonism):
   - excessive attempts to attract and be the focus of others' attention
   - admiration seeking

Note. From *Diagnostic and Statistical Manual of Mental Disorders* (5th ed., pp. 767–768), 2013, American Psychiatric Association (https://doi.org/10.1176/appi.books.9780890425596). Copyright 2013 by the American Psychiatric Association. Reprinted with permission.

interpersonal functioning; and manifestations of emotional, cognitive, and behavioral personality dysfunction, which can be helpful in identifying the specific pathology of narcissistic personality functioning. AMPD assesses identity, self-direction, empathy, and intimacy. Both systems share the trait domains of negative affectivity, detachment, and disinhibitions; *ICD-11* also includes dissociality and anankastia, whereas *DSM-5* refers to antagonism and psychoticism.

The criteria-based diagnosis of NPD in *DSM-5* Section II (see Exhibit 16.2), which has had only minor changes made since its inclusion in 1980, provides an insufficient conceptualization of NPD and does not cover the ranges of PN with different degrees of severity, including both high-functioning as well as severely dysfunctional and malignant narcissism. Neither does it cover the contrasting phenotypes of PN, including grandiose versus vulnerable, thick skinned versus thin skinned, overt versus covert, or arrogant versus shy. Expressions of PN (i.e., overt/external/interpersonal vs. covert/internal/intrapersonal) and self-regulatory fluctuations in self-esteem, emotions, empathy, and interpersonal

Narcissistic Personality Disorder 377

EXHIBIT 16.2

Diagnostic Criteria for Narcissistic Personality Disorder in *DSM-5* Section II

A pervasive pattern of grandiosity (in fantasy or behavior), need for admiration, and lack of empathy, beginning by early adulthood and present in a variety of contexts, and indicated by five (or more) of the following:

1. Grandiose sense of self-importance (e.g., exaggerates achievements and talents, expects to be recognized as superior without commensurate achievements).
2. Preoccupied with fantasies of unlimited success, power, brilliance, beauty or ideal love.
3. Believes that he or she is "special" and unique and can only be understood by, or should associate with, other special or high-status people (or institutions).
4. Requires excessive admiration.
5. Sense of entitlement (i.e., unreasonable expectations of especially favorable treatment or automatic compliance with his or her expectations).
6. Interpersonally exploitive (i.e., takes advantage of others to achieve his or her own ends).
7. Lacks empathy; is unwilling to recognize or identify with the feelings and needs of others.
8. Envious of others or believes that others are envious of him or her.
9. Shows arrogant, haughty behaviors or attitudes.

Note. From *Diagnostic and Statistical Manual of Mental Disorders* (5th ed., pp. 669–670), 2013, American Psychiatric Association (https://doi.org/10.1176/appi.books.9780890425596). Copyright 2013 by the American Psychiatric Association. Reprinted with permission.

relations are not included. In addition, the diagnostic criteria for PN and NPD do often not capture the complex interaction between internal and interpersonal functioning or between the often-subtle underlying interactions between neurobiological, cognitive, and psychophysiological processes.

Empirical studies and clinical accounts over the past 20 years have pointed to different factors that can cause and influence emotion dysregulation and self-esteem fluctuations in patients with PN or NPD, such as temperament, hypersensitivity and reactivity, attachment patterns, and early psychological trauma (Diamond et al., 2014; Maldonado, 2006; Ronningstam, 2017; Simon, 2002; Thomaes et al., 2009; Tritt et al., 2009). Furthermore, several features and functional patterns central to PN are not included, such as compromised ability to recognize, tolerate, and process emotions, especially rage, shame, and fear; hypervigilance and hypersensitivity; a need for control and fear of losing control; perfectionism; aggressivity with critical, resentful, or retaliating interpersonal behavior; avoidance and dismissive interpersonal patterns; underlying narcissistic trauma; and potential suicidality.

One of the major challenges in identifying and treating PN and NPD has involved the range of presentations and levels of functioning in individuals who struggle with these conditions. High levels of functioning, which include significant competence and accomplishments with the ability to maintain relationships, can seem counterintuitive to personality pathology, which usually is associated with the opposite (i.e., fluctuating or low functioning). On the other hand, strikingly provocative interpersonal patterns with an inability to maintain close relationships, and the co-occurrence of an enhanced/grandiose and a devalued/vulnerable and insecure sense of self, is also representative of

NPD, especially on lower levels of functioning. Nevertheless, maintaining control and accessing a sense of agency and direction are core components in pathological narcissistic functioning. Efforts to win attention, approval, and recognition are important for some individuals' self-esteem regulation, whereas distance, avoidance, or even isolation, with interactions taking place only under very controlled conditions, such as in virtual video games, are central to others'. Co-occurring mental conditions, such as substance use, mood disorder, obsessive-compulsive disorder, eating disorders, or other characterological features or personality disorders, such as borderline personality disorder and psychopathy or antisocial behavior, can either conceal or exaggerate narcissistic pathology (Fulford et al., 2008; Gordon & Dombeck, 2010; Russell et al., 2022; Stinson et al., 2008; Vaglum, 1999; Widiger, 2011). In addition, sudden or prolonged external circumstances or specific life stages can have a significant impact on the individual's narcissistic stability and balance, affecting both self-perception and sense of self-worth (Caligor et al., 2015; Gabbard & Crisp-Han, 2016, 2018; Yakeley, 2018). The aim of this chapter is to provide a guideline for diagnostic assessment and an overview of treatment modalities for NPD.

AT THE CROSSROADS OF DIAGNOSTIC APPROACHES

The introduction in *DSM-5* of the AMPD (*DSM-5* Section III; see Exhibit 16.1), which integrates dimensional and trait aspects of personality functioning, in addition to the traditional trait model (*DSM-5* Section II; see Exhibit 16.2), is a major step forward in providing access to and describing PN and NPD. This alternative model was developed in response to substantial criticism directed toward the categorical trait-based system, and its introduction contributed to many necessary improvements and corrections in the diagnosis of NPD. The dimensions of personality functioning, including identity, self-direction, empathy, and intimacy, are all relevant to NPD functioning and provide appropriate guidance for diagnostic assessment and choice of treatment modality and focus. In addition to the dimensions of personality functioning, at least one of two pathological traits related to specific domains has to be present. For NPD, the trait facets related to the trait domain of antagonism are *grandiosity* (feelings of entitlement, either overt or covert, self-centeredness; firmly holding the belief that one is better than others; and being condescending toward others), and *attention seeking* (excessive attempts to attract and be the focus of the attention of others; admiration seeking; American Psychiatric Association, 2013, p. 768).

The AMPD promotes a regulatory, dynamic approach to the diagnostic assessment and formulation of NPD. It captures a broader range of narcissistic personality functioning, including fluctuations and variability, as well as the complex range of phenotypic and clinical presentations. It incorporates central concepts, such as self-direction related to self-agency, competence, decision making, and sense of control (internal or external). In addition, the AMPD attends to self-regulation in interpersonal relations and how self-regulation is influenced by emotions; empathic capability; and self-esteem, with its range and fluctuations. In line with recent research, empathy is considered a capability with *impairment* and *fluctuations*, affected by deficits in emotional processing as well as by motivation (Baskin-Sommers et al., 2014; Ritter et al., 2011). This is one of the major clarifications and changes in the specification of PN (i.e., that individuals with NPD have fluctuating empathic capability with usually intact cognitive empathic functioning but limited or oscillating emotional empathic functioning). In addition, their motivation for empathic engagement can vary significantly. In other words, NPD is associated not with a lack of empathy but with individually specific and compromised empathic functioning that needs careful assessment. An additional advantage is that the AMPD in general applies a language that is more diagnostically meaningful and informative and less one-sided and derogatory.

A dimensional conceptualization of the self-regulatory nature of PN can help identify the patient's fluctuating self-esteem and the co-occurrence of self-enhancing grandiosity and self-diminishing vulnerability. It can also help differentiate temporary fluctuations or externally evoked features and patterns from consistent enduring indications of PN. Most important, it enables clinicians and therapists to recognize narcissistic individuals' internal struggles related to insecurity, self-criticism, anxiety, shame, and fear, which can often stand in sharp contrast to the external and often-domineering or provocatively assertive surface and interpersonal presentation (Ronningstam, 2020).

Conceptualizing narcissistic personality functioning and its co-occurrence with other mental conditions in terms of a dimensional range has several advantages. First, narcissism can range from healthy and proactive to pathological and malignant functioning. Normal aspects of narcissism with healthy self-esteem and emotion regulation can co-occur with PN and even severe forms of NPD either consistently or in specific life contexts (Stone, 1998). Second, self-enhancing grandiosity, arrogance, and aggressivity usually co-occur with vulnerability, including insecurity and inferiority in people diagnosed with PN and NPD (Pincus et al., 2014; Russ et al., 2008). Although one form of narcissism can be more phenotypically prevailing than the other, in assessment, and especially in treatment, it is important to attend to the interactions and fluctuations between the two. Third, individuals with NPD often present with a range of symptoms, from overtly striking and provocative to covertly hidden, unnoticeable narcissistic patterns and features (Akhtar, 1989). Protective patterns, such as controlling, hiding, and avoiding, along with shame, denial, and limited self-disclosure, can contribute to diagnostic misinterpretations and the bypassing of significant narcissistic features and personality functioning. On the other hand, the dominance of extreme extrovert symptoms, with bluntly provocative, critical, manipulative, controlling, or competitive personality patterns, can also lead to neglect of underlying narcissistic fragility and insecurity. Fourth, narcissistic personality functioning is highly influenced by life context and specific events that can either enhance the severity of narcissistic pathology or contribute to a corrective organizing impact on pathological narcissistic patterns (Ronningstam et al., 1995). Fifth, mood disorders, such as depressive disorder or bipolar II, are often comorbid with NPD and readily contribute to the redirection of assessment and treatment away from personality pathology. It is important, however, to distinguish biochemically based mood disorders from characterological, emotional depression and self-esteem–related mood fluctuations, which in NPD are connected to intense self-negativity (i.e., feeling inferior, devalued, undeserving, and hopeless, especially in the context of unreachable enhanced aspirations or superior envisions of oneself; Huprich, 2020; Huprich et al., 2018). Similarly, excitement related to actual or envisioned achievements and acknowledgments can co-occur with mood elevation.

In addition to the typical diagnostic traits included in *DSM-5*, some other common features and underlying denominators are central to PN and hence diagnostically useful. Perfectionism can both serve to enhance self-esteem as well as being a reason for failure and accompanying self-criticism. A need for control, both internally and interpersonally, is a strong indicator of PN and often is associated with hypervigilance and fears related to losing control. Similarly, hiding and avoiding are also effective ways of maintaining control and steering clear of intolerable emotional or interpersonal issues. Aggression and shame are closely related and often intertwined so that signs of anger can evoke shame, or shame can trigger aggressive reactions or behavior. Underlying psychological trauma and early attachment patterns, such as avoidant, dismissive, or preoccupied, can set the tone for the individual's specific interpersonal functioning and experiences (Diamond & Mehan, 2013; Glickauf-Hughes & Wells, 1995; Kernberg, 1992; Maldonado, 2006; Pincus et al., 2014; Roepke & Vater, 2014; Ronningstam, 2011, 2012).

DIMENSIONAL ASSESSMENT OF PATHOLOGICAL NARCISSISM AND NARCISSISTIC PERSONALITY DISORDER

When diagnosing and initiating treatment with patients with NPD, it is especially informative for clinicians and psychotherapists to keep in mind that the patient's external presentations and interactive patterns can be quite different from their internal experiences and processing. In other words, compartmentalization and fragmentation contributing to identity diffusion and different appearance in different presentations and interactive styles in various contexts are common; as a consequence, an important part of the assessment process is pointing out and exploring when such discrepancies become obvious. For example, "I notice that you are smiling when you are talking about how your manager at work humiliates and aggravates you with his comments. How come?"

Because PN and NPD are identified primarily by self-esteem regulation (i.e., self-enhancement, and grandiosity in particular), it is important in diagnostic assessment to thoroughly differentiate and evaluate the many aspects of this as it relates to the dimension of self-direction. Moments and areas of real competence, or even exceptional abilities, which can provide a foundation for high, stable, and positive self-esteem and a sense of agency, are different from a self-aggrandizing and inflated personality style with self-focused bragging, haughtiness, confidence, assertiveness, and arrogance, which often are accompanied by overt or covert condescending, critical devaluation of others or an intolerance of others' weaknesses. Nevertheless, they can often coexist and surface in different contexts. This must be differentiated from lesser or non-reality-anchored grandiose or enhancing self-evaluation, with fantasies about achievement or personal talents that expand beyond the person's real abilities and accomplishments. An additional aspect of self-esteem that is important to attend to in the assessment of NPD is the actual potential capabilities and personal assets hidden behind grandiose fantasies and low self-esteem, insecurity, self-criticism or perfectionist ideals, avoidance, and fear of failure. Experiences of a sudden loss of competence can contribute to chronic insecurity, self-criticism, internal fear of failure, or self-hatred.

Interpersonal dominance, aggression, and competitiveness can also co-occur with tendencies to avoid and hide. Most challenging is the confusion in sense of self and direction to which these fluctuations can contribute, which is especially relevant to the assessment of impairment in one's sense of identity. Individuals with NPD can present with difficulties or an inability to integrate and regulate experiences of challenges, failures, and limitations with actual competence, goals, and aspirations and thus be excessively dependent on external cues or references to others for motivation and a sense of ability to function and achieve. Despite their preoccupation with and need for attention from (or connections to) specific others, the ability of persons with NPD to engage in mutual close relationships is limited given that it can evoke an overwhelming sense of dependency with a concomitant fear of losing control, facing weaknesses, or being rejected.

Another paradox relates to the co-occurrence in individuals with NPD of hypersensitivity versus impaired emphatic ability or motivation to attend to the feelings and needs of others. This combined hypervigilant other-orientation and self-serving self-focus can be complicated to assess. The individual may appear attuned and interpersonally competent but indeed struggles with significant detachment and loneliness due to a fear of or inability to access mutuality and genuine interest in others. For example, insecurity, vulnerability to criticism and losses, and tendencies to assign negative subjective meaning to events, can activate or relate to internalized early challenging or trauma-related experiences (Maldonado, 2006; Ronningstam & Baskin-Sommers, 2013; Simon, 2002). This contributes to difficulties with tolerating closeness and intimacy and with handling conflicts and disagreements, which leads to a range of typical narcissism-related interpersonal reactions or maneuvers.

CASE VIGNETTE

Joanne, a woman in her early 20s, dropped out of college as she was close to graduating and was hospitalized for a range of problems.[1] The admitting clinician took notes on Joanne's anxiety, obsessive preoccupation with perfectionism

---

[1]This vignette has been modified to protect the identity of the subject.

regarding her studies and future aspirations, racing thoughts, social anxiety, avoidance, and suicidal preoccupation. The case manager obtained information from family members and one of Joanne's friends, all of whom described her as very focused on her own achievements and as having the ability to get top grades and awards. However, she was also perceived as critical and demeaning, readily becoming dismissive or envious of others. On the other hand, with a small group of friends with whom she shared music performance and yoga, she was considered collaborative and friendly but distant and difficult to get to know. To her assigned individual psychotherapist, Joanne described herself as struggling with internal agony caused by what she perceived as inconsistent cognitive intellectual functioning and feelings of being overwhelmed by insecurity and internal self-criticism. She often felt frustrated with other people and found them stupid, unpredictable, and difficult to understand. Foremost, however, she was concerned about how she was or would be perceived by others and extremely worried about her future after graduating from college because she believed that, although she had top grades, she could not fully trust her faculties and had trouble envisioning herself pursuing and managing the academic track to which she had long aspired.

Joanne's grandmother was a highly renowned physician, and her mother, who had struggled with substance dependency and major depressive disorder since Joanne's childhood, had been moody, critical, and unreliable. Consequently, Joanne felt divided between becoming a failure, like her mother, or a success, like her grandmother. She felt ashamed of her mother but at the same time doubtful of whether she herself could, or even deserved to, do well, and although she sincerely wanted to please her grandmother and meet her expectations, Joanne also feared that she would fail and disappoint her if she tried. In diagnostic testing with a self-report screening for personality disorders, she met eight of the nine *DSM* criteria for NPD (not exploitive). In follow-up testing with the Diagnostic Interview for Narcissism (3rd ed.; Ronningstam & Gunderson, 1997) she met criteria for a high level of PN in the areas of self-experiences, interpersonal relations, reactivity, and affects and mood states, and she met the diagnosis of NPD.

After discussing this rather diverse picture with her psychotherapist, Joanne said,

> I do not know from one day to another whether I can rely on my thinking and capability, access my knowledge, and communicate and perform. I struggle inside myself with dreadful self-scolding, constantly comparing and criticizing myself. I am a perfectionist, and I know that I can be very good, but it does not help because it does not hold up. Thinking of my mother, I should not aspire to become a medical doctor because she hated her mother, but my grandmother has been like a role model for me, always looked at me with a smile and told me, "You will become a medical doctor like me." I don't know who I am or what I want. All this has also taken up so much of my time. I have not been able to date, and I don't know what love is, and I feel extremely afraid of the future and ashamed of having to be in treatment.

COMMENTS ON THE CASE VIGNETTE

Joanne had reached a point where her functional fluctuations and problems with her self-esteem, sense of identity, and direction had become so overwhelming that she could not tolerate her life or see a future, and she had doubt about and resistance to starting treatment because she did not know where it would lead.

Her case highlights both the presence of features typical for NPD as well as dimensions related to personality pathology (i.e., sense of identity, goals and direction in life, empathy, emotional tolerance, and interpersonal relations and intimacy). Obviously, Joanne had high intelligence and cognitive functioning with areas of solid competence, as well as areas of exceptional accomplishment. She could also connect with and commit to a group with shared interest in a less competitive context, but she did not engage in deep friendships. She struggled with enhanced self-evaluation and fantasies or visions of becoming successful like her grandmother, but she also presented with age-adequate accomplishments and with a sudden loss of competence. In addition, she showed interpersonal avoidance, aggressivity, competitiveness, internal fear, agony, insecurity, self-criticism, and identity diffusion.

In sum, from a self-esteem perspective, Joanne was unable to integrate and regulate perceptions of expectations, challenges, failures, and limitations in regard to her actual competence, goals, and aspirations. As a consequence, she struggled with severe identity diffusion, which was affected both by her fluctuations in self-esteem and her detachment from closer relationships. In addition, self-preoccupation and self-centeredness impaired her interest in and ability to engage in close, mutual, and intimate relationships, at the same time as she was extremely preoccupied with gaining (vs. not gaining) her grandmother's approval and sustaining herself vis-à-vis her mother. Suicidal ideation and intent can, especially in the context of challenging life stages like graduation, be escalated by fear, shame, underlying rage, or extreme aloneness (Ronningstam et al., 2008). Foremost, however, was that Joanne had also long-standing, complexly divided experiences of herself in relationship to her grandmother and mother, who each had come to represent two totally incompatible female role models and attachment patterns. As a consequence, her pathological grandiose self with internalized self–object relations (Kernberg, 1975) included both enhanced and desired, as well as devalued, undesired, and even threatening, aspects of herself and others. At the same time, Joanne had been able to access her own sense of agency and organize her competence (Fonagy & Target, 1997). This is a central aspect of self-functioning in patients with PN or NPD. It contributes to both balance and fluctuations in real life between an ability for direction, agency, and aspirations (i.e., aspects that can contribute to sustaining or enhancing self-esteem in line with the individual's adaptive competence) and a range of defensive patterns that vary in level of severity. These defensive patterns are noticeable in Joanne's more severe impairments in interpersonal and empathic functioning and in her avoidance

TREATMENT MODALITIES FOR NARCISSISTIC PERSONALITY DISORDER

There are by now several treatment modalities that have been specifically adjusted to PN and NPD and can be useful. Patients' subjective experiences of their problems, as well as their agreement to and level of engagement in treatment, are highly dependent on their motivation to change. Similarly, their curiosity about their own functioning and the causes of problems provides important guidance regarding choice of treatment modality. Their ability to relate and reflect may initially be inhibited, but it is vital for long-term engagement and change. Likewise, their tolerance and understanding of emotions are essential, in particular, those that evolve within the therapeutic alliance, which can be challenging to identify and process. The patient's life situation may also influence motivation for and ability to engage in treatment.

Transference-focused psychotherapy (TFP) for NPD is an object relations–focused modality that attends to the patient's way of relating and to the unfolding narcissistic pathology in relationship to the therapist, especially entitlement, grandiosity, humiliation, shame, envy, and anger. It uses primarily active and interactive exploration with interpretations that focus on identifying and changing internal representations of the self and others and the accompanying emotional and interpersonal dysregulation. Patients who can commit to and engage in an active interactive therapeutic relationship and tolerate intense emotions can benefit from this treatment modality, which also can be flexible and adaptable to patients with more fragile personality functioning (Diamond & Hersh, 2020).

Mentalization-based therapy (MBT) for NPD focuses on attachment-related inhibition of mentalization, nonmentalizing modes, and the narcissistic alien self (i.e., an aspect of the self that was forced on the individual in early development and remained incongruent with their state of mind and identity). The therapist's use of empathic validation and clarification can encourage the patient's reflective ability to further understand the interaction between their life circumstances and their emotional states and reactions. Another step involves the patient's observations and understanding of others' states and intentions and explorations of the impact of their assumptions. In particular, the often rigid, critical, or blaming state of mind in patients with NPD requires extensive exploration and validation and shifts between attention to one's own perspective and experience versus others'. This modality offers a supportive, nonauthoritative strategy for treatment of PN that can be especially useful for attending to narcissistic vulnerability and hypervigilance. Balancing the patient's need to feel understood with active exploration and attention to goals and change makes this modality specifically useful for patients with NPD (Drozek & Unruh, 2020).

Schema-focused therapy for NPD attends to the patient's schema modes as they unfold in relationships both within and outside therapy. It is an integrative modality that incorporates cognitive–behavioral as well as object relations and psychodynamic strategies to challenge the patient's maladaptive schemas related to self and others. The aim is to encourage the patient to change narcissistic modes and promote more adult modes of functioning. Empathic confrontations as well as cognitive behavioral strategies and reparenting are used to change typical schemas, including perfectionism, black-or-white perceptions, and devaluations (Behary & Dieckmann, 2011).

Metacognitive interpersonal therapy (MIT) is a manual-based treatment modality that starts with an autobiographical mode that aims to identify and outline an understanding of the patient's problems. By attending to maladaptive patterns in self-states and self–other schemas, a diminished sense of agency, and impaired metacognition and empathy, this modality promotes perspective taking and an understanding of causalities related to grandiosity, perfectionism, wishful thinking, and poor agency. Movement toward reality-anchored perspective taking and distancing from behaviors involving unhealthy narcissism will promote change, especially in autonomy and interpersonal relationships (Dimaggio & Attinà, 2012).

Cognitive behavior therapy (CBT) can be useful for patients who prefer strategies that focus on identifying and gaining control of behaviors and thoughts. Using validation, psychoeducation, and specifying target behaviors, this treatment can help stabilize self-esteem and emotion dysregulation in patients with NPD, especially because it encourages long-term goals, behavioral responsibility, and change in attitudes The initial clinical objectives include the development of a collaborative relationship, introduction of a cognitive approach to treatment, and establishment of agreements regarding the patient's cognitive and behavioral problems and the treatment approach. Three strategies—psychoeducation, validation, and identifying target behaviors—can be useful in reaching long-term goals related to changing behavior and attitudes. Treatment interventions focus on increasing behavioral responsibility, decreasing cognitive distortions and affect dysregulation, and implementing new attitudes (Beck et al., 1990; Cukrowicz et al., 2011).

Dialectical behavioral therapy (DBT) also identifies target behaviors and symptoms specifically related to emotion intolerance and dysregulation central to NPD, such as self-criticism, shame, anger, and insecurity. Exploration, validation, and implementation of skills can help the patient improve their sense of agency, self- and emotion regulation, and internal control. This modality can be useful for patients who prefer to focus on specific problems and seek clear evidence of progress and change (Reed-Knight & Fischer, 2011).

Group therapy can, in conjunction with individual treatment, attend to interpersonal problems, specifically, difficult patterns of avoidance, shame, dismissiveness, self-sufficiency, and competitiveness. The group setting can encourage both other-oriented attention and self-exposure as well as increased tolerance and understanding of self and others. Nevertheless, balancing self- versus group-related interests can be challenging both for patients and group therapists (Roth, 1998).

Psychoeducation builds on the principles of dialectical behavior therapy, and for patients with NPD this modality can help decrease a fear of the incomprehensible and an anticipated loss of control. The aim is to enhance the patient's sense of agency, control, and directive motivation to change pathological narcissistic patterns and mental processes. Psychoeducation can encourage patients to formulate a purpose and goals for treatment and to explore complex challenges, emotions, and patterns.

Psychopharmacological treatment is considered when patients with NPD have a comorbid Axis I disorder, such as bipolar disorder, major depressive disorder, or anxiety disorder. Attention to possible side effects is important because these patients are sensitive to and readily affected by side effects that influence intellectual and sexual functioning as well as level of energy. Noncompliance with or rejection of psychopharmacological treatment is common, as are expectations of being given the perfect pharmacological treatment. There is no specific pharmacotherapy for PN or NPD; however, specific medications may temporarily help alleviate certain symptoms, such as insomnia due to extreme worries or self-negativity, instability in mood related to self-esteem fluctuation, or depression related to excessive self-negativity. The characterological aspects of the symptoms have to remain the focus in therapy.

CONCLUSION

This chapter has identified the nature of PN and NPD in terms of dimensions that include fragility in self-regulation, self-esteem, and sense of agency accompanied by strong self-protective reactivity and a range of self-enhancing, self-serving behaviors and attitudes. Consequently, the patient's sense of identity can be fragmented and dependent on external approval or appreciation, and the ability for interpersonal relations, empathy, and closeness is impaired. PN and narcissistic personality functioning can take on a variety of phenotypic presentations, ranging from overt and interpersonal pretentiousness, arrogance, and assertiveness to covert and internal vulnerability, insecurity, shyness, and hypersensitivity. It often co-occurs with occasional or consistent high levels of functioning accompanied by sense of agency and competence, or with real special qualities, capabilities, or social skills. It can also contribute to compromised or lost working capacity, hostility and detachment in relationships, reactivity to unmet needs and expectations, or deceptive and deceitful behavior, as well as to occasional criminal and violent acts. Co-occurring self-negativity and depressivity with harsh self-criticism and low self-esteem is common. In some individuals the residual effects of early psychological trauma and trauma associated with symptoms that relate to and affect narcissistic personality functioning can be present (Simon, 2002). Changes in life experiences or actual circumstances may lead to a sudden unfolding of fragility with gradual impairments in personality functioning and aggravations of pathological narcissistic patterns and features. Functional fluctuations can be dependent on interpersonal, as well as social, vocational, or general, life contexts. NPD can also be either enhanced or concealed by comorbid substance use, a mood disorder, or suicidality. Advances in identifying and understanding PN and NPD have led to increased interest in developing optimal treatment strategies, and by now there is an increasing availability of different treatment modalities that can be adjusted to individual patients' needs and abilities.

REFERENCES

Akhtar, S. (1989). Narcissistic personality disorder: Descriptive features and differential diagnosis. *Psychiatric Clinics of North America, 12*(3), 505–529. https://doi.org/10.1016/S0193-953X(18)30411-8

American Psychiatric Association. (2013). *Diagnostic and statistical manual of mental disorders* (5th ed.). https://doi.org/10.1176/appi.books.9780890425596

Baskin-Sommers, A., Krusemark, E., & Ronningstam, E. (2014). Empathy in narcissistic personality disorder: From clinical and empirical perspectives. *Research and Treatment, 5*(3), 323–333. https://doi.org/10.1037/per0000061

Beck, A. T., Freeman, A., Pretzer, J., Davis, D. D., Fleming, B., Ottaviani, R., Beck, J., Simon, K. M., Padesky, C., Meyer, J., & Trexler, L. (1990). *Cognitive therapy of the personality disorders*. Guilford Press.

Behary, W. T., & Dieckmann, E. (2011). Schema therapy for narcissism: The art of empathic confrontation, limit-setting, and leverage. In W. K. Campbell & J. D. Miller (Eds.), *The handbook of narcissism and narcissistic personality disorder: Theoretical approaches, empirical findings, and treatments* (pp. 445–456). Wiley. https://doi.org/10.1002/9781118093108.ch40

Caligor, E., Levy, K. N., & Yeomans, F. E. (2015). Narcissistic personality disorder: Diagnostic and clinical challenges. *The American Journal of Psychiatry, 172*(5), 415–422. https://doi.org/10.1176/appi.ajp.2014.14060723

Cukrowicz, K. C., Poindexter, E. K., & Joiner, T. E., Jr. (2011). Cognitive behavioral approaches to the treatment of narcissistic personality disorder. In W. K. Campbell & J. D. Miller (Eds.), *The handbook of narcissism and narcissistic personality disorder: Theoretical approaches, empirical findings, and treatments* (pp. 457–465). Wiley. https://doi.org/10.1002/9781118093108.ch41

Diamond, D., & Hersh, R. G. (2020). Transference-focused psychotherapy for narcissistic personality disorder: An object relations approach. *Journal of Personality Disorders, 34*(Suppl.), 159–176. https://doi.org/10.1521/pedi.2020.34.supp.159

Diamond, D., Levy, K. N., Clarkin, J. F., Meehan, K. B., Cain, N. M., Yeomans, F. E., & Kernberg, O. F. (2014). Change in attachment and reflective function in borderline patients with or without narcissistic personality disorder in transference focused psychotherapy. *Contemporary Psychoanalysis, 50*(1-2), 175–210. https://doi.org/10.1080/00107530.2014.880316

Diamond, D., Mehan, K. B. (2013). Attachment and object relations in patients with narcissistic personality disorder: Implications for therapeutic process and outcome. *Journal of Clinical Psychology, 69*(11), 1148–1159. https://doi.org/10.1002/jclp.22042

Dimaggio, G., & Attinà, G. (2012). Metacognitive interpersonal therapy for narcissistic personality disorder and associated perfectionism. *Journal of Clinical Psychology, 68*(8), 922–934. https://doi.org/10.1002/jclp.21896

Drozek, R. P., & Unruh, B. T. (2020). Mentalization-based treatment for pathological narcissism. *Journal of Personality Disorders, 34*(Suppl.), 177–203. https://doi.org/10.1521/pedi.2020.34.supp.177

Fonagy, P., & Target, M. (1997). Attachment and reflective function: Their role in self-organization. *Development and Psychopathology, 9*(4), 679–700. https://doi.org/10.1017/S0954579497001399

Fulford, D., Johnson, S. L., & Carver, C. S. (2008). Commonalities and differences in characteristics of persons at risk for narcissism and mania. *Journal of Research in Personality, 42*(6), 1427–1438. https://doi.org/10.1016/j.jrp.2008.06.002

Gabbard, G. O., & Crisp-Han, H. (2016). The many faces of narcissism. *World Psychiatry, 15*(2), 115–116. https://doi.org/10.1002/wps.20323

Gabbard, G. O., & Crisp-Han, H. (2018). *Narcissism and its discontents: Diagnostic dilemmas and treatment strategies with narcissistic patients.* American Psychiatric Publishing. https://doi.org/10.1176/appi.pn.2018.5b12

Glickauf-Hughes, C., & Wells, M. (1995). Narcissistic characters with obsessive features: Diagnostic and treatment considerations. *American Journal of Psychoanalysis, 55*(2), 129–143. https://doi.org/10.1007/BF02741961

Gordon, K. H., & Dombeck, J. J. (2010). The associations between two facets of narcissism and eating disorder symptoms. *Eating Behaviors, 11*(4), 288–292. https://doi.org/10.1016/j.eatbeh.2010.08.004

Huprich, S. K. (2020). Critical distinctions between vulnerable narcissism and depressive personalities [Commentary]. *Journal of Personality Disorders, 34*(Suppl.), 207–209. https://doi.org/10.1521/pedi.2020.34.supp.207

Huprich, S. K., Nelson, S., Sohnleitner, A., Lengu, K., Shankar, S., & Rexer, K. (2018). Are malignant self-regard and vulnerable narcissism different constructs? *Journal of Clinical Psychology, 74*(9), 1556–1569. https://doi.org/10.1002/jclp.22599

Kernberg, O. (1975). *Borderline conditions and pathological narcissism.* Jason Aronson.

Kernberg, O. F. (1992). *Aggression in personality disorders and perversions.* Yale University Press.

Maldonado, J. L. (2006). Vicissitudes in adult life resulting from traumatic experiences in adolescence. *The International Journal of Psycho-Analysis, 87*(5), 1239–1257. https://doi.org/10.1516/4VUN-32CV-BPW9-8QBF

Pincus, A. L., Cain, N. M., & Wright, A. G. (2014). Narcissistic grandiosity and narcissistic vulnerability in psychotherapy. *Personality Disorders, 5*(4), 439–443. https://doi.org/10.1037/per0000031

Reed-Knight, B., & Fischer, S. (2011). Treatment of narcissistic personality disorder symptoms in a dialectical behavior therapy framework: A discussion and case example. In W. K. Campbell & J. D. Miller (Eds.), *The handbook of narcissism and narcissistic personality disorder: Theoretical approaches, empirical findings, and treatments* (pp. 466–475). Wiley. https://doi.org/10.1002/9781118093108.ch42

Ritter, K., Dziobek, I., Preissler, S., Rüter, A., Vater, A., Fydrich, T., Lammers, C. H., Heekeren, H. R., & Roepke, S. (2011). Lack of empathy in patients with narcissistic personality disorder. *Psychiatry Research, 187*(1-2), 241–247. https://doi.org/10.1016/j.psychres.2010.09.013

Roepke, S., & Vater, A. (2014). Narcissistic personality disorder: An integrative review of recent empirical data and current definitions. *Current Psychiatry Reports, 16*(5), 445. https://doi.org/10.1007/s11920-014-0445-0

Ronningstam, E. (2011). Narcissistic personality disorder: A clinical perspective. *Journal of Psychiatric Practice, 17*(2), 89–99. https://doi.org/10.1097/01.pra.0000396060.67150.40

Ronningstam, E. (2012). Alliance building and narcissistic personality disorder. *Journal of Clinical Psychology, 68*(8), 943–953. https://doi.org/10.1002/jclp.21898

Ronningstam, E. (2017). Intersect between self-esteem and emotion regulation in narcissistic personality disorder—Implications for alliance building and treatment. *Borderline Personality Disorder and Emotion Dysregulation, 4*(3), 3. https://doi.org/10.1186/s40479-017-0054-8

Ronningstam, E. (2020). Internal processing in patients with pathological narcissism or narcissistic personality disorder: Implications for alliance building and therapeutic strategies. *Journal of Personality Disorders, 34*(Suppl.), 80–103. https://doi.org/10.1521/pedi.2020.34.supp.80

Ronningstam, E., & Baskin-Sommers, A. R. (2013). Fear and decision-making in narcissistic personality disorder—A link between psychoanalysis and neuroscience. *Dialogues in Clinical Neuroscience, 15*(2), 191–201. https://doi.org/10.31887/DCNS.2013.15.2/eronningstam

Ronningstam, E., & Gunderson, J. (1997). *The Diagnostic Interview for Narcissism* (3rd ed.). McLean Hospital, Harvard Medical School, Cambridge, MA.

Ronningstam, E., Gunderson, J., & Lyons, M. (1995). Changes in pathological narcissism. *The American Journal of Psychiatry, 152*(2), 253–257. https://doi.org/10.1176/ajp.152.2.253

Ronningstam, E., Weinberg, I., & Maltsberger, J. T. (2008). Eleven deaths of Mr. K.: Contributing factors to suicide in narcissistic personalities. *Psychiatry, 71*(2), 169–182. https://doi.org/10.1521/psyc.2008.71.2.169

Roth, B. E. (1998). Narcissistic patients in group psychotherapy: Containing affects in the early group. In E. Ronningstam (Ed.), *Disorders of narcissism—Diagnostic, clinical, and empirical implications* (pp. 221–238). American Psychiatric Press.

Russ, E., Shedler, J., Bradley, R., & Westen, D. (2008). Refining the construct of narcissistic personality disorder: Diagnostic criteria and subtypes. *The American Journal of Psychiatry, 165*(11), 1473–1481. https://doi.org/10.1176/appi.ajp.2008.07030376

Russell, T., Holdren, S., & Ronningstam, E. (2022). Narcissistic personality disorder and deviant behavior. In C. Garofalo & J. J. Sijtsema (Eds.), *Clinical forensic psychology: Development, psychopathology, and treatment* (pp. 241–268). Palgrave Macmillan/Springer Nature. https://doi.org/10.1007/978-3-030-80882-2_13

Simon, R. I. (2002). Distinguishing trauma-associated narcissistic symptoms from post-traumatic stress disorder: A diagnostic challenge. *Harvard Review of Psychiatry, 10*(1), 28–36. https://doi.org/10.1080/10673220216206

Stinson, F. S., Dawson, D. A., Goldstein, R. B., Chou, S. P., Huang, B., Smith, S. M., Ruan, W. J., Pulay, A. J., Saha, T. D., Pickering, R. P., & Grant, B. F. (2008). Prevalence, correlates, disability, and comorbidity of *DSM-IV* narcissistic personality disorder: Results from the Wave 2 National Epidemiologic Survey on Alcohol and Related Conditions. *The Journal of Clinical Psychiatry, 69*(7), 1033–1045. https://doi.org/10.4088/JCP.v69n0701

Stone, M. (1998). Normal narcissism: An etiological and ethological perspective. In E. Ronningstam (Ed.), *Disorders of narcissism—Diagnostic, clinical, and empirical implications* (pp. 7–28). American Psychiatric Press.

Thomaes, S., Bushman, B. J., Orobio de Castro, B., & Stegge, H. (2009). What makes narcissists bloom? A framework for research on the etiology and development of narcissism. *Development and Psychopathology, 21*(4), 1233–1247. https://doi.org/10.1017/S0954579409990137

Tritt, S. M., Ryder, A. G., Ring, A. J., & Pincus, A. L. (2009). Pathological narcissism and the depressive temperament. *Journal of Affective Disorders, 122*(3), 280–284. https://doi.org/10.1016/j.jad.2009.09.006

Vaglum, P. (1999). The narcissistic personality disorder and addiction. In J. Derksen, C. Maffei, & H. Groen (Eds.), *Treatment of personality disorders* (pp. 241–253). Kluwer Academic/Plenum Press. https://doi.org/10.1007/978-1-4757-6876-3_17

Widiger, T. (2011). The comorbidity of narcissistic personality disorder with other *DSM-IV* personality disorders. In W. K. Campbell & J. D. Miller (Eds.), *The handbook of narcissism and narcissistic personality disorder: Theoretical approaches, empirical findings, and treatments* (pp. 248–250). Wiley.

World Health Organization. (2019). *International statistical classification of diseases and related health problems* (11th ed.). https://icd.who.int/

Yakeley, J. (2018). Current understanding of narcissism and narcissistic personality disorder. *BJPsych Advances, 24*(5), 301–315. https://doi.org/10.1192/bja.2018.20

17

Antisocial Personality Disorder

Daniel Mark, Sandeep Roy, Hannah Walsh, and Craig S. Neumann

Psychopathic personality is a disorder associated with substantial impacts on mental health and the criminal justice systems (Hare et al., 2018). In addition to the significant emotional cost of the disorder to people with this personality profile and those around them, researchers have estimated the financial costs resulting from psychopathic behavior to be $400 billion in the United States alone (Brazil et al., 2018). This highlights the need to develop effective diagnostic criteria, assessment methodology, and treatment modalities to assess and treat psychopathy. However, the difficulties of instantiating psychopathy into the diagnostic nosology of the *Diagnostic and Statistical Manual of Mental Disorders* (5th ed.; *DSM-5*; American Psychiatric Association, 2013) and the *International Statistical Classification of Diseases and Related Health Problems* (11th ed.; *ICD-11*; World Health Organization, 2019) unintentionally introduced a similar disorder, antisocial personality disorder (ASPD), that may have some utility in distinguishing subsets of criminal offenders (Brazil et al., 2018; Crego & Widiger, 2015). In this chapter, we review the traits associated with psychopathy and ASPD across conceptual models, discuss the clinical assessment tools used to reliably assess these disorders, present a clinical case, and provide an overview of recent developments in treating psychopathy and ASPD. Finally, we discuss areas for future research on these diagnoses.

---

https://doi.org/10.1037/0000310-018
Personality Disorders and Pathology: Integrating Clinical Assessment and Practice in the DSM-5 *and* ICD-11 *Era*, S. K. Huprich (Editor)
Copyright © 2022 by the American Psychological Association. All rights reserved.

CONCEPTUAL MODELS OF PSYCHOPATHY

Conceptualizations of psychopathy and ASPD have consistently appeared throughout psychiatric history under various labels or as subtypes of other disorders. The earliest descriptions of the construct, at least those that align with modern conceptualizations, have been traced as far back as Pinel's (1806, cited in Lynam & Vachon, 2012) *manie sans delire*, translated as "insanity without delusion," which is characterized by repeated engagement in impulsive, destructive actions despite intact reasoning. Although other early clinicians and theorists have contributed to modern conceptualizations of psychopathy (for a review, see Hare et al., 2018), the work of Hervey Cleckley has been particularly influential. Cleckley initially provided a diagnostic list of 21 features (Lilienfeld et al., 2018) that were reduced to 16 (Cleckley, 1976, pp. 338–339):

1. Superficial charm and good "intelligence"
2. Absence of delusions and other signs of irrational thinking
3. Absence of "nervousness" or psychoneurotic manifestations
4. Unreliability
5. Untruthfulness and insincerity
6. Lack of remorse or shame
7. Inadequately motivated antisocial behavior
8. Poor judgment and failure to learn by experience
9. Pathological egocentricity and incapacity of love
10. General poverty in major affective reactions
11. Specific loss of insight
12. Unresponsiveness in general interpersonal relations
13. Fantastic and uninviting with drink and sometimes without
14. Suicide rarely carried out
15. Sex life impersonal, trivial, and poorly integrated
16. Failure to follow any life plan

Across his 15 classic case studies, Cleckley (1976) described chronically antisocial patients who presented with narcissistic tendencies (i.e., egocentricity, deceptive tendencies, exploitative interpersonal relationships), lack of empathy and remorse, impulsivity and unreliability, and difficulties learning from previous experiences. He also identified traits that researchers have termed *positive adjustment* traits (i.e., Patrick, 2006), such as low internalizing propensities (e.g., low fear, anxiety, suicidality) and superficial charm and good intelligence. The importance of Cleckley's writings to various conceptual models of psychopathic personality has been well established (for a review, see Lilienfeld et al., 2018); however, prominent models of psychopathy show varying degrees of allegiance to Cleckley's writings as well as empirical support. The conceptual model currently proposed by Hare and colleagues (Hare et al., 2018) and operationalized in the Psychopathy Checklist and its revisions (PCL and PCL-R; Hare, 1991, 2003) has received the most empirical support. A synthesis of seminal clinical insights by various early psychopathy theorists and clinicians with empirical research conducted by Hare and colleagues, the PCL-R, a 20-item construct rating scale, conceptualizes psychopathic personality as a dimensional, superordinate construct underpinned by four correlated dimensions: (a) *Interpersonal* (glibness/superficial charm, grandiose sense of self-worth, pathological deception, conning/manipulative), (b) *Affective* (lack of remorse or guilt, shallow affect, callous/lack of empathy, failure to accept responsibility for actions), (c) *Lifestyle* (need for stimulation/proneness to boredom, parasitic lifestyle, lack of realistic long-term goals, impulsivity, irresponsibility), and (d) *Antisocial* (poor behavioral control, early behavior problems, juvenile delinquency, revocation of conditional release, criminal versatility). Two other items, reflecting relationship instability (many short-term relationships, promiscuous sexual behavior), also contribute to the PCL-R total score. Although psychopathy varies continuously, a 20-item score of 30 is used as a diagnostic indicator of psychopathy for research and forensic decision making (Hare, 2003). The PCL-R is strongly correlated with clinical ratings using Cleckley's criteria ($r = .80-.90$; Hare, 2003); advanced the field by providing a common metric to assess the disorder; and has robust relationships with a wide variety of external correlates theoretically and empirically linked to psychopathic personality, such as antisocial conduct (e.g., violent and nonviolent offenses, recidivism; Leistico et al., 2008), instrumental and reactive aggression (Blais et al., 2014), fearlessness/low anxiety (Neumann, Johansson, et al., 2013), diminished cortical gray-matter volume (Baskin-Sommers et al., 2016), and corporate misbehavior (Babiak et al., 2010).

Lynam and Widiger (2007, cited in Lynam & Miller, 2015) translated the PCL-R items into the language of the five-factor model of personality (FFM; McCrae & Costa, 1990, cited in Lynam & Miller, 2015) and found the interpersonal and affective items were largely defined by low Agreeableness (i.e., antagonism), whereas the lifestyle and antisocial items were characterized by a mixture of low Conscientiousness (i.e., disinhibition) and antagonism. Select facets of Neuroticism (i.e., high hostility, high impulsivity, low depression) and Extraversion (i.e., low warmth, low positive emotions, high excitement seeking) were also evident in the PCL-R-to-FFM translation. Lynam and colleagues have validated this personality profile across expert ratings of psychopathy on general personality traits, profiles on FFM measures, and in a psychopathy self-report measure anchored in the FFM (Lynam & Miller, 2015).

In addition to the PCL-R and FFM models of psychopathy, other researchers have proposed different conceptual models to capture the positive adjustment features Cleckley identified that were omitted from the PCL-R framework (for responses to these concerns, see Crego & Widiger, 2015, and Neumann, Johansson, et al., 2013). Most prominent among these alternative models is Patrick and colleagues' triarchic psychopathy model (TPM; Patrick & Drislane, 2015), operationalized in the Triarchic Psychopathy Measure (TriPM; Patrick, 2010, cited in Patrick & Drislane, 2015). In this framework, psychopathy is a compound trait that emerges from the interaction among three distinct but intersecting symptomatic constructs: (a) disinhibition, (b) meanness, and (c) boldness. *Disinhibition* indexes impulsiveness, weak restraint, hostility and mistrust, and difficulties in regulating emotion. *Meanness* captures deficient empathy, lack of affiliative capacity, contempt toward others, predatory exploitativeness, and empowerment through cruelty or destructiveness. *Boldness*, proposed to capture the positive adjustment features in Cleckley's (1976) profile and in other psychopathy measures (e.g., the Psychopathic Personality Inventory; Lilienfeld & Andrews, 1996, cited in Roy et al., 2021b), indexes tendencies toward confidence, social assertiveness, emotional resiliency, and venturesomeness (Patrick & Drislane, 2015). In this model, individuals high in disinhibition with elevations in *either* boldness *or* meanness would warrant a diagnosis of psychopathy. Although the TPM has become a popular framework for the study of psychopathic personality, meta-analytic and structural investigations of the TriPM (Collison et al., 2021; Roy et al., 2021b; Sleep et al., 2019) have raised several concerns, such as the limited discriminant validity between meanness and disinhibition, the significant multidimensionality of each triarchic domain, and the divergence of the TriPM statistical measurement model from the theoretical TPM (see Patrick et al., 2021, for a response to these concerns and Roy et al., 2021a, for a rejoinder). Taken together, the works of Cleckley, Hare, Lynam, and Patrick have provided distinct yet overlapping conceptualizations and diagnostic criteria for identifying and differentiating psychopathic personality from other disorders.

DSM-5 DIAGNOSTIC CRITERIA AND LIMITATIONS

The development of the diagnostic profile for ASPD for the *DSM* and *ICD* occurred in parallel with the work of prominent psychopathy theorists and researchers. Because a review of the development of ASPD criteria across iterations of the *DSM* and *ICD* (for a thorough review, see Crego & Widiger, 2015) is beyond the scope of this chapter, only the diagnostic criteria for Sections II and III of *DSM-5* and the criteria of *ICD-11* are reviewed. Table 17.1 displays the diagnostic criteria for ASPD across both sections of *DSM-5*, arranged in a manner to show concordance with and divergence between the two symptom profiles.

Both models describe individuals with calloused and deceptive interpersonal styles as well as impulsive and hostile tendencies, although Section III does not include failure to conform to social and legal norms as a diagnostic indicator of the disorder. Section II of *DSM-5* retains the criteria initially developed and refined through *DSM–III* (American Psychiatric Association, 1980) and *DSM-IV* (American Psychiatric Association, 1994; see Crego & Widiger, 2015). In addition to having at least three of the seven symptoms in Criterion B, an individual must be over age 18, meet the criteria for conduct disorder before age 15, and not have these tendencies attributed to other diagnoses. Although *DSM-5* claims this pattern of symptoms and "has also been referred to as psychopathy, sociopathy, or dyssocial personality disorder" (American Psychiatric Association, 2013, p. 659), evaluation of the empirical literature suggests otherwise; specifically, the diagnostic profile of Section II ASPD is overrepresented in forensic populations, with rates ranging from 50% to 80% relative to the 15% to 25% prevalence of PCL-R psychopathy (Hare, 2003), suggesting limited

TABLE 17.1. *DSM-5* Criteria for Antisocial Personality Disorder

DSM-5 Section II Criterion A symptoms	*DSM-5* Section III Criterion B symptoms
Failure to conform to social norms with respect to lawful behaviors, as indicated by repeatedly performing acts that are grounds for arrest	
Deceitfulness, as indicated by repeated lying, use of aliases, or conning others for personal profit or pleasure	Manipulativeness (an aspect of antagonism): Frequent use of subterfuge to influence or control others; use of seduction, charm, glibness, or ingratiation to achieve one's ends
	Deceitfulness (an aspect of antagonism): Dishonesty and fraudulence; misrepresentation of self; embellishment of fabrication when relating events
Impulsivity or failure to plan ahead	Impulsivity (an aspect of disinhibition): Acting on the spur of the moment in response to immediate stimuli, acting on a momentary basis without a plan or consideration of outcomes, difficulty establishing and following plans
Irritability and aggressiveness, as indicated by repeated physical fights or assaults	Hostility (an aspect of antagonism): Persistent or frequent angry feelings; anger or irritability in response to minor slights and insults; mean, nasty, or vengeful behavior
Reckless disregard for safety of self or others	Risk taking (an aspect of disinhibition): Engagement in dangerous, risky, and potentially self-damaging activities, unnecessarily and without regard for consequences; boredom proneness and thoughtless initiation of activities to counter boredom; lack of concern for one's limitations and denial of the reality of personal danger
Consistent irresponsibility, as indicated by repeated failure to sustain consistent work behavior or honor financial obligations	Irresponsibility (an aspect of disinhibition): Disregard for—and failure to honor—financial and other obligations or commitments; lack of respect for—and lack of follow-through on—agreements and promises
Lack of remorse, as indicated by being indifferent to or rationalizing having hurt, mistreated, or stolen from another	Callousness (an aspect of antagonism): Lack of concern for feelings or problems of others, lack of guilt or remorse about the negative or harmful effects of one's actions on others, aggression, sadism

Note. While this table is an original compilation using information from the *Diagnostic and Statistical Manual of Mental Disorders* (*DSM-5*), the idea to compare the models in this format comes from Lynam and Vachon (2012).

diagnostic utility. Poythress and colleagues (2010) used model-based cluster analysis in a large sample of offenders diagnosed with *DSM-IV* criteria for ASPD and found subgroups that scored high and low on the PCL-R. Poythress et al. suggested that their findings provide "the most compelling empirical support to date for the contention that ASPD is heterogeneous and not isomorphic with . . . psychopathy" (p. 398). Furthermore, Kosson and colleagues (2006; Riser & Kosson, 2013) have found that offenders who met criteria for both ASPD and psychopathy, as measured by the PCL-R, engaged in more severe criminal behavior and showed less emotional facilitation in a lexical decision task than did those with ASPD alone. They concluded that offenders with and without comorbid psychopathy represent distinct syndromes and that psychopathy is not a more extreme version of ASPD. Venables and colleagues (2014) used a triarchic framework to compare the PCL-R factor scores and the *DSM-IV* criteria for ASPD on the three facets of the TPM as indexed by variants of the TriPM scales. They found negligible to moderate–large associations between the PCL-R ($r = .07–.40$) and ASPD symptoms ($r = .17–.47$) with the scales. Given that boldness was marginally associated with ASPD symptoms, Venables et al. opined that it is boldness that distinguishes psychopathy from ASPD.

A reason for this divergence between ASPD and psychopathy may be that the preponderance of traits in Section II of *DSM-5* index the lifestyle and antisocial traits of the PCL-R with limited coverage of the interpersonal and affective traits, which are hypothesized to differentiate the constructs (Hare, 2003; Hare et al., 2018; Patrick & Drislane, 2015). Given these concerns, the *DSM-5* Personality and Personality Disorders Work Group aimed to shift the diagnosis of ASPD toward PCL-R or Cleckley psychopathy (Crego & Widiger, 2015). Toward this end, the work group developed a new hybrid model, combining deficits in sense of self and interpersonal relatedness with maladaptive personality traits obtained from a five-domain dimensional trait model to diagnose personality disorders (Krueger & Markon, 2014). For ASPD, the hybrid diagnostic profile consisted of four deficits in interpersonal functioning (Criterion A) and seven maladaptive personality traits (Criterion B in Table 2). More specifically, at least two of the four Criterion A deficits, which are (a) impairments in identity (i.e., egocentrism), (b) self-direction (i.e., goal setting based on personal gratification, absence of prosocial internal standards), (c) empathy (i.e., lack of remorse), and (d) intimacy (i.e., exploitation is a primary means of relating to others), and at least six of the seven maladaptive traits in Criterion B are required for a diagnosis of ASPD using the hybrid model of Section III of *DSM-5*. The conduct disorder criterion was also removed from the diagnostic profile of ASPD in Section III. Of interest is that a psychopathy specifier has been added to the ASPD Section III criteria that indexes low levels of anxiousness and withdrawal and high levels of attention seeking (American Psychiatric Association, 2013). These traits were influenced by the boldness traits captured by the TPM (Crego & Widiger, 2015; Wygant et al., 2016).

Researchers comparing the two models of ASPD in the *DSM-5* have found support for the Section III conceptualization over the Section II criteria. Multiple studies across university, community, and offender samples have found that the Criterion B alternative model ASPD traits accounted for more variance in (or correlated more robustly with) several self-report (e.g., TriPM, Psychopathic Personality Inventory) and clinician-rated (i.e., PCL-R) psychopathy measures and externalizing propensities relative to the Section II *DSM-5* ASPD traits (Anderson et al., 2014; Few et al., 2015; Wygant et al., 2016). The psychopathy specifier was also found to predict the boldness traits across a variety of psychopathy measures, though not much else beyond those traits (Anderson et al., 2014; Few et al., 2015; Wygant et al., 2016). Although Few and colleagues (2015) raised concerns with the limited utility of the *DSM-5* Alternative *DSM-5* Model of Personality Disorders (AMPD) Criterion A impairment ratings in predicting scores on psychopathy measures, Wygant and colleagues (2016) found the impairment ratings to be robustly correlated with psychopathy measures and incrementally predicted psychopathy scores above and beyond the contributions of the Section III Criterion B traits. In sum, emerging research indicates that the *DSM-5* Section III ASPD criteria are more effective in bringing the construct closer in alignment with conceptualizations of psychopathic personality relative to *DSM-5* Section II.

Despite these strides forward, there are notable concerns with the Section III *DSM-5* approach to ASPD. A salient concern was the limited concordance between *DSM-5* ASPD and the personality profile of ASPD and psychopathy as delineated through the FFM (Lynam & Vachon, 2012). Given that the *DSM-5* AMPD in Section III is a new model that is not anchored in the FFM, Lynam and Vachon (2012) argued that it provides limited coverage of all the traits associated with psychopathy. Of the 18 traits they identified to be relevant to the construct through the lens of the FFM, six are not represented in the *DSM-5* AMPD, four are assigned to other personality disorders, and one trait (i.e., distractibility) was not assigned to any personality disorder. Thus, only 38% of the traits associated with psychopathic personality (from a general personality framework) are represented in the Section III *DSM-5* criteria. Furthermore, Lynam and Vachon argued that the *DSM-5* work group missed an opportunity to bring ASPD more in line with conceptual models of psychopathy. Crego and Widiger (2015) expanded on this by noting that the work group referred to the more recent TPM in revising the ASPD criteria and psychopathy specifier instead of the influential work of Cleckley and Hare. It is important to note that the relevance of boldness traits to psychopathic personality, which form the basis of the *DSM-5* psychopathy specifier, has been extensively debated (Lilienfeld et al., 2012; Miller & Lynam, 2012; Neumann, Johansson, et al., 2013; Neumann, Uzieblo, et al., 2013; Roy et al., 2021b; Sleep et al., 2019). Although proponents of the TPM argue that such traits are represented in Cleckley's profile and in other psychopathy measures to varying degrees, others have argued these traits reflect psychological well-being, do not differentiate psychopathic offenders from nonpsychopathic offenders (Neumann, Uzieblo, et al., 2013); do not have relationships with key correlates in the nomological network of psychopathy (Sleep et al., 2019); and are measured by reverse-keyed items in *DSM-5*, which have problematic psychometric and conceptual properties (Crego & Widiger, 2014).

Researchers have also shown that boldness, whether operationalized by the *DSM-5* specifier (Miller et al., 2018) or the TriPM (Roy et al., 2021b), is multidimensional, with lower order facets evidencing divergent relationships with external correlates, indicating limited utility. Thus, how this constellation of traits differentiates those with psychopathic personality from those with antisocial traits and tendencies remains unclear. Although the traits and tendencies identified in the *DSM-5* sections have utility in differentiating a subset of individuals of concern to the mental health and criminal justice system, the current empirical literature suggests that these diagnostic profiles should not be conflated with psychopathy and that further work is needed to realign these conditions that have unintentionally diverged.

ICD-11 DIAGNOSTIC CRITERIA

Although not as popular as the *DSM-5*, the *ICD-11* has proposed another novel approach to conceptualizing personality disorders and ASPD in particular. In contrast to the hybrid model of Section III of *DSM-5*, all personality dysfunction is rated on a single dimension of severity that is inferred by interpersonal dysfunction, impact on social and occupational roles, cognitive and emotional experiences, and the risks of harm to self or others (Tyrer et al., 2019). Differences in the expression of personality were addressed by introducing domain traits that had been recognized in all personality systems that qualified but did not replace the severity level of diagnosis (Tyrer et al., 2019). These trait domains are negative affectivity, anankastia, detachment, dissociality, and disinhibition. Further deviating from *DSM-5* Section II and more consistent with *DSM-5* Section III, the time of onset was made to be more flexible to allow for the diagnosis of personality disorder to be made at any age (Tyrer et al., 2019). For ASPD and psychopathy, the antagonistic domain was conceptualized as including many of the features across both diagnostic criteria (Tyrer, 2013); however, considering the consistent role of externalizing behaviors across models of psychopathy (Hare et al., 2018; Lynam & Miller, 2015; Patrick & Drislane, 2015), the trait domain of disinhibition would also likely play a role in specifying a severe personality profile consistent with the theoretical and empirical literature on psychopathic personality. Because the *ICD-11* model and assessment tool were recently released, there are limited empirical investigations of how ASPD and psychopathy relate to both the severity and trait domain profiles in this model. Sellbom and colleagues (2020), however, found that the *ICD-11* (derived from a measure indexing *DSM-5* AMPD) dimensions of dissociality and disinhibition were modestly associated with (though robustly predictive of) *DSM-5* Section II ASPD symptom counts. Further research with more diverse measures of psychopathy is needed to compare the utility of this diagnostic framework with *DSM-5*.

ASSESSMENT CONSIDERATIONS

In addition to being familiar with the diagnostic criteria, there are other considerations practitioners must be aware of when assessing patients with traits consistent with ASPD and psychopathy. To gain a sense of how ASPD might present, it is informative to contrast the base rates at which it is found in different settings. In the community, between 0.2% and 3.3% of individuals are diagnosed with ASPD, whereas in institutions rates as high as 70% have been observed (American Psychiatric Association, 2013; Hare, 2003). A notable exception to this rough guideline are settings with large populations of people with substance use disorders, in which rates of ASPD can run as high as approximately one in five or higher (Galen et al., 2000).

How ASPD is diagnosed and presents also differs on the basis of gender. In a structured review that included 23,000 prisoners, 47% of men and 21% of women were diagnosed with ASPD (Fazel & Danesh, 2002). In general, ASPD is diagnosed in a 3:1 ratio of men to women (Alegria et al., 2013). Although research on the gender differences in this population is relatively sparse, several trends have emerged. Compared with men, women with ASPD demonstrate higher rates of irritability and aggressiveness, financial and parental neglect, and elevated rates of running away from home as children. However, women diagnosed with ASPD are less likely than men to be violent, have used weapons, vandalized property, shown cruelty to animals, or started fires as children, and to have fewer run-ins with the police (Sher et al., 2015). Taken together, it appears that there are multiple domains in which men and women with ASPD differ from one another. Although this remains an area in need of additional research, many have hypothesized that some of the differences reflect socialization pressures on the individual. Thus, clinicians should be mindful of how these socialization factors influence symptom presentation.

In contrast to the *ICD-11* or *DSM-5* Section III, a diagnosis of ASPD using *DSM-5* Section II requires evidence of conduct disorder before age 15. Therefore, practitioners will need to establish a solid means of evaluating the individual's history, whether through self-report (the considerations of which we discuss later in this chapter), secondary reporters (e.g., family members), and collateral or institutional records. This is a point of emphasis because the diagnostic criteria for ASPD include frequent deceit and manipulation. When evaluating the individual's tendency to lie or deceive, one must look beyond just statements made about substance use and criminal history. With both of these areas, it is normative (even for those without ASPD) to present as defensive or dishonest, especially if the professional is not well known to the individual. This tendency is further magnified if their reporting to the professional may have direct negative consequences for the individual (e.g., forensic evaluations). Thus, finding a larger pattern of deception outside of these areas will allow the professional to assess these traits more accurately. Practitioners must keep this potential trait in mind as they evaluate reported symptoms and behaviors. Conversely, when considering secondary reporters, those with ASPD can cause significant emotional and physical harm to those around them, and thus it is not uncommon to come across exasperated reporters who overstate their claims as a means of displaying their distress. By remaining cognizant of these considerations, practitioners can take a more even-handed and cautious approach to the evaluation of individuals who potentially have ASPD while avoiding the potential for overpathologizing.

COMMON ASSESSMENT MEASURES

In this section, we provide a brief overview of several popular measures and their expected profiles or relevant scales/portions.

Multiscale Inventories

Personality Assessment Inventory

Assessing traits relevant to ASPD can be accomplished with the Personality Assessment Inventory. The Antisocial Features (ANT) scale is designed to measure personality features and behavior related to both psychopathy and ASPD (Morey, 1991). This scale also has three subscales (a) the Antisocial Behavior scale (ANT-A), which assesses problematic behavior across adolescence and adulthood; (b) the Egocentricity (ANT-E) scale, which measures diminished empathy and callousness in interactions with others; and (c) the Stimulus Seeking (ANT-S) scale, which indexes a desire for novelty, sensation seeking, and related behaviors. In addition to elevations on the Stimulus Seeking scale, one would expect to see an elevation on the Aggression (AGG) scale. For both ASPD and psychopathy, one could also see elevations in Alcohol Problems (ALC) and Drug Problems (DRG) scales, reflecting the tendency for substance use and high comorbidity of SUDs with these disorders. Individuals high in psychopathic traits (less so with ASPD) would also be expected to score high in interpersonal dominance (the DOM scale) and low in warmth (the WARM scale). We must emphasize that elevations on these scales are not sufficient for a diagnosis of ASPD or psychopathy because they focus on distinguishing features and traits, not comprehensive diagnostic criteria.

Minnesota Multiphasic Inventory—Second Edition and Restructured Form

On the original Minnesota Multiphasic Personality Inventory–2 (MMPI-2; Butcher et al., 1989) scales, the Psychopathic Deviate (Pd) scale has relatively little to do with modern conceptualizations of ASPD or psychopathy and is a poor predictor of either (Hare et al., 2018). The Antisocial Practices (ASP) content scale correlates moderately with external measures of ASPD and psychopathy. It is more closely associated with antisocial attitudes (ASP$_1$; e.g., fearlessness, callousness, aggression) than behaviors (ASP$_2$), but it has items that cover both. The Harris–Lingoes Authority Problems (Pd2) subscale has the strongest relationship with ASPD and psychopathy global scores, appearing to capture aspects of callousness (Lilienfeld, 1999). On the MMPI-2–Restructured

Form (Ben-Porath & Tellegen, 2008/2011), antisocial personality and behavioral tendencies consistent with ASPD and psychopathy are captured by the Behavioral/Externalizing Dysfunction (BXD), Disconstraint-revised (DISC-r), Antisocial Behavior (RC4), Juvenile Conduct Problems (JCP), and Substance Use (SUB) scales. In addition, elevated scores on the Aggression (AGG), Hypomanic Activation (RC9), Anger Proneness (ANP), Disaffiliativeness (DSF) scales as well as low scores on Interpersonal Passivity (IPP), Shyness (SHY) and Dysfunctional Negative Emotions (RC7) are consistent with ASPD and psychopathy trait profiles.

Personality Inventory for *DSM-5*

The Personality Inventory for *DSM-5* (Krueger et al., 2012) assesses the Section III model of ASPD and the psychopathy specifier. The Antagonism and Disinhibition scales have some of the most pertinent facets, but overall profiles align with those described in the proposed diagnostic criteria. These profiles align well with external measures of psychopathy but have only modest overlap with Section II–based conceptualizations of ASPD.

Millon Clinical Multiaxial Inventory

The Millon Clinical Multiaxial Inventory–Fourth Edition (Millon et al., 2015) assesses an Antisocial Personality pattern (6A), with three facet subscales: (a) Interpersonally Irresponsible (6A.1), (b) Autonomous Self-Image (6A.2), and (c) Acting-Out Dynamics (6A.3). Unfortunately, perhaps because of its relatively recent publication, there is a dearth of research linking performance on these scales to external measures of ASPD or psychopathy.

Diagnostic Interviews

Structured Clinical Interview for *DSM-5* Personality Disorders and Alternative Model for Personality Disorders

Both the Structured Clinical Interview for *DSM-5* Personality Disorders (First et al., 2015) and the Structured Clinical Interview for *DSM-5* AMPD (First et al., 2018) offer the ability to directly assess specific traits and diagnostic criteria from their respective sections of the *DSM-5* in an interview format. This structured and direct approach offers the most straightforward way of assessing ASPD with *DSM* criteria. These items are generally face valid and clustered by disorder; thus, if the practitioner has concerns related to the interviewee's response style, these measures may not be ideal.

Structured Interview for *DSM-IV* Personality

Although written for the *DSM-IV*, the Structured Interview for *DSM-IV* Personality (Pfohl et al., 1997) is still an effective assessment for Section II *DSM-5* personality disorders. It has a number of advantages, including that it is written in a more conversational and nonpejorative manner and aids in differential diagnoses between personality disorders. Its seven items correspond to each of the Criterion A symptoms of Section II ASPD.

Structured Interview for the Five-Factor Model of Personality

Whereas other semistructured interviews more focused on ASPD criteria are indicated for diagnosis, the Structured Interview for the Five-Factor Model of Personality (Stepp et al., 2005) uses the dimensional approach of the FFM to assess personality disorders. An advantage of this is that it allow clinicians to evaluate all the FFM-identified traits associated with ASPD beyond those within the *DSM-5* Sections II and III diagnostic criteria to inform treatment planning and assessment considerations.

Psychopathy Checklist Revised

The PCL-R and its derivatives (see Hare et al., 2018) are regarded as the most widely used instruments in the assessment of psychopathic traits. Although the PCL-R was designed to measure a clinical construct, it is now frequently used in a number of contexts (often in forensic settings). The PCL-R is a 20-item clinician rating scale based on a semistructured interview and file review. It requires specialized training to administer. The assessment of psychopathic traits is an active, ongoing research pursuit in which multiple different research measures have been introduced (Patrick, 2018), but further discussion falls outside the purview of this chapter. Suffice it to say that the PCL-R allows an evaluator to assess psychopathic traits in an effective and comprehensive manner. Although some of these traits are related to ASPD, this measure is not recommended for the assessment of ASPD.

CASE PRESENTATION

Mr. Jones is a man in his mid-30s who presented to a community clinic seeking diagnostic testing to investigate possible personality pathology.[1] He reported that he wanted to understand why he was not able to connect with others. During the intake, Mr. Jones reported that he was born in the United States. His parents divorced when he was nearly finished with high school, reportedly because of his father's infidelity. Mr. Jones described previous problems in his relationship with his mother, explaining he "could not stand [her] growing up." Although he described their relationship as "good" currently, and he lived in a camper on her property, he noted his mother can become "upset super easily" and is "always yelling." Mr. Jones stated that she had been recently diagnosed with breast cancer and that he had "no reaction" to that news. He reported that his father was physically abusive when he was growing up, noting that his father frequently used corporal punishment, which he described as an "overreaction." Mr. Jones stated that he and his father had gotten into physical fights several times. He described his current relationship with his father as "good" but that he did not care for his stepmother because she was "too nice."

---

[1]This vignette has been altered to protect the identity of the subject.

Mr. Jones reported that, growing up, he did not have much structure and that he was not close to his family then. He described not having many friends because he had "high standards" and got into fights at school. Mr. Jones stated that he frequently got into trouble as school, which led to discipline from his father at home. In high school, he was suspended several times. He shared that he ran away from home several times and often broke curfew. Mr. Jones described "getting drunk almost every weekend" starting at the age of 15. He had to repeat two grades in junior high and high school. Mr. Jones eventually dropped out and later earned his general equivalency diploma. As a child, he shot small animals with a BB gun and carried weapons on a regular basis. He began vandalizing property and breaking into homes. As a teenager, he was caught shoplifting on several occasions. After he began driving, he received multiple tickets, including for driving with an open alcohol container. Mr. Jones was never detained as a juvenile and was always able to talk down his difficulties without being charged.

Mr. Jones reported that he began viewing pornographic materials when he was 7 years old. He began having sexual contact with similar-age peers at 9 and penetrative sex at age 15. Mr. Jones reported that he had been sexually active, with more than 70 female partners. He reported being in the midst of his second divorce and that each of his significant relationships ended by him having an affair. When discussing his infidelity, he stated he could not "help [himself]" and explained he often used it to cause the relationship to end faster. Furthermore, Mr. Jones described identifying his partners' insecurities and engaging in verbal and psychological abuse. He had two previous charges of domestic violence charges, and one for false imprisonment, from former romantic partners. However, in each case he was able to persuade the victim to not appear in court; thus, each of these charges was eventually dropped. Mr. Jones has one daughter with a former partner. His contact with his daughter has varied from daily contact to multiple consecutive months without contact.

Mr. Jones joined the military shortly after turning 18. He got into multiple physical fights with other recruits during boot camp. Mr. Jones reported that he "hated" his time in the military because of the structure and hierarchy but discussed enjoying the travel and "action" during deployment, as well as being given authority over others. Mr. Jones discussed losing close team members and that it made him "emotional." However, when asked to describe it further, he likened it to having to replace an old vehicle. Across his time in service, Mr. Jones received multiple commendations but also received several non-judicial punishments and lost multiple ranks for various infractions (although he was never court martialed). Mr. Jones was eventually "chaptered out" of the military after 5 years because of these infractions.

After leaving the military, Mr. Jones worked a series of jobs across multiple fields. The longest he held a single job was just under 1 year. He voluntarily left some jobs and was fired from others. He attributed his difficulty with these jobs to factors such as not being paid as much as he thought he deserved and "hating" his bosses. In his late 20s, Mr. Jones acquired disability benefits from the military related to medical conditions developed during his service.

Mr. Jones laughed while explaining that he feigned and exaggerated symptoms during his initial evaluations, but over time many of the symptoms had increased to the point that they were causing him authentic impairment. Because of his disability payments, Mr. Jones had no plans to seek full-time employment, and he stated, "I don't have much of a direction."

Currently, he was working toward an undergraduate degree. When asked about his academic strengths, Mr. Jones stated that he was "pretty good at everything." He reported having the highest test grades in each of his courses but generally failing because he "hates homework." He described disliking a range of courses and subjects because he found them "tedious and boring." Furthermore, Mr. Jones stated that his grades fall during the semester as he grows bored with his classes and begins to skip them.

Mr. Jones reported that he had a small number of close friends; however, he went on to describe sporadic contact with them and was unable to provide much detail about their personal lives. Mr. Jones tells people that he is a lawyer or real estate dealer and displays a business card with his falsified credentials. He explained that he was good at "knowing what [others] want to hear" and thus was able to "win people over quickly." Mr. Jones reported that his hobbies include snowboarding, rock climbing, shooting rifles, and other extreme sports.

He reported that at least once a year he gets into serious physical altercations when others "ruin [his] good mood" but that he is able to "calm down fast" after these incidents. None of these fights resulted in legal charges, although police were reportedly called on more than one occasion. Mr. Jones was being sued by a car rental company over a car that he totaled. He explained that "it was not [his] fault" and stated that it should have been covered by insurance. Mr. Jones reported that he did not plan on responding to the subpoena that he had been issued or making payments toward the car. He has been charged several times for driving under the influence but reported he hired an "expensive lawyer" who was able to reduce the charges and allow him to keep his license and serve only probation.

Mr. Jones reported that his history of substance use started at age 9. He stated that he had used a wide range of substance and was "willing to try anything once." Mr. Jones most frequently consumed alcohol, stating that he typically has 10 to 14 drinks in a night, multiple times a week.

During testing, Mr. Jones presented as suspicious at times and with low frustration tolerance. At multiple points he balled his hands into fists and appeared to be clenching his jaw. After being told the clinician was taking notes for one measure, Mr. Jones smiled and began to give noticeably elongated responses.

On the Structured Interview for the Five-Factor Model of Personality, Mr. Jones scored very low in Neuroticism, noting that he does not often worry or feel self-conscious. He had high trait hostility and low frustration tolerance scores, and his Extraversion score was high, despite his difficulty maintaining friendships. Mr. Jones indicated that he gravitates toward leadership positions and does not like to stay in the background of social situations. He scored more moderately in Openness to experience. He reported engaging in a wide variety of experiences and seeking adventure. Mr. Jones also described himself as intellectually curious; however, later in the interview he discussed frequently being called racist and sexist because of his views, which he was unwilling to change. Mr. Jones was low in Agreeableness. Although he is able to make a good impression, he frequently lies, cheats, and manipulates. He has little regard for others and can become hostile quickly. He scored very low in altruism and compliance facets. Finally, Mr. Jones scored low in Conscientiousness. He very rarely plans out his behavior and rarely works consistently toward his goals. Mr. Jones expressed a feeling of being "in it for [himself]" and feeling little obligation to others.

Mr. Jones met all criteria for *DSM-5* Section II ASPD, in addition to having evidence of Conduct Disorder before age 15. He also met criteria for *DSM-5* Section II Narcissistic Personality Disorder.

TREATMENT OF ANTISOCIAL PERSONALITY DISORDER AND PSYCHOPATHY

There historically has been considerable pessimism regarding the treatment amenability of individuals with ASPD and psychopathy. Given claims by prominent theorists on the disorder, and early research exploring treatment response (see Salekin, 2002, for a review), clinicians and researchers have initially labeled ASPD and psychopathy as treatment-resistant disorders. However, the results of scientific studies and meta-analyses present a more optimistic clinical picture than would be expected on the basis of historical conceptualization and traditional clinical lore. Although the literature provides evidence of greater treatment amenability than previously theorized, there is no identified gold standard treatment for individuals with ASPD and psychopathy. For example, in his meta-analysis, Salekin (2002) examined the efficacy of a variety of therapeutic approaches in the treatment of psychopathy and found that psychoanalytic, cognitive behavior, and eclectic interventions were effective, with average success rates of 59%, 62%, and 82%, respectively. Of note is that the intervention programs that were found to be most successful in treating adults with psychopathic personality traits tended to be intensive (i.e., involve an average of four individual therapy sessions per week for at least 1 year), include individual and group psychotherapy, and incorporate family members into treatment. A noteworthy treatment benefit of effective intervention programs was a reduction in psychopathic traits (e.g., a decrease in lying and manipulation behaviors, an increase in expressed remorse and empathy, improved interpersonal relationships per patient report). Salekin described four specific psychotherapy interventions and techniques that were found to decrease psychopathic traits: (a) rational therapy, (b) action-oriented therapies, (c) interventions that involved fixed-role therapy, and (d) psychodrama. Finally, with regard to potential moderator effects on treatment efficacy, Salekin found that a greater proportion of youth with psychopathic traits benefited from treatment as compared with adults. Furthermore, psychopathic individuals were more likely to benefit from long-term (> 6 months) as compared with short-term (< 6 months) treatment.

Another promising line of work has come from Anthony Bateman and colleagues involving mentalization-based treatment. This treatment increases an individual's ability to understand both their own actions and those of other people through recognizing thoughts, feelings, desires, and so on, as being intentional (Bateman & Fonagy, 2019). This intervention has shown promise for both ASPD and other personality disorders in stabilizing affect and improving personal relationships.

Brazil and colleagues (2018) provided a more recent summary of the literature surrounding treatment amenability of ASPD and psychopathy. They reported that treatment studies using cognitive–behavioral interventions found limited or no evidence of efficacy, in particular in individuals with high levels of psychopathic traits; specifically, cognitive behavior therapy (CBT) intervention studies have found that psychopathy is negatively correlated with clinical improvements in forensic samples (Brazil et al., 2018); offenders with high levels of psychopathic traits, relative to those with low levels, were more likely to recidivate despite demonstrating symptom improvement due to treatment (Olver & Wong, 2009; Olver et al., 2013), and sex offenders with high as compared with low levels of psychopathy were more likely to prematurely terminate services and recidivate (Olver & Wong, 2009). It is important to note, however, that integrative forms of CBT incorporated into *milieu therapy* (i.e., an approach in therapeutic communities in which the environment is manipulated to promote behavioral change) have demonstrated efficacy in reducing relapse in substance use and criminal recidivism in offenders with comorbid substance use disorders and ASPD (Messina et al., 1999). Brazil and colleagues further presented evidence regarding the limited efficacy of milieu therapy interventions in the treatment of psychopathy, although they have demonstrated efficacy in treating ASPD.

Brazil et al. (2018) highlighted findings regarding *contingency management* (CM; a therapeutic intervention based on the principles of instrumental learning and involving the use of both negative and positive reinforcement to modify behaviors) as an effective intervention for the treatment of ASPD with comorbid substance use disorders. They emphasized, however, that no study to date has examined the efficacy of CM approaches in the treatment of psychopathy. Although CM has not been specifically examined in psychopathic populations, support for the use of behavioral interventions as efficacious treatments for psychopathy can be found in the work of Mark Olver and his colleagues. In a sample of Canadian high-risk violent offenders with psychopathic traits, Olver et al. (2013) examined the efficacy of a high-risk violence reduction program (i.e., the Aggressive Behavior Control program) that is based on social learning principles and using cognitive–behavioral interventions guided by the "what works" principles of effective correctional treatment. The results indicated that positive therapeutic change (i.e., operationalized as reduced dynamic risk ratings and lower rates of violent recidivism) was negatively associated with higher PCL-R scores, in particular with regard to traditional Factor 1 and affective facet traits, and was associated with clinically significant reductions in violence risk when controlling for psychopathic traits. However, Olver and colleagues found that the association between positive therapeutic change and violence recidivism decreased when controlling for the affective traits of psychopathy. Such findings highlight the role of traditional Factor 1 traits in terms of weakening potential therapeutic gains for the treatment of offenders with psychopathy.

Brazil and colleagues (2018) argued that, taken together, the findings regarding the efficacy of psychological and behavioral interventions for the treatment of antisocial individuals are mixed. They further emphasized that, although some studies have suggested that medications such as antipsychotics, anticonvulsants, and selective serotonin reuptake inhibitors may decrease impulsive aggressive behaviors, there is no direct evidence suggesting that pharmacotherapy is an effective approach to the treatment of patients with ASPD and psychopathy. They argued that research regarding the effectiveness of interventions in antisocial populations may be limited by the considerable heterogeneity of these disorders and discrepancies in conceptualizations and measurement of these disorders between researchers and clinicians, as well as a failure to incorporate into treatment knowledge regarding the etiological factors contributing to these disorders.

FUTURE DIRECTIONS

Although there has been significant progress in terms of researchers' and clinicians' understanding of the assessment of, identification of, and differentiation between ASPD and psychopathy, as well as professionals' understanding of treatment of these disorders, further research is necessary to hone evidence-based evaluation and treatment. Of note is that emerging research is parsing the heterogeneity of PCL-R–measured psychopathy profiles by using person-centered analyses, such as latent profile analysis and cluster analysis (see Neumann et al., 2016). These profiles have been shown to have differential risk characteristics and treatment responsiveness (Hare et al., 2018; Klein Haneveld et al., 2018), which may have implications for the assessment and treatment of ASPD. Furthermore, more work is needed to assess the generalizability and symptom presentation of ASPD across multicultural groups and gender. More research is also needed to examine the differential utility of *ICD-11* diagnostic approaches as compared with *DSM-5* Section III in terms of their alignment with various conceptual models of psychopathy. Finally, continued longitudinal, behavioral–genetic, and neuroimaging work will continue to help elucidate the etiological factors that give rise to these disorders (Brazil et al., 2018). Despite the conceptual drift from psychopathy to ASPD in Section II of *DSM-5*, the theoretical and empirical literature indicates that both constructs have utility in identifying different personality profiles that place significant stress on the mental health and criminal justice systems.

REFERENCES

Alegria, A. A., Blanco, C., Petry, N. M., Skodol, A. E., Liu, S.-M., Grant, B., & Hasin, D. (2013). Sex differences in antisocial personality disorder: Results from the National Epidemiological Survey on Alcohol and Related Conditions. *Personality Disorders, 4*(3), 214–222. https://doi.org/10.1037/a0031681

American Psychiatric Association. (1980). *Diagnostic and statistical manual of mental disorders* (3rd ed.).

American Psychiatric Association. (1994). *Diagnostic and statistical manual of mental disorders* (4th ed.).

American Psychiatric Association. (2013). *Diagnostic and statistical manual of mental disorders* (5th ed.). https://doi.org/10.1176/appi.books.9780890425596

Anderson, J. L., Sellbom, M., Wygant, D. B., Salekin, R. T., & Krueger, R. F. (2014). Examining the associations between *DSM-5* Section III antisocial personality disorder traits and psychopathy in community and university samples. *Journal of Personality Disorders, 28*(5), 675–697. https://doi.org/10.1521/pedi_2014_28_134

Babiak, P., Neumann, C. S., & Hare, R. D. (2010). Corporate psychopathy: Talking the walk. *Behavioral Sciences and the Law, 28,* 174–193. https://doi.org/10.1002/bsl.925

Baskin-Sommers, A. R., Neumann, C. S., Cope, L. M., & Kiehl, K. A. (2016). Latent-variable modeling of brain gray-matter volume and psychopathy in incarcerated offenders. *Journal of Abnormal Psychology, 125*(6), 811–817. https://doi.org/10.1037/abn0000175

Bateman, A., & Fonagy, P. (2019). Mentalization-based treatment for borderline and antisocial personality disorder. In D. Kealy & J. S. Ogrodniczuk (Eds.), *Contemporary psychodynamic psychotherapy: Evolving clinical practice* (pp. 133–148). Elsevier. https://doi.org/10.1016/B978-0-12-813373-6.00009-X

Ben-Porath, Y. S., & Tellegen, A. (2011). *MMPI-2-RF (Minnesota Multiphasic Personality Inventory–2–Restructured Form): Manual for administration, scoring, and interpretation.* University of Minnesota Press. (Original work published 2008)

Blais, J., Solodukhin, E., & Forth, A. E. (2014). A meta-analysis exploring the relationship between psychopathy and instrumental versus reactive violence. *Criminal Justice and Behavior, 41*(7), 797–821. https://doi.org/10.1177/0093854813519629

Brazil, I. A., van Dongen, J. D. M., Maes, J. H. R., Mars, R. B., & Baskin-Sommers, A. R. (2018). Classification and treatment of antisocial individuals: From behavior to biocognition. *Neuroscience and Biobehavioral Reviews, 91,* 259–277. https://doi.org/10.1016/j.neubiorev.2016.10.010

Butcher, J. N., Dahlstrom, W. G., Graham, J. R., Tellegen, A. M., & Kreammer, B. (1989). *The Minnesota Multiphasic Personality Inventory–2 (MMPI-2) manual for administration and scoring.* University of Minneapolis Press.

Cleckley, H. (1976). *The mask of sanity* (5th ed.). Mosby.

Collison, K. L., Miller, J. D., & Lynam, D. R. (2021). Examining the factor structure and validity of the Triarchic Model of Psychopathy across measures. *Personality Disorders: Theory, Research, and Treatment, 12*(2), 115–126. https://doi.org/10.1037/per0000394

Crego, C., & Widiger, T. A. (2014). Psychopathy, *DSM-5,* and a caution. *Personality Disorders: Theory, Research, and Treatment, 5*(4), 335–347. https://doi.org/10.1037/per0000078

Crego, C., & Widiger, T. A. (2015). Psychopathy and the *DSM. Journal of Personality, 83*(6), 665–677. https://doi.org/10.1111/jopy.12115

Fazel, S., & Danesh, J. (2002). Serious mental disorder in 23 000 prisoners: A systematic review of 62 surveys. *The Lancet, 359*(9306), 545–550. https://doi.org/10.1016/S0140-6736(02)07740-1

Few, L. R., Lynam, D. R., Maples, J. L., MacKillop, J., & Miller, J. D. (2015). Comparing the utility of *DSM-5* Section II and III antisocial personality disorder diagnostic approaches for capturing psychopathic traits. *Personality Disorders: Theory, Research, and Treatment, 6*(1), 64–74. https://doi.org/10.1037/per0000096

First, M., Skodol, A., Bender, D., & Oldham, J. (2018). *Structured Clinical Interview for the* DSM-5 *Alternative Model for Personality Disorders (SCID–AMPD)*. New York State Psychiatric Institute.

First, M. B., Williams, J., Benjamin, L. S., & Spitzer, R. L. (2015). *User's guide for the SCID-5-PD (Structured Clinical Interview for* DSM-5 *Personality Disorder)*. American Psychiatric Association.

Galen, L. W., Brower, K. J., Gillespie, B. W., & Zucker, R. A. (2000). Sociopathy, gender, and treatment outcome among outpatient substance abusers. *Drug and Alcohol Dependence, 61*(1), 23–33. https://doi.org/10.1016/S0376-8716(00)00125-3

Hare, R. D. (1991). *Manual for the Revised Psychopathy Checklist*. Multi-Health Systems.

Hare, R. D. (2003). *The Hare Psychopathy Checklist–Revised* (2nd ed.). Multi-Health Systems.

Hare, R. D., Neumann, C. S., & Mokros, A. (2018). The PCL-R assessment of psychopathy: Development, properties, debates, and new directions. In C. J. Patrick (Ed.), *Handbook of psychopathy* (2nd ed., pp. 58–88). Guilford Press.

Klein Haneveld, E., Neumann, C. S., Smid, W., Wever, E., & Kamphuis, J. H. (2018). Treatment responsiveness of replicated psychopathy profiles. *Law and Human Behavior, 42*(5), 484–495. https://doi.org/10.1037/lhb0000305

Kosson, D. S., Lorenz, A. R., & Newman, J. P. (2006). Effects of comorbid psychopathy on criminal offending and emotion processing in male offenders with antisocial personality disorder. *Journal of Abnormal Psychology, 115*(4), 798–806. https://doi.org/10.1037/0021-843X.115.4.798

Krueger, R. F., Derringer, J., Markon, K. E., Watson, D., & Skodol, A. E. (2012). Initial construction of a maladaptive personality trait model and inventory for *DSM-5*. *Psychological Medicine, 42*(9), 1879–1890. https://doi.org/10.1017/S0033291711002674

Krueger, R. F., & Markon, K. E. (2014). The role of the *DSM-5* personality trait model in moving toward a quantitative and empirically based approach to classifying personality and psychopathology. *Annual Review of Clinical Psychology, 10*(1), 477–501. https://doi.org/10.1146/annurev-clinpsy-032813-153732

Leistico, A. M., Salekin, R. T., DeCoster, J., & Rogers, R. (2008). A large-scale meta-analysis relating the Hare measures of psychopathy to antisocial conduct. *Law and Human Behavior, 32*(1), 28–45. https://doi.org/10.1007/s10979-007-9096-6

Lilienfeld, S. O. (1999). The relation of the MMPI-2 Pd Harris–Lingoes subscales to psychopathy, psychopathy facets, and antisocial behavior: Implications for clinical practice. *Journal of Clinical Psychology, 55*(2), 241–255. https://doi.org/10.1002/(SICI)1097-4679(199902)55:2<241::AID-JCLP12>3.0.CO;2-I

Lilienfeld, S. O., Patrick, C. J., Benning, S. D., Berg, J., Sellbom, M., & Edens, J. F. (2012). The role of fearless dominance in psychopathy: Confusions, controversies, and clarifications. *Personality Disorders, 3*(3), 327–340. https://doi.org/10.1037/a0026987

Lilienfeld, S. O., Watts, A. L., Smith, S. F., Patrick, C. J., & Hare, R. D. (2018). Hervey Cleckley (1903–1984): Contributions to the study of psychopathy. *Personality Disorders: Theory, Research, and Treatment. 9*, 520–520. https://doi.org/10.1037/per0000306

Lynam, D. R., & Miller, J. D. (2015). Psychopathy from a basic trait perspective: The utility of a Five-Factor Model approach. *Journal of Personality, 83*(6), 611–626. https://doi.org/10.1111/jopy.12132

Lynam, D. R., & Vachon, D. D. (2012). Antisocial personality disorder in *DSM-5*: Missteps and missed opportunities. *Personality Disorders: Theory, Research, and Treatment, 3*(4), 483–495. https://doi.org/10.1037/per0000006

Messina, N. P., Wish, E. D., & Nemes, S. (1999). Therapeutic community treatment for substance abusers with antisocial personality disorder. *Journal of Substance Abuse Treatment, 17*(1-2), 121–128. https://doi.org/10.1016/S0740-5472(98)00066-X

Miller, J. D., Lamkin, J., Maples-Keller, J. L., Sleep, C. E., & Lynam, D. R. (2018). A test of the empirical profile and coherence of the *DSM-5* psychopathy specifier. *Psychological Assessment, 30*(7), 870–881. https://doi.org/10.1037/pas0000536

Miller, J. D., & Lynam, D. R. (2012). An examination of the Psychopathic Personality Inventory's nomological network: A meta-analytic review. *Personality Disorders: Theory, Research, and Treatment, 3*(3), 305–326. https://doi.org/10.1037/a0024567

Millon, T., Grossman, S., & Millon, C. (2015). *MCMI-IV: Millon Clinical Multiaxial Inventory Manual* (4th ed.). NCS Pearson.

Morey, L. C. (1991). *The Personality Assessment Inventory: Professional manual.* Psychological Assessment Resources.

Neumann, C. S., Johansson, P. T., & Hare, R. D. (2013). The Psychopathy Checklist–Revised (PCL-R), low anxiety, and fearlessness: A structural equation modeling analysis. *Personality Disorders: Theory, Research, and Treatment, 4*(2), 129–137. https://doi.org/10.1037/a0027886

Neumann, C. S., Uzieblo, K., Crombez, G., & Hare, R. D. (2013). Understanding the Psychopathic Personality Inventory (PPI) in terms of the unidimensionality, orthogonality, and construct validity of PPI-I and -II. *Personality Disorders: Theory, Research, and Treatment, 4*(1), 77–79. https://doi.org/10.1037/a0027196

Neumann, C. S., Vitacco, M. J., & Mokros, A. S. (2016). Using both variable-centered and person-centered approaches to understanding psychopathic personality. In C. B. Gacono (Ed.), *The clinical and forensic assessment of psychopathy: A practitioner's guide* (2nd ed., pp. 14–31). Routledge.

Olver, M. E., Lewis, K., & Wong, S. C. P. (2013). Risk reduction treatment of high-risk psychopathic offenders: The relationship of psychopathy and treatment change to violent recidivism. *Personality Disorders: Theory, Research, and Treatment, 4*(2), 160–167. https://doi.org/10.1037/a0029769

Olver, M. E., & Wong, S. C. (2009). Therapeutic responses of psychopathic sexual offenders: Treatment attrition, therapeutic change, and long-term recidivism. *Journal of Consulting and Clinical Psychology, 77*(2), 328–336. https://doi.org/10.1037/a0015001

Patrick, C. J. (2006). Back to the future: Cleckley as a guide to the next generation of psychopathy research. In C. J. Patrick (Ed.), *Handbook of psychopathy* (pp. 605–617). Guilford Press.

Patrick, C. J. (Ed.). (2018). *Handbook of psychopathy* (2nd ed.). Guilford Press.

Patrick, C. J., & Drislane, L. E. (2015). Triarchic Model of Psychopathy: Origins, operationalizations, and observed linkages with personality and general psychopathology. *Journal of Personality, 83*(6), 627–643. https://doi.org/10.1111/jopy.12119

Patrick, C. J., Joyner, K. J., Watts, A. L., Lilienfeld, S. O., Somma, A., Fossati, A., Donnellan, M. B., Hopwood, C. J., Sellbom, M., Drislane, L. E., Edens, J. F., Verona, E., Latzman, R. D., Sica, C., Benning, S. D., Morey, L. C., Hicks, B. M., Fanti, K. A., Blonigen, D. M., . . . Krueger, R. F. (2021). Latent variable modeling of item-based factor scales: Comment on *Triarchic or Septarchic? Uncovering the Triarchic Psychopathy Measure's (TriPM) Structure,* by Roy et al. *Personality Disorders: Theory, Research, and Treatment, 12*(1), 16–23. https://doi.org/10.1037/per0000424

Pfohl, B., Blum, N., & Zimmerman, M. (1997). *Structured Interview for DSM-IV® Personality (SDIP).* American Psychiatric Press.

Poythress, N. G., Edens, J. F., Skeem, J. L., Lilienfeld, S. O., Douglas, K. S., Frick, P. J., Patrick, C. J., Epstein, M., & Wang, T. (2010). Identifying subtypes among offenders with antisocial personality disorder: A cluster-analytic study. *Journal of Abnormal Psychology, 119*(2), 389–400. https://doi.org/10.1037/a0018611

Riser, R. E., & Kosson, D. S. (2013). Criminal behavior and cognitive processing in male offenders with antisocial personality disorder with and without comorbid psychopathy. *Personality Disorders: Theory, Research, and Treatment, 4*(4), 332–340. https://doi.org/10.1037/a0033303

Roy, S., Vize, C., Uzieblo, K., van Dongen, J. D. M., Miller, J. D., Lynam, D. R., Brazil, I., Yoon, D., Mokros, A., Gray, N. S., Snowden, R., & Neumann, C. S. (2021a). The perils of untested assumptions in theory testing: A reply to Patrick et al. (2020). *Personality Disorders, 12*(1), 24–28. https://doi.org/10.1037/per0000461

Roy, S., Vize, C., Uzieblo, K., van Dongen, J. D. M., Miller, J., Lynam, D., Brazil, I., Yoon, D., Mokros, A., Gray, N. S., Snowden, R., & Neumann, C. S. (2021b). Triarchic or septarchic? Uncovering the Triarchic Psychopathy Measure's (TriPM) structure. *Personality Disorders, 12*(1), 1–15. https://doi.org/10.1037/per0000392

Salekin, R. T. (2002). Psychopathy and therapeutic pessimism: Clinical lore or clinical reality? *Clinical Psychology Review, 22*(1), 79–112. https://doi.org/10.1016/S0272-7358(01)00083-6

Sellbom, M., Solomon-Krakus, S., Bach, B., & Bagby, R. M. (2020). Validation of Personality Inventory for *DSM-5* (PID-5) algorithms to assess *ICD-11* personality trait domains in a psychiatric sample. *Psychological Assessment, 32*(1), 40–49. https://doi.org/10.1037/pas0000746

Sher, L., Siever, L. J., Goodman, M., McNamara, M., Hazlett, E. A., Koenigsberg, H. W., & New, A. S. (2015). Gender differences in the clinical characteristics and psychiatric comorbidity in patients with antisocial personality disorder. *Psychiatry Research, 229*(3), 685–689. https://doi.org/10.1016/j.psychres.2015.08.022

Sleep, C. E., Weiss, B., Lynam, D. R., & Miller, J. D. (2019). An examination of the Triarchic Model of psychopathy's nomological network: A meta-analytic review. *Clinical Psychology Review, 71*, 1–26. https://doi.org/10.1016/j.cpr.2019.04.005

Stepp, S. D., Trull, T. J., Burr, R. M., Wolfenstein, M., & Vieth, A. Z. (2005). Incremental validity of the Structured Interview for the Five-Factor Model of Personality (SIFFM). *European Journal of Personality, 19*(4), 343–357. https://doi.org/10.1002/per.565

Tyrer, P. (2013). The classification of personality disorders in *ICD-11*: Implications for forensic psychiatry. *Criminal Behaviour and Mental Health, 23*(1), 1–5. https://doi.org/10.1002/cbm.1850

Tyrer, P., Mulder, R., Kim, Y. R., & Crawford, M. J. (2019). The development of the *ICD-11* classification of personality disorders: An amalgam of science, pragmatism, and politics. *Annual Review of Clinical Psychology, 15*(1), 481–502. https://doi.org/10.1146/annurev-clinpsy-050718-095736

Venables, N. C., Hall, J. R., & Patrick, C. J. (2014). Differentiating psychopathy from antisocial personality disorder: A triarchic model perspective. *Psychological Medicine, 44*(5), 1005–1013. https://doi.org/10.1017/S003329171300161X

World Health Organization. (2019). *International statistical classification of diseases and related health problems* (11th ed.). https://icd.who.int/

Wygant, D. B., Sellbom, M., Sleep, C. E., Wall, T. D., Applegate, K. C., Krueger, R. F., & Patrick, C. J. (2016). Examining the *DSM-5* Alternative Personality Disorder Model operationalization of antisocial personality disorder and psychopathy in a male correctional sample. *Personality Disorders: Theory, Research, and Treatment, 7*(3), 229–239. https://doi.org/10.1037/per0000179

18

Higher Level Personality Disorders

Benjamin McCommon, Julia F. Sowislo, and Eve Caligor

Much research and clinical attention has been focused on the severe personality disorders, in particular, borderline, antisocial, schizotypal, and, more recently, narcissistic personality disorders (PDs). In contrast, only limited attention in the clinical and research literature has been devoted to PDs that present with lower severity, despite their frequent presentation in clinical practice (Mullins-Sweatt et al., 2012; Zimmerman et al., 2005). This chapter focuses on what we refer to as the *higher level personality disorders* (HLPDs). PDs that fall in this group are defined on the basis of severity of pathology rather than on the basis of presenting traits or personality style; specifically, HLPDs are characterized by relatively low severity while meeting full criteria for a PD diagnosis with clinically significant functional impairment. The clinical presentation of HLPDs is highly variable and spans the avoidant, dependent, histrionic, and obsessive-compulsive categorical personality disorders of Section II of the *Diagnostic Statistical Manual of Mental Disorders* (5th ed.; *DSM-5*; American Psychiatric Association, 2013), as well as the various presentations of mild, syndromal personality pathology not fitting any of these traditional categories (Other Specified Personality Disorder in *DSM-5*).

Categorical systems of classification of PDs based on traits, maladaptive behaviors, and symptoms, such as *DSM-5* Section II, traditionally have not identified HLPDs as a group because these systems of classification do not consider the crucial dimension of severity. Instead, attention is directed toward defining the different personality disorder presentations, highlighting distinctions among them, and obscuring shared and defining features of the HLPDs.

https://doi.org/10.1037/0000310-019
Personality Disorders and Pathology: Integrating Clinical Assessment and Practice in the DSM-5 *and* ICD-11 *Era*, S. K. Huprich (Editor)
Copyright © 2022 by the American Psychological Association. All rights reserved.

In contrast, dimensional models of classification of PDs, such as the Alternative *DSM-5* Model of Personality Disorders (AMPD; American Psychiatric Association, 2013), the *International Statistical Classification of Diseases and Related Health Problems* (11th ed.; *ICD-11*; World Health Organization, 2019) classification of PDs, and the object relations theory (ORT)–based model[1] of levels of personality organization (Caligor et al., 2018) anchor classification in the severity of impairment of self- and interpersonal functioning. From the vantage point of these diagnostic systems, HLPDs emerge clearly as a cohort, with the shared essential feature of mild impairment in self- and interpersonal functioning despite manifest differences in terms of personality styles, traits, and symptoms. These classification systems enable clinicians and researchers to distinguish between HLPDs and more severe personality pathology on the one hand, and between HLPDs and subsyndromal presentations of personality pathology on the other, while also highlighting continuity across all of the PDs along the dimension of severity of self and interpersonal functioning.

In this chapter, we discuss diagnostic and treatment approaches to HLPDs. We begin by providing an overview of the AMPD, *ICD-11*, and ORT models of classification and their approach to the HLPD diagnosis. We then address the clinical presentation, differential diagnosis, and treatment of HLPDs. A clinical vignette provides further illustration. Identifying HLPD as a diagnostic classification can be seen to lead to a more coherent approach to treatment than is offered by categorical approaches to diagnosis; because we address treatment of HLPDs, we point to the relationship among diagnosis, prognosis, and treatment planning. In discussing clinical presentation and treatment, we highlight contributions from the ORT model because it is unique in offering a theory-guided approach to personality pathology and treatment.

EVOLVING FROM CATEGORICAL TO DIMENSIONAL APPROACHES TO PERSONALITY DISORDER DIAGNOSIS

The decades since 1980, when the current *DSM* classification of PDs was introduced in the *DSM-III* (American Psychiatric Association, 1980), have seen rapid advancement of our knowledge of PDs and evolution of our systems of classification. The *DSM* system adopted and has retained a *categorical*, polythetic approach to diagnosis, emphasizing symptoms and maladaptive behaviors to define 10 discrete disorders. To make the diagnosis, these features must be relatively stable and pervasive and lead to clinically significant distress or impairment in social, occupational, or other important areas of functioning. The *ICD-10* (World Health Organization, 1993) identified the same

---

[1]*ORT* refers to a group of psychoanalytic and psychodynamic models that view the internalization of early patterns of relating to others as a central feature of psychological functioning. In this formulation the term "object" is used as a historical, psychoanalytic term to refer to a person with whom the subject has a relationship. We include the ORT approach in this chapter because it preceded other, more contemporary models in classifying PDs along a dimension of severity of self- and interpersonal dysfunction (Caligor et al., 2018).

group of categorical diagnoses as does the *DSM*, with the exception of schizo-typal personality disorder, which is classified as a schizophrenia spectrum illness. Grouping within the *DSM* model relies on descriptive similarities (Clusters A, B, and C). Although HLPDs are not identified as a group, the categorical diagnoses best characterized as falling within the HLPD diagnosis are the obsessive-compulsive, avoidant, dependent, and histrionic personality disorders.

Both the research and clinical literature have extensively documented the significant limitations of the categorical approach to PD classification (e.g., Widiger & Samuel, 2005). Perhaps most central is the failure to define what is essential to and shared by all PDs and to identify which features are most central to determining prognosis, clinical course, and outcome. These limitations have resulted in a failure to provide a diagnostic framework that could organize coherent approaches to treatment (Caligor et al., 2018; Clarkin et al., 2015). Although much remains controversial, there is convergence across the field on a number of central issues, reflecting developing knowledge and study of PDs. There is general acceptance that PDs are best described *dimensionally* rather than categorically and that the dimension of severity (however it may be defined) is perhaps the most powerful predictor of prognosis and clinical outcome (Crawford et al., 2011). This consensus is taken into account by the dimensional models of personality classification that we describe in more detail in the next section. When we turn to the issue of identifying core and defining features of PDs, there is an emerging consensus across varying perspectives that these lie in the domains of self- and interpersonal functioning (Bender & Skodol, 2007; Hopwood et al., 2013; Kernberg & Caligor, 2005; Sharp et al., 2015) and that different presentations of PD can be most usefully classified in terms of these shared features characterized across a continuum of severity.

DIMENSIONAL CLASSIFICATION OF PERSONALITY DISORDERS: AMPD, *ICD-11*, AND ORT

Convergence of expert opinion in relation to the centrality of impairment of self- and interpersonal functioning across the continuum of severity in the classification of PDs is formally recognized in the *DSM-5* Section III AMPD (American Psychiatric Association, 2013) and in the *ICD-11* (World Health Organization, 2019) classification of PDs. This approach closely corresponds to the psychodynamic ORT model (Kernberg, 1984) of PD, which preceded the dimensional shift in the *DSM* and *ICD* classifications. These three models all characterize syndromal PDs dimensionally, across three continuous levels of severity, reflecting degree of impairment of self- and interpersonal functioning. Although using different terminology—and, in the case of ORT, a different theoretical framework—the three diagnostic systems identify and characterize the HLPDs similarly as the mildest form of PD, presenting with syndromal but relatively low severity impairment in self- and interpersonal functioning.

AMPD AND *ICD-11*: DESCRIPTIVE CLASSIFICATION OF PERSONALITY PATHOLOGY AND HLPDs

In the AMPD and *ICD-11*, evaluation of self- and interpersonal functioning is combined to determine a single overall level of severity. Thus, although they are conceptualized as separate domains, self- and interpersonal functioning are understood to be intimately linked. In the AMPD self-functioning is conceptualized in terms of *identity* (subdomains: unique sense of self, stable and accurate self-esteem, and adequate-self regulation) and *self-direction* (subdomains: meaningful short-term and life goals, prosocial standards of behavior, and self-reflection). Interpersonal functioning is conceptualized in terms of *empathy* (subdomains: comprehension of others, tolerance of different perspectives, and understanding of the impact of one's behavior on others) and capacity for *intimacy* (subdomains: depth and duration of meaningful connections with others, the desire and capacity for closeness, and mutuality of regard for others).

The AMPD Levels of Personality Functioning Scale (LPFS) focuses on self- and interpersonal functioning and outlines five levels of personality functioning, spanning from LPFS 0 (*normal*) to LPFS 1 (*some impairment*), representing subsyndromal pathology, followed by three levels of syndromal PD: (a) LPFS 2 (*moderate impairment*), (b) LPFS 3 (*severe impairment*), and (c) LPFS 4 (*extreme impairment*). LPFS 2 corresponds with the HLPDs. Using a similar framework, the *ICD-11* also identifies three levels of syndromal personality pathology: (a) mild personality disorder, (b) moderate personality disorder, and (c) severe personality disorder, corresponding to AMPD LPFS Levels 2, 3, and 4, respectively. *ICD-11* also includes the classification "personality difficulty," to describe pathology that is subsyndromal, characterized by difficulties that may be intermittent or limited to specific settings and do not cause notable disruption in functioning. The *ICD-11* mild personality disorder classification corresponds with the HLPDs. Table 18.1 summarizes defining features of HLPDs in the AMPD and *ICD-11*.

ORT-Based Classification: Structural Classification of Personality Pathology and HLPDs

The ORT-based approach to PD classification (Caligor et al., 2018; Clarkin et al., in press; Kernberg, 1984) long predates and is compatible with both the AMPD and *ICD-11* systems while adding a psychodynamic perspective. As in both the AMPD and *ICD-11*, the essential nature of personality health and disorder is conceptualized and characterized in relation to self- and interpersonal functioning across a range of severity levels. In contrast to the purely descriptive classification adopted in the AMPD and *ICD-11*, the ORT model combines assessment of descriptive aspects of functioning with attention to underlying psychological processes, or mental structures, seen to organize self- and interpersonal functioning, to yield an overall rating of severity. To be

Higher Level Personality Disorders 417

TABLE 18.1. Defining Higher Level Personality Disorders in the AMPD and *ICD-11*

AMPD Levels of Personality Functioning Scale (LPFS)	*ICD-11* essential features of personality disorder severity
LPFS Level 2: Moderate level of impairment. Threshold for personality disorder diagnosis, defined on basis of clinically significant disruption of personality functioning	Mild personality disorder: Threshold for personality disorder diagnosis, defined on the basis of clinically significant disruptions of personality functioning
Dimensional diagnosis based on degree of impairment in self-functioning and interpersonal functioning	Dimensional diagnosis based on degree of impairment in self-functioning and degree and pervasiveness of interpersonal dysfunction across various contexts and relationships

Self-functioning: Domains

Identity • Unique sense of self, clear boundaries between self and others • Stability of self-esteem, accuracy of self-appraisal • Capacity for adequate self-regulation Self-directedness • Pursuit of coherent and meaningful short-term and life goals • Utilization of prosocial standards of behavior • Ability to self-reflect	Identity • Self-worth • Accuracy of self-view • Self-direction

Self-functioning: Defining HLPD

• Depends excessively on external sources for identity definition • Vulnerable self-esteem • Goals are a means of gathering others' approval, and thus may lack coherence and or stability • Self-standards may be exceptionally high or low	Disturbances affect some areas of personality functioning (e.g., problems with self-direction in the absence of problems with stability and coherence of identity or self-worth) and may not be apparent in some contexts

Interpersonal functioning: Domains

Empathy • Comprehension of others • Tolerance of different perspectives • Understanding the impact of one's behavior on others Capacity for intimacy • Depth and duration of meaningful connections with others • Desire and capacity for closeness • Capacity for mutuality of regard for others reflected in interpersonal behavior	• Interest in engaging in relationships with others • Ability to develop and maintain close and satisfying relationships • Ability to understand others' perspectives • Ability to manage conflict in relationships

(continues)

TABLE 18.1. Defining Higher Level Personality Disorders in the AMPD and ICD-11 (Continued)

AMPD Levels of Personality Functioning Scale (LPFS)	ICD-11 essential features of personality disorder severity
Interpersonal functioning: Defining HLPD	
• Desire and capacity to form relationships, but connections may be largely superficial • Tends to predominantly view intimate relations in terms of meeting self-regulatory needs • Tends not to view relationships in reciprocal terms • Compromised capacity to value and understand others' experience and to consider alternative perspectives	Problems in many interpersonal relationships and/or in performance of expected occupational and social roles, but some relationships are maintained and/or some roles are carried out

Note. AMPD = Alternative *DSM-5* Model for Personality Disorders; *ICD-11* = *International Statistical Classification of Diseases and Related Health Problems* (11th ed.); HLPD = higher level personality disorders. Data from American Psychiatric Association (2013) and World Health Organization (2019).

specific, the ORT model identifies six structural domains (see Table 18.2) central to personality health and pathology: (a) identity (experience of self and others in interactions), (b) object relations (working models of relationships and interpersonal relations), (c) predominant defensive style (customary ways of coping with external stress and internal conflict), (d) moral functioning (ethical behavior, ideals, and values), (e) aggression, and (f) reality testing (appreciation of conventional notions of reality).

Assessment of these six domains will lead to determination of *level of personality organization,* namely, normal personality, subsyndromal personality pathology ("neurotic level of personality organization"), and borderline personality organization (BPO), with the latter encompassing all syndromal PDs. Normal personality and neurotic levels of personality organization are characterized by a consolidated identity; the predominance of higher level, mature and repression-based defenses; a capacity for object relations marked by mutuality and concern for the needs of the other independent of the needs of the self; and consistent, internalized value systems. In contrast, BPO[2] is characterized by pathology of identity formation and the predominance of lower level, splitting-based defenses, in conjunction with variable pathology of object relations, moral functioning, and poorly integrated aggression.

The borderline level of personality organization covers a relatively broad spectrum of personality pathology, and distinctions within the range of BPOs are highly clinically significant.

---

[2]It is important to appreciate the distinction between *DSM-5* Borderline Personality Disorder (BPD) and BPO. BPD is a specific personality disorder, diagnosed on the basis of a constellation of descriptive features. BPO is a much broader category based on structural features—in particular, pathology of identity formation. The BPO diagnosis subsumes the *DSM-5* BPD diagnosis as well as all of the severe PDs.

TABLE 18.2. Levels of Personality Organization According to the Object Relations Theory Model

Level of organization	Core structural domains and definitions					
	Identity: Experience of self and others in interaction, confers capacity for self-regulation and mentalization, capacity to invest in and pursue long-term goals	**Object relations: Working models of relationships, reflected in quality of interpersonal relations and capacity for intimacy**	**Predominant defensive style: Customary ways of coping with external stress and internal conflict**	**Moral functioning: Value systems, ethical behavior and ideals**	**Aggression: Quality of internal aggression and nature of aggressive behavior; may be self-directed or other-directed**	**Reality testing: Capacity to distinguish between internal and external reality**
Normal personality organization	Consolidated, with stable and integrated sense of self and others	Deep, mutual relations; capacity for concern	Mature and repression based	Internalized, consistent, flexible	Modulated, appropriate	Intact and stable
Neurotic personality organization	Consolidated, with stable and integrated sense of self and others	Deep, mutual relations; capacity for concern; some conflict	Repression based[a]	Internalized, consistent, but rigid or demanding	Modulated, inhibited	Intact and stable
High-level borderline personality organization	Mild–moderate identity pathology with some instability and distortion in sense of self and others	Some capacity for dependent relations, highly conflictual or distant	Repression and splitting based	Variable across individuals, may see marked rigidity combined with focal deficits	Verbal aggression, temper outbursts, self-directed aggression in the form of self-neglect	Intact

(continues)

	Core structural domains and definitions					
Level of organization	Identity: Experience of self and others in interaction, confers capacity for self-regulation and mentalization, capacity to invest in and pursue long-term goals	Object relations: Working models of relationships, reflected in quality of interpersonal relations and capacity for intimacy	Predominant defensive style: Customary ways of coping with external stress and internal conflict	Moral functioning: Value systems, ethical behavior and ideals	Aggression: Quality of internal aggression and nature of aggressive behavior; may be self-directed or other-directed	Reality testing: Capacity to distinguish between internal and external reality
Middle borderline personality organization	Severe identity pathology with polarized and affectively charged, distorted, and unstable experience of self and others	Relations are based on need fulfillment with limited interest in the needs of the other independent of the needs of the self, limited to no capacity for dependent relations	Splitting based[b]	Moderate pathology with failure of internalized values, inconsistent or deficient moral functioning, may see circumscribed antisocial behavior	Poorly integrated and poorly modulated; potential for aggression against self and others; outbursts, threats, and self-injurious behavior	Vulnerable to extreme stress-related transient loss of reality testing; altered mental states without loss of reality testing such as dissociation, depersonalization
Low-level borderline personality organization	Severe identity pathology with polarized and highly affectively charged, distorted, and unstable experience of self and others	Relations based on frank exploitation, others are used as a means to an end, no capacity for dependency	Splitting based	Extreme pathology with absent or corrupt moral system, prominent antisocial traits with frank antisocial behavior	Severe aggression against self and others; assault, intimidation, and self-mutilation	Vulnerable to stress-related transient loss of reality testing; altered mental states without loss of reality testing such as dissociation, depersonalization

[a]Repression-based defenses include intellectualization, isolation of affect, reaction formation, displacement, and repression proper. [b]Splitting-based defenses include projective identification, idealization, devaluation, omnipotence, lower level denial, and splitting proper.

The ORT model identifies three continuous levels of PD severity ranging from the least severe (high BPO) to the middle BPO to the most severe (low BPO). All are characterized by identity disturbance and splitting-based defenses. As pathology becomes more severe, poorly integrated and dysregulated aggression plays an increasingly central role in psychological functioning. In this setting, splitting and related defenses of projective identification, omnipotent control, and idealization–devaluation become more extreme, leading to gross distortion and instability of interpersonal experience often associated with paranoid states. As the sense of self and of significant others become increasingly distorted, extreme, superficial, and unstable, the quality of relatedness and capacity for empathy deteriorate; the capacity for mutuality and dependency are lost; and relationships become, at best, organized around need fulfillment and at worst, around frank exploitation. At the same time, increasing severity of PD brings deterioration of internalized value systems and ethically driven behavior. Table 18.2 provides an overview of the five levels of personality organization and their defining features.

HLPDs fall into the high–BPO category as defined within the framework of ORT. The characteristic impairments in self- and interpersonal functioning that define the HLPDs can be understood as an expression of mild–moderate identity pathology, reflecting incomplete identity consolidation in the setting of a combination of splitting-based and higher level defenses. The impact of this defensive constellation leads to distortions and instability in the experience of self and others that are clinically significant but relatively mild, less extreme, and less pervasive, and as a result less disruptive of functioning, than the more flagrant distortion and gross instability characterizing the sense of self and others in the more severe PDs. Also, manifestations of identity disturbance and splitting typically present as vulnerability to mild distortion and/or instability in the sense of self and others, often limited to areas of conflict. As a result, expression of identity pathology tends to be context dependent, most pronounced in areas of psychological conflict—often dependency, intimacy, autonomy, or self-valuation—while less likely to be in evidence in other areas of functioning. From the perspective of defensive operations, individuals with HLPDs rely on a combination of lower level, splitting-based, and higher level, mature and repression-based, defenses. Lower level defenses of splitting, idealization, and denial and less dangerous forms of acting out tend to be especially prominent, whereas higher level defenses of rationalization and reaction formation tend to support repression. In contrast to what is seen in more severe pathology, where conflicts in relation to poorly integrated aggression tend to be central and splitting-based defenses predominate, in the HLPDs conflicts around dependency and self-esteem ("narcissistic conflicts") tend to be most prominent, with pathological expression or inhibition of aggression most typically secondary to frustration of dependency and narcissistic needs. Aggression is often self-directed and can include self-defeating behaviors, self-neglect, and inhibited expressions of aggression.

As outlined in Table 18.2, the ORT description of this group of disorders adds to the AMPD and *ICD-11* descriptions by highlighting features that help

TABLE 18.3. Crosswalk Among the *DSM-5* AMPD, *ICD-11*, and Object Relations Theory Classifications of Personality Pathology

DSM-5 AMPD Level of Personality Functioning Scale (LPFS)	*ICD-11* severity of personality dysfunction	Object relations theory level of personality organization
LPFS 0: No impairment	None	Normal personality organization
LPFS 1: Some impairment (subsyndromal)	Personality difficulty (subsyndromal)	Neurotic level of personality organization (subsyndromal)
LPFS 2: Moderate impairment (threshold for PD)	Mild personality disorder (PD; threshold for PD)	High BPO (threshold for PD)
LPFS 3: Severe impairment	Moderate personality disorder	Mid-BPO
LPFS 4: Extreme impairment	Severe personality disorder	Low BPO

Note. Severity increases as you move down the table. The higher level personality disorder designation corresponds with LPFS 2, mild personality disorder, and high borderline level of personality organization (BPO), respectively, in the *DSM-5* AMPD, *ICD-11*, and object relations theory systems. *DSM-5* = *Diagnostic and Statistical Manual of Mental Disorders* (5th ed.); *ICD-11*= International Statistical Classification of Diseases and Related Health Problems (11th ed.).

distinguish HLPDs from subsyndromal personality pathology on the one hand and more severe PDs on the other. In particular, the presence of (a) identity disturbance that is clinically significant albeit relatively mild and (b) the presence of an admixture of higher level and splitting-based defenses both help to distinguish HLPDs from subsyndromal personality pathology; similarly, the following three features emphasized in the ORT model help distinguish HLPDs from the more severe PDs: (a) some capacity for dependent relations; (b) the presence of internalized value systems that are relatively intact, with an absence of antisocial features; and (c) relatively mild pathology of aggression. Table 18.3 provides a crosswalk among AMPD (LPFS), *ICD-11*, and ORT classifications of personality pathology and points to the similarities among the three models.

CLINICAL PRESENTATION OF HLPDs

In HLPDs, pathology of self- and interpersonal functioning, though clinically significant, are relatively mild, such that functioning may be significantly compromised but not severely disrupted, often relatively preserved in some domains of functioning while more severely affected in others. Individuals with HLPDs typically come to clinical attention with complaints of problems with self-esteem and self-valuation, interpersonal conflicts that may interfere with social or work functioning, instability or distance in their intimate relations, and/or inadequate self-care. Associated feelings of dysphoria and anxiety are common, and many individuals with HLPDs initially come to clinical attention for treatment of symptoms of anxiety and/or depression rather than for treatment of personality dysfunction.

In contrast to what is seen in normal self functioning, individuals with HLPDs are excessively dependent on external factors, in particular, relationships with others, for maintaining self-definition and for supporting self-esteem. Mild instability and distortion in the sense of self typically manifest in problems with self-valuation; individuals with HLPDs often undervalue themselves, or they may fluctuate between under– and over–self-valuation depending on external circumstances. Similarly, they may have idealized or devalued views of others, often with some stability interspersed with shifts in perception, or with distortion and instability limited to their most intimate or significant relations. Although individuals with HLPDs typically are able to identify and sustain shorter and longer term life goals; those goals may be organized in relation to gathering external approval rather than internally driven, and as a result they may lack coherence, stability, and depth, or the individual may gradually lose interest in what had initially felt like deeply held aspirations. Personal standards may be unreasonably high or unreasonably low, or standards may alternate between the two. Severely aggressive and self-destructive behaviors and antisocial features are lacking.

Although pathology of interpersonal functioning may cause problems in many relationships and in performance of expected occupational and social roles, in the HLPDs some relationships are maintained and some roles are successfully carried out. They are able to develop and sustain interpersonal relationships, which may be long lasting, and they typically demonstrate at least some capacity for dependent relations. At the same time, connections with significant others tend to be somewhat distant and superficial or marked by conflict, and they are often characterized by idealization, excessive dependency, and a need-fulfilling orientation. Individuals with HLPDs tend not to consistently view relationships in reciprocal terms, a capacity that is a hallmark of the mature relationships of the subsyndromal disorders and normal personality, and they demonstrate a compromised ability to consistently appreciate and understand others' experience and to consider alternative perspectives.

Internalized values are present and moral functioning is generally intact, although it may be uneven or inconsistent, for example, extreme rigidity and holding the self to unreasonably high standards coexisting with focal deficits such as cheating in athletics, or infidelity. Similarly, excessively harsh feelings of self-recrimination may alternate with tolerance of deceptive or manipulative behavior. There is a notable absence of the prominent unethical behavior or frank antisocial features that characterize more extreme pathology. Reality testing is generally intact and stable. At the same time, individuals with HLPDs may demonstrate subtle deficits of *social reality testing*, with difficulties interpreting social cues and demonstrating social tact.

DIAGNOSIS ILLUSTRATION

Ms. A is a 30-year-old married woman with long-standing anxiety who has not previously sought treatment.[3] Trained as an architect, she lost her job 12 months ago when the firm where she had been employed was dissolved.

---

[3] This vignette has been altered to protect the identity of the subject.

She presents with feelings of depression and anxiety in relation to her unemployment: "Without my job I don't know how to define myself." She worries that she may never work again, explaining, "I am unworthy, ineffective and socially awkward. . . . Who would want to hire me?" She maintains this view despite a history of steady employment until now with positive performance reviews that made note of her conscientiousness, exacting standards, and seeming investment in her work. She has been reluctant to apply for jobs since a painful interview 10 months earlier that she continues to play over in her mind. She described how during the interview she felt tongue tied and "humiliated," distracted by worries that the interviewer was looking down on her, and then imagining the interviewer laughing at her with colleagues as soon as she was gone. She quickly assured the evaluating clinician that she understood this was unlikely—"I'm not paranoid"—but did admit to being profoundly troubled by these thoughts, nevertheless.

Ms. A looks up to her husband and describes him as "Perfect, everything anyone would want in a husband . . . I don't know where I'd be without him." At the same time, she acknowledges that she is very reserved in their relationship and is chronically worried about making a fool of herself in his eyes. When they socialize, she feels self-conscious and that she has little to say that would be of interest to others, and as a result she tends to withdraw. She has one close friend from high school who now lives in another city, but with whom she stays in regular contact, and one college friend whom she sees occasionally. She describes herself as shy, inept, and passive. Ms. A drinks two to three glasses of wine each night with her husband to help her relax. When asked whether she had considered cutting back on alcohol, she somewhat defensively insists that it was not a problem.

Ms. A illustrates many of the features of HLPDs outlined in this chapter. According to *DSM-5* Section II categorical diagnoses, she meets criteria for avoidant personality disorder, defined on the basis of the personality traits of social inhibition, feelings of inadequacy, and hypersensitivity to negative evaluation.

The AMPD would classify Ms. A as LPFS Level 2, indicating moderate impairment in self- and interpersonal functioning. Moderate impairment in identity is evidenced by excessively negative self-appraisal and low self-esteem. She relies on her job and on her role as her husband's wife to define herself. Goal directedness is mildly impaired; she has been sufficiently goal directed to complete her architectural training and pursue employment, although she has not been able to find her footing after losing her job. Moderate impairment in empathy is evident in her misreading others, misattributing to them negative views of herself, and a lack of awareness of the impact of her withdrawal at social gatherings on the experience of others. Intimacy is also moderately impaired; she does have a few friendships and a stable marriage, but relationships are marked by reserve and fear of humiliation. *ICD-11* would classify Ms. A as presenting with a mild PD, identifying features similar to those highlighted in the AMPD assessment. *ICD-11* would emphasize not only the relatively mild severity but also the lack of pervasiveness in her impaired functioning—for example, although self-valuation is distinctly impaired, she has demonstrated a capacity for self-directedness, and despite clear difficulties in her more intimate relationships, in her job she was able to perform in role without great difficulty. *ICD-11* would also specifically identify the distortions in her self-perception as part of assessment of "accuracy of situational and interpersonal appraisals, especially under stress," included in *ICD-11* in the overall rating of personality functioning.

From the perspective of ORT, Ms. A illustrates many of the cardinal features of the high BPO. Identity is characterized by mild failure of consolidation with distortions in her sense of self characterized by negative self-valuation and some distortion in her sense of others. Object relations are characterized by a capacity for dependency but with conflict, and there is evidence of superficiality and impaired closeness reflecting a reliance on idealization. A combination of splitting-based (largely idealization) and repression-based (remaining unaware of her own hostility and criticism of others) defenses allows her to sustain stable relationships with significant others, while hostility and criticism of those she sees as superior are managed through projection (she imagined the man who interviewed her was hostile and critical). Moral functioning is intact, but she demonstrates standards for herself that are overly rigid, especially in social interactions ("If I am not funny and entertaining, no one is interested in hearing from me"). Aggression is largely self-directed and typically not overt, expressed predominantly as a hostile, critical attitude toward herself (and, more covertly, toward others) and withdrawal. Conflicts in relation to dependency and self-esteem result in painful narcissistic vulnerability (in the absence of narcissistic personality disorder).

ASSESSMENT AND DIFFERENTIAL DIAGNOSIS

For purposes of treatment planning in the clinical setting it is necessary to distinguish HLPDs from both milder, subsyndromal personality pathology and more severe PDs. HLPDs are relatively easily distinguished from more severe PDs on the basis of capacity for dependent relations, relatively intact moral functioning, and limited pathology of aggression. HLPDs are perhaps more easily confused with subsyndromal or neurotic disorders on initial, superficial assessment, especially when individuals present with complaints of anxiety or disturbances of mood rather than problems in personality functioning. In this setting it can be easy to miss more subtle impairments in personality functioning. However, as illustrated by Ms. A, careful evaluation of identity formation, focusing on the experience of self and others and goal-directedness, as well as interpersonal functioning, focusing on intimacy, empathy, and working models of relationships, will reveal characteristic features of the HLPDs.

We endorse clinical interviews to evaluate personality functioning, focusing on quality of relationships and intimacy, work history and work satisfaction, personal interests and hobbies, and emotional investment and goal-directedness in these domains of functioning. Identity can be assessed efficiently by asking the patient to provide a self-description and a description of a significant other. Responses can be evaluated on the basis of superficiality versus depth, specificity and coherence versus vagueness and inconsistency, black-and-white thinking versus complexity, and shades of gray in descriptions of self and other. Assessment of defensive style can be informed by attention to the interviewer's experience during the interview; when evaluating a patient who uses higher level defenses, presenting problems and relevant history tend to unfold in a coherent manner, and the interviewer generally does not have difficulty feeling comfortably engaged. In contrast, a patient's use of lower level, splitting-based defenses can make obtaining a coherent and specific history somewhat challenging. The interviewer may be left feeling somewhat confused, with only a vague understanding of relevant information. In addition, lower level defenses may leave the interviewer feeling in some way controlled during the interaction with the patient. For example, during her interview with Ms. A, the interviewer recognized at times feeling overly fearful of offending her, overly solicitous, and avoiding exploration of potentially important areas of functioning that Ms. A was reluctant to address.

In addition to the clinical interview, a number of structured assessments are available for evaluating personality pathology. The Structured Clinical Interview for the *DSM-5* Alternative Model of Personality Disorders (SCID-AMPD; Bender et al., 2018) assesses personality functioning within the framework of the *DSM-5* AMPD. The interview covers the four domains and 12 subdomains of the LPFS through ratings made on 5-point scales. The interview starts with eight screener questions that inquire about how the individual relates to the self and to significant others (e.g., "How would you describe yourself as a person?" or "What are your relationships with other people like?"). This level of inquiry provides a preliminary impression and rating of level of personality functioning. This preliminary rating is explored through follow-up questions corresponding to increasing levels of dysfunction. In addition to the SCID-AMPD, several other structured interviews and screening questionnaires have been developed to assess PD according to the LPFS; an overview of those can be found in Zimmermann et al. (2019). Assessment tools for the *ICD-11* classification are currently under development, but diagnoses made through the SCID-AMPD can be translated into *ICD-11* diagnoses (Bach & First, 2018; cf. Table 5). With regard to the ORT model, the Structured Interview for Personality Organization (Clarkin et al., 2016; Stern et al., 2010) provides a semistructured tool to reliably assess personality psychology. The instrument focuses on the five domains of functioning described by the ORT model: (a) identity (subdomains: capacity to invest in work and recreation, sense of self, sense of others), (b) quality of object relations (subdomains: interpersonal relations, intimate relations and sexuality, internal working models of relationships), (c) defenses (subdomains: primitive defenses, coping and rigidity), (d) aggression (subdomains: self-directed and other-directed aggression), and (e) moral values. These domains are assessed by 55 individual items (e.g., that address satisfaction in work, closeness in friendships, idealization and devaluation, self-harm, capacity for guilt). Each item provides standardized questions and follow-up probes.

TREATMENT OF HIGHER LEVEL PERSONALITY DISORDERS

Treatment of HLPDs can be targeted toward symptomatic relief (improvement in anxiety, depression) or behavioral improvement (increased assertiveness, decreased impulsivity), or they may be targeted more generally toward personality change (changes in identity, self-direction, empathy, and intimacy). HLPDs generally have a good prognosis in treatment if appropriate structure is provided to address possible self-destructive or treatment-interfering behaviors, such as inconsistent attendance, frequent lateness, failure to adaptively pursue work or relationships, or misuse of alcohol or marijuana. Indications of a particularly positive prognosis include the presence of intact moral functioning; low levels of aggression; and a relatively well-developed capacity to form stable, dependent relationships.

The research literature provides limited guidance for the treatment of HLPDs. Most studies have been case reports or based on longitudinal observation (Dixon-Gordon et al., 2011; Leichsenring et al., 2015; Porcerelli et al., 2009). A few randomized controlled trials are available to guide treatment. One study of 62 patients with avoidant personality disorder found that patients who received 20 weeks of cognitive behavior therapy showed significantly more improvement than patients who received brief dynamic therapy or were assigned to a wait list control group, and no difference was found between the brief dynamic and wait-list groups (Emmelkamp et al., 2006). Two other randomized controlled trials included a mixed group of patients with avoidant, dependent, and obsessive-compulsive personality disorders (previously known as Cluster C PDs). In one trial, significant improvement in symptoms, interpersonal problems, and personality functioning during treatment and at a 2-year follow-up were found in 50 patients who received 40 weeks of treatment with either short-term dynamic psychotherapy or cognitive therapy (Svartberg et al., 2004). In another trial, 323 patients were randomized to receive 50 sessions of schema therapy, clarification-oriented therapy (a client-centered psychotherapy for PDs), or treatment as usual (Bamelis et al., 2014). Significantly greater recovery from PD after 3 years was found in the group that received schema therapy, but all three groups showed significant improvement in secondary outcome measures.

Given this limited guidance, it is reasonable to consider adapting evidence-supported treatments for more severe PDs for use in HLPDs, selected on the basis of the patient's presenting difficulties. We include here dialectical behavioral therapy (Linehan, 2018), schema therapy (Young et al., 2003), good psychiatric management for borderline personality disorder (Gunderson, 2014), mentalization-based therapy (Bateman & Fonagy, 2004), and transference-focused psychotherapy (TFP; Yeomans et al., 2015). It may be most useful to use general evidence-based principles of psychotherapy common to a variety of these evidence-based treatments, including the following:

- complete assessment of the patient's presenting difficulties, symptoms, and personality functioning, with careful attention to severity of pathology, to guide treatment planning;

- diagnostic sharing, including explicit discussion of the problems to be treated and psychoeducation;

- discussion of treatment options and how treatments work, as part of informed consent;

- establishment of an explicit treatment frame and treatment agreement, including patient and therapist responsibilities;

- determination of treatment goals;

- a coherent theory of technique to guide therapists in treatments that may at times include significant confusion;

- attention to the therapeutic relationship, especially the patient's negative experiences of the therapist; and

- plans for handling intersession contact and urgent issues.

Compared with borderline personality disorder and other severe PDs, patients with HLPDs may not require as much planning for emergencies and crises or as much focus on treatment-interfering behaviors, although attention to these problems may be needed at times. At the same time, compared with patients with subsyndromal personality pathology, patients with HLPDs benefit from a more structured treatment frame and attention to concrete treatment goals. If the patient has a history of prior treatment, discussions with former clinicians will provide valuable information about problems likely to again emerge as the patient reenters treatment, for example, irregular attendance, less than full and open communication, or precipitous dropout. Anticipating the risk of such problems enables the clinician to discuss them with the patient before beginning, along with plans for how to manage such difficulties should they emerge.

Our own preferred treatment approach is derived from TFP, a psychodynamic, evidence-based treatment grounded in ORT that helps effectively treat borderline personality disorder. TFP has been adapted to provide a well-defined approach to treatment of personality pathology across the range of severity (TFP–Extended [TFP-E]; Caligor et al., 2018), with special attention to general principles applicable to treatment of patients across the spectrum of severity as well as to modifications that help clinicians tailor treatment to the individual patient. TFP-E relies on an explicitly agreed-on treatment frame outlining the need for consistent attendance at sessions; consistent engagement in structured activity outside of the therapy, be it at work or school; and free and open communication on the part of the patient. The frame outlines procedures for the handling of intersession contact, cancellations and payment, and management of urgent issues should they arise. Attention to the treatment frame discourages destructive and treatment-interfering behaviors, and the potential for secondary gain is restricted by the requirement for structured activity. As these behaviors are limited, the patient's dominant areas of difficulty and underlying conflicts are brought into the treatment. Explicit treatment goals, such as better work performance or improved marital relations, are agreed on before the treatment begins and serve both to anchor the treatment in the patient's outside functioning and to organize the therapist's listening and interventions. The TFP-E therapist's stance is active, empathic, and positive, supporting the development of a therapeutic alliance and patient motivation for change.

The overarching objective of treatment of HLPDs within the framework of TFP-E is to promote identity consolidation and a shift from splitting-based to higher level defenses, leading to increased coherence and differentiation in the experience of the self and others and improved self- and interpersonal functioning. Identity integration is understood in terms of the coalescence of polarized views of the self and other as splitting is diminished. Integrative processes are supported by the therapist providing affect containment while promoting self-observation, reflection, and consideration of alternative perspectives on the part of the patient. These objectives are achieved through exploration of the polarized and distorted internalized relationship patterns organizing the patient's interpersonal relationships and the relationship with the therapist. The therapeutic focus is on what is affectively dominant, or emotionally salient, in each session and includes careful attention to the patient's life situation outside of therapy. The emergence of treatment-interfering behaviors or other acts of noncompliance with the agreed-on treatment frame, when they occur, will take priority in determining the dominant issue to be addressed in the session. Interventions focus on the here and now of the patient's experience in session; their current functioning; and their relationships, including the relationship with the therapist. There is less emphasis on the past and on childhood relations with caretakers than is characteristic of traditional psychoanalytic therapy.

In each session, the TFP-E therapist attends to three channels of communication coming from the patient: (a) verbal communications, (b) nonverbal behavior and attitudes, and (c) countertransference elicited in the therapist. In the treatment of PDs as a group, nonverbal communications—including the patient's behavior outside the session—and countertransference tend to play a particularly central role in psychotherapeutic process relative to what the patient is saying. In the treatment of HLPDs verbal communications tend to be more salient than in the treatment of more severe PDs, with the therapist's attention often equally drawn to verbal channels, nonverbal channels, and countertransference, integrating the three to form an understanding of the patient's current psychological experience. This can be contrasted with the treatments of patients with subsyndromal personality pathology, for whom verbal communication generally serves as the dominant channel of communication and nonverbal communications and countertransference play a less central role.

Standard psychodynamic techniques of *clarification, confrontation, interpretation,* and *transference analysis* using countertransference are used in exploring the dominant issue of a session. Clarification helps address areas of vagueness or omission ("I'm having difficulty understanding exactly what happened; you said your boss was critical and you felt humiliated. Can you take me through what happened step by step?"); confrontation points to contradictions and inconsistences introduced by the patient's defenses ("You're telling me your boss was critical and callous, but until now you have consistently described him to me as supportive and kind"). Repeated cycles of clarification and confrontation serve to promote the patient's capacity for self-observation, reflection, and entertaining of alternative perspectives, and they prepare the patient for more formal interpretations of the unconscious fears and motivations that may be driving defensive operations. Interpretations are likely to focus on wishes or fears in relation to relationships, often idealized or, at times, somewhat paranoid and colored by mistrust. In the setting of high BPO, transference interpretations may be especially valuable in addressing negative transferences (Høglend, 2014). Initial transferences are often idealizing; negative and more paranoid transferences are expected to eventually emerge, although they will be less extreme than those seen in the more severe PDs.

TREATMENT ILLUSTRATION

We return to Ms. A, the 30-year-old unemployed architect described earlier. During her initial consultation, she identified a treatment goal of returning to work, although she was fearful that her year-long unemployment would be difficult to explain and make her an undesirable candidate for any position. The therapist agreed that returning to work would be a reasonable treatment goal and further explained that engaging in meaningful productive activity was necessary for a treatment focused on understanding and changing avoidant behavior. As another part of their treatment agreement, Ms. A grudgingly agreed to limit her alcohol to one drink per day and to discuss with the therapist any increases in her alcohol intake.

When treatment started, Ms. A initially made only superficial efforts to resume her job search. The therapist tactfully confronted her behavior as not meeting their treatment agreement and as possibly interfering with treatment being helpful. After that, Ms. A began more actively to look for work, and within 3 months she found a part-time position as a contract employee at a small architecture firm. The glowing terms in which she described the two partners who ran the firm reminded the therapist of Ms. A's idealized description of her husband. Ms. A was interested in full-time work, and the firm quickly increased her employment to 40 hours per week. This continued for an extended period on a contractual basis with no mention of Ms. A being hired for a salaried, permanent position.

After discussing this unsatisfying work situation over several sessions, Ms. A tentatively admitted that she wondered whether the two partners were taking advantage of her. She shared that she suspected that they saw her as inadequate and would want to get rid of her. She also blamed herself for not being assertive enough to inquire about a salaried position, saying that she was fearful that asking for anything more would lead to her being dismissed. Avoiding eye contact, Ms. A went on to say that she probably seemed foolish in her fears about being more assertive. After a pause she fearfully added that if she lost her job, perhaps the therapist would no longer be willing to work with her. The therapist noted feeling protective of her.

The therapist described a possible relationship pattern, or object relation, playing out between Ms. A and her employers, that of a weak, incompetent childlike figure at the mercy of negligent, potentially rejecting, and possibly even abusive powerful parental figures, linked to feelings of fear and unworthiness. Ms. A nodded in agreement and seemed reflective, so the therapist went on to say that a similar pattern might be being played out between them: a weak patient fearful of not doing what is required by a demanding, dismissive, and rejecting therapist. In response, Ms. A apologized, saying that she could not help feeling that way even though she knew that was not the whole story and that it might be possible that this could be true at work as well. Guided by her countertransferential feelings of protectiveness toward Ms. A, the therapist described another possible, wished-for object relation: a patient who is well cared for and feels secure with a helpful, protective therapist. The therapist commented that perhaps Ms. A might want this to be offered without even having to own it, let alone ask for it, similar to how she might be wanting her employers to act positively toward her without her having to take a chance of asking for something. Softly, Ms. A replied by acknowledging how hard it is to ask for things and how powerfully she anticipated painful rejection.

This clinical vignette demonstrates how TFP adapted for high BPO is useful in the treatment of HLPDs. The structure provided by the treatment agreement allows the therapist and patient to be comfortable in psychodynamic exploration of self- and interpersonal problems by setting limits around possible destructive behavior, such as misuse of alcohol, or more subtle treatment-interfering behavior, such as the lack of meaningful productive activity. Once a secure treatment setting is established, repeated identification and exploration of affectively dominant relationship patterns can take center stage in the therapy, contributing over time to accomplishing the overarching treatment goal of promoting integration of idealized and more paranoid experiences of self in relation to other. In the case of Ms. A, the therapist began by identifying a fearful and somewhat paranoid object relation played out in a significant relationship outside of the treatment relationship, and once this was accepted and understood by the patient the therapist extended exploration to the patient's experience with the therapist. The therapist used their own countertransference to complement the patient's verbal and nonverbal communications, leading to a hypothesis about a less evident, positive object relation with an idealized version of the therapist, a relationship that represented a change in affective valence from the more obvious negative one initially discussed. The repeated identification and exploration of such positively and negatively valanced core object relations, both in the transference and in the patient's important relationships, is oriented toward the promotion of identity consolidation. In the process, the therapist will at the same time address Ms. A's interpersonal difficulties, focusing in particular, in light of her treatment goals, on her interactions with her employers, with the objective of enabling her to consider the possibility of being more assertive in the workplace.

CONCLUSION

In this chapter, we have outlined an approach to the diagnosis and treatment of HLPDs. With the recent ascendence of dimensional understanding and classification of personality pathology focusing on degree of impairment in self- and interpersonal functioning, the HLPDs emerge as a clearly defined and well-described form of syndromal personality pathology across the AMPD, *ICD-11*, and ORT models of PD diagnosis and classification. Representing the mildest form of syndromal PD, HLPDs carry a favorable prognosis in treatments that make use of evidence-based principles for treatment of personality pathology.

REFERENCES

American Psychiatric Association. (1980). *Diagnostic and statistical manual of mental disorders* (3rd ed.).

American Psychiatric Association. (2013). *Diagnostic and statistical manual of mental disorders* (5th ed.). https://doi.org/10.1176/appi.books.9780890425596

Bach, B., & First, M. B. (2018). Application of the *ICD-11* classification of personality disorders. *BMC Psychiatry, 18*(1), 351. https://doi.org/10.1186/s12888-018-1908-3

Bamelis, L. L., Evers, S. M., Spinhoven, P., & Arntz, A. (2014). Results of a multicenter randomized controlled trial of the clinical effectiveness of schema therapy for personality disorders. *The American Journal of Psychiatry, 171*(3), 305–322. https://doi.org/10.1176/appi.ajp.2013.12040518

Bateman, A. W., & Fonagy, P. (2004). Mentalization-based treatment of BPD. *Journal of Personality Disorders, 18*(1), 36–51. https://doi.org/10.1521/pedi.18.1.36.32772

Bender, D. S., & Skodol, A. E. (2007). Borderline personality as a self–other representational disturbance. *Journal of Personality Disorders, 21*(5), 500–517. https://doi.org/10.1521/pedi.2007.21.5.500

Bender, D. S., Skodol, A. E., First, M. B., & Oldham, J. (2018). *Structured clinical interview for the DSM-5® Alternative Model for Personality Disorders (SCID-5-AMPD) Module I Level of Personality Functioning scale.* American Psychiatric Association.

Caligor, E., Kernberg, O. F., Clarkin, J. F., & Yeomans, F. E. (2018). *Psychodynamic therapy for personality pathology: Treating self and interpersonal functioning.* American Psychiatric Association.

Clarkin, J. F., Cain, N. M., & Livesley, W. J. (2015). The link between personality theory and psychological treatment: A shifting terrain. In S. K. Huprich (Ed.), *Personality disorders: Toward a theoretical and empirical integration in diagnosis and assessment* (pp. 413–434). American Psychological Association. https://doi.org/10.1037/14549-018

Clarkin, J. F., Caligor, E., & Sowislo, J. F. (in press). Transference-focused psychotherapy for levels of personality pathology severity. In H. Crisp & G. Gabbard (Eds.), *Gabbard's textbook of psychotherapeutic treatments* (2nd ed.). American Psychiatric Publishing.

Clarkin, J. F., Caligor, E., Stern, B. L., & Kernberg, O. F. (2016). *Structured Interview of Personality Organization (STIPO-R)*. Personality Disorders Institute, Weill Medical College of Cornell University.

Crawford, M. J., Koldobsky, N., Mulder, R., & Tyrer, P. (2011). Classifying personality disorder according to severity. *Journal of Personality Disorders, 25*(3), 321–330. https://doi.org/10.1521/pedi.2011.25.3.321

Dixon-Gordon, K. L., Turner, B. J., & Chapman, A. L. (2011). Psychotherapy for personality disorders. *International Review of Psychiatry, 23*(3), 282–302. https://doi.org/10.3109/09540261.2011.586992

Emmelkamp, P. M., Benner, A., Kuipers, A., Feiertag, G. A., Koster, H. C., & van Apeldoorn, F. J. (2006). Comparison of brief dynamic and cognitive–behavioural therapies in avoidant personality disorder. *The British Journal of Psychiatry, 189*(1), 60–64. https://doi.org/10.1192/bjp.bp.105.012153

Gunderson, J. G. (2014). *Handbook of good psychiatric management for borderline personality disorder*. American Psychiatric Publishing.

Høglend, P. (2014). Exploration of the patient–therapist relationship in psychotherapy. *The American Journal of Psychiatry, 171*(10), 1056–1066. https://doi.org/10.1176/appi.ajp.2014.14010121

Hopwood, C. J., Wright, A. G., Ansell, E. B., & Pincus, A. L. (2013). The interpersonal core of personality pathology. *Journal of Personality Disorders, 27*(3), 270–295. https://doi.org/10.1521/pedi.2013.27.3.270

Kernberg, O. F. (1984). *Severe personality disorders: Psychotherapeutic strategies*. Yale University Press.

Kernberg, O. F., & Caligor, E. (2005). A psychodynamic theory of personality disorders. In M. F. Lenzenweger & J. F. Clarkin (Eds.), *Major theories of personality disorder* (2nd ed., pp. 114–156). Guilford Press.

Leichsenring, F., Leweke, F., Klein, S., & Steinert, C. (2015). The empirical status of psychodynamic psychotherapy—An update: Bambi's alive and kicking. *Psychotherapy and Psychosomatics, 84*(3), 129–148. https://doi.org/10.1159/000376584

Linehan, M. M. (2018). *Cognitive–behavioral treatment of borderline personality disorder*. Guilford Press.

Mullins-Sweatt, S. N., Bernstein, D. P., & Widiger, T. A. (2012). Retention or deletion of personality disorder diagnoses for *DSM-5*: An expert consensus approach. *Journal of Personality Disorders, 26*(5), 689–703. https://doi.org/10.1521/pedi.2012.26.5.689

Porcerelli, J., Dauphin, B., Ablon, J. S., Leitman, S., & Bambery, M. (2009). Psychoanalysis of avoidant personality disorder: A systematic case study of process and outcome. *Journal of the American Psychoanalytic Association, 57*(2), 444–449. https://doi.org/10.1177/00030651090570020906

Sharp, C., Wright, A. G., Fowler, J. C., Frueh, B. C., Allen, J. G., Oldham, J., & Clark, L. A. (2015). The structure of personality pathology: Both general ('g') and specific ('s') factors? *Journal of Abnormal Psychology, 124*(2), 387–398. https://doi.org/10.1037/abn0000033

Stern, B. L., Caligor, E., Clarkin, J. F., Critchfield, K. L., Horz, S., MacCornack, V., Lenzenweger, M. F., & Kernberg, O. F. (2010). Structured Interview of Personality Organization (STIPO): Preliminary psychometrics in a clinical sample. *Journal of Personality Assessment, 92*(1), 35–44. https://doi.org/10.1080/00223890903379308

Svartberg, M., Stiles, T. C., & Seltzer, M. H. (2004). Randomized, controlled trial of the effectiveness of short-term dynamic psychotherapy and cognitive therapy for cluster C personality disorders. *The American Journal of Psychiatry, 161*(5), 810–817. https://doi.org/10.1176/appi.ajp.161.5.810

Widiger, T. A., & Samuel, D. B. (2005). Diagnostic categories or dimensions? A question for the *Diagnostic and Statistical Manual of Mental Disorders. Journal of Abnormal Psychology, 114*(4), 494–504. https://doi.org/10.1037/0021-843X.114.4.494

World Health Organization. (1993). *The* ICD-10 *classification of mental and behavioural disorders: Clinical descriptions and diagnostic guidelines.*

World Health Organization. (2019). *International statistical classification of diseases and related health problems* (11th ed.). https://icd.who.int

Yeomans, F. E., Clarkin, J. F., & Kernberg, O. F. (2015). *Transference-focused psychotherapy for borderline personality disorder: A clinical guide.* American Psychiatric Publishing.

Young, J. E., Klosko, J., & Weishaar, M. (2003). *Schema therapy.* Guilford Press.

Zimmerman, M., Rothschild, L., & Chelminski, I. (2005). The prevalence of *DSM-IV* personality disorders in psychiatric outpatients. *The American Journal of Psychiatry, 162*(10), 1911–1918. https://doi.org/10.1176/appi.ajp.162.10.1911

Zimmermann, J., Kerber, A., Rek, K., Hopwood, C. J., & Krueger, R. F. (2019). A brief but comprehensive review of research on the Alternative *DSM-5* Model for Personality Disorders. *Current Psychiatry Reports, 21*(9), 92. https://doi.org/10.1007/s11920-019-1079-z

INDEX

A

Abraham, P. F., 196
ACC. *See* Anterior cingulate cortex
Acceptance, in DBT, 260
Acceptance and commitment therapy, 192
Accuracy
  diagnostic, of *ICD-11* model, 34
  of informant report measures, 87–88
Achievement of identity consolidation, 213
Acting-Out Dynamics (6A.3) subscale,
  MCMI-IV, 401
"Action man or person" mode, 252. *See also*
  Teleological mode
Action-oriented therapy, 405
Active dependency, 142
Active listening, for validation, 267
Active phase, of TFP, 217–219
Acute clinical care settings, TFP principles
  in, 224
Adaptive coping behaviors, 287
Adaptive significance, of traits, 191
ADHD. *See* Attention-deficit/hyperactivity
  disorder
Adolescents. *See also* Personality assessment
  for youth
  DBT with, 269
  informant report measures for, 88
  LPF assessments for, 115–116
  mentalization-based treatment with,
    254, 255
  nonsuicidal self-injury by, 363
  psychotherapy with, 405–406

subthreshold personality difficulty for, 35
  TFP principles in treatment for, 225
Affective dimension, of psychopathy, 393
Affective path of social cognition, 334
Affective Quality of Representations (AFF)
  subscale, SCORS-G, 164, 169, 173
Affective ToM, 336, 337
Affect regulation
  in BPD vs. bipolar disorder, 359–360
  pharmacotherapy for, 195, 196, 310,
    311, 315
  in PTSD vs. BPD, 362
  skills acquisition for, 153
Affiliative Reward-Rejection Sensitivity
  reaction surface, 62
AFF subscale. *See* Affective Quality of
  Representations (AFF) subscale,
  SCORS-G
Aggression
  in antisocial personality disorder, 395
  impulsive, 195, 196
  instrumental, 393
  in narcissistic personality disorder, 381
  neurobiological studies of, 329, 339
  in ORT-based classification of personality,
    418–421
  in pathological narcissism, 380, 381
  pharmacotherapy to reduce, 308
  provocation-induced, 339
  and psychopathy, 393
  reactive, 339, 393

436 *Index*

Aggression (AGG) scale, MMPI-2-RF, 401
Aggression (AGG) scale, PAI, 400
Aggressive Behavior Control program,
406–407
AGG subscale, SCORS-G. *See* Experience
and Management of Aggressive
Impulses subscale, SCORS-G
Agreeableness
and Antagonism, 14, 227, 356
and Dissociality, 193
and psychopathy, 393
AIDA. *See* Assessment of Identity
Development in Adolescence
Alcohol Problems (ALC) scale, PAI, 400
Alcohol use, 148, 152, 153, 269. *See also*
Substance use
Alexander, J., 41
Alexithymia, 35
Alliance. *See* Therapeutic alliance
Allport, G. W., 159
Alternative *DSM-5* Model for Personality
Disorders (AMPD), 3–4, 9–21, 159–177
about, 10–11
and Anankastia in *ICD-11* model, 33
antisocial personality disorder in, 394–398
assessment methods to inform diagnosis
with, 168–170
borderline personality disorder in, 355–356
borderline personality organization and,
224
case example of diagnosis and treatment
planning with, 170–176
and categorical thinking by clinicians, 57
clinical direction from, 59
clinical interviews using, 78
in clinical practice, 18–20
clinical staging framework based on,
121–125
clinical utility of, 53, 56, 62
Criterion A in. *See* Criterion A, in AMPD
model
Criterion B in. *See* Criterion B, in AMPD
model
and dialectical behavior psychotherapy,
272–274
dimensionalization of diagnosis with, 77,
166–167
discriminative power of, 59–60
efficiency and complexity of, 61
future research directions, 20–21
higher level personality disorders in,
414, 416–418
ICD-11 model and, 27, 28, 30–33, 53–54,
184, 375–376
if–then contingencies in diagnosis with, 58
learning to apply, 162–165
and mentalization-based treatment, 238,
255
method of diagnosis with, 160–161

mode profiles associated with PDs in,
285, 286
narcissistic personality disorder in, 375–380
neurobiological research supporting,
323, 330
overlap between criteria in, 17–18, 166–167
personality assessment for youth based on,
112, 115–120
and pharmacotherapy, 314
psychodiagnosis and treatment planning
with, 167–168
reliability of diagnosis with, 356
and schema therapy, 300
severity measures for, 35, 36, 135
trait domains in *ICD-11* vs., 37
and transference-focused psychotherapy,
215, 225–227
transtheoretical model for assessment
related to, 96–97
treatment planning with, 20, 65–66, 135,
167–168, 170–176
Álvarez-Tomás, I., 365
Amantadine, 308
American Psychiatric Association, 3, 9, 29,
116, 195, 237–238, 309–310, 353–355,
364, 375, 391
American Psychological Association, 268
Amitriptyline, 308
AMPD. *See* Alternative *DSM-5* Model for
Personality Disorders
AMPD Levels of Personality Functioning
Scale (LPFS). *See* Level of Personality
Functioning Scale (LPFS)
D-Amphetamine, 307
Amygdala
dissociation and, 327
empathy and, 331, 334, 335
facial emotion recognition and, 331–333
impact of TFP on, 223
intimacy/trust and, 339
self- and other-referential processing in,
325
self-control and, 328–330
theory of mind and, 336, 337
Anankastia
empirical support for delineating, 39, 40
in *ICD-11* model, 4, 33–34, 37, 54
and mortality risk, 43
in multimethod assessment, 97
Orderliness and, 39
PDs characterized by overlapping
domains with, 197
pharmacotherapy to reduce, 196
PID5BF+ items related to, 41, 42
SASPD items related to, 36
treatments to reduce, 194–195
Anger
DBT to reduce, 268
facial emotion recognition of, 332, 333

neurobiological studies of, 329
pharmacotherapy to reduce, 310, 311
Anger Proneness (ANP) scale, MMPI-2-RF, 401
Anger rumination, 328
Angry Child mode, 287, 288
Angular gyrus, 220
Anhedonia, 14
ANP (Anger Proneness) scale, MMPI-2-RF, 401
Antagonism
  and Agreeableness, 14
  with antisocial personality disorder, 398
  with borderline personality disorder, 356
  and Criterion B, 227, 356
  dialectical behavior psychotherapy to reduce, 273
  and Dissociality, 54
  in multimethod assessment, 96
  with psychopathy, 393, 398
Antagonism scale, PID-5, 401
Antagonism subscale, PID-5-BF, 164, 172–173
ANT-A (Antisocial Behavior) scale, PAI, 400
Ant colony optimization, 41
Anterior cingulate cortex (ACC), 223
  empathy and, 331, 334, 335
  facial emotion recognition and, 333
  intimacy/trust and, 338
  self-awareness and, 326
  self-control and, 328–329
  self-functioning and, 325
  theory of mind and, 336
ANT-E (Egocentricity) scale, PAI, 400
Anticonvulsants, 407
Antidepressants, 306, 308–310, 313
Antiepileptics, 308, 311–312
Antipsychotics
  for antisocial personality disorder, 407
  for borderline personality disorder, 310, 311
  and ICD-11 model for treatment, 195
  for paranoid PD, 306
  for schizotypal personality disorder, 307
Antisocial Behavior (ANT-A) scale, PAI, 400
Antisocial Behavior (RC4) scale, MMPI-2-RF, 401
Antisocial conduct, psychopathy and, 393, 396
Antisocial Features (ANT) scale, PAI, 400
Antisocial personality disorder (ASPD), 391–407
  in AMPD model, 3, 10, 356
  assessment considerations for, 399–400
  assessment measures, 400–402
  case example, 402–405
  comorbidities with, 308, 378, 396, 399
  and conceptual models of psychopathy, 392–394
  DBT for treatment of, 270
  diagnostic criteria for, 10, 227, 394–398

differential diagnosis of, 59
DSM-5 diagnostic criteria for, 394–398
empathy deficits with, 334
Extreme impairment with/Severe, 139
facial emotion recognition deficits with, 333–334
future research directions, 407
ICD-11 diagnostic criteria for, 398
interpersonal functioning deficits with, 330
MBT for treatment of, 250, 254, 255
mentalization deficits in, 239
mode profiles associated with, 286
with narcissistic personality disorder, 378
neurobiological research on, 324
not-knowing stance in treatment of, 250
overlapping trait domains in, 197
PAQ-11 scores of individuals with, 42
pharmacotherapy for treatment of, 305, 308
self-control deficits with, 328–330
self-referential processing deficits with, 327
TFP-based diagnostic criteria for, 227
TFP for treatment of, 215
theory of mind deficits with, 337
treatment of, 139, 215, 250, 254, 255, 270, 405–407
Antisocial Personality pattern, on MCMI-IV, 401
Antisocial Practices (ASP) content scale, MMPI-2, 400
ANT (Antisocial Features) scale, PAI, 400
ANT-S (Stimulus Seeking) scale, PAI, 400
Anxiety
  about termination of TFP, 219–220
  in higher level personality disorders, 422, 425
  for youth, 112
Anxiety disorder(s)
  with borderline personality disorder, 357, 358
  differentiating borderline personality disorder from, 358
  misdiagnosis of Mild PD as, 145
  with narcissistic personality disorder, 309
  with obsessive-compulsive PD, 313
  with schizoid personality disorder, 306
  self-concept of individuals with, 221
Anxiousness, in Criterion B, 14
Aripiprazole, 196
Arntz, A., 222, 285, 290
Asenapine, 311
ASP (Antisocial Practices) content scale, MMPI-2, 400
ASPD. See Antisocial personality disorder
Assessment of Identity Development in Adolescence (AIDA), 116, 117, 122, 125
At-risk mental state, in clinical staging framework, 121

438   *Index*

At-risk mothers, MBT with, 254
Attachment security
  LPFS score and, 13
  MBT focusing on, 253–254
  and pathological narcissism, 380
  TFP's impact on, 222–223
Attachment theory, Criterion A and, 11
Attentional bottleneck hypothesis of
    psychopathy, 335
Attentional problems, in ADHD vs. BPD, 362
Attention-deficit disorder, 357, 362
Attention-deficit/hyperactivity disorder
    (ADHD), 194, 358, 362
Attention Seeking
  and Criterion B of AMPD, 14
  in *ICD-11* algorithm for PID-5, 38
  with narcissistic personality disorder,
    376, 378
Autonomous Self-Image (6A.2) subscale,
    MCMI-IV, 401
Autonomy stage, of schema therapy, 290
Avoidance, 148–149, 381
Avoidant personality disorder (AvPD)
  in AMPD model, 3, 10, 356
  comorbidities with, 306, 312, 313
  diagnostic criteria for, 10
  differential diagnosis of, 59, 60
  and early maladaptive schemas, 282, 300
  as higher level personality disorder, 413,
    415
  Intimacy Avoidance with, 58
  mode profiles associated with, 285, 286
  overlapping trait domains in, 197
  PAQ-11 scores of individuals with, 42
  pharmacotherapy for treatment of, 313
  RO-DBT for treatment of, 270
  Severe impairment with/Moderate, 142
  skills acquisition for individuals with, 153
  ST for treatment of, 290, 291
  TFP–Extended for treatment of, 215
  TFP for treatment of, 215
  treatment of, 215, 270, 290, 291, 313, 427
Avoidant Protector mode, 283, 285
AvPD. *See* Avoidant personality disorder
Axis I disorders
  comorbidity of PD and, for youth, 121
  DBT for treatment of, 268
  pharmacotherapy for NPD with, 386

B

Bach, B., 38, 41, 43, 60, 61, 170, 184, 198,
    281, 285
Bagby, R. M., 15, 16
Bamelis, L. L., 427
Barroilhet, S. A., 43
BASC–3 (Behavior Assessment System for
    Children, third edition), 122
Baseline measures, for EMA, 92–93

Bateman, A., 254, 406
Beck, A. T., 214
Beeney, J. E., 220
Behavioral activation, 225
Behavioral chain analysis, 262–263
Behavioral/Externalizing Dysfunction
    (BXD) scale, MMPI-2-RF, 401
Behavioral interventions, in schema
    therapy, 288
Behavioral manifestations, of personality
    dysfunction, 30, 33, 185
Behavioral regulation, 153, 427
Behavioral Styles Questionnaire (BSQ),
    122, 124
Behavioral therapy, 194, 260
Behavioral therapy skills training, 193
Behavior Assessment System for Children,
    third edition (BASC–3), 122, 124
Bender, D. S., 11, 63, 225
Benzodiazepines, 196, 310
Bernstein, B. P., 285
Bias
  and clinical interviews, 79
  with informant report methods, 88
  negativity, 332–333
  recall, 92
  response, on PID-5, 15–16
Bieling, A. E., 43
Big Five Inventory, 64
Big Five Personality Traits, 112, 166. *See also*
    Five-factor model (FFM)
Binge-eating disorder, 270
Biologically-oriented psychiatry, 144
Biological vulnerabilities, 261, 324
Biosocial theory, 260–262
Bipolar disorder
  with borderline personality disorder, 357,
    358
  with dependent personality disorder, 312
  differentiating BPD from, 359–360
  with narcissistic personality disorder, 309
  with schizoid personality disorder, 306
Birkeland, S. F., 306
Black and white thinking, 214
Blais, M. A., 55, 96
Blashfield, R. K., 160, 309
Blatt, S. J., 215, 226
Body ownership, 326
Bogenschutz, M. P., 311
Boldness, 16, 394, 398
Bonding and emotional regulation stage, of
    schema therapy, 290
"Boom brain" mode. *See* Psychic equivalence
    mode
Borderline Pattern Scale, 198
Borderline pattern specifier
  clinical utility of, 198–200
  in *ICD-11* model, 4, 27, 183, 198–200, 314
  schema therapy for PDs with, 300

transference-focused psychotherapy for
PDs with, 215
Borderline personality disorder (BPD),
353–367
in adolescence, 111
in AMPD model, 3, 10, 356
assessment and diagnosis of, 363–364
biosocial theory on, 261
borderline personality organization vs.,
418n2
clinical staging framework for, 121, 122,
124, 125
comorbidities with, 306, 357–359, 361, 378
conceptualization of, in DBT, 263
countertransference for patients with,
154–155
DBT for treatment of, 260, 268–269
diagnostic criteria for, 10, 354–357
differential diagnosis of, 59, 355,
358–363
and early maladaptive schemas, 282, 300
effectiveness of treatments for, 238
empathy deficits with, 334–336
epistemic trust for individuals with, 248
Extreme impairment with/Severe, 139
facial emotion recognition deficits with,
332–333
global severity measure for, 35
harm management for patients with, 152
historical perspective on diagnosis of,
354–355
in *ICD-11* model, 30, 198
identity difficulties for individuals with,
220–221
interpersonal functioning deficits with, 330
intimacy/mutually satisfying relationships
for individuals with, 337–339
MBT for treatment of, 249–255
mentalizing model of, 239, 241–243, 250
metacognitive reorganization in
treatment of, 237
mode model for, 285
mode profiles associated with, 285, 286
with narcissistic personality disorder, 378
neurobiological research on, 324, 326–327
in object relations model, 214–216, 225
overlapping trait domains in, 197
PAQ-11 scores of individuals with, 42
personality structure framework for, 95
pharmacotherapy for, 195–196, 305,
309–312
PID-5 as screening tool for, 16, 64
premature dropout risk for clients with,
265
prevalence rates of, 357
self-control deficits with, 328, 329
self-referential processing deficits with, 328
ST for treatment of, 290–299
TFP for treatment of, 211–213, 221–223

theory of mind deficits with, 336
treatment of, 195–196, 211–213, 221–223,
238, 249–255, 260, 268–269, 290–299,
305, 309–312, 364–366. *See also*
Dialectical behavior therapy (DBT)
treatment planning based on diagnosis
of, 58–59
treatments for HLPDs vs., 428
Borderline Personality Disorder Severity
Index–IV (BPDSI-IV), 111, 112
Borderline Personality Features Scale for
Children (BPFS-C), 111–113
Borderline Personality Features Scale for
Children–parent report 11-item
version (BPFS-P-11), 122
Borderline Personality Features Scale for
Children–self report 11-item version
(BPFS-C-11), 113, 122
Borderline Personality Features Scale–parent
report (BPFS-P), 111–113
Borderline personality organization (BPO)
borderline personality disorder vs., 418n2
conceptualization of, in TFP-based
model, 226–227
Criterion B and, 227
for higher level personality disorders, 421
high-level, 419, 421
and history of BPD, 354
low-level, 420, 421
middle, 420, 421
in ORT-based classification, 137, 418–421
TFP–Extended for individuals with,
428–432
TFP for individuals with, 215, 224
Borderline schizophrenia, 355
Borderline Symptom List (BSL), 263
Bornovalova, M. A., 362
Bornstein, R. F., 56–57, 95, 142
Bowlby, J., 282
Bozzatello, P., 311
BPD. *See* Borderline personality disorder
BPDSI-IV (Borderline Personality Disorder
Severity Index–IV), 111, 112
BPFS-C (Borderline Personality Features
Scale for Children), 111–113
BPFS-C-11 (Borderline Personality
Features Scale for Children–self report
11-item version), 113, 122
BPFS-P (Borderline Personality Features
Scale–parent report), 111–113
BPFS-P-11 (Borderline Personality Features
Scale for Children–parent report
11-item version), 122
BPO. *See* Borderline personality organization
Brain functioning
changes in, with TFP, 223
research on. *See* Neurobiological research
Brainstem, 326
Brazil, I. A., 406, 407

440 *Index*

Bridler, R., 310
Brief dynamic therapy, 427
Bromocriptine, 308
Bromperidol, 306
Brown, T. A., 198
BSL (Borderline Symptom List), 263
"Bubble" mode. *See* Pretend mode
Buchheim, A., 223
Build Mastery skills, in DBT, 274
Bulimia nervosa, 269–270
"Bullshit" mode. *See* Pretend mode
BXD (Behavioral/Externalizing Dysfunction)
    scale, MMPI-2-RF, 401

C

CAFAS (Child and Adolescent Functional
    Assessment Scale), 122, 124
Cailhol, L., 111
Cain, N. M., 19, 20
Calabrese, J. R., 196
Caligor, E., 137, 149
Callousness, 14, 333, 334, 395
Campbell, D. T., 94
Capozzi, F., 331
CAPS (cognitive affective personality
    system) framework, 226
Carbamazepine, 308, 313
Carnovale, M., 39
Carr, A. C., 95
Case examples, for training on dimensional
    models, 63
Case formulation
    in mentalization-based treatment,
        244–245, 248
    in schema therapy, 287
    in transference-focused psychotherapy,
        217
Case history, 77
CAT (computer adaptive testing), 90–91
Categorical model of personality disorder
    assessment and diagnosis, 3, 9
    clinical direction given by, 58–59
    clinical utility of, 55–56
    higher level personality disorders in,
        413–415
    integrating dimensional models with, 64–65
    limitations of, 28
    and mentalization-based treatment,
        237–238
    neurobiological research based on,
        323–324
    reliability of BPD diagnosis with, 356
    treatment planning with, 20
Categorical thinking, by clinicians, 56–57
CATI (Coolidge Axis II Inventory), 16–17
CAT-PD. *See* Computerized Adaptive Test of
    Personality Disorder
CBCL (Child Behavior Checklist), 122, 124

CBQ (Child Behavior Questionnaire), 122,
    124
CBT. *See* Cognitive behavior therapy
Chang, B., 113
Change process, in MBT, 243–244
Child and Adolescent Functional Assess-
    ment Scale (CAFAS), 122, 124
Child Behavior Checklist (CBCL), 122, 124
Child Behavior Questionnaire (CBQ), 122,
    124
Childhood Interview for *DSM-IV* Borderline
    Personality Disorder (CI-BPD), 122
Childhood Interview for *DSM-IV-TR*
    Borderline Personality Disorder
    (CI-BPD), 111–113
Childhood maltreatment, 326
Childhood trauma, 362
Children
    CS model stages for, 121, 122, 124
    personality assessment for, 112
    pre-mentalizing modes for, 243
    TFP principles in treatment for, 225
Christensen, S., 43
Chronically suicidal patients, DBT with, 260
CI-BPD (Childhood Interview for *DSM-IV*
    Borderline Personality Disorder), 122
CI-BPD (Childhood Interview for *DSM-IV-TR*
    Borderline Personality Disorder),
    111–113
Cingulum, 329
Citalopram, 313
Clarification, in TFP–Extended, 430
Clarification-oriented therapy, 427
Clark, L. A., 91, 161
Clarkin, J. F., 20, 59, 167, 220, 221
Cleckley, H., 392–394, 396, 397
Clinical direction
    as clinical utility criterion, 55
    improving dimensional models', 65–66
    and pathological traits used in dimensional
        models, 61–62
    and treatment planning based on diagnosis,
        58–59
Clinical interviews, 78–80
    advantages and disadvantages of, 79–80
    assessing BPO with, 354
    assessing HLPDs with, 425–426
    to inform AMPD diagnosis, 169
    for personality assessment for youth,
        127–128
    reliability and validity of, 80
    structured vs. unstructured, 78–79
Clinical practice
    AMPD model in, 18–20
    considerations with treating PDs in,
        146–155
    of HLPD presentation in, 422–423
    MBT implementation in, 243–254
    PD assessment for youth in, 126–129

Clinical significance, 161
Clinical staging (CS) framework, 115, 116, 121–126
Clinical utility (generally)
of AMPD, 18–20
of BPD diagnosis, 366
construct validity and, 54–55, 160
of severity measure, 34–35, 138, 184–189
Clinical utility of dimensional models, 53–68
and categorical thinking by clinicians, 56–57
and complexity–efficiency balance in models, 60–61
and construct validity approach to clinical utility, 54–55
and diagnosis as treatment determiner, 58–59
and discriminative power of models, 59–60
and ICD-11 model vs. AMPD, 53–54
and if–then contingency patterns in PDs, 57–58
improving, 62–67
one-size-fits-all approach to, 67–68
and pathological traits used in models, 61–62
research on, 55–56
Clinician bias, 79
Clinician Rating Personality Disorder Level and Traits Form, 169
Clinician-report measures, of ICD-11 trait domains, 42–43
Cloitre, M., 361–362
Cluster analysis, 407
Cluster A personality disorders, 139, 306–307
Cluster-based classifications of personality disorders, 313–314
Cluster B personality disorders, 270–271, 308–312
Cluster C personality disorders
pharmacotherapy for, 312–313
self-control deficits with, 329
Severe impairment with/Moderate, 142
treatment for, 427
CM (contingency management), 406–407
Cognitive-affective mentalizing, 241–242
Cognitive affective personality system (CAPS) framework, 226
Cognitive and Perceptual Dysregulation, in Criterion B, 14
Cognitive behavior therapy (CBT)
alignment of AMPD with, 20
for borderline personality disorder, 364
for higher level personality disorders, 427
for narcissistic personality disorder, 385
for psychopathy, 405, 406
Cognitive empathy, 331
Cognitive interventions, in schema therapy, 288
Cognitive manifestations, of personality dysfunction, 30, 185

Cognitive processing
multimethod assessment of, 96
pharmacotherapy to improve, 195, 196
with schizotypal personality disorder, 307
Cognitive route, of social cognition, 336
Cognitive self-control, 328–330, 339
Cognitive theory of mind, 336
Cognitive therapy, 253, 260
Coherence, in psychosocial interventions for PD, 237
Collaborative therapeutic approach, 191
College students, TFP principles for treatment of, 224
COM (Complexity of Representation of People), 169
Communication
professional, 55–57
in psychosocial interventions for PD, 237
in TFP–Extended, 429
Community mental health settings, DBT in, 268–269
Comorbidity(-ies)
for antisocial personality disorder, 308, 378, 396, 399
for avoidant personality disorder, 306, 312, 313
for borderline personality disorder, 306, 357–359, 361, 378
in categorical model, 9
complex, 125, 357–358
global PD severity and, 35
for narcissistic personality disorder, 306, 309, 310, 378–380, 386
neurobiological research on, 324
and severity scale of ICD-11 model, 35, 60
for youth, 121, 126, 128
Compartmentalization, in NPD, 380
Compassion-focused therapy, 195
Competitiveness, in NPD and PN, 381
Completed suicide rates, for individuals with BPD, 363
Complex comorbidity, 125, 357–358
Complex depression, TFP principles for treatment of, 224–225
Complexity–efficiency balance, in models, 60–61
Complexity of Representation of People (COM), 169
Complex posttraumatic stress disorder, 360–361
Complex trauma, 241, 291
Compliant Surrenderer mode, 283
Comprehensive System (CS), 82–83
Compulsive work, 148
Compulsivity, Anankastia and, 33
Computer adaptive testing (CAT), 90–91
Computerized Adaptive Test of Personality Disorder (CAT-PD), 17, 39, 91
Comtois, K. A., 266

Concrete thinking, 241
Conduct disorder criterion, for ASPD, 396, 399
Confidence, in diagnostic decisions, 62–63
Conform, failure to, in ASPD, 394, 395
Confrontation
    in TFP, 218
    in TFP–Extended, 430
Conscientiousness, 227
    and Anankastia, 194
    and Disinhibition, 14, 194, 356
    and psychopathy, 393
Consistency
    internal, 13, 15, 86, 88
    in psychosocial interventions for PD, 237
Consolidated identity, 32, 213
Construct validity, clinical utility and, 54–55, 160
Contingency management (CM), 406–407
Continuity, in psychosocial interventions for PD, 237
Control, need for, 380
Convergent validity, 13, 17, 80, 83
Coolidge Axis II Inventory (CATI), 16–17
Coping behaviors and strategies, 97, 191, 287
Corporate misbehavior, psychopathy and, 393
Corpus callosum, 329
Countdown method, 90
Countertransference, 154–155, 187, 429–430
Cramer, P., 149
Crawford, M. J., 312
Crego, C., 39, 397
Crick, N. R., 113
Criminal history, deceitfulness about, 399
Criminal offenders. *See* Forensic populations; Prison populations
Criterion A, in AMPD model, 3–4
    about, 10
    alignment of *ICD-11* model with, 28
    and antisocial personality disorder, 396, 397
    and borderline personality disorder, 356
    in clinical staging model, 122, 123, 125
    clinical utility of, 18–19
    complexity of, 162
    and diagnosis, 160, 161
    in diagnosis case example, 171–172
    diagnostic efficiency for decisions related to, 63
    diagnostic efficiency of decisions related to, 63
    and dialectical behavior psychotherapy, 273–274
    efficiency and complexity of, 61
    future research directions, 20–21
    and identity diffusion, 215
    incremental validity of, 18
    informant report measures of, 169

interrater reliability for, 63
and level of personality functioning, 54
mentalizing and, 255–256
overlap between Criterion B and, 17–18, 166–167
performance-based measures of, 169–170
in personality assessment for youth, 112, 115, 116
for psychodiagnosis, 167
research findings on, 11–13
self-report measures for, 168–169
structured clinical interviews for assessing, 169
and TFP model of personality, 227
treatment planning based on, 20
Criterion B, in AMPD model, 4. *See also specific traits*
    about, 10
    alignment of *ICD-11* model with, 28
    and antisocial personality disorder, 395–397
    and borderline personality disorder, 356
    in clinical staging model, 122
    clinical utility of, 18
    complexity of, 162
    and diagnosis, 160, 161
    in diagnosis case example, 172–173
    diagnostic efficiency of, 64
    and five-factor model, 166
    future research directions, 20–21
    incremental validity of, 18
    informant report measures of, 169
    overlap between Criterion A and, 17–18, 166–167
    in personality assessment for youth, 112, 115, 116
    research findings on, 13–17
    self-report measures of, 168
    and TFP model of personality, 227
    treatment planning based on, 20, 167–168
Criterion C, in AMPD model, 10
Criterion-count method of diagnosis, 159, 162
Criterion D, in AMPD model, 10
Criterion E, in AMPD model, 10
Criterion F, in AMPD model, 10
Criterion G, in AMPD model, 11
Criterion validity
    for computer adaptive testing, 91
    of Criterion A, 13
    of Criterion B, 16
    for informant report methods, 89
    for self-report methods, 87
Cross-informant correlation, 88
CS (Comprehensive System), 82–83
CS framework. *See* Clinical staging framework
Cultural differences, in self-report measures, 85

Cuneus, 327, 335
Curiosity, in psychosocial interventions for
    PD, 248
Cyberball Paradigm, 338

D

DAPP-BQ (Dimensional Assessment of
    Personality Pathology–Basic
    Questionnaire), 39
DAPP-BQ-A (Dimensional Assessment
    of Personality Pathology–Basic
    Questionnaire for Adolescents), 116,
    118
DAPP-SF-A (Dimensional Assessment of
    Personality Pathology–Short Form for
    Adolescents), 119
Davis, K. L., 195
Day hospitals, MBT in, 255
DBT. *See* Dialectical behavior therapy
DBT-Linehan Board of Certification
    (DBT-LBC), 264
DBT skills groups, 367
DBT-WCCL (Dialectical Behavior Therapy
    Ways of Coping Checklist), 263
Deceitfulness, 14, 395, 399
Decision-making
    confidence in diagnostic, 62–63
    for gray area cases, 66–67
De Clercq, B., 119
Decuyper, M., 119
Default mode network (DMN), 325
    empathy and, 335
    self-referential processing and, 327–328
    theory of mind and, 336
Defense Mechanism Rating Scale, 149
Defensive style and functioning
    clinical interviews to assess, 426
    with higher level personality disorders,
        421
    in ORT-based classification, 418–421
    treatment centering on, 148–150
Degree of differentiation, identity
    representations, 214
Degree of integration, identity
    representations, 214
Demanding Critic mode, 283
Dependent personality disorder (DPD)
    differential diagnosis of, 59
    and early maladaptive schemas, 282
    as higher level personality disorder, 413,
        415
    mode profiles associated with, 285, 286
    PAQ-11 scores of individuals with, 42
    pharmacotherapy for, 312–313
    Severe impairment with/Moderate, 142
    ST for treatment of, 290
    TFP–Extended for treatment of, 215
    treatment for, 215, 290, 427

Depression. *See also* Major depressive
        disorder (MDD)
    differentiating BPD from, 358–359
    MBT for treatment of, 255
    misdiagnosis of Mild PD as, 144–145
    ST for treatment of, 291
    in youth, 112
Depressive personality disorder, 145
Depressivity, 14, 15, 166
Depue, R. A., 62
DERS (Difficulties in Emotion Regulation
        Scale), 264
Descriptive classification, of higher level
        personality disorders, 416–418
Desipramine, 308
Detached Protector mode, 285
Detachment
    adaptive significance of, 191
    in AMPD model, 14, 54
    and Criterion B, 227, 356
    and Depressivity, 166
    and Extraversion, 14, 39
    in *ICD-11* model, 4, 37, 54
    PDs characterized by overlapping domains
        with, 197
    PID5BF+ items related to, 42
    prevalence of, for hospital inpatients, 43
    SASPD items related to, 36
    scores for, in multimethod assessment, 96
    treatments focused on modulating, 190,
        193
Determinants of reactions, in treatment of
        PDs, 147
Deutsch, H., 354
Developmental history, 126–127
Developmental model for personality
        pathology, 115. *See also* Clinical
        staging (CS) framework
Developmental stage, 11, 111–114
Diagnosis, treatment planning based on,
        58–59
Diagnostic accuracy, of *ICD-11* model, 34
*Diagnostic and Statistical Manual of Mental
        Disorders*, 2nd ed. *(DSM-II)*, 28, 354,
        394, 397
*Diagnostic and Statistical Manual of Mental
        Disorders*, 3rd ed. *(DSM-III)*
    antisocial personality disorder in, 394
    borderline personality disorder in, 224,
        355, 357
    categories of personality disorders in, 9
    definition of PD syndromes in, 159
    and higher level personality disorders,
        414
    identity disturbance in, 215
*Diagnostic and Statistical Manual of Mental
        Disorders*, 3rd ed., rev. *(DSM-III-R)*,
        10, 355

Diagnostic and Statistical Manual of Mental Disorders, 4th ed. *(DSM-IV)*
  and AMPD, 11, 18
  antisocial personality disorder in, 394, 396
  and borderline pattern specifier, 198
  borderline personality disorder in, 224, 263, 357
  categorical model of personality disorders in, 10
  defense mechanism scale in, 149
  narcissistic personality disorder in, 19
  severity estimations for PDs using, 29
Diagnostic and Statistical Manual of Mental Disorders, 4th ed., text rev. *(DSM-IV-TR)*, 10, 55, 149
Diagnostic and Statistical Manual of Mental Disorders, 5th ed. *(DSM-5)*, 3
  antisocial personality disorder in, 394–398
  borderline personality disorder in, 224, 263, 353, 355–357
  categorical model of PD in, 10
  components of personality disorders in, 136
  ease of implementation with, 60
  higher level personality disorders in, 413
  levels of personality functioning in, 136–138
  linking performance-based assessments to, 81
  and mentalization-based treatment, 237–238
  narcissistic personality disorder in, 19, 376–380
  Other Specified Personality Disorder code in, 10, 160
  and personality assessment for youth, 111–114
  personality inventory for. *See* Personality Inventory for *DSM-5* (PID-5)
  pharmacotherapy recommendations in, 196
  psychopathy in, 391
  Section III of. *See* Alternative *DSM-5* Model for Personality Disorders (AMPD)
  Structured Interview for *DSM-IV* Personality and ASPD in, 401
  and transference-focused psychotherapy, 215
Diagnostic criteria
  for antisocial personality disorder, 10, 227, 394–398
  for avoidant personality disorder, 10
  for borderline personality disorder, 10, 354–357
  for narcissistic personality disorder, 10, 227
  for obsessive-compulsive personality disorder, 10
  for PD-Trait Specified, 10, 11
  for schizotypal personality disorder, 10, 227

Diagnostic efficiency, 60–61, 63–64
Diagnostic functionality, 55, 59–62
Diagnostic Interview for Borderlines (DIB), 263, 354
Diagnostic interviews, for antisocial personality disorder, 401–402
Diagnostic precision, 92, 121
Dialectical behavior therapy (DBT), 259–275
  assessment in, 262–264
  biosocial theory in, 260–262
  for borderline personality disorder, 364–366
  case examples, 259–269, 271–272
  for conditions other than BPD, 269–271
  and dimensional models of PD, 272–275
  empirical support for, 268–271
  harm management in, 152
  for higher level personality disorders, 427
  lowering Negative Affectivity with, 192
  mentalization-based treatment vs., 254–255
  for narcissistic personality disorder, 385
  neurobiological studies of response to, 330
  for obsessive-compulsive personality disorder, 195
  self-awareness in, 327
  severity-based treatment strategies in, 188
  skills acquisition in, 150, 153
  stages of, 265
  structure of, 264–265
  therapeutic techniques in, 266–268
  therapist training for, 264
  transference-focused psychotherapy vs., 221, 222
  and treatment planning based on diagnosis, 59
Dialectical Behavior Therapy Ways of Coping Checklist (DBT-WCCL), 263
Dialectics, 266–267
Diamond, D., 223
Diary cards, DBT, 262
DIB (Diagnostic Interview for Borderlines), 263, 354
DIF (differential item functioning), in self-report measures, 85
Differential diagnosis
  of antisocial personality disorder, 59
  of borderline personality disorder, 59, 355, 358–363
  of dependent personality disorder, 59
  of higher level personality disorders, 425–427
  of narcissistic personality disorder, 59
  of obsessive-compulsive personality disorder, 59, 60
Differential item functioning (DIF), in self-report measures, 85
Difficulties in Emotion Regulation Scale (DERS), 264
Dihydrexidine, 307

Dimensional assessment
  and multivariate paradigm, 84
  of NPD and pathological narcissism,
    380–381
Dimensional Assessment of Personality
    Pathology–Basic Questionnaire
    (DAPP-BQ), 39
Dimensional Assessment of Personality
    Pathology–Basic Questionnaire for
    Adolescents (DAPP-BQ-A), 116, 118
Dimensional Assessment of Personality
    Pathology–Short Form for Adolescents
    (DAPP-SF-A), 119
Dimensionalization of diagnosis, with AMPD,
    166–167
Dimensional model of drug effects, 195
Dimensional models of personality disorder
    assessment and diagnosis. *See also*
    Alternative *DSM-5* Model for Personality
    Disorders (AMPD); *ICD-11* personality
    disorder classification model
  clinical utility of, 53–68
  and dialectical behavior therapy, 272–275
  higher level personality disorders in,
    414–415
  integrating categorical models with, 64–65
  and mentalization-based treatment,
    255–256
  movement to, 3–4
  and neurobiological research, 323–325
  and personality assessment for youth,
    112, 115
  and pharmacotherapy, 313–314
  and schema therapy, 299–301
  and transference-focused psychotherapy,
    225–228
  treatment principles based on, 135–155
Dimensional Personality Symptom Item
    Pool (DIPSI), 116, 119, 122, 124, 125
Dimensions of personality functioning, with
    NPD, 378
Disaffiliativeness (DSF) scale, MMPI-2-RF, 401
Disconstraint-revised (DISC-r) scale,
    MMPI-2-RF, 401
Discriminant validity, 13, 17
Discriminative power, of dimensional
    models, 59–60
DISC-r (Disconstraint-revised) scale,
    MMPI-2-RF, 401
Disease model of mental illness, 84
Disinhibition
  in AMPD, 14, 54
  Anankastia and, 33–34
  with antisocial personality disorder, 398
  with borderline personality disorder, 356
  and Conscientiousness, 14
  and Criterion B, 227, 356
  dialectical behavior psychotherapy to
    reduce, 273

externalizing disorders in youth and, 112
  in *ICD-11* model, 4, 37, 54
  and mortality risk, 43
  in multimethod assessment, 97
  Negative Affectivity and, 29
  Orderliness and, 39
  PDs characterized by overlapping
    domains with, 197
  pharmacotherapy for reduce, 196
  PID5BF+ items related to, 42
  PID-5 items related to, 16
  with psychopathy, 393, 394, 398
  SASPD items related to, 36
  treatments focused on modulating, 190,
    194, 196
Disinhibition scale, of PID-5, 401
Disinhibition subscale, PID-5-BF, 164, 173
Disorganized attachment, 35, 244
Dispositional trait constructs, Criterion B
    and, 166
Dissociality
  and Antagonism, 54
  in *ICD-11* model, 4, 37
  and Insensitivity, 39
  PDs characterized by overlapping
    domains with, 197
  pharmacotherapy to reduce, 196
  PID5BF+ items related to, 42
  SASPD items related to, 36
  treatments to reduce, 193–194, 196
Dissociation, 311, 327
Dissociative identity disorder, 291
Distractibility, 14
Distress, in severity measure, 185
Distress Tolerance module, DBT, 266, 270, 273
Diverse populations, performance-based
    assessments with, 82
DLPFQ. *See DSM-5* Levels of Personality
    Functioning Questionnaire
DMN. *See* Default mode network
Doering, S., 221–223
"Doing time" mode. *See* Teleological mode
Dominance, 381
DOM (Interpersonal Dominance) scale, PAI,
    400
Dopamine agonists, 307, 308
DPD. *See* Dependent personality disorder
Draguns, J. G., 160
Drislane, L. E., 16
Drive theory, 211
Dropout risk. *See* Premature termination of
    therapy
Drug Problems (DRG) scale, PAI, 400
Drug use, 148, 152, 153. *See also* Substance
    use
DSF (Disaffiliativeness) scale, MMPI-2-RF,
    401
*DSM-II. See Diagnostic and Statistical Manual
    of Mental Disorders,* second ed.

DSM-III. See Diagnostic and Statistical Manual of Mental Disorders, 3rd ed.

DSM-III-R. See Diagnostic and Statistical Manual of Mental Disorders, 3rd ed., rev.

DSM-IV. See Diagnostic and Statistical Manual of Mental Disorders, 4th ed.

DSM-IV-TR. See Diagnostic and Statistical Manual of Mental Disorders, 4th ed., text rev.

DSM-5. See Diagnostic and Statistical Manual of Mental Disorders, 5th ed.

DSM-5 Level of Personality Functioning Scale. *See* Level of Personality Functioning Scale (LPFS)

DSM-5 Levels of Personality Functioning Questionnaire (DLOPFQ), 12, 84, 168, 169, 226

DSM-5 Personality and Personality Disorders Work Group, 10, 14, 396, 397

Duloxetine, 310

Dynamic deconstructive psychotherapy, 366

Dysfunctional Critic modes, 283, 284, 288

Dysfunctional Negative Emotions (RC7) scale, MMPI-2-RF, 401

Dysphoria, 309, 422

E

Early maladaptive schemas (EMSs), 281, 282, 300–301

Ease of implementation
balance of goodness of fit and, 60–61
as clinical utility criterion, 55
and if–then contingency patterns in PDs, 57–58

EAS Temperament Survey (EAS), 122, 124

Eating disorders
with borderline personality disorder, 357
DBT for treatment of, 269–270
differentiating BPD from, 358
MBT for treatment of, 255
with narcissistic personality disorder, 378
with obsessive-compulsive personality disorder, 313

Eccentricity, 14

Eclectic interventions, 405

Ecological momentary assessment (EMA), 92–94

EEG (electroencephalography) studies, 324

Egocentricity (ANT-E) scale, PAI, 400

EIM (Emotional Investment in Values and Moral Standards), 169

EIR (Emotional Investment in Relationships), 169

Electroencephalography (EEG) studies, 324

Elementary-school age children, clinical staging model for, 121, 122, 124

EMA (ecological momentary assessment), 92–94

Emmelkamp, P. M., 427

Emotional activity, treatment to increase, 190

Emotional empathy, 332, 334–335

Emotional expression, in schema therapy, 287

Emotional Investment in Relationships (EIR), 169

Emotional Investment in Values and Moral Standards (EIM), 169

Emotional Lability
adaptive significance of, 191
in BPD vs. bipolar disorder, 360
in Criterion B, 14, 167
in multimethod assessment, 96

Emotional manifestations, of personality dysfunction, 30, 185

Emotional processing, multimethod assessment of, 96

Emotional regulation
biosocial theory on, 260–262
capacity for, in *ICD-11* model, 33
neurobiological studies of, 328, 329
with NPD and PN, 377
pharmacotherapy to improve, 195–196
provocation-induced aggression and, 339
schema therapy to improve, 290
and self-awareness, 326
theory of mind and, 336
transference-focused psychotherapy to improve, 215, 223
treatment focused on, 190

Emotional stability, Negative Affectivity vs., 356

Emotion regulation group therapy, 367

Emotion Regulation module, DBT, 266, 270, 273, 274

Empathic validation, in MBT, 249–250, 384

Empathy
in AMPD, 31, 416
with antisocial personality disorder, 327
cognitive, 332
countertransference reactions based in, 154
dialectical behavior psychotherapy to improve, 274
emotional, 332, 334–335
and facial emotion recognition, 331, 332
in *ICD-11* models, 31
in interpersonal functioning, 330
on Level of Personality Functioning Scale, 161
with narcissistic personality disorder, 376
neurobiological research on, 331–332, 334–336
with NPD and PN, 379, 381

Empathy scale, LPFS-SR, 164, 171–172

Empirical paradigm, 19, 84

EMSs. *See* Early maladaptive schemas

Epistemic trust, 248
Erikson, E. H., 215
European Society for the Study of
    Personality Disorders, 30
Expected outcomes, of BPD treatments, 365
Experience and Management of Aggressive
    Impulses (AGG) subscale, SCORS-G,
    164, 169–170, 173
Experiential antidotes, in mode healing, 289
Experiential interventions, 288
Explicit processes, in transtheoretical model
    of personality, 96
Exploration of mentalizing model, 250–254
Exploratory (expressive) psychotherapy. *See*
    Transference-focused psychotherapy
    (TFP)
External features, mentalizing with regard
    to, 242
External focus, threat hypersensitivity and,
    332
Externalization, of ineffective mentalizing
    modes, 243
Externalizing problems, 112, 122, 124
External perspective, on defensive
    functioning, 148
Extraversion
    and Detachment, 14, 39, 193, 356
    and psychopathy, 393
Extreme impairment (AMPD model), 32,
    138–140
Eysenck's trait model, 39

F

Facial emotion recognition, 331–334
Factor 1 traits of psychopathy, 328, 334–335,
    407
Factor 2 traits of psychopathy, 328
Factor analysis, 61
"Fake news" mode. *See* Pretend mode
False-belief situations, individuals with
    BPD in, 336
Farrell, J. M., 290
Fast emotional action tendencies, overriding,
    329
FDA (U.S. Food and Drug Administration),
    305
Fear
    of abandonment, 220
    facial recognition of, 333
Fearlessness, psychopathy and, 393
Few, L. R., 397
FFiCD (Five-Factor Personality Inventory
    for *ICD-11*), 40, 189
FFM. *See* Five-factor model
First, M. B., 38, 60, 61, 184
Fischer, S., 271
Fiske, F. W., 94

Five-factor model (FFM)
    clinical utility of, 55–56
    and Criterion B of AMPD, 13–14, 166,
        227, 356, 397
    and DBT theory, 273
    and *ICD-11* trait domains, 38–41
    psychopathy and ASPD in, 393, 397
    Structured Interview for the Five-Factor
        Model of Personality, 402
    treatment planning based on, 191
Five-Factor Personality Inventory for *ICD-11*
    (FFiCD), 40, 189
Fixed-role therapy, 405
Flesch–Kincaide readability index values, 162
Flight into health, 220
Fluoxetine, 306
Flupentixol, 306
Flynn, D., 268–269
(f)MRI (functional magnetic resonance
    imaging) studies, 324
Forensic populations. *See also* Prison
    populations
    ASPD and psychopathy prevalence in,
        394, 396
    BPD prevalence in, 357
    dialectical behavior psychotherapy with,
        269, 270
    empathy impairments in, 334–335
    schema therapy with, 290, 291
    treatment of psychopathy with, 406
Four-cell model of interpersonal dependency,
    95
Four Cs of psychosocial interventions for PD,
    237, 254
Fowler, J. C., 16, 64
Fragmentation, of identity, 380
Frankenburg, F. R., 312, 363
Freud, Anna, 226
Freud, Sigmund, 211, 214
Frontal cortex, 330, 331
Frontal gyri, 327, 329, 334
Frontal lobes, 325, 329
Frontoparietal regions, 328–329
Frustration tolerance, 138
Full Scores on Elevated Scales (FSES)
    method, 90
Functional analysis, in DBT, 262–263
Functional magnetic resonance imaging
    (fMRI) studies, 324
Fusiform face area, 331–333, 336, 337
Fusiform gyrus, 327

G

Gabapentin, 313
Gabbard, G. O., 139
Gaebel, W., 34
Garcia, D. J., 170
Gelso, 212

448 *Index*

Gender differences, in PD prevalence, 357, 399
General factor for personality pathology (*g*-PD)
    and borderline pattern specifier, 198–199
    dimensional models of PD and, 356, 366
    as target for intervention, 184–185, 187
    TFP model and, 227
General psychopathology evaluation, for youth, 126
General psychopathology (p) factor, 366
German Society for Psychiatry, Psychotherapy, and Psychosomatics, 213
GIVE method, 274
Global functioning
    in clinical staging model, 122, 124
    dialectical behavior psychotherapy and, 268
    for individuals with NPD/PN, 377–378
Global PD severity, 33–36
Glover, N. G., 56
Goals
    for individuals with HLPDs, 423
    for patients high in Anankastia, 194
    for patients high in Dissociality, 193–194
    of schema therapy, 287–288, 290, 296
    of transference-focused psychotherapy, 213–215
Goldstein, E. G., 95
Good, E. W., 171
"Good enough" personality assessment for youth, 126–129
Goodman, M., 362
Goodness of fit
    as clinical utility criterion, 55
    and discriminative power of dimensional models, 59
    ease of use and, 60–61
    and pathological traits in dimensional models, 61–62
"Good parent," in schema therapy, 287, 299
Goth, K., 117
g-PD. *See* General factor for personality pathology
Grandiosity
    in Criterion B, 14
    narcissistic, 19, 143, 376, 378
Gratz, K. L., 362
Gray area cases, 66–67
Gray matter volume
    psychopathy and, 393
    self-control deficits and, 329, 330
Grinke, R., 354, 355
Group psychotherapy
    dialectical behavior therapy in, 264–265
    mentalization-based treatment in, 248–249
    for narcissistic personality disorder, 385–386
Guanfacine, 307
Gunderson, J. G., 354, 355
Gutiérrez, F., 39

H

Haloperidol, 307, 311
Hansen, S. J., 34
Happy Child mode, 283, 288
Harassment, of therapists, 153
Hare, R. D., 392, 397
Harm management, 152–153
Harm to others, risk of
    and PD severity, 33
    reducing, 152–153
Harm to self. *See* Self-harm
Harned, M. S., 268, 269
Harris–Lingoes Authority Problems (Pd2) subscale, MMPI-2, 400
Health care actions, poor compliance with, 152
Health records, trait domain information in, 43
Healthy Adult mode, 283, 285, 287, 289
Healthy modes, 283, 284
Healthy personality function (AMPD model), 32, 115, 422
Heffernan, K., 361
Heterogeneity, in categorical model, 9
Hierarchical organization, for identity representations, 214
Hierarchical Personality Inventory for Children (HiPIC), 122, 124
Hierarchical Taxonomy of Psychopathology (HiTOP), 226, 274, 314
Higher level personality disorders (HLPDs), 413–432
    assessment and differential diagnosis of, 425–427
    case example, 423–425, 430–432
    and categorical vs. dimensional models of PD, 414–415
    clinical presentation of, 422–423
    descriptive classification of, 416–418
    ORT-based structural classification of, 416, 418–422
    treatment of, 427–432
High-level borderline personality organization, 419, 421
HiPIC (Hierarchical Personality Inventory for Children), 122, 124
Hippocampus, 223, 329
Histrionic personality disorder (HPD)
    as higher level personality disorder, 413, 415
    mode profiles associated with, 286
    PAQ-11 scores of individuals with, 42
    pharmacotherapy for, 308–309
    Severe impairment with/Moderate, 142–143
    transference-focused psychotherapy for, 215
HiTOP. *See* Hierarchical Taxonomy of Psychopathology

HLPDs. *See* Higher level personality disorders
Hoch, P., 354
Hollander, E., 311–312
Hopwood, C. J., 19–21, 34, 58, 95, 167, 171
Hostility, 14, 15, 300, 395
HPD. *See* Histrionic personality disorder
Huband, N., 308
Huprich, S. K., 57, 59, 61, 95–96
Hybrid categorical–dimensional diagnostic
    model. *See also* Alternative *DSM-5* Model
    for Personality Disorders (AMPD)
    antisocial personality disorder in, 396–398
    characteristics of, 10
    diagnosis with, 160–161
Hypermentalization, 242, 326–327, 336
Hypersensitivity, 381
    rejection, 338
    social threat, 339
    threat, 332–334
Hypervigilance, 332
Hypomanic Activation (RC9) scale,
    MMPI-2-RF, 401
Hypothalamus, 339
Hysteroid dysphoria, 309

I

ICD-9 (International Statistical Classification of
    Diseases and Related Health Problems,
    9th ed.), 28
ICD-10. See International Statistical Classification
    of Diseases and Related Health Problems,
    10th ed.
ICD-11. See International Statistical Classification
    of Diseases and Related Health Problems,
    11th ed.
ICD-11 Clinical Descriptions and Diagnostic
    Guidelines for Mental and Behavioural
    Disorders (WHO), 27
ICD-11 personality disorder classification
    model, 4, 27–44, 183–202
    AMPD model and, 27, 28, 30–33, 53–54,
        184, 375–376
    Anankastia trait domain in, 33–34
    antisocial personality disorder in, 407
    borderline pattern specifier in, 198–200
    case example of diagnosis and treatment
        with, 200–202
    clinical direction from, 59
    clinical utility of, 53, 62, 184–189
    complexity and efficiency of, 60
    and dialectical behavior psychotherapy,
        273
    dimensionalization of diagnosis with, 77
    discriminative power of, 60
    final approval of, 29–30
    higher level personality disorders in,
        414, 416–418
    interpersonal functioning in, 330

levels of personality functioning in,
    136–138
links between treatment planning and,
    65–66
mentalization-based treatment and, 256
neurobiological research supporting, 323
and pharmacotherapy, 195–197, 314
reasons for developing, 28–29
and schema therapy, 285, 300–301
severity classification in, 34–36, 141,
    184–189
trait domains in, 37–43, 187, 189–191
transference-focused psychotherapy and,
    215, 226–228
transtheoretical model for assessment
    related to, 96–97
treatment based on specific trait domains
    in, 191–195
treatment for patients with blends of traits
    in, 197–198
Identity
    with ADHD vs. BPD, 362
    in AMPD, 31, 416
    with borderline personality disorder, 359,
        362
    clinical interviews to assess, 426
    consolidated, 32, 213
    fragmentation of, 380
    with higher level personality disorders,
        421
    in *ICD-11* model, 31
    on Level of Personality Functioning Scale,
        161
    with narcissistic personality disorder, 376
    in ORT-based classification, 418–421
    for patients with Mild PD, 145
    with PTSD vs. BPD, 362
    TFP–Extended for integration of, 429
    in transference-focused psychotherapy,
        213–214, 226
Identity and Coherence of Self (ISC), 170
Identity diffusion
    empirical support for, 220–221
    in object relations model, 216, 225
    resolution of, 213
    in transference-focused psychotherapy,
        215, 216
Identity scale, LPFS-SR, 164, 171, 172
If–then contingency patterns, 57–58
IIP-SC (Inventory of Interpersonal
    Problems–Short Circumplex), 164, 173
Imagery rescripting, 298–299
Impairment of functioning, severity of PD
    vs., 166
Implantation phase, of TFP, 217–219
Implicit methods. *See* Performance-based
    methods
Implicit motivation, 150–152
Implicit processes, in transtheoretical model
    of personality, 96

450   *Index*

Impulsive aggression, 195, 196
Impulsive Child mode, 287, 288
Impulsivity
    in antisocial personality disorder, 395
    in BPD vs. bipolar disorder, 360
    and Criterion B, 14
    dialectical behavior psychotherapy to
        reduce, 268
    neurobiological studies of, 329, 330
    pharmacotherapy to reduce, 308, 310
    and schema modes, 300
    TFP to reduce, 223
Incentive-Anxiety reaction surface, 62
Inconsistency scale, PID-5, 16, 86
Incremental validity, 17–18, 80, 89
Individual psychotherapy
    dialectical behavior psychotherapy in,
        264–265
    mentalization-based treatment in, 248–249
    schema therapy with, 291
Inflexibility, in AMPD model, 10
Informant-Personality Inventory for *ICD-11*
    (IPiC), 87, 96, 97
Informant report methods, 87–89. *See also*
    specific measures
    advantages and limitations of, 87–88
    to inform AMPD diagnosis, 169
    with self-report methods, 89
    validity and reliability of, 88–89
    for youth, 127
Information integration, 323
Inhibitory control, neurobiological studies
    of, 328
Innate Child modes, 283, 284
Inpatient settings, 255, 357
Insensitivity, 39
Insight-oriented treatment, 153–154
Instrumental aggression, 393
Insula
    empathy and, 331, 334, 335
    intimacy/trust and, 338
    mentalization and, 331
    self-awareness and, 326
    self-control and, 328–329
    theory of mind and, 337
Integrated modular treatment, 150, 153, 225
Integrated sense of self, in TFP, 213
Intellectual evaluation, for youth, 127
Internal consistency, 13, 15, 86, 88
Internalizing problems, 122, 124
Internalizing vs. externalizing dimension,
    object relations model, 225
Internal representations of self and others,
    in BPD, 214–216
International Society for Schema Therapy,
    287
International Society for the Study of
    Personality Disorders, 30
International Society for Transference-
    Focused Therapy (ISTFP), 216

*International Statistical Classification of Diseases
    and Related Health Problems*, 9th ed.
    (ICD-9), 28
*International Statistical Classification of Diseases
    and Related Health Problems*, 10th ed.
    (ICD-10), 29, 196, 356, 414–415
*International Statistical Classification of Diseases
    and Related Health Problems*, 11th ed.
    (ICD-11), 4, 238. *See also ICD-11*
    personality disorder classification model
    antisocial personality disorder in, 398
    borderline personality disorder in, 353,
        356–357
    description of personality disorders in, 136
    narcissistic personality disorder in, 375
    psychopathy in, 391
    SCID-5-AMPD and diagnostic criteria in,
        426
    severity and trait domain specifiers in, 27
    and treatment of personality disorders, 135
Interpersonal dependency, 13, 95
Interpersonal dimension, of psychopathy, 393
Interpersonal Dominance (DOM) scale,
    PAI, 400
Interpersonal Effectiveness module, DBT,
    266, 273, 274
Interpersonal functioning
    in AMPD model, 3–4, 31
    with borderline personality disorder, 356
    Criterion A assessment of, 10–12
    dialectical behavior psychotherapy to
        improve, 274
    with higher level personality disorders,
        415–417, 421–423
    in *ICD-11* model, 31
    on Level of Personality Functioning Scale,
        13, 161
    neurobiological research on, 330–339
    in ORT-based classification, 416
    overlap between brain processes related
        to self and, 324–325
    for patients with Mild PD, 144, 145
    for patients with Moderate PD, 142
    for patients with Severe PD, 138–139
    PD-related impairment in, 136
    and severity determination, 185
    severity ratings based on, 54
Interpersonally Irresponsible (6A.1) subscale,
    MCMI-IV, 401
Interpersonal paradigm, 19
Interpersonal Passivity (IPP) scale,
    MMPI-2-RF, 401
Interpersonal psychotherapy, Criterion A
    and, 11
Interpersonal Sensitivities Circumplex (ISC),
    164, 173
Interpretations of relational patterns
    in TFP, 218–219
    in TFP–Extended, 430

Index 451

Interrater reliability
  of clinical interviews, 80
  for Criterion A, 12, 162
  defined, 80
  of performance-based methods, 82, 83
Interviews. *See* Clinical interviews
Intimacy
  in AMPD, 31, 416
  with higher level personality disorders,
    422, 423
  in *ICD-11* model, 31
  and interpersonal functioning, 330
  on Level of Personality Functioning
    Scale, 161
  with narcissistic personality disorder, 376
  neurobiological research on, 337–339
  for patients with Severe PD, 139
  treatment focused on increasing, 190
Intimacy Avoidance, 14, 58
Intimacy scale, LPFS-SR, 164, 171
Introductory group, mentalization-based
    treatment, 248
Introversion, 226–227
Invalidation, in biosocial model, 261–262
Inventories, CAT, 91
Inventory of Interpersonal Problems, 66
Inventory of Interpersonal Problems–Short
    Circumplex (IIP-SC), 164, 173
Inventory of Personality Organization (IPO),
    169, 226
IPiC. *See* Informant-Personality Inventory
    for *ICD-11*
IPO (Inventory of Personality Organization),
    169, 226
IPP (Interpersonal Passivity) scale,
    MMPI-2-RF, 401
Irresponsibility, 14, 395
Irritability, 360, 395
ISC (Identity and Coherence of Self), 170
ISC (Interpersonal Sensitivities Circumplex),
    164, 173
ISTFP (International Society for Transference-
    Focused Therapy), 216
Item response theory, 90

J

Jariani, M., 310
JCP (Juvenile Conduct Problems) scale,
    MMPI-2-RF, 401
Johnson, T., 29
Joint Attention Task, 338
Juvenile Conduct Problems (JCP) scale,
    MMPI-2-RF, 401

K

Keeley, J. W., 16
Kerber, A., 41, 87

Kernberg, O. F., 30, 138, 154, 159, 166, 184,
    211, 214–216, 224–227, 245, 354, 355
Kernberg, Paulina, 225
Keshavan, M., 307
Kety, S. S., 355
Khalifa, N. R., 308
Kim, Y.-R., 41
Klonsky, E. D., 362
Knight, R., 354
Koenigsberg, H. W., 307
Kohut, H., 163
Koot, H. M., 118, 119
Kosson, D. S., 396
Kotov, R., 20–21
Kraepelin, Emil, 84
Krause-Utz, A., 327
Krueger, R. F., 9, 14, 15
Kunst, H., 282

L

Lamotrigine, 196, 312
Larstone, R., 137
Latent profile analysis, 407
Latent schizophrenia, 354
Lei, H., 327
Lenzenweger, M. F., 62
Level of personality functioning (LPF).
    See also Criterion A, in AMPD model
  attending to fluctuations in, 168
  for higher level personality disorders, 416
  to inform diagnosis with AMPD, 161
  interplay of maladaptive trait expression
    and, 167
  interrater reliability for assessments of,
    62–63
  linking PD symptoms to, 64–65
  as moderator, 93
  performance-based methods of assessing,
    81
  preventing reification of assessment of, 65
  severity in *ICD-11* model vs., 30–33, 35, 398
  treatment based on, 135
  for youth, 112, 115–116
Level of Personality Functioning Scale (LPFS)
  assessing Criterion A with, 11–13
  correlations of self- and informant report
    versions of, 88–89
  and diagnosis with AMPD, 161
  informant report versions of, 88–89, 169
  Kernberg's model of personality
    organization and, 225
  and SCID-5-AMPD, 426
  scores of individuals with higher level
    personality disorders on, 416–418, 422
  and SCORS-G, 170
  sensitivity and specificity of, 63
Level of Personality Functioning Scale–Brief
    Form (LPFS-BF), 12, 36, 84, 168, 169

452 *Index*

Level of Personality Functioning Scale–Self Report (LPFS-SR), 84
  assessing Criterion A with, 12
  correlation of informant report version of LPFS and, 88–89
  in diagnosis case example, 164, 171–172
  to inform AMPD diagnosis, 168, 169
  Kernberg's model of personality organization and, 225
  and predictive validity of Criterion B, 16–17
Level of personality organization, in ORT-based classification, 418
Levels of Personality Functioning Questionnaire (LoPF-Q 12–18), 116, 117, 122, 125
Levy, K. N., 220, 221, 223, 361
Lifestyle dimension, of psychopathy, 393, 396
Limited reparenting, 187, 288–290, 293, 295
Lind, M., 117
Linde, J. A., 120
Linehan, M. M., 152, 260–262, 266
Linehan Risk Assessment and Management Protocol (LRAMP), 263
Lingual gyri, 327
Linked diversion, in MBT, 251–252
Livesley, W. J., 135, 137, 153, 191
Longitudinal fasciculus, 329
LoPF-Q 12–18. *See* Levels of Personality Functioning Questionnaire
Lowe, J. R., 55
Low-level borderline personality organization, 420, 421
LPF. *See* Level of personality functioning
LPFS. *See* Level of Personality Functioning Scale
LPFS-BF. *See* Level of Personality Functioning Scale–Brief Form
LPFS-SR. *See* Level of Personality Functioning Scale–Self Report
LRAMP (Linehan Risk Assessment and Management Protocol), 263
Lucidity, 356
Lynam, D. R., 392, 393, 397
Lynch, T. R., 270

M

MAFS (Multidimensional Adolescent Functioning Scale), 122, 124
Magnetic encephalography, 324
Magnetic resonance imaging (MRI) studies, 324
Major depressive disorder (MDD)
  with borderline personality disorder, 357, 358
  differentiating BPD from, 359
  pharmacotherapy for PDs with, 309, 312, 313
Maladaptive Coping modes, 283, 284, 287, 288

Maladaptive traits. *See also* Pathological traits
  assessment of, 189
  in clinical staging model, 121, 122, 124
  and diagnosis of PD in youth, 116
  in diagnosis with AMPD, 161
  focusing treatment planning with, 190
  interplay of LPF and expression of, 167
  treatment of expression of, 190–191
  treatment planning based on, 167
  use of, in therapeutic process, 191
Malda-Castillo, J., 254
Mandated treatment programs, BPD prevalence in, 357
Manie sans delire (insanity without delusion), 392
Manipulativeness, 14, 395
Marcia, J. E., 215
Mayer, J. D., 96
MBT. *See* Mentalization-based treatment
McAdams, D. P., 159–160, 166, 215
McCabe, G. A., 40, 87
McCann, R. A., 270
McClure, M. M., 307
MCMI-III (Millon Clinical Multiaxial Inventory–III), 86
McWilliams, N., 138, 139
MDD. *See* Major depressive disorder
MDPF (Measure of Disordered Personality Functioning), 40
Meanness, 16, 393–394
Measure of Disordered Personality Functioning (MDPF), 40
Mechanical model of mental illness, 84
Medial prefrontal cortex (mPFC), 325–327
Medical model of *DSM*, 11
Meehan, K. B., 59
Meehl, P. E., 54
Menninger Foundation's Psychotherapy Research Project, 16, 211, 224
Mentalization
  and Criterion A, 255–256
  defining, 239–240
  dimensions of, 239
  DSM-5 definition of, 238
  and facial emotion recognition, 331
  and *ICD-11* model, 256
  neurobiological research on, 336–337
  TFP's impact on, 222, 223
  as transdiagnostic mental process, 255
Mentalization-based treatment (MBT), 237–256
  about, 240–241
  for antisocial personality disorder, 337, 406
  assessment and formulation in, 244–248
  for borderline personality disorder, 364, 366
  case example, 245–247, 251–253
  and categorical approach to PDs, 237–238
  clinical implementation of, 243–254

clinical utility of severity in, 185
defining mentalization, 239–240
Dissociality as target in, 194
exploration of mentalizing model in, 250–254
for higher level personality disorders, 427
identifying ineffective mentalizing modes in, 241–243
in individual and group psychotherapy, 248–249
introductory group in, 248
for narcissistic personality disorder, 384
Negative Affectivity as target in, 192
not-knowing stance in, 249–250
outcome research on, 254–255
severity-based treatment strategies in, 188
Mentalizing functional analysis, 253–254
Mentalizing model, exploration of, 250–254
Mentalizing modes, ineffective, 241–243
Mentalizing profile, 244
Menton, W. H., 39
Meta-analytic reviews
of mentalization-based treatment, 254–255
of transference-focused psychotherapy, 222
Metacognitive disorganization, 237, 244
Metacognitive interpersonal therapy (MIT), 385
Methadone maintenance therapy, 310
Middle borderline personality organization, 420, 421
Middle cingulate cortex, 336
Middle Eastern culture, 38
Mild identity pathology, on STIPO, 32
Mild PD (*ICD-11* model)
defined, 32, 141, 186
and higher level personality disorders, 416
and LPFS level, 416–418
manifestations of, 33
as threshold for diagnosis, 137, 138
treatments for patients with, 144–146, 188–189
Milieu therapy, 406
Miller, J. D., 227, 393
Millon, T., 355
Millon Clinical Multiaxial Inventory–Fourth Edition, 401
Millon Clinical Multiaxial Inventory–III (MCMI-III), 86
Mindfulness-based interventions, 192, 327
Mindfulness module, DBT, 266, 273
Minnesota Multiphasic Personality Inventory (MMPI), 84
Minnesota Multiphasic Personality Inventory—Second Edition (MMPI-2), 86, 91, 400
Minnesota Multiphasic Personality Inventory–2–Restructured Form (MMPI-2-RF), 400–401
internal consistency of, 86
overreporting scale of, 16

and PiCD, 39
and PID-5, 17, 168
Minnesota Multiphasic Personality Inventory for Adolescents, the Restructured Form (MMPI-A-RF), 111, 112
Mirror neuron system, 334
Mischel, W., 57
MIT (metacognitive interpersonal therapy), 385
Mixed PD groups, treatment of, 291
MMPI (Minnesota Multiphasic Personality Inventory), 84
MMPI-2. *See* Minnesota Multiphasic Personality Inventory—Second Edition
MMPI-2-RF. *See* Minnesota Multiphasic Personality Inventory–2–Restructured Form
MMPI-A-RF (Minnesota Multiphasic Personality Inventory for Adolescents, the Restructured Form), 111, 112
Mode awareness interventions, 289, 295, 297
Mode healing, 289, 297–299
Model Management Plans, 289, 297
Mode management, 289, 297
Mode model
conceptualization of personality disorders in, 284–286
goals of schema therapy in, 287–288
schema therapy interventions based on, 288–290
treating PDs with, 285, 287–290
Moderate identity pathology, on STIPO, 32
Moderate impairment (AMPD model)
defined, 32
as threshold for diagnosis, 137, 138
treatments for patients with, 144–146
Moderate PD (*ICD-11* model)
defined, 32, 141, 186
diagnostic accuracy for, 34
and LPFS level, 416
treatments for patients with, 142–144, 188–189, 215
Monoamine oxidase inhibitors, 195
Mood disorders
differentiating BPD from, 358–359
with narcissistic personality disorder, 378–380
symptoms of HLPDs and, 425
Mood reactivity, with BPD, 359
Mood stabilizers
for antisocial personality disorder, 308
for borderline personality disorder, 310–312
and *ICD-11* model for treatment, 195, 196
for obsessive-compulsive personality disorder, 313
Moral functioning, 418–421, 423
Morey, L. C., 13, 18–19, 34, 56, 63, 114, 171
Motivation, treatment and, 150–152

454 *Index*

Motive-oriented therapeutic relationship, 367
Movie for Assessment of Social Cognition Task, 336
Moyer, A., 362
mPFC (medial prefrontal cortex), 325–327
MRI (magnetic resonance imaging) studies, 324
Mulay, A. L., 19, 166
Mulder, R., 198
Mulder, R. T., 37, 306
Müller, L. E., 326
Mullins-Sweatt, S. N., 18, 20, 56, 61, 65
Multidimensional Adolescent Functioning Scale (MAFS), 122, 124
Multidisciplinary Directive for Personality Disorders, 213
Multimethod AMPD formulation, 174–176
Multimethod clinical assessment, 94–97, 173–174
Multiscale inventories, 400–401
Multivariate paradigm, 19, 84–85
Murray, A. M., 266
Mutually satisfying relationships, 337–339

N

Narcissism, 227, 375. *See also* Pathological narcissism (PN)
Narcissistic conflicts, 421
Narcissistic grandiosity, 19, 143, 376, 378
Narcissistic personality disorder (NPD), 330, 375–387
  in AMPD model, 3, 10, 356
  case example, 381–384
  categorical diagnosis of, 19
  comorbidities with, 306, 309, 310, 378–380, 386
  conceptualization of, 375
  DBT for treatment of, 270–271
  differential diagnosis of, 59
  difficulties in diagnosing, 375–378
  dimensional assessment of PN and, 380–381
  in *DSM-5* vs. AMPD, 378–380
  empathy deficits with, 335
  if–then contingencies in diagnosis of, 57
  interpersonal functioning deficits with, 330
  intimacy/mutually satisfying relationships with, 338
  mentalization deficits with, 239, 240
  mode profiles associated with, 286
  neurobiological research on, 324
  PAQ-11 scores of individuals with, 42
  pharmacotherapy for treatment of, 309
  self-images of individuals with, 221
  Severe impairment with/Moderate, 142, 143

  skills acquisition by patients with, 153–154
  termination of therapy by individuals with, 220
  TFP for treatment of, 211, 215, 224, 227
  treatment modalities for, 384–386
Narcissistic vulnerability, 19, 143
National Health and Medical Research Council (NHMRC), 196, 213
National Institute for Health and Care Excellence (NICE), 196, 212–213, 310
National Institute of Mental Health (NIMH), 29, 274
Naturalistic treatment settings, DBT in, 268–269
Needs, unmet, 281–283, 288–289, 292
Needs analysis, 62
Negative Affectivity
  in AMPD model, 14, 54
  with borderline personality disorder, 356
  and cognitive self-control, 329
  and Criterion B, 227, 356
  DBT to reduce, 273
  depression/anxiety as variant of, 112
  Depressivity and, 166
  Disinhibition and, 29
  in *ICD-11* model, 4, 37, 54
  in multimethod assessment, 96
  Neuroticism and, 14, 39
  PDs characterized by overlapping domains with, 197
  Perseveration and, 41
  pharmacotherapy to reduce, 196
  PID5BF+ items related to, 42
  SASPD items related to, 36
  treatment focused on modulating, 190
  treatments for individuals high in, 192–193
Negative Affectivity subscale, PID-5-BF, 164, 172
Negativity bias, in facial emotion recognition, 332–333
Nelson, S. M., 56, 57
NEO Personality Inventory–Revised (NEO-PI-R), 86, 91
Neural Constraint reaction surface, 62
Neurobiological research, 323–340
  and dimensional models of PD, 62, 323–325
  on empathy, 334–336
  on facial emotion recognition, 332–334
  on interpersonal functioning, 330–339
  on intimacy and mutually satisfying relationships, 337–339
  on self-awareness, 326–327
  on self-control, 328–330
  on self-functioning, 325–330
  on self-referential processing, 327–328
  on ToM/mentalizing, 336–337
Neurosis, 354

Neuroticism
and Criterion B, 227
and Negative Affectivity, 14, 39, 192
and psychopathy, 393
Neurotic level of personality organization
Criterion B and, 227
distinguishing HLPDs from, 425
in ORT-based classification, 418, 419
in TFP model, 226
treatment for, 137
Neurotransmitters, 315
Neurovegetative symptoms, of BPD, 359
NHMRC (National Health and Medical
Research Council), 196, 213
NICE. *See* National Institute for Health and
Care Excellence
Nidotherapy, 193
NIMH (National Institute of Mental
Health), 29, 274
No dysfunction (*ICD-11* model), 32, 422
No impairment (AMPD model), 32, 115, 422
Nonsuicidal self-injury (NSSI)
borderline personality disorder with, 353,
363
as defensive functioning, 148
in differential diagnosis of BPD, 362
global PD severity and risk of, 35
harm management to reduce, 152
Nonverbal communication, 429
Normal personality, in ORT-based
classification, 137, 418, 419
Norman, P., 254
Nortriptyline, 306
Not-knowing stance, in MBT, 249–250, 254
NPD. *See* Narcissistic personality disorder
NSSI. *See* Nonsuicidal self-injury
Nucleus accumbens, 328
Nurnberg, H. G., 311

O

Obesity, polypharmacy and, 366
Object relations, 418–421
Object relations theory (ORT)-based model
of personality organization
and AMPD, 225
empirical support for, 220–221
higher level personality disorders in, 416,
418–422
origins of BPD in, 214
structured assessments for, 426–427
and transference-focused psychotherapy,
211, 216
treatment based on, 137
Obsessive-compulsive disorder, 313, 378
Obsessive-compulsive personality disorder
(OCPD)
in AMPD model, 3, 10, 356
countertransference for patient with, 154
differential diagnosis of, 59, 60

and early maladaptive schemas, 282, 300
as higher level personality disorder, 413,
415
Mild, 145
mode profiles associated with, 286
overlapping trait domains in, 197
PAQ-11 scores of individuals with, 42
pharmacotherapy for treatment of, 313
RO-DBT for treatment of, 195, 270
self-referential processing deficits with, 327
ST for treatment of, 290
TFP–Extended for treatment of, 215
treatment of, 195, 215, 270, 290, 313, 427
Occipital areas, 331
OCPD. *See* Obsessive-compulsive personality
disorder
OFC. *See* Orbitofrontal cortex
Olajide, K., 63–64
Olanzapine, 196, 307, 310, 311
Older adults
predictive validity of Criterion B for, 16–17
schema therapy with, 291
Oltmanns, J. R., 36, 38, 40, 198
Olver, Mark, 406–407
Omega-3-fatty acids, 310, 312
One-size-fits-all approach to clinical utility,
67–68
Openness, 14, 15
Opposite action, in DBT, 273
Orbitofrontal cortex (OFC), 223, 325, 336
Orderliness, 39
Ordinal scaling of personality organization,
166
Orthogenetic principle, 214
Other Specified Personality Disorder, 10, 160
Outcome monitoring, in DBT, 262–264
Outcome research
on dialectical behavior therapy, 268–271
on global PD severity, 35
on mentalization-based treatment, 249,
254–255
on psychotherapy for BPD, 365
on schema therapy, 290–291
on transference-focused psychotherapy,
212–213, 221–223
Outpatient settings, BPD prevalence in, 357
Overcompensator mode, 283
Overreporting scale, PID-5, 16, 86
Oxcarbazepine, 308
Oxytocin, 333–336

P

PAG (periaqueductal gray), 339
PAI. *See* Personality Assessment Inventory
PAI-A (Personality Assessment Inventory–
Adolescent), 112
PAI-A-BOR (Personality Assessment
Inventory–Adolescent–Borderline
Scale), 113, 122

456 *Index*

Pain sensitivity, BPD and, 363
Pals, J. L., 166
PAQ-11 (Personality Assessment
  Questionnaire for *ICD-11*), 41–42, 189
Parahippocampus, 223, 330
Paralimbic system, 334–335
Paranoid ideation, 311
Paranoid personality disorder (PPD)
  countertransference with, 154
  mode profiles associated with, 286
  PAQ-11 scores of individuals with, 42
  pharmacotherapy for treatment of, 306
  RO-DBT for treatment of, 270
  Severe, 139
Parental input, in personality assessment
  for youth, 126, 127
Parent modes (Dysfunctional Critic modes),
  283, 284, 288
Parietal cortices, 327
Parietal lobes, 328–329, 336
PAS (Personality Assessment Schedule), 29,
  41
Pathological narcissism (PN)
  assessment of, 379–381
  categorical diagnosis of, 19
  conceptualization of, 375
  in *DSM-5*, 376–377
  treatment modalities for, 384–386
Pathological traits. *See also* Maladaptive traits
  diagnostic efficiency of, 64
  in dimensional models, 54, 61–62, 136
  linking PD symptoms to, 64–65
  preventing reification of assessment of, 65
  as treatment targets, 66
Patient-specific methods, 89–94
PCC. *See* Posterior cingulate cortex
PCL (Psychopathy Checklist), 392
PCL-R. *See* Psychopathy Checklist Revised
PCPs (primary care providers), 67–68, 153
Pd2 (Harris–Lingoes Authority Problems)
  subscale, MMPI-2, 400
PDD (Personality Dynamics Diary), 93
PDNOS. *See* Personality Disorder Not
  Otherwise Specified
Pd (Psychopathic Deviate) scale, MMPI-2,
  400
PDS-ICD-11 scale. *See* Personality Disorder
  Severity *ICD-11* scale
PD-TS. *See* Personality Disorder—Trait
  Specified
Pellegrini, A. M., 43
Perceptual distortions
  pharmacotherapy to reduce, 195, 196
  self-report measures on, 86
Perceptual Dysregulation, in Criterion B, 14
Perceptual Thinking Index (PTI), 33
Perez, D. L., 223
Perfectionism, 380. *See also* Rigid Perfectionism
Performance-based methods, 81–84,
  169–170

Pergolide, 307
Periaqueductal gray (PAG), 339
Peripubertal period, clinical staging model
  in, 124, 125
Perry, J. C., 149
Perseveration, 14, 41
Persistent depressive disorder, 306, 357
Personality
  conceptualization of, 159–160
  HLPD treatments targeting change in, 427
Personality assessment (generally), 77–97
  adapting adult measures for youth,
    111–114
  clinical interview methods, 78–80
  informant report methods, 87–89
  multimethod, 94–97
  patient-specific methods, 89–94
  performance-based methods, 81–84
  self-report methods, 84–87
Personality assessment for youth
  with adapted adult personality measures,
    111–114
  AMPD-based, 112, 115–120
  case example, 109–111, 125–126, 128–129
  clinical considerations with, 126–129
  clinical staging framework for, 116,
    121–126
Personality Assessment Inventory (PAI), 86,
  168, 400
Personality Assessment Inventory–Adolescent
  (PAI-A), 112
Personality Assessment Inventory–
  Adolescent–Borderline Scale
  (PAI-A-BOR), 113, 122
Personality Assessment Questionnaire for
  ICD-11 (PAQ-11), 41–42, 189
Personality Assessment Schedule (PAS),
  29, 41
Personality difficulty (*ICD-11* model), 32,
  35, 186, 416
Personality Disorder Not Otherwise
  Specified (PDNOS), 35, 60n1, 161
Personality Disorder Severity *ICD-11*
  (PDS-ICD-11) scale, 36, 184, 198
Personality Disorders Institute of Cornell
  University, 211–212
Personality disorder (PD) symptoms
  linking LPF and pathological traits to,
    64–65
  neurotransmitters and, 315
  pharmacotherapy targeting, 195–196
  treatments for HLPDs to relieve, 427
  for youth, 121
Personality Disorder—Trait Specified
  (PD-TS), 10, 11, 59, 160–161, 314
Personality Dynamics Diary (PDD), 93
Personality Inventory for *DSM-5* (PID-5),
  85, 116, 401
  assessing Criterion B with, 14–17
  in clinical staging framework, 122, 125

correlations of self- and informant report versions for, 89
diagnostic efficiency of, 64
discriminant validity of, 59–60
to inform AMPD diagnosis, 168
internal consistency of, 86
measuring *ICD-11* trait domains with, 38–40, 189
in multimethod assessment based on transtheoretical model, 96, 97
and quantification of trait level, 161
Personality Inventory for *DSM-5*, Brief Form Plus (PID5BF+), 41
Personality Inventory for *DSM-5* and *ICD-11* Brief Form–Modified, 189
Personality Inventory for *DSM-5*–Brief Form (PID-5-BF), 14, 116, 168
Personality Inventory for *DSM-5*–Informant Report Form (PID-5-IRF), 87
in AMPD diagnosis case example, 164, 172–173
assessing Criterion B with, 15
correlations of self-report version of PID-5 with, 89
to inform AMPD diagnosis, 169
measuring *ICD-11* trait domains with, 38
Personality Inventory for *DSM-5*–Intermediate Form, 168
Personality Inventory for *ICD-11* (PiCD), 85
assessing trait domains with, 38–40, 189
clinician-report form of, 43
correlations of self- and informant report versions of, 89
internal consistency of, 86
in multimethod assessment based on transtheoretical model, 96, 97
Personality organization, in TFP model, 225–226
Personality Psychopathology 5 (PSY-5), 39, 168
Personality system, 137
Personality Trait Rating Form, 169
Personological approach to personality assessment, 11, 19
P (general psychopathology) factor, 366
PFC. *See* Prefrontal cortex
Pharmacotherapy, 305–315
and AMPD, 167
for antisocial personality disorder, 407
for borderline personality disorder, 366
for Cluster A personality disorders, 306–307
for Cluster B personality disorders, 308–312
for Cluster C personality disorders, 312–313
and dimensional models of PD, 313–314
and *ICD-11* model, 195–197
for narcissistic personality disorder, 386
TFP principles for treatment with, 224
Phenelzine, 309
Phenytoin, 308
Piaget, J., 214

PiCD. *See* Personality Inventory for *ICD-11*
PID-5. *See* Personality Inventory for *DSM-5*
PID-5-BF. *See* Personality Inventory for *DSM-5*–Brief Form
PID5BF+ (Personality Inventory for *DSM-5*, Brief Form Plus), 41
PID-5-IRF. *See* Personality Inventory for *DSM-5*–Informant Report Form
Pincus, A. L., 12, 20
PN. *See* Pathological narcissism
Point Subtraction Aggression Paradigm, 339
Polatin, P., 354
Pompili, M., 363
Pornography use, 148
Positive adjustment traits, 392, 393
Positive affect, MBT focusing on, 253
Positron emission tomography, 324
Postcentral gyrus, 330
Posterior cingulate cortex (PCC), 220
dissociation and, 327
intimacy/trust and, 338
self-functioning and, 325
theory of mind and, 336
Postpubertal period, clinical staging model in, 124, 125
Posttraumatic stress disorder (PTSD)
with borderline personality disorder, 357
complex, 360–361
DBT for treatment of, 269
differentiating BPD from, 358, 360–362
Poythress, N. G., 396
PPD. *See* Paranoid personality disorder
Precision, diagnostic, 92, 121
Precuneus, 220
cognitive empathy and, 331
empathy and, 334
self-control and, 329
self-functioning and, 325
self-referential processing and, 327
theory of mind and, 336
Predictive validity, of Criterion B, 16–17
Prefrontal cortex (PFC), 223
aggression and, 339
anger rumination and, 328
cognitive empathy and, 331
empathy and, 334, 335
facial emotion recognition and, 333
intimacy/trust and, 338
self-control and, 328–330
theory of mind and, 336, 337
Premature termination of therapy
countertransference and, 155
global PD severity and, 35
LPFS scores and, 13
by patients with psychopathy, 406
severity of dysfunction and, 187
Prementalizing modes, 243
Prepubertal period, clinical staging model in, 124

458　*Index*

Preschoolers, clinical staging model for, 122, 124
Presupplementary motor area, 328
Pretend mode, 241, 242
Pretreatment stage, of DBT, 265
Primary care providers (PCPs), 67–68, 153
Prison populations. *See also* Forensic populations
　mentalization-based treatment with, 255
　prevalence of ASPD in, 399
　self-referential processing deficits for, 327–329
　theory of mind deficits for, 337
Problem analysis, in schema therapy, 295
Problematic behaviors
　chain analysis of, 263
　as treatment targets, 66
Professional communication, 55–57
Projective methods. *See* Performance-based methods
Prolonged exposure therapy, DBT with, 269
Promazine, 306
Protective patterns, 379
Protocol compliance, EMA, 93–94
Provocation-induced aggression, 339
PSY-5 (Personality Psychopathology 5), 39, 168
Psychiatric management
　for borderline personality disorder, 364, 366
　for higher level personality disorders, 427
　TFP principles in, 225
Psychiatric residents, training in TFP principles for, 225
Psychiatry, biologically-oriented, 144
Psychic equivalence mode, 241–242, 251
Psychoanalytic approach, 137, 405
Psychobiographies, 77
Psychodiagnosis, with AMPD, 167
Psychodrama, 405
Psychodynamic Diagnostic Manual, Second Edition (PDM-2), 137
Psychodynamic Diagnostic Manual–Version 2 (PDM-2), 215, 226
Psychodynamic therapy
　alignment of AMPD with, 20
　for borderline personality disorder, 364
　and Criterion A, 11, 19
　and mentalization-based therapies, 253
　and ORT-based classification of personality functioning, 137
　supportive, 221, 225
　and TFP–Extended, 430
　and transference-focused psychotherapy, 211
Psychoeducation, 385, 386
Psychological conflict, 421
Psychological trauma, pathological narcissism and, 380
Psychopathic Deviate (Pd) scale, MMPI-2, 400

Psychopathy
　aggression and, 339
　with antisocial personality disorder, 324, 396
　assessment of, 399–400
　conceptual models of, 392–394
　empathy deficits with, 334–335
　facial emotion recognition deficits with, 333
　future research directions, 407
　with narcissistic personality disorder, 378
　neurobiological studies of, 328, 329
　self-referential processing deficits with, 327–328
　Severe, 139
　theory of mind deficits with, 337
　treatment of, 405–407
Psychopathy Checklist (PCL), 392
Psychopathy Checklist Revised (PCL-R)
　assessing psychopathy with, 402
　and diagnostic criteria for ASPD, 392–394, 396, 402
　heterogeneity of profiles on, 407
Psychopathy specifier, in AMPD model, 396–398
Psychopharmacological treatment. *See* Pharmacotherapy
Psychosis, 121, 255, 354
Psychosocial functioning, 13, 35
Psychosocial interventions
　common mechanisms in, 184, 185
　four Cs of, 237, 254
Psychotherapist, mode profile of, 286
Psychotherapy
　AMPD model and integration of, 20
　intimate relationships as focus of, 339
　for treatment of BPD, 330, 364–365
　for treatment of personality disorders, 147–148
Psychoticism
　in AMPD model, 14, 54
　and Criterion B, 227, 245
　in multimethod assessment, 96
　Openness to Experience and, 14
Psychoticism subscale, PID-5-BF, 164, 173
Psychotic level of personality organization, 137, 226
PTI (Perceptual Thinking Index), 33
PTSD. *See* Posttraumatic stress disorder
Punitive Critic mode, 283

Q

Quetiapine, 311

R

Radical genuineness, 267
Radically open dialectical behavior therapy (RO-DBT), 197, 270
Radical Openness module, RO-DBT, 270

Rapaport, D., 354
Rapport building, 79–80, 193
Rational therapy, 405
RC4 (Antisocial Behavior) scale, MMPI-2-RF, 401
RC7 (Dysfunctional Negative Emotions) scale, MMPI-2-RF, 401
RC9 (Hypomanic Activation) scale, MMPI-2-RF, 401
Reactive aggression, 339, 393
Reactivity
  in biosocial theory, 261
  and ecological momentary assessment, 94
  mood, 359
  reciprocal, 249
  therapist, 148
  treatment focused to reduce, 148, 190
Reading-the-Mind-in-the-Eyes Task, 334
Reality testing
  for individuals with HLPDs, 423
  in ORT-based classification, 418–420
  of transference, 212, 226
Real relationship, transference and, 212
Recall bias, 92
Recidivism rates, psychopathy and, 406
Reciprocal reactivity, 249
Reckless disregard for safety, 395
Reed, G. M., 198
Reed-Knight, B., 271
Rehearsals, in MBT, 252–253
Rejection hypersensitivity, 338
Relational assessment, before MBT, 240
Relational patterns
  interpretations of, in TFP, 218–219
  MBT focusing on, 253
Relationship difficulties. See also Interpersonal functioning
  with psychopathy, 393
  with PTSD vs. BPD, 362
Reliability
  of clinical interviews, 80
  of computer adaptive testing, 91
  of Criterion A assessments, 12–13
  of Criterion B assessments, 15–17
  of ecological momentary assessment, 93–94
  of informant report methods, 88
  interrater, 12, 80, 82, 83, 162
  and multimethod clinical assessment, 94
  of performance-based methods, 82, 83
  of personality assessments for youth, 111
  of self-report measures, 86
Remorse, lack of, 395
Repeated invalidation, in biosocial model, 261–262
Repression-based defenses, 149
Resolution of identity diffusion, 213
Response bias, on PID-5, 15–16
Resting state magnetic resonance imaging ((rs)MRI) studies, 324

Restricted Affectivity, 14, 15
Reverse correlation method, 221
Revised Neuroticism, Extraversion, Openness Personality Inventory, 15
Ridolfi, M. E., 363
Rigid Perfectionism, 14, 15, 41, 145
Risk Taking, 14, 395
Risperidone, 307
Ristic, J., 331
RO-DBT (radically open dialectical behavior therapy), 197, 270
Rodriguez-Seijas, C., 18
Ronningstam, E., 167
Roper, B. L., 91
Rorschach inkblot method, 81, 96, 97
Rorschach Performance Assessment System (R-PAS), 82, 83, 170
Rottman, B. M., 56
(rs)MRI (resting state magnetic resonance imaging) studies, 324
Rumination, 328

S

Saccades, 332, 339
Safer, D. L., 269–270
Safety, reckless disregard for, 395
Salekin, R. T., 405–406
Samuel, D. B., 55, 56, 80
Santamarina-Perez, P., 269
SAPAS (Standardized Assessment of Personality–Abbreviated Scale), 29
SASPD. See Standardized Assessment of Severity of Personality Disorder
SC (Understanding of Social Causality), 169
Scala, J. W., 221
Schedule for Nonadaptive and Adaptive Personality (SNAP), 39
Schedule for Nonadaptive and Adaptive Personality (SNAP-CAT), 91
Schedule for Nonadaptive and Adaptive Personality–Youth Version (SNAP-Y), 116, 118
Schema flipping, 214
Schema mode change stage, of schema therapy, 290
Schema Mode Inventory (SMI), 282, 284
Schema modes, 282–284, 300
Schemas, 282, 300
Schema therapy (ST), 281–301
  for borderline personality disorder, 366
  case example, 291–299
  clinical utility of severity in, 185
  and dimensional models of PD, 299–301
  Dissociality as target of, 194
  evidence for treatment effectiveness of, 290–291
  for higher level personality disorders, 427
  for narcissistic personality disorder, 385

460 *Index*

Negative Affectivity as target of, 193
personality disorders in mode model, 284–286
schemas and schema modes in, 282–284
severity-based treatment strategies in, 189
transference-focused psychotherapy vs., 222
treating PDs with mode model in, 285, 287–290
and treatment planning based on diagnosis, 59
Schizoid personality disorder (ScPD), 42, 139, 306
Schizophrenia, 307
Schizotypal personality disorder (SPD)
in AMPD model, 3, 10, 356
borderline personality disorder vs., 355
in *ICD-10* vs. *DSM*, 415
pharmacotherapy for, 305, 307
Psychoticism and, 54
Severe, 139
transference-focused psychotherapy for treatment of, 215, 227
Schmideberg, M., 354
Schmitgen, M. M., 330
Schneider, I., 333
School age children, clinical staging model for, 121, 122, 124
Schools, mentalization-based treatment in, 255
Schulz, S. C., 311
SCID-II. *See* Structured Clinical Interview for *DSM-IV* Axis II Personality Disorders
SCID-5-AMPD. *See* Structured Clinical Interview for the *DSM-5* Alternative Model for Personality Disorders
SCORS-G. *See* Social Cognition and Object Relations Scale-Global Rating Method
ScPD. *See* Schizoid personality disorder
Screener questions, SCID-5-AMPD, 426
SDQ (Strengths and Difficulties Questionnaire), 122, 124
Segal, D. L., 16–17
Selective norepinephrine reuptake inhibitors (SNRIs), 310, 313
Selective serotonin reuptake inhibitors (SSRIs), 195, 196, 310, 313, 407
Self, mentalization of others vs., 239–240
Self and Interpersonal Functioning Scale, 168, 225–226
Self-appraisal, 85
Self-awareness, 81, 325–327
Self-care, promoting, 153
Self-concept, of individuals with BPD, 221
Self-control
cognitive, 328–330, 339
neurobiological research on, 325–326, 328–330
in obsessive-compulsive personality disorder, 327

Self-destructive activities, 139
Self-direction
in AMPD, 31, 416
dialectical behavior psychotherapy to improve, 274
in *ICD-11* model, 31
for individuals with NPD, 376
on Level of Personality Functioning Scale, 161
for patients with Mild PD, 145
for patients with Moderate PD, 142
Self-Direction scale, LPFS-SR, 164, 171
Self-esteem
in higher level personality disorders, 422, 423
in NPD and pathological narcissism, 377, 380–381
Self-Esteem (SE) subscale, SCORS-G, 164, 170, 173
Self-functioning
in AMPD model, 3, 31
Criterion A assessment of, 10–12
in *ICD-11* model, 31, 33
for individuals with BPD, 356
for individuals with HLPDs, 415–417, 421, 422
for individuals with Mild PD, 144
on Level of Personality Functioning Scale, 161
multimethod assessment of, 96
neurobiological research on, 325–330
in ORT-based classification, 416
overlap between interpersonal functioning and, 324–325
on SASPD, 36
in severity determination, 54, 136, 185
Self-harm. *See also* Nonsuicidal self-injury (NSSI)
DBT to reduce, 268
harm management to reduce, 152–153
linking LPF and pathological traits to, 64–65
MBT to reduce, 253–255
and PD severity, 33
Self-images, of individuals with BPD, 221
Self-referential processing, 325, 327–328
Self-reflection, capacity for, 167
Self-regulation, 122, 124, 378
Self-report measures, 84–87. *See also specific measures by name*
advantages and disadvantages of, 85–86
assessing Criterion A with, 12
and computer adaptive testing, 90
correlation of informant report measures and, 88–89
for DBT outcome monitoring, 263–264
to inform AMPD diagnosis, 168–169
informant report methods in combination with, 89

limitations on utility of, 65
in multimethod AMPD formulation, 174, 176
reliability and validity of, 86–87
for youth, 127–128
Self-valuation, in higher level personality disorders, 422, 423
Sellbom, M., 16, 38, 398
Semi-Structured Interview for Personality Functioning *DSM-5* (STiP-5.1), 78
assessing Criterion A with, 12
in clinical staging framework, 122, 125
for youth, 116, 118
Semistructured interviews
advantages and disadvantages of, 79
for AMPD diagnosis, 169
defined, 78
reliability and validity of, 80
for youth, 127–128
Sensitivity, in biosocial theory, 260
Separation anxiety disorder, 312
Separation Insecurity, 14, 166, 167, 300
Sertraline, 310, 313
SE subscale, SCORS-G. *See* Self-Esteem subscale, SCORS-G
Severe identity pathology, on STIPO, 32
Severe impairment (AMPD model), 32, 142–144
Severe PD (*ICD-11* model)
adapting treatments for, 427–428
defined, 32, 141, 184, 186
differentiating higher level personality disorders from, 421–422, 425
LPFS level correlated to, 416
managing countertransference with patients who have, 187
situational and interpersonal appraisals by individuals with, 31, 33
transference-focused psychotherapy for treatment of, 211, 215
treatments for patients with, 138–140, 188–189, 211, 215
Severity
in AMPD. *See* Level of personality functioning (LPF)
in assessment of PD, 183, 184
and borderline pattern specifier, 198
clinical utility of measure for, 54, 184–189
and comorbidity, 35, 60
contributors to, 185
diagnostic efficiency of decisions related to, 63
empirical foundation for *ICD-11* measure of, 34–36
and Healthy Adult mode, 285
of higher level personality disorders, 413, 414, 416
in *ICD-11* model vs. AMPD, 30–33, 398
impairment of functioning vs., 166

interrater reliability of LPF and ratings of, 62–63
measures of, in clinical staging model, 122, 123
in ORT-based classification, 225, 416, 418–421
preventing reification of assessment of, 65
Severity framework for treatment of personality disorders, 135–155, 190
about, 136–138
clinical considerations in, 146–155
countertransference in, 154–155
defensive functioning in, 148–150
harm management in, 152–153
and *ICD-11* severity classification, 141
patients with extreme impairment or Severe PD, 138–140
patients with moderate impairment or Mild PD, 144–146
patients with severe impairment or Moderate PD, 142–144
skill acquisition in, 153–154
therapeutic action of, 147–148
unconscious and implicit motivation in, 150–152
Severity Indices of Personality Problems (SIPP-118), 116, 169
Sex, loss of interest in, 359
s-factors. *See* Specific factors for personality pathology
Shafti, S. S., 311
Shahveisi, B., 311
Shame, 380
Sharp, C., 113, 114, 225–227, 356
Shedler, J., 18, 95
Shedler–Westen Assessment Procedure (SWAP-200-A), 61, 111, 112
Shoda, Y., 57
Shyness (SHY) scale, MMPI-2-RF, 401
Siever, L. J., 195
Simms, L. J., 91
Simonsen, E., 3
SIPP-118 (Severity Indices of Personality Problems), 116, 169
Situational stresses, maladaptive trait expression and, 167
6A.1 (Interpersonally Irresponsible) subscale, MCMI-IV, 401
6A.2 (Autonomous Self-Image) subscale, MCMI-IV, 401
6A.3 (Acting-Out Dynamics) subscale, MCMI-IV, 401
Skills acquisition, in treatment of personality disorders, 153–154
Skills training, DBT with, 266, 269, 270
Skinner, B. F., 262
Skodol, A. E., 63
Slight deficit, on STIPO, 32
SMI (Schema Mode Inventory), 282, 284

462   *Index*

Smith, S. R., 96
SNAP (Schedule for Nonadaptive and Adaptive Personality), 39
SNAP-CAT (Schedule for Nonadaptive and Adaptive Personality), 91
SNAP-Y (Schedule for Nonadaptive and Adaptive Personality–Youth Version), 116, 118
SNRIs (selective norepinephrine reuptake inhibitors), 310, 313
Social adjustment, DBT and, 268
Social anxiety disorder, 313
Social cognition, 334, 336
Social Cognition and Object Relations Scale-Global Rating Method (SCORS-G), 82–84
   in diagnosis case example, 164, 173–174
   to inform AMPD diagnosis, 169–170
   in multimethod assessment based on transtheoretical model, 96, 97
Social-cognitive approach, Criterion A and, 11
Social exchange, 338
Social learning, 248, 252
Social phobia, 291
Social reality testing, 423
Social support, in youth, 126
Social threat hypersensitivity, 339
Society of Clinical Psychology Committee on Science and Practice, 212–213
Sociocultural environment, Criterion G and, 11
Soloff, P. H., 195
Solution analysis, 263
Somatic examination, for youth, 126
Somatosensory cortices, 325, 331, 334
Some impairment (AMPD model), 32
Somma, A., 39–40
SPD. *See* Schizotypal personality disorder
Specific factors for personality pathology (s-factors), 227, 356, 366
Spitzer, R. L., 55
Splitting-based defenses, 149, 421, 426, 429
Sprock, J., 55
SSRIs. *See* Selective serotonin reuptake inhibitors
ST. *See* Schema therapy
Stability across time, in AMPD model, 10
Stage 0, in clinical staging framework, 121, 122, 124
Stage 1a, in clinical staging framework, 122, 124
Stage 1b, in clinical staging framework, 122, 124–125
Stage 2, in clinical staging framework, 122, 125
Stage 3a, in clinical staging framework, 123, 125
Stage 3b, in clinical staging framework, 123, 125

Stage 3c, in clinical staging framework, 123, 125
Stage 4, in clinical staging framework, 123, 125
Stalking, 153
Standardized Assessment of Personality–Abbreviated Scale (SAPAS), 29
Standardized Assessment of Severity of Personality Disorder (SASPD), 84–85
   in clinical staging framework, 123, 125
   internal consistency of, 86
   as measure of PD complexity, 35–36
   SAPAS and, 29n1
   sensitivity and specificity of, 63–64
Standardized scoring systems
   for clinical interviews, 79
   for performance-based assessments, 82–84
Steinberg, L., 114
Steiner, T. G., 221
STEPPS therapy, 364
Stern, B. L., 354
Stimulus attribution methods. *See* Performance-based methods
Stimulus Seeking (ANT-S) scale, PAI, 400
STiP-5.1. *See* Semi-Structured Interview for Personality Functioning *DSM-5*
STIPO. *See* Structured Interview for Personality Organization
Stoffers-Winterling, J. M., 196
Stone, L. E., 16–17
Stone, M. H., 355
Storebø, O. J., 254
Strengths and Difficulties Questionnaire (SDQ), 122, 124
Striatum, 223, 325
Structural aspects, of representations of identity, 213–214
Structural personality changes, with TFP, 222–223
Structured Clinical Interview for *DSM-5* Personality Disorders, 401
Structured Clinical Interview for *DSM-IV* Axis II Personality Disorders (SCID-II), 16, 29, 61
Structured Clinical Interview for the *DSM-5* Alternative Model for Personality Disorders (SCID-5-AMPD), 78
   assessing antisocial personality disorder with, 401
   assessing higher level personality disorders with, 426
   Module II of, 38
   Module I of, 36
   validity of, 80
Structured Clinical Interview for the Level of Personality Functioning Scale, 12
Structured interventions, MBT, 249
Structured Interview for *DSM-IV* Personality, 401

Structured Interview for Personality Organization (STIPO), 32, 78, 80, 426–427
Structured Interview for the Five-Factor Model of Personality, 402
Structured interviews
    advantages and disadvantages of, 79–80
    for AMPD diagnosis, 169
    assessing Criterion A with, 12
    assessing Criterion B with, 15
    in diagnosis of BPD, 364
    in diagnosis of HLPDs, 426
    reliability and validity of, 80
    unstructured vs., 78–79
Submissiveness, 14, 15
SUB (Substance Use) scale, MMPI-2-RF, 401
Substance abuse
    and borderline personality disorder, 357, 358
    DBT for treatment of, 269
    MBT for treatment of, 254
    with narcissistic personality disorder, 309
Substance use
    and Criterion F of AMPD, 10
    deceitfulness about, 399
Substance use disorder (SUD)
    with antisocial personality disorder, 399, 406
    with avoidant personality disorder, 313
    MBT for treatment of, 255
    with narcissistic personality disorder, 378
Substance Use (SUB) scale, MMPI-2-RF, 401
Subsyndromal pathology, 35, 416, 425, 428
Subsyndromal personality, 418. See also Neurotic level of personality organization
Subthreshold personality difficulty. See Personality difficulty (ICD-11 model)
SUD. See Substance use disorder
Suicidality
    borderline personality disorder with, 362–363
    DBT to reduce, 260, 268
    global PD severity and, 35
    harm management to reduce, 152
    MBT to reduce, 255
Supportive psychodynamic therapy, 221, 225
Supramarginal gyrus, 334
Suspiciousness, 14, 15, 38, 300
Svartberg, M., 427
SWAP-200-A. See Shedler–Westen Assessment Procedure
Swiss Association for Psychiatry and Psychotherapy, 213
Syndromal personality pathology, as HLPD, 413
Systems training for emotional predictability and problem-solving, 367

T

"Talk the talk but not walk the walk" mode. See Pretend mode
Tarasoff v. Regents of the University of California et al., 152
Tarescavage, A. M., 39
Target behaviors, in CBT for NPD, 385
TAT (Thematic Apperception Test), 83–84, 173–174
Teacher input, in personality assessment for youth, 127
Teacher's Report Form (TRF), 122, 124
Technology, 89
Telch, C. F., 270
Teleological mode, 241–243
Temperament
    in clinical staging model, 122–124
    in schema therapy model, 281, 293
Temporal cortex, 331, 336
Temporal gyrus, 329, 336, 338
Temporal lobes, 325, 329, 336
Temporal pole, 331
Temporal sulcus
    empathy and, 334, 335
    facial emotion recognition and, 331–333
    theory of mind and, 336, 337
Temporoparietal junction
    cognitive empathy and, 331
    empathy and, 334, 335
    intimacy/trust and, 338
    mentalization and, 331
    self-referential processing deficits and, 328
    theory of mind and, 336
Termination, of TFP, 219–220. See also Premature termination of therapy
Test–retest reliability
    of clinical interviews, 80
    for Comprehensive System, 82
    for computer adaptive testing, 91
    defined, 80
    for self-report methods, 86
Test security, with computer adaptive testing, 90
TFP. See Transference-focused psychotherapy
TFP-E. See Transference-Focused Psychotherapy–Extended
Thalamus, 325, 326
Thematic Apperception Test (TAT), 83–84, 173–174
Theory of mind (ToM)
    affective, 336, 337
    cognitive, 336
    and empathy, 334
    and facial emotion recognition, 331
    measures of, in clinical staging framework, 122, 124
    neurobiological research on, 336–337
Therapeutic action, of treatments for PDs, 147–148

Therapeutic alliance, 147
  and Criterion A, 18
  and global PD severity, 35
  and identity diffusion, 220
  in mentalization-based treatment, 244,
    248, 253
  for patients with Severe PD, 138, 139
  and severity of dysfunction, 187
Therapeutic process, use of patient traits in,
  191
Therapeutic relationship, transference in,
  212
Therapist reactivity, 148
Therapist training
  in dialectical behavior therapy, 264
  in dimensional model use, 62–63
  in performance-based assessment, 81
  in psychotherapy for BPD, 365
  to use AMPD, 162–165
Thiothixene, 307
Threat approach, 333, 334
Threat hypersensitivity, 332–334, 339
Thresholds
  in AMPD, 161
  in categorical model, 9
  and clinical staging framework, 121
ToM. *See* Theory of mind
Topiramate, 196, 312
TPM. *See* Triarchic psychopathy model
Trait callousness, 333, 334
Trait domains. *See also specific domains*
  in AMPD model, 10, 15, 54, 161
  assessment of, 189
  clinician-report measures of, 42–43
  FFiCD for measuring, 40
  and five-factor model, 356
  in *ICD-11* model, 37–43, 54, 136, 183, 187,
    189–191, 398
  PAQ-11 for measuring, 41–42
  pharmacotherapy based on, 196–197
  PiCD for measuring, 38–40
  PID-5 algorithm for measuring, 38
  PID5BF+ for measuring, 41
  treatment planning based on, 191–195
  treatments for patients with blends of
    traits, 197–198
Trait facets. *See also specific facets*
  in AMPD, 10, 40, 54
  development of, 14
  and if–then contingencies in diagnosis, 58
  reliability of, 15
  validity of, 17
Transference, 212, 260, 430
Transference-focused psychotherapy (TFP),
  211–228
  about, 211–213
  adapting, for HLPDs, 428–429
  for borderline personality disorder, 366

and dimensional models of PD, 225–228
Dissociality as target in, 194
empirical support for, 220–223
goals of, 213–215
harm management in, 152
indications for use, 215–216
mentalization-based treatment vs.,
  253–254
for narcissistic personality disorder, 384
recent clinical and theoretical
  developments, 224–225
severity-based treatment strategies in,
  188
structure and techniques of, 216–220
and treatment planning based on
  diagnosis, 59
underlying theory for, 216
Transference-Focused Psychotherapy–
  Extended (TFP-E), 215, 428–432
Transtheoretical model of personality,
  96–97
Trauma
  borderline personality disorder and,
    360–361
  complex, 241, 291
  pathological narcissism and, 380
  TFP principles for treatment of, 224
Treatment contract, TFP, 217
Treatment effectiveness
  dialectical behavior psychotherapy, 268
  schema therapy, 290–291
  transference-focused psychotherapy,
    221–222
Treatment efficacy, 221–222, 268–269
Treatment engagement, global PD severity
  and, 35
Treatment frame, in TFP, 217
Treatment Guidelines for Personality Disorders
  (German Society for Psychiatry,
  Psychotherapy, and Psychosomatics),
  213
Treatment length
  of psychotherapy for BPD, 365
  of schema therapy, 291
  of transference-focused psychotherapy,
    219
Treatment planning
  with AMPD, 20, 65–66, 167–168, 170–176
  diagnosis in, 58–59
  five-factor model as basis for, 191
  focusing, with traits, 190
  global PD severity for, 34
  with *ICD-11* model, 190–195, 197–198,
    200–202
  linking dimensional models to, 65–66
  for patients with blends of traits, 197–198
  specific trait domains as basis for, 191–195
  for treatment of maladaptive trait
    expressions, 190–191

TRF (Teacher's Report Form), 122, 124
Triarchic Psychopathy Measure (TriPM), 393, 394, 396, 398
Triarchic psychopathy model (TPM), 393–394, 396, 397
Tricyclic antidepressants, 196
TriPM. *See* Triarchic Psychopathy Measure
Tromp, N. B., 118, 119
Trull, T. J., 3, 4
Trust, epistemic, 248
Tull, M. T., 362
Tyrer, P., 4, 29, 41

U

Ultimatum Game, 339
Uncinate fasciculus, 335
Unconscious motivation, 150–152
Understanding of Social Causality (SC), 169
Undisciplined Child mode, 287, 288
Unified Protocol for Transdiagnostic Treatment of Emotional Disorders (UP), 192, 197
Unmet childhood needs, 281–283, 288–289, 292
Unpacking defensive functioning, 149–150
Unstructured interviews, 78–80, 169
Unusual Beliefs and Experiences, 14
UP (Unified Protocol for Transdiagnostic Treatment of Emotional Disorders), 192, 197
U.S. Food and Drug Administration (FDA), 305

V

Vachon, D. D., 396, 397
Vaillant, G. E., 149, 226
Validation
    in biosocial model, 261–262
    in CBT for NPD, 385
    in DBT, 267–268
Validity
    of clinical interviews, 79, 80
    of computer adaptive testing, 91
    construct, 54–55, 160
    convergent, 13, 17, 80, 83
    criterion, 13, 16, 87, 89, 91
    of Criterion A, 13
    of Criterion B, 15–16
    defined, 80
    discriminant, 13, 17
    of ecological momentary assessment, 93–94
    incremental, 17–18, 80, 89
    of informant report methods, 88–89
    and multimethod clinical assessment, 94

of performance-based methods, 83–84
    of personality assessments for youth, 111
    predictive, 16–17
    of self-report measures, 86–87
Validity indices, for self-report measures, 86–87
Valproate, 196, 308, 311–312
Valuation
    self-, 422, 423
Venables, N. C., 396
Venta, A., 114
Verbal communication, 429
Visual cortices, 332
Vogt, K. S., 254
Vulnerable Child mode, 287–289
Vygotsky, L., 214

W

Wachtel, P. L., 191
Warmth (WARM) scale, PAI, 400
"Watching others in pain" paradigm, 334
Watters, C. A., 15, 59
Waugh, M. H., 10, 11, 19, 169
Weekers, L. C., 118, 170
Weijers, J., 255
"We-ness," in MBT, 240–241
Werner, H., 214
White matter volume, self-control deficits and, 329, 330
WHO. *See* World Health Organization
WHODAS 2.0 (World Health Organization Disability Assessment Schedule 2.0), 123, 125
Widiger, T. A., 3, 4, 36, 38–40, 55, 56, 65, 87, 198, 227, 397
Winter, D., 327
Wise mind, 266
Withdrawal, 14
Woodbridge, J., 365
Woods, W. C., 93
World Federation of Societies of Biological Psychiatry, 195–196
World Health Assembly, 28, 30
World Health Organization (WHO), 4, 27–29, 34, 35, 183, 215, 238, 353, 375, 391
World Health Organization Disability Assessment Schedule 2.0 (WHODAS 2.0), 123, 125
World Psychiatric Association Section on Personality Disorders, 29
Wright, A., 225, 227, 356
Wygant, D. B., 397

Y

Yeomans, F. E., 152
Young, J. E., 281, 283, 285

466 *Index*

Young adults, clinical staging model for, 124, 125
Young Schema Questionnaire (YSQ), 282
Young Schema Questionnaire-third version (YSQ-S3), 282
Youth, personality assessment for. *See* Personality assessment for youth
Youth Self-Report (YSR), 122, 124
YSQ (Young Schema Questionnaire), 282

YSQ-S3 (Young Schema Questionnaire-third version), 282
YSR (Youth Self-Report), 122

Z

Zanarini, M. C., 113, 311, 312, 357, 363
Zilboorg, G., 354
Zimmermann, J., 11–13, 17, 87, 93, 167, 426

ABOUT THE EDITOR

Steven K. Huprich, PhD, is a professor of psychology at the University of Detroit Mercy in Detroit, Michigan, and owner of Steven K. Huprich, PhD & Associates. He is past president of the International Society for the Study of Personality Disorders, past editor of the *Journal of Personality Assessment*, and a fellow of the American Psychological Association (APA) and the Society for Personality Assessment. He was awarded the 2013 Theodore Millon Award for Mid-Career Excellence in Personality Psychology by APA.

Dr. Huprich has published six professional texts and more than 120 peer-reviewed publications. He also has made more than 225 conference presentations. His interests have focused on the diagnosis, assessment, and classification of personality disorders and pathology, with a major focus on the historical depressive personality disorder and the development of the malignant self-regard construct. Dr. Huprich has had faculty appointments at Baylor, Eastern Michigan, and Wichita State Universities as well as adjunct appointments with the University of Kansas School of Medicine and Michigan State University College of Human Medicine. He has an active private practice in Northville, Michigan.